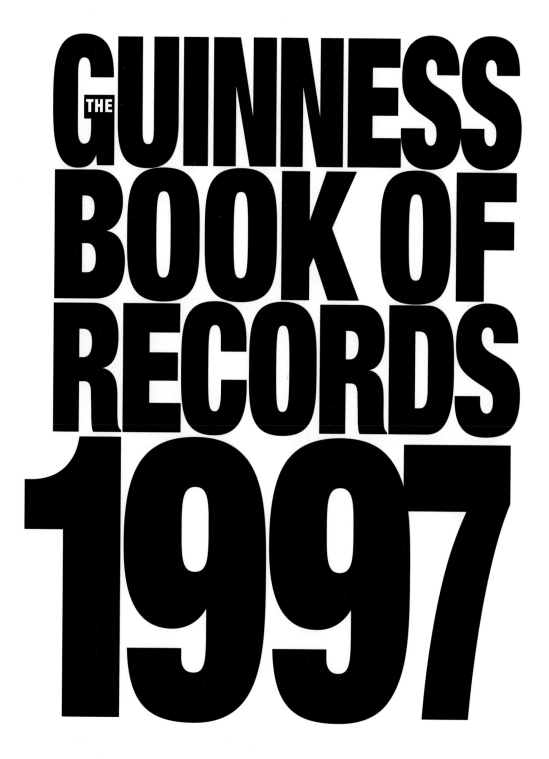

THE GUINNESS BOOK OF RECORDS 1997

Welcome to Guinness

The big news this year is: we've gone digital.
The fabulous book you're holding was put together using the latest digital production technology. Records are now derived from an automated database which allows us to be as up to date as the day the book was printed. The pictures in the book came to us as digital files; you can see the result—vibrant colours and ultra crisp definition. The Olympic pictures on pages 328–339 came to us via ISDN line from Atlanta just a few hours after they were taken— and delivered in a matter of seconds.

Being digital is allowing Guinness to enter new territories. In the near future we will be launching the *Guinness Book of Records* Internet Club. Much more than a web site, we see this as a major new communication channel for all of you as fascinated as we are by records and record-breaking. You will be able to chat live to other record-breakers worldwide. We will break news of new records as they happen and much much more. So why not register now? At the end of the book—on page 352—you will find the registration form which you can freepost, fax or e-mail to us here at Guinness.

THE GUINNESS BOOK OF RECORDS 1997

World Copyright Reserved
Copyright © 1996 Guinness Publishing Ltd

No part of this book may be reproduced or transmitted in any form or by any means electronic, chemical or mechanical, including photocopying, any information storage or retrieval system without a licence or other permission in writing from the copyright owners. Reviewers are welcome to quote brief passages should they wish.

British Library Cataloguing in Publication Data A catalogue record for this book is available from the British Library
ISBN 0-85112-693-6

'Guinness' is a registered trade mark of Guinness Publishing Ltd

Colour origination
Graphic Facilities, London

Printing and binding
Printer Industria Grafica S.A., Barcelona

Paper
Printed on woodfree, chlorine free and acid free paper

Cover
Cover printed with Holofoil manufactured by Astor Universal, UK

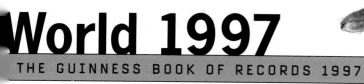

World 1997

THE GUINNESS BOOK OF RECORDS 1997

Digital doesn't end there.
Look at page 118 and see the latest
Guinness Challenge. We wish to include
you games and computer fanatics in a
whole new digital records category. So read the rules and get in touch, take
the challenge and maybe see your name included in the 1998 edition.
The new design was also inspired by the digital world—for instance the
flash strips which highlight key records. It is also intended to make the
book even clearer and easier to use—open it anywhere and you know
exactly where you are. All of this needed better indexing and more
pages—you've got them, 352 in total to be precise.

That's enough of us. We've had fun putting this new edition together: now it's
time for you to enjoy the 1997 *Guinness Book of Records*.

Joint Publishing Directors

THE GUINNESS BOOK OF RECORDS 1997   THE GUINNESS BOOK OF RECORDS 1997

Managing Editor
Elizabeth Wyse

Designer
Karen Wilks

Editorial
Rhonda Carrier

Senior Researcher
Clive Carpenter

Research Assistant
Simon Gold

**Page Make-up and
Pre-Production**
Jo Brewer

Digital Production
Andrzej Michalski
Steve Tagg

Fulfilment
Mary Hill

Records Editors
Nick Heath-Brown
Stewart Newport

Research
Michael Russoff

Copy Editor
Kevin McRae

**Correspondence
Editor**
Amanda Brooks

Index
Connie Tyler

Picture Research
Anna Calvert
Richard Philpott

Print Production
Chris Lingard

Cover Design
Ron Callow at
Design 23

Joint Publishing Directors
Ian Castello-Cortes and Michael Feldman

Managing Director
Christopher Irwin

How to use this book

Running heads: these show the spread's title and, in capital letters, the title of the section in which the spread appears.

Sub-headings: these are used to divide the records that appear on each spread into thematic subject areas.

Mini-headings: these are used to identify the individual records listed on each spread.

Side bars: for each spread an outstanding record or extraordinary superlative has been chosen for the black side bar.

Icons: a number of icons appear throughout the book (see below). The icon shown here is used when an image is at actual size.

Coloured information bars: each spread contains up to four coloured information bars highlighting interesting records that can be found, in more detail, in the spread itself.

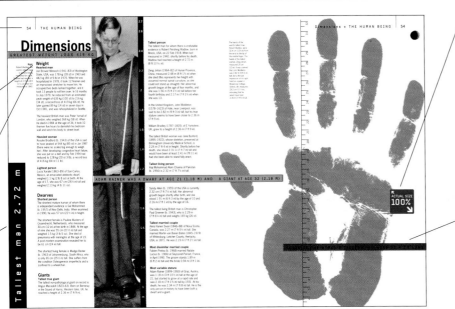

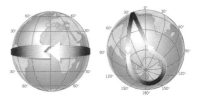

How the book is organized

This edition of *The Guinness Book of Records* is organized on a double-page spread basis. It is divided into 11 sections, and the information is arranged thematically within each section. Interesting records and superlatives are highlighted in a number of ways. Photographs and artworks are used to illustrate the records, while a number of 'icons' are used throughout the book to highlight information about certain records.

There are 11 section openers throughout the book and these are used to introduce each of the chapters. The abstract design highlights some of the records that are to be found in the ensuing pages.

The 12-page Olympic section celebrates the 1996 Atlanta Olympics, listing the results for all the events and highlighting new record-breaking achievements. All new records that are set in Atlanta in 1996 will be found in this section only.

The Index has been divided into two sections: a Subject Index and Name Index. The Name Index includes the names of people, of pets and of animals that are used in sports such as horse racing.

General warning

Attempting to break records or set new records can be dangerous. Appropriate advice should be taken first and all record attempts are undertaken entirely at the participant's risk. In no circumstances will Guinness Publishing Ltd have any liability for death or injury suffered in any record attempts. Guinness Publishing Ltd has complete discretion over whether or not to include any particular records in the book.

Icons

The following icons have been used throughout the book:

Flick-book icons

These appear on the top right-hand corner of each spread. Three images have been used; the Moon, the Earth and a clock. When the pages of the book are flicked, the images appear to move: the Moon waxes and wanes; the Earth rotates on its axis; the hands move around the clock.

Actual size icon This icon is used to show that an image has been reproduced at actual size.

Guinness man icon This icon is used to indicate that objects or phenomena are very large. The human figure represents a man of average height: 1.82 m (6 ft).

Circumnavigation icon

A number of records in the book concern circumnavigation of the globe: by boat, aeroplane, train and even on foot. Two globes are used to indicate the two circumnavigation routes, equatorial and polar. An agreed definition of circumnavigation is as follows: the start and return points are the same; all meridians of longitude and the Equator must be crossed; some, but not all, meridians can be crossed more than once.

Olympic icons

The following icons have been used in the Olympic section (pp. 328–339) to highlight record-breaking achievements:

Olympic record

world record

British record

Abbreviations and measurements

The Guinness Book of Records uses both metric and imperial measurements (imperial in brackets). The only exception to this rule is for some scientific data, where metric measurements only are universally accepted.

Where possible, the sterling equivalent for foreign currency values is given in brackets after the figure. Where a specific date is given the sterling equivalent is calculated according to the exchange rates that were in operation at the time. Where only a year date is given the exchange rate is calculated from December of that year. The billion conversion is one thousand million.

Acknowledgements

Founder Editor
Norris McWhirter

Editorial Consultant
Peter Matthews

Consultants
Andrew Adams, John Arblaster, Brian Bailey, Amanda Bailieu, Howard Bass, Dennis Bird, Richard Braddish, Robert Brooke, Tony Brown, Ian Buchanan, Mark Carwardine, Chris Cavey, Andy Chipling, Graham Coombs, Alan Dawson, Peter Day, Graham Dymott, Colin Dyson, Clive Everton, John Flynn, Brian Ford, Paulette Foyle, Bill Frindall, Tim Furniss, Ian Goold, Stan Greenberg, Liz Hawley, Ron Hildebrant, Rick Hogben, Elizabeth Hussey, Sir Peter Johnson, Ove Karlsson, Raymond Keene, Bernard Lavery, Stephanie McCullough, Loren McIntyre, John Marshall, Carol Michaelson, Andy Milroy, Michael Minges, Ray Mitchell, Raymond Monelle, John Moody, Patrick Moore, Bill Morris, Ron Moulton, Barry Norman, Michael Orr, Enzo Paci, Greg Parkinson, John Randall, Elfan ap Rees, Chris Rhys, Jonathan Rice, Dan Roddick, Peter Rowan, Joshua Rozenberg, Steven Salberg, Irvin Saxton, Jack Schofield, Alexander Schwartz, Screaming Lord Sutch, Ian Smith, Neil Somerville, Martin Stone, James Varley, Juhani Virola, Tony Waltham, David Wells, Dave Whitehouse, Rick Wilson

Guinness Publishing Ltd would like to thank the following:
American Miniature Horse Association; American Miniature Horse Registry; Anthony D'Offay Gallery; Bank of England; BBC; BRECSU Building Research Establishment; British Horse Society; British Standards Institute; Christie's; Council for Tall Buildings; Crucible, Sheffield; FBI; *Garden News*; General Post Office, Nassau, Bahamas; German Ministry of Transport; Goethe-Institut; *The Guardian*; *Guatemala Weekly*; William Hill; Indian Embassy, London; Lloyd's Shipping Registry; London Research Centre; National Museum of Cartoon Art; Natural History Museum; Network Wizards (http://www.nw.com/); Nevada State Prison; *New York Post*; Cesar Pelli & Associates Inc.; Permanent Committee of Geographical Names; The Reference Centre (U.S.A. Information Service); Reuter News Service; Royal Entomological Society; Shire Horse Society; Sotheby's, *Toy Horse International*; Western Deep Levels Mine; *Yeddah News*

Picture Acknowledgements
t=top; c=centre; b=bottom; l=left; r=right
All diagrams by Line + Line
6t Tony Duffy/Allsport; 6b Buddy Mays/Corbis; 7 Paul Rogers; 8/10 Space Telescope Science Institute/Corbis; 11/12 NASA/Corbis; 13t US Naval Observatory (PAO)/ Corbis; 13c US Naval Observatory (PAO)/Corbis; 13b/14t NASA/Corbis; 14b Space Telescope Science Institute/Corbis; 15/17t NASA/Corbis; 17b Galen Rowell/Corbis; 18 David Muench/Corbis; 19 Burt Jones/Maurine Shimlock/ Secret Sea; 20 David Muench/Corbis; 22 Galen Rowell/Corbis; 23 Richard List/Corbis; 24t Roger Ressmeyer/ Corbis; 24c Frank Lane Picture Agency; 24bl Dieter & Mary Plage/ Survival Anglia/Oxford Scientific Films; 24/25 F. Stuart Westmorland/Corbis; 25l Giboux/Liaison/Frank Spooner Pictures; 25r Michael T. Sedam/ Corbis; 26t Perry Conway/Corbis; 26bl Scott T. Smith/Corbis; 26br Jeremy Horner/Corbis; 27tl Perry Conway/Corbis; 27tr NASA/Corbis; 27b Rick Price/Corbis; 28/29 F. Stuart Westmorland/Corbis; 30 Sunset; 31t/b The Natural History Museum, London; 32t Wolfgang Kaehler/Corbis; 32bl Perry Conway/Corbis; 32br Brandon Cole/Corbis; 33t Nick Garbutt/Planet Earth Pictures; 33b/t Perry Conway/ Corbis; 34b Ned Middleton/Planet Earth Pictures; 35t Jamie Harron; Papilio/Corbis; 35bl Wolfgang Kaehler/Corbis; 35br Perry Conway/ Corbis; 36 Mr Sombat Raksakul; 37t John Feltwell; 37b Bruce Coleman; 38/39 Hulton Deutsch/Corbis; 38 Perry Conway/Corbis; 39 Robert A. Tyrrell/Oxford Scientific Films; 40t David H. Northcott/Corbis; 40b Wolfgang Kaehler/Corbis; 41 Buddy Mays/Corbis; 42t Stephen Frink/Corbis; 42b F. Stuart Westmorland/Corbis; 43t Brandon Cole/Corbis; 43b F. Stuart Westmorland/Corbis; 44 Perry Conway/Corbis; 45 The Natural History Museum, London; 46/47 J. A. L. Cooke /Oxford Scientific Films; 46 Robert Pickett/Corbis; 47t Hulton Deutsch/ Corbis; 47b Robert Gill; Papilio/Corbis; 48/49 Corbis–Bettmann; 50/51t Lester V. Bergman/Corbis; 51c Science Pictures Ltd/Corbis; 51b/52t Lester V. Bergman/Corbis; 52c Pamela Singh/ Gamma; 52b Philip Reeve/Rex Features; 53l Arriti/Gamma; 53r Philip Reeve/Rex Features; 54 Corbis–Bettmann; 56/57 Hulton Deutsch/ Corbis; 56 Scottish Daily Record & Sunday Mail Limited; 58 Stanford University Medical Center; 59 National Medical Slide Bank; 60/61 Peter Crowther; 62/63 Robert Clifford; 65t NASA/Corbis; 65c Morton Beebe–S.F./Corbis; 65b Stephen Frink/Corbis; 66l Ffyona Campbell; 66r Michael Maslan Historic Photographs/Corbis; 67l Phil Schermeister/Corbis; 67r Russell Cheyne/Allsport; 68/69 City of Aberdeen; 68 Kurita/Frank Spooner Pictures; 69 Sams/Fuji; 70 Norman Johnson; 71 David A. Breen; 72t Jean Luc Petit/Gamma; 72b Hulton Deutsch/Corbis; 73 Gary Norman; 74t BBC Television; 74b Kobal Collection; 75 Brian Cook; 76 Paul Rogers; 77t Paul Farrell; 77b Sam MacAdam/GMTV Ltd; 78 Philip Gold/Corbis; 79t Tony Arruza/Corbis; 79b Paul Souders/Corbis; 80/81 Courtesy of Nanyang Technological University Student's Union, Singapore; 80 Bon Delong, University of Maine; 81 M. N. Azwad/WWF Malaysia Photo Library; 82 Owen Morse; 83t Rhonda L. Swafford; 83b Mike Southern; Eye Ubiquitous/Corbis; 84 Egremont Crab Fair Committee; 85t Ben Block; 85b Lupe C. Mora; 86 Rex Features; 87t/c Bernard Lavery Marketing Ltd; 87b Corbis–Bettmann/UPI; 88 A/S Svindlands Pølsefabrik; 89t/92t Robert Clifford; 92b Peter Gough Photography Pty. Ltd.; 93t Steve Miller; Eye Ubiquitous/Corbis; 93b David Lees/ Corbis; 94/95 Courtesy of Naha City; 95 Citroën; 96t Robert Clifford; 96b Morton Beebe/Corbis; 97t Cableworld & Multichannel News; 97b Robert Clifford; 98/99 Michael W. Davidson/ Science Photo Library; 100l/r Roger Ressmeyer, Starlight/Science Photo Library; 101l Cern/Science Photo Library; 101r Michael W. Davidson/ Science Photo Library; 102 Morton Beebe/Corbis; 103 Paul Souders/Corbis; 104t Hulton Deutsch/Corbis; 104 Paul Souders/Corbis; 105t David Bartruff/Corbis; 105b The Natural History Museum, London; 106l Robert Harding Picture Library; 106r Haydn Jones; 107t Bassignac/Deville/ Gaillard/Frank Spooner Pictures; 107b Karen Wilks; 108 Charles E. Rotkin/Corbis; 109 The Purcell Team/Corbis; 110/111l Sander/ Liaison/Gamma; 111r Lester V. Bergman/Corbis; 112t NASA/Corbis; 112c US Naval Observatory (PAO)/ Corbis; 112b Science Telescope Science Institute/Corbis; 113 NASA/ Science Photo Library; 114 NASA/ Corbis; 115t Real Time Strategies Inc.; 115b Barzilay Public Relations; 116t/b Corbis–Bettmann/UPI; 118 Nintendo; 119t Sega Europe Limited, 1996; 119c Sony; 119b Nintendo; 120/121 Eastlight Vienna/Rex Features; 122 Stena Line Limited; 123t Hulton Deutsch/Corbis; 123b Tim Thompson/ Corbis; 124 Sea and See; 126t Emilio Sciotto; 126b Honda (UK); 127 Matsuhiro Wada/Gamma; 128t Darren Heath; 128b Jay Ohrberg; 129 Jaguar Cars Limited; 130 NASA; 131 David Taylor/Sipa Press/Rex Features; 132/133 Aerofilms; 133 Eastlight Vienna/Rex Features; 134l Wolfgang Kaehler/Corbis; 134r Buu Alain/Gamma; 135 Richard Nowitz/Corbis; 136 Hulton Deutsch/ Corbis; 137t British Airways Image Library; 137b Sander/Gamma-Liaison; 138t British Airways Image Library; 138b Corbis–Bettmann; 139 Christy B. Krieg; 140/141 Jim Corwin/Corbis; 140 Jerry Edwards, Austin Jet; 141t/b Virgin Management Ltd; 142t Robert Harding Picture Library; 142b Peter Aaron/Arcaid; 143 William Bake/Corbis; 144/145 David Lees/ Corbis; 146t David Lees/Corbis; 146b/147l Wolfgang Kaehler/Corbis; 147r Hulton Deutsch/Corbis; 148 Wolfgang Volz/Bilderberg Archiv der Fotografen; 149t Karen Wilks; 149b Kevin Fleming/Corbis; 150l AKG London; 150r Retrograph; 151r The British Library; 150/151 "Crown copyright is reproduced with the permission of the Controller of HMSO"; 151l Retrograph; 152l The Royal Society; 152r The Lancet, October 5 1823 Vol. 1 No. 1; 152/153 United Feature Syndicate, Inc; 153 Foulsham; 154l Rex Features; 154l/r Hulton Deutsch/Corbis; 155r Rex Features; 156 Robert Holmes/Corbis; 157l Countrywide Communications London; 157r Corbis–Bettmann/UPI; 158 David Lees/Corbis; 159t Corbis–Bettmann; 159b Rex Features; 160/161 Robert Harding Picture Library; 163t Douglas Peebles/Corbis; 163c/b Robert Holmes/Corbis; 164t Robert Harding Picture Library; 164b Hulton Deutsch/Corbis; 165 Michael St. Maur Sheil/Colorific!; 166 BBC Television; 167 Ron Wingham/ Simon Cocker; 168t Wolfgang Kaehler/ Corbis; 168b Corbis; 169t J. Levy/ AFP/Bettmann/Corbis; 169b/170t Robert Clifford; 170b Phil Schermeister/Corbis; 171/172t Hulton Deutsch/Corbis; 172b Hulton Deutsch/ Corbis; 173l Rex Features; 173r/174l Hulton Deutsch/Corbis; 174r Corbis–Bettmann/Reuter; 175 Corbis–Bettmann/UPI; 176 David Sandison/ *The Independent*; 177a Philip Ollerenshaw/RCA; 177b Sony Music; 177c Creation Records; 177d WEA Records; 177e Mercury; 177f Columbia; 177g RCA; 177h London Records; 177i A&M Records Limited; 177j Arista; 178 Harpo Inc.; 179 Paul Farrell; 180/181 Bill Bachman/ Colorific!; 182 Jeremy Horner/Corbis; 183t Tim Hawkins; Eye Ubiquitous/ Corbis; 183b The Purcell Team/Corbis; 184t Japan National Tourist Organisation; 184b J. Apicella/Cesar Pelli & Associates; 184/185 Ken Champlin/Cesar Pelli & Associates; 185t David W. Hamilton/The Image Bank; 185b Zooid Pictures; 188 Arvind Garg/Corbis; 189l Tom Sobolik/Black Star/Colorific!; 189r Hulton Deutsch/ Corbis; 190t Chromosohm Media, Inc./ Corbis; 190b Bill Mackenzie/ GlaxoWellcome; 191 Bank of England; 192 Robert Clifford; 193t/c Hulton Deutsch/Corbis; 193b Morton Beebe–S.F./Corbis; 194 Corbis–Bettmann; 195l Frank Spooner Pictures; 195c Nils Jorgensen/Rex Features; 195r Mike Walmseley/Rex Features; 196l Paul Souders/Corbis; 196r David Muench/Corbis; 197t Yorkshire Agricultural Society; 197bl William A. Bake/Corbis; 197br Bill Bachman/ Colorific!; 198 Robert Dowling/Corbis; 199t Hulton Deutsch/Corbis; 199b Robert Dowling/Corbis; 200/201 Shout Picture Company; 202 Sarah Leen/Matrix/Colorific!; 203 David Lees/Corbis; 204/205 Jeffrey W. Myers/Corbis; 206t Randy Brandon/Sipa/Rex Features; 206b/207t Sipa/Rex Features; 207b Rex Features; 208t Kevin R. Morris/Corbis; 208b Galen Rowell/Corbis; 209 Ric Ergenbright/Corbis; 210l Sipa Press/ Rex Features; 210r M. Ginies/Alix/Sipa Press/Rex Features; 211t John Wallace; 211b GPL; 212 Vic Feazell; 213 Rex Features; 214/215 Shout Picture Company; 214 SIPA–Press; 216/217t Popperfoto; 217b Associated Press; 218l Paul Almasy/ Corbis; 218r Michael T. Sedam/Corbis; 219l Wolfgang Kaehler/Corbis; 219r Ric Ergenbright/Corbis; 221t Hulton Deutsch/Corbis; 221c The National Archives/Corbis; 221b Chromosohm Media, Inc./Corbis; 222 Moment in Time Photography; 223 Sipa Press/Rex Features; 224/225 Robert Clifford; 226 Robert Holmes/Corbis; 227l Paul Almasy/Corbis; 227r Dave G. Houser/Corbis; 229t Richard T. Nowitz/Corbis; 229c Ric Ergenbright/Corbis; 229b David G. Houser/Corbis; 230/231 Anton Want/Allsport; 232/233l Hulton Deutsch/Corbis; 233r Corbis–Bettmann; 234l Simon Bruty/Allsport; 234r Mike Powell/Allsport; 235l Bob Martin/ Allsport; 235r Mike Powell/Allsport; 236l Gray Mortimore/Allsport; 236r Allsport; 237l Gary M. Prior/Allsport; 237r Mike Powell/Allsport; 238l Clive Mason/Allsport; 238r Simon Bruty/ Allsport; 239r Clive Mason/Allsport; 239l Mike Cooper/Allsport; 240 Darrell Ingham/Allsport; 241 Hulton Deutsch/ Corbis; 242 Pascal Rondeau/Allsport; 243 Dan Smith/Allsport; 244 Chris Cole/Allsport; 246l/r Galen Rowell/ Corbis; 247 The Military Picture Library/Corbis; 248t Vandystadt/ Allsport; 248b Allsport/Hulton Deutsch; 249 Allsport; 250t Al Bello/Allsport; 250b Scott Halleran/Allsport; 252 Kevin R. Morris/Corbis; 253 Allsport/Hulton Deutsch; 254t Jonathan Daniel/Allsport; 254b Andrew Bernstein/NBA/Allsport; 255 Tim Defrisco/Allsport; 256t Shaun Botterill/Allsport; 256b/257l Hulton Deutsch/Corbis; 257r Mike Hewitt/ Allsport; 258 Chris Cole/Allsport; 259/260l Hulton Deutsch/Corbis; 260r Corbis–Bettmann–Reuters; 261l Clive Brunskill/Allsport; 261r Stu Forster/Allsport; 262t Clive Brunskill/Allsport; 262c Allsport/MSI; 262b Tony Duffy/ Allsport; 263 Shaun Butterill/Allsport; 264 Mark Thompson/Allsport; 265t Jon Nicholson/Allsport; 265b Anton Want/Allsport; 266t Shaun Botterill/Allsport; 266b Ken Levine/Allsport; 267 David Rogers/Allsport; 268 Mike Cooper/Allsport; 269t Mike Hewitt/Allsport; 269b David Cannon/Allsport; 270 Allsport; 271t Pascal Rondeau/ Allsport; 271c Mike Powell/Allsport; 271b Al Bello/Allsport; 272t Clive Brunskill/Allsport; 272b Allsport/Hulton Deutsch; 273t/b Hulton Deutsch/Corbis; 274t/275t Clive Brunskill/Allsport; 275b Jon Nicholson/Allsport; 276t Associated Press; 276b Stu Foster/Allsport; 277l Mike Powell/Allsport; 277r Bob Martin/Allsport; 278 David Cannon/Allsport; 279t Allsport/Hulton Deutsch; 279b Stephen Munday/Allsport; 280 David Cannon/Allsport; 281 Allsport/Hulton Deutsch; 282 Kevin R. Morris/Corbis; 283t Hulton Deutsch/Corbis; 283b David S. Robbins/Corbis; 284 Dave G. Houser/Corbis; 285t Gary M. Prior/Allsport; 285b Anton Want/Allsport; 286t Kevin R. Morris/Corbis; 286b Sylain Cazenave/Vandystadt/ Allsport; 287 Tony Duffy/Allsport; 288 Anton Want/Allsport; 289l Anton Want/Allsport; 289r Shaun Botterill/Allsport; 291t David Lees/Corbis; 291c Corbis–Bettmann; 291b Richard Hamilton Smith/Corbis; 292/293 Stuart Westmorland/Corbis; 292 Simon Bruty/Allsport; 293 Steve Powell/ Allsport; 294 Howard Boylan/Allsport; 295t Bob Martin/Allsport; 295b Vandystadt/Allsport; 296t Pascal Rondeau/Allsport; 296b Chris Cole/Allsport; 297 Clive Brunskill/ Allsport; 298t/b Rick Stewart/Allsport; 299 Christopho Guibbaud/Agence Vandystadt/Allsport; 300l Pascal Rondeau/Allsport; 300r Bob Martin/ Allsport; 301 Chris Cole/Allsport; 302 Allsport/Hulton Deutsch; 303t/b Holly Stein/Allsport; 304/305 Simon Bruty/Allsport; 304 Chris Cole/Allsport; 305 Russell Cheyne/Allsport; 306 Dave Cannon/Allsport; 308l Corbis–Bettmann/UPI; 308r Mike Hewitt/ Allsport; 309 Kit Houghton/Corbis; 310t Jack Fields/Corbis; 310b Simon Bruty/Allsport; 311t Hulton Deutsch/ Corbis; 311b Kit Houghton/Corbis; 312t Simon Bruty/Allsport; 312b Shaun Botterill/Allsport; 313 Bob Martin/Allsport; 314t The International Game Fish Association ; 314b Ferry-Liaison/Gamma/Frank Spooner Pictures; 315 The International Game Fish Association; 316t Gray Mortimore/ Allsport; 316b John Downer/Planet Earth Pictures; 317l Jeffrey W. Myers/ Corbis; 317r Ken Levine/Allsport; 318l Allsport/Hulton Deutsch; 318r Pascal Rondeau/Allsport; 319l Mike Hewitt/Allsport; 319r Mike Hewitt/Allsport; 320t Anton Want/ Allsport; 320b/321 Allsport; 322 Richard Martin/Allsport; 323l Allsport/Hulton Deutsch; 323r Corbis/Bettmann; 324/326b Vandystadt/Allsport; 327 US Department of Defense/Corbis; 328/339 Allsport; 340 Kevin Brown; 341 BBC Television

Contents

MORE THAN 150 SPREADS OF RECORDS AND SUPERLATIVES

008
009
010
011
012
013
014
015
016
017
018
019
020
021
022
023
024
025
026
027

Earth

MAXIMUM POSSIBLE DURATIO

GREATEST LAND MOUNTAIN RANGE, THE HIMALAYA–KARAKORA

JUPITER IS THE LARGEST PLANET AND HAS THE SHORTEST DAY, AT 9 HR 50 MIN 30.003 SE

LONGEST-LASTING RAINBOW WAS VISIBLE FOR SIX HOURS

GREATEST NUMBER OF TORNADOES IN 24 HOURS WAS 1

HIGHEST SHADE TEMPERATURE EVER RECORDED WAS 58°C

KILAUEA ON HAWAII, THE WORLD'S MOST ACTIVE VOLCANO, HAS BEEN CONTINUOUSLY ERUPTING SINCE 1983

MORE THAN 460 M

WAIMANGU GEYSER IN NEW ZEALAND ERUPTED TO A HEIGHT OF

IAN SEA BASIN WHICH COVERS 518,000 KM²

LARGEST EXPOSED DEPRESSION IN THE WORLD, THE CASP

F AN ECLIPSE OF THE SUN IS 7 MIN 31 SEC

NEAREST STAR IS THE VERY FAINT PROXIMA CENTAURI

ONTAINS 96 OF THE 109 PEAKS OVER 7,315 M

LARGEST ZODIACAL CONSTELLATION IS VIRGO

and Space

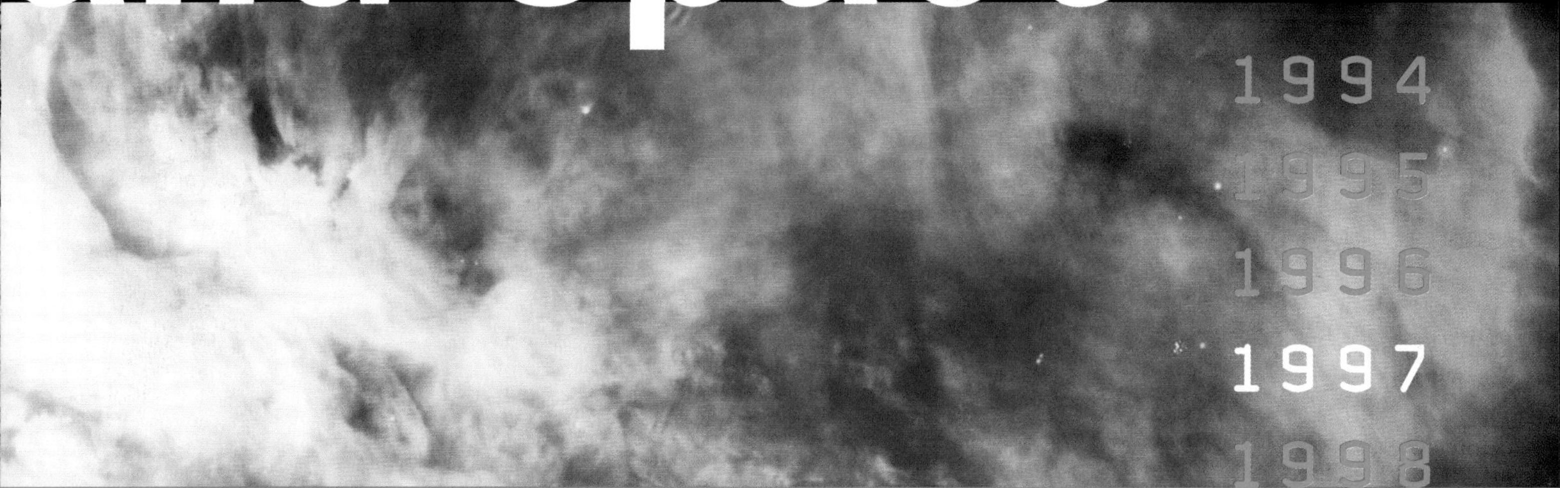

1994

1995

1996

1997

1998

RTHEST OBJECT VISIBLE TO THE NAKED EYE, MESSIER 31, IS 2,310,000 LIGHT YEARS AWAY

The Universe

Right
The Great Nebula of Orion contains sufficient gas to produce thousands of stars and has a cluster of hot young stars at its centre. The constellation Orion contains the largest star, the M-class supergiant Betelgeuse, which has a diameter 500 times greater than that of the Sun.

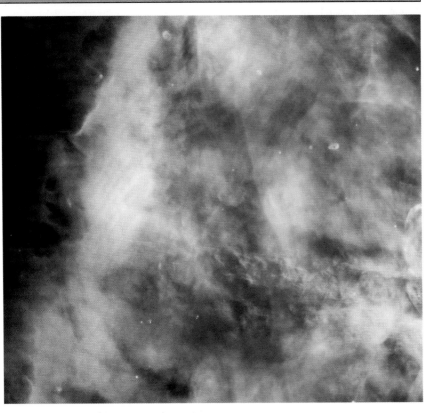

Most luminous galaxy
The highest recorded luminosity for a galaxy is 4.7×10^{14} times that of the Sun, for the hyperluminous IRAS (Infra Red Astronomy Satellite) galaxy FSC 10214+4724 (identified in 1990) which has a red shift of 2.282, equivalent to a distance of 11,600 million light years. This value has been magnified 10–100 times by the lensing effect of at least one and probably two intervening galaxies, so the brightest galaxy could be the hyperluminous IRAS F15307+3252 (discovered in 1990), which has a luminosity 1.0×10^{13} times that of the Sun. Although it has a red shift of only 0.926, equivalent to a distance of 8,100 million light years, the possibility remains that the luminosity of this galaxy could also be enhanced by lensing.

Farthest object visible to the naked eye
The Great Galaxy in Andromeda (mag. 3.47), known as Messier 31, is a rotating nebula in spiral form at a distance of about 2,310,000 light years. Our galaxy is moving towards it.

Under good observation conditions, Messier 33, the Spiral in Triangulum (mag. 5.79), can be glimpsed by the naked eye at a distance of 2,530,000 light years.

Remotest object
Quasi-stellar radio sources (quasars or QSOs) are believed to be the active centres of distant galaxies. The record red shift is 4.897 for the quasar PC1247+3406, announced in

The Cosmos

Largest structure in the Universe
The largest structure found in the Universe to date is a cocoon-shaped shell of galaxies about 650 million light years across, which surrounds the Local Supercluster. This discovery was made by a team of French astronomers led by Georges Paturel and announced in June 1994.

First galaxies
In April 1992, it was announced that the Cosmic Background Explorer (COBE) satellite, launched by NASA on 18 Nov 1989, had detected minute fluctuations from the cosmic microwave background temperature of −270.424°C (−454.763°F). This has been interpreted as the initial formation of galaxies within the first billion years of the Big Bang.

Largest galaxy
The central galaxy of the Abell 2029 galaxy cluster, 1,070 million light years distant in Virgo, has a major diameter of 5,600,000 light years—80 times the diameter of the

Milky Way—and a light output equivalent to 2 trillion (2×10^{12}) Suns. The discovery was announced in July 1990 by Juan M. Uson, Stephen P. Boughn and Jeffrey R. Kuhn, all of the USA.

Closest galaxy to the Milky Way
The closest object outside our galaxy is the Sagittarius Dwarf galaxy, at a distance of 82,000 light years.

Furthest galaxy from the Milky Way
The remotest galaxy to have been definitely established is the radio galaxy 8C 1435+635, the discovery of which was announced by a Dutch/British/US team in May 1994. It has a red shift of 4.25, equivalent to a distance of 13,000 million light years.

In 1994, a European Southern Observatory (ESO) team obtained tentative evidence for a galaxy of red shift 4.38, equivalent to a distance of 13,100 million light years, obscuring the even more distant quasar BRI 1202–0725, which has a red shift of 4.68.

May 1991. If it is assumed that there is an 'observable horizon', where the speed of recession is equal to the speed of light, i.e. at 14,000 million light years or 1.32×10^{23} km (8.23×10^{22} miles), a simple interpretation would place this quasar at 94.4% of this value or 13,200 million light years.

Most luminous object in the sky
The quasar HS1946+7658 is at least 1.5×10^{15} times more luminous than the Sun. Its discovery was announced in July 1991. It has a red shift of 3.02 and is therefore 12,400 million light years away.

Most violent outburst seen in a quasar
On 13 Nov 1989, a joint US-Japanese team noted that the energy output of the quasar PKS0558–504 (about 2,000 million light years away) increased by two-thirds in three minutes. This is equivalent to all the energy released by the Sun in 340,000 years.

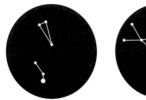

Aries

Taurus

Gemini

Cancer

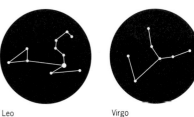

Leo

Virgo

Stars

Nearest star
Except for our own Sun, the nearest star is the very faint Proxima Centauri, discovered in 1915, at a distance of 4.225 light years (4.00×10^{13} km or 2.48×10^{13} miles).

The nearest 'star' visible to the naked eye is the southern-hemisphere binary alpha Centauri, at 4.35 light years distant.

Largest star
The M-class supergiant Betelgeuse (alpha Orionis, the top left star of Orion), which is 310 light years distant, has a diameter of 700 million km (400 million miles)—about 500 times greater than that of the Sun. It is surrounded by a dust 'shell' and by an outer tenuous gas halo up to 8.5×10^{11} km (5.3×10^{11} miles) in diameter.

Most massive star
The variable eta Carinae, 9,100 light years away in the Carina Nebula, is estimated to have a mass 150–200 times that of the Sun.

Among stars whose masses have been directly determined, the two stars of the binary known as Plaskett's Star both have masses 60 to 100 times that of the Sun.

Smallest stars
Neutron stars, which may have a mass up to three times that of the Sun, have a diameter of only 10–30 km (6–19 miles).

Least massive stars
The mass of the white dwarf companion to the millisecond pulsar PSR B1957+20 has been reduced to only 0.02 that of the Sun (20 Jupiter masses), owing to the fact that it is being evaporated by the neutron star.

The brown dwarf star Gliese 229B has a mass estimated at between 20 and 50 times that of Jupiter.

Most luminous star
If all the stars could be viewed at the same distance, eta Carinae would be the most luminous, with a total luminosity 6,500,000 times that of the Sun. In 1843, its absolute luminosity temporarily increased to 60 million times that of the Sun.

Visually brightest star
The hypergiant Cygnus OB2 No. 12, which is 5,900 light years distant, has an absolute visual magnitude of –9.9 (810,000 times that of the Sun). This may be matched by the supergiant IV b 59 in the nearby galaxy Messier 101.

Brightest star seen from Earth
Sirius A (alpha Canis Majoris), which is 8.64 light years distant, is the brightest star in the sky, with an apparent magnitude of –1.46. At 2.33 million km (1.45 million miles) in diameter, it has a mass 2.14 times that of the Sun and is 24 times visually brighter.

Dimmest star
The brown dwarf Gliese 229B, discovered in Oct 1994 orbiting at 6,600 million km (4,100 million miles) from the main star Gliese 229A, is at a distance of 18.6 light years and has a luminosity 500,000 times less than that of the Sun and a visual brightness 500 million times less. Its surface temperature of less than 700°C (1,300°F) is the lowest observed stellar temperature.

Youngest stars
Two protostars known as IRAS–4 in the nebula NGC1333 (1,100 light years distant), appear to be the youngest stars. Announced in May 1991, they will not be fully fledged stars for at least 100,000 years.

Oldest stars
The oldest stars in the galaxy are in the halo, high above the disc of the Milky Way. A group led by Timothy Beers (USA) had discovered

70 such stars by Jan 1991 but expect to detect 500. Such stars would have been formed c.1 billion years after the Big Bang.

Pulsars
Of pulsars that have been accurately measured, the fastest-spinning is PSR B1937+214, discovered by a group led by Donald C. Backer in Nov 1982. It is located in the minor constellation Vulpecula (the Little Fox), 11,700 light years distant, and has a pulse period of 1.5578064949 milliseconds, which is equivalent to a spin rate of 641.9282518 revolutions per second.

The pulsar with the slowest spin-down rate (and therefore the most accurate stellar clock) is PSR J0034–0534 at only 6.7×10^{-21} seconds per second. Its discovery was announced in Sept 1993.

Brightest supernova
The brightest supernova seen in recorded history is believed to be SN 1006, noted in April 1006 near Beta Lupi. It flared for two years and attained a magnitude of –9 to –10. The remnant is believed to be the radio source G327.6+14.5, almost 3,000 light years distant. Others occurred in 1054, 1604, 1885 and on 23 Feb 1987, when Ian Shelton sighted SN 1987A in the Large Magellanic Cloud 170,000 light years distant. It was visible to the naked eye when at its brightest in May 1987.

Largest constellations
The largest of the 88 constellations is Hydra (the Sea Serpent), which covers 3.16% of the entire sky and contains at least 68 stars that are visible to the naked eye.

The constellation Centaurus (Centaur) ranks only ninth in area but embraces at least 94 stars that are visible to the naked eye.

Smallest constellation
Crux Australis (Southern Cross) covers only 0.16% of the whole sky.

Zodiacal constellations
Virgo is the largest zodiacal constellation, with an area of 1294.428 square degrees.

The smallest zodiacal constellation is Capricornus (Capricorn), which has an area of 413.947 square degrees.

Taurus has the most bright stars of any zodiacal constellation, with 125 down to magnitude 6, while Aries, Capricornus and Libra have the fewest, with only 50 each.

Left
The closest object outside our own galaxy is the Sagittarius Dwarf galaxy, which was discovered by R. A. Ibata, G. Gilmore and M. J. Irwin of the United Kingdom and announced in April 1994.

Libra

Scorpio

Sagittarius

Capricornus

Aquarius

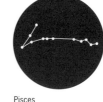

Pisces

The Solar System

Right
Solar flares occur above sunspots and can eject atomic particles at a speed of up to 1,000 km/sec (600 miles/sec). These can disturb the Earth's magnetic field and cause radio blackouts and auroras. A typical star classified as a yellow dwarf (type G2 V), the Sun is at the centre of a solar system extending up to 50,000 times the distance of the Earth from the Sun to the 'Oort Cloud'—a 'halo' of comets, some of which are swept into the inner Solar System from time to time.

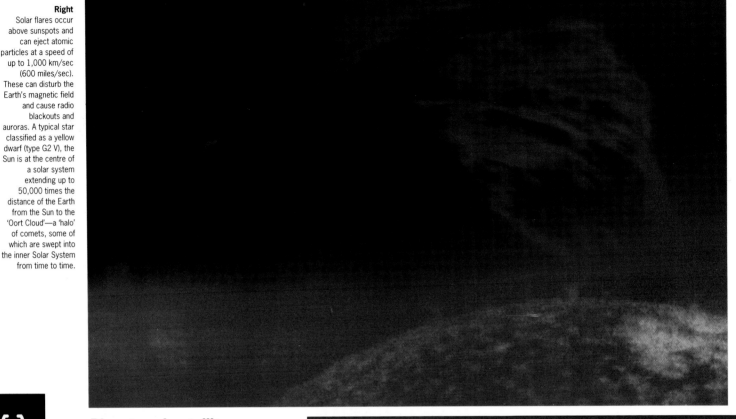

Hottest planet 462°C

Planet and satellites

Largest major planet
Jupiter has an equatorial diameter of 142,984 km (88,846 miles) and a polar diameter of 133,708 km (83,082 miles). Its mass and volume are 317.828 times and 1,323.3 times that of the Earth respectively. It also has the shortest period of rotation, resulting in a Jovian day of 9 hr 50 min 30.003 sec in the equatorial zone.

Smallest and coldest planet
Pluto is 2,320 km (1,442 miles) in diameter and has a mass 0.0021 times that of the Earth. Its surface composition suggests that it has a surface temperature close to the −235°C (−391°F) measured for Neptune's moon Triton—the lowest recorded for any natural body in the Solar System.

Hottest planet
The Soviet *Venera* and American *Pioneer* surface probes recorded a surface temperature of 462°C (864°F) on Venus.

Outermost planets
The Pluto–Charon system orbits at a mean distance of 5,914 million km (3,675 million miles) from the Sun for 248.54 years, but because of orbital eccentricity it is closer to the Sun than Neptune between 23 Jan 1979 and 15 March 1999.

Nearest planet
Venus can come within 38 million km (24 million miles) of the Earth, but its average is 41,400,000 km (25,700,000 miles) inside the Earth's orbit.

Fastest planet
Mercury orbits the Sun at an average distance of 57,909,200 km (35,983,100 miles) and has an orbital period of 87.9686 days, giving the highest average speed in orbit of 172,248 km/h (107,030 mph).

Brightest planet
Viewed from Earth, the brightest of the five planets that are normally visible to the naked eye (Jupiter, Mars, Mercury, Saturn and Venus) is Venus, which has a maximum magnitude of −4.4.

Faintest planet
Uranus, which has a magnitude of 5.5, can only be seen with the naked eye under certain favourable conditions.

The faintest of the nine planets as seen from Earth is Pluto (mag. 15.0), which can only be viewed through a telescope.

Densest and least dense planet
Earth is the densest planet, with an average density 5.515 times that of water.

Saturn has an average density only about one-eighth the density of Earth, or 0.685 times that of water.

Most spectacular surface feature
The volcano Olympus Mons on Mars has a diameter of 500–600 km (310–370 miles) and an estimated height of 26 km (16 miles).

Most dramatic conjunctions
On 5 Feb 1962, 16° covered all seven principal members of the Solar System besides the Earth (Sun, Moon, Mercury, Venus, Mars, Jupiter and Saturn) during an eclipse in the Pacific area.

Extrasolar planets
Indirect evidence suggests that 70 Virginis B is the most massive extrasolar planet. It has a mass 6.5 times that of Jupiter, and is orbiting at a distance of 64 million km (40 million miles) from the star 70 Virginis, which is 49 light years away from Earth.

The least massive extrasolar planet is at a distance of 28 million km (18 million miles) from the millisecond pulsar PSR B1257+12, which is 2,000 light years distant. It has a mass roughly equal to that of the Moon.

Most and least satellites
Saturn has at least 18 satellites, while Mercury and Venus have none.

Largest satellite
The largest and most massive satellite is Ganymede (Jupiter III), which is 2.017 times

as heavy as the Moon and has a diameter of 5,268 km (3,273 miles).

Smallest satellite
The smallest satellite to have had its diameter measured is Deimos, the outer moon of Mars. Although irregularly shaped, it has an average diameter of 12.5 km (7¾ miles).

Asteroids

Furthest from and closest to the Sun
The orbits of only about 7,200 of the estimated 45,000 asteroids have been computed. Most orbit between Mars and Jupiter, and distances from the Sun vary between 17,910,000 km (11,130,000 miles) for the Aten asteroid 1995 CR at perihelion, and 7,939 million km (4,933 million miles) for the Kuiper belt object 1994 JS at aphelion.

Largest and smallest asteroids
With an equatorial diameter of 959 km (596 miles) and a polar diameter of 907 km (564 miles), the largest asteroid is 1 Ceres.

The smallest asteroid is $1993KA_2$, with a diameter of approximately 5 m (16 ft).

Brightest and dimmest asteroids
The only asteroid visible to the naked eye is 4 Vesta, with an absolute magnitude of 3.16.

The dimmest asteroid and the faintest object ever detected is $1993KA_2$, with an absolute magnitude of 29.

N ORBIT OF 172,248 KM/H

Closest approach
The asteroid $1994XM_1$ was discovered by James Scotti (USA) on 9 Dec 1994, just 14 hours before it came within 100,000 km (62,000 miles) of Earth.

Comets

Earliest recorded comet
Records of comets appear as early as the 7th century BC, and appearances of Halley's Comet can be traced back to 240 BC. The first prediction of its return, by Edmund Halley (1656–1742), proved true on Christmas Day 1758, 16 years after his death.

Largest comets
The object 2060 Chiron, discovered in 1977, is 182 km (113 miles) in diameter and is now regarded as the largest comet. It does not show spectacular cometary behaviour, however, because its closest approach to the Sun is 1,273 million km (791 million miles).

The largest coma (the luminous cloud around the nucleus in the head of the comet) to have been observed formed part of the comet of 1811, which had a diameter of approximately 2 million km (1¼ million miles).

The tail of the brilliant Great Comet of 1843 trailed for a distance of about 330 million km (205 million miles).

Brightest comet
The brightest comet is considered to be either the Cruls Comet of 1862 or the Ikeya-Seki Comet of 1965.

Shortest orbital period
Encke's Comet has an orbital period of 1,198 days (3 years 103 days) and a closer approach to the Sun than any other comet. At perihelion, it comes within a distance of 49,500,000 km (30,800,000 miles) of the Sun, and attains a speed of 254,000 km/h (158,000 mph). First identified in 1786, the comet has been missed on only eight of its subsequent 63 returns to perihelion. Due to modern advances in instrumentation, scientists are now able to track it over most of its orbit.

Left
Ikeya-Seki appeared in 1965 and vies for the title of brightest ever comet with the Cruls Comet that appeared in 1862.

Left
Halley's comet, which orbits the Sun every 76 years or so, is the brightest periodic comet and the earliest comet on record, with reports dating back to more than 2,000 years ago.

CLOSEST ASTEROID CAME WITHIN 100,000 KM OF EARTH IN 1994

Longest orbital period
The comet with the longest confirmed orbital period is Herschel-Rigollet, at 156 years. The comet was discovered by Caroline Herschel in 1788 and re-observed in 1939.

Longer orbital periods have been calculated, for example the 1,550 years computed for Comet McNaught-Russell (1993v), which was discovered by Robert H. McNaught and Kenneth S. Russell on 17 Dec 1993. The comet's mean distance from the Sun is 20 billion km (12 billion miles) and its aphelion distance is 40 billion km (25 billion miles). Both figures are the largest for any known object in the Solar System.

Closest approach
On 1 July 1770, Lexell's Comet, travelling at 138,600 km/h (86,100 mph) relative to the Sun, came within a distance of 1,200,000 km (745,000 miles) of the Earth. More recently the Earth is believed to have passed through the tail of Halley's Comet on 19 May 1910.

Left
A montage of Saturn and six of the planet's moons is shown here, created from images taken by Voyager 1. Saturn has at least 18 of the 61 satellites that are known to exist in the Solar System. A further four or five possible Saturn satellites were detected on images taken by Voyager 2 in 1981, and Hubble Space Telescope observations during the ring plane crossings of May and Aug 1995 suggested the existence of a further three satellites.

The Earth in Space

MAXIMUM DISTANCE OF THE EARTH FROM THE SUN (APHELION) IS 152,097,800 KM

Longest solar eclipse 7 min 31 sec

The Earth and the Moon

Minimum and maximum distance
The Moon orbits at a mean distance from the Earth of 384,399.1 km (238,854½ miles) centre-to-centre. In this century, the closest approach was 356,375 km (221,441 miles) centre-to-centre, on 4 Jan 1912. The farthest distance between the two was 406,711 km (252,718 miles) on 2 March 1984.

Craters and maria
The largest wholly visible crater is the walled plain Bailly near the Moon's South Pole. It is 295 km (183 miles) across and has walls rising to 4,250 m (14,000 ft).

The largest lunar impact basin is the far-side South Pole-Aitken, which has a diameter of 2,500 km (1,550 miles) and an average depth of 12,000 m (39,000 ft) below its rim. It is the largest and deepest such crater known in the Solar System.

The largest regular mare or 'sea' is the Mare Imbrium, which has a diameter of 1,300 km (800 miles).

Highest mountains
In the absence of a sea level, lunar altitudes are measured relative to an adopted radius of 1,738 km (1,079 miles 1,660 yd). On this basis the highest elevation is the highlands north of the Korolev Basin on the lunar far-side, at 8,000 m (26,000 ft).

Temperature extremes
When the Sun is overhead, the temperature on the lunar equator reaches 117°C (243°F) (17°C [31°F] above the boiling point of water). After nightfall it sinks to –163°C (–261°F).

The Earth and the Sun

Minimum and maximum distance
The Earth's distance from the Sun varies between a minimum of 147,098,200 km (91,402,600 miles) and a maximum of 152,097,800 km (94,509,200 miles). This is due to its elliptical orbit.

Left
The total eclipse of the Sun of 7 March 1970, as seen from Morgan's Corner, North Carolina, USA. There are between two and five solar eclipses each year, and a maximum of five lunar eclipses.

MAXIMUM POSSIBLE DURATION OF AN ECLIPSE O

Minimum and maximum orbital velocity
The Earth's average orbital velocity is 107,220 km/h (66,620 mph), but this varies between 105,450 km/h (65,520 mph) at aphelion (maximum distance from the Sun) and 109,030 km/h (67,750 mph) at perihelion (minimum distance from the Sun).

Eclipses and sunspots

Earliest recorded eclipses
Computer programs can calculate eclipses far back into history, but there is no firm evidence for eclipses prior to the partial eclipse observed in Nineveh, Assyria, on 15 June 763 BC.

The first definite evidence for a total eclipse comes from Chu-fu, China, where one was observed on 17 July 709 BC.

The first description of a solar eclipse in the United Kingdom occurs in the *Anglo-Saxon Chronicle*, which describes a two-thirds solar eclipse in London in AD 538.

Longest duration
The maximum possible duration of an eclipse of the Sun is 7 min 31 sec. The longest of recent date lasted for 7 min 8 sec. It occurred on 20 June 1955 west of the Philippines.

The maximum possible duration of a lunar eclipse is 1 hr 47 min. This will occur on 16 July 2000.

The duration of eclipses can be 'extended' if observers are airborne. The total eclipse of the Sun on 30 June 1973 was extended to 1 hr 14 min for observers on a Concorde that took off from Toulouse, France, and stayed in the Moon's shadow over the Atlantic from 10:51 to 12:05 GMT before landing in Chad.

The longest possible eclipse in the United Kingdom is 5 min 30 sec. In recent times, an eclipse on 3 May 1715 lasted 4 min 4 sec.

Most and least eclipses
The highest number of eclipses possible in a year is seven, as in 1935, when there were five solar and two lunar eclipses. In 1982 there were four solar and three lunar eclipses.

The lowest possible number of eclipses in a year is two, both of which must be solar. This took place in 1944 and 1969.

The only recent example of three total solar eclipses at a single location was at a point east of the Aral Sea in Kazakhstan (44°N, 67°E). These took place on 21 Sept 1941, 9 July 1945 and 25 Feb 1952.

Largest sunspots
To be visible to the protected naked eye, a sunspot must cover an area of approximately 1,300 million km² (500 million miles²).

Below
This small meteorite fell in Western Australia in 1960. Meteorites vary widely in size: the largest discovered so far—in Namibia—was 2.7 m (9 ft) long.

ACTUAL SIZE
100%

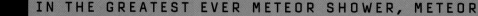

IN THE GREATEST EVER METEOR SHOWER, METEOR

The largest sunspot ever recorded was seen in the southern hemisphere of the Sun on 8 April 1947. It covered a total area of about 18,000 million km^2 (7,000 million $miles^2$), and had an extreme longitude of 300,000 km (187,000 miles) and an extreme latitude of 145,000 km (90,000 miles).

Meteorites

Oldest meteorite
In 1981, a revision of the estimated age of meteorites that have remained essentially undisturbed after their formation suggests that the oldest to have been accurately dated is the Krähenberg meteorite, at 4,600±20 million years (just within the initial period of Solar System formation).

Dust grains in the Murchison meteorite, which fell at Murchison, Victoria, Australia, in Sept 1969, may be older than the Solar System.

Largest known meteorite
A block 2.7 m (9 ft) long and 2.4 m (8 ft) wide, estimated to weigh 59 tonnes, was found near Grootfontein in Namibia in 1920.

The largest piece of stony meteorite recovered weighs 1,770 kg (3,902 lb) and

HE MOON IS 1 HR 47 MIN

was part of a 4-tonne shower that struck Jilin (formerly Kirin), China, on 8 March 1976.

The heaviest of the 23 meteorites known to have fallen on the United Kingdom since 1623 weighed at least 46 kg (102 lb). It fell at Barwell, Leics, at around 4:15 p.m. on 24 Dec 1965.

Greatest explosion
The explosion over the Podkamennaya Tunguska River basin on 30 June 1908 was equivalent to 10–15 megatons of high explosive and resulted in the devastation of an area of 3,900 km^2 (1,500 $miles^2$). The shock wave was felt up to 1,000 km (620 miles) away. The cause is thought to be the energy released when a stony meteoroid 30 m (98 ft) in diameter travelling at hypersonic velocity at an incoming angle of 45° totally disintegrated at an altitude of 10 km (6 miles).

Meteor shower
On the night of 16–17 Nov 1966, the Leonid meteors, which recur every 33¼ years, were visible between western North America and eastern Russia (then the USSR). It was calculated that the meteors passed over Arizona, USA, at a rate of 2,300 per minute for 20 minutes from 5 a.m. on 17 Nov 1966.

Lunar meteorites
There are 12 meteorites that are believed to be of lunar origin. All were found in Antarctica except the most recently discovered, which is only 3 cm (1 in) in diameter and weighs 19 g

($^{67}/_{100}$ oz). It was found at Calcalong Creek on the Nullarbor Plain to the north of the Great Australian Bight by D. H. Hill, W. V. Boynton and R. A. Haag of the USA. Their discovery was announced in Jan 1991.

Largest craters
In 1962, a crater with an approximate depth of 800 m (½ mile) and a diameter of 240 km (150 miles) in Wilkes Land, Antarctica, was attributed to a meteorite. To create a crater of this size the meteorite would have had to weigh approximately 13 billion tonnes and strike the Earth at a speed of 70,800 km/h (44,000 mph).

In Dec 1970, Soviet scientists reported an astrobleme (an impression left on the Earth's surface by a large ancient meteorite) with a diameter of 95 km (60 miles) and a maximum depth of 400 m (1,300 ft) in the basin of the River Popigai.

There is a crater-like formation or astrobleme 442 km (275 miles) in diameter on the eastern shore of Hudson Bay, Canada.

The largest and best-preserved crater to have definitely been formed by a meteorite is Coon Butte (or Barringer Crater), which was discovered near Winslow, Arizona, USA, in 1891. It has a diameter of 1,265 m (4,150 ft) and is about 175 m (575 ft) deep, with a parapet rising 40–48 m (130–155 ft) above the surrounding plain. It has been estimated that an iron-nickel mass of 2 million tonnes and a diameter of 61–79 m (200–260 ft) gouged this crater c. 25,000 BC.

Above
The Moon is the Earth's closest neighbour, and its only natural satellite. Only 59% of its surface is directly visible from the Earth, because it is in 'captured rotation' (the period of rotation is equal to the period of orbit).

The Earth's surface

OLDEST FRAGMENTS OF THE EARTH'S CRUST ARE 4,276 MILLION YEARS OLD

The Earth's crust
Oldest rocks
The age of the Earth is generally considered to be within the range of 4,540±40 million years, but no rocks of this age have been found. They have presumably been destroyed by geological processes.

The greatest age of any scientifically dated rock is 3,962 million years. Acasta Gneisses were discovered about 320 km (200 miles) north of Yellowknife, Northwest Territories, Canada, by Dr Samuel Bowring of the USA in May 1984, during an ongoing Canadian geology survey mapping project.

Oldest fragments of the Earth's crust
Some zircon crystals discovered by Bob Pidgeon and Simon Wilde in the Jack Hills, 700 km (430 miles) north of Perth, Western Australia, in Aug 1984, were found to be 4,276 million years old.

Smallest continent
The Australian mainland, with an area of 7,614,500 km^2 (2,939,960 miles^2), is the smallest continent.

Islands
Largest islands
Discounting the Australian mainland, which is generally regarded as a continental land mass, the largest island in the world is Greenland, which covers an area of about 2,175,000 km^2 (840,000 miles^2).

The largest sand island in the world is Fraser Island, Queensland, Australia, which has a sand dune 120 km (75 miles) long.

The largest island that is surrounded mostly by fresh water is the Ilha de Marajó in the mouth of the Amazon River, Brazil, with an area of about 48,000 km^2 (18,500 miles^2).

The remotest British islet is Rockall, 307 km (191 miles) west of St Kilda, Western Isles. The rock is 21 m (70 ft) high and 25 m (83 ft) across, and was not formally annexed until 18 Sept 1955.

The remotest British island ever inhabited is North Rona, which is 71 km (44 miles) from the nearest land at Cape Wrath and the Butt of Lewis. It was evacuated c. 1844.

The remotest currently inhabited British island is Fair Isle, which lies 38.5 km (24 miles) south-west of Sumburgh Head, Shetland, and has a population of some 80 people.

Newest island
An as yet unnamed island halfway between the islands of Kao and Late in Tonga's Ha'apai

NEWEST ISLAND WAS FORME

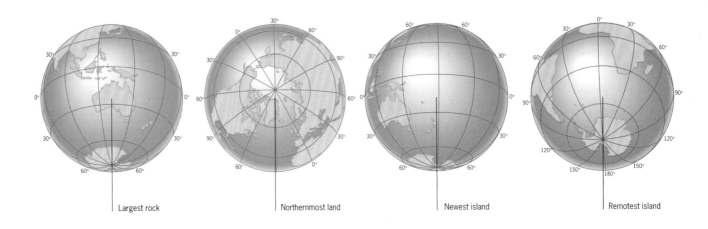

Largest rock	Northernmost land	Newest island	Remotest island

Largest rocks
The largest exposed monolith is Ayers Rock, known to Aborigines as *Uluru*, which rises 348 m (1,143 ft) above the desert plain in Northern Territory, Australia. It is 2.5 km (1½ miles) long and 1.6 km (1 mile) wide.

It was estimated in 1940 that La Gran Piedra, a volcanic plug located in the Sierra Maestra, Cuba, weighs 61,355 tonnes.

Continents
Largest continent
The Eurasian land mass is the largest, with an area (including islands) of 53,698,000 km^2 (20,733,000 miles^2).

The Afro-Eurasian land mass, separated artificially only by the Suez Canal, covers an area of 84,702,000 km^2 (32,704,000 miles^2), and thus constitutes 57.2% of the Earth's total land mass.

The largest inland island (land surrounded by rivers) is Ilha do Bananal, Brazil, which covers 20,000 km^2 (7,700 miles^2).

The largest island within a lake is Manitoulin Island, covering 2,766 km^2 (1,068 miles^2) in the Canadian section of Lake Huron.

Remotest island
Bouvet Island (Bouvetøya), discovered in the South Atlantic by J. B. C. Bouvet de Lozier on 1 Jan 1739, is an uninhabited Norwegian dependency located about 1,700 km (1,050 miles) north of the uninhabited coast of Queen Maud Land, Antarctica.

The remotest inhabited island is Tristan da Cunha in the South Atlantic, discovered by Portuguese admiral Tristão da Cunha in March 1506. It has an area of 98 km^2 (38 miles^2). The nearest inhabited land is the island of St Helena, located 2,435 km (1,315 nautical miles) to the north-east.

group in the south-west Pacific was formed as a result of submarine volcanic activities that were first observed on 6 June 1995. It covers an area of 5 ha (12 acres) and has a maximum height of 40 m (131 ft).

Largest archipelago
The world's greatest archipelago is the 5,600-km (3,500-mile) crescent of more than 17,000 islands that forms Indonesia.

Largest atoll
The largest atoll in the world is Kwajalein in the Marshall Islands, in the central Pacific Ocean. Its slender coral reef is 283 km (176 miles) long and encloses a lagoon of 2,850 km^2 (1,100 miles^2).

The atoll that covers the largest land area is Christmas Atoll, situated in the Line Islands in the central Pacific Ocean. It covers an area of 649 km^2 (251 miles^2), of which 321 km^2 (124 miles^2) is land.

LONGEST GLACIER IS UP TO 64 KM WIDE AND AT LEAST 700 KM LONG WIT

Longest reef 2,027 km

Land

Northernmost land
On 26 July 1978, Uffe Petersen of the Danish Geodetic Institute observed the remote islet of Odaaq Ø, located 1.36 km (1,478 yd) north of Kaffeklubben Ø, off Pearyland, Greenland, and 706.4 km (439 miles) from the North Pole. The islet measures 30 m (100 ft) across.

Southernmost land
The South Pole, unlike the North Pole, is on land. The ice sheet at the South Pole is drifting 10 m (33 ft) per year from the pole along the 40th meridian west of Greenwich.

Land furthest from the sea
A point in the Dzungarian Basin in north-west China's Xinjiang Uygur autonomous region (at 46°16.8'N, 86°40.2'E) is at a great-circle distance of 2,648 km (1,645 miles) from the nearest open sea—Baydaratskaya Guba to the north (Arctic Ocean), Feni Point to the south (Indian Ocean) and Bohai Wan to the east (Yellow Sea).

The highest cliffs in the United Kingdom are the Conachair cliffs on St Kilda, Western Isles, which are 400 m (1,300 ft) high.

Y VOLCANIC ACTIVITIES FIRST OBSERVED ON 6 JUNE 1995

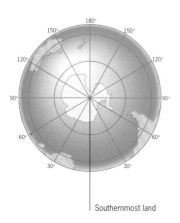

Southernmost land

Natural features

Deserts
The largest desert is the Sahara in North Africa, with a maximum length of 5,150 km (3,200 miles) from east to west. It is 1,280–2,250 km (800–1,400 miles) from north to south and covers an area of about 9,269,000 km² (3,579,000 miles²).

Sand dunes
The highest measured sand dunes are in the Saharan sand sea of Isaouane-N-Tifernine in east-central Algeria, at 26°42'N, 6°43'E. They have a wavelength of 5 km (3 miles) and attain a height of 465 m (1,526 ft).

Cliffs
The highest known sea cliffs are on the north coast of east Moloka'i, Hawaii, near Umilehi Point. They descend 1,010 m (3,300 ft) at an average angle of inclination of more than 55° and an average gradient of more than 1.428.

TS SEAWARD EXTENSION

The highest sheer sea cliffs on the British mainland are located at Clo Mor, 5 km (3 miles) to the south-east of Cape Wrath, Sutherland. They drop 281 m (921 ft).

Natural arches
The two longest natural arches in the world are both in Utah, USA. Landscape Arch, in Arches National Park, and Kolob Arch, in Zion National Park, stand over openings 94.5 m (310 ft) wide. The first spans an open gully and narrows to 5 m (16 ft); the second is close to a high cliff face.

Glaciers
The world's longest glacier is the Lambert Glacier, which was discovered by an Australian aircraft crew in Australian Antarctic Territory in 1956–57. Draining about 20% of the East Antarctic ice sheet, it is up to 64 km (40 miles) wide and, with its seaward extension (the Amery Ice Shelf), is at least 700 km (440 miles) long.

The fastest-moving major glacier in the world is the Columbia Glacier, between Anchorage and Valdez, in Alaska, USA. It flows at an average rate of 20 m (65 ft) per day.

Peninsulas
Arabia is the largest peninsula, covering about 3,250,000 km² (1,250,000 miles²).

Reefs
The longest reef is the Great Barrier Reef off Queensland, north-eastern Australia, which is 2,027 km (1,260 miles) in length and actually consists of thousands of separate reefs. Between 1962 and 1971, and 1979 and 1991, corals on large areas of the central section of the reef, between Cooktown and Proserpine, were devastated by the crown-of-thorns starfish (*Acanthaster planci*). In 1995, devastation of the reef began again.

Above
The Earth seen from Space. The Sahara, the world's largest desert, is clearly visible.

Left
The South Pole, indicated by a marker, is the world's most southerly point.

Terrain and landscape

THE YARLUNG ZANGBO VALLEY IN EASTERN TIBET IS A RECORD 5,075 M DEEP

Largest gorge 446 km long

Mountains

Highest mountain
Peak XV on the Tibet–Nepal border in the eastern Himalayas was found to be the highest mountain by the Survey Department of the Government of India in 1856, from theodolite readings taken in 1849 and 1850. Its height was calculated at 8,840 m (29,002 ft) and it was named Mt Everest after Col. Sir George Everest, formerly Surveyor-General of India. There have been several surveys since then, and 8,848 m (29,029 ft) is now the most widely accepted height.

Furthest summit from the Earth's centre
The Andean peak of Chimborazo is 6,267 m (20,562 ft) high and lies 158 km (98 miles) south of the Equator. The summit is 2,150 m (7,054 ft) further away from the Earth's centre than that of Mt Everest, because the Earth's radius in Ecuador is longer than its radius at the latitude of Everest.

Highest mountain on the Equator
The Cayambe volcano in Ecuador (77°58'W), is 5,790 m (18,996 ft) high. A mountaineer on its summit would move at 1,671 km/h (1,038 mph) relative to the Earth's centre, due to the Earth's rotation.

Highest insular mountain
A survey carried out by the Australian Universities' Expedition in 1973 gave a height of 4,884 m (16,023 ft) for Puncak Jaya on Irian Jaya, Indonesia.

Highest mountain in the United Kingdom
Ben Nevis is 1,343.6 m (4,408 ft 2 in) above sea level excluding the cairn at its peak, which is 3.65 m (12 ft) high.

Tallest mountain
When measured from its submarine base, at 6,000 m (3,280 fathoms) in the Hawaiian Trough, to its peak, Mauna Kea ('White Mountain') on the island of Hawaii is 10,205 m (33,480 ft) high. Of this, 4,205 m (13,796 ft) are above sea level.

Largest mountain ranges
The submarine Mid-Ocean Ridge stretches 65,000 km (40,000 miles) from the Arctic Ocean to the Atlantic Ocean, around Africa, Asia and Australia, and under the Pacific Ocean to the west coast of North America. Its greatest height is 4,200 m (13,800 ft) above the base ocean depth.

On land, the Himalaya–Karakoram range contains 96 of the 109 peaks in the world that are over 7,315 m (24,000 ft) high.

The longest range is the Andes of South America, at 7,600 km (4,700 miles) in length.

LONGEST MOUNTAIN RANG

Longest lines of sight
Vatnajökull in Iceland is 2,119 m (6,952 ft) high and has been seen from the Faeroes 550 km (340 miles) away by refracted light.

In Alaska, Mt McKinley, at a height of 6,194 m (20,320 ft), has been sighted from Mt Sanford, which is 4,949 m (16,237 ft) tall and situated 370 km (230 miles) away.

Greatest plateau
The most extensive high plateau is the Tibetan Plateau in Central Asia. Its average altitude is 4,900 m (16,000 ft) and it covers an area of 1,850,000 km^2 (715,000 miles^2).

Caves
Longest cave
The most extensive cave system is beneath Mammoth Cave National Park, Kentucky, USA. Interconnected passages beneath the Flint, Mammoth Cave and Toohey ridges have a total mapped length of 565 km (351 miles).

Largest cave
The largest cave chamber is the Sarawak Chamber, Lubang Nasib Bagus, in the Gunung Mulu National Park, Sarawak, discovered and surveyed by the British–Malaysian Mulu Expedition in 1980. It is 700 m (2,300 ft) long with an average width of 300 m (980 ft) and a minimum height of 70 m (230 ft).

Deepest cave
The Réseau Jean Bernard in France descends to a record depth of 1,602 m (5,256 ft).

Longest stalactite
The longest free-hanging stalactite in the world is believed to be one that is more than 12 m (40 ft) long in the Gruta do Janelão, in Minas Gerais, Brazil.

Tallest stalagmite
The tallest indisputable stalagmite, at 32 m (105 ft) in height, is located in Krásnohorská cave near Rožňava, Slovakia.

Underwater cave
The longest explored underwater cave in the world is the Nohoch Nah Chich cave system in Quintana Roo, Mexico, which has 51.31 km (31 miles 1,540 yd) of mapped passages.

Other features
Deepest valley
The Yarlung Zangbo Valley attains a record depth of 5,075 m (16,650 ft) where it turns through the Himalayas in eastern Tibet. The peaks of Namche Barwa and Jala Peri, which are 7,753 m (25,436 ft) and 7,282 m (23,891 ft) high respectively, are 21 km (13 miles) apart on either side of the River Yarlung Zangbo, which is at an elevation of 2,440 m (8,000 ft) at that point.

Largest gorge
The Grand Canyon on the Colorado River in north-east Arizona, USA, extends over 446 km (277 miles) from Marble Gorge to the Grand Wash Cliffs. It averages 16 km (10 miles) in width and 1.6 km (1 mile) in depth.

The submarine Labrador Basin canyon, between Greenland and Labrador, Canada, is 3,440 km (2,140 miles) long.

Deepest canyon
The Vicos Gorge in the Pindus Mountains of north-west Greece is 900 m (2,950 ft) deep and only 1,100 m (3,600 ft) between its rims.

The deepest submarine canyon discovered is situated 40 km (25 miles) south of Esperance, Western Australia, and is 1,800 m (6,000 ft) deep and 32 km (20 miles) wide.

Depressions
Largest depression
The largest exposed depression is the Caspian Sea basin in Azerbaijan, Russia, Kazakhstan, Turkmenistan and Iran. It covers more than 518,000 km^2 (200,000 miles^2), of which 371,800 km^2 (143,550 miles^2) is lake.

Deepest depression
The bedrock of the Bentley subglacial trench in Antarctica is located at 2,538 m (8,326 ft)

TALLEST STALAGMITE IS FOUND IN SLOVAKIA AND IS 32 M IN HEIGHT

below sea level and is the deepest known depression in the world.

The greatest submarine depression is an area of the north-west Pacific floor that has an average depth of 4,600 m (15,000 ft).

The deepest exposed depression on land is the shore surrounding the Dead Sea, which is now 400 m (1,310 ft) below sea level. The deepest point of this seabed is 728 m (2,388 ft) below sea level. The rate of fall in the lake surface has been 350 mm (13¾ in) per annum since 1948.

The deepest part of the bed of Lake Baikal in Russia is 1,181 m (3,875 ft) below sea level.

The lowest-lying area in the United Kingdom is in the Holme Fen area east of Stilton, Cambs, which has a lowest point of 2.2 m (7 ft 3 in) below sea level.

Water

Right
The coast of Kauai in the Hawaii Islands is washed by the Pacific, which is the world's largest ocean and home to both the deepest point of any ocean and the spot farthest from land.

Oceans

Largest ocean
The Pacific is the largest ocean in the world. Excluding adjacent seas, it represents 45.9% of the world's oceans and covers a total area of 166,241,700 km^2 (64,186,300 miles^2). Its average depth is 3,940 m (12,925 ft).

Smallest ocean
The Arctic, which covers an area of 13,223,700 km^2 (5,105,700 miles^2), is the world's smallest ocean. It has an average depth of 1,038 m (3,407 ft).

Deepest ocean
The deepest point of any of the world's oceans is in the Marianas Trench in the Pacific Ocean. It was pinpointed in 1951 by HM Survey Ship *Challenger*, and on 23 Jan 1960, the manned US Navy bathyscaphe *Trieste* became the first vessel to descend to the bottom of the trench. The unmanned Japanese probe *Kaiko* also reached the bottom, on 24 March 1995, and recorded the most accurate measurement to date, a depth of 10,911 m (35,797 ft).

Furthest spot from land
A point in the South Pacific Ocean, at 47°30'S 120°W, is about 2,575 km (1,600 miles) from the nearest land masses—Pitcairn Island, Ducie Island and Peter I Island. Centred on this spot is a circle of water that covers an area considerably larger than Russia—some 20,826,800 km^2 (8,041,200 miles^2).

Most southerly ocean point
The most southerly part of the oceans is the snout of the Scott Glacier in the Southern Ocean, 320 km (200 miles) from the South Pole at 87°S, 151°W.

Largest sea
The largest sea in the world is the South China Sea, which covers an area of 2,974,600 km^2 (1,148,500 miles^2).

Highest seamount
The highest known seamount (submarine mountain) is near the Tonga Trench between Samoa and New Zealand. It rises 8,700 m (28,500 ft) from the seabed, and its summit is 365 m (1,200 ft) below the surface.

Highest sea wave 34 m

Sea temperature
Water temperature at the sea's surface can be as low as −2°C (28°F) in the White Sea in the Arctic Ocean and as high as 36°C (96°F) in shallow areas of the Persian Gulf in summer.

The highest temperature recorded in the ocean is 404°C (759°F), measured in 1985 at a hot spring 480 km (300 miles) off the American west coast.

Largest bay
The largest bay in the world in terms of shoreline length is Hudson Bay in Canada,

Narrowest straits
The narrowest navigable strait in the world is the Strait of Dofuchi between Shodoshima Island and Mae Island, Japan, which is just 9.93 m (32 ft 7 in) wide at the bridge that links the two islands.

Waves
Highest waves
The highest officially recorded sea wave was calculated to have reached a height of 34 m (112 ft) from trough to crest. It was measured by Lt. Frederic Margraff of the US Navy from

Currents
Fastest-flowing current
The Antarctic Circumpolar Current, also known as the West Wind Drift, is the fastest-flowing current in the Earth's oceans. On the basis of four measurements that were taken in Drake Passage, which lies between South America and Antarctica, in 1982, the current was found to be flowing at a rate of approximately 130 million m³ (4.3 billion ft³) per second. Results that were obtained by computer modelling in 1990 estimated a higher figure of about 195 million m³ (6.9 billion ft³) per second.

which has a shoreline of 12,268 km (7,623 miles) and covers an area of about 1,233,000 km² (476,000 miles²).

The Bay of Bengal in the Indian Ocean is the world's largest bay in terms of total area. It covers approximately 2,172,000 km² (839,000 miles²).

Largest gulf
The Gulf of Mexico covers 1,544,000 km² (596,000 miles²) and has a shoreline that stretches 5,000 km (3,100 miles) from Cape Sable, Florida, USA, to Cabo Catoche, Mexico.

Longest fjord
The Nordvest Fjord arm of Scoresby Sund, eastern Greenland, extends inland to a point 313 km (195 miles) from the sea.

The longest fjord in Norway is the Sognefjord, which extends 204 km (127 miles) inland from the island of Sogneoksen to the head of the Lusterfjord arm at Skjolden. It ranges from 2.4 to 5.1 km (1½ to 3¼ miles) in width.

Clearest sea
The Weddell Sea off Antarctica has the clearest water of any sea. A 30-cm-diameter (1-ft) white 'Secchi' disc—for measuring water clarity—was visible to a depth of 80 m (262 ft) when measured by Dutch researchers at the German Alfred Wegener Institute on 13 Oct 1986. Such clarity corresponds to that of distilled water.

Straits
Longest strait
The world's longest strait is the Tartar Strait between Sakhalin Island and the Russian mainland, running 800 km (500 miles) from the Sea of Japan to Sakhalinsky Zaliv.

Broadest strait
The broadest named strait is the Davis Strait between Greenland and Baffin Island, Canada, with a minimum width of 338 km (210 miles).

Drake Passage between the Diego Ramirez Islands, Chile, and the South Shetland Islands is 1,140 km (710 miles) wide.

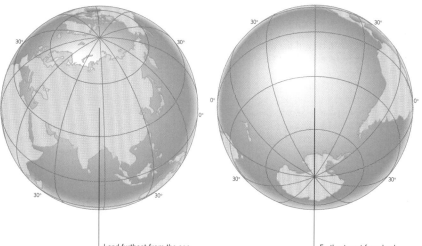

Land furthest from the sea

Furthest spot from land

the USS *Ramapo* as it proceeded from Manila, Philippines, to San Diego, California, USA, on the night of 6–7 Feb 1933, during a hurricane which reached a speed of 126 km/h (68 knots).

The highest wave to have been measured by an instrument reached a height of 26 m (86 ft). It was recorded on 30 Dec 1972 by the British ship *Weather Reporter* in the North Atlantic at 59°N, 19°W.

Highest tsunamis
On 9 July 1958, a landslip on land caused a wave that was moving at a speed of 160 km/h (100 mph) to wash a record 524 m (1,720 ft) high along the fjord-like Lituya Bay in Alaska, USA.

The highest tsunami to have been triggered by a submarine landslide struck the island of Lanai in the Hawaiian Islands approximately 105,000 years ago. It deposited sediment up to an altitude of about 375 m (1,230 ft).

The highest tsunami to have been caused by an offshore earthquake appeared off Ishigaki Island in the Ryukyu volcanic island chain, Japan, on 24 April 1771. The wave, which may have reached a height of 85 m (279 ft), tossed a 750-tonne block of coral more than 2.5 km (1½ miles) inland.

Strongest current
The most powerful currents in the world can be found in the Nakwakto Rapids in Slingsby Channel, British Columbia, Canada, where the flow may reach a rate of 30 km/h (16 knots).

Ice
Thickest ice
The greatest thickness of ice on record is 4.78 km (2 miles 1,704 yd). This measurement was achieved by radio echo soundings emitted from a US Antarctic research aircraft situated 440 km (270 miles) from the coast in Wilkes Land, Antarctica (at 69°56'17"S, 135°12'9"E) on 4 Jan 1975.

Northernmost ice in southern hemisphere
The most northerly location in the southern hemisphere where the seas are normally closed by ice for part of each year is in the South Atlantic, at a point approximately 600 km (370 miles) east of South Georgia (roughly 54°S).

Southernmost ice in northern hemisphere
The most southerly location in the northern hemisphere where the seas are normally closed by ice for part of the year is the Bo Hai (Gulf of Chihli) off the coast of China at roughly 37° 48'N—about the same latitude as Athens, Greece.

Inland water

Longest single drop 807 m

Rivers

Longest rivers

The world's longest rivers are the Nile, in Africa, and the Amazon, in South America. Which is the longer is more a matter of definition than of measurement.

The Amazon begins in Peru with a number of lakes and brooks that converge to form the Apurimac. This joins other streams to become the Ene, the Tambo and then the Ucayali. From the confluence of the Ucayali and the Marañón, the river is called the Amazon for the final 3,700 km (2,300 miles). It has several mouths, so it is not clear precisely where it ends. If the most distant mouth is counted, the river is about 6,750 km (4,080 miles) long.

NILE EXTENDED 6,670 KM FROM BURUNDI TO THE MEDITERRANEAN BUT LOST A FE

The River Nile—which stretches from Burundi to the Mediterranean Sea—was 6,670 km (4,145 miles) long before the loss of a few kilometres of meanders when Lake Nasser formed behind the Aswan High Dam.

Longest river in the United Kingdom

The Severn is 354 km (220 miles) long and its basin covers an area of 11,419 km² (4,409 miles²). It has the most tributaries of any British river, at 17.

Shortest river

The candidates for the shortest named river are the North Fork Roe River near Great Falls, Montana, USA, and the D River, at Lincoln City, Oregon, USA. The 17.7-m-long (58-ft) North Fork Roe River is the shorter of two forks that make up the Roe River. The D River connects Devil's Lake to the Pacific Ocean. Its official length is 37±1.5 m (120±5 ft).

Longest transcontinental waterway

The waterway linking the Beaufort Sea in northern Canada with the Gulf of Mexico in the southern United States has a total length of 10,682 km (6,637 miles). It has its source in the north, at Tuktoyaktuk on the Mackenzie River, and ends at Port Eads on the Mississippi delta. The final link was formed in 1976, with the completion of the South Bay Diversion Channel in Manitoba, Canada, joining the Churchill and Nelson river systems.

Largest river basin

The river basin drained by the Amazon covers about 7,045,000 km² (2,720,000 miles²). Of its countless tributaries, the Madeira is the longest tributary in the world, at 3,380 km (2,100 miles) in length, and is surpassed by only 17 rivers.

Largest delta

The delta created by the Ganges and the Brahmaputra rivers in Bangladesh and West Bengal, India, covers a total area of about 75,000 km² (30,000 miles²).

Greatest flow

The Amazon discharges an average of 200,000 m³/sec (7,100,000 cusec) into the Atlantic Ocean. This increases to more than 340,000 m³/sec (12 million cusec) in full flood—60 times more than the Nile.

Largest swamp

The largest tract of swamp is the Pantanal in Mato Grosso and Mato Grosso do Sul states in Brazil. It covers an area of about 109,000 km² (42,000 miles²).

Greatest river bores

The bore (abrupt rise of tidal water) on the Qiantong Jiang (Hangzhou He) River in eastern China is the most remarkable of the 60 river bores in the world. At spring tides, the wave attains a height of up to 7.5 m (25 ft) and a speed of 24–27 km/h (13–15 knots). It can be heard advancing from 22 km (14 miles).

The annual downstream flood wave on the Mekong River in South-east Asia can reach a height of 14 m (46 ft).

The Furo do Guajarú, a shallow channel that splits Ilha Caviana in the mouth of the Amazon, has the greatest recorded volume of any tidal bore.

Waterfalls

Highest waterfall

The Salto Angel (Angel Falls) on a branch of the Carrao River, an upper tributary of the Caroní River, in Venezuela, has a total drop of 979 m (3,212 ft). The longest single drop is 807 m (2,648 ft). First reported by Ernesto Sánchez la Cruz in 1910, the falls are named after US pilot Jimmie Angel, who recorded them in his log book on 16 Nov 1933, but are known to the Indians as Churun-Meru.

Largest waterfall

The greatest waterfall in the world on the basis of average annual flow is the Boyoma Falls in Zaïre, which have a mean flow rate of 17,000 m³/sec (600,000 cusec).

Above right
Lake Baikal in Siberia is fed by more than 300 rivers and has the greatest volume of any freshwater lake, containing roughly 20% of the Earth's total supply of freshwater. It is also both the deepest and the oldest lake in the world, dating back almost 25 million years.

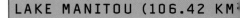

The Guaíra (Salto das Sete Quedas) on the Alto Paraná River between Brazil and Paraguay is known to have occasionally attained a flow rate of 50,000 m³/sec (1,750,000 cusec) before the closing of the Itaipú dam gates in 1982.

Widest waterfall

The Khône Falls in Laos in South-east Asia are 10.8 km (6¾ miles) wide and have a flood flow of 42,500 m³/sec (1,500,000 cusec). They are 15–21 m (50–70 ft) in height.

Lakes and inland seas

Largest lake

The largest inland sea or lake is the Caspian Sea, in Azerbaijan, Russia, Kazakhstan, Turkmenistan and Iran. The sea is 1,225 km (760 miles) long and covers a total area of 371,800 km² (143,550 miles²), some 143,200 km² (55,280 miles²), or 38.5%, of which is in Iran. It has a maximum depth of 1,025 m (3,360 ft), an estimated volume of 89,600 km³ (21,500 miles³) of saline water, and a surface that is 28.5 m (93 ft) below sea level.

Deepest lakes

Lake Baikal in eastern Siberia, Russia, is 620 km (385 miles) long and 32–74 km (20–46 miles) wide. In 1974, its Olkhon Crevice was measured by the Hydrographic Service of the Soviet Pacific Navy and found to have a depth of 1,637 m (5,371 ft), of which 1,181 m (3,875 ft) is below sea level.

The deepest lake in the United Kingdom is Loch Morar, Highland. Its surface is 9 m (30 ft) above sea level and it has an extreme depth of 310 m (1,017 ft).

The British lake with the greatest mean depth is Loch Ness, at 130 m (427 ft).

Highest lakes

The highest lake in the world is an unnamed lake in Tibet, at 34°16'N, 85°43'E. Located at

The largest lake in the United Kingdom is Lough Neagh, at 14.6 m (48 ft) above sea level in Northern Ireland. It is 29 km (18 miles) long, 17.7 km (11 miles) wide, and has an area of 381.73 km² (147⅖ miles²) and an extreme depth of 31 m (102 ft).

Largest lake within a lake

Covering 106.42 km² (41 1/10 miles²), Lake Manitou is situated on the world's largest lake island, Manitoulin Island, which has a total area of 2,766 km² (1,068 miles²) in the Canadian part of Lake Huron. Lake Manitou itself contains a number of islands.

Largest underground lake

The largest known underground lake is located within the Drachenhauchloch cave near Grootfontein, Namibia, and was discovered in 1986. A survey in April 1991 revealed the surface area of the lake to be 2.61 ha (6 45/100 acres). The lake is 66 m (217 ft) underground at its surface, and has a depth of 84 m (276 ft).

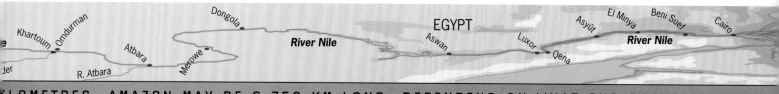

Dongola · EGYPT · El Minya · Beni Suef · Cairo · Asyût · River Nile · Aswan · Luxor · Qena · River Nile · Khartoum · Omdurman · Atbara · Merowe · R. Atbara

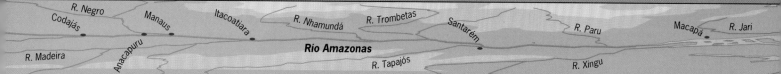

...ILOMETRES. AMAZON MAY BE 6,750 KM LONG, DEPENDING ON WHAT END POINT IS TAKEN

R. Negro · Codajás · Manaus · Itacoatiara · R. Nhamundá · R. Trombetas · Santarém · R. Paru · Macapá · R. Jari · R. Madeira · Anacapuru · Río Amazonas · R. Tapajós · R. Xingu

an altitude of about 5,800 m (19,000 ft), it has a maximum length of 8 km (5 miles) and a maximum width of 5 km (3 miles).

Burog Co, the world's highest named lake, lies just to the north of the highest lake, at an altitude of about 5,600 m (18,400 ft). Its maximum length is 17.7 km (11 miles) and its maximum width is 8 km (5 miles).

The highest lake in the United Kingdom is Lochan Buidhe, which is located at 1,100 m (3,600 ft) above sea level in the Cairngorms, Aberdeenshire. It covers an area of 7,600 m² (81,800 ft²).

Largest freshwater lake

Lake Superior, one of the North American Great Lakes, has a total surface area of 82,350 km² (31,800 miles²). Of this, 53,600 km² (20,700 miles²) are in the US states of Minnesota, Wisconsin and Michigan, and 27,750 km² (11,100 miles²) are in Ontario, Canada. The lake is 180 m (600 ft) above sea level.

The freshwater lake with the greatest volume is Lake Baikal in eastern Siberia, Russia, which has an estimated volume of 23,000 km³ (5,500 miles³).

Largest freshwater lochs

The largest lake in the United Kingdom, and the largest inland loch in Scotland, is Loch Lomond, which is situated in West Dunbartonshire, Argyll and Bute and Stirling, and is located approximately 7 m (23 ft) above sea level. The lake is 36.44 km (22 miles 1,126 yd) long and has a surface area of 71.2 km² (27½ miles²). Its greatest depth is 190 m (623 ft).

The British lake or loch with the greatest volume is Loch Ness, at 7,443 million m³ (262,845 million ft³). It reaches a depth of 240 m (788 ft).

Loch Ness is also the longest lake or loch in the United Kingdom, extending for a distance of 38.99 km (24 miles 405 yd). The three arms of the Y-shaped Loch Awe in Argyll and Bute, however, have a total length of 40.99 km (25 miles 827 yd).

Largest lagoon

Lagoa dos Patos, situated in Rio Grande do Sul in Brazil, is 280 km (174 miles) long, and covers an area of 9,850 km² (3,803 miles²) and has a maximum width of 70 km (44 miles). It is separated from the Atlantic Ocean by long sand strips.

Left
The Angel Falls, whose white waters tumble a distance of some 979 m (3,212 ft), is the highest waterfall in the world.

Dynamic Earth

KILAUEA CONSTANTLY DISCHARGES LAVA AND IS THE WORLD'S MOST ACTIVE VOLCANO

Right and below far right
Kilauea on Hawaii is the world's most active volcano, with a continuous extrusion of magma. Violent explosions are rare among the volcanoes of Hawaii.

Below centre
Shield volcanoes such as Mauna Loa in Hawaii consist of gentle slopes constructed from hundreds or thousands of successive lava flows and can extend for tens of kilometres. Mauna Loa is the largest active volcano.

Below
The greatest volcanic explosion in historic times occurred on Krakatoa in 1883. It was heard four hours later on the island of Rodrigues, 4,776 km (2,968 miles) away, as distinctly as "the roar of heavy guns".

Volcanoes

Greatest volcanic explosion

The greatest explosion in historic times occurred on 27 Aug 1883, when Krakatoa, an island in the Sunda Strait between Sumatra and Java, Indonesia, erupted, causing a tidal wave that wiped out 163 villages and killed a total of 36,380 people. Pumice was thrown 55 km (34 miles) high and dust fell 5,330 km (3,313 miles) away 10 days later. The explosion was heard over 8% of the Earth's surface and is estimated to have been approximately 26 times as powerful as the largest H-bomb test.

Greatest eruptions

The total volume of matter discharged during the eruption of Tambora, a volcano on the island of Sumbawa, Indonesia, on 5–10 April 1815, was 150–180 km³ (36–43 miles³). This compares with 20 km³ (5 miles³) ejected by Krakatoa. The energy of the eruption, which reduced the height of the island from 4,100 m (13,450 ft) to 2,850 m (9,350 ft) and formed a crater 8 km (5 miles) across, was 8.4×10^{19} joules.

The most violent of all documented volcanic events is the Taupo eruption in New Zealand *c.* AD 130, which is estimated to have ejected 30,000 million tonnes of pumice at 700 km/h (400 mph). It flattened an area of 16,000 km² (6,200 miles²). Less than 20% of the pumice

HIGHEST DEATH TOLL IN AN EARTHQUAKE IS AN ESTIMATED 830,000 PEOPLE IN

Largest volcanic crater 1,775 km²

carried up into the air fell within 200 km (125 miles) of the vent.

Longest lava flows
The longest lava flow in historic times was a mixture of *pahoehoe* ropey lava (twisted cord-like solidifications) and *aa* blocky lava that resulted from the eruption of Laki, south-east Iceland, in 1783. It flowed for a distance of 65–70 km (40½–43½ miles).

The largest known prehistoric flow is the Roza basalt flow in North America *c.* 15 million years ago. It was 300 km (190 miles) long, with an area of 40,000 km^2 (15,400 miles^2) and a volume of 1,250 km^3 (300 miles^3).

Most active volcano
Kilauea, on Hawaii, USA, has erupted continuously since 1983. Lava is discharged at a rate of 5 m^3 (7 yd^3) per second.

Largest active volcano
Mauna Loa, on Hawaii, is 4,170 m (13,680 ft) high, 120 km (75 miles) long and 50 km (31 miles) wide. It has a total volume of 42,500 km^3 (10,200 miles^3), 84.2% of which is below sea level. It averaged one eruption every 4½ years between 1843 and 1984. Mokuaweoweo, its volcano crater, covers 10.5 km^2 (4 miles^2) and descends to a depth of 150–180 m (500–600 ft).

Highest active volcano
Ojos del Salado, which reaches a height of 6,887 m (22,595 ft) on the frontier between Chile and Argentina, has fumaroles and can therefore be regarded as active.

Northernmost volcanoes
Mt Beerenberg, on the island of Jan Mayen at 71°05′N in the Greenland Sea, is the world's most northerly volcano. When it erupted in 1970, the 39 inhabitants, all men working on whaling stations, were evacuated.

The Ostenso seamount, situated just 556 km (346 miles) from the North Pole at 85°10′N, 133°W, was once volcanic.

Southernmost volcano
The world's southernmost active volcano is Mt Erebus on Ross Island in the Antarctic Ocean's Ross Sea.

Largest volcanic crater
Toba in north-central Sumatra, Indonesia, has the world's largest caldera, or volcanic crater, covering an area of 1,775 km^2 (685 miles^2).

Earthquakes
Strongest earthquake on the M_w scale
The Chilean shock of 22 May 1960 measured 9.5 on the M_w, or Kanamori, scale.

Highest death tolls
There were an estimated 830,000 fatalities in an earthquake that shook the Shaanxi, Shanxi and Henan provinces of China on 2 Feb 1556.

The highest death toll caused by an earthquake in modern times was the result of the Tangshan earthquake (Mag. M_s = 7.9) in eastern China on 28 July 1976. On 4 Jan 1977, the official death toll stood at 655,237, but this figure was subsequently adjusted to 750,000. In Nov 1979, the New China News Agency inexplicably reduced the toll to 242,000.

Highest British death toll
The record undisputed death toll in an earthquake in the United Kingdom is two. Apprentice Thomas Grey was struck by masonry falling from Christ's Hospital Church, near Newgate, London, at 6 p.m. on 6 April 1580. A young woman, Mabel Everet, died of her injuries four days later.

Material damage
The greatest physical devastation to have been caused by an earthquake was on 1 Sept 1923, on the Kanto plain, Japan (Mag. M_s = 8.2). In the cities of Tokyo and Yokohama, approximately 575,000 dwellings were destroyed. The official toll of people killed and missing in the earthquake and its resultant fires was 142,807.

Avalanches and landslides
Greatest avalanches
The greatest natural avalanches occur in the Himalayas, but they are rarely observed and there have been no estimates of their volume.

An estimated 3.5 million m^3 (120 million ft^3) of snow fell during an avalanche in the Italian Alps in 1885.

The eruption of Mt St Helens in Washington State, USA, on 18 May 1980 triggered an avalanche that was estimated to measure 2,800 million m^3 (96,000 million ft^3) and to travel at 400km/h (250 mph).

Worst avalanche
On 31 May 1970, approximately 18,000 people were killed by an avalanche in Yungay, Huascarán, Peru.

Worst landslide
A landslide triggered off by an earthquake in Gansu Province, China, on 16 Dec 1920, claimed the lives of 180,000 people.

Geysers
Tallest geysers
In 1903, the Waimangu ('black water') geyser in New Zealand erupted to a height of more than 460 m (1,500 ft) every 30–36 hours. In Aug 1903, four people were killed during a violent eruption, but the geyser fell inactive in late 1904 and has remained so ever since.

The world's tallest active geyser is Steamboat Geyser in Yellowstone National Park, Wyoming, USA. During the 1980s, it erupted at intervals of between 19 days and more than four years. There were periods in the 1960s when it erupted every 4–10 days. Its maximum height is 115 m (380 ft).

Greatest measured water discharge
The Giant Geyser in Yellowstone National Park, Wyoming, USA, was estimated to be emitting approximately 28,000–38,000 hl (616,000–836,000 gal) in the 1950s.

Below left
The surface-wave magnitude (M_s), commonly known as the Richter scale, is the most commonly used measure of the size (energy release) of an earthquake. However, this scale only measures one particular frequency of the vibrations caused by an earthquake. This frequency reaches a saturation point at a reading of about 8.6 M_s, causing all earthquakes over a this size to give similar readings. To remedy this the Japanese seismologist Hiroo Kanamori developed a scale for measuring earthquakes which takes into account the full spectrum of frequencies emitted by an earthquake— illustrated by the symbol M_w.

Below
Yellowstone National Park, the largest nature reserve in the USA, is situated on a wide plateau in the Rocky Mountains and contains more than 3,000 geysers and hot springs, including Morning Glory Geyser, shown here, and the record-breaking Steamboat Geyser and Giant Geyser.

OLONGED QUAKE IN THE SHAANXI, SHANXI AND HENAN PROVINCES OF CHINA, IN 1556

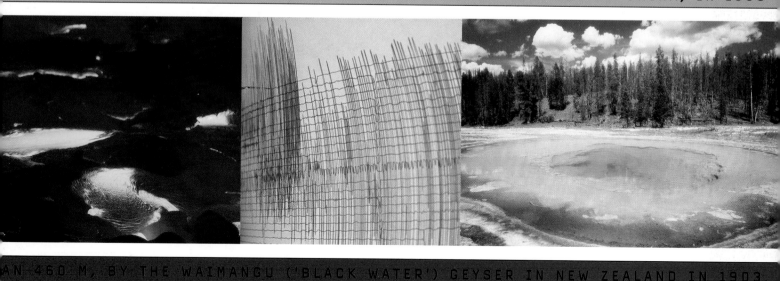

AN 460 M, BY THE WAIMANGU ('BLACK WATER') GEYSER IN NEW ZEALAND IN 1903

Weather

GREATEST TEMPERATURE VARIATION IN A SINGLE DAY IS 56°C

Right and below right
Death Valley, California, USA, is one of the hottest and driest places on Earth. The temperature often rises above 51.7°C (125°F), and temperatures in excess of 49°C (120°F) were sustained over a record 43 consecutive days.

Below far right
The Atacama Desert in Chile experiences virtually no rain and is the location of the world's longest drought.

The coldest permanently inhabited place in the world is the Siberian village of Oymyakon (63°16'N, 143°15'E) in Russia, which is at an altitude of 700 m (2,300 ft) and has a population of around 4,000. The temperature there reached –68°C (–90°F) in 1933. More recently, an unofficial report cited a new low of –72°C (–98°F).

The lowest temperature recorded in the United Kingdom was –27°C (–17°F), on 11 Feb 1895 and on 10 Jan 1982. Both instances were at Braemar, Aberdeenshire. The –31°C (–23°F) that was recorded at Blackadder, Scottish Borders, on 4 Dec 1879, and the –29°C (–20°F) recorded at Grantown-on-Spey, Highland, on 24 Feb 1955, were not recorded to official standards.

Polyus Nedostupnosti or 'Pole of Inaccessibility' (78°S, 96°E) in Antarctica is the coldest location in the world, with an extrapolated annual mean of –58°C (–72°F).

The coldest measured mean is –57°C (–70°F), at Plateau Station, Antarctica.

The coldest mean temperature recorded in the United Kingdom is 6.3°C (43.4°F), at Braemar, Aberdeenshire (based on readings taken between 1952 and 1981).

58°	54°	50°	46°	42°	38°	34°	30°	26°	22°	18°	14°	10°	6°

Temperature

Smallest temperature range
Between 1927 and 1935, the lowest temperature recorded at Garapan, on Saipan in the Mariana Islands, was 19.6°C (67.3°F). The highest was 31.4°C (88.5°F), giving an extreme range of 11.8°C (21.2°F).

Greatest temperature range
Temperatures in Verkhoyansk around the Siberian 'cold pole' in the east of Russia (67°33'N, 133°23'E) have ranged 105°C (188°F), from –68°C (–90°F) to 37°C (98°F).

The greatest temperature variation recorded in a single day is 56°C (100°F), in a fall from 7°C (44°F) to –49°C (–56°F) at Browning, Montana, USA, on 23–24 Jan 1916.

Highest shade temperature
At Al'Azīzīyah, Libya, a temperature of 58°C (136°F) was recorded on 13 Sept 1922.

In the United Kingdom, a temperature of 37.1°C (98.8°F) was recorded at Cheltenham, Glos, on 3 Aug 1990. The 38°C (100°F) reported from Tonbridge, Kent, was not recorded to official standards. It is estimated to be equivalent to 36–37°C (97–98°F).

Hottest place
The average mean temperature recorded at Dallol, Ethiopia, between 1960 and 1966 was 34°C (94°F).

In Death Valley, California, USA, maximum temperatures in excess of 49°C (120°F) were recorded on 43 consecutive days between 6 July and 17 Aug 1917.

Marble Bar, Western Australia, has had a maximum temperature of 49.2°C (120.5°F). Temperatures of 37.8°C (100°F) or higher were recorded there on a total of 160 consecutive days between 31 Oct 1923 and 7 April 1924.

At Wyndham, Western Australia, the temperature reached 32.2°C (90°F) or more on 333 days in 1946.

Lowest temperature
On 21 July 1983, a record low temperature of –89.2°C (–128.6°F) was registered in Vostok, Antarctica, at an altitude of 3,420 m (11,220 ft).

Sunshine and rain

Most sunshine
The annual average at Yuma, Arizona, USA, is 4,055 out of 4,456 possible hours of sun.

St Petersburg, Florida, USA, recorded 768 consecutive sunny days from 9 Feb 1967 to 17 March 1969.

Highest rainfall
A record 1,870 mm (73⅔ in) of rain fell within a 24-hour period at Cilaos, at an altitude of 1,200 m (3, 940 ft), on Réunion Island in the Indian Ocean, on 15 and 16 March 1952. This figure is equivalent to 7,554 tonnes of rain per acre.

The greatest rainfall within a 12-month period was at Cherrapunji, Meghalaya, India, where 26,461 mm (1,041¾ in) fell between 1 Aug 1860 and 31 July 1861.

WORLD'S SUNNIEST PLACE IS YUMA, ARIZONA, USA, WITH SUNSHINE F

WORLD'S COLDEST PLACE HAS AN AVERAGE TEMPERATURE OF -58°C

By average annual rainfall, the wettest place is Mawsynram, Meghalaya State, India, which has 11,873 mm (467½ in) of rain per annum.

Most rainy days
Mt Wai-'ale-'ale on Kauai, Hawaii, has had as many as 350 rainy days per annum.

Least rainfall
The annual mean rainfall on the Pacific coast of Chile between Arica and Antofagasta is less than 0.1 mm (1/250 in).

Longest drought
The Atacama Desert in northern Chile experiences virtually no rain, although several times a century a squall strikes a small area.

Longest-lasting rainbow
A rainbow was visible for six hours over Sheffield, S Yorkshire, UK, on 14 March 1994, from 9 a.m. to 3 p.m.

Wind
Windiest place
Gales in Commonwealth Bay, Antarctica, can reach a speed of 320 km/h (200 mph).

Snow and hail
Greatest snowfall
Between 19 Feb 1971 and 18 Feb 1972, 31,102 mm (1,224½ in) of snow fell at Paradise, Mt Rainier, Washington State, USA.

The record snowfall in a single snowstorm is the 4,800 mm (189 in) that fell at Mt Shasta Ski Bowl, California, USA, between 13 and 19 Feb 1959.

The greatest snowfall within 24 hours is 1,930 mm (76 in) at Silver Lake, Colorado, USA, on 14–15 April 1921.

The greatest depth of snow ever recorded was 1,146 cm (37 ft 7 in) at Tamarac, California, USA, in March 1911.

Hail
The heaviest hailstones on record, weighing up to 1 kg (2 lb 3 oz), are reported to have killed 92 people in the Gopalganj district of Bangladesh on 14 April 1986.

The worst hailstorm on record claimed the lives of 246 people in Moradabad, Uttar Pradesh, India, on 20 April 1888.

White Christmases
It has snowed on eight Christmas days in London, UK, since 1900: in 1906, 1917, 1923, 1927, 1938, 1956, 1970 and 1981.

Storms
Thunder
In Tororo, Uganda, an average of 251 days of thunder per year was recorded in 1967–76.

The record number of days of thunder in a specific place in a calendar year in the United Kingdom is 38. The first time was in 1912, at Stonyhurst, Lancs; the second was in 1967, at Huddersfield, W Yorkshire.

Lightning
Ex-park-ranger Roy C. Sullivan of Virginia, USA, was struck by lightning a total of seven times. In 1942 he lost a big toe nail, in July 1969 he lost his eyebrows, in July 1970 he seared his left shoulder, in April 1972 his hair was set on fire, in Aug 1973 his hair was set alight again and his legs seared, and in June 1976 he injured his ankle. On 25 June 1977, Sullivan was sent to Waynesboro Hospital with chest and stomach burns after being struck

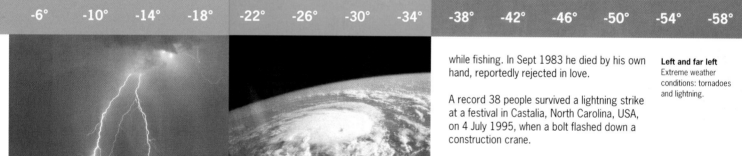

-6° -10° -14° -18° -22° -26° -30° -34° -38° -42° -46° -50° -54° -58°

while fishing. In Sept 1983 he died by his own hand, reportedly rejected in love.

A record 38 people survived a lightning strike at a festival in Castalia, North Carolina, USA, on 4 July 1995, when a bolt flashed down a construction crane.

The most devastating lightning strike killed 81 passengers on a Boeing 707 jet liner downed near Elkton, Maryland, USA, on 8 Dec 1963.

Left and far left
Extreme weather conditions: tornadoes and lightning.

Highest surface wind speed
A record surface wind speed of 371 km/h (231 mph) was recorded at Mt Washington, New Hampshire, USA, on 12 April 1934.

The highest wind speed at a low altitude was registered on 8 March 1972 at the USAF base at Thule in Greenland, when a peak speed of 333 km/h (207 mph) was recorded.

Tornadoes
The most tornadoes to have occurred within 24 hours is 148 in the southern and mid-western states of the USA on 3–4 April 1974.

A tornado in Shaturia, Bangladesh, on 26 April 1989, killed around 1,300 people.

The highest speed measured in a tornado is 450 km/h (280 mph) at Wichita Falls, Texas, USA, on 2 April 1958.

Left
Antarctica is the world's coldest continent. A record low temperature of −89.2°C (−128.6°F) was registered in Vostok in July 1983.

% OF POSSIBLE HOURS

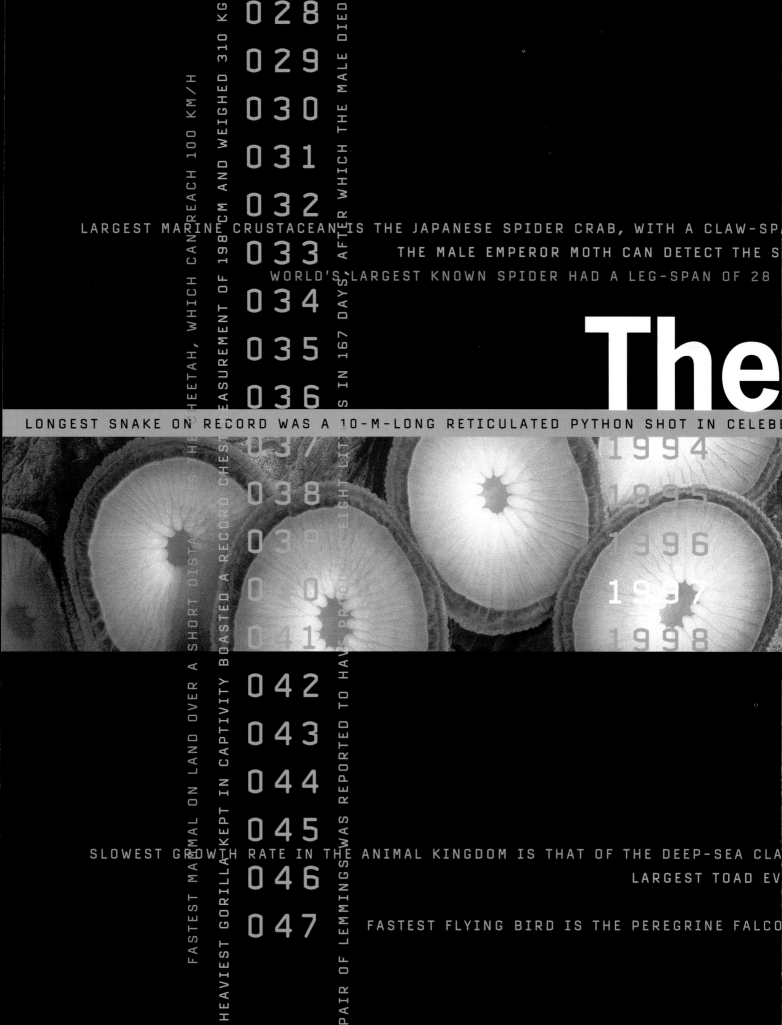

028
029
030
031
032
033
034
035
036
037
038
039
040
041
042
043
044
045
046
047

The

1994
1995
1996
1997
1998

LARGEST MARINE CRUSTACEAN IS THE JAPANESE SPIDER CRAB, WITH A CLAW-SPA

THE MALE EMPEROR MOTH CAN DETECT THE S

WORLD'S LARGEST KNOWN SPIDER HAD A LEG-SPAN OF 28

LONGEST SNAKE ON RECORD WAS A 10-M-LONG RETICULATED PYTHON SHOT IN CELEB

SLOWEST GROWTH RATE IN THE ANIMAL KINGDOM IS THAT OF THE DEEP-SEA CLA

LARGEST TOAD EV

FASTEST FLYING BIRD IS THE PEREGRINE FALCO

CHEETAH, WHICH CAN REACH 100 KM/H

EASUREMENT OF 198 CM AND WEIGHED 310 KG

AFTER WHICH THE MALE DIED

S IN 167 DAYS

FASTEST MAMMAL ON LAND OVER A SHORT DISTA

HEAVIEST GORILLA KEPT IN CAPTIVITY BOASTED A RECORD CHEST

EIGHT BROUG

PAIR OF LEMMINGS WAS REPORTED TO HAVE

living world

Dinosaurs and prehistoric life

LARGEST KNOWN DINOSAUR EGGS WERE ABOUT 30 CM LONG AND 25.5 CM IN DIAMETER

Right
Long believed to be the largest ever predatory dinosaur, *Tyrannosaurus rex* has been superseded by the newly discovered *Carcharodontosaurus saharicus.*

Largest footprints 1.36 m

Dinosaurs

First scientifically described dinosaur
The bipedal flesh-eater *Megalosaurus bucklandi* ('great fossil lizard') was described in 1824 after remains were found by workmen in a slate quarry near Woodstock, Oxon, UK.

Earliest dinosaur
Eoraptor lunensis ('dawn stealer') was named in 1993 from a skeleton found in rocks dated at 228 million years old in the Andes foothills in Argentina. The dinosaur was 1 m (39 in) long and the most primitive of the theropods (meat-eaters), lacking the dual-hinged jaw present in other members.

Largest dinosaur
The largest ever land animals were sauropod dinosaurs—long-necked, long-tailed, four-legged plant-eaters that lumbered around most of the world in the Jurassic and Cretaceous periods, 208–65 million years ago.

Largest predatory dinosaur
Skeletal parts and a huge skull measuring 1.62 m (5 ft 3¾ in), recently discovered in the Moroccan Sahara, establish *Carcharodontosaurus saharicus* ('shark-toothed reptile from the Sahara') as the largest flesh-eating dinosaur. The new finds suggest that the creature, which lived during the Cretaceous Period (100–65 million years ago), was about 13.7 m (45 ft) long.

Heaviest dinosaurs
The largest known sauropods appear to have weighed 50–80 tonnes, but this may not be the upper limit for a land vertebrate. Calculations suggest that some dinosaurs approached the maximum weight possible for a terrestrial animal of 120 tonnes. At weights greater than this, the animals would have needed such massive legs that they would not have been able to move.

The heaviest dinosaurs were probably the titanosaurid

Antarctosaurus giganteus ('Antarctic lizard') from Argentina and India (at 40–80 tonnes); the brachiosaurid *Brachiosaurus altithorax* (at 45–55 tonnes); and the diplodocids *Seismosaurus halli* ('earthquake lizard') and *Supersaurus vivianae* (50–100 tonnes). A new titanosaurid from Argentina, *Argentinocaurus*, was estimated in 1994 to have weighed up to 100 tonnes, based on its vast vertebrae.

Tallest dinosaur
The tallest and largest dinosaur species known from a complete skeleton is *Brachiosaurus brancai* ('arm lizard') from the Tendaguru site in Tanzania, dated as Late Jurassic (150–144 million years old).

A skeleton was constructed from the remains of several individuals and displayed in 1937. Now in the Museum de Naturkunde, Berlin, Germany, it is the largest mounted dinosaur skeleton with a length of 22.2 m (72 ft 9½ in) and a raised-head height of 14 m (46 ft).

Longest dinosaurs
Footprints suggest that the brachiosaurid *Breviparopus* may have been the longest vertebrate, at 48 m (157 ft) in length.

In 1994, a diplodocid named *Seismosaurus halli* from New Mexico, USA, was estimated to be 39–52 m (128–170 ft) long, based on comparisons of individual bones.

The longest dinosaur known from a complete skeleton is *Diplodocus carnegii* ('double beam'), assembled from remains found in Wyoming, USA, in 1899. It was 26.7 m (87 ft 6 in) long and probably weighed 12 tonnes.

On the evidence of a haemal arch (the bone running beneath the vertebrae of the tail)

GIANT MOA MAY HAVE BEEN THE TALLEST PREHISTOR[

found on the Isle of Wight, UK, the brachiosaur *Pelorosaurus* ('monstrous lizard') may be the longest British dinosaur, at 24 m (80 ft).

Smallest dinosaur
The chicken-sized *Compsognathus* ('pretty jaw') of southern Germany and south-east France, and an undescribed plant-eating fabrosaurid from Colorado, USA, were both 70–75 cm (27½–29½ in) in length from the snout to the tip of the tail and weighed approximately 3 kg (6 lb 10 oz) and 6.8 kg (15 lb) respectively.

Fastest dinosaur
The size of and distance between footprints found in the Morrison formation from the Late Jurassic Period in Texas, USA, in 1981, allowed scientists to calculate that a carnivorous dinosaur had been moving at 40 km/h (25 mph).

Some ornithomimids moved at speeds in excess of 40 km/h (25 mph), and the large-brained, 100-kg (220-lb) *Dromiceiomimus* ('emu mimic lizard') of the Late Cretaceous of Alberta, Canada, could probably outsprint an ostrich, which has a top speed of more than 60 km/h (37.3 mph).

Largest footprints
In 1932, gigantic footprints of a large bipedal hadrosaurid ('duckbill') 1.36 m (53½ in) in length and 81 cm (32 in) wide were discovered in Salt Lake City, Utah, USA.

Largest skull
The skulls of the long-frilled ceratopsids were the largest of all known land animals. The long-frilled *Torosaurus* ('piercing lizard'), a herbivore about 7.6 m (25 ft) in total length and weighing up to 8 tonnes, had a skull that was up to 3 m (9 ft 10 in) in length (including fringe) and weighed up to 2 tonnes. It ranged from Montana to Texas, USA.

Left
Diplodocus and *Triceratops* skeletons stand side by side, on display at the Natural History Museum, London. *Diplodocus* is perhaps the dinosaur most commonly displayed in museums.

FASTEST DINOSAURS ARE THOUGHT TO HAVE MOVED AT MORE THAN 60 KM/H

Largest claws
The therizinosaurids ('scythe lizards') from the Late Cretaceous of the Nemegt Basin, Mongolia, had the largest claws of any known animal. In the case of *Therizinosaurus cheloniformis* they measured up to 91 cm (36 in) along the outer curve.

In the United Kingdom, a 30-cm-long (12-in) claw-bone was found by amateur fossil collector William Walker near Dorking, Surrey, in Jan 1983. The claw was later identified as having possibly belonged to a spinosaur with an overall length of more than 9 m (29 ft 6 in), an estimated weight of 2 tonnes, and a bipedal height of 3–4 m (9–13 ft). It was also distinguished from other theropods by having 128 teeth instead of the usual 64. This enigma, said to be the most important dinosaur fossil found in Europe this century, was named *Baryonyx walkeri* ('heavy claw').

IRD, AT UP TO 3.7 M HIGH

Largest eggs
The largest known dinosaur eggs are those of *Hypselosaurus priscus* ('high ridge lizard'), a 12-m-long (40-ft) titanosaurid which lived about 80 million years ago. Examples found in the Durance valley near Aix-en-Provence, France, in Oct 1961 would have been about 30 cm (12 in) long (about the height of this page), with a diameter of 25.5 cm (10 in) and a capacity of 3.3 litres (5⅘ pt).

Prehistoric life
Largest predator
The largest ever land predator may have been an alligator found in rocks dated at 8 million years old on the banks of the River Amazon. Estimates from a skull 1.5 m (5 ft) long, complete with 10-cm-long (4-in) teeth, indicate a length of 12 m (40 ft) and a weight of about 18 tonnes, making it larger than the fearsome *Tyrannosaurus rex*. The creature was subsequently identified as a giant example of *Purussaurus brasiliensis*, a species named in 1892 on the basis of smaller specimens.

Largest mammal
The largest land mammal on record is *Indricotherium* (*Baluchitherium* or *Paraceratherium*), a long-necked, hornless rhinocerotid that roamed across western Asia and Europe about 35 million years ago. A restoration in the American Museum of Natural History, New York City, USA, measures 5.41 m (17 ft 9 in) to the top of the shoulder hump and has a total length of 11.27 m (37 ft). The most likely maximum weight of this browser was revised from 34 tonnes to 11–20 tonnes in 1993.

Largest prehistoric bird
The flightless *Dromornis stirtoni*, a huge emu-like creature that lived in central Australia between 15 million and 25,000 years ago, may have been the largest prehistoric bird. Fossil leg bones found near Alice Springs in 1974 indicate that the bird must have stood approximately 3 m (10 ft) tall and weighed about 500 kg (1,100 lb).

The giant moa *Dinornis maximus* of New Zealand may have been taller than *Dromornis stirtoni*, possibly attaining a height of 3.7 m (12 ft). It weighed about 227 kg (500 lb).

The largest known flying bird was the giant teratorn (*Argentavis magnificens*), which lived in Argentina 6–8 million years ago. Fossil remains at a site 160 km (100 miles) west of Buenos Aires in 1979 indicate that this vulture-like bird had a wingspan of between 6 m (19 ft 8 in) and 7.6 m (25 ft) and weighed about 80 kg (176 lb).

Largest prehistoric fish
No prehistoric fish larger than living species has yet been discovered. Modern estimates suggest that the largest fish in prehistoric times was the great shark *Carcharodon megalodon*, which abounded in middle and late Tertiary seas 50–4.5 million years ago. Recent studies suggest that it attained a maximum length of 13.7 m (45 ft).

Longest prehistoric snake
The python-like *Gigantophis garstini* inhabited what is now Egypt about 38 million years ago. Parts of a spinal column and a small piece of jaw discovered at Fayum in the Western Desert indicate an approximate length of 11 m (36 ft), which is 1 m (3 ft 3 in) longer than the longest present-day snake.

Left
The longest complete dinosaur skeleton is a 26.7-m (87-ft 6-in) *Diplodocus carnegii*.

Mammal dimensions

Right
The world's tallest mammal is the giraffe, which inhabits sub-Saharan Africa.

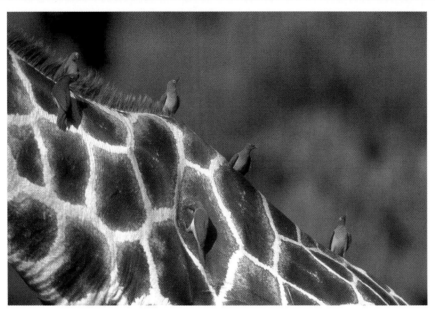

Mammals

Largest mammal
The blue whale (*Balaenoptera musculus*) is the heaviest and longest animal on earth. Female adults have an average length of 26.2 m (86 ft) and body weights of 90–120 tonnes. Newborn calves are 6–8 m (20–26 ft) long and weigh up to 3 tonnes. After a year, they weigh 26 tonnes.

The largest mammal in the United Kingdom is the red deer (*Cervus elaphus*). Stags stand up to 1.22 m (4 ft) tall at the shoulder and weigh 104–113 kg (230–250 lb). The heaviest on record was a stag weighing 238 kg (525 lb), killed at Glenfiddich, Moray, in 1831.

Heaviest mammal
A female blue whale 190 tonnes in weight and 27.6 m (90 ft 6 in) in length was caught in the Southern Ocean on 20 March 1947.

Longest mammal
A female blue whale measuring 33.58 m (110 ft 2½ in) landed in 1909 at Grytviken, South Georgia, in the South Atlantic.

Largest land mammal
The average bull of the African bush elephant (*Loxodonta africana africana*) is between 3 and 3.7 m (9 ft 10 in and 12 ft 2 in) tall at the shoulder and weighs between 4 and 7 tonnes. The largest specimen on record is a bull shot near Mucusso, Angola, in Nov 1974, which had an overall length of 10.67 m (35 ft) and a weight calculated to be 12.24 tonnes.

Largest carnivorous land mammals
The largest carnivorous land mammals are polar bears (*Ursus maritimus*). Adult males typically weigh 400–600 kg (880–1,320 lb), and have a nose-to-tail length of 2.4–2.6 m (7 ft 10 in–8 ft 6 in).

The male Kodiak bear (*Ursus arctos middendorffi*), found on Kodiak Island and the adjacent islands of Afognak and Shuyak in the Gulf of Alaska, USA, is usually shorter than the polar bear but is more robustly built.

In 1960, a polar bear estimated to weigh around 1,000 kg (2,210 lb) was shot in the Chukchi Sea, west of Kotzebue, Alaska, USA. It was said to measure 3.4 m (11 ft 6 in) from nose to tail over the contours of the body, 1.5 m (4 ft 11 in) around the body and 43 cm (17 in) around the paws. It is probably the heaviest bear taken in the wild.

A Kodiak bear named Goliath at the Space Farms Zoo in Sussex, New Jersey, USA, reportedly exceeded 900 kg (1,900 lb) in weight in the early 1980s.

Tallest mammal
Adult male giraffes (*Giraffa camelopardalis*)—found in sub-Saharan Africa—have an average height of between 4.7 and 5.3 m (15 ft 5 in and 17 ft 5 in). The tallest recorded specimen is a Masai bull (*G. c. tippelskirchi*) named George, brought to Chester Zoo, Cheshire, UK, from Kenya in 1959. His 'horns' almost grazed the roof of the 6.1-m-high (20-ft) Giraffe house when he was nine years old.

THE PAWS OF THE SIBERIA

Largest toothed mammal
The 5-m-long (16-ft 5-in) lower jaw of a sperm whale (*Physeter macrocephalus*), exhibited in the British Museum, belonged to a bull that was reputedly almost 25.6 m (84 ft) long.

The longest officially measured specimen was a male sperm whale measuring 20.7 m (67 ft 11 in), captured in the summer of 1950 off the Kurile Islands in the north-west Pacific.

LARGEST RODENT WAS A CAGE-FAT CAPYBARA WEIGHING 113 KG

The capybara has a head-and-body length of 1.0–1.4 m (3 ft 3 in–4 ft 6 in).

The southern elephant seal is the largest known species of pinniped in the world.

Smallest mammal

Bumblebee bats—or Kitti's hog-nosed bats—(*Craseonycteris thonglongyai*), live in caves on the Kwae Noi River, Kanchanaburi Province, south-west Thailand. They have a head-and-body length of 29–33 mm (1⁷⁄₅₀–1³⁄₁₀ in), a wingspan of 150–160 mm (5⁹⁄₁₀–6³⁄₁₀ in) and weigh 1.7–2.0 g (³⁄₅₀–⁷⁄₁₀₀ oz).

The smallest non-flying mammal is Savi's white-toothed, or pygmy, shrew (*Suncus etruscus*). It has a head-and-body length of

In July 1970, a weight of 375 kg (827 lb) and a shoulder height of 1.11 m (3 ft 8 in) was reported for a black-maned lion named Simba at Colchester Zoo, Essex, UK.

Primates

Largest primate

The male gorilla (*Gorilla gorilla*) of eastern Zaïre has a bipedal standing height of up to 1.8 m (5 ft 11 in) and can weigh as much as 175 kg (386 lb).

3.7 m (12 ft) and weigh between 2,000 and 3,500 kg (4,400 and 7,720 lb). The largest accurately measured specimen was a bull that weighed at least 4 tonnes and was 6.5 m (21 ft 4 in) long after flensing (stripping of the blubber or skin).

The largest reported live pinniped is a bull nicknamed Stalin recorded off Georgia, USA, on 14 Oct 1989. It weighs 2,662 kg (5,869 lb) and is 5.10 m (16 ft 9 in) long.

Smallest pinniped

The smallest pinniped is the Galapagos fur seal (*Arctocephalus galapagoensis*). Adult females average 1.2 m (3 ft 11 in) in length and weigh about 27 kg (60 lb). Males are usually larger, averaging 1.5 m (4 ft 11 in) in length and weighing around 64 kg (141 lb).

Rodents

Largest rodent

The capybara (*Hydrochoerus hydrochaeris*) of northern South America has a head-and-body length of 1.0–1.4 m (3 ft 3 in–4 ft 7 in) and can weigh up to 66 kg (145 lb). One cage-fat specimen reached 113 kg (250 lb).

Smallest rodent

The Baluchistan pygmy jerboa (*Salpingotus michaelis*) from Pakistan has a head-and-body length of as little as 3.6 cm (1⁷⁄₁₆ in), and a tail length of 7.2 cm (2¹³⁄₁₆ in). Its 1.8–1.9-cm-long (¾-in) hind feet (an adaptation for jumping) are enormous in relation to its size.

Left
At only 24.5–38 g (1⁷⁄₂₀–1³⁄₂₀ oz) in weight, the western rufous mouse lemur—the world's smallest primate—is only slightly larger than an overweight mouse. It tends to freeze when it is spotted, and is therefore easy to approach in the wild.

Below
The paws of the Siberian tiger—the largest member of the cat family—measure 100 mm across the pad and 150 mm across the width of the toes.

...GER ARE 100 MM ACROSS THE PAD AND 150 MM ACROSS THE WIDTH OF THE TOES

36–52 mm (1⁷⁄₁₆–2¹⁄₁₆ in), a tail length of 24–29 mm (1⁵⁄₁₆–1¹⁄₁₆ in) and weighs 1.5–2.5 g (¹⁄₂₀–⁹⁄₁₀₀ oz). It lives along the coast of the Mediterranean, as far east as Sri Lanka and as far south as Cape Province, South Africa.

Felines

Largest feline

The male Siberian tiger (*Panthera tigris altaica*) averages 3.15 m (10 ft 4 in) in length from the nose to the tip of the extended tail, stands 99–107 cm (39–42 in) at the shoulder and weighs about 265 kg (585 lb).

An Indian tiger (*Panthera tigris tigris*) shot in northern Uttar Pradesh State, India, in 1967, weighed 389 kg (858 lb). An average male weighs 190 kg (420 lb).

Smallest feline

The rusty-spotted cat (*Prionailurus rubiginosus*) of southern India and Sri Lanka has a head-and-body length of 35–48 cm (13¾–18⅞ in), and an average weight of 1.1 kg (2 lb 7 oz) for the female and 1.5–1.6 kg (3 lb 5 oz–3 lb 8 oz) for the male.

Heaviest lion

The heaviest wild African lion (*Panthera leo leo*) on record was shot in South Africa in 1936. It weighed 313 kg (690 lb).

Tallest primate

The greatest height (top of crest to heel) recorded for a wild gorilla is 1.95 m (6 ft 5 in) for an eastern lowland bull shot in the eastern Congo (now Zaïre) on 16 May 1938.

Heaviest primate

The heaviest gorilla kept in captivity was N'gagia, a male from an unidentified subspecies who died in San Diego Zoo, California, USA, in Jan 1944, at the age of 18. His peak weight was 310 kg (683 lb) in 1943. He was 1.72 m (5 ft 7¾ in) tall and boasted a record chest measurement of 198 cm (78 in).

Smallest primate

The western rufous mouse lemur of eastern Madagascar was thought to be extinct until its rediscovery in 1993. These tiny creatures have a head-and-body length of 6.2 cm (2⅖ in) and a tail length of 13.6 cm (5⅓ in).

Pinnipeds

Largest pinniped

The largest of the 34 known species of pinniped is the southern elephant seal (*Mirounga leonina*), found mainly on subantarctic islands. Bulls typically grow to a length of 5.8 m (19 ft) from the tip of the inflated snout to the tips of the outstretched tail flippers. They have a maximum girth of

Mammals

A RUNAWAY RED DEER REGISTERED 67.5 KM/H ON A POLICE RADAR SPEED-TRAP

Right
At certain times of the year, polar bears have a higher fat intake than any other mammal. They are also the most carnivorous bears, subsisting almost entirely on seals.

Sound and motion

Loudest animal sound

The low-frequency pulses that blue whales (*Balaenoptera musculus*) and fin whales (*B. physalus*) make when communicating with one another have been measured at up to 188 decibels, making them the loudest sounds emitted by any living source. Specialist equipment has detected the pulses from a distance of 850 km (530 miles).

Deepest dives

A bull sperm whale (*Physeter macrocephalus*) was killed 160 km (100 miles) south of Durban, South Africa, in 1969 after surfacing from a dive lasting 1 hr 52 min. Inside its stomach were two small sharks swallowed an hour earlier, of a type found only on the seafloor. As the water in the area is more than 3,193 m (10,473 ft) deep for a radius of 48–64 km (30–40 miles), it may be that the sperm whale can descend to a depth of more than 3,000 m (9,800 ft) when seeking food.

The deepest authenticated dive was to a depth of 2,000 m (6,560 ft), by a bull sperm whale off the coast of Dominica in the Caribbean in 1991. It lasted 1 hr 13 min.

Fastest marine mammal

In 1958, a bull killer whale (*Orcinus orca*) was registered travelling at a speed of 55.5 km/h (34.5 mph) in the eastern North Pacific. Similar speeds have been reported in Dall's porpoises (*Phocoenoides dalli*) when moving in short bursts.

Fastest land mammals

Up to a distance of 550 m (600 yd), the cheetah (*Acinonyx jubatus*), which lives on the open plains of east Africa and parts of Asia, has a probable maximum speed of 100 km/h (60 mph) on level ground.

The pronghorn antelope (*Antilocapra americana*) of the western USA, south-western Canada and parts of northern Mexico, is the fastest land animal over a long distance. It

BIGGEST MAMMAL COLONY EVAR (MOST POPULOUS)

has been seen to travel at 56 km/h (35 mph) for 6 km (4 miles), at 67 km/h (42 mph) for 1.6 km (1 mile) and at 88.5 km/h (55 mph) for 0.8 km (½ mile).

The roe deer (*Capreolus capreolus*) is the fastest land mammal in the United Kingdom. It can cruise at 40–48 km/h (25–30 mph) for more than 32 km (20 miles), with occasional bursts of up to 64 km/h (40 mph).

In Oct 1970, a red deer (*Cervus elaphus*) charging through Stalybridge, Greater Manchester, UK, registered 67.5 km/h (42 mph) on a police radar speed-trap.

Slowest mammal

The three-toed sloth (*Bradypus tridactylus*) of tropical South America has an average ground speed of 1.8–2.4 m (6–8 ft) per minute or 0.1–0.16 km/h (0.07–0.1 mph), but in the trees it can accelerate to 4.6 m (15 ft) per minute or 0.27 km/h (0.17 mph).

Sleepiest mammals

Some armadillos (Dasypodidae), opossums (Didelphidae) and sloths (Bradypodidae and Megalonychidae) spend up to 80% of their lives sleeping or dozing. The least active of all mammals are probably the three species of three-toed sloths in the genus *Bradypus*.

Most fearless mammal

The ratel or honey badger (*Mellivora capensis*) will defend itself against animals of any size, especially if they dare to wander too close to its breeding burrow. It has good reason to be brave: its skin is so tough that it is impervious to the stings of bees, the quills of porcupines and the bites of most snakes. It is also so loose that if the creature is held by the scruff of the neck, by a hyena or leopard for example, it can turn inside its skin and bite the attacker until it lets go.

Habitat and distribution

Highest altitude

The large-eared pika (*Ochtona macrotis*) has been recorded at a record height of 6,130 m (20,106 ft) in mountain ranges in Asia.

The yak (*Bos mutus*) of Tibet and the Sichuanese Alps, China, climbs to an altitude of 6,100 m (20,000 ft) when foraging.

Lowest altitude

A colony of 1,000 little brown bats (*Myotis lucifugus*) spends the winter at a record depth of 1,160 m (3,805 ft) in a zinc mine in New York, USA. The species normally roosts at a depth of about 200 m (660 ft).

Largest colony

The black-tailed prairie dog (*Cynomys ludovicianus*), a rodent of the family Sciuridae

Killer whales are perhaps the world's fastest marine mammals, reaching speeds of up to 55.5 km/h (34.5 mph).

Fastest land mammal 100 km/h

from the western USA and northern Mexico, builds exceptionally large colonies. A 'town' discovered in 1901 contained approximately 400 million individuals and covered about 61,440 km² (24,000 miles²)—almost the size of the Republic of Ireland. It is the largest mammal colony ever recorded.

Diet

Most fatty diet
The diet of the polar bear (*Ursus maritimus*) in spring and early summer consists of recently weaned ringed seal pups, which can be up to 50% fat. From April to July, the seals are in such plentiful supply that the bears sometimes feed only on the fat below the skin and leave the rest of the carcass untouched.

Fussiest eater
The koala (*Phascolarctos cinereus*) of eastern Australia feeds almost exclusively on eucalyptus leaves. It browses regularly on only half a dozen of the 500 species and prefers certain individual trees above others. It is even choosy when it comes to specific leaves, sometimes sifting through up to 9 kg

THE REPUBLIC OF IRELAND

(20 lb) of leaves every day to find the 0.5 kg (1¼ lb) that it consumes.

Birth and life

Longest gestation period
The Asiatic elephant (*Elephas maximus*) has a gestation period averaging 609 days (over 20 months), and sometimes lasting for as long as 760 days—more than 2½ times that of humans.

Shortest gestation period
A gestation period of just 12–13 days is common in several species, including the Virginia opossum (*Didelphis virginiana*) of North America and the water opossum or yapok (*Chironectes minimus*) of South America. Gestation periods of eight days have been recorded in some of these species.

Earliest pregnancy
The female Norway lemming (*Lemmus lemmus*) of Scandinavia can become pregnant at the age of 14 days. The gestation period is 16 to 23 days, and litter size varies from one to 13. A single pair of these prolific animals was reported to have produced eight litters in 167 days, after which the male died.

Most dangerous love life
The male brown antechinus (*Antechinus stuartii*), a marsupial mouse that inhabits eastern Australia, has an insatiable sexual appetite. Every year, the entire adult male population goes on the rampage for two weeks in a desperate bid to mate with as many females as possible. They are so busy chasing females and fighting rival males that they do not eat, and all die within days, due to starvation, ulcers or infection.

Oldest mammals
No land mammals live as long as human beings (*Homo sapiens*), but the Asiatic elephant (*Elephas maximus*) probably comes closest. The greatest verified age is 78 years, for a cow elephant named 'Modoc', who died at Santa Clara, California, USA, on 17 July 1975, of complications following surgery for an ingrowing toenail.

Bowhead whales (*Balaena mysticetus*) may live for more than 100 years. The evidence for this is provided by a hunted bowhead in Alaska, which was recently found to have two stone harpoon blades embedded in its blubber. The use of such harpoons ended a century ago, so the animal must have been at least a few years old when it cheated death the first time, and more than 100 years old when it succumbed the second time.

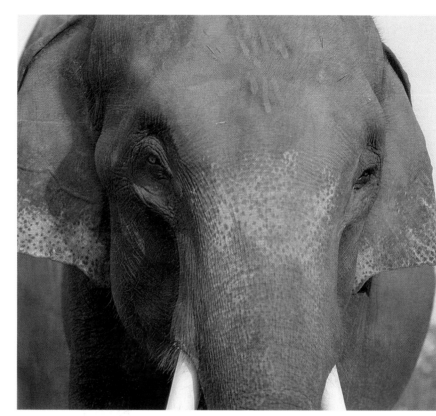

Left
The Asiatic elephant is probably the longest-lived terrestrial mammal after human beings and has the longest gestation period of any mammal. Most Asian elephants live to the age of 55–70 and there are credible reports of specimens living for longer than 80 years.

FEMALE NORWAY LEMMING CAN GET PREGNANT AT THE AGE OF 14 DAYS

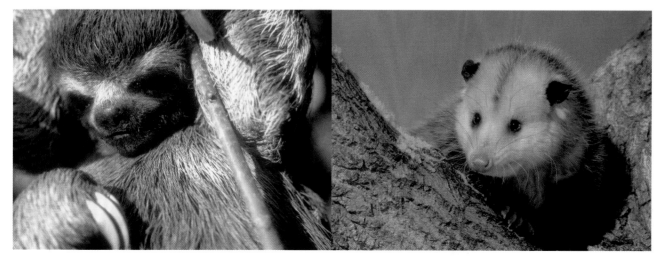

Far left
Certain sloth species are among the least active mammals, with a metabolic rate only 40–45% of that expected for their size. They spend more of their lives upside down than any other mammal, eating, sleeping, travelling, mating and giving birth while hanging down from branches.

Left
Opossums are among the world's sleepiest mammals. Some species spend as much as 80% of their lives asleep.

Domestic animals

Dogs

Largest dogs
The heaviest breeds of domestic dog (*Canis familiaris*) are the Old English mastiff and the St Bernard. Males of both species often weigh 77–91 kg (170–200 lb).

Tallest dog
The tallest dog on record is *Shamgret Danzas* (b. 1975), a great Dane owned by Wendy and Keith Comley of Milton Keynes, Bucks, UK. He stood 105.4 cm (41½ in) tall, or 106.6 cm (42 in) with hackles raised, and had a peak weight of 108 kg (238 lb).

Smallest dogs
A matchbox-sized Yorkshire terrier owned by Arthur Marples, of Lancs, UK, stood 6.3 cm (2½ in) at the shoulder and was 9.5 cm (3¾ in) long from the tip of its nose to the root of its tail. It weighed 113 g (4 oz) and died in 1945, at almost two years old.

The smallest living dog is 'Big Boss', a Yorkie owned by Dr Chai Khanchanakom of Bangkok, Thailand. On his first birthday on 7 Dec 1995, he was 11.94 cm (4⁷⁄₁₀ in) tall and 12.95 cm (5¹⁄₁₀ in) long, and weighed 481 g (1 lb 1 oz).

Oldest dogs
The greatest reliably recorded age for a dog is 29 years 5 months, for an Australian cattle-dog by the name of 'Bluey', owned by Les Hall of Rochester, Victoria, Australia.

The oldest dog in the United Kingdom was a Welsh collie named 'Taffy', which was owned by Evelyn Brown of West Bromwich, W Midlands, and lived for 27 years 313 days.

Richest dog
Ella Wendel of New York, USA, left £15 million to her standard poodle 'Toby' in 1931.

Longest-serving guide dog
'Cindy-Cleo', a Labrador-retriever owned by Aron Barr of Tel Aviv, Israel, served as a guide dog for 14 years and eight months.

Largest dog walk
The 4.8-km (3-mile) 'Great North Dog Walk' held on 19 May 1996 in South Shields, UK, involved 672 dogs of 103 breeds.

Largest dog show
The centenary of the annual Crufts show in 1991 was held at the National Exhibition Centre, Birmingham, W Midlands, UK, and attracted a record 22,993 entries.

Top show dogs
The greatest number of Challenge Certificates won by one dog in all-breed shows is 275, by German shepherd bitch *Altana's Mystique* (b. 1987), formerly owned by Mrs Jane Firestone, and now owned and trained by James A. Moses of Alpharetta, Georgia, USA.

The greatest number of 'Best-in-Show' awards won by one dog in all-breed shows is 203, by Scottish terrier bitch *Ch. Braeburn's Close Encounter* (b. 1978), owned by Sonnie Novick of Plantation Acres, Florida, USA.

Cats

Largest cats
The heaviest reliably recorded domestic cat is a tabby named 'Himmy', who weighed 21.3 kg (46 lb 15 oz) at his death in 1986. He was owned by Thomas Vyse of Redlynch, Cairns, Queensland, Australia, and had an 83.8-cm (33-in) waist, and was 96.5 cm (38 in) long.

An 11-year-old tabby called 'Poppa', owned by Gladys Cooper of Newport, UK, weighed 20.19 kg (44 lb 8 oz) in Nov 1984.

Smallest cat
A male blue point Himalayan–Persian cat called 'Tinker Toy', owned by Katrina and Scott Forbes of Taylorville, Illinois, USA, is 7 cm (2¾ in) tall and 19 cm (7½ in) long.

Oldest cats
The oldest cat on record is the female tabby 'Ma', who was put to sleep in Nov 1957 at the age of 34. She was owned by Alice St George Moore of Drewsteignton, Devon, UK.

The tabby 'Puss', owned by Mrs T. Holway of Clayhidon, Devon, UK, is said to have died the day after his 36th birthday in Nov 1939.

Most prolific cat
A tabby named 'Dusty' (b. 1935) of Bonham, Texas, USA, produced 420 kittens during her breeding life. She gave birth to her last litter (a single kitten) on 12 June 1952.

Oldest mother
In May 1987, 'Kitty', owned by George Johnstone of Croxton, Staffs, UK, gave birth to two kittens at the age of 30. She died just short of her 32nd birthday in June 1989. She had produced a known total of 218 kittens.

Best climber
In 1950, a four-month-old kitten belonging to Josephine Aufdenblatten of Geneva, Switzerland, reached an altitude of 4,478 m

ACTUAL SIZE
100%

Smallest dog 113 g

(14,690 ft) when it followed climbers to the summit of the Matterhorn in the Alps.

Rabbits and hares
Largest rabbit
In April 1980, a five-month-old French lop doe weighing 12 kg (26 lb 7 oz) was exhibited at the Reus Fair in north-east Spain.

Smallest rabbit
Both the Netherland dwarf and the Polish dwarf have a weight range of 0.9–1.13 kg (2 lb–2 lb 8 oz). In 1975, Jacques Bouloc of Coulommière, France, announced that a new hybrid of these had been created, weighing 396 g (14 oz).

Longest ears
Sweet Majestic Star, a champion black English lop owned and bred by Therese and Cheryl Seward of Exeter, Devon, UK, had ears that were 72.4 cm (28½ in) long and 18.4 cm (7¼ in) wide. He died in Oct 1992. The ears of his grandson, *Sweet Regal Magic*, are equally long.

WORLD'S BIGGEST DOG WALK INVOLVED 672 DOGS OVER 4.8 KM

Horses and ponies
Smallest horse
The stallion 'Little Pumpkin', owned by J. C. Williams Jr of Dell Terra Mini Horse Farm, Inman, South Carolina, USA, stood 35.5 cm (14 in) and weighed 9 kg (20 lb) in Nov 1975.

IE TOP OF THE MATTERHORN

Largest horse
The tallest and heaviest horse on record is a shire gelding called 'Sampson' (later 'Mammoth'), bred by Thomas Cleaver of Toddington Mills, Beds, UK. It was 21.2½ hands (2.19 m or 7 ft 2½ in) tall in 1850, and is said to have weighed 1,520 kg (3,360 lb).

Oldest horse
The greatest reliably recorded age for a horse is 62, for 'Old Billy' (b. 1760), bred by Edward Robinson of Woolston, Lancs, UK.

Oldest ponies
The greatest reliable recorded age for a pony is 54, for a stallion owned by a farmer in central France. He died in 1919.

In the United Kingdom, a moorland pony called 'Joey' owned by June and Rosie Osborne of the Glebe Equestrian Centre, Wickham Bishop, Essex, died aged 44 in 1988.

Largest litters
Dogs
Litters of 23 were produced by: an American foxhound owned by W. Ely of Ambler, Pennsylvania, USA, in 1944; a St Bernard owned by R. and A. Rodden of Lebanon, Missouri, USA, in 1975 (14 of them survived); and a great dane owned by M. Harris of Little Hall, Essex, UK, in 1987 (16 survived).

Cats
In 1970 a Burmese/Siamese cat owned by V. Gane, of Church Westcote, Kingham, Oxon, UK, produced a litter of 19 (15 survived).

Domestic ferrets
A litter of 15 was produced by a ferret belonging to J. Cliff of Denstone, Uttoxeter, Staffs, UK, in 1981.

Gerbils
A litter of 15 was recorded in the 1960s for a gerbil belonging to George Meares, the owner of a gerbil-breeding farm in St Petersburg, Florida, USA. He used a special food formula.

A Mongolian gerbil owned by S. Kirkman of Bulwell, Notts, UK, had a litter of 14 in 1983.

Hamsters
A golden hamster owned by L. and S. Miller of Louisiana, USA, produced a litter of 26 (of which 18 were killed by the mother) in 1974.

Mice
In 1982 a house mouse kept by M. Ogilvie of Blackpool, Lancs, UK, produced 34 offspring.

Rabbits
The most prolific domestic breeds produce five or six litters of 8–12 kittens a year during their breeding life. In 1978, a New Zealand white owned by J. Filek of Cape Breton, Nova Scotia, Canada, produced 24 young.

Oldest caged pets
Birds
'Prudle', a parrot that was captured in 1958 and kept by I. Frost of E Sussex, UK, lived to the age of 35.

A budgerigar called 'Charlie', kept by J. Dinsey of Stonebridge, London, UK, died in 1977 at the age of 29.

Gerbil
A Mongolian gerbil called 'Sahara', owned by Aaron Milstone of Lathrup Village, Michigan, USA, was eight years old when it died in 1981.

Guinea pig
'Snowball', owned by M. A. Wall of Bingham, Notts, UK, was almost 15 years of age when it died in 1979.

Mouse
'Fritzy', a mouse that was kept by Bridget Beard of West House School, Edgbaston, Birmingham, W Midlands, UK, died at the age of seven in 1985.

Rabbit
'Flopsy', a wild rabbit caught in 1964 and kept by L. B. Walker of Tasmania, Australia, died in 1983, having lived to the age of almost 19.

Goldfish
A goldfish named 'Fred', owned by A. R. Wilson of Worthing, W Sussex, UK, died on 1 Aug 1980 aged 41 years.

Left
Miniature Horses, the world's smallest horses, have always been popular and were often kept as pets by European royal households. There are many different blood lines, including Falabella and Toyhorse, and amongst these are some incredibly tiny horses. *Toyhorse Princess Snowdrop*, pictured here with five-year-old Bryony Heaver, was born on 23 April 1996 and is currently 53 cm (21 in) high. Breeder Tikki Adorian expects 'Snowdrop' to reach an adult height of probably no more than 66 cm (26 in). The smallest horse on record was 'Little Pumpkin', at 35.5 cm (14 in) in height.

Left
Sweet Majestic Star had the longest ears of any rabbit, equalled only by his grandson, *Sweet Regal Magic*.

Extreme left
The smallest dogs in the world are Yorkshire terriers. *Big Boss* stands just 11.97 cm (4⁷⁄₁₀ in) tall at the shoulder.

Birds

Largest wingspan 3.63 m

FASTEST LIVING CREATUR

Largest and smallest

Largest living bird

Male specimens of the flightless North African ostrich (*Struthio c. camelus*) have been recorded at heights of up to 2.74 m (9 ft).

Heaviest birds

Struthio c. australis, the southern African ostrich, is reputed to reach weights of up to 160 kg (353 lb).

The heaviest flying birds are the Kori bustard or paauw (*Ardeotis kori*) of north-east and southern Africa and the great bustard (*Otis tarda*) of Europe and Asia. Weights of 19 kg (42 lb) have been reported for the former. The heaviest reliably recorded great bustard weighed 18 kg (39 lb 11 oz), but there is an unconfirmed record of 21 kg (46 lb 4 oz) for a male great bustard that was too heavy to fly, shot in Manchuria.

On rare occasions, the mute swan (*Cygnus olor*), which is resident in the United Kingdom, can reach a weight of 18 kg (40 lb). There is a record of a cob (male) in Poland that had temporarily lost the power of flight and weighed 22.5 kg (49 lb 10 oz).

The heaviest individual bird of prey on record is a female harpy eagle (*Harpia harpyja*) from Guyana, weighing 12.3 kg (27 lb). The mean weight for this species is 4.5 kg (10 lb).

There are some subspecies of condor (often grouped with birds of prey) in which the largest males weigh 9–12 kg (20–27 lb).

Tallest bird

The tallest flying birds are cranes, which are waders from the family *Gruidae*. Some stand slightly more than 1.5 m (5 ft) high.

Smallest birds

Males of the bee hummingbird (*Mellisuga helenae*) of Cuba and the Isle of Pines weigh 1.6 g ($^7/_{125}$ oz) and are 5.7 cm (2¼ in) long. Half of this length is the bill and tail. Females are slightly larger.

The smallest regularly breeding British bird is the goldcrest (*Regulus regulus*), which is 8.5–9 cm (3⅓–3½ in) long and weighs 3.8–4.5 g ($^{13}/_{100}$–$^4/_{25}$ oz)—half the weight of the common wren (*Troglodytes troglodytes*).

The smallest birds of prey are the black-legged falconet (*Microhierax fringillarius*) of South-east Asia and the white-fronted, or Bornean, falconet (*M. latifrons*) of north-western Borneo. Both species have an average length of 14–15 cm (5½–6 in), including a 5-cm-long (2-in) tail, and weigh about 35 g (1¼ oz).

Fastest and slowest

Fastest land bird

Despite its bulk, the ostrich can reach a speed of 72 km/h (45 mph) when necessary.

Fastest flying birds

The peregrine falcon (*Falco peregrinus*) is the fastest living creature, reaching record speed levels when stooping from great heights during territorial displays or catching prey in mid-air. Speeds, recorded in German experiments, of up to 350 km/h (217 mph) at a 45° angle of stoop have been disputed, but there is little doubt that its maximum speed is at least 200 km/h (124 mph).

The fastest level flight is achieved by powerful duck and geese (*Anatidae*). Species such as the red-breasted merganser (*Mergus serrator*), the eider (*Somateria mollissima*), the canvasback (*Aythya valisineria*) and the spur-winged goose (*Plectropterus gambiensis*), can probably reach speeds of 90–100 km/h (56–62 mph).

Slowest flying bird

The American woodcock (*Scolopax minor*) and the Eurasian woodcock (*S. rusticola*) have been timed at speeds of 8 km/h (5 mph) without stalling during their courtship displays.

Above
The wandering albatross has the largest wingspan of any living bird.

Below
The peregrine falcon reaches record speeds of at least 200 km/h (124 mph) during territorial displays or when catching prey.

GREATEST DISTANCE TO HAVE BEEN COVERED BY

Birth and life

Largest eggs

Ostrich eggs are normally 15–20 cm (6–8 in) long, 10–15 cm (4–6 in) in diameter and 1–1.78 kg (2 lb 3 oz–3 lb 14 oz) in weight. Each egg is equivalent in volume to around 24 hens' eggs. The shell is 1.5 mm (³⁄₅₀ in) thick but can support the weight of an adult human.

The largest egg on record weighed 2.3 kg (5 lb 1 oz) and was laid on 28 June 1988 by a two-year-old northern/southern ostrich hybrid (*Struthio c. camelus* x *S. c. australis*) at the Kibbutz Ha'on collective farm, Israel.

Smallest eggs

The vervain hummingbird (*Mellisuga minima*), which inhabits Jamaica, lays the smallest eggs. The tiniest specimens are less than 1 cm (²⁄₅ in) long, and can weigh as little as 0.365 g (¹⁶⁄₁₂₅ oz).

Largest breeding populations

The red-billed quelea (*Quelea quelea*)—a seed-eating weaver that lives in the drier parts of sub-Saharan Africa—in densely packed flocks of hundreds of thousands of birds—has an estimated breeding population of 1.5 billion birds. The annual slaughter of at least 200 million of these 'feathered locusts' has no impact on this number.

The commonest species of wild bird in the United Kingdom is the blackbird (*Turdus merula*), which has a breeding population of approximately 5 million pairs.

Oldest birds

A Siberian white crane (*Grus leucogeranus*) named 'Wolf', which was kept at the International Crane Foundation in Baraboo, Wisconsin, USA, was reported to have lived to the age of 82. The bird died in late 1988, after breaking his bill while repelling a visitor near his pen.

The greatest irrefutable age for any bird is more than 80 years, for a male sulphur-crested cockatoo (*Cacatua galerita*), 'Cocky', who died at London Zoo, UK, in 1982.

Excluding the ostrich, which is known to live for up to 68 years, the longest-lived domesticated bird is the goose (*Anser a. domesticus*), which has a normal life-span of about 25 years. On 16 Dec 1976, a gander named 'George', owned by Florence Hull of Thornton, Lancs, UK, died at the age of 49 years 8 months.

Flight

Highest flying birds

The highest confirmed altitude to have been reached by a bird is 11,300 m (37,000 ft), by a Ruppell's griffon vulture (*Gyps rueppellii*) that collided with a commercial aircraft over Abidjan, Ivory Coast, on 29 Nov 1973. The impact caused one of the engines to shut down, but the plane landed safely. Feather remains allowed the US Museum of Natural History, Washington, to make a positive identification. The species is rarely seen above 6,000 m (19,700 ft).

On 9 Dec 1967, around 30 whooper swans (*Cygnus cygnus*) were reported at an altitude of just over 8,200 m (27,000 ft) as they flew in from Iceland to winter at Lough Foyl, on the Northern Ireland–Republic of Ireland border.

Longest flights

The greatest distance to have been covered by a ringed bird is 22,500 km (14,000 miles), by an Arctic tern (*Sterna paradisaea*) that had been banded as a nestling on 5 July 1955, in the Kandalaksha Sanctuary on the White Sea coast of Russia, and was captured alive by a fisherman 13 km (8 miles) south of Fremantle, Western Australia, on 16 May 1956. It had probably flown south via the Atlantic Ocean and then circled Africa before crossing the Indian Ocean. The bird did not survive to make the return journey.

Most airborne birds

After leaving their nesting grounds as youngsters, sooty terns (*Sterna fuscata*) are reputed to stay aloft continuously for between three and 10 years whilst maturing, before returning to land to breed as adults.

The most airborne land bird, the common swift (*Apus apus*), remains aloft for two to four years, during which time it sleeps, eats and mates on the wing. It has been calculated that a young swift completes a non-stop flight of about 500,000 km (310,700 miles) between being fledged and landing at a potential nesting site two years later.

Largest wingspan

Unconfirmed measurements of up to 4.22 m (13 ft 10 in) have been claimed in specimens of the wandering albatross (*Diomedea exulans*). The largest accurately measured span is 3.63 m (11 ft 11 in), for a very old male caught by members of the Antarctic research ship USNS *Eltanin* in the Tasman Sea on 18 Sept 1965.

HE PEREGRINE FALCON, HAS A MAXIMUM SPEED OF AT LEAST 200 KM/H

Right
Male bee hummingbirds are the smallest birds in the world.

ACTUAL SIZE
100%

Fastest wing beat

The horned sungem (*Heliactin cornuta*), a hummingbird from tropical South America, has a wing beat of 90 beats/sec. At this speed, the wings make the humming sound that gives hummingbirds their family name.

Sight and speech

Keenest vision

It has been calculated that a large bird of prey can see at least three times further than humans. Under ideal conditions, a peregrine falcon (*Falco peregrinus*) can spot a pigeon from a distance of more than 8 km (5 miles).

Largest field of vision

The eyes of the woodcock (*Scolopax rusticola*) are set so far back on its head that it has a 360° field of vision.

Best talking bird

A female African grey parrot (*Psittacus erithacus*) named 'Prudle' won the 'Best talking parrot-like bird' title at the National Cage and Aviary Bird Show in London, UK, for 12 consecutive years, retiring undefeated in 1976. 'Prudle', who had a vocabulary of almost 800 words, was taken from a nest in Jinja, Uganda, in 1958.

Largest vocabulary

'Puck', a budgerigar owned by Camille Jordan of Petaluma, California, USA, had a vocabulary of an estimated 1,728 words at its death in Jan 1994.

INGED BIRD IS 22,500 KM

Above
Ostriches lay the largest eggs of any bird—the size of 24 hen eggs. Vervain hummingbirds lay eggs less than 1 cm (²⁄₅ in) long.

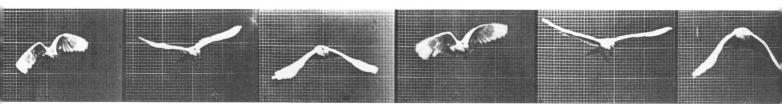

Underwater life

Right
The taka-ashi-gani, or Japanese spider crab, is the largest marine crustacean in the world. The largest specimen on record had a claw-span of 3.7 m (12 ft 1½ in).

Fish

Largest fish
The world's largest fish is the rare plankton-feeding whale shark (*Rhincodon typus*), found in warmer areas of the Atlantic, Pacific and Indian oceans. The largest scientifically recorded specimen was 12.65 m (41 ft 6 in) long, measured 7 m (23 ft) around the thickest part of its body and weighed an estimated 15–21 tonnes. It was captured off Baba Island, near Karachi, Pakistan, in 1949.

The largest fish recorded in British waters was a basking shark (*Cetorhinus maximus*) measuring 11.12 m (36 ft 6 in) and weighing an estimated 8 tonnes, washed ashore at Brighton, E Sussex, in 1806.

Largest freshwater fish
The largest fish to spend its entire life in fresh or brackish water is the pla buk or pa beuk (*Pangasianodon gigas*), found in the Mekong River and its major tributaries. The largest

Molluscs, such as this Giant Pacific Octopus (*Octopus doeflini*), grow to enormous sizes. The largest is the Atlantic giant squid with tentacles that can stretch over 10 m (33 ft).

specimen, captured in the River Ban Mee Noi in Thailand, was reportedly 3 m (9 ft 10¼ in) long and weighed 242 kg (533 lb 8 oz).

The largest fish caught in a British river was a common sturgeon (*Acipenser sturio*) weighing 230 kg (507 lb) and measuring 2.74 m (9 ft). It was accidentally netted in the River Severn at Lydney, Glos, UK, on 1 June 1937.

Smallest fish
The shortest recorded fish, and the shortest known vertebrate, is the marine dwarf goby (*Trimmatom nanus*) of the Chagos Archipelago in the Indian Ocean. Average lengths in a series of specimens collected by the 1978/79 Joint Services Chagos Research Expedition of the British Armed Forces were 8.6 mm (¹⁷⁄₅₀ in) for males and 8.9 mm (⁷⁄₂₀ in) for females.

Smallest freshwater fish
The shortest and lightest freshwater fish is the dwarf pygmy goby (*Pandaka pygmaea*), a colourless, almost transparent species found in streams and lakes on Luzon, Philippines. Males are 7.5–9.9 mm (⁷⁄₂₅–¹⁹⁄₅₀ in) long and weigh 4–5 mg.

The smallest commercial fish is the sinarapan (*Mistichthys luzonensis*), an endangered goby found only in Lake Buhi, Luzon, Philippines. Males are 10–13 mm (²⁄₅–½ in) long.

Deepest-living fish
Brotulids of the genus *Bassogigas* are generally regarded as the deepest-living vertebrates. The greatest depth from which a

specimen has been recovered is 8,300 m (27,230 ft) in the Puerto Rico Trench in the Atlantic Ocean, by Dr Gilbert L. Voss of the US research vessel *John Elliott* in April 1970.

Most ferocious fish
Razor-toothed piranhas of the genera *Serrasalmus* and *Pygocentrus* are generally considered to be the fiercest freshwater fish. They live in South American rivers, and attack any creature, regardless of size, if it is injured or making a commotion in the water. On 19 Sept 1981, more than 300 people were reportedly eaten when a boat sank while docking at the Brazilian port Obidos.

Largest predatory fish
Adult specimens of the rare great white shark (*Carcharodon carcharias*) usually grow to between 4.3 and 4.6 m (14–15 ft) in length and weigh 520–770 kg (1,150–1,700 lb). There is circumstantial evidence to suggest that some grow to more than 6 m (20 ft).

Most valuable fish
The world's most valuable fish is the Russian sturgeon (*Huso huso*). A 1,227-kg (2,706-lb) female caught in the Tikhaya Sosna River in 1924 yielded 245 kg (540 lb) of best-quality caviar, worth almost £200,000 today.

The 76-cm-long (30-in) ginrin showa koi, which won the supreme championship in nationwide Japanese koi shows between 1976 and 1980, was sold for 17 million yen (about £50,000) in 1982. In March 1986, this ornamental carp (*Cyprinus carpio*) was acquired by Derry Evans of the Kent Koi

Centre near Sevenoaks, Kent, UK, for an undisclosed sum, but died five months later.

Starfish

Largest starfish
The largest of the 1,600 known species of starfish is the fragile brisingid *Midgardia xandaros*. A specimen collected by the Texas A&M University research vessel *Alaminos* in the Gulf of Mexico in 1968 was 1.38 m (4 ft 6 in) long from tip to tip, but its disc was only 26 mm (1¹⁄₅₀ in) in diameter.

Smallest starfish
The smallest known starfish is the asterinid sea star *Patiriella parvivipara*, discovered on the west coast of the Eyre peninsula, South Australia, by Wolfgang Zeidler in 1975. It has a maximum radius of 4.7 mm (⁹⁄₅₀ in) and a diameter of less than 9 mm (⁷⁄₂₀ in).

Deepest-living starfish
The greatest depth from which a starfish has been recovered is 7,584 m (24,881 ft). A *Porcellanaster ivanovi* specimen was collected by the Soviet research ship *Vityaz* in the Marianas Trench, west Pacific, c. 1962.

Crustaceans
Largest marine crustacean
The largest crustacean is the taka-ashi-gani, or Japanese spider crab (*Macrocheira kaempferi*). One specimen had a 3.7-m (12-ft 1½-in) claw-span and weighed 18.6 kg (41 lb).

The heaviest crustacean is the American, or North Atlantic, lobster (*Homarus americanus*). In Feb 1977, a specimen weighing 20.14 kg (44 lb 6 oz) and measuring 1.06 m (3 ft 6 in) from the end of the tail-fan to the tip of the largest claw was caught off Nova Scotia, Canada, and sold to a New York restaurant.

Largest freshwater crustacean
The crayfish or crawfish (*Astacopsis gouldi*), found in streams in Tasmania, Australia, has been measured at lengths of 61 cm (2 ft) and can weigh up to 4.1 kg (9 lb).

Largest concentration of crustaceans
A swarm of shrimp-like krill (*Euphausia superba*) estimated to weigh 10 million tonnes was tracked by US scientists off Antarctica in March 1981.

ROWS TO ABOUT 4.5 M

Molluscs
Largest invertebrate
On 2 Nov 1878, an Atlantic giant squid (*Architeuthis dux*) ran aground in Thimble Tickle Bay, Newfoundland, Canada, on 2 Nov 1878. Its body was 6.1 m (20 ft) long, and one of its tentacles measured 10.7 m (35 ft).

Oldest mollusc
The longest-lived mollusc is the ocean quahog (*Arctica islandica*), a thick-shelled clam found in the Atlantic and the North Sea. A specimen with 220 annual growth rings was collected in 1982, but not all biologists accept these rings as an accurate measure of age.

Slowest growth
The deep-sea clam (*Tindaria callistiformis*), found in the North Atlantic, has the slowest growth rate in the animal kingdom, taking around 100 years to grow to 8 mm (⅓ in).

Largest clam
The largest bivalve shell is found on the marine giant clam *Tridacna gigas*, which lives on Indo-Pacific coral reefs. A specimen 1.15 m (3 ft 9¼ in)

long and weighing 333 kg (734 lb) was collected off Ishigaki Island, Okinawa, Japan, in 1956, but was not scientifically examined until 1984. Alive, it probably weighed just over 340 kg (750 lb). The soft parts weighed 9.1 kg (20 lb).

Most venomous mollusc
Hapalochlaena maculosa and *H. lunulata*, two species of blue-ringed octopus found around the coast of Australia and parts of south-east Asia, carry a neurotoxic venom so potent that their relatively painless bite can kill in minutes.

Jellyfish
Largest jellyfish
An Arctic giant (*Cyanea capillata arctica*) from the north-eastern Atlantic that washed up in Massachusetts Bay, USA, in 1870, had a bell diameter of 2.28 m (7 ft 6 in) and tentacles measuring 36.5 m (120 ft).

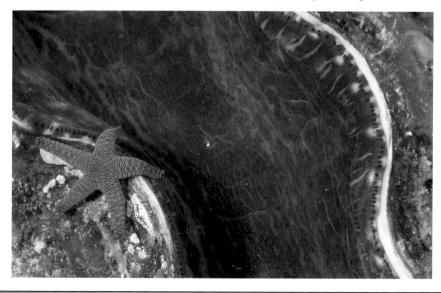

Most venomous jellyfish
The cardiotoxic venom of the Australian sea wasp or box jellyfish (*Chironex fleckeri*) has killed at least 70 people off the coast of Australia in the last century. An effective defence is women's hosiery—outsize tights were once worn by Queensland lifesavers.

Marine gastropods
Most venomous gastropod
Cone shells can deliver a fast-acting neurotoxic venom. The geographer cone (*Conus geographus*) of the Indo-Pacific is considered to be one of the most dangerous.

Largest gastropod
The largest known gastropod is the trumpet or baler conch (*Syrinx aruanus*). In 1979, a specimen collected off Western Australia weighed almost 18 kg (40 lb).

Above
The sandtiger shark is one of 400 species of shark. In May 1986, a sandtiger shark weighing 144.24 kg (318 lb) was caught off Nags Head, North Carolina, USA.

Left
The marine giant clam, here providing a home for a starfish, has the largest bivalve shell.

Reptiles and amphibians

Right
The bright colours of poison arrow frogs warn potential predators that they are highly poisonous. Several species produce some of the most deadly biological toxins known to science—their secretions are so toxic that a tiny smear would kill a horse.

Fastest lizard
The highest recorded speed achieved by a reptile on land is 34.9 km/h (21.7 mph), by a spiny-tailed iguana (*Ctenosaura* sp) from Costa Rica, in a series of experiments carried out by Prof. Raymond Huey of the University of Washington, USA, and colleagues at the University of California, Berkeley.

Oldest lizard
A male slow worm (*Anguis fragilis*) that was kept in the Zoological Museum, Copenhagen, Denmark, from 1892 to 1946 lived for more than 54 years.

Tortoises and turtles
Largest turtle
The leatherback turtle (*Dermochelys coriacea*), which can weigh up to 450 kg (1,000 lb), averages between 1.8 and 2.1 m (6 and 7 ft) from the tip of its beak to the end of its tail and 2.1 m (7 ft) across the front flippers. A male found dead at Harlech, Gwynedd, UK, in 1988, was 2.91 m (9 ft 5½ in) long over the carapace and 2.77 m (9 ft) across the front flippers, and weighed 961.1 kg (2,120 lb).

Crocodilians
Largest crocodilian
The estuarine, or saltwater, crocodile (*Crocodylus porosus*), which lives in tropical regions of Asia and the Pacific, is the largest reptile. At the Bhitarkanika Wildlife Sanctuary in Orissa State, India, there are four protected specimens that are more than 6 m (19 ft 8 in) long. The largest exceeds 7 m (23 ft).

Smallest crocodilian
The maximum length of the dwarf caiman (*Paleosuchus palpebrosus*) of northern South America is rarely more than 1.5 m (4 ft 11 in) for males and 1.2 m (4 ft) for females.

Oldest crocodilian
The greatest authenticated age is 66 years, for a female American alligator (*Alligator mississippiensis*) that arrived at Adelaide Zoo, South Australia, on 5 June 1914 as a two-year-old and died there on 26 Sept 1978.

Lizards
Largest lizard
The Komodo dragon (*Varanus komodoensis*), also known as the Komodo monitor or ora, is found on the Indonesian islands of Komodo, Rintja, Padar and Flores. Males average about 2.25 m (7 ft 5 in) in length and 59 kg (130 lb) in weight. The largest accurately measured specimen was a male given to an American zoologist by the Sultan of Bima in 1928. In 1937, it was 3.10 m (10 ft 2 in) long and weighed 166 kg (365 lb).

Smallest lizard
Sphaerodactylus parthenopion, a tiny gecko native to Virgin Gorda, British Virgin Islands, is known from 15 specimens found between 10 and 16 Aug 1964. The three largest females were 18 mm (⁷⁄₁₀ in) long from snout to vent, with a tail of roughly the same length.

Longest lizard
The slender Salvadori or Papuan monitor (*Varanus salvadori*) of Papua New Guinea can reach up to 4.75 m (15 ft 7 in) long. Its tail accounts for almost 70% of its total length.

Largest tortoise
The largest living tortoise on record is a Galapagos giant tortoise (*Geochelone nigra*) named 'Goliath', who has lived at the Life Fellowship Bird Sanctuary in Sessner, Florida, USA, since 1960. He is 135.5 cm (4 ft 5⅝ in) long, 102 cm (3 ft 4½ in) wide, 68·5 cm (2 ft 3 in) high, and weighs 385 kg (849 lb).

Smallest chelonian (turtle or tortoise)
Several species vie for the title of smallest chelonian in the world: the stinkpot, or common musk, turtle (*Sternotherus odoratus*);

The world's largest lizard is the Komodo dragon. Males of the species grow to an average length of 2.25 m (7 ft 5 in).

the bog turtle (*Clemmys muhlenbergi*); and the small speckled, or rock, tortoise (*Homopus signatus*). The male rock tortoise, which inhabits Cape Province, South Africa, has an average carapace length of 7.4 cm (2⁹⁄₁₀ in) and typically weighs approximately 65 g (2¼ oz). In a study carried out on 27 males, the largest individual was found to have a carapace length of 8.75 cm (3⁷⁄₁₆ in) and to weigh 96 g (3⅜ oz).

sensitive recording device had reached a depth of 1,200 m (3,973 ft) off the Virgin Islands in the West Indies.

Amphibians

Largest frog

The world's largest known frog is the African goliath frog (*Conraua goliath*). A specimen captured on the Sanaga River in Cameroon in April 1989, had a snout-to-vent length of 36.83 cm (1 ft 2½ in), and an overall length of 87.63 cm (2 ft 10½ in) with its legs extended. The animal weighed 3.66 kg (8 lb 1 oz) on 30 Oct 1989.

Smallest frog

The smallest frog, and the smallest known amphibian, is *Sminthillus limbatus* of Cuba, which is 8.5–12 mm (¹⁷⁄₅₀–½ in) long from snout to vent when fully grown.

Smallest toad

The smallest toad is the subspecies *Bufo taitanus beiranus* of Africa, the largest known specimen of which was 24 mm (¹⁵⁄₁₆ in) long.

Largest amphibians

Giant salamanders (family Cryptobranchidae), of which there are three species, are the world's largest amphibians. The record-holder is the Chinese giant salamander (*Andrias davidianus*), which lives in the mountain

Below
The estuarine, or saltwater, crocodile is the world's largest reptile. The biggest known specimen is over 7 m (23 ft) long.

ARAPACE AND 2.77 M ACROSS THE FRONT FLIPPERS

Oldest chelonian

The greatest authenticated age to have been reached by a chelonian is at least 188 years, by a Madagascar radiated tortoise (*Astrochelys radiata*) that was presented to the royal family of Tonga by Captain Cook in either 1773 or 1777. The animal was called 'Tui Malila' and remained in the care of the Tongan royal family until its death in 1965.

Fastest chelonian

The highest speed at which a reptile is said to have travelled in water is 35 km/h (22 mph), by a frightened Pacific leatherback turtle.

Deepest dive

In May 1987, Dr Scott Eckert reported that a leatherback turtle fitted with a pressure-

Largest toad

The largest known toad in the world is the cane or marine toad (*Bufo marinus*) of South America and Australia. Average specimens weigh approximately 450 g (1 lb). In 1991, a male named 'Prinsen' ('The Prince'), owned by Håkan Forsberg of Åkers Styckebruk, Sweden, was found to weigh 2.65 kg (5 lb 13½ oz) and measured 38 cm (1 ft 3 in) from snout to vent, or 53.9 cm (1 ft 9¼ in) when fully extended.

The largest toad in the United Kingdom is the common toad (*Bufo bufo*), which grows to a length of between 8 and 10 cm (3 and 4 in).

streams of north-eastern, central and southern China. A specimen collected in Hunan Province was 1.8 m (5 ft 11 in) long and weighed 65 kg (143 lb).

Most poisonous

The brightly coloured poison-arrow frogs (*Dendrobates* and *Phyllobates*) of South and Central America secrete some of the deadliest biological toxins known, and are the world's most poisonous animals. The skin secretion of the golden poison arrow frog (*Phyllobates terribilis*) of western Colombia is the most poisonous.

Spiders, snakes and scorpions

Right
The reticulated python (*Python reticulatus*) of South-east Asia, Indonesia and the Philippines is the largest snake in the world, regularly exceeding 6.25 m (20 ft 6 in) in length. A record 10-m (32-ft 10-in) specimen was shot on the north coast of Celebes in 1912 and was accurately measured with a surveying tape by civil engineers from a nearby mining camp.

Largest scorpion 29.2 cm

Spiders

Largest spider
A male goliath bird-eating spider (*Theraphosa leblondi*) collected at Rio Cavro, Venezuela, in 1965 had a 28-cm (11-in) leg-span—large enough to cover a dinner plate.

The cardinal spider (*Tegenaria gigantea*) has the greatest average leg-span of a British spider. In 1994 Lynda and John Culley of Wantage, Oxon, found a specimen with a span of 14.9 cm (5⅞ in) in their bathroom sink.

Greatest size difference between sexes
In some species of the golden orb-web spider (genus *Nephila*), females weigh almost 1,000 times more than their mates, but the latter are below the minimum size of the females' normal prey and are not eaten by them.

Fastest spider
A female house spider (*Tegenaria atrica*) reached a speed of 1.9 km/h (1.2 mph) over short distances during British experiments in 1970 and covered a distance equivalent to 330 times her own body length in 10 seconds.

Longest fangs
The fangs of the bird-eater *Theraphosa leblondi* reach a length of 1.2 cm (½ in), while those of the much more poisonous black widow (*Latrodectus mactans*) are only 0.4 mm (²⁄₁₂₅ in) long.

Most venomous spiders
The Brazilian wandering spiders of the genus *Phoneutria*, particularly the Brazilian huntsman *P. fera*, have the most active neurotoxic venom. These aggressive creatures often hide in clothing, and bite furiously when disturbed. An antivenom is now available.

Largest webs
The biggest webs are built by tropical orb-web spiders of the genus *Nephila*. A web found in the Karrakpur Hills near Nonghyr, Bihar, India, was 1.5 m (5 ft) in circumference and had supporting guy-lines up to 6.1 m (20 ft) long.

The largest communal webs, built by *Ixeuticus socialis* from Australia, can be 3.7 m (12 ft 2 in) long and 1.2 m (3 ft 11 in) wide.

Snakes

Longest snake
The record length is 10 m (32 ft 10 in), for a reticulated python (*Python reticulatus*) shot in 1912 in Celebes, Indonesia.

Shortest snake
The shortest snake is the thread snake (*Leptotyphlops bilineata*), known only from Martinique, Barbados and St Lucia. The longest specimen on record was 10.8 cm (4¼ in) in length and had a matchstick-thin body that could have fitted inside the lead hole in a standard pencil.

Heaviest snake
The mean length of the anaconda (*Eunectes murinus*) of tropical South America and Trinidad is 5.5–6.1 m (18–20 ft). A female shot in Brazil c. 1960 was 8.45 m (27 ft 9 in) long with a 111-cm (44-in) girth, and must have weighed almost 227 kg (500 lb).

Fastest snake
The aggressive black mamba (*Dendroaspis polylepis*) of eastern tropical Africa probably the world's fastest land snake. Top speeds of 16–19 km/h (10–12 mph) may be possible in short bursts over level ground.

Oldest snake
A common boa (*Boa constrictor constrictor*) named 'Popeye' lived for 40 years 104 days. He died at Philadelphia Zoo, Pennsylvania, USA, on 15 April 1977.

Longest venomous snake
The king cobra (*Ophiophagus hannah*), or hamadryad, averages 3.65–4.5 m (12–15 ft) in length and lives in South-east Asia and India. A 5.54-m (18-ft 2-in) specimen was captured in Negri Sembilan, Malaysia, in 1937 and grew to 5.71 m (18 ft 9 in) in London Zoo, UK. It was destroyed at the outbreak of war in 1939 to avoid the risk of its escape.

Most venomous snakes
The *Hydrophis belcheri* species of sea snake, found in parts of the Australo-Pacific region, has a myotoxic venom many times more effective than that of any land snake, but is friendly, so human fatalities are rare.

The world's most venomous land snake is the small-scaled, or fierce, snake (*Oxyuranus microlepidotus*), which is found mainly in the Diamantina River and Cooper's Creek drainage basins in Channel County, Queensland, and western NSW, Australia. One specimen yielded 110 mg of venom after milking—

enough to kill 250,000 mice—but no human fatalities have been reported.

Snakebites
More people die of snakebites in Sri Lanka than in any comparable area. Over 95% of the 800 fatalities that occur annually on the island are caused by the common krait (*Bungarus caeruleus*), the Sri Lankan cobra (*Naja n. naja*) and Russell's viper (*Vipera russelli pulchella*).

The saw-scaled or carpet viper (*Echis carinatus*), which ranges from West Africa to India, probably bites and kills more people than any other species.

The only venomous snake in the United Kingdom is the adder, or viper (*Vipera berus*), which has caused 10 human deaths, including six children, since 1890. The most recent death on record occurred in 1975, when a five-year-old was bitten at Callander, Perthshire, and died 44 hours later.

Longest fangs
The highly venomous gaboon viper (*Bitis gabonica*), which lives in tropical Africa, has the longest fangs of any snake. One 1.83-m (6-ft) specimen had fangs up to 5 cm (2 in) in length.

Scorpions

Largest scorpions

Males of the *Heterometrus swannerdami* species from southern India often grow to more than 18 cm (7 in) from the tips of the pedipalps or 'pincers' to the end of the sting. A specimen found during WWII was 29.2 cm (11½ in) long overall.

The tropical emperor, or imperial, scorpion (*Pandinus imperator*) of West Africa also grow to at least 18 cm (7 in). A male from Sierra Leone reached a length of 22.9 cm (9 in).

Smallest scorpions

Microbothus pusillus, which is found on the Red Sea coast, has an overall length of about 13 mm (½ in).

Most venomous scorpion

The Palestine yellow scorpion (*Leiurus quinquestriatus*), which ranges from eastern North Africa through the Middle East to the Red Sea, is the most venomous scorpion, but delivers a tiny amount of venom (typically 0.255 mg). Adult lives are seldom endangered, but it has killed a number of children under the age of five.

Most deaths from scorpion stings

Mexico had a toll of 1,933 in 1946. Control measures, education and improved medical treatment have lowered the toll, but as many as 1,000 people still die every year. The main culprits are from the genus *Centruroides*, and most victims are youngsters.

PIDER WAS BIG ENOUGH TO COVER A DINNER PLATE

ACTUAL SIZE 100%

Left
The world's largest known spider is the goliath bird-eating spider (*Theraphosa leblondi*). It inhabits the coastal rainforests of Surinam, Guyana and French Guiana, and isolated specimens have been reported in Venezuela and Brazil. The largest goliath on record, which had a leg-span of 28 cm (11 in), was found by members of the Pablo San Martin Expedition in Venezuela in 1965.

Insects

WHEN JUMPING 130 TIMES THEIR OWN HEIGHT, FLEAS ENCOUNTER A FORCE OF 200 G

Largest and smallest

Longest
The longest insect on record is *Pharnacia kirbyi*, a stick insect from the rainforests of Borneo. A specimen in the Natural History Museum in London, UK, has a body length of 32.8 cm (12⁹⁄₁₀ in) and a total length, including the legs, of 54.6 cm (21½ in).

Smallest
The 'feather-winged' beetles of the family Ptiliidae (or Trichopterygidae) and the battledore-wing fairy flies (parasitic wasps) of the family Mymaridae are smaller than some species of protozoa (single-celled animals).

Heaviest
The heaviest insects are the Goliath beetles (family Scarabaeidae) of equatorial Africa. In measurements of a series of males (females are smaller), the lengths from the tips of the small frontal horns to the end of the abdomen were up to 11 cm (4⅓ in). The specimens weighed 70–100 g (2½–3½ oz).

The heaviest insect in the United Kingdom is the stag beetle (*Lucanus cervus*), which is widely distributed over southern England. The largest specimen on record is a male 8.74 cm (3⁷⁄₁₆ in) in length (body and mandibles), which probably weighed over 6 g (⅕ oz) when alive.

On 2 June 1994, 10-year-old Ryan Morris and his friends James Simpson, Scott Cowan and Ross Cowan found a 8.9-cm-long (3½-in) stag beetle near their homes in Sheppey, Kent, UK. It was later identified as *Odontolabis delessertii*, a species that does not naturally occur in the United Kingdom.

Lightest
The male bloodsucking banded louse (*Enderleinellus zonatus*) and the parasitic wasp (*Caraphractus cinctus*) may each weigh as little as 0.005 mg (equal to 5,670,000 creatures to an oz).

Strongest
In proportion to their size, the strongest animals in the world are the larger beetles of

A TROPICAL COCKROACH SPECIMEN MOVED AT A RATE OF 50 TIMES ITS OWN BOI

Cockroaches are among the most primitive living insects. They have existed relatively unchanged for 320 million years.

the family Scarabaeidae, which are found mainly in the tropics.

Largest cockroach
The biggest cockroach in the world is *Megaloblatta longipennis*, which is found in Colombia. A preserved female in the collection of Akira Yokokura of Yamagata, Japan, measures 9.7 cm (3¹³⁄₁₆ in) in length and 4.5 cm (1¾ in) across.

Largest fly
Specimens of *Mydas heros* from tropical South America have been found with a body length of 6 cm (2⅜ in) and a wingspan of about 10 cm (3¹⁵⁄₁₆ in). The fly tackles bees and wasps by biting them on the neck.

Largest dragonfly or damselfly
Specimens of the damselfly *Megaloprepus caeruleata*, which lives in Central and South America, have been measured at lengths of up to 12 cm (4¾ in) and wingspans of as much as 19.1 cm (7½ in).

Smallest dragonfly
Agriocnemis naia of Myanmar (Burma) is the smallest dragonfly in the world. A specimen in the Natural History Museum, UK, had a wing spread of 1.76 cm (⁶⁹⁄₁₀₀ in) and a body length of 1.8 cm (7¹⁄₁₀₀ in).

Largest flea
The world's largest known variety of flea is *Hystrichopsylla schefferi*, which has been described from a single specimen that was taken from the nest of a mountain beaver (*Aplodontia rufa*) at Puyallup, Washington, USA, in 1913. Females can reach a length of 8 mm (⅓ in).

MALARIAL PARASITES CARRI

Largest butterfly
The largest known species of butterfly in the world is the Queen Alexandra's birdwing (*Ornithoptera alexandrae*), which lives in Papua New Guinea. Females can have a wingspan of more than 28 cm (11 in) and weigh in excess of 25 g (⁹⁄₁₀ oz).

The largest butterfly in the United Kingdom is the monarch butterfly (*Danaus plexippus*),

NGTH PER SECOND IN 1991

which has a wingspan of up to 12.7 cm (5 in) and weighs approximately 1 g (¹⁄₂₅ oz).

Smallest butterfly
A micro-moth called *Stigmella ridiculosa*, found in the Canary Islands, has a wingspan of 2 mm (¹⁄₁₆ in) and a similar body length.

Birth and life
Most fertile
With unlimited food and no predators, a single cabbage aphid (*Brevicoryne brassicae*) could give rise to a mass of descendants weighing 822 million tonnes—more than three times the weight of the total human population. This makes it the world's most fertile animal.

Longest lives
The longest-lived insects are the splendour beetles (family Buprestidae). On 27 May

1983, a *Buprestis aurulenta* specimen appeared from the staircase in the home of Mr W. Euston of Prittlewell, Southend-on-Sea, Essex, UK, after at least 47 years as a larva.

Shortest lives
Mayflies, of the family Ephemeroidea, may spend two to three years as nymphs at the bottom of lakes and streams and then live for as little as an hour as winged adults.

Speed and activity
Fastest moving
The world's fastest insects on land are certain large tropical cockroaches of the family Dictyoptera. In 1991 a record speed of 5.4 km/h (3.4 mph), or 50 body lengths per second, was achieved by a *Periplaneta americana* specimen at the University of California in Berkeley, USA.

Longest flea jump
The cat flea (*Ctenocephalides felis*) has been known to reach a height of 34 cm (13½ in) in a single jump, and the common flea (*Pulex irritans*) is capable of similar feats. In a 1910 American experiment, a specimen allowed to leap at will performed a long jump of 33 cm (13 in) and a high jump of 19.7 cm (7¾ in). In jumping 130 times its own height, a flea subjects itself to a force of 200 g.

Longest migration
A tagged female monarch, or milkweed, butterfly (*Danaus plexippus*) released by Donald Davis at Presqu'ile Provincial Park near Brighton, Ontario, Canada, on 6 Sept 1986 was recaptured 3,432 km (2,133 miles) away on a mountain near Angangueo, Mexico, on 15 Jan 1987. (This is the linear distance from the release site to the place where it was recaptured; the actual distance travelled may have been much larger.)

Most destructive
The single most destructive insect is the desert locust (*Schistocerca gregaria*) from the dry and semi-arid regions of Africa, the Middle East and western Asia. Individuals are

only 4.5–6 cm (1¾–2⅜ in) long but can eat their own weight in food every day. Certain weather conditions induce unimaginable numbers to gather in huge swarms that devour almost all vegetation in their path. In a single day, a 'small' swarm of about 50 million locusts can eat food that would sustain 500 people for a year.

Most dangerous
Malarial parasites of the genus *Plasmodium* carried by mosquitoes of the genus *Anopheles* have probably been responsible for 50% of all human deaths since the Stone Age (excluding wars and accidents). According to 1993 World Health Organization estimates, 1.4–2.8 million people die from malaria each year in sub-Saharan Africa alone.

Left
Fleas are the best jumpers in the animal kingdom in relation to their size. Their huge leaps are achieved not only through muscle power, but also through a triggered click mechanism that involves generating and then storing energy, up to 97% of which can then be released for a leap or a series of leaps. Many fleas can jump non-stop for hours or even days on end. It is this resilience that allowed flea circus managers to put on up to 50 10-minute shows a day—with the fleas performing such acts as pulling miniature carriages or walking the tightrope—for two weeks at a stretch.

Strangest defence
The bombardier beetle (genus *Brachinus*) stores two relatively benign chemicals in a special chamber in its abdomen. When it feels threatened, they are released into a second chamber and mix with an enzyme, resulting in a violent chemical reaction and the release of considerable heat (up to 100°C or 212°F) from the anus. This spray of irritating gas can be turned on and off 500 times a second.

Most acute sense of smell
According to German experiments that were carried out in 1961, the male emperor moth (*Eudia pavonia*) is capable of detecting the sex attractant of the virgin female from a distance of 11 km (6⁷⁄₁₀ miles).

Far left
A rhinoceros beetle of the family Dynastinae (a sub-family of the family Scarabaeidae, the world's strongest animals in relation to their size) was found to be capable of supporting 850 times its own weight on its back. (In a trestle lift, human beings can support 17 times their own body weight.)

Loudest insect
At 7,400 pulses per minute, the tymbal organs of the male cicada (family Cicadidae) produce a noise (officially described by the US Department of Agriculture as 'Tsh-ee-EEEE-e-ou') that is detectable from a distance of more than 400 m (¼ mile).

048
049
050
A BABY BORN IN 1921 HAD A RECORD 14 FINGERS AND 15 TO
051
GREATEST AUTHENTICATED AGE TO WHI
052
LONGEST INTERVAL BETWEEN THE BIRTH OF TWINS WAS 84 DAYS
053
IN THE LONGEST CARDIAC ARREST, JAN EGIL REFSDAHL'S HEA
054
055
056

The

AT HIS PEAK WEIGHT WALTER HUDSON HAD THE WORLD'S LARGEST WAIST, MEASURING 30 2

058
059
061

GREATEST NUMBER OF CHILDREN BORN TO ONE MOTHER IS 69
SMALLEST BONE, THE STAPES, IS 2.6-3.4 MM L

UPLE HAD A HEIGHT DIFFERENCE OF 95 CM

AIR ON RECORD WAS 4.23 M IN LENGTH IN FEB 1994

MOST...UPLE...MARRI

Y HUMAN BEING HAS EVER LIVED IS 121 YEARS

OPPED BEATING FOR FOUR HOURS

MOST OPERATIONS ENDURED BY ONE PERSON IS 970

THE HEAVIEST PERSON IN MEDICAL HISTORY WEIGHED 442 KG

human being

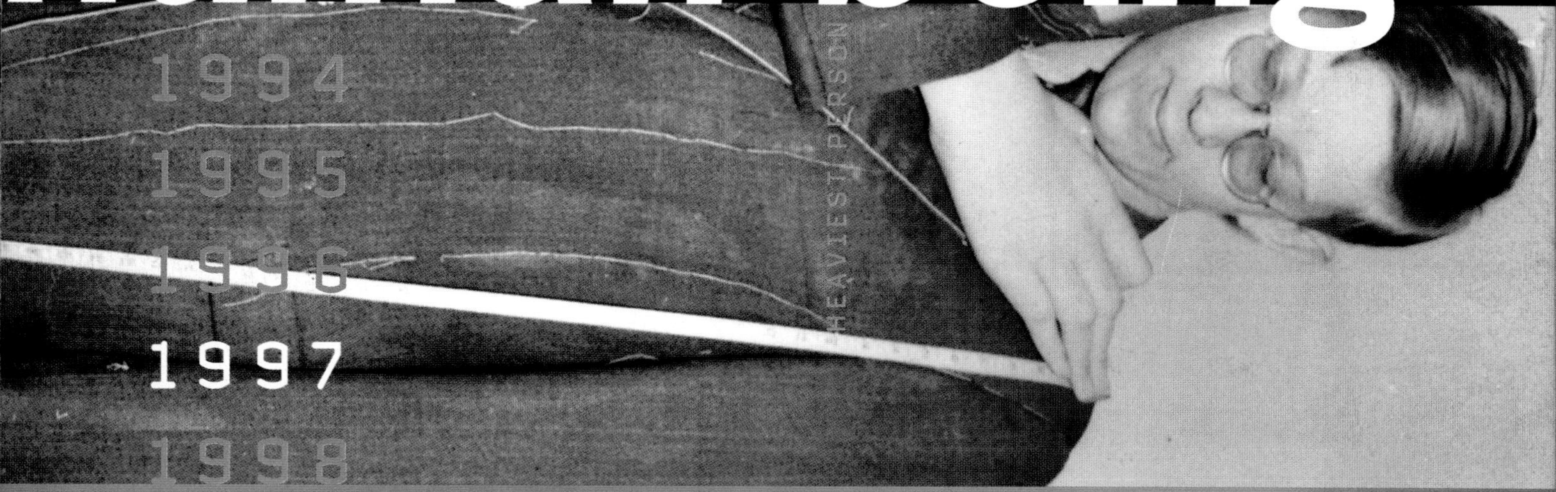

1994

1995

1996

1997

1998

LLEST MAN IN THE WORLD WAS 2.72 M IN HEIGHT WHEN HE WAS LAST MEASURED IN 1940

Anatomy: internal

Right
Megakaryocyte cells, found in the bone marrow, are the largest cells.

Longest cells 1.3 m

Cells

Largest cells
The megakaryocyte, a blood cell, has a diameter of 0.2 mm ($\frac{1}{125}$ in). Found in the bone marrow, it produces the 'stickiest' particles in the human body—the platelets, which play an important role in blood clotting.

Longest cells
Motor neurons (nerve cells) are 1.3 m (4 ft 3 in) long. They have cell bodies in the lower spinal cord, with axons that carry nerve impulses from the spinal cord to the big toe. The cell systems that carry sensations back from the big toe to the brain are even longer. Their uninterrupted length is roughly equal to body height.

Smallest cells
The brain cells in the cerebellum are approximately 0.005 mm in diameter.

Fastest turnover of cells
The cells with the shortest life are those in the lining of the alimentary tract (gut), which are shed every three to four days.

Commonest cells
The body contains approximately 30,000 billion red blood cells (erythrocytes)—about 5×10^{12} in every litre of blood. Their function is to carry oxygen around the body.

Longest life of a cell
The brain cells last for life, and can be up to three times as old as bone cells, which may live for 10–30 years.

Blood

Commonest blood group
On a worldwide basis, 46% of people have blood that belongs to Group O, but in some areas, such as Norway, Group A is the commonest group.

The full description of the commonest British sub-group is O MsNs, P+, Rr, Lu(a–), K–, Le(a–b+), Fy(a+b+), Jk(a+b+). It occurs in one in every 270 people.

Rarest blood group
There is a type of Bombay blood (sub-type h-h) that has so far been found only in a Czech nurse in 1961, and in a brother (Rh positive) and sister (Rh negative) in Massachusetts, USA, in 1968.

Recipient of most blood
A 50-year-old haemophiliac, Warren C. Jyrich, required 2,400 donor units (1,080 litres) of blood during open-heart surgery at the Michael Reese Hospital, Chicago, Illinois, USA, in Dec 1970.

Largest artery
The aorta has a diameter of 3 cm ($1\frac{3}{16}$ in) where it leaves the heart. By the time it ends at the level of the fourth lumbar vertebra, it is approximately 1.75 cm ($1\frac{1}{16}$ in) in diameter.

Largest vein
The largest vein is the inferior vena cava, the function of which is to return the blood from the lower half of the body to the heart. It is slightly larger than the aorta.

Bones

Longest bone
The thigh bone, or femur, is the longest bone in the human body. It normally constitutes 27.5% of a person's stature, and it is likely to be about 50 cm (19¾ in) long in a man 1.82 m (6 ft) tall.

Smallest bone
The stapes, or stirrup bone, which is one of the three auditory ossicles in the middle ear, is 2.6–3.4 mm ($\frac{1}{10}$–$1\frac{3}{100}$ in) long and weighs 2.0–4.3 mg ($\frac{15}{500}$–$\frac{33}{500}$ oz). Its function is to conduct sound towards the inner ear.

Joints

Largest and smallest joints
The body's largest joint is the knee, and involves the body's two longest bones, the femur and tibia.

Not surprisingly, the smallest joint is between the smallest bone, the stapes, and the incus bone in the middle ear. The joint is so small that it is unnamed.

Strongest joint
The hip joint is the strongest in the human body. It is also one of the most stable joints, because the head of the femur fits almost perfectly into the socket of the pelvis.

Most mobile joint
The shoulder joint is the body's most mobile, and, consequently, the easiest to dislocate.

Muscles

Largest muscle
The bulkiest of the 639 named muscles in the human body is usually the gluteus maximus or buttock muscle, which extends the thigh.

During pregnancy, the uterus or womb (which is a pear-shaped muscular organ) can increase in weight from about 30 g (1 oz) to more than 1 kg (2 lb 3 oz).

Longest muscle
The longest muscle in the body is the sartorius, which runs from the pelvis, across the front of the thigh, to the top of the tibia below the knee. Its function is to draw the lower limb into the cross-legged position.

Smallest muscle
The stapedius, which controls the stapes in the ear, is less than 0.127 cm ($\frac{1}{20}$ in) long.

Strongest muscle
The strongest muscle in the human body is the masseter, which is responsible for the action of biting. There is one such muscle on either side of the mouth.

In Aug 1986, Richard Hofmann of Lake City, Florida, USA, achieved a bite strength of

442 kg (975 lb) for a duration of approximately two seconds in a research test using a gnathodynamometer that was undertaken at the College of Dentistry, University of Florida. This is more than six times the normal biting strength.

Most active muscle

It has been estimated that the muscles of the human eye move in excess of 100,000 times a day. A large number of these rapid eye movements (REM) take place during the dream phase of sleep, which occupies about 25% of total sleep time.

LLIE JONES OF ATLANTA

Largest chest measurements

Robert Earl Hughes of the USA (1926–58) had the largest ever chest measurement, at 315 cm (124 in).

The largest chest measurement ever recorded in the United Kingdom was 244 cm (96 in), for William Campbell. Among muscular subjects (mesomorphs) of normal height, expanded chest measurements in excess of 142 cm (56 in) are extremely rare.

The world record for the largest muscular chest measurement is 188 cm ($74\frac{1}{16}$ in). It is held by Isaac Nesser of Greensburg, Pennsylvania, USA.

Largest biceps

The right biceps of Denis Sester of Bloomington, Minnesota, USA, measure 77.8 cm ($30\frac{5}{8}$ in) cold.

Body temperature

Hottest and coldest body parts

The standard temperature of the body is 37°C (98.6°F), but there are small variations. The coolest parts of the body are the hands and feet, and the hottest area is the centre of the brain.

Highest body temperature

Willie Jones, aged 52, was admitted to Grady Memorial Hospital, Atlanta, Georgia, USA, with heatstroke on 10 July 1980, when the temperature reached 32°C (90°F) with 44% humidity. His own temperature was found to be 46.5°C (115.7°F). He was discharged after 24 days.

Lowest body temperature

Human beings can die of hypothermia with a body temperature of 35°C (95°F). The lowest authenticated body temperature on record is a rectal temperature of 14.2°C (57.5°F) for two-year-old Karlee Kosolofski of Regina, Saskatchewan, Canada, on 23 Feb 1994. She had been accidentally locked outside her home for six hours in a temperature of −22°C (−8°F). Despite severe frostbite, which necessitated the amputation of her left leg above the knee, she has made a full recovery.

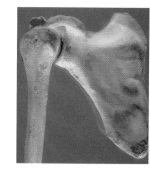

Left
The shoulder joint is the most mobile in the human body.

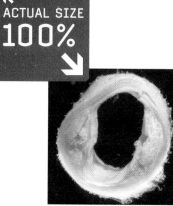

ACTUAL SIZE
100%

Left
The aorta is the largest of the body's arteries. From it branch smaller arteries that supply all bodily organs.

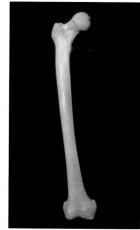

Left
The longest bone is the thigh bone or femur, which is typically about 50 cm ($19\frac{3}{4}$ in) long in a man 1.82 m (6 ft) tall.

Anatomy: external

LONGEST MOUSTACHE EVER CULTIVATED HAD A TOTAL SPAN OF 3.39 M IN 19

Most valuable tooth £730

Right
The retina covers the back two-thirds of the eyeball and contains the rod and cone cells that convert light into nervous signals, which are transmitted to the brain. In 1942, Maurice H. Pirenne exhibited acute light sensitivity when he detected a flash of blue light of 500 nm in total darkness.

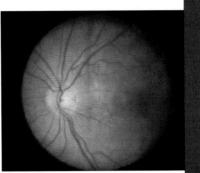

Right
The maximum recorded extension of the neck achieved by the successive fitting of copper coils, as practised by the women of the Padaung or Kareni tribe of Myanmar (Burma), is 40 cm (15¾ in).

Right
Fingernails grow four times faster than toenails, at a rate of about 0.05 cm (1/50 in) a week. The longest fingernails are those of Shridhar Chillal of India. His thumbnail was 135 cm (53 in) long in 1996.

Hair

Most valuable hair
On 18 Feb 1988, a bookseller from Cirencester, Glos, UK, paid £5,575 for a lock of hair that had belonged to Vice Admiral Lord Nelson (1758–1805).

Hair splitting
The greatest hair splitter on record was Briton Alfred West (1901–85), who split a single human hair lengthways 17 times with a razor blade, creating 18 strands of hair.

Longest beard
The beard of Hans N. Langseth (1846–1927) from Norway was 5.33 m (17 ft 8 in) long at the time of his burial at Kensett, Iowa, USA. It was presented to the Smithsonian Institution, Washington DC, in 1967.

Longest beard on a woman
The 'bearded lady' Janice Deveree (b. 1842) of Bracken County, Kentucky, USA, had a 36-cm-long (14-in) beard in 1884.

Longest moustache
The moustache grown by Kalyan Ramji Sain of Sundargarth, India, since 1976, had reached a span of 3.39 m (11 ft 1½ in) by July 1993. The right side was 1.72 m (5 ft 7¾ in) long and the left side was 1.67 m (5 ft 5¾ in).

John Roy (1910–88) of Weeley, near Clacton, Essex, boasted the longest moustache to have been cultivated by a British man. It began to grow in 1939 and attained a peak span of 1.89 m (6 ft 2½ in) on 2 April 1976. In 1984, it was shortened by 42 cm (16½ in) when Roy accidentally sat on it in the bath. He removed an equal amount from the other side to even the moustache.

Ted Sedman of St Albans, Herts, has grown a 1.6-m (5-ft 3-in) handlebar moustache and is the current holder of the British record.

Eyes

Highest hyperacuity
In April 1984, Dr Dennis M. Levi of the College of Optometry, University of Houston, Texas, USA, repeatedly identified the relative position of a thin bright green line within 0.85 seconds of arc. This is equivalent to a displacement of some 6 mm (¼ in) at a distance of 1.6 km (1 mile).

Light sensitivity
Working in Chicago, Illinois, USA, in 1942, Maurice H. Pirenne detected a flash of blue light of 500 nm in total darkness, when as few as five quanta or photons of light were available to be absorbed by the rod photoreceptors of the retina.

LARGEST AND SMALLEST WAI

Teeth

Earliest teeth
The first deciduous or milk teeth normally appear in infants at the age of between five and eight months, but there have been many cases of children born with teeth. Sean Keaney of Newbury, Berks, UK, was born on 10 April 1990 with 12 teeth. They were extracted to prevent feeding problems.

Molars usually appear at the age of 24 months, but in Pindborg's case (published in Denmark in 1970), a baby that was born six weeks prematurely had eight teeth at birth, four of them in the molar region.

Most sets of teeth
The growth of a third set of teeth in late life has been recorded several times. A case of a fourth dentition, known as Lison's case, was published in France in 1896.

Most valuable tooth
In 1816, a tooth that had belonged to Sir Isaac Newton (1642–1727) was sold in London, UK, for £730. It was purchased by a nobleman, who had the tooth set into a ring.

Most dedicated dentist
Brother Giovanni Battista Orsenigo of the Ospedale Fatebenefratelli, Rome, Italy, was a dentist by profession, and kept all 2,000,744 teeth that he extracted during his career, which lasted from 1868 to 1904. This gives an average of 185 teeth, or almost six total extractions, per day.

Hands and feet

Longest fingernails
The combined measurement of the nails of the left hand of Shridhar Chillal of India (b. 1937) was 587 cm (231 in) on 12 March 1996. The thumbnail was 135 cm (53 in) long, and the nails of his first, second, third and fourth fingers were 104 cm (41 in), 112 cm (44 in), 119 cm (47 in), and 117 cm (46 in) long respectively. Chillal last cut his nails in 1952.

Most and least fingers and toes
An inquest held on a baby boy at Shoreditch in the East End of London, UK, in Sept 1921 reported that he had 14 fingers and 15 toes.

The two-toed syndrome exhibited by some members of the Wadomo tribe of the Zambezi Valley, Zimbabwe, and the Kalanga tribe of the eastern Kalahari Desert, Botswana, is hereditary via a single mutated gene.

Largest feet
Excluding cases of elephantiasis, the biggest feet currently on record belong to Matthew McGrory (b. 1973) of Pennsylvania, USA, who wears US size 26 shoes (UK size 25½).

John Thrupp (b. 1964) of Stratford-upon-Avon, Warks, has the largest feet of any British person. He wears a size 21 shoe and is 2.11 m (6 ft 11 in) tall.

Necks and waists

Longest neck
Women of the Padaung, or Kareni, tribe of Myanmar (Burma) extend their necks by fitting increasing numbers of copper coils around them. The maximum recorded neck extension achieved in this manner is 40 cm (15¾ in).

Largest waist
Walter Hudson (1944–91) of New York, USA, had a record waist measurement of 3.02 m (119 in) when he was at his peak weight of 545 kg (85 st 7 lb).

Smallest waist
Ethel Granger (1905–82) of Peterborough, Cambs, UK, had the smallest waist of a person of normal stature. She reduced from a natural 56 cm (22 in) to 33 cm (13 in) between 1929 and 1939.

A measurement of 33 cm was also claimed for French actress Mlle Polaire (Emile Marie Bouchand) who lived from 1881 to 1939.

HANS LANGSETH'S BEARD GREW TO A RECORD LENGTH OF 5.33 M

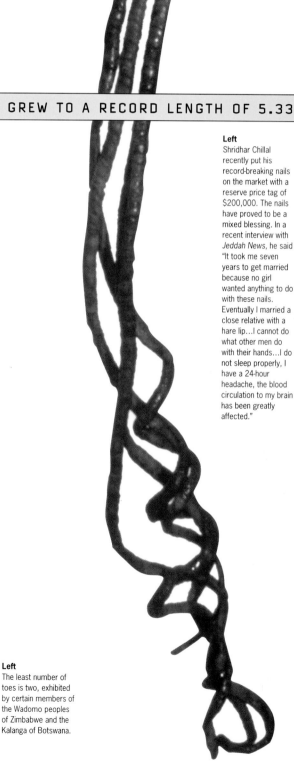

Left
Shridhar Chillal recently put his record-breaking nails on the market with a reserve price tag of $200,000. The nails have proved to be a mixed blessing. In a recent interview with *Jeddah News*, he said "It took me seven years to get married because no girl wanted anything to do with these nails. Eventually I married a close relative with a hare lip...I cannot do what other men do with their hands...I do not sleep properly, I have a 24-hour headache, the blood circulation to my brain has been greatly affected."

Left
The least number of toes is two, exhibited by certain members of the Wadomo peoples of Zimbabwe and the Kalanga of Botswana.

Dimensions

GREATEST WEIGHT LOSS 419 KG

Right
Robert Wadlow, the world's tallest man, is pictured being measured for a suit. Wadlow had reached a height of 2.72 m (8 ft 11¹⁄₁₀ in) when last measured in 1940.

Weight

Heaviest man
Jon Brower Minnoch (1941–83) of Washington State, USA, was 178 kg (28 st) in 1963 and 442 kg (69 st 9 lb) in 1976. When he was hospitalized in 1978, it took 12 firemen and an improvised stretcher to move him. He occupied two beds lashed together, and it took 13 people to roll him over. In 16 months to July 1979, he reduced from an estimated peak weight of 635 kg (100 st) to 216 kg (34 st), a record loss of 419 kg (66 st). He later gained 89 kg (14 st) in seven days in Oct 1981, and was rehospitalized in Seattle.

The heaviest British man was Peter Yarnall of London, who weighed 368 kg (58 st). When he died in 1984 at the age of 34, it took 10 firemen five hours to demolish his bedroom wall and winch his body to street level.

Heaviest woman
Rosalie Bradford (b. 1943) of the USA is said to have peaked at 544 kg (85 st) in Jan 1987 (there were no scales big enough to weigh her). After developing congestive heart failure, she was put on a diet and by Feb 1994 had reduced to 128 kg (20 st 3 lb), a record loss of 416 kg (64 st 11 lb).

Lightest person
Lucia Xarate (1863–89) of San Carlos, Mexico, an emaciated ateleiotic dwarf, weighed 1.1 kg (2 lb 8 oz) at birth. At the age of 17, she was 67 cm (26½ in) tall and weighed 2.13 kg (4 lb 11 oz).

Dwarves

Shortest person
The shortest mature human of whom there is independent evidence is Gul Mohammed (b. 1957) of New Delhi, India. When examined in 1990, he was 57 cm (22½ in) in height.

The shortest female is Pauline Musters of Ossendrecht, Netherlands, who measured 30 cm (12 in) at her birth in 1846. At the age of nine she was 55 cm (21½ in) tall and weighed 1.5 kg (3 lb 5 oz). She died of pneumonia with meningitis at the age of 19. A post mortem examination revealed her to be 61 cm (24 in) tall.

The shortest living female is Madge Bester (b. 1963) of Johannesburg, South Africa, who is only 65 cm (25½ in) tall. She suffers from the condition Osteogenesis imperfecta and is confined to a wheelchair.

Giants

Tallest true giant
The tallest non-pathological giant on record is Angus Macaskill (1823–63). Born on Berneray in the Sound of Harris, Western Isles, UK, he reached a height of 2.36 m (7 ft 9 in).

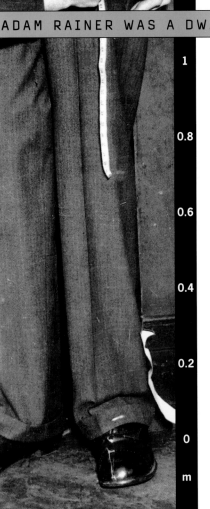

ADAM RAINER WAS A DWARF AT AGE 21 (1.18 M) AN

Tallest person
The tallest man for whom there is irrefutable evidence is Robert Pershing Wadlow, born in Illinois, USA, on 22 Feb 1918. When last measured in 1940, shortly before his death, Wadlow had reached a height of 2.72 m (8 ft 11¹⁄₁₀ in).

Zeng Jinlian (1964–82) of Hunan Province, China, measured 2.48 m (8 ft 1¾ in) when she died (this represents her height with assumed normal spinal curvature, as she could not stand up straight). Her abnormal growth began at the age of four months, and she was 1.56 m (5 ft 1½ in) tall before her fourth birthday and 2.17 m (7 ft 1½ in) when she was 13.

In the United Kingdom, John Middleton (1578–1623) of Hale, near Liverpool, was said to be 2.82 m (9 ft 3 in) tall, but his true stature seems to have been closer to 2.36 m (7 ft 9 in).

William Bradley (1787–1820), of E Yorkshire, UK, grew to a height of 2.36 m (7 ft 9 in).

The tallest British woman was Jane Bunford, (1895–1922), whose skeleton, preserved at Birmingham University Medical School, is 2.24 m (7 ft 4 in) in height. Shortly before her death, she stood 2.31 m (7 ft 7 in) tall and would have been at least 2.41 m (7ft 11 in) had she been able to stand fully erect.

Tallest living person
Haji Mohammad Alam Channa of Pakistan (b. 1956) is 2.32 m (7 ft 7¼ in) tall.

Sandy Allen (b. 1955) of the USA is currently 2.32 cm (7 ft 7¼ in) tall. Her abnormal growth began shortly after birth, and she stood 1.91 m (6 ft 3 in) by the age of 10 and 2.16 m (7 ft 1 in) by the age of 16.

The tallest living British man is Christopher Paul Greener (b. 1943), who is 2.29 m (7 ft 6¼ in) tall and weighs 165 kg (26 st).

Tallest married couple
Anna Hanen Swan (1846–88) of Nova Scotia, Canada, was 2.27 m (7 ft 5½ in) tall. She married Martin van Buren Bates (1845–1919) of Whitesburg, Letcher County, Kentucky, USA, in 1871. He was 2.19 m (7 ft 2½ in) tall.

Most dissimilar married couple
Fabien Pretou (b. 1968) married Natalie Lucius (b. 1966) at Seyssinet-Pariset, France, in April 1990. The groom stands 1.89 m (6 ft 2 in) tall and the bride 0.94 m (3 ft 1 in).

Most variable stature
Adam Rainer (1899–1950) of Graz, Austria, was 1.18 m (3 ft 10½ in) tall at the age of 21, but started to grow at a rapid rate and was 2.18 m (7 ft 1¾ in) tall by 1931. At his death, he was 2.34 m (7 ft 8 in) tall. He is the only person in history to have been both a dwarf and a giant.

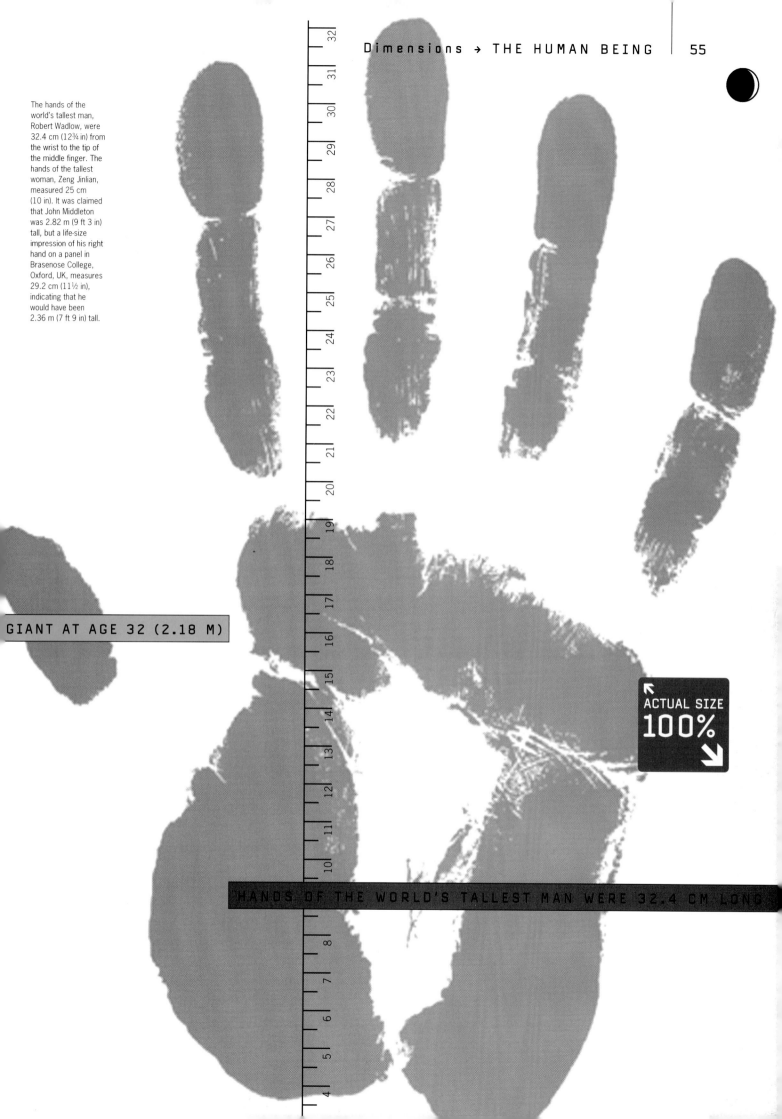

The hands of the world's tallest man, Robert Wadlow, were 32.4 cm (12¾ in) from the wrist to the tip of the middle finger. The hands of the tallest woman, Zeng Jinlian, measured 25 cm (10 in). It was claimed that John Middleton was 2.82 m (9 ft 3 in) tall, but a life-size impression of his right hand on a panel in Brasenose College, Oxford, UK, measures 29.2 cm (11½ in), indicating that he would have been 2.36 m (7 ft 9 in) tall.

GIANT AT AGE 32 (2.18 M)

ACTUAL SIZE
100%

HANDS OF THE WORLD'S TALLEST MAN WERE 32.4 CM LONG

Birth and life

MRS VASSILYEV HAD 69 CHILDREN IN 27 CONFINEMENTS

Right
Margaret McNaught, who along with Mabel Constable has produced more children than any other woman in the United Kingdom this century, is seen here with 20 of her 22 offspring.

Reproduction

Most children

The greatest officially recorded number of children that have been born to one mother is 69. The wife of Feodor Vassilyev (b. 1707), a peasant from Shuya, Russia, gave birth to 16 pairs of twins, seven sets of triplets and four sets of quadruplets in 27 confinements. Only two of the children, born between 1725 and 1765, failed to survive their infancy.

In the United Kingdom, Elizabeth Greenhille of Abbots Langley, Herts, who died in 1681, is alleged to have had 39 children (seven sons, 32 daughters) in a record 38 confinements.

The British record for the most number of children to one mother this century is 22. Margaret McNaught (b. 1923) of Balsall Heath, Birmingham, had 12 boys and 10 girls in single confinements, while the 22 offspring of Mabel Constable (b. 1920), of Long Itchington, Warwicks, included one set of triplets and two sets of twins.

Oldest mother

Rosanna Dalla Corta (b. 1931) of Viterbo, Italy, was reported to have given birth to a baby boy in July 1994, at the age of 63, after fertility treatment.

Heaviest single birth

The heaviest baby on record is a boy of 10.2 kg (22 lb 8 oz), born to Carmelina Fedele of Aversa, Italy, in Sept 1955.

In Jan 1879, Anna Bates of Canada (1846–88), who was 2.27 m (7 ft 5½ in) tall, gave birth to a boy weighing 10.8 kg (23 lb 12 oz) at her home in Seville, Ohio, USA, but the baby died 11 hours later.

Guy Warwick Carr, the eighth child of Andrew and Nicola Carr of Kirkby-in-Furness, Cumbria, UK, weighed 7 kg (15 lb 8 oz) when he was born on 9 March 1992.

Heaviest twins

Twins weighing 12.6 kg (27 lb 12 oz) were born to Mrs Haskin of Arkansas, USA, on 20 Feb 1924.

Heaviest triplets

The heaviest triplets in the United Kingdom, weighing 10.9 kg (24 lb), were born to Mary McDermott of Bearpark, Co Durham, on 18 Nov 1914.

Heaviest quadruplets

Two girls and two boys weighing 10.426 kg (22 lb 15¾ oz) were born to Tina Saunders at St Peter's Hospital, Chertsey, Surrey, UK, in Feb 1989.

Heaviest quintuplets

A weight of 11.35 kg (25 lb) was recorded in June 1953 for quintuplets born to Liu Saulian of Zhejiang, China, and in 1956 for quintuplets born to Mrs Kamalammal of Pondicherry, India.

Lightest single births

A premature baby girl weighing 280 g (9⁹⁄₁₀ oz) was reported to have been born on 27 June 1989 at the Loyola University Medical Center, Illinois, USA.

The lowest birthweight officially recorded for a surviving infant in the United Kingdom is 283 g (10 oz), for Marian Taggart (1938–83), who was six weeks premature. She was nursed by Dr D. A. Shearer, who fed her hourly for the first 30 hours with brandy, glucose and water through a fountain-pen filler. At three weeks she weighed 821 g (1 lb 13 oz) and by her first birthday 6.3 kg (13 lb 14 oz).

Lightest twins

A combined weight of 860 g (30⅓ oz) was recorded for: Roshan Maralyn and Melanie Louise, weighing 490 g (17⁷⁄₂₅ oz) and 370 g (13¹⁄₂₀ oz) respectively, born to Katrina Gray in the Royal Women's Hospital, Brisbane, Australia, in 1993; and Anne Faith Sarah and John Alexander, weighing 420 g (14⅘ oz) and 440 g (15½ oz) respectively, born to Wendy Kay Morrison in Ottawa General Hospital, Canada, in 1994.

CONJOINED TWINS CHAN

Heaviest baby 10.2 kg

Longest interval between births
Pegge Lynn of Huntingdon, Pennsylvania, USA, gave birth to a girl, Hanna, on 10 Nov 1995, but was not delivered of the twin, Eric, until 84 days later, on 2 Feb 1996, at the Geisinger Medical Center, Danville.

Most premature baby
James Elgin Gill was born 128 days premature to Brenda Gill in Ottawa, Ontario, Canada in May 1987. He weighed 624 g (1 lb 6 oz).

British baby Rukaya Bailey was born 122 days premature to Joanne Bailey in Salford, Greater Manchester, in June 1989.

CHANG AND ENG BUNKER FATHERED A TOTAL OF 22 CHILDREN

Multiple births
'Siamese' twins
Conjoined twins are termed 'Siamese' after Chang and Eng ('Left' and 'Right' in Thai) Bunker, born of Chinese parents at Meklong in 1811 and joined by a cartilaginous band at the chest. They married Sarah and Adelaide Yates of North Carolina, USA, and fathered 10 and 12 children respectively. They died within three hours of each other in 1874.

The most extreme form of the syndrome is *dicephales tetrabrachius dipus* (two heads, four arms and two legs). The only fully reported example is Masha and Dasha Krivoshlyapovy, born in the USSR in Jan 1950.

The earliest successful separation of Siamese twins was performed on 14 Dec 1952 on xiphopagus girls (joined at the sternum) at Mount Sinai Hospital, Cleveland, Ohio, USA, by Dr Jac S. Geller.

Greatest single pregnancies
Dr Gennaro Montanino of Rome, Italy, claimed to have removed the foetuses of 10 girls and five boys from the womb of a 35-year-old housewife who was four months pregnant in July 1971. A fertility drug was responsible for this unique instance of quindecaplets.

Cases of decaplets (two males, eight females) were reported in Bacacai, Brazil, in April 1946, in Spain in 1924, and in China in May 1936.

The greatest number of children in a single birth on medical record is nine (nonuplets), born to Geraldine Brodrick at the Royal Hospital for Women, Sydney, Australia, in June 1971. Of the five boys and four girls, none lived for more than six days.

Nonuplets were also reported in Philadelphia, Pennsylvania, USA, in May 1971 and Bagerhat, Bangladesh, in May 1977. In both cases, none of the babies survived.

The British record is septuplets (four boys, three girls), born to Susan Halton (b. 1960) at Liverpool Maternity Hospital in Aug 1987. None of the children survived.

Most multiple births in one family
Mrs Vassilyev of Shuya, Russia, bore 16 sets of twins, seven sets of triplets and four sets of quadruplets.

Barbara Zulu of Barberton, South Africa, bore six sets of twins in seven years, to 1973. Anna Steynvaait of Johannesburg, South Africa, had two sets in 10 months in 1960.

Maddalena Granata (b. 1839) of Italy gave birth to 15 sets of triplets.

Descendants
Greatest number of descendants
In polygamous countries, the number of a person's descendants can become incalculable. The Emperor of Morocco, Moulay Ismail (1672–1727), was reputed to have fathered 525 sons and 342 daughters by 1703 and achieved a 700th son in 1721.

At his death at the age of 96 in 1992, Samuel S. Mast of Fryburg, Pennsylvania, USA, had 824 living descendants (11 children, 97 grandchildren, 634 great-grandchildren and 82 great-great-grandchildren).

Family spanning seven generations
Augusta Bunge (b. 1879) of Wisconsin, USA, became a great-great-great-great-grandmother when her great-great-great-granddaughter gave birth to a son, Christopher John Bollig, on 21 Jan 1989.

Most living ascendants
Megan Sue Austin (b. 1982) of Bar Harbor, Maine, USA, had 19 direct ascendants (a full set of grandparents and great-grandparents and five great-great-grandparents) at her birth.

Longest family tree
The lineage of K'ung Ch'iu, or Confucius (551–479 BC), can be traced back to his great-great-great-great grandfather K'ung Chia in the 8th century BC and forward to K'ung Chia's 86th lineal descendants, seven of whom are alive today.

Longevity
Oldest authenticated centenarian
The greatest fully authenticated age to which a human has lived is 121. Jeanne Louise Calment was born on 21 Feb 1875 and currently lives in Arles, France.

Lucy Askew (b. 8 Sept 1883), of Buckhurst Hill, Essex, is the oldest living person in the United Kingdom.

Vinson Gulliver (b. 28 Nov 1887) of Altrincham, Cheshire, UK, is the oldest living man.

Oldest twins
Eli Shadrack and John Meshak Phipps were born on 14 Feb 1803 at Affington, Virginia, USA. The first to die was Eli, on 23 Feb 1911.

Identical twins Mildred Widman Philippi and Mary Widman Franzini of St Louis, Missouri, USA, celebrated their 104th birthday on 17 June 1984. Mildred was the first to die, 44 days short of their 105th birthday.

Oldest triplets
Faith, Hope and Charity Cardwell were born on 18 May 1899 at Elm Mott, Texas, USA. Faith died first, on 2 Oct 1994, aged 95.

The oldest British triplets were Faith Alice, Hope Fanny and Charity Sarah Stockdale (b. 1857) of N Yorkshire. Charity died first, on 30 July 1944.

Oldest quadruplets
Adolf, Anne-Marie, Emma and Elisabeth Ottman of Munich, Germany, were born on 5 May 1912. Adolf was the first to die, on 17 March 1992, at the age of 79.

Disease and medicine

OLDEST PERSON EVER TO UNDERGO AN OPERATION WAS 111 YEARS 105 DAYS OLD

Right
Prof. Katherine O'Hanlan frees the last of the adhesions to the abdominal wall, before rolling the largest tumour ever to be removed intact onto a stretcher.

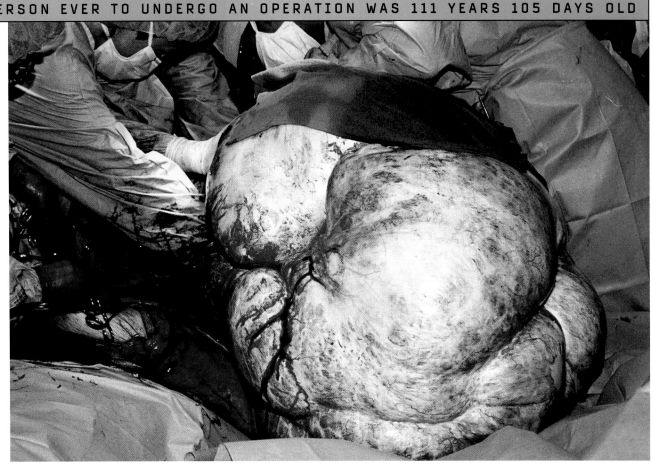

Largest tumour 137.6 kg

Death and disease
Commonest diseases
Periodontal diseases such as gingivitis (inflammation of the gums) are the commonest non-contagious diseases. The most common contagious disease is coryza, or the common cold.

Most fatal diseases
A number of diseases, such as AIDS and rabies encephalitis, are generally considered to be universally fatal.

The pneumonic form of plague (a bacterial infection) was fatal to all who caught it: the Black Death of 1347–51 claimed a quarter of the population of Europe and 75 million people worldwide.

Leading cause of death
In industrialized countries, diseases of the heart and the blood vessels account for more than half of all deaths. The commonest of these are heart attacks and strokes.

Operations
Longest operation
An operation lasting 96 hours was performed from 4 to 8 Feb 1951 in Chicago, Illinois, USA, on Gertrude Levandowski. During the removal of an ovarian cyst, her weight fell from 280 kg (44 st) to 140 kg (22 st).

Most operations endured and performed
From 22 July 1954 to the end of 1994, Charles Jensen of Chester, South Dakota, USA, had 970 operations to remove tumours associated with basal cell naevus syndrome.

Dr M. C. Modi, a pioneer of mass eye surgery in India since 1943, has performed up to 833 cataract operations in one day. By 1993, he had visited 46,120 villages and 12,118,630 patients, and performed 610,564 operations.

Oldest to undergo an operation
James Henry Brett Jr of Houston, Texas, USA, underwent a hip operation on 7 Nov 1960 at the age of 111 years 105 days.

The oldest Briton to be operated on was Miss Mary Wright, who died during a thigh operation at Boston, Lincs, on 22 April 1971, aged 109 years 53 days.

Transplants
First heart transplant
The first heart transplant was performed on 55-year-old Louis Washkansky at the Groote Schuur Hospital, Cape Town, South Africa, from 1 a.m. to 6 a.m. on 3 Dec 1967, by a team of 30 led by Prof. Christiaan Neethling Barnard. The donor was 25-year-old Denise Ann Darvall. Washkansky lived for 18 days.

The first British heart transplant took place at the National Heart Hospital, London, on 3 May

A MUNCHAUSEN'S SUFFER

1968. The patient, Frederick West, survived for 46 days.

Longest-surviving heart transplant patient
Dirk van Zyl of Cape Town, South Africa, survived for 23 years 57 days after receiving a heart at the Groote Schuur Hospital, Cape Town, on 10 May 1971.

The longest-surviving transplant patient in the United Kingdom is Derrick Morris, who underwent surgery at Harefield Hospital, Greater London, on 23 Feb 1980.

Youngest heart transplant patient
Olivia Maize of Murphy, North Carolina, USA, underwent a heart transplant at Loma Linda Hospital in California, USA, on 1 July 1994 at the age of 1 hr 40 min. She died one month later, following rejection complications.

THE BLACK DEATH OF 1347–51 CLAIMED THE LIVES OF 75 MILLION PEOPLE

The youngest British recipient was Hollie Roffey, who received a heart at the age of 10 days at the National Heart Hospital, London, on 29 July 1984. She survived for 10 days.

First heart-lung-liver transplant
The first triple transplant took place on 17 Dec 1986 at Papworth Hospital, Cambridge, UK, when Davina Thompson of Rawmarsh, S Yorkshire, underwent surgery for seven hours by a team of 15 headed by surgeon John Wallwork and Prof. Sir Roy Calne.

Kidney
The longest surviving kidney transplant patient is Johanna Leanora Rempel of Red Deer, Alberta, Canada, who was given a kidney from her identical twin sister Lana Blatz on 28 Dec 1960, at the Peter Bent Brigham Hospital, Boston, Massachusetts, USA.

First transplantee to give birth
Johanna Rempel, who received a donor kidney from her twin in Dec 1960, gave birth to a baby boy at Winnipeg General Hospital, Manitoba, Canada, on 7 Sept 1967.

Medical oddities

Longest tracheostomy
Winifred Campbell of Wanstead, London, UK, breathed through a silver tube in her throat from the age of four in 1906 until her death 86 years later, in 1992.

Longest haemodialysis treatment
Brian Wilson of Edinburgh, Lothian, UK, suffered kidney failure from the age of 24, and began dialysis at the Royal Infirmary of Edinburgh on 30 May 1964. He averages three visits per week to the hospital.

Munchausen's syndrome
The most extreme known case of the rare and incurable condition known as Munchausen's syndrome, characterized by a continual desire for medical treatment, was William McIlroy, who cost the British National Health Service an estimated £2.5 million during his 50-year career as a hospital patient. During that time he had 400 major and minor operations, and stayed at 100 different hospitals under 22 aliases. The longest period he was ever out of hospital was six months. In 1979, McIlroy hung up his bedpan for the last time, saying that he was sick of hospitals. He retired to an old people's home in Birmingham, W Midlands, where he died in 1983.

Largest tumour
The largest recorded tumour was an ovarian cyst weighing about 148.7 kg (23 st 6 lb). It was drained before the shell was removed by Dr Arthur Spohn in Texas, USA, in 1905.

The largest tumour ever removed intact was a multicystic mass of the right ovary weighing 137.6 kg (303 lb) and measuring 1 m (3 ft) in diameter. The operation, which lasted more than six hours, was performed by Prof. Katherine O'Hanlan of Stanford University Medical Center, California, USA, in Oct 1991. The 34-year-old patient weighed 95 kg (210 lb) after the operation and has made a full recovery. She left the operating theatre on one stretcher and the cyst left on another.

Largest gall bladder
Prof. Bimal C. Ghosh removed an enlarged gall bladder weighing 10.4 kg (23 lb) from a 69-year-old woman complaining of increasing swelling around the abdomen, at the National Naval Medical Center in Bethesda, Maryland, USA, on 15 March 1989. After the removal of this gall bladder, which had a weight more than three times that of the average newborn baby, the patient made a full recovery.

Gallstones
The largest gallstone reported in medical literature weighed 6.29 kg (13 lb 14 oz). It was removed from an 80-year-old woman by Dr Humphrey Arthure at Charing Cross Hospital, London, UK, on 29 Dec 1952.

In Aug 1987, it was reported that a total of 23,530 gallstones had been removed from an 85-year-old woman by Dr K. Whittle Martin at Worthing Hospital, W Sussex, UK, after the patient complained of severe abdominal pain.

Treatment

Most hospitals
The country with the greatest number of hospitals is China, with 60,784 in 1993.

Most and least hospital beds
Monaco has the greatest number of hospital beds per person (168 for every 10,000 people), and Afghanistan, Bangladesh, Ethiopia and Nepal have the fewest (three per 10,000 people).

The hospital with the greatest number of beds is Baragwanath Hospital, in Soweto, South Africa, which has a total of 3,294 beds.

Most doctors
The country with the greatest number of doctors is China, which had a total of 1,832,000 in 1993, including dentists and those practising traditional Chinese medicine.

Least doctors
Niger has the highest number of people per doctor, at 54,472.

Most mental health practitioners
The USA has the most psychiatrists and psychologists. The American Psychological Association had 142,000 registered members in early 1996, and the American Psychiatric Association had 39,450.

Most dentists
The country with the greatest number of dental practitioners is the USA, where there

...TH AN OBSESSIVE DESIRE FOR TREATMENT HAD 400 OPERATIONS UNDER 22 ALIASES

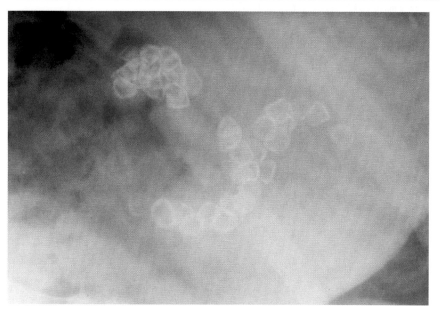

Gallstones are small pebble-like objects that form in the gall bladder. The largest ever reported weighed 6.29 kg (13 lb 14 oz).

were a total of 141,412 registered members of the American Dental Association at the end of 1995.

Youngest doctor
Balamurali Ambati (b. 29 July 1977) of Hollis Hills, New York, USA, was the youngest ever person to become a doctor when he graduated from the Mount Sinai School of Medicine in New York on 19 May 1995 at the age of 17.

Most doctors in one family
The eight sons and two daughters of Dr William and Beryl Waldron of Knocknacarra, Co. Galway, Republic of Ireland, all qualified as doctors from University College, Galway, between 1976 and 1990.

Oldest family medical practice
The Barcia family of Valencia, Spain, have owned the same medical practice for seven generations since 1792.

Medical extremes

LONGEST EVER COMA LASTED FOR 37 YEARS 111 DAYS

Longest sneezing fit 978 days

Medical emergencies

Longest cardiac arrest

When fisherman Jan Egil Refsdahl fell overboard off Bergen, Norway, in Dec 1987, his temperature fell to 24°C (75°F) and his heart stopped beating for four hours. He made a full recovery after being connected to a heart-lung machine at Haukeland Hospital.

Longest post-mortem birth

The longest gestation interval in a post-mortem birth was 84 days, in the case of a baby girl delivered of a brain-dead woman at Roanoke, Virginia, USA, on 5 July 1983.

Longest coma

Elaine Esposito (b. 1934) of Florida, USA, fell into a coma during an appendectomy on 6 Aug 1941. She died on 25 Nov 1978, after a coma lasting 37 years 111 days.

Endurance

Highest g forces

In a crash at Silverstone race circuit, Northants, UK, in July 1977, racing driver David Purley survived a deceleration from 173 km/h (108 mph) to zero in 66 cm (26 in). He endured 179.8 g and suffered a total of 29 fractures, three dislocations and six heart stoppages.

The highest g value to have been voluntarily endured is 82.6 g for a duration of 0.04 seconds, by Eli L. Beeding Jr on a water-braked rocket sled at Holloman Air Force Base, New Mexico, USA, on 16 May 1958. He was hospitalized for three days.

Longest hospital stay

Martha Nelson was admitted to the Columbus State Institute for the Feeble-Minded in Ohio, USA, in 1875. She died in the Orient State Institution, Ohio, in Jan 1975, aged 103, after spending more than 99 years in hospitals.

Highest air temperature

The highest dry-air temperature to have been endured by naked men during US Air Force experiments in 1960 was 205°C (400°F). A temperature of 260°C (500°F) was endured by heavily clothed men. Air temperatures of 140°C (284°F) have been found quite bearable in saunas.

Most injections

Samuel L. Davidson (b. 1912) of Glasgow, UK, has had—at a conservative estimate—78,900 insulin injections since 1923.

Longest in an iron lung

Dorothy Stone (b. 1928) of Liss, Hants, UK, has used a negative pressure respirator ever since 1947.

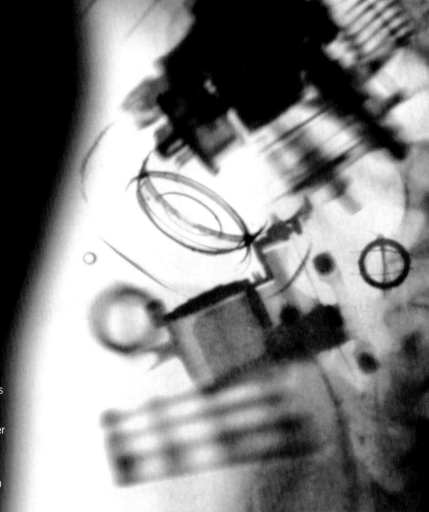

'MONSIEUR MANGETOUT' HAS DEVOURED BICYCLES

LONGEST PERIOD WITHOUT FOOD OR WATER IS 18 DAYS, WHEN ANDREAS MIHAVE

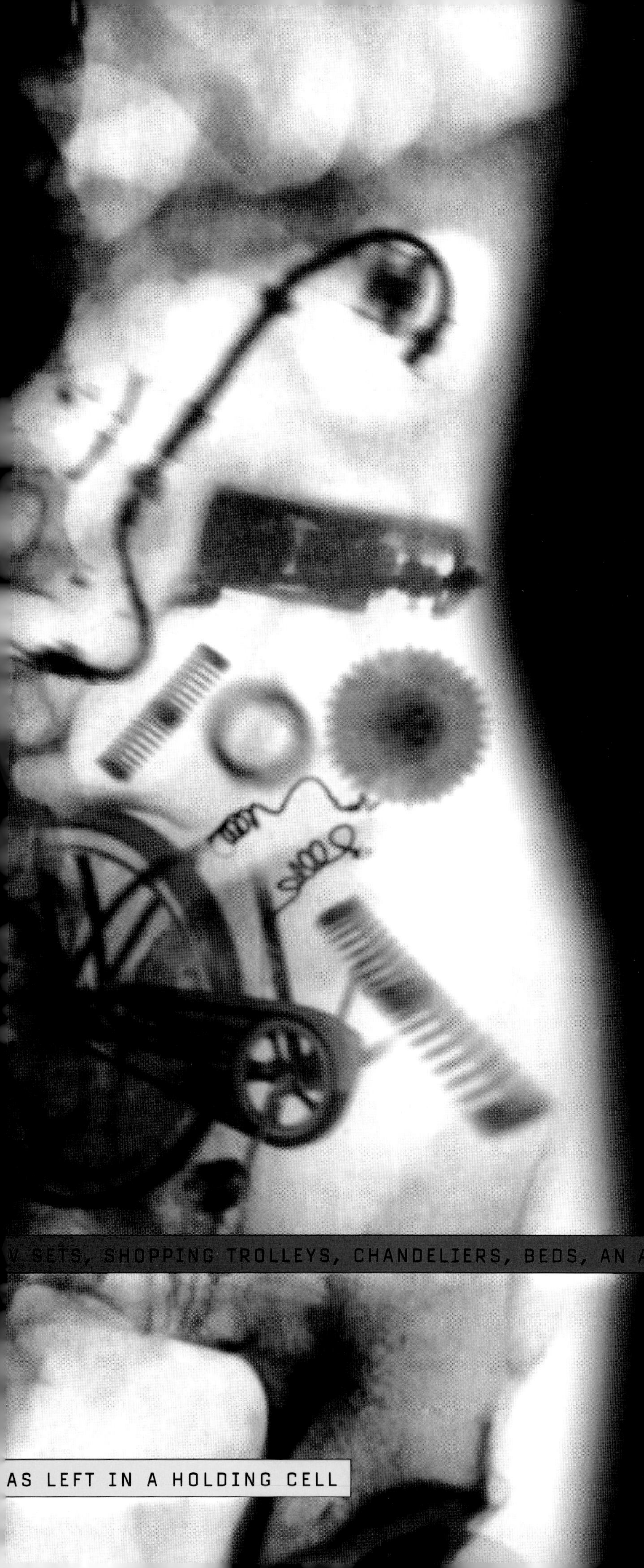

John Prestwich (b. 1938) of Kings Langley, Herts, UK, has been dependent on a respirator since 24 Nov 1955.

Most pills taken
The highest recorded number of pills to have been taken by a single individual is 565,939 between 9 June 1967 and 19 June 1988 by C. H. A. Kilner of Bindura, Zimbabwe.

Longest without food and water
Andreas Mihavecz of Bregenz, Austria, was put into a holding cell in a local government building in Höchst on 1 April 1979, but was totally forgotten by the police. On 18 April he was discovered close to death. Mihavecz had been a passenger in a crashed car.

Longest underwater submergence
In 1986, two-year-old Michelle Funk of Salt Lake City, Utah, USA, made a full recovery after spending 66 minutes underwater having fallen into a swollen creek.

Medical anomalies
Hiccoughing
Charles Osborne of Anthon, Iowa, USA, began to hiccough in 1922 while weighing a hog before slaughtering it. He led a normal life, marrying twice and fathering eight children, and stopped hiccoughing in 1990.

Sneezing
Donna Griffiths of Pershore, Hereford and Worcester, UK, began to sneeze on 13 Jan 1981. She sneezed an estimated 1 million times in the first 365 days, and stopped after 978 days.

Snoring
Kåre Walkert (b. 1949) of Kumala, Sweden, who suffers from the breathing disorder apnea, recorded peak levels of 93 dBA at the Örebro Regional Hospital on 24 May 1993.

Swallowing
A 42-year-old compulsive swallower who complained of 'slight abdominal pain' in June 1927 was found to have 2,533 objects, including 947 bent pins, in her stomach.

The heaviest object to have been extracted from a human stomach is a ball of hair weighing 2.35 kg (5 lb 3 oz), from a 20-year-old female compulsive swallower in the South Devon and East Cornwall Hospital, UK, on 30 March 1895.

V SETS, SHOPPING TROLLEYS, CHANDELIERS, BEDS, AN AEROPLANE, A COMPUTER AND A COFFIN

Michel Lotito (b. 1950), or 'Monsieur Mangetout', of Grenoble, France, has eaten metal and glass since 1959. Experts have x-rayed his stomach and described his ability to consume 900 g (2 lb) of metal per day as unique. His diet since 1966 has included 18 bicycles, 15 supermarket trolleys, seven TV sets, six chandeliers, two beds, a pair of skis, a Cessna light aircraft and a computer. He is said to provide the only example of a coffin (handles and all) ending up inside a man.

AS LEFT IN A HOLDING CELL

062 084

063 085

064 086   IN 1990 BERNAI

065 087

066 088

067 089

LARGEST MASS WEDDING CEREMONY INVOLVED ABOUT 35,000 COUPLES

068 090

Human

069 091

070 092

MOST BAKED BEANS EATEN ONE BY ONE WITH A COCKTAIL STICK IN 30 MINUTES IS 2,78

1994   071 093

1995   072 094

1996   073 095

1997   074 096

1998   075 097

076   MOST TRAVELLED HITCHHIKER HA

077

078   HIGHEST SPEE

079

080

FASTEST TIME ATTAINED IN A 1-MILE WHEELBARROW RACE IS 4 MIN 48.51 SEC

DANCE PICKED 50 SHELLS IN 1 MIN 30.55 SEC

WORLD'S FASTEST WINKLE PICKER, SHEILA

AVERY CULTIVATED A PARSNIP THAT GREW TO A RECORD LENGTH OF 4.36 M

achievements

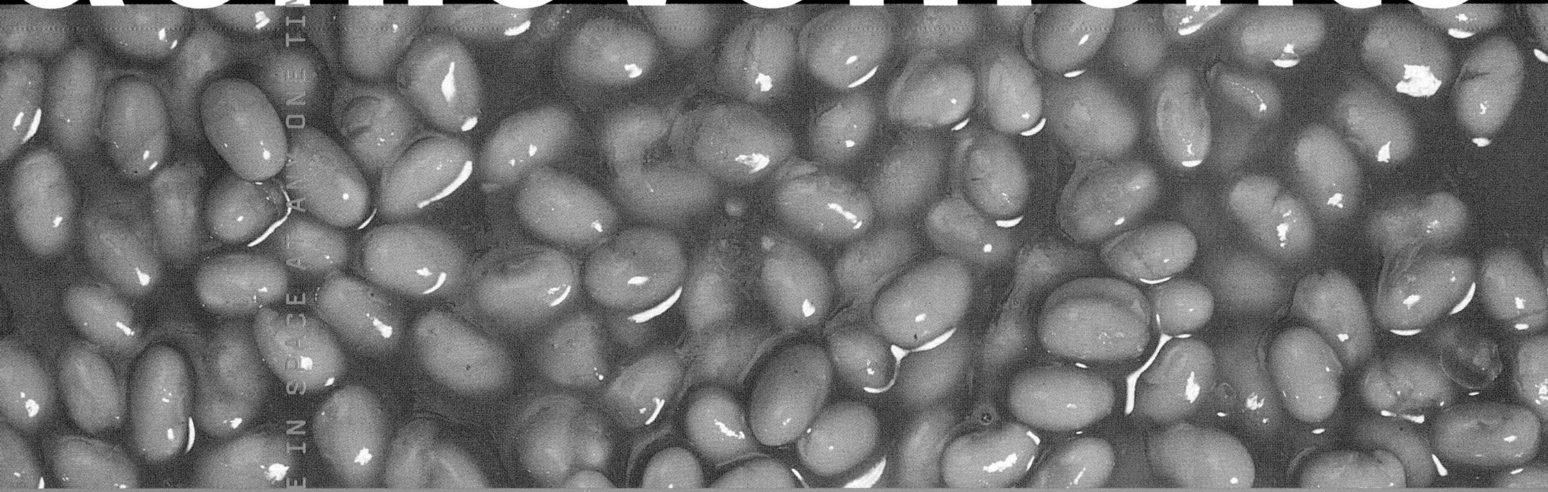

GREATEST NUMBER OF PEOPLE IN SPACE AT ONE TIME WAS 13

ERRY COLE BALANCED A RECORD-BREAKING 29 MILK CRATES ON HIS CHIN FOR 10 SECONDS

BTAINED FREE RIDES OVER A DISTANCE OF 776,955 KM

GREATEST DISTANCE THAT A COW PAT HAS BEEN TOSSED IS 81.1 M

ABOUT 99.2% OF TOM LEPPARD'S BODY IS COVERED WITH A LEOPARD SKIN TATTOO

T WHICH HUMANS HAVE TRAVELLED IS 39,897 KM/H

MOST PEOPLE TO KISS SIMULTANEOUSLY WAS 1,420

OUNGEST PERSON TO HAVE VISITED BOTH POLES WAS 11 YEARS OF AGE

Exploration

Longest spaceflight 437 days · **Longest spaceflight 437 days**

Polar exploration

North Pole conquest
The first people to have indisputably reached the North Pole at ground level—exactly 90°00'00"N (±300 m)—were Pavel Afanasyevich Geordiyenko, Pavel Kononovich Sen'ko, Mikhail Mikhailovich Somov and Mikhail Yemel'yanovich Ostrekin (USSR), on 23 April 1948.

South Pole conquest
The South Pole was first reached at 11 a.m. on 14 Dec 1911 by a Norwegian party of five men led by Capt. Roald Engebereth Gravning Amundsen (1872–1928) after a 53-day march with dog sledges from the Bay of Whales.

First to visit both poles
Dr Albert Paddock Crary of the USA reached the North Pole in a Dakota aircraft on 3 May 1952. On 12 Feb 1961 he arrived at the South Pole by Sno Cat.

Oldest to visit both poles
Major Will Lacy went to the North Pole on 9 April 1990 at the age of 82 and the South Pole on 20 Dec 1991 at the age of 84, both times by light aircraft.

Youngest to visit both poles
Robert Schumann went to the North Pole by air on 6 April 1992 at the age of 10 and the South Pole on 29 Dec 1993 at the age of 11. On the second trip he arrived by mountain bike after flying to within a short distance of the pole.

Pole-to-pole circumnavigation
Sir Ranulph Fiennes and Charles Burton of the British Trans-Globe Expedition travelled south from Greenwich (2 Sept 1979), crossed the South Pole (15 Dec 1980) and the North Pole (10 April 1982), and returned to Greenwich, arriving on 29 Aug 1982 after a 56,000-km (35,000-mile) trek.

First to walk to both poles
Robert Swan (b. 1956) led the three-man Footsteps of Scott expedition, which reached the South Pole on 11 Jan 1986. He also led the eight-man Icewalk expedition, which arrived at the North Pole on 14 May 1989.

Longest polar sledge journeys
The six-member International Trans-Antarctica Expedition sledged 6,040 km (3,750 miles) in 220 days from Seal Nunataks on 27 July 1989 to Mirnyy on 3 March 1990. They were supported by aircraft throughout, and accompanied by a team of 40 dogs.

The longest totally self-supporting polar sledge journey was undertaken by Sir Ranulph Fiennes and Dr Michael Stroud, who covered the 2,170 km (1,350 miles) from Gould Bay to the Ross ice shelf in Antarctica in 94 days between 9 Nov 1992 and 16 Jan 1993.

Submarine exploration

Greatest ocean descent
The Swiss-built US-Navy bathyscaphe *Trieste*, manned by Dr Jacques Piccard (b. 1922) of Switzerland and USN Lt. Donald Walsh, reached a depth of 10,911 m (35,797 ft) on 23 Jan 1960 in the Challenger Deep of the Marianas Trench, 400 km (250 miles) south-west of Guam in the Pacific Ocean.

Deep-diving records
The record depth for the ill-advised activity of breath-held diving is 130 m (428 ft), by Francisco 'Pipín' Ferreras (Cuba) off Cabo San Lucas, Mexico, on 10 March 1996. He was underwater for 2 min 11 sec.

The record dive with scuba (self-contained underwater breathing apparatus used without surface air hoses) is 133 m (437 ft), by John J. Gruener and R. Neal Watson of the USA off Freeport, Grand Bahama, on 14 Oct 1968.

Submergence
The continuous duration record for scuba is 212 hr 30 min, by Michael Stevens of Birmingham in a Royal Navy tank at the National Exhibition Centre, Birmingham, UK, from 14–23 Feb 1986.

Deepest underwater escape
Roger R. Chapman and Roger Mallinson were trapped for 76 hours when the *Pisces III* sank to a depth of 480 m (1,575 ft) at a point 240 km (150 miles) south-east of Cork, Republic of Ireland, on 29 Aug 1973. The vessel was hauled to the surface on 1 Sept by the cable ship *John Cabot* after work by *Pisces V*, *Pisces II* and the remote-control recovery vessel *Curv* (Controlled Underwater Recovery Vehicle).

The greatest depth from which an escape without equipment has been made is 68.6 m (225 ft), by Richard A. Slater from the rammed submersible *Nekton Beta* off Catalina Island, California, USA, on 28 Sept 1970.

The record for an escape with equipment is by Norman Cooke and Hamish Jones, who escaped from the submarine HMS *Otus* at a depth of 183 m (601 ft) during a naval exercise in Bjørnefjorden, off Bergen, Norway, on 22 July 1987. They were wearing standard suits with built-in lifejackets.

Deepest salvage
The greatest depth at which salvage has been carried out is 5,258 m (17,251 ft), after a helicopter crashed into the Pacific Ocean in Aug 1991 with the loss of four lives. Crew of the USS *Salvor* and personnel from Eastport International managed to raise the wreckage to the surface on 27 Feb 1992.

Space exploration

Earliest manned satellites
The earliest manned spaceflight ratified by the governing body, the Fédération Aéronautique Internationale (FAI), was by Cosmonaut Flight Major (later Col.) Yuri Alekseyevich Gagarin (1934–68) in *Vostok 1* on 12 April 1961.

Most spaceflights
Of the 188 manned spaceflights undertaken by 1 April 1996, 106 were American flights.

Astronauts
By 1 April 1996, the oldest of the 345 people to have been in Space was Vance DeVoe Brand of the USA (b. 1931). He was 59 when he took part in the space shuttle mission aboard the STS 35 *Columbia* on 2 Dec 1990.

The oldest female astronaut is Shannon Lucid of the USA, who was 53 when she took part in the space shuttle mission STS 76 *Atlantis* in March 1996.

The youngest astronaut is Major (later Lt-Gen.) Gherman Stepanovich Titov, who was aged 25 when launched in *Vostok 2* in Aug 1961.

The youngest, and first, woman in Space was Valentina Tereshkova, aged 26, in *Vostok 6* on 16 June 1963.

Most experienced astronauts
Russian doctor Valeriy Poliyakov clocked up 678 days 16 hr 33 min 16 sec on two spaceflights in 1988–89 and 1994–95.

Capt. John Watts Young completed his sixth spaceflight on 8 Dec 1983, when he relinquished command of *Columbia* STS 9/Spacelab after a space career lasting 34 days 19 hr 41 min 53 sec.

The most flights by Soviet/Russian cosmonauts is five, by Vladimir Dzhanibekov between 1978 and 1985, and by Gennadiy Strekalov in 1980 and 1995.

The most flights by a woman is five, by Shannon Lucid (flights STS 51G, 34, 43, 58 and 76).

Longest manned spaceflight
Russian doctor Valeriy Poliyakov was launched to the *Mir* space station aboard *Soyuz TM18* on 8 Jan 1994 and landed in *Soyuz TM20* on 22 March 1995, after a spaceflight of 437 days 17 hr 58 min 16 sec.

Shortest manned spaceflight
The suborbital mission by Comdr. Alan Bartlett Shepard aboard *Mercury-Redstone 3* on 5 May 1961 lasted 15 min 28 sec.

Largest crew
The record for a single space mission is the crew of eight launched on space shuttle STS 61A *Challenger* on 30 Oct 1985.

Most people in Space at one time
On 14 March 1995, seven Americans were aboard the space shuttle STS 67 *Endeavour*, three CIS cosmonauts were aboard the *Mir* space station and two cosmonauts and a US astronaut were aboard *Soyuz TM21*.

On 31 July 1992, five countries had astronauts or cosmonauts in Space at the same time: four CIS cosmonauts and one Frenchman were aboard *Mir* and five US astronauts, one Swiss and one Italian were aboard STS 46 *Atlantis*.

Most isolated human being
The farthest a human has been from another is 3,596.4 km (2,234¾ miles). Alfred M. Worden was command module pilot on the US *Apollo 15* lunar mission of 30 July–1 Aug 1971 while David Scott and James Irwin were exploring the Moon's surface.

Speed
The fastest speed at which human beings have travelled is 39,897 km/h (24,791 mph). The command module of *Apollo 10*, carrying Col. Thomas Patten Stafford, USAF, Comdr. Eugene Andrew Cernan and Comdr. John Watts Young, USN, reached this maximum speed on 26 May 1969, when travelling at 11.08 km/sec (6⅞ miles/sec).

Lunar conquests
Neil Armstrong, command pilot of the *Apollo 11* mission, was the first man to set foot on the Moon, on 21 July 1969.

Capt. Eugene Cernan and Dr Harrison Hagen 'Jack' Schmitt were on the Moon's surface for 74 hr 59 min during the longest lunar mission, *Apollo 17*, which lasted 12 days 13 hr 51 min from 7 to 19 Dec 1972.

JURNEY COVERED A DISTANCE OF 2,170 KM

EEPEST BREATH-HELD DIVE IS 130 M, BY FRANCISCO FERRERAS IN 1996

Spacewalks
The greatest number of spacewalks undertaken is 10, by the Russian cosmonaut Aleksandr Serebrov (b. 1944), during two missions in 1990 and 1993.

The longest spacewalk, by Pierre Thuot, Rick Hieb and Tom Akers of STS 49 *Endeavour* on 13 May 1992, lasted 8 hr 29 min.

Heaviest space object
The combined Russian *Mir 1* space station and US space shuttle *Atlantis*, which docked on 29 June 1995, weighed 223 tonnes.

Largest space object
The Italian Tethered Satellite deployed from the space shuttle STS 75 *Columbia* extended 19.7 km (12¼ miles) on 26 Feb 1996, before the tether snapped. The satellite and the length of tether continued to orbit until 19 March 1996.

Top
The first American to walk in Space was Edward White, during the *Gemini 4* mission in June 1965.

Middle
A mean annual temperature of -25°C (-13°F) at the North Pole creates bitter conditions for Arctic explorers.

Bottom
Grand Bahama was the site of the record scuba dive of 133 m (437 ft).

Travel and tourism

LONGEST 'ROUND THE WORLD' WALK HAS COVERED 50,559 KM TO DATE

Travellers

Most active travellers

The most travelled person is John D. Clouse from Evansville, Indiana, USA, who has visited all the sovereign countries and all but six of the non-sovereign or other territories that existed in early 1996.

The most travelled person in the horseback era is believed to have been Methodist bishop Francis Asbury, who travelled 425,000 km (264,000 miles) in North America from 1771 to 1815, preaching 16,000 sermons and ordaining almost 3,000 ministers.

Most travelled couple

Dr Robert and Carmen Becker of East Northport, New York, USA, have visited all of

The greatest distance claimed for a 'round the world walker' is 50,559 km (31,416 miles), by Arthur Blessitt of North Fort Myers, Florida, USA, in more than 26 years since 25 Dec 1969. He has been to all seven continents, carrying a 3.7-m (12-ft) cross and preaching throughout his walk.

Solo walker Steven Newman of Bethel, Ohio, USA, spent a total of four years (from 1 April 1983 to 1 April 1987) walking a distance of 24,959 km (15,509 miles) around the world, at a faster rate than Schilling, Kunst or Blessitt. He visited 20 different countries and five continents.

The record for the 6,057-km (3,764-mile) trans-Canada (Halifax to Vancouver) walk is 96 days by Clyde McRae, between 1 May and 4 Aug 1973.

John Lees of Brighton, E Sussex, UK, walked 4,628 km (2,876 miles) across the USA from City Hall, Los Angeles, California, to City Hall, New York, in 53 days 12 hr 15 min, averaging 86.49 km (53 miles 1,314 yd) a day, between 11 April and 3 June 1972.

FASTEST EVER FLIGHT FROM CENTRAL LONDON

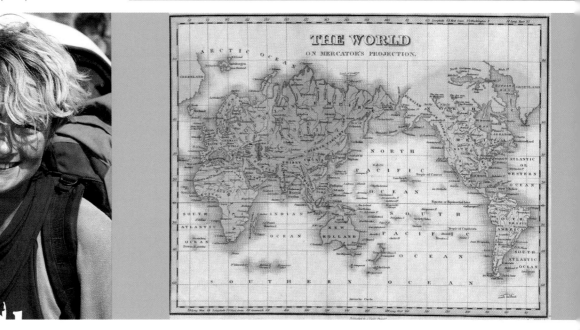

GERMAN HITCH-HIKER STEPHAN SCHLEI HAS COVERED A TOTAL OF 776,955 K

the sovereign countries and all but seven of the non-sovereign or other territories.

Most travelled hitchhiker

Stephan Schlei of Ratingen, Germany, can lay claim to the title of world-champion hitchhiker, having obtained free rides over a distance of 776,955 km (482,777 miles) since 1960.

Walking

Longest walks

The first person reputed to have 'walked round the world' is George Matthew Schilling (USA), from 1897 to 1904.

The first verified walk round the world was achieved by David Kunst (USA), who walked a distance of 23,250 km (14,450 miles) through four continents from 20 June 1970 to 5 Oct 1974.

The longest walk by a woman was 31,521 km (19,586 miles), by Ffyona Campbell of Dartmouth, Devon, UK, who walked round the world in five phases, covering four continents and 20 countries. She left John O' Groats, Highland, UK, on 16 Aug 1983 and returned there on 14 Oct 1994.

The first crossing of the Americas and the western hemisphere was by George Meegan from Rainham, Kent, UK, who walked 30,431 km (19,019 miles) from Ushuaia, the southern tip of South America, to Prudhoe Bay in northern Alaska, in 2,426 days from 26 Jan 1977 to 18 Sept 1983.

Sean Eugene McGuire (USA) covered 11,791 km (7,327 miles) from the Yukon River north of Livengood, Alaska, to Key West, Florida, USA, in 307 days, from 6 June 1978 to 9 April 1979.

The longest walk round the coast of the British Isles was 15,239 km (9,469 miles), by John Westley of Kessingland, Suffolk, UK, from 5 Aug 1990 to 20 Sept 1991. His walk began and ended at Tower Bridge, London.

Vera Andrews completed the longest walk on the British mainland, covering a distance of 11,777 km (7,318 miles) between 2 Jan and 24 Dec 1990, and taking in all the British Gas showrooms. She started and finished her walk at her home town of Clacton-on-Sea, Essex.

Rick Hansen, who was paralysed from the waist down in 1973 as a result of a motor accident, wheeled his wheelchair for a distance of 40,075.2 km (24,901 miles 880 yd) through four continents and 34 countries. He started out from Vancouver, Canada, on 21 March 1985 and returned on 22 May 1987.

Cycle touring

Greatest distances covered on bicycles

Itinerant lecturer Walter Stolle covered more than 646,960 km (402,000 miles) from Jan 1959 to Dec 1976. He set out from Romford, Essex, UK, and visited 159 countries.

John W. Hathaway of Vancouver, Canada, covered 81,430 km (50,600 miles) and visited every continent from 10 Nov 1974 to 6 Oct 1976.

Greatest distances covered on tandems

Laura Geoghegan and Mark Tong travelled 32,248 km (20,155 miles) from London, UK, to Sydney, Australia, from 21 May 1994 to 11 Nov 1995.

Veronica and Colin Scargill, of Bedford, UK, travelled 29,000 km (18,020 miles) around the world, from 25 Feb 1974 to 27 Aug 1975.

time of 64 hr 2 min from 2 to 5 May 1995. He began his journey in London, UK, and flew to Madrid, Spain, then to Napier, New Zealand, via Heathrow, Singapore and Auckland. From Napier he travelled by helicopter to Ti Tree Point on Highway 52 (the point exactly opposite Madrid airport). He returned via Los Angeles, USA, having covered a total distance of 41,709 km (25,917 miles).

Brother Michael Bartlett of Sandy, Beds, UK, an 'Eccentric Globetrotter', achieved a record time for flying around the world on scheduled flights, taking in only the airports closest to antipodal points, when he flew via Shanghai, China and Buenos Aires, Argentina, in 58 hr 44 min. Bartlett set out on his journey from Zürich, Switzerland, on 13 Feb 1995, and travelled a total distance of 41,547 km (25,816 miles) before arriving back in Zürich on 16 Feb 1995.

Sandy, Beds, UK, who made 42 passenger flights with Heli Transport of Nice, southern France, between Nice, Sophia Antipolis, Monaco and Cannes in a time of 13 hr 33 min on 13 June 1990.

David Beaumont of Wimbledon, London, UK, visited all 15 countries belonging to the European Union on scheduled passenger flights in a time of 35 hr 8 min on 2 and 3 May 1995.

Tourism

Highest income from tourism

The USA earned a record $60 billion (£38.4 billion) from tourism in 1994.

Highest expenditure on tourism

The Germans spent a record $47.3 billion (£30.4 billion) on trips abroad in 1995.

Far left
The Chinese invented the compass, an invaluable aid for travellers, around the time of Christ, but were using pieces of magnetic rock as simple compasses by 2,500 BC.

Left
In 1995 David Sole, best known for his exploits as the Scotland Rugby Union captain, broke the record for flying around the world taking in points that are exactly opposite to each other in just over 64 hours. He did the trip to raise funds for the Gordon Highlanders' museum.

FREE RIDES SINCE 1960

Flying

Oldest pilot to circumnavigate the world

Fred Lasby was 82 when he completed a solo round-the-world flight in his single-engined Piper Comanche. Leaving Fort Myers, Florida, USA, on 30 June 1994 he flew 37,366 km (23,218 miles) westwards with 21 stops, arriving back at Fort Myers on 20 Aug 1994.

Fastest circumnavigation

The fastest circumnavigation under FAI regulations using scheduled flights is 44 hr 6 min, by David J. Springbett of Taplow, Bucks, UK. He flew 37,124 km (23,068 miles) from Los Angeles, California, USA, via London, Bahrain, Singapore, Bangkok, Manila, Tokyo and Honolulu from 8 to 10 Jan 1980.

Former Scottish Rugby Union captain David Sole travelled around the world on scheduled flights, taking in exact antipodal points, in a

Fastest London–New York flight

The shortest time ever taken to fly from central London, UK, to downtown New York City, New York, USA, is 3 hr 59 min 44 sec by helicopter and Concorde, with a return journey of 3 hr 40 min 40 sec. It was set by David J. Springbett and David Boyce on 8 and 9 Feb 1982.

Paris-London

The fastest time taken to cover the 344 km (214 miles) from central Paris, France, to central London (BBC TV centre), UK, is 38 min 58 sec, by David Boyce of Stewart Wrightson (Aviation) Ltd on 24 Sept 1983. Boyce travelled by motorcycle and helicopter to Le Bourget, France, then by Hawker Hunter jet (piloted by the late Michael Carlton) to Biggin Hill, Kent, UK, and finally by helicopter to the TV centre car park.

Scheduled flight records

The record for the most scheduled flights in 24 hours is held by Brother Michael Bartlett of

Most popular destination

The most popular destination is France, with a total of 60,584,000 foreign tourists in 1995. It was also the most popular overseas destination for Britons, receiving more than a fifth of all British trips abroad.

Visitors to the United Kingdom

A record 23.6 million foreign tourists visited the United Kingdom in 1995, spending a record £11.7 billion.

The country that sent the most visitors to the United Kingdom was the USA; Americans made almost 3 million visits in 1994 and spent a total of £1.8 billion.

Of all visitors to the United Kingdom in 1994, the highest spending visitors were Icelanders, with an average daily expenditure of £116. The French spent the least money on average, at £170 per visit, while New Zealanders had the lowest average daily expenditure, at £29.40.

Marriage and celebrations

WORLD CHAMPION 'BEST MAN' HAS OFFICIATED AT A TOTAL OF 1,035 WEDDINGS

Right
In the world's largest mass wedding, 35,000 couples were married by Sun Myung Moon in the Olympic Stadium in Seoul, South Korea in Aug 1995. An additional 325,000 couples took part via a satellite link.

Longest engagement 67 years

Marriage

Most marriages
The greatest number of marriages contracted by one person in the monogamous world is 28, by former Baptist minister Glynn 'Scotty' Wolfe (b. 1908) of Blythe, California, USA, who first married in 1927. He is currently separated from his 28th wife, is hoping to marry again, and thinks that he has a total of 41 children.

The most monogamous marriages by a woman is 22, by Linda Essex of Anderson, Indiana, USA, who has had 15 husbands since 1957. Her most recent marriage was in Oct 1991, and ended in divorce.

The greatest number of bigamous marriages is 104, by Giovanni Vigliotto, one of many aliases used by either Fred Jipp (b. New York City, 1936) or Nikolai Peruskov (b. Siracusa, Sicily, 1929), between 1949 and 1981 in 27 US states and 14 other countries. In 1983, he was sentenced to 28 years for fraud and six years for bigamy, and fined $336,000.

The only woman in the United Kingdom to have contracted eight legal marriages is Olive Joyce Wilson of Marston Green, Birmingham,

W Midlands, who has been Mrs John Bickley, Mrs Don Trethowan, Mrs George Hundley, Mrs Raymond Ward, Mrs Harry Latrobe, Mrs Leslie Harris, Mrs Ray Richards and Mrs John Grassick. She was left a widow when Mr Hundley died, but the other marriages all ended in divorce.

Pat Hinton of Burton-on-Trent, Staffs, UK, has been married 10 times since 1971, although four of these unions were bigamous. She married her 10th husband in 1991.

Most married couple
Richard and Carole Roble of South Hempstead, New York, USA, have married each other 56 times since 1969. They have chosen a different location each time and have had ceremonies in every US state.

Oldest brides
The oldest bride on record is Minnie Munro, who was 102 years old when she married Dudley Reid, aged 83, at Point Clare, NSW, Australia, on 31 May 1991.

Mrs Winifred Clark (b. 1871) became the oldest recorded bride in the United Kingdom when she married Albert Smith, aged 80, at

LARGEST BIRTHDAY PAR

St Hugh's Church, Cantley, S Yorkshire, on the eve of her 100th birthday.

Oldest bridegrooms
The oldest bridegroom on record is Harry Stevens, aged 103, who married Thelma Lucas, 84, at the Caravilla Retirement Home, Wisconsin, USA, on 3 Dec 1984.

The oldest British bridegroom was George Jameson aged 102, who married Julie Robinson, 53, at Honiton, Devon, UK, on 10 March 1995.

OLDEST BRIDEGROOM ON RECORD MARRIED AT THE AGE OF 103

Longest marriages

Cousins Sir Temulji Bhicaji Nariman and Lady Nariman were married for 86 years, from 1853 to 1940. Both were five years old when the marriage took place. Sir Temulji died in Aug 1940 in Bombay, India, at the age of 91.

Lazarus Rowe and Molly Webber, both born in 1725, were recorded as marrying in 1743. Molly died in June 1829 at Limington, Maine, USA, after 86 years of marriage.

The duration of the longest British marriage is 82 years, by James Frederick Burgess (1861–1966) and Sarah Ann (1865–1965), who were married on 21 June 1883 at St James's, Bermondsey, London. Sarah Ann died on 22 June 1965.

Longest engagement

Octavio Guillén and Adriana Martínez were engaged for 67 years before finally taking the plunge in June 1969 in Mexico City. Both were 82 years old.

Most golden weddings

The most 50th wedding anniversaries in one family is 10, by the six sons and four daughters of Joseph and Sophia Gresl of Manitowoc, Wisconsin, USA, between 1962 and 1988; and by the six sons and four daughters of George and Eleonora Hopkins of Patrick County, Virginia, USA, between 1961 and 1988.

The British record is seven. The three sons and four daughters of Mr and Mrs F. Stredwick of E Sussex, all celebrated their golden wedding anniversaries between May 1971 and April 1981.

Best man

The person who has most frequently been a best man is Ting Ming Siong of Sibu, Sarawak, Malaysia, who served at 1,035 weddings between 1975 and March 1996.

Oldest divorced couple

The record combined age for a divorced couple is 188, set when a divorce was granted to Simon Stern who was 97 years old, and his wife, Ida, 91, in Milwaukee, Wisconsin, USA, on 2 Feb 1984.

The British record is 166, set on 21 Nov 1980, when 101-year-old Harry Bidwell from Brighton, E Sussex, UK, divorced his 65-year-old wife.

Dining out

The world champion for eating out is Fred E. Magel of Chicago, Illinois, USA, who dined out 46,000 times in 60 countries during his 50 years as a restaurant grader. His favourite dishes were South African rock lobster and mousse of fresh English strawberries.

The greatest altitude at which a formal meal has been held is 6,768 m (22,205 ft), at the top of Mt Huascarán, Peru, by nine members of the Ansett Social Climbers from Sydney, Australia, on 28 June 1989. The diners climbed the mountain carrying a dining table, chairs, wine and the components of a three-course meal.

Parties

The International Year of the Child children's party in Hyde Park, London, UK, on 30–31 May 1979 was attended by the royal family and 160,000 children.

The biggest birthday party was attended by an estimated 100,000 people in the centre of Aberdeen, UK, on 24 July 1994. It celebrated the 200th birthday of the city's main street, Union Street.

The largest birthday party held for a person who was present was attended by an estimated 35,000 people at Louisville, Kentucky, USA, on 8 Sept 1979. It celebrated the 89th birthday of Col. Harland Sanders, the founder of Kentucky Fried Chicken.

The largest birthday party held in the British Isles was attended by an estimated 10,000 people on 5 Aug 1989 at Douglas, Isle of Man. It marked the 50th birthday of Trevor Baines, a well-known local businessman.

On 29 Sept 1995, 438,552 people attended 13,080 coffee mornings throughout the United Kingdom as part of the Macmillan Nurse Appeal. They raised £1¼ million.

The largest teddy bears' picnic was attended by 33,573 bears and their owners at Dublin Zoo, Republic of Ireland, on 24 June 1995.

R ONE PERSON WAS ATTENDED BY 35,000 GUESTS

Biggest wedding ceremony

Some 35,000 couples were married by Sun Myung Moon (b. 1920) of the Holy Spirit Association for the Unification of World Christianity in the Olympic Stadium, Seoul, South Korea, on 25 Aug 1995. A further 325,000 couples around the world took part via a satellite link.

Most expensive wedding ceremony

The wedding of Mohammed, son of Shaik Rashid Bin Saeed Al Maktoum, to Princess Salama in Dubai in May 1981, lasted for a total of seven days and cost an estimated £22 million. It was held in a purpose-built stadium for 20,000 people.

Feasts and celebrations
Banquets

The most lavish menu ever served was at the main banquet at the Imperial Iranian 2,500th Anniversary gathering at Persepolis in Oct 1971. The feast comprised quails' eggs stuffed with Iranian caviar, a mousse of crayfish tails in Nantua sauce, stuffed rack of roast lamb, roast peacock stuffed with foie gras, fig rings and raspberry sweet champagne sherbet, and the very best wines.

The largest feast—attended by 150,000 guests—was at Ahmedabad, India, on 2 June 1991. It marked the renunciation ceremony of Atul Dalpatlal Shah, when he became a monk.

Individual speed

Right
Norman Johnson, formerly a lecturer in hotel management and catering, shows the skills that brought him the title of the world's fastest cucumber slicer.

Magic
Eldon D. Wigton, alias Dr Eldoonie, performed 225 different tricks in two minutes at Kilbourne, Ohio, USA, on 21 April 1991.

Noodle making
Simon Sang Koon Sung of Singapore made 8,192 noodle strings (2^{13} in 13 movements) from a single piece of noodle dough in 59.29 seconds during the Singapore Food Festival on 31 July 1994. This equals more than 138 noodles per second.

Omelette making
The greatest recorded number of two-egg omelettes made in 30 minutes is 427, by Howard Helmer at the International Poultry Trade Show held at Atlanta, Georgia, USA, on 2 Feb 1990.

Oyster opening
The record for opening oysters is 100 in a time of 2 min 20.07 sec, by Mike Racz at Invercargill, New Zealand, on 16 July 1990.

All speed records were made by individuals in less than one hour.

Baton twirling
The greatest number of complete spins achieved between tossing a baton into the air and catching it again is 10, by Donald Garcia on the BBC *Record Breakers* programme on 9 Dec 1986.

Bed making
The shortest recorded time taken by one person to make a bed is 28.2 seconds, by Wendy Wall of Hebersham, Sydney, Australia, on 30 Nov 1978.

Beer stein carrying
Duane Osborn covered a distance of 15 m (49 ft 2½ in) in 3.65 seconds with five full steins in each hand in a contest at Cadillac, Michigan, USA, on 10 July 1992.

Coal carrying
David Jones of Huddersfield, W Yorkshire, UK, set the record for the annual race at Gawthorpe when he carried a 50-kg (110-lb) bag over the 1,012.5-m (1,107-yd 7-in) course in 4 min 6 sec on 1 April 1991.

Coal shovelling
The record for filling a 508-kg (1,120-lb) hopper with coal is 26.59 seconds, by Wayne Miller at Wonthaggi, Victoria, Australia, on 17 April 1995.

Crochet
Barbara Jean Sonntag of Craig, Colorado, USA, crocheted a total of 330 shells plus five stitches (equivalent to 4,412 stitches) in

30 minutes at a rate of 147 stitches per minute on 13 Jan 1981.

Cucumber slicing
Norman Johnson of Blackpool College, Lancs, UK, set a world record of 13.4 seconds for slicing a 30.5-cm (12-in) cucumber with a diameter of 3.8 cm (1½ in), at 22 slices to the inch (a total of 264 slices) at the Westdeutsche Rundfunk studios in Cologne, Germany, on 3 April 1983.

Drumming
Making a strong claim to be the world's fastest and most manic drummer, Rory Blackwell of Starcross, Devon, UK, played a total of 400 separate drums in 16.2 seconds at Finlake Leisure Park, near Chudleigh, Devon, UK, on 29 May 1995.

Knitting
The world's fastest ever hand-knitter is Gwen Matthewman of Featherstone, W Yorkshire, UK, who attained a speed of 111 stitches per minute in a test carried out at Phildar's Wool Shop, Central Street, Leeds, W Yorkshire, on 29 Sept 1980.

Knot-tying
The fastest recorded time taken to tie the six knots explained in the *Boy Scout Handbook* (square knot, sheet bend, sheep shank, clove hitch, round turn and two half hitches, and bowline) on individual ropes is 8.1 seconds, by Clinton R. Bailey Sr of Pacific City, Oregon, USA, on 13 April 1977.

Pancake tossing
The greatest recorded number of times a pancake has been tossed in two minutes is 349, by Dean Gould at Felixstowe, Suffolk, UK, on 14 Jan 1995.

Sheep shearing
Godfrey Bowen of New Zealand sheared a Cheviot ewe in 46 seconds at the Royal Highland Show in Dundee, UK, in June 1957.

Somersaults
The greatest number of somersaults completed on a trampoline in one minute is 75, by Richard Cobbing of Lightwater, Surrey, UK, at BBC Television Centre, London, for *Record Breakers* on 8 Nov 1989.

Speed march
Paddy Doyle covered a distance of 1.6 km (1 mile) with a rucksack weighing 18.1 kg (40 lb) on his back in a time of 5 min 35 sec at Ballycotton, Co. Cork, Republic of Ireland, on 7 March 1993.

Stair climbing
The 100-storey record for stair climbing was set by Dennis W. Martz in the Detroit Plaza Hotel, Detroit, Michigan, USA, on 26 June 1978, in a time of 11 min 23.8 sec.

The record for the 1,760 steps (with a vertical height of 342 m or 1,122 ft) in the world's tallest free-standing structure, Toronto's CN Tower in Canada, is 7 min 52 sec, by Brendan Keenoy on 29 Oct 1989.

The fastest time ever recorded for ascending the 1,336 stairs of the world's tallest hotel, the Westin Stamford Hotel, Singapore, is 6 min 55 sec, by Balvinder Singh, in the hotel's Third Annual Vertical Marathon held on 4 June 1989.

Sunil Tamang of the 7th Gurkha Rifles ascended the 50 storeys of Canary Wharf, the tallest building in the United Kingdom, in a time of 7 min 3.44 sec on 22 Aug 1992.

Stamp licking
Dean Gould of Felixstowe, Suffolk, UK, licked and affixed 450 stamps in four minutes outside Tower Ramparts Post Office, Ipswich, Suffolk, on 24 Nov 1995.

Stilt walking
The fastest stilt walker on record is Roy Luiking, who covered 100 m (328 ft) on 30.5-cm-high (1-ft) stilts in 13.01 seconds at Didam, Netherlands, on 28 May 1992.

Over a long distance, the fastest stilt walker on record was M. Garisoain of Bayonne, France, who walked the 8 km (5 miles) from Bayonne to Biarritz in a time of 42 minutes in 1892, maintaining an average speed of 11.42 km/h (7.1 mph).

Window cleaning
Terry Burrows of South Ockendon, Essex, UK, cleaned three standard 114.3 x 114.3 cm (45 x 45 in) office windows set in a frame with a 30-cm-long (11¾-in) squeegee and 9 litres (2 gal) of water in 19.4 seconds at the Holiday Inn, Maidenhead, Berks, UK, on 20 April 1996.

A RECORD RATE OF MORE THAN 138 PER SECOND

Tree climbing
The record for climbing up and down a 30.5-m (100-ft) fir spar pole is 24.82 seconds, by Guy German of Sitka, Alaska, USA, on 3 July 1988 at the World Championship Timber Carnival in Albany, Oregon, USA.

Typewriting
In an official test in 1946, Stella Pajunas, now Mrs Garnand, typed 216 words in a minute on an IBM machine in Chicago, Illinois, USA.

Gregory Arakelian of Herndon, Virginia, USA, set a speed record of 158 wpm, with two errors, on a PC in the Key Tronic World Invitational Type-Off. He recorded this speed in the semi-final on 24 Sept 1991.

Michael Shestov set a numerical record by typing spaced numbers from 1 to 801 on a PC without any errors in five minutes at Baruch College, New York City, USA, on 2 April 1996.

Walking on hands
Mark Kenny of Norwood, Massachusetts, USA, completed a 50-m (164-ft) inverted sprint in 16.93 seconds on 19 Feb 1994.

Walking on water
Rémy Bricka of Paris, France, 'walks on water' with ski-floats attached to his feet, moving in the same way as in cross-country skiing but using a double-headed paddle instead of ski poles. He set a speed record in the Olympic Pool, Montreal, Quebec, Canada, by walking 1 km (1,094 yd) in 7 min 7.41 sec.

Winkling
The world's fastest winkle picker is Sheila Bance, who picked a total of 50 shells with a straight pin in 1 min 30.55 sec at the European Food and Drink Fair at Rochester, Kent, UK, on 7 May 1993.

Left
Mark Kenny, a former wrestler and now an aide to an American state senator by profession, started walking on his hands as a change from lifting weights during his training. After years of practising, he beat the world 50-m record by more than half a second.

0 DRUMS IN 16.2 SECONDS

Sustained speed, persistence

YOGESH SHARMA SHOOK HANDS WITH A RECORD 31,118 PEOPLE IN A TIME OF EIGHT HOURS

Right
Baths have been used as boats—both sailing and motor— on many occasions. At Grafton in Australia, a bath tub race that originally started out as a bit of fun has now become an annual festival and the acknowledged World Championships.

Below
The egg-and-spoon race may have its roots in the traditional school sports day, but adults enjoy it too. In 1990 Dale Lyons ran the London Marathon holding a spoon with an egg on it in a time of 3 hr 47 min.

Sustained speed

All speed records were set by individuals or pairs in times of one hour or more.

Apple picking
A record-breaking 7180.3 kg (15,830 lb) of apples was picked in a time of eight hours by George Adrian of Indianapolis, Indiana, USA, on 23 Sept 1980.

Baling
On 30 Aug 1989 Svend Erik Klemmensen of Trustrup, Djursland, Denmark, baled 200 tonnes of straw in 9 hr 54 min, using a Hesston 4800 baling machine.

Bath tub racing
The record for a 36-mile (57.9-km) motorized bath tub race (with the bath used as a boat) is 1 hr 22 min 27 sec, by Greg Mutton at the Grafton Jacaranda Festival, NSW, Australia, in Nov 1987.

IN A TIME OF ONE HOUR, BARBER TOM RODDEN SHAVED

Most eggs shelled 1,050 dozen

Bricklaying
Gary Lovegrove of Wisbech, Cambs, UK, laid 872 bricks, each weighing 2 kg (4 lb 7 oz), in 60 minutes at the East of England Show at Peterborough, Cambs, on 18 July 1995.

Coal carrying
Brian Newton of Leicester, UK, covered the marathon distance (42.195 km or 26 miles 385 yd) carrying 1 cwt (50.8 kg) of coal in an open bag in 8 hr 26 min on 27 May 1983.

Combine harvesting
Philip Baker of Merton, Oxon, UK, harvested 165.6 tonnes of wheat in eight hours using a Massey Ferguson MF 38 combine on 8 Aug 1989.

Cow milking by hand
Joseph Love of Kilifi Plantations Ltd, Kenya, milked 531 litres (117 gal) from 30 cows in 12 hours on 25 Aug 1992.

Egg shelling
Blind kitchen hands Harold Witcomb and Gerald Harding shelled 1,050 dozen eggs in a 7¼-hour shift at Bowyers, Trowbridge, Wilts, UK, on 23 April 1971.

Egg-and-spoon racing
On 23 April 1990, Dale Lyons of Meriden, W Midlands, UK, ran the London Marathon carrying a dessert spoon with a fresh egg on it in 3 hr 47 min.

Handshaking
Yogesh Sharma shook hands with a total of 31,118 people in eight hours during the Gwalior Trade Fair, Madhya Pradesh, India, on 14 Jan 1996.

Hedge laying
Steven Forsyth and Lewis Stephens of Sennybridge, Powys, UK, hedged 280.7 m (920 ft 11 in) in 11 hours by the 'stake and pleach' method on 23 April 1994.

Kissing
Alfred A. E. Wolfram of Minnesota, USA, kissed a world record 10,504 people in eight hours—about one person every 2.7 seconds—at the Minnesota Renaissance Festival on 19 Aug 1995.

Ploughing
The greatest recorded area ploughed with a six-furrow plough to a depth of 25 cm (9¾ in) in 24 hours is 91.37 ha (225¾ acres), by Matthias Robrahn of Pogeez, Germany, in a John Deere Type 4955 (228 PS) from 23 to 24 Sept 1992.

Riveting
The world record for riveting is 11,209 rivets in nine hours, by John Moir at the Workman Clark Ltd shipyard, Belfast, UK, in June 1918. His best hour was his seventh, with 1,409 rivets, representing an average of more than 23 per minute.

Shaving
Denny Rowe shaved a total of 1,994 men in 60 minutes with a retractor safety razor at Herne Bay, Kent, UK, on 19 June 1988, taking an average 1.8 seconds per volunteer and drawing blood four times.

Tom Rodden of Chatham, Kent, UK, shaved 278 volunteers in one hour with a cut-throat razor on 10 Nov 1993 for *Record Breakers*, averaging 12.9 seconds per face. He drew blood seven times.

Shearing

The highest speed for sheep-shearing in a working day was achieved by Alan MacDonald, who machine-sheared 805 lambs in nine hours (an average of 89.4 per hour) at Waitnaguru, New Zealand, on 20 Dec 1990.

A record 817 lambs were sheared by Philip Evans at Pant Farm, Merthyr Cynog, Powys, UK, on 20 July 1991. (Although this exceeds the world record set in New Zealand, the attempts are not directly comparable because of differing rules.)

Peter Casserly of Christchurch, New Zealand, achieved a solo-blade (hand-shearing) record of 353 lambs in a time of nine hours on 13 Feb 1976.

In a 24-hour shearing marathon, Alan MacDonald and Keith Wilson machine-sheared 2,220 sheep at Warkworth, Auckland Province, New Zealand, on 26 June 1988.

Speed march

Flt Sgt Chris Chandler set an individual speed march record in the RAF Swinderby Marathon at Swinderby, Lincs, UK, on 25 Sept 1992,

in one hour on 24 May 1996, using a 38.1-cm (15-in) high exercise bench.

Three-legged race

Dale Lyons and David Pettifer set a three-legged running record in the London Marathon, with a time of 3 hr 58 min 33 sec on 2 April 1995. They were tied together both at ankle and wrist.

Turkey plucking

Vincent Pilkington of Cootehill, Co. Cavan, Republic of Ireland, killed and plucked 100 turkeys in 7 hr 32 min on 15 Dec 1978. His record for a single turkey is 1 min 30 sec, set on RTE television in Dublin on 17 Nov 1980.

Typewriting

The official typing record for one hour on an electric typewriter is 9,316 words (40 errors) on an IBM machine, giving a net rate of 149 words per minute, by Margaret Hamma, now Mrs Dilmore, in Brooklyn, New York, USA, on 20 June 1941.

Yo-yo-ing

'Fast' Eddy McDonald of Toronto, Canada, completed 21,663 loops with a yo-yo in a

Crocheting

On 14 July 1986, Rita van der Honing of Wormerveer, Netherlands, completed a crochet chain a record 62.5 km (38 mile 1,471 yd) long.

Escapology

Since 1954 Nick Janson of Benfleet, Essex, UK, has escaped from handcuffs locked onto him by more than 1,500 police officers.

French knitting

Ted Hannaford of Sittingbourne, Kent, UK, began work on a piece of French knitting in 1989. It is now a record-breaking 10.39 km (6 miles 840 yd) in length.

Grave digging

Johann Heinrich Karl Thieme, sexton of Aldenburg, Germany, is reported to have dug a total of 23,311 graves during a 50-year career. On his death in 1826 his own grave was dug by his understudy.

Snake milking

Over a 14-year period ending in Dec 1965, Bernard Keyter, a supervisor at the South African Institute for Medical Research in Johannesburg, South Africa, personally milked a total of 780,000 venomous snakes and obtained 3,960 litres (870 gallons) of venom. He was never bitten.

TAL OF 278 VOLUNTEERS WITH A CUT-THROAT RAZOR

with a pack weighing 18.1 kg (40 lb). His time was 3 hr 56 min 10 sec.

Stair climbing

Brian McCauliff ran a vertical mile on the stairs of the Westin Hotel, Detroit, Michigan, USA, in a time of 1 hr 38 min 5 sec on 2 Feb 1992, ascending and descending eight times.

Russell Gill climbed the 835 steps of the Rhodes State Office Tower in Columbus, Ohio, USA, 53 times in a time of 9 hr 16 min 24 sec on 20 Feb 1994. He climbed a total of 44,255 steps to a total vertical height of 8,141.8 m (26,712 ft) and descended by lift each time.

Step-ups

Terry Cole of Walthamstow, London, UK, completed a record-breaking 2,970 step-ups

time of three hours on 14 Oct 1990 at Boston, Massachusetts, USA. He had previously set a speed record of 8,437 loops in one hour at Cavendish, Prince Edward Island, Canada, on 14 July 1990.

Persistence

Apple peeling

The longest single unbroken apple peel on record was 52.51 m (172 ft 4 in) in length. It was peeled by Kathy Wafler of Wolcott, New York, USA, in a time of 11 hr 30 min at Long Ridge Mall, Rochester, New York, on 16 Oct 1976. The apple weighed 167 g (20 oz).

Bubble-blowing

Alan McKay of Wellington, New Zealand, created a record-breaking 19.45-m-long (63-ft 10-in) bubble on 30 July 1995.

Stair climbing

In his job as a tour guide Brian Davis has mounted 334 of the 364 steps of the tower in the Houses of Parliament, London, UK, a total of 5,914 times in 12 years to 19 April 1996—equal to 36 ascents of Mt Everest.

String ball

Between 1989 and 1992, J. C. Payne of Valley View, Texas, USA, put together the largest ball of string on record, measuring 4.03 m (13 ft 2½ in) in diameter and 12.65 m (41 ft 6 in) in circumference.

Typewriting

By 11 April 1996 Les Stewart of Mudjimba Beach, Queensland, Australia, had typed the numbers 1 to 894,000 in words on 17,770 quarto sheets. He aims to reach 1 million.

Left
The world's largest bubble, made using a bubble wand, washing-up liquid, glycerine and water, was 19.45 m (63 ft 10 in) long. Alan McKay, its creator, chose a clear frosty day for his successful attempt on the record. One of the adjudicators, who can just be seen through the end of the bubble, was 1.83 m (6 ft) tall.

BERNARD KEYTER MILKED A RECORD 780,000 VENOMOUS SNAKES IN 14 YEARS

Endurance

Right
Roy Castle spent more than three hours 'wing-walking' on a flight from England to France in 1990.

Below right
Simon of the Desert, directed by Luis Buñuel, depicted the life of St Simeon the Younger, who lived at the top of a pillar for 45 years.

(870 miles) from Aligarh to Jamma, India, to appease his revered Hindu goddess, Mata.

Debating
Students and staff of University College Galway, together with special guest speakers, debated the motion that 'This House has all the Time in the World' for exactly 28 days, from 2 Feb to 2 March 1995 at Galway, Republic of Ireland.

Escalator riding
The record distance travelled on a pair of 'up' and 'down' escalators is 214.34 km (133 miles 325 yd), by David Beattie and Adrian Simons at Top Shop, Oxford Street, London, UK, from 17 to 21 July 1989. Each completed 7,032 circuits.

Fashion shows
The greatest distance covered by a model on a catwalk is 133.7 km (83 miles 176 yd), by Eddie Warke at Parke's Hotel, Dublin, Republic of Ireland, from 19 to 21 Sept 1983.

The record for a female model is 114.4 km (71 miles 176 yd), by Roberta Brown and Lorraine McCourt on the same occasion.

Footbag
The world record for keeping a footbag airborne is 51,155 consecutive kicks, by Ted

Army drill
On 8 and 9 July 1987, a 90-man squad of the Queen's Colour Squadron, RAF, performed a total of 2,722,662 drill movements (2,001,384 rifle and 721,278 foot) from memory and without a word of command in 23 hr 55 min at RAF Uxbridge, Middx, UK.

Balancing on one foot
The longest recorded time a person has spent balancing on one foot is 71 hr 40 min, by Amresh Kumar Jha at Bihar, India, from 13 to 16 Sept 1995. The disengaged foot may not be rested on the standing foot nor may any object be used for support or balance.

Bed pushing
The greatest distance covered by a team of bed pushers is 5,204 km (3,233 miles 1,144 yd), by nine employees of Bruntsfield Bedding Centre, Edinburgh, UK, pushing a wheeled hospital bed. The effort took them from 21 June to 26 July 1979.

Brick carrying
The greatest distance covered while carrying a brick weighing 4.08 kg (9 lb) in a nominated ungloved hand in an uncradled downward pincher grip is 114.3 km (71 miles 45 yd), by Ashrita Furman of Jamaica, New York, USA, on 3 and 4 June 1995.

Camping out
The silent Indian *fakir* Mastram Bapu ('contented father') remained on the same spot by the roadside in the village of Chitra for 22 years, from 1960 to 1982.

Cardiopulmonary resuscitation
Brent Shelton and John Ash completed a CPR marathon (cardiopulmonary resuscitation—15 compressions alternating with two breaths) of 130 hours from 28 Oct to 2 Nov 1991 at Regina, Saskatchewan, Canada.

Charity fundraising
The greatest recorded amount raised by a charity walk or run is $Can24.7 million (£9.1 million), by Terry Fox (1958–81) of Canada. Fox, who had an artificial leg, ran from St John's, Newfoundland, to Thunder Bay, Ontario, in 143 days from 12 April to 2 Sept 1980. He covered 5,373 km (3,339 miles).

Clapping
The duration record for continuous clapping (sustaining an average of 160 claps per minute, audible from 110 m or 120 yd) is 58 hr 9 min, by V. Jeyaraman of Tamil Nadu, India, from 12 to 15 Feb 1988.

Crawling
The longest continuous voluntary crawl (progression with one or the other knee in unbroken contact with the ground) is 50.65 km (31 miles 827 yd), by Peter McKinlay and John Murrie, who covered 115 laps of an athletics track at Falkirk, UK, on 28 and 29 March 1992.

Over 15 months, ending on 9 March 1985, Jagdish Chander crawled a total of 1,400 km

Most pogo jumps 177,737

Martin (USA) at Chicago, Illinois, USA, on 29 May 1993.

The doubles record is 123,456 kicks, by Gary Lautt and Tricia George (USA), at Chico, California, USA, on 11 and 12 Nov 1995.

Land rowing
The greatest distance covered on a land rowing machine is 5,278.5 km (3,280 miles), by Rob Bryant of Fort Worth, Texas, USA, who rowed across the USA. He left Los Angeles, California, on 2 April 1990 and reached Washington DC on 30 July.

Leap-frogging
The greatest distance covered was 1,603.2 km (996 miles 352 yd), by 14 students from Stanford University, California, USA, who started on 16 May 1991 and stopped 244 hr 43 min later on 26 May.

Milk bottle balancing
The greatest distance walked while balancing a milk bottle on the head is 113.76 km (70 miles 282 yd), by Ashrita Furman at Jamaica, New York, USA, on 1 and 2 Aug 1993. It took him a total of 18 hr 46 min.

Pedal-boating
Kenichi Horie of Kobe, Japan, set a pedal-boating distance record of 7,500 km

LANCING ON ONE FOOT

(4,660 miles), leaving Honolulu, Hawaii, USA, on 30 Oct 1992 and arriving at Naha, Okinawa, Japan, on 17 Feb 1993.

Pogo stick jumping
The most jumps achieved is 177,737, by Gary Stewart at Huntington Beach, California, USA, on 25 and 26 May 1990.

Ashrita Furman of Jamaica, New York, USA, set a distance record of 25.75 km (16 miles) in a time of 6 hr 40 min on 8 Oct 1993 at Gotemba, Japan.

Pole sitting
Modern records do not compare with that of St Simeon the Younger (c. AD 521–97), called Stylites, a monk who spent his final 45 years living at the top of a stone pillar on the Hill of Wonders near Antioch in Syria.

The 'standards of living' at the top of poles can vary widely. Mellissa Sanders lived in a shack measuring 1.8 x 2.1 m (6 x 7 ft) at the top of a pole in Indianapolis, Indiana, USA, for a total of 516 days, from 26 Oct 1986 to 24 March 1988.

Rob Colley stayed in a barrel (maximum capacity 150 gal or 682 litres) at the top of a pole 13.1 m (43 ft) high at Dartmoor Wildlife Park near Plymouth, Devon, UK, for 42 days 35 min from 13 Aug to 24 Sept 1992.

Quizzes
A record 41,599 questions were answered correctly in a quiz at the Oak 'n' Ash pub at

Walmley, W Midlands, UK, from 9 to 15 June 1994. Team A scored 20,245 and Team B 21,354, and 10,366 answers were incorrect.

Riding in armour
The longest recorded ride in armour is by Dick Brown, who left Edinburgh, UK, on 10 June 1989 and arrived in Dumfries four days later. He had covered 334.7 km (208 miles) in a total riding time of 35 hr 25 min.

Stilt-walking
The greatest distance ever walked on stilts is 4,804 km (3,008 miles), from Los Angeles, California, to Bowen, Kentucky, USA, by Joe Bowen from 20 Feb to 26 July 1980.

In 1891, Sylvain Dornon stilt-walked from Paris, France, to Moscow, Russia, covering 2,945 km (1,830 miles). It is said that this took either 50 or 58 days.

Tightrope walking
The world tightrope endurance record is 205 days, by Jorge Ojeda-Guzman of Orlando, Florida, USA, on a wire 11 m (36 ft) long, which was 10.7 m (35 ft) above the ground. He was there from 1 Jan to 25 July 1993, and entertained crowds by walking, balancing on a chair and dancing. His main luxury was a wooden cabin measuring 91 x 91 cm (3 x 3 ft) at one end of the tightrope.

Tree sitting
The duration record for staying in a tree is more than 25 years, by Bungkas, who climbed a palm tree in the Indonesian village of Bengkes in 1970 and has been there ever since. He lives in a nest that he made from branches and leaves. Efforts to persuade him to come down have been unsuccessful.

Walking on hands
The distance record for walking on one's hands is 1,400 km (870 miles), by Johann Hurlinger, who walked from Vienna, Austria, to Paris, France, in 55 daily 10-hour stints in 1900, averaging 2.54 km/h (1.58 mph).

Walking on water
Rémy Bricka of Paris, France, 'walked' across the Atlantic Ocean on skis 4.2 m (13 ft 9 in) long in 1988. Leaving Tenerife, Canary Islands, on 2 April 1988, he covered a distance of 5,636 km (3,502 miles), arriving at Trinidad on 31 May 1988.

Wall of death
The greatest endurance feat on a 'wall of death' was 7 hr 0 min 13 sec, by Martin Blume at Berlin, Germany, on 16 April 1983. He rode a Yamaha XS 400 over 12,000 laps on a wall with a diameter of 10 m (33 ft), averaging 45 km/h (30 mph) for the 292 km (181 miles 775 yd).

Wing walking
Roy Castle (1932–94), host of the BBC TV *Record Breakers* programme from 1972 to 1993, flew on the wing of a Boeing Stearman biplane for 3 hr 23 min on 2 Aug 1990, taking off from Gatwick, W Sussex, UK, and landing at Le Bourget, near Paris, France.

Left
A group of 14 American students leap-frogged 1,603.2 km (996 miles 352 yd) in shifts in May 1991—an effort that resulted in sore backs, knees and feet for the participants.

Strength and bravery

Longest motorcycle jump 76.5 m

Right
The record for the most bricks balanced on the head is 75, by Terry Cole, in May 1996. Here former record-holder John Evans, who balanced 67 bricks in 1995, demonstrates the technique. Evans still holds the record for balancing milk crates on his head—a total of 92—and has even managed to balance the shell of a car on his head.

Strength

Barrow pushing
The heaviest loaded one-wheeled barrow pushed for a minimum 61 level m (200 level ft) weighed a gross 3.75 tonnes (8,275 lb). Loaded with bricks, it was pushed a distance of 74.1 m (243 ft) by John Sarich at London, Ontario, Canada, on 19 Feb 1987.

Beer keg lifting
George Olesen raised a keg weighing 62.9 kg (138 lb 11 oz) above his head 737 times in six hours (an average of more than twice a minute) at Horsens, Denmark, on 1 May 1994.

Brick balancing
Terry Cole of Walthamstow, London, UK, balanced 75 bricks on his head for 19 seconds, on 15 May 1996.

Brick lifting
On 14 June 1992, Russell Bradley of Worcester, UK, lifted a record 31 bricks—laid side by side—from a table and then held them at chest height for two seconds.

The greatest weight of bricks lifted was 91.76 kg (202 lb 5 oz), by Fred Burton of Cheadle, Staffs, UK, who held 20 heavier bricks for two seconds on 4 May 1996.

Cigar box balancing
Terry Cole balanced 220 unmodified cigar boxes on his chin for nine seconds on 24 April 1992.

Demolition work
Fifteen members of the Aurora Karate Do demolished a seven-room house in Prince Albert, Saskatchewan, Canada, in 3 hr 9 min 59 sec on 16 April 1994, using only feet and empty hands.

Field gun pull
Three teams of eight from 72 Ordnance Company (V) RAOC pulled a 25-pounder gun over 177.98 km (110 miles 1,041 yd) in 24 hours at Donnington, Shrops, UK, in April 1993.

Glass balancing
Ashrita Furman balanced 57 pint glasses on his chin for 11.5 seconds on 18 May 1996.

Hod carrying
Russell Bradley of Worcester, UK, carried bricks weighing 164 kg (361 lb 9 oz) up a 3.65-m (12-ft) ladder on 28 Jan 1991 at Worcester City Football Club. As the hod weighed 43 kg (94 lb 13 oz), the total weight carried was 207 kg (456 lb 6 oz). On 20 Nov 1993 he carried bricks weighing 264 kg (582 lb) in a 48-kg (105-lb 13-oz) hod for a distance of 5 m (16 ft 5 in) on the flat, before ascending a runged

ramp to a height of 2.49 m (8 ft 2 in). This gave a total weight of 312 kg (687 lb 13 oz).

Lifting and pulling with teeth
Walter Arfeuille of Ieper-Vlamertinge, Belgium, lifted weights totalling 281.5 kg (620 lb 10 oz) 17 cm (6¾ in) off the ground with his teeth in Paris, France, on 31 March 1990.

Robert Galstyan of Armenia pulled two railway wagons coupled together, weighing a total of 219,175 kg (483,198 lb), for 7 m (23 ft) along a rail track with his teeth at Shcherbinka, Moscow, Russia, on 21 July 1992.

Lung power
Nicholas Mason of Cheadle, Greater Manchester, UK, inflated a standard 1,000-g

(35-oz) meteorological balloon to a diameter of 2.44 m (8 ft) in 45 min 2.5 sec for *Record Breakers* on 26 Sept 1994.

Milk crate balancing
John Evans of Marlpool, Derbys, UK, balanced 92 crates (each weighing 1.36 kg or 3 lb) on his head for 10 seconds at Birmingham, W Midlands, UK, on 27 March 1996.

Terry Cole balanced 29 crates on his chin in a single stack for the minimum specified time of 10 seconds on 16 May 1994.

Plane pulling
A team of 60 people pulled a British Airways Boeing 747 weighing 205 tonnes 100 m (328 ft) in 61 seconds at Heathrow airport, near London, UK, on 25 May 1995.

Rope slide
The greatest distance recorded in a rope slide is 1,746.5 m (5,730 ft), by L/Cpl Peter Baldwin of the Royal Marines, based at Plymouth, Devon, UK, and Stu Leggett of the Canadian School of Rescue Training. The slide took place from the top of Mount Gibraltar, near Calgary, Canada, down to level ground on 31 Aug 1994, and the successful attempt was subsequently shown on the BBC *Record Breakers* programme.

Speed march
A team of nine representing II Squadron RAF Regiment from RAF Hullavington, Wilts, UK, completed the London marathon in a time of 4 hr 33 min 58 sec on 21 April 1991. Each man was carrying a pack weighing at least 18.1 kg (40 lb) and including a rifle.

Static wall 'sit'
Rajkumar Chakraborty stayed in an unsupported sitting position against a wall for 11 hr 5 min at Panposh Sports Hostel, Rourkela, India, on 22 April 1993.

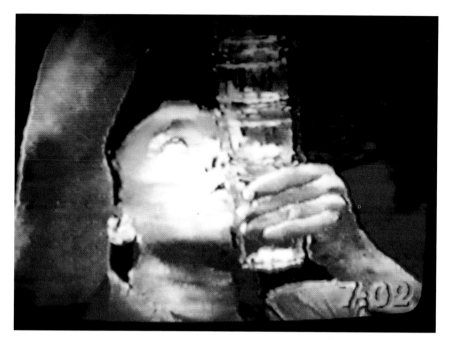

Tyre supporting
The greatest number of motor tyres to have been supported in a free-standing 'lift' is 96, by Gary Windebank of Romsey, Hants, UK, in Feb 1984. The tyres that he used were Michelin XZX 155 x 13 and the total weight was 653 kg (1,440 lb).

Wood cutting
All records were set at the Lumberjack World Championships at Hayward, Wisconsin, USA (founded in 1960).

The record for the power saw (three slices of a 51-cm or 20-in diameter white-pine log with a single-engine saw from a dead start) is 7.45 seconds, by Rick Halvorson (USA) in 1994.

The one-man bucking record (one slice from a 51-cm or 20-in diameter white-pine log with a crosscut saw) is 16.05 seconds, by Melvin Lentz (USA) in 1994. The two-man record is 6.67 seconds, by Mike Slingerland and Matt Bush (both USA) in 1994.

The record for the standing block chop (chopping through a vertical 35.5-cm or 14-in diameter white-pine log 76 cm or 30 in in length) is 22.05 seconds, by Melvin Lentz (USA) in 1988.

The underhand block chop record (chopping through a horizontal 35.5-cm or 14-in diameter white-pine log 76 cm or 30 in long) is 17.84 seconds by Laurence O'Toole (Australia) in 1985.

The springboard chopping record (scaling a 2.7-m or 9-ft spar pole on springboards and chopping a 35.5-cm or 14-in diameter white-pine log) is 1 min 18.45 sec, by Bill Youd (Australia) in 1985.

Bravery
Bungee jumping
The longest ever bungee was 249.9 m (820 ft) in length and was used by Gregory Riffi, who made a jump from a helicopter above the Loire Valley, France, in Feb 1992. His cord stretched to 610 m (2,000 ft) during the jump.

Crate climbing
Philip Bruce stacked 38 beer crates in a single column and climbed up them to a height of 9.65 m (31 ft 8 in) at Sowerby Bridge, W Yorkshire, UK, on 26 Aug 1991.

High diving
Col. Harry A. Froboess (Switzerland) jumped 120 m (394 ft) into Lake Constance from the airship *Hindenburg* on 22 June 1936.

The highest regularly performed head-first dives in the world are those made by professional divers from La Quebrada ('the break in the rocks') at Acapulco, Mexico, which is 26.7 m (87 ft 6 in) high. The water there is 3.65 m (12 ft) deep.

The world record high dive from a diving board is 53.9 m (176 ft 10 in), by Olivier Favre (Switzerland) at Villers-le-Lac, France, on 30 Aug 1987.

The greatest height reported for a dive into an air bag is 99.4 m (326 ft), by stuntman Dan Koko, who jumped from the top of Vegas World Hotel and Casino in Las Vegas, Nevada, USA, onto a 6.1 x 12.2 x 4.2-m (20 x 40 x 14-ft) target on 13 Aug 1984. His impact speed was 141 km/h (88 mph).

Ramp jumping (car)
The longest ever ramp jump in a car (with the car landing on its wheels and being driven on) is 70.73 m (232 ft), by Jacqueline De Creed in a 1967 Ford Mustang at Santa Pod Raceway, Beds, UK, on 3 April 1983.

Ramp jumping (motorcycle)
The longest ever motorcycle jump is 76.5 m (251 ft), by Doug Danger on a 1991 Honda CR500 at Loudon, New Hampshire, USA, on 22 June 1991.

Tightrope walking
The greatest ever drop over which a person has walked on a tightrope is 3,150 m (10,335 ft) above the French countryside, by Michel Menin of Lons-le-Saunier, France, on 4 Aug 1989.

On 1 Nov 1985, tightrope walker Ashley Brophy of Neilborough, Victoria, Australia, took a total of 3½ hours to walk a distance of 11.57 km (7 miles 329 yd) on a wire that was 45 m (147 ft 8 in) long and located 10 m (32 ft 10 in) above the ground at the Adelaide Grand Prix, Australia.

The world's oldest ever tightrope walker was 'Professor' William Ivy Baldwin (1866–1953), who crossed the South Boulder Canyon, Colorado, USA, on a 97.5-m (320-ft) wire with a 38.1-m (125-ft) drop on his 82nd birthday on 31 July 1948.

Left
On 6 Oct 1994, Terry Cole set a new record for glass balancing on *The Big Breakfast* television programme, when he balanced 50 pint glasses on his chin. He subsequently improved on his own record, with 51 glasses, only to see it beaten by Ashrita Furman from the USA, who managed 57 glasses on 18 May 1996. Both Cole and Furman hold a number of records, and they both have often made attempts on each other's records.

Left
The team record for pulling an aeroplane was set on 25 May 1995, when 60 people pulled a British Airways Boeing 747 a distance of 100 m (328 ft) in 61 seconds.

Teamwork

RECORD FOR STRETCHER BEARING IS 270.15 KM WITH A 63.5-KG BODY IN 41 HR 3 MIN

Right
Piet Pitzer and Jaco Erasmus set a 1-mile barrow-racing record of 4 min 48.51 sec in 1987, taking it in turns to push each other for stretches of a quarter of a mile.

Bale rolling
Michael Priestley and Marcus Stanley of Heckington Young Farmers' Club rolled a cylindrical bale 1.2 m (3 ft 11 in) wide over a course 50 m (164 ft) long in 18.06 seconds at the Lincolnshire Federation of Young Farmers' Clubs annual sports day at Sleaford, Lincs, UK, on 25 June 1989.

Barrel rolling
The record for rolling a full 1.64-hl (36-gal) metal beer barrel over a measured mile (1.6 km) is 8 min 7.2 sec, by Phillip Randle, Steve Hewitt, John Round, Trevor Bradley, Colin Barnes and Ray Glover of Haunchwood Collieries Institute and Social Club, Nuneaton, Warks, UK, on 15 Aug 1982.

A team of 10 people from TEcza Sports Club, Łódź, Poland, rolled a 63.5-kg (140-lb) barrel 200.11 km (124 miles 603 yd) in 24 hours from 1 to 2 Sept 1995.

Barrow racing
The fastest time attained in a wheelbarrow race over a distance of 1 mile (1.6 km) is 4 min 48.51 sec, by Piet Pitzer and Jaco Erasmus at Transvalia High School, Vanderbijlpark, South Africa, on 3 Oct 1987.

Bath tub racing
The greatest distance covered while paddling a hand-propelled bath tub on still water in 24 hours is 145.6 km (90½ miles), by 13 members of Aldington Prison Officers Social Club, near Ashford, Kent, UK, from 28 to 29 May 1983.

Bed making
The pair record for making a bed with one blanket, two sheets, an undersheet, an uncased pillow, one counterpane and 'hospital' corners is 14 seconds, by Sister Sharon Stringer and Nurse Michelle Benkel of the Royal Masonic Hospital, London, UK, at the launch of the 1994 edition of *The Guinness Book of Records*, which was held at Canary Wharf, London, on 26 Nov 1993.

Bed racing
The record time for the annual Knaresborough Bed Race (established 1966), N Yorkshire, UK, is 12 min 9 sec for a 3.27-km (2-mile 63-yd) course crossing the River Nidd. It was set by the Vibroplant team on 9 June 1990.

Bridge building
A team of British soldiers from 21 Engineer Regiment, which is based at Nienburg, Germany, constructed a bridge across a gap 8 m (26 ft 3 in) wide using a five-bay single-storey MGB (medium girder bridge). They achieved this in a time of 8 min 44 sec at Hameln, Germany, on 3 Nov 1995.

Coal shovelling
The record for filling a 508-kg (1,120-lb) hopper with coal by a team of two is 15.01 seconds, by Brian McArdle and Rodney Spark, both of Middlemount, Queensland, Australia, at the Fingal Valley Festival in Fingal, Tasmania, Australia, on 5 March 1994.

Combine harvesting
On 9 Aug 1990, an international team from CWS Agriculture harvested a record 358.09 tonnes of wheat in eight hours from an area of 44 ha (108¾ acres) at Cockayne Hatley Estate, Sandy, Beds, UK. The equipment consisted of a Claas Commandor 228 combine fitted with a Shelbourne Reynolds SR 6000 stripper head.

TOP DISTANCE CLIMBED ON

Field to loaf
The fastest time taken to produce 13 loaves (a baker's dozen) from growing wheat is 8 min 13.6 sec, by representatives from Wheat Montana Farms & Bakery at Three Forks, Montana, USA, on 19 Sept 1995. They used 13 microwaves to bake the loaves.

Using a traditional baker's oven to bake the bread, the record time for producing 13 loaves from growing wheat is 19 min 14 sec, by a team led by John Haynes and Peter Rix at Alpheton, Suffolk, UK, on 22 Aug 1993.

Fire pumping
The greatest volume of water to have been stirrup-pumped by a team of eight in 80 hours is 143,459 litres (31,557 gal), by firefighters based at Knaresborough Fire Station, N Yorkshire, UK, from 25 to 28 June 1992.

Glass blowing
A bottle standing 2.3 m (7 ft 8 in) high with a capacity of approximately 712 litres (157 gal) was blown at Wheaton Village, Millville, New Jersey, USA, on 26 Sept 1992 by a team led by glass artist Steve Tobin. The attempt was made during the 'South Jersey Glass Blast', which forms part of a celebration of the local glassmaking heritage.

Handpumped railcars
A five-man team (one pusher and four pumpers) achieved a speed of 33.12 km/h (20.58 mph) while moving a handpumped railcar over a 300-m (984-ft) course at Rolvenden, Kent, UK, on 21 Aug 1989, recording a time of 32.61 seconds.

Field to loaf 8 min 13.6 sec

MOST POTATOES PEELED BY FIVE PEOPLE WITHIN 45 MINUTES IS 482.8 KG

Ladder climbing
These records are shown in the order in which they have been set since their introduction to *The Guinness Book of Records* in 1993. All were set on a standard fire-service ladder in a time of 24 hours.

A team from the Royal Berkshire Fire & Rescue Service, based at Dee Road Fire Station, climbed a vertical height of 48.17 km (29 miles 1,639 yd) at Reading, Berks, UK, from 13 to 14 Aug 1993.

A team from the Wholetime Recruit Course 67 of the Derbyshire Fire & Rescue Service climbed a vertical height of 51.20 km (31 miles 1,433 yd) at Derby, UK, from 1 to 2 April 1994.

A team from Somerset Fire Brigade, based at Frome Fire Station, climbed 54.31 km (33 miles 1,314 yd) at Frome, UK, from 24 to 25 June 1994.

A team from Gwent Fire Brigade, based at Malpas Fire Station, climbed 61.68 km (38 miles 574 yd) at Newport, UK, from 26 to 27 Aug 1994.

Kent, UK, with an adult 'baby', in 24 hours from 22 to 23 Nov 1990.

Sheep to shoulder
A team of eight people using commercial machinery produced a jumper in a record time of 2 hr 28 min 32 sec (the time taken from shearing the sheep to achieving the finished article) on 3 Sept 1986 at Ilkley, W Yorkshire, UK.

Stretcher bearing
The longest distance that a stretcher with a 63.5-kg (10-st) 'body' has been carried is 270.15 km (167 miles 1,520 yd), in a time of 49 hr 2 min from 29 April to 1 May 1993. This was achieved by two teams of four from CFB (Canadian Forces Base) Trenton in and around Trenton, Ontario, Canada.

Tailoring
The highest speed at which the manufacture of a three-piece suit has ever been executed, from sheep to finished article, is 1 hr 34 min 33.42 sec, by 65 members of the Melbourne College of Textiles, Pascoe Vale, Victoria, Australia, on 24 June 1982. Catching and fleecing took 2 min 21 sec.

...ANDARD FIRE-SERVICE LADDER IN A TIME OF 24 HOURS IS 76.56 KM, IN 1995

A West Yorkshire Fire Service team, based at Batley Fire Station, climbed 62.66 km (38 miles 1,646 yd), at Heckmondwike, W Yorkshire, UK, from 29 to 30 Sept 1994.

A team from the Isle of Man Fire & Rescue Service climbed a total of 74.92 km (46 miles 973 yd) at Douglas, Isle of Man, from 25 to 26 Nov 1994.

The current record was set by a team of 10 firefighters from the Royal Berkshire Fire & Rescue Service, based at Dee Road Fire Station, who climbed a vertical height of 76.56 km (47 miles 1,007 yd), at Reading, Berks, UK, from 28 to 29 April 1995.

Potato peeling
The greatest quantity of potatoes peeled by five people to an institutional cookery standard with standard kitchen knives in 45 minutes is 482.8 kg (1,064 lb 6 oz) net, by Marj Killian, Terry Anderson, Barbara Pearson, Marilyn Small and Janene Utkin at Shelley, Idaho, USA, on 19 Sept 1992.

Pram pushing
The greatest distance covered pushing a pram in 24 hours is 563.62 km (350 miles 382 yd), by 60 members of the Oost-Vlanderen branch of Amnesty International at Lede, Belgium, on 15 Oct 1988.

A distance of 437.27 km (271 miles 1,240 yd) was covered by a team of 10 from the Royal Marines School of Music, Deal,

Left
Tremendous fitness and a good head for heights are necessary for setting records at ladder climbing. The keen rivalry between fire services helps to spur the teams on to cover ever greater distances in the 24 hours allowed.

Below left
Sheep feature in a number of record attempts, with people trying to shear them as quickly as possible, and make jumpers or three-piece suits from their wool in the shortest possible time. In 1982 a suit was produced in just over an hour and a half, starting with the catching of the sheep.

Mass participation

Below right
Valentine's Day provided an appropriate occasion for the largest mass kissing, at the University of Maine, on 14 Feb 1996.

Balloon release
The largest mass balloon release ever held involved a total of 1,592,744 balloons. It was staged by Disney Home Video at Longleat House, Wilts, UK, on 27 Aug 1994.

Balloon sculpture
The world's largest balloon sculpture was a reproduction of Van Gogh's *Fishing Boats on the Beach of Les Saintes Maries*, constructed from 25,344 coloured balloons. Students from Haarlem Business School created the picture at a harbour in Ouddorp in the Netherlands on 28 June 1992.

Bucket chain
The longest ever fire-service bucket chain stretched a distance of 3,496.4 m (11,471 ft), with 2,271 people passing 50 buckets along the complete course at the Centennial Parade and Muster held at Hudson, New York, USA, on 11 July 1992.

Column of coins
The most valuable column of coins was worth 39,458 punt (£37,458) and was 1.88 m (6 ft 2 in) high. It was built by St Brigid's Family and Community Centre at Waterford, Republic of Ireland, on 20 Nov 1993.

Daisy chain
The villagers of Good Easter, Chelmsford, Essex, UK, made a 2.12-km (6,980-ft 7-in) daisy chain in seven hours, on 28 May 1985.

Dancing dragon
The longest dancing dragon measured 1,691.64 m (5,550 ft). It consisted of 610 people, who danced for more than five minutes at Tiantan (Temple of Heaven), Beijing, China, on 19 May 1995.

Domino toppling
Thirty students at Delft, Eindhoven and Twente Technical Universities in the Netherlands set up 1.5 million dominoes to represent all of the European Community member countries. Of these, 1,382,101 were toppled by one push on 2 Jan 1988.

Gymnastic display
The most participants in an aerobic/gymnastic display is 30,517, for the Great Singapore Workout, Singapore, on 27 Aug 1995.

Human centipede
The largest 'human centipede' to move 30 m (98 ft 5 in) consisted of 1,601 students from Nanyang Technological University, Singapore, on 29 July 1995. Participants' ankles were firmly tied together and not one person fell over in the course of the walk.

Human logos
The largest logo ever formed from human beings was the Human US Shield, consisting of some 30,000 officers and men at Camp Custer, Battlecreek, Michigan, USA, on 10 Nov 1918.

Jumble sales
The most money made at a jumble sale was $427,935.21 (£285,786), at the USA White Elephant Sale at the Cleveland Convention Center, Ohio, USA, on 18 and 19 Oct 1983.

The most money raised in one day is $214,085.99 (£142,686), at the 62nd one-day rummage sale organized by the Winnetka Congregational Church, Winnetka, Illinois, USA, on 12 May 1994.

The largest jumble sale ever to have been held in the United Kingdom was Jumbly '79, in aid of the Save the Children Fund. It was sponsored by the magazine *Woman's Own* and held at Alexandra Palace, London, from 5 to 7 May 1979. The total attendance was 60,000 and the gross takings were in excess of £60,000.

Kissing
The greatest number of couples to have kissed simultaneously in the same place was 1,420, at the University of Maine at Orono, USA, on 14 Feb 1996.

Line of coins
The world's most valuable line of coins was made up of a total of 1,724,000 US quarters to a value of $431,000 (£226,860). The line, which was 41.68 km (25 miles 1,584 yd) in length, was laid at the Atlanta Marriott Marquis Hotel, Atlanta, Georgia, USA, by members of the National Exchange Club on 25 July 1992.

The longest line of coins on record had a total length of 55.63 km (34 miles 998 yd) and was made in Kuala Lumpur, Malaysia, using

Most kissing couples 1,420

2,367,234 20-sen coins. It was laid by representatives of WWF (World Wide Fund for Nature) Malaysia and Dumex Sdn Bhd on 6 Aug 1995.

Litter collection
A total of 50,405 volunteers gathered along the Californian coast, USA, on 2 Oct 1993, in order to collect litter in conjunction with the International Coastal Cleanup.

Musical chairs
The largest game on record began with 8,238 participants, and ended with Xu Chong

Pile of coins
The most valuable pile of coins comprised 1,000,298 American coins of various denominations, with a total value of $126,463.61 (£70,030). It was constructed by the YWCA of Seattle-King County, Washington, USA, at Redmond, Washington, on 28 May 1992.

Quizzes
The greatest number of participants to contest a quiz was 80,799, in the All-Japan High-School Quiz Championship televised by NTV on 31 Dec 1983.

Sand castle
The tallest sand castle on record, constructed only with hands, buckets and shovels, stood 6.56 m (21 ft 6 in) high when completed. It was made by a team led by Joe Maize, George Pennock and Ted Siebert at Harrison Hot Springs, British Columbia, Canada, on 26 Sept 1993.

The longest ever sand castle extended over 8.37 km (5 miles 352 yd). It was made by the staff and pupils of Ellon Academy, Aberdeenshire, UK, on 24 March 1988.

Tree planting
The greatest number of trees ever to have been planted in a single week by an unlimited number of volunteers is 24,159. The trees were planted by 9,084 volunteers, mostly students, in Guaratinguetá, São Paulo, Brazil, on 10 April 1996.

The greatest number of trees ever planted in a week by no more than 300 volunteers is 3,100. A total of 270 pupils from Eton Park Junior School and members of the general public planted the saplings at Eton Road Community Park, Burton upon Trent, Staffs, UK, during the week beginning 19 Nov 1995.

Unsupported circle
The highest number of people on record to have demonstrated the physical paradox of being seated without a chair is an unsupported circle of 10,323 employees of the Nissan Motor Co. at Komazawa Stadium, Tokyo, Japan, on 23 Oct 1982.

Left
The longest ever 'human centipede' consisted of 1,601 people, who managed to advance 30 m (98 ft 5 in) across an enormous field in Singapore in 1995.

VAN GOGH PAINTING MADE OUT OF 25,344 BALLOONS

Wei occupying the last chair. It was held at the Anglo-Chinese School, Singapore, on 5 Aug 1989.

Origami
A paper crane with a wingspan of 35.7 m (117 ft 2 in) was folded by residents of the district of Gunma at Maebashi, Japan, on 28 Oct 1995. It was 16 m (52 ft 6 in) high and took six hours to make.

Paper chain
A paper chain 59.05 km (36 miles 1,218 yd) long was made by 60 students from University College Dublin, Republic of Ireland, as part of UCD Science Day, from 11 to 12 Feb 1993. The chain consisted of almost 400,000 links, and took 24 hours to make.

Paper clip chain
A chain of paper clips 6.93 km (4 miles 539 yd) long was constructed by 53 students from Mount Vernon High School, Washington, USA, in 12 hr 20 min on 30 March 1996.

Pass the parcel
The largest game of pass the parcel ever held took place at Alton Towers, Staffs, UK, on 8 Nov 1992. It involved 3,464 people, who took a total of two hours to remove the 2,000 wrappers covering a parcel that initially measured 1.5 x 0.9 x 0.9 m (5 x 3 x 3 ft). The event was organized by Parcelforce International and the final present was an electronic keyboard, won by Sylvia Wilshaw.

Left
Great enthusiasm from a large number of volunteers in Kuala Lumpur resulted in a single line of coins stretching for more more than 55 km (34 miles).

Juggling, projectiles, balance

A RECORD 826 JUGGLERS KEPT 2,478 OBJECTS IN THE AIR SIMULTANEOUSLY

Right
Owen Morse demonstrates his skills at joggling. He holds the five-object record for 100 m with a time of 13.8 seconds, as well as the three-object record with a time of 11.68 seconds—faster than the winning time for the 100 m at the first modern Olympic Games in 1896.

'Juggled' means that the number of catches made is equal to the number of objects thrown multiplied by the number of hands.

'Flashed' means the number of catches made equals at least the number of objects, but less than a juggle.

Juggling
* Historically accepted but not fully substantiated.

Rings
Eleven rings were juggled by Albert Petrovski* (USSR) in 1963, Eugene Belaur* (USSR) in 1968, and Sergei Ignatov* (USSR) in 1973.

Twelve rings were flashed by Anthony Gatto (USA) in 1993 and Albert Lucas (USA) in 1995.

Clubs
Seven clubs were juggled by Albert Petrovski* (USSR) in 1963, Sorin Munteanu* (Romania) in 1975, Jack Bremlov* (Czechoslovakia) and Albert Lucas* in 1985, Anthony Gatto (USA) in 1988, and Bruce Tiemann (USA) in 1995.

Eight clubs were flashed by Anthony Gatto in 1989 and Scott Sorensen (USA) in 1995.

Balls
Ten balls were juggled by Enrico Rastelli* (Italy) in the 1920s and Bruce Sarafian (USA) in 1996.

Twelve balls were flashed by Bruce Sarafian (USA) in 1995.

Ten balls were bounce juggled by Tim Nolan* (USA) in 1988.

Nine balls were spun on one hand by François Chotard (France) in 1990.

Five balls were juggled by Bobby May (USA) while he was standing on his head, in 1953.

A total of seven ping pong balls were flashed with the mouth by Tony Ferko (Czechoslovakia) in 1987, and Wally Eastwood (USA).

Plates
Eight plates were juggled by Enrico Rastelli* (Italy) in the 1920s.

Eight plates were flashed by Albert Lucas (USA) in 1993.

Torches
Seven flaming torches were juggled by Anthony Gatto (USA) in 1989.

Passing
Eleven clubs were juggled by Owen Morse and John Wee (USA) in 1995.

Fifteen balls were flashed by Peter Kaseman and Rob Vancko (USA) in 1995.

Duration (without a drop)
Five clubs were juggled for 45 min 2 sec by Anthony Gatto (USA) in 1989.

Three objects were juggled for 11 hr 4 min 22 sec by Terry Cole (GB) in 1995.

Most pirouettes with cigar boxes
Kris Kremo (Switzerland) did a quadruple turn with three cigar boxes in mid air in 1977.

Most objects kept aloft
A total of 826 people, juggling at least three objects each, kept 2,478 objects in the air at Glastonbury, Somerset, UK, on 26 June 1994.

'Joggling'
The world record times for running while juggling three objects are held by: Owen Morse (USA) over 100 m in 11.68 seconds (1989) and 400 m in 57.32 seconds (1990); Kirk Swenson (USA), over 1 mile in 4 min 43 sec (1986) and 5,000 m in 16 min 55 sec (1986); Ashrita Furman (USA) over a marathon distance in 3 hr 22 min 32.5 sec (1988) and 50 miles in 8 hr 52 min 7 sec (1989); Michael Hout (USA) over the 110 m hurdles in 18.9 seconds (1993); Albert Lucas (USA) over the 400 m hurdles in 1 min 7 sec (1993); and Owen Morse, Albert Lucas,

Tuey Wilson and John Wee (USA) in the 1-mile relay in 3 min 57.38 sec (1990).

The world record times for running while juggling five objects are held by: Owen Morse (USA) over 100 m in 13.8 seconds (1988), and Bill Gillen (USA) over 1 mile in 7 min 41.01 sec (1989) and 5,000 m in 28 min 11 sec (1989).

Projectiles
Throwing
In the longest authenticated throw of an inert object heavier than air, a lead weight with a long string tail was thrown 385.8 m (1,265 ft 9 in) by David Engvall at El Mirage, California, USA, on 17 Oct 1993.

The longest throw of an object without a velocity-aiding feature was on 8 July 1986, when a flying ring was thrown 383.13 m (1,257 ft) by Scott Zimmerman, at Fort Funston, California, USA.

Boomerang throwing
The most consecutive two-handed catches is 817, by Michael Girvin (USA) on 17 July 1994 at Oakland, California, USA.

The longest out-and-return throw is 149.12 m (489 ft 3 in), by Michel Dufayard (France) on 5 July 1992 at Shrewsbury, Shrops, UK.

The longest flight duration (with self-catch) is 2 min 59.94 sec by Dennis Joyce on 25 June 1987 at Bethlehem, Pennsylvania, USA.

Yannick Charles (France) caught 76 boomerang throws in five minutes. He also

made 555 catches using two boomerangs simultaneously. He achieved both feats at Strasbourg, France, on 4 Sept 1995.

Brick throwing
On 19 July 1978, Geoff Capes threw a standard 2.27-kg (5-lb) brick 44.54 m (146 ft 1 in) at Orton Goldhay, Cambs, UK.

Card throwing
Jim Karol threw a standard playing card 61.26 m (201 ft) at Newton Centre, Massachusetts, USA, on 18 Oct 1992.

Cow pat tossing
The greatest distance thrown under the 1970 'non-sphericalization and 100% organic' rule, which forbids the moulding of the projectile into a spherical shape, is 81.1 m (266 ft), by Steve Urner (USA), on 14 Aug 1981.

ALEKSANDR BENDIKOV STACKED 522 DOMINOES O

GREATEST DISTANCE THA

Longest 'Wellie wang' 56.7 m

Egg throwing

The longest authenticated throw of a fresh hen's egg without breaking it is 98.51 m (323 ft 2½ in) by Johnny Dell Foley to Keith Thomas in Jewett, Texas, USA, in Nov 1978.

Flying disc throwing (formerly Frisbee)

The distance records are: 200.01 m (656 ft 2 in) for men, by Scott Stokely (USA) on 14 May 1995; and 136.31 m (447 ft 3 in) for women, by Anni Kreml (USA) on 21 Aug 1994. Both were at Fort Collins, Colorado, USA.

The records for the throw, run and catch are: 92.64 m (303 ft 11 in) for men, by Hiroshi Oshima (Japan) at San Francisco, California, USA, on 20 July 1988; and 60.02 m (196 ft 11 in) for women, by Judy Horowitz (USA) on 29 June 1985 at La Mirada, California, USA.

The 24-hour distance records for a pair are: 592.15 km (367 miles 1,663 yd) for men, by Conrad Damon and Pete Fust (USA) from 24 to 25 April 1993 at San Marino, California, USA; and 186.12 km (115 miles 1,143 yd) for women, by Jo Cahow and Amy Berard (USA) from 30 to 31 Dec 1979 at Pasadena, California, USA.

The maximum times aloft are: 16.72 seconds for men, by Don Cain (USA) on 26 May 1984 at Philadelphia, Pennsylvania, USA; and 11.81 seconds for women, by Amy Bekken (USA) on 1 Aug 1991 at Santa Cruz, California, USA.

Gumboot throwing

The longest recorded distance for 'Wellie wanging' is 56.7 m (186 ft), by Olav Jensen at Fagernes, Norway, on 10 July 1988.

SINGLE DOMINO IN 1994

The women's record is 40.70 m (133 ft 6 in), by Mette Bergmann, also at Fagernes, on 10 July 1988.

Haggis hurling

The longest recorded throw of a haggis (minimum weight allowed is 680 g or 1 lb 8 oz) is 55.11 m (180 ft 10 in) by Alan Pettigrew at Inchmurrin, Argyll, UK, in May 1984.

Rolling pin throwing

The longest throw of a rolling pin weighing 907 g (2 lb) is 53.47 m (175 ft 5 in), by Lori La Deane Adams at Iowa State Fair, Iowa, USA, on 21 Aug 1979.

Spear throwing

The record throw of a spear is 258.63 m (848 ft 6½ in), by David Engvall at Aurora, Colorado, USA, on 15 July 1995.

Catapulting

The longest catapult shot on record is 415 m (1,362 ft), by James M. Pfotenhauer, using a patented 5.22-m (17-ft 1½-in) Monarch IV Supershot and lead ball at Escanaba, Michigan, USA, on 10 Sept 1977.

Slinging

The greatest distance an object has been hurled from a sling is 477.10 m (1,565 ft 4 in), using a 127-cm-long (50-in) sling and a 62-g (2¼-oz) dart, by David Engvall at Baldwin Lake, California, USA, on 13 Sept 1992.

Grape catching

The furthest from which a grape thrown from level ground has been caught in the mouth is 99.82 m (327 ft 6 in), by Paul J. Tavilla at East Boston, Massachusetts, USA, on 27 May 1991. It was thrown by James Deady.

Spitting

The greatest distance for a cherry stone is 28.98 m (95 ft 1 in), by Horst Ortmann at Langenthal, Germany, on 27 Aug 1994.

The record for spitting a water-melon seed is 22.91 m (75 ft 2 in) by Jason Schayot at De Leon, Texas, USA, on 12 Aug 1995.

David O'Dell spat a tobacco wad 15.07 m (49 ft 5½ in) at the 19th World Tobacco Spitting Championships at Calico Ghost Town, California, USA, on 26 March 1994.

Left
David Engvall threw a spear 258.63 m (848 ft 6½ in) in July 1995. To achieve such a distance he used an atlatl, or spear thrower. This ancient hunting implement is a hand-held device that fits onto the spear.

Coin balancing and snatching

Aleksandr Bendikov (Belarus) stacked a pyramid of 880 coins on the edge of a coin free-standing vertically on the base of a coin that was on a table on 15 Nov 1995.

The tallest column of coins stacked on the edge of a coin consisted of 253 Indian one-rupee pieces on top of a vertical five-rupee coin, built by Dipak Syal (India) on 3 May 1991.

The most new 10-pence pieces clean-caught after being flipped from the back of a forearm into the same downward palm is 328, by Dean Gould (UK) on 6 April 1993.

Domino stacking

Aleksandr Bendikov stacked 522 dominoes on a supporting domino in Sept 1994.

Golf ball balancing

Lang Martin balanced seven golf balls vertically without adhesive at Charlotte, North Carolina, USA, on 9 Feb 1980.

House of cards

The most storeys achieved without adhesive in a house of playing cards is 100, to a height of 5.85 m (19 ft 2½ in). It was completed by Bryan Berg (USA) in Copenhagen, Denmark, between 1 and 10 May 1996.

Balance

Beer mat flipping

Dean Gould flipped 111 mats (1.2-mm-thick 490-gsm wood pulp board) through 180° and caught them at Edinburgh, UK, in Jan 1993.

The human being

Right
Gurning, which means 'to snarl like a dog, look savage, distort the countenance', is one of the highlights of the annual Egremont Crab Fair and Sports, Cumbria, UK. Contestants have to pull a grotesque face through a horse collar, a practice that is thought to have originated in mockery of the village idiot. The townsfolk would throw a horse's collar over him and make him pull funny faces for a few pints of ale.

Top yodel 22 tones in a second

Body decoration

Most tattooed people

Tom Leppard of the Isle of Skye, UK, has had about 99.2% of his body tattooed with a leopard skin design. All the skin between the dark spots is tattooed saffron yellow.

Bernard Moeller of Pennsylvania, USA, had 14,002 individual tattoos by 1 April 1996.

Canadian strip artiste 'Krystyne Kolorful' has a 95% body suit that took 10 years to complete.

The most decorated British woman, Rusty Field, has had 85% of her body tattooed.

Most pierced person

Alex Lambrecht (Belgium) has 137 piercings on his face and body.

Faces and mouths

Bubble-gum blowing

A record bubble diameter of 58.4 cm (23 in) was achieved by Susan Montgomery Williams of Fresno, California, USA, at the ABC-TV studios, New York City, USA, on 19 July 1994.

Gurning

The World Gurning Competition has been won a record 10 times by Gordon Mattinson, from 1967 to 1972 and 1974 to 1977.

The human voice

Greatest voice range

The normal intelligible range of the male human voice in still air is 180 m (200 yd). *Silbo*, the whistled language of La Gomera, Canary Islands, can be heard at 8 km (5 miles).

Screaming

The highest scientifically measured scream is 128 dbA at 2.5 m (8 ft 2 in), by Simon Robinson in 'The Guinness Challenge' at Adelaide, Australia, on 11 Nov 1988.

Whistling

Roy Lomas whistled at 122.5 dbA at 2.5 m (8 ft 2 in) in the Deadroom at the BBC studios in Manchester, UK, on 19 Dec 1983.

Shouting

Annalisa Wray shouted at 121.7 dbA at Belfast, Co. Antrim, UK, on 16 April 1994.

Fastest yodel

Thomas Scholl of Germany achieved 22 tones (15 falsetto) in one second on 9 Feb 1992.

Fastest talker

Steve Woodmore of Orpington, Kent, UK, said 595 words in 56.01 seconds (637.4 words per minute) on the ITV programme *Motor Mouth* on 22 Sept 1990.

Mind and memory

'Mastermind'

British civil servant Kevin Ashman scored a record-breaking 41 points in his heat of the TV programme 'Mastermind', which was transmitted on 21 May 1995. Ashman went on to win the 1995 title.

'KRYSTYNE KOLORFUL' HAS A TATTOO SUIT COVERING 95% OF HER BODY

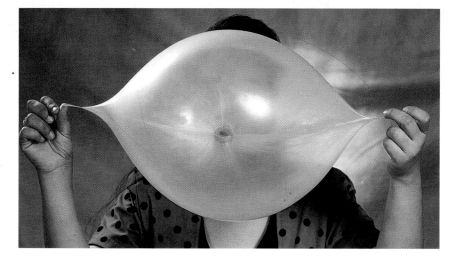

Memory skills

In May 1974, Bhanddanta Vicittabi Vumsa recited a total of 16,000 pages of Buddhist canonical texts in Yangon (Rangoon), the capital of Myanmar (Burma).

Card memorizing (40 packs)

On a single sighting Dominic O'Brien (GB) memorized a random sequence of 40 packs of cards (2,080 in total) that had been shuffled together at the BBC Studios, Elstree, Herts, UK, on 26 Nov 1993. He made just one error.

Memorizing π

Hiroyuki Goto (b. 1973) of Tokyo, Japan, recited from memory to a record-breaking 42,195 places at the NHK Broadcasting Centre, Tokyo, on 18 Feb 1995.

Left
Susan Montgomery Williams displays the skills that have made her the record-holder for bubble-gum blowing. She was once hauled before a judge for popping bubbles in the corridor outside a courtroom. The usher thought that it was the sound of gunfire, and the judge put her on probation for disrupting a trial.

Fruit and vegetable growing

A GIANT STRAWBERRY WEIGHING 231 G WAS GROWN BY GEORGE ANDERSEN IN 1983

Gargantuan gardening

Giant fruit and vegetable growing is a competitive and cut-throat affair. After months of careful nurturing, some growers stay up all night to guard their exhibits from the threat of sabotage. One record-holder reports how he returned to his garden on the morning of a show to find all of his prize cucumbers snapped in half. Enthusiasm for growing big vegetables began in the USA, but the activity has now become popular in Canada, Europe, Africa and Australasia. The highlight of the British grower's calendar is the *Garden News* UK Giants' Championship, an annual event at which large fruit and vegetables from all over the country compete for various coveted titles.

World's largest specimens

Apple
1.47 kg (3 lb 4 oz), Hanners family, Hood Rivers, Oregon, USA, 1994.

Beetroot
18.37 kg (40 lb 8 oz), Ian Neale, Newport, UK, 1994.

Broccoli
15.87 kg (35 lb), John and Mary Evans, Palmer, Alaska, USA, 1993.

Cabbage
56.24 kg (124 lb), Bernard Lavery, Llanharry, UK, 1989.

Cantaloupe melon
28.12 kg (62 lb), Gene Daughtridge, Rocky Mount, North Carolina, USA, 1991.

Carrot
7.13 kg (15 lb 11½ oz), Bernard Lavery, Llanharry, UK, 1996.

Celery
20.89 kg (46 lb 1 oz), Bernard Lavery, Llanharry, UK, 1990.

Corn cob
92 cm (36¼ in), Bernard Lavery, Llanharry, UK, 1994.

Largest carrot 7.13 kg

LARGEST ONION IN TH

Courgette
29.25 kg (64 lb 8 oz), Bernard Lavery,
Llanharry, UK, 1990.

Cucumber
Two specimens each weighing 9.1 kg (20 lb
1 oz), Bernard Lavery, Llanharry, UK, 1991.

A 1.83-m-long (6-ft) Vietnamese specimen
was reported by L. Szabó of Hungary in
1976.

Garlic
1.19 kg (2 lb 10 oz), Robert Kirkpatrick,
Eureka, California, USA, 1985.

Grapefruit
3.065 kg (6 lb 12 oz), Debbie Hazleton,
Queensland, Australia, 1995.

Grapes (bunch)
9.4 kg (20 lb 11½ oz), Bozzolo y Perut Ltda,
Santiago, Chile, 1984.

Green beans
121.9 cm (48 in), B. Rogerson, Robersonville,
North Carolina, USA, 1994.

Leek (pot)
5.5 kg (12 lb 2 oz), Paul Harrigan, Linton,
Northumberland, UK, 1987.

Lemon
3.88 kg (8 lb 8 oz), Charlotte and Donald
Knutzen, Whittier, California, USA, 1983.

Marrow
49.04 kg (108 lb 2 oz), Bernard Lavery,
Llanharry, UK, 1990.

Onion
5.55 kg (12 lb 4 oz), Mel Ednie, Anstruther,
Fife, UK, 1994.

Parsnip
4.36 m (171¾ in), Bernard Lavery, Llanharry,
UK, 1990.

Pepper
34.29 cm (13½ in), J. Rutherford, Hatch,
New Mexico, 1975.

Pineapple
8.06 kg (17lb 12 oz), Ermand Kamuk, Ais
Village, WNBP, Papua New Guinea, 1994.

Potato
Three specimens of 3.5 kg (7 lb 13 oz), Ken
Sloane, Patrick, Isle of Man, 1994.

A specimen weighing 8.275 kg (18 lb 4 oz) is
reported to have been dug up by Thomas
Siddal in his garden in Chester, UK, on 17
Feb 1795.

Radish
17.2 kg (37 lb 15 oz), Litterini family,
Tanunda, South Australia, 1992.

Rhubarb
2.67 kg (5 lb 14 oz), Eric Stone,
E Woodyates, Wilts, UK, 1985.

Runner bean
100.3 cm (39½ in), J. Taylor, Shifnal,
Shrops, UK, 1986.

Squash
408.5 kg (900 lb 8 oz), John and Chris
Lyons, Baltimore, Ontario, Canada, 1994.

Strawberry
231 g (8.17 oz), George Andersen,
Folkestone, Kent, UK, 1983.

Swede
28.27 kg (62 lb 3 oz), Norman Craven,
Stouffville, Ontario, Canada, 1996.

Tomato
3.51 kg (7 lb 12 oz), Gordon Graham,
Edmond, Oklahoma, USA, 1986.

Tomato plant
16.3 m (53 ft 6 in), Gordon Graham,
Edmond, Oklahoma, USA, 1985.

Watermelon
118.84 kg (262 lb), Bill Carson, Arrington,
Tennessee, USA, 1990.

Largest British specimens
Cantaloupe melon
9.91 kg (21 lb 13½ oz), Bernard Lavery,
Llanharry, 1995.

Gooseberry
61.04 g (2.18 oz), Kelvin Archer, Scholar
Green, Cheshire, 1993.

Grapefruit
1.67 kg (3 lb 11 oz), Willington Garden
Centre Club, Bedford, 1986.

Lemon
2.13 kg (4 lb 11 oz), Pershore College,
Pershore, Hereford and Worcester, 1986.

Peach
411 g (14½ oz), Jean Bird, London, 1984.

Squash
252.4 kg (556 lb 7 oz) Richard Hope,
Shevington, near Wigan, Lancs, 1995.

Tomato
2.54 kg (5 lb 9½ oz), R. Burrows,
Huddersfield, W Yorkshire, 1985.

Tomato plant
13.96 m (45 ft 9½ in), Chosen Hill School,
Glos, 1981.

Watermelon
52.98 kg (116 lb 13 oz), Bernard Lavery,
Llanharry, 1995.

Top and middle
Grower and seed
breeder Bernard
Lavery makes a living
selling 30 different
varieties of giant seed.
This year, he reports
a strong surge of
interest from the
Japanese—an unusual
development for a
country with a history
of miniaturizing plants.
Lavery is seen here
(top) with his heaviest
carrot, the largest
ever specimen, and
with an impressive
sweet melon
specimen (middle).

Left
Emanuel Antonilli with
specimens of giant
unknown vegetables
that grow in his
garden in St
Petersburg, Florida,
USA. The Antonillis
believe that the plants
are Spanish squash,
and cook and eat
them accordingly.

Food

Below right
The world's longest salami was made at Flekkefjord, Norway, between 6 and 16 July 1992. At 20.95 m (68 ft 9 in) in length, it had a circumference of 63.4 cm (25 in) and weighed 676.9 kg (1,492 lb 5 oz).

Bread, cheese and meat

Loaves
On 6 Jan 1996, a 9,200-m-long (30,184-ft) Rosca de Reyes (twisted loaf) was baked in Acapulco, Mexico.

The largest pan loaf weighed 1.43 tonnes (3,163 lb 10 oz) and measured 3 x 1.25 x 1.1 m (9 ft 10 in x 4 ft 1 in x 3 ft 7 in). It was baked by staff of Sasko in Johannesburg, South Africa, on 18 March 1988.

Cheese
A 26.09-tonne (57,508-lb 8-oz) cheddar was made in 1995 by Loblaws Supermarkets and Agropur Dairies at Granby, Quebec, Canada.

Meat pie
The largest meat pie was a chicken pie made by KFC in New York City, USA, in Oct 1995. It weighed 10.06 tonnes (22,178 lb) and was 3.66 m (12 ft) in diameter.

Haggis
The largest known haggis weighed 303.2 kg (668 lb 7 oz) and was made from 80 ox stomachs by the Troon Round Table, Burns Country Foods and a team of chefs at the Hilton Hotel in Glasgow, UK, on 24 May 1993.

Hamburger
The largest hamburger on record weighed 2.5 tonnes (5,520 lb) and was made at the Outagamie County Fairgrounds, Seymour, Wisconsin, USA, on 5 Aug 1989.

Kebab

An 880.6-m-long (2,889-ft 3-in) kebab was made by the West Yorkshire Family Service Units, the Trade Association of Asian Restaurant Owners and National Power at Bradford, W Yorkshire, UK, on 19 June 1994.

Salami
A 20.95-m (68-ft 9-in) salami was made by A/S Svindlands Pølsefabrikk, Norway, in 1992.

Sausage
In 1995, a 46.3-km-long (28¾-mile) sausage was made by M & M Meat Shops and J. M. Schneider Inc. at Kitchener, Ontario, Canada.

Biggest barbecues
The highest attendance at a one-day barbecue was 44,158, at Warwick Farm Racecourse, Sydney, Australia, on 10 Oct 1993.

The greatest known meat consumption at a barbecue was 19.96 tonnes (44,010 lb), or 31,500 chicken halves, in eight hours at Lancaster Sertoma Club's Chicken Bar-B-Que, Pennsylvania, USA, on 21 May 1994.

Dishes and fast food

Lasagne
A 21.33 x 2.13-m (70 x 7-ft) lasagne was made by the Food Bank for Monterey County at Salinas, California, USA, on 14 Oct 1993.

Omelette
The largest ever omelette covered 128.5 m² (1,383 ft²) and contained 160,000 eggs.

It was cooked by representatives of Swatch at Yokohama, Japan, on 19 March 1994.

Paella
A paella 20 m (65 ft 7 in) in diameter was made by Juan Carlos Galbis and helpers in Valencia, Spain, on 8 March 1992.

Pizza
A pizza made at Norwood Hypermarket, South Africa, on 8 Dec 1990 was a record 37.4 m (122 ft 8 in) in diameter.

Popcorn
The most popped corn put in a container occupied 211.41 m³ (7,466 ft³) in a box filled at Pittsville Elementary School, Wisconsin, USA, in March 1996.

Spice
The hottest spice is believed to be Red 'Savina' Habanero (1994 special) of the genus capsicum. A single dried gram will produce 'heat' in 577 kg (1,272 lb) of bland sauce.

Yorkshire pudding
A 42-m² (452-ft²) pudding was made by caterers at Rotherham Council, S Yorkshire, UK, in Aug 1991 to celebrate Yorkshire Day.

Desserts

Banana split
A 7.32-km-long (4-mile 964-yd) split was made by residents of Selinsgrove, Pennsylvania, USA, on 30 April 1988.

Christmas pudding
A 3.28-tonne (7,231-lb 1-oz) pudding was made by the villagers of Aughton, Lancs, UK, and unveiled at the Famous Aughton Pudding Festival in July 1992.

Left
In 1991 a stick of rock weighing a record 413.6 kg (911 lb 13 oz) was made by the Coronation Rock Company of Blackpool. It was 43.2 cm (17 in) in diameter.

Pastry
In 1992 a 1,037.25-m (3,403-ft) mille-feuille was made by staff of Pidy, Ypres, Belgium.

Confectionery
Chocolate model
In 1991 a 13 x 8.5 x 2.5-m (42-ft 8-in x 27-ft 10½-in x 8-ft 2½-in) model of a ship was made by Gremi Provincial de Pastisseria, Confiteria i Bolleria school, Barcelona, Spain.

Easter egg
A 4.76-tonne (10,482-lb 14-oz) Easter egg was made at Cadbury Red Tulip at Ringwood, Victoria, Australia, in April 1992.

Lollipops
The largest lollipop weighed 1.37 tonnes (3,011 lb 5 oz) and was made by BonBon at Holme Olstrup, Denmark, in 1994.

The largest ice lolly weighed 8.78 tonnes (19,357 lb) and was made by Augusto Ltd at Kalisz, Poland, from 18 to 29 Sept 1994.

Stick of rock
A 413.6-kg (911-lb 13-oz), 5.03-m-long (16-ft 6-in) stick of rock was made by the Coronation Rock Company of Blackpool, Lancs, UK, on 20 July 1991.

Below
The largest box of popcorn was 12.19 m (40 ft) long, 8.53 m (28 ft) wide and 2.03 m (6 ft 8 in) high, and was filled by students from Pittsville Elementary School, Wisconsin, USA, with help from local residents, over five days from 22 to 26 March 1996.

LARGEST HAGGIS ON RECORD WAS MADE FROM A TOTAL OF 80 OX STOMACHS

Ice cream sundae
A sundae made by Palm Dairies Ltd at Edmonton, Alberta, Canada, in July 1988 had 20.27 tonnes (44,689 lb 8 oz) of ice cream, 4.39 tonnes (9,688 lb 2 oz) of syrup and 243.7 kg (537 lb 3 oz) of topping.

Jelly
A 35,000-litre (7,700-gal) watermelon jelly, made by Paul Squires and Geoff Ross, was set in a tank at Roma Street Forum, Brisbane, Queensland, Australia, on 5 Feb 1981.

Pancake
A pancake 15.01 m (49 ft 3 in) in diameter was made and flipped at Rochdale, Greater Manchester, UK, in Aug 1994.

Pies
TV chef Glynn Christian made a 12.2 x 7-m (40 x 23-ft) apple pie at Hewitts Farm, Chelsfield, Kent, UK, from 25 to 27 Aug 1982.

A cherry pie with a diameter of 6.1 m (20 ft) and containing 16.69 tonnes (36,800 lb) of

Waterloo, Ontario, Canada, in June 1993. The strawberries were picked at Joe Moss Farms.

Trifle
A 3.13-tonne (6,896-lb) trifle containing 91 litres (20 gal) of sherry was made by students of Clarendon College of Further Education, Nottingham, UK, on 26 Sept 1990.

Biscuits, cakes and pastries
Biscuit
A 487-m² (5,242-ft²) cookie containing 2.5 tonnes of chocolate was made at Christchurch, New Zealand, on 2 April 1996.

Cakes
The largest cake weighed 58.08 tonnes (128,238 lb 8 oz), including 7.35 tonnes (16,209 lb) of icing. It was baked in the shape of Alabama to celebrate the 100th birthday of Fort Payne, Alabama, USA, in Oct 1989.

The tallest cake was 30.85 m (101 ft 2½ in) high, with 100 tiers, and was made by Beth

Sweets
The largest sweet on record was a 1.85-tonne (4,078-lb 8-oz) marzipan chocolate made at the Ven International Fresh Market, Diemen, Netherlands, in May 1990.

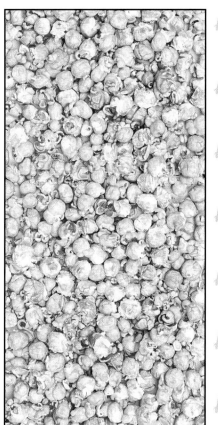

SINGLE BARBECUE WAS 31,500 CHICKEN HALVES

---

cherry filling was baked by Oliver Rotary Club members, British Columbia, Canada, in 1990.

A 6.1 x 1.5-m (20 x 5-ft) mince pie was baked at Ashby-de-la-Zouch, Leics, UK, in Oct 1932.

Strawberry bowl
A bowl of strawberries with a net weight of 2.39 tonnes (5,266 lb) was filled at Kitchener-

Cornell Trevorrow and helpers at Shiawassee County Fairgrounds, Michigan, USA, in 1990.

Doughnut
A 1.7-tonne (3,739-lb) jam doughnut with a diameter of 4.9 m (16 ft) was made by representatives of Hemstrought's Bakeries, Donato's Bakery and the radio station WKLL-FM at Utica, New York, USA, on 21 Jan 1993.

Gluttony

World's greatest trencherman
Edward Abraham ('Bozo') Miller of Oakland, California, USA, used to consume up to 25,000 calories a day—more than 11 times the recommended quantity. He stood 1.71 m (5 ft 7½ in) tall with a 144-cm (57-in) waist and his weight varied from 127 to 139 kg (20 st to 20 st 7 lb). He was undefeated in eating contests and once ate 28 907-g (2-lb) pullets at a single sitting at Trader Vic's, San Francisco, USA, in 1963.

Baked beans
Karen Stevenson of Wallasey, Merseyside, UK, ate 2,780 cold baked beans one by one with a cocktail stick in 30 minutes—a rate of 1.54 beans per second—on 4 April 1981.

Bananas
Dr Ronald L. Alkana ate 17 bananas, with an edible weight of at least 128 g (4½ oz) each, in two minutes at the University of California, Irvine, USA, on 7 Dec 1973.

Eggs
In May 1984 Peter Dowdeswell ate 13 raw eggs in a second at Kilmarnock, Ayrshire, UK.

In April 1987 John Kenmuir ate 14 eggs in 14.42 seconds on Scottish TV's *Live at 1.30.*

Frankfurters
Reg Morris ate 30 frankfurters in 64 seconds at the Miners Rest, Burntwood, Staffs, UK, on 10 Dec 1986.

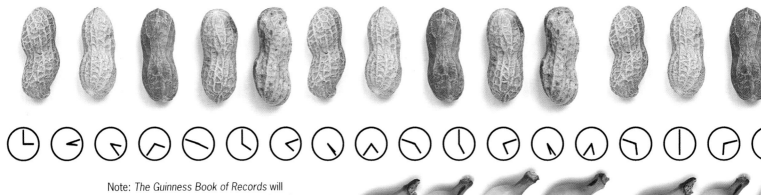

Note: *The Guinness Book of Records* will accept new baked bean eating records using a cocktail stick, but attempts must be made in the presence of a doctor, in addition to the other required independent witnesses, and should only last five minutes.

1 2 3 4 5 6 7

Grapes
The world record for grape-eating is held by Jim Ellis of Montrose, Michigan, USA, who ate 1.39 kg (3 lb 1 oz) of grapes in 34.6 seconds on 30 May 1976.

Ice cream
Tony Dowdeswell ate 1.53 kg (3 lb 6 oz) of ice cream in a time of 31.67 seconds at the Guinness Museum of World Records, New York, USA, on 16 July 1986. (The ice cream was unmelted.)

Kippers
The record for eating the greatest number of kippers is held by Reg Morris, who filleted and ate a total of 27 fish in a time of 16 min 52.66 sec at Walsall, W Midlands, UK, on 30 May 1988.

13 raw eggs in one second

'BOZO' MILLER ONCE A

PAT DONAHUE ATE 91 PICKLED ONION

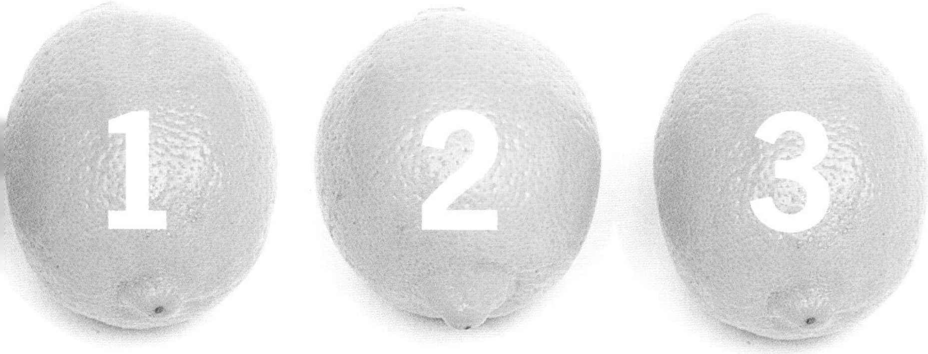
1
2
3

HEALTH WARNING!
Attempts to break these records or set new records for eating or drinking can be dangerous to health or even fatal and medical advice should always be taken first. In no circumstances will Guinness Publishing Ltd have any liability for death or for injury suffered in record attempts. Guinness Publishing Ltd has complete discretion whether or not to include any particular records in the book.

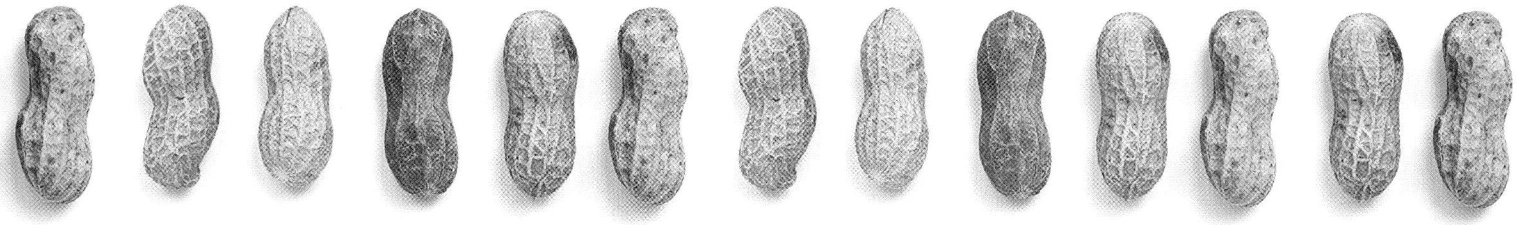

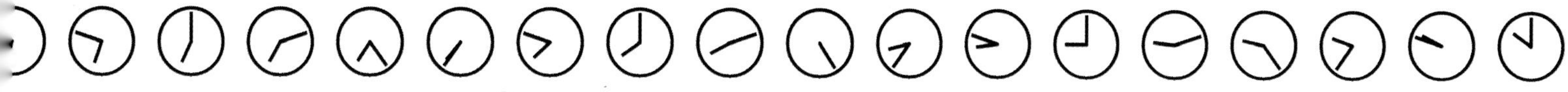

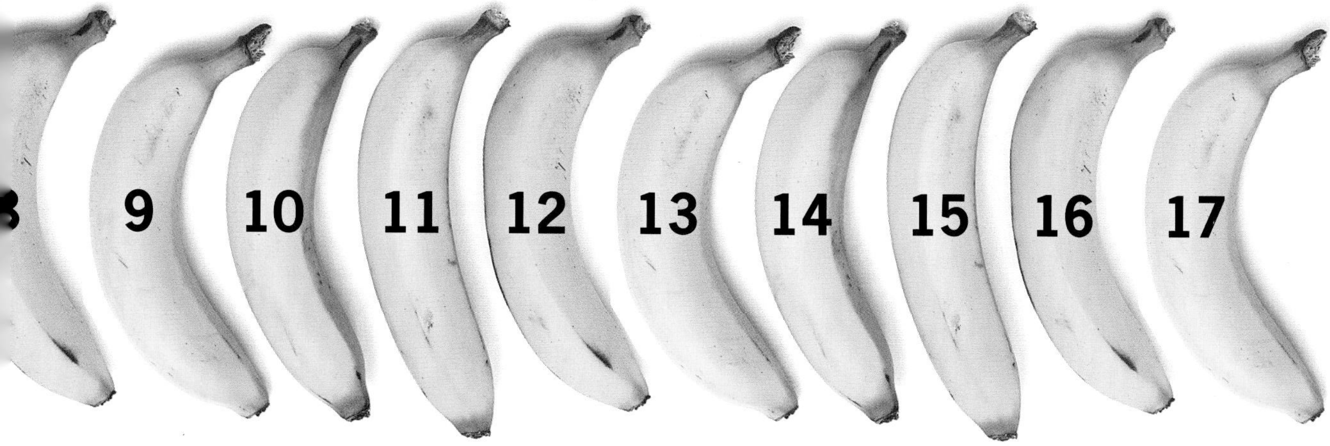
9
10
11
12
13
14
15
16
17

TOTAL OF 28 PULLETS AT A SINGLE SITTING

Lemons
Bobby Kempf of Roanoke, Virginia, USA, ate three whole lemons, including skin and pips, in 15.3 seconds on 2 May 1979.

Peanuts
In Aug 1979, 100 whole unshelled peanuts were eaten one at a time in 46 seconds by Jim Kornitzer at Brighton, E Sussex, UK.

Pickled onions
In 1978, 91 onions weighing a total of 850 g (30 oz) were eaten in 1 min 8 sec by Pat Donahue at Victoria, British Columbia, Canada.

Pizza
John Kenmuir ate a 907-g (2-lb) pizza in 32 seconds at Confettis Nightclub, Derby, UK, on 18 March 1988.

Prunes
Peter Dowdeswell ate 144 prunes in a time of 31.27 seconds at Silver Stadium, Rochester, New York, USA, on 20 June 1986.

Sausage meat
Reg Morris ate 2.72 kg (6 lb) of sausage meat in 3 min 10 sec at Spring Cottage, Shelfield, Walsall, W Midlands, UK, on 28 Dec 1986.

Spaghetti
Peter Dowdeswell ate 91.44 m (100 yd) of spaghetti in 12.02 seconds at 42nd St Disco, Halesowen, W Midlands, UK, in 1986.

N 1 MIN 8 SEC IN 1978

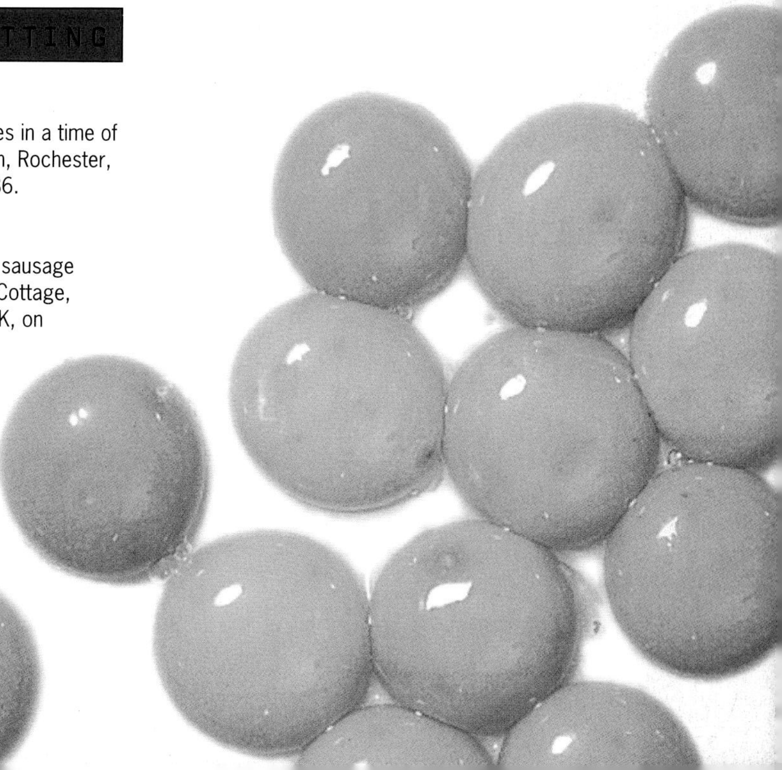

Drink

Fastest yard of ale five seconds

Right
The smallest liquor bottle on sale at the present time contains 1.3 ml of White Horse Scotch Whisky. A mini case of 12 bottles, distributed by Cumbrae Supply Co., Linwood, Renfrewshire, UK, costs about £8 and measures 5.3 x 4.8 x 3.4 cm (2⅟₁₆ x 1⅞ x 1⅟₁₆ in). They were originally designed to be jokingly handed over to retailers who had been promised a free case of Scotch.

Below right
The world's largest bottle was made by Schweppes to celebrate the company's 200th anniversary in 1994. Filled with 2,250 litres (495 gal) of lemonade, it is 1,000 times the size of a standard bottle of Schweppes, and a perfect replica.

ACTUAL SIZE 100%

Drinking

Highest alcohol consumption
Russia has the highest consumption of spirits per person, with every Russian consuming on average 4.4 litres (7¾ pints) of pure alcohol in 1994.

The Czechs are the world's leading beer consumers, with 160 litres (281½ pints) per person in 1994.

The highest consumption of wine is in France, at 62.5 litres (110 pints) per person in 1994.

Highest alcohol content
When Estonia was independent between the two world wars, the Estonian Liquor Monopoly marketed 98% alcohol distilled from potatoes.

Fastest yard of ale
Peter Dowdeswell from Earls Barton, Northants, UK, drank a yard of ale (1.42 litres or 2½ pints) in a record five seconds at RAF Upper Heyford, Oxon, UK, on 4 May 1975.

Largest wine tasting
The largest wine tasting on record was sponsored by KQED, a TV station, in San Francisco, California, USA, on 22 Nov 1986. Approximately 4,000 tasters consumed a total of 9,360 bottles of wine.

Beer

Earliest
Written references to beer dating to as far back as c. 5000 BC have been found. It formed part of the daily wages of workers at the Temple of Erech in Mesopotamia.

Evidence of beer dating from c. 3500 BC has been detected in the remains of a jug found at Godin Tepe, Iran, in 1973 during a Royal Ontario Museum expedition. In 1991, analysis of the remains revealed that residues in deep grooves in the jug were calcium oxalate, which is also known as beerstone and is still created in barley-based beers.

Most expensive
In the United Kingdom, a 3,000-year-old beer recipe has been resurrected after a six-year collaboration between Scottish and Newcastle Breweries and archaeologists from the Egypt Exploration Society, who uncovered the remains of ancient Egyptian beer preserved in near-perfect condition by the desert climate. A limited edition of 1,000 bottles of the beer, which is made from modern emmer wheat and flavoured with coriander, was sold at Harrods, London, UK, in July 1996 for the record price of £5,000 for the first bottle and £50 for the rest, with proceeds to Egyptology.

Strongest
Baz's Super Brew, brewed by Barrie Parish and on sale at The Parish Brewery, Somerby, Leics, UK, has an alcohol volume of 23%. It is only sold in ⅓ measures.

Largest bottle
A 2.54-m-tall (8-ft 4-in) beer bottle with a circumference of 2.17 m (7 ft 1½ in) was unveiled at the Shepherd Neame Brewery at Faversham, Kent, UK, on 27 Jan 1993. It took 13 minutes to fill the bottle with 625.5 litres (137½ gal) of Kingfisher beer.

Brewers
The oldest brewery in the world is the Weihenstephan Brewery in Freising, near Munich, Germany, founded in AD 1040.

Schweppes Lemonade
Schweppervescence for your Refreshment.
2250 Litres

Wine

Earliest
It is thought that wine may have been produced as early as 8000 BC, during the Stone Age, and definite physical evidence of wine has been detected in the remains of an ancient pottery jar dating back to c. 5000 BC. The latter were found at Hajji Firuz Tepe, Iran, and following analysis it was announced, in June 1996, that the yellowish residue on them contained two of the hallmarks of wine. One of these was tartaric acid, a chemical naturally abundant in grapes.

Oldest
The oldest bottle of wine ever to have been sold at auction was a bottle of 1646 Imperial Tokay, which was bought by John A. Chunko of Princeton, New Jersey, USA, and Jay Walker of Ridgefield, Connecticut, USA, for the sum of Sw.Fr.1,250 (including buyer's premium) at Sotheby's, Geneva, Switzerland, on 16 Nov 1984. At the time the sum paid was equivalent to £405.

Oldest vintners
The world's oldest champagne firm is Ruinart Père et Fils, founded in 1729.

The oldest cognac firm is Augier Frères & Cie, established in 1643.

Champagne cork flight
The longest flight of a cork from an untreated and unheated champagne bottle 1.22 m (4 ft) from level ground is 54.18 m (177 ft 9 in). The feat was achieved by Prof. Emeritus Heinrich Medicus at the Woodbury Vineyards Winery, New York, USA, on 5 June 1988.

Champagne fountain
The greatest number of storeys achieved in a champagne fountain, successfully filled from the top and using traditional long-stem glasses, is 47 (to a height of 7.85 m or 25 ft 9 in). It was constructed from 23,642 glasses by Moet & Chandon Champagne at Caesar's Palace in Las Vegas, Nevada, USA, between 19 and 23 July 1993.

Far left
Even by accident, a champagne cork can travel a few metres when exploded from a bottle. In June 1988, however, Heinrich Medicus was trying to launch a cork as far as possible, and achieved a distance of 54.18 m (177 ft 9 in)—more than twice the length of a tennis court.

MOST EXPENSIVE BOTTLE OF WINE IN THE WORLD FETCHED £105,000 IN 1985

The largest single brewing organization in the world is Anheuser-Busch Inc. of St Louis, Missouri, USA, with 13 breweries in the USA. In 1995 the company sold 10.27 billion litres (2.26 billion gal). This included the world's top-selling brand, Budweiser, at 4.40 billion litres (968 million gal).

The largest brewery on a single site is the Coors Brewing Co. at Golden, Colorado, USA, where 2.22 billion litres (488.8 million gal) were produced in 1995. At the same location is the largest aluminium can manufacturing plant in the world, which can produce more than 4 billion cans annually.

Left
The largest ever wine-tasting event took place in 1986 in San Francisco, USA, when 9,360 bottles of wine were consumed. It was sponsored by KQED, a local TV station, who had first organized such an event in 1978. The wine tasting is held nearly every year, although the 1986 record still stands.

Spirits and cocktails

Most expensive spirits
A bottle of 50-year-old Glenfiddich whisky was sold for the record price of 99,999,999 lire (about £45,200) to an anonymous Italian businessman at a postal charity auction in Milan, Italy, from Oct to Dec 1992.

The most expensive spirit currently on sale is Springbank 1919 Malt Whisky, one bottle of which costs £6,750 (inc. VAT) at Fortnum & Mason in London, UK.

Smallest bottles
The smallest bottles of liquor currently sold are bottles of White Horse Scotch Whisky, which are produced by United Distillers. They are just over 5 cm (2 in) in height and contain 1.3 ml (22 minims).

Cocktail
The largest cocktail on record was a 11,102.6-litre (2,442¼-gal) Finlandia Sea Breeze made at Maui Entertainment Center in Philadelphia, Pennsylvania, USA, on 5 Aug 1994. The ingredients used in the drink were Finlandia vodka, cranberry juice, grapefruit juice and ice.

Most expensive
A record £105,000 was paid for a bottle of 1787 Château Lafite claret, which was sold to Christopher Forbes (USA) at Christie's, London, UK, on 5 Dec 1985. The bottle was engraved with 'Th J', the initials of Thomas Jefferson, third president of the United States—a factor that greatly affected the bidding. In Nov 1986, the bottle's cork was dried out by exhibition lights and slipped, making the wine undrinkable.

The highest price paid for one glass of wine is Fr.8,600 (£982), for the first glass of Beaujolais Nouveau 1993 released (by Maison Jaffelin) in Beaune in the wine region of Burgundy, France. It was bought by Robert Denby at Pickwick's, a British pub in Beaune, on 18 Nov 1993.

Largest auction
The largest single sale of wine was conducted by Christie's of London, UK, from 10 to 11 July 1974 at Quaglino's Ballroom, London, when 2,325 lots comprising 432,000 bottles realized the price of £962,190.

Soft drinks

Largest beverage companies
PepsiCo of Purchase, New York, USA, had overall sales of $30.4 billion (£19.6 billion) in 1995, compared to $18 billion (£11.6 billion) for The Coca-Cola Company of Atlanta, Georgia, USA. However, Coca-Cola sells more drinks, as PepsiCo's sales include revenue from restaurants and snack foods amounting to $19.9 billion (£12.8 billion).

Most popular soft drink
Sales of Coca-Cola in 1995 were 573 million drinks per day.

Largest milk shake
A 7,400.4-litre (1,627⅞-gal) chocolate milk shake was made by the Nelspruit and District Child Welfare Society and the Fundraising Five at Nelspruit, South Africa, on 5 March 1994.

Largest bottle
A 3.11-m-tall (10-ft 2-in) plastic bottle with a circumference of 3.5 m (11 ft 6 in) was made for Schweppes in Melbourne, Victoria, Australia, on 17 March 1994.

Manufactured articles

LARGEST FIREWORK EVER PRODUCED BURST TO A DIAMETER OF 1.2 KM

Household items

Basket
The largest handwoven basket measures 14.63 x 7.01 x 5.79 m (48 x 23 x 19 ft), and was made by the Longaberger Company of Dresden, Ohio, USA, in 1990.

Blanket
A blanket covering 17,289 m² (186,108 ft²), hand-knitted, machine-knitted and crocheted by Knitting and Crochet Guild members worldwide, was assembled at Dishforth Airfield, N Yorkshire, UK, on 30 May 1993.

Chandeliers
The largest set of chandeliers, created by the Kookje Lighting Co. Ltd of Seoul, South Korea, is 12 m (39 ft) high, weighs 10.67 tonnes and has 700 bulbs. Completed in Nov 1988, it occupies three floors of the Lotte Chamshil Department Store, Seoul.

The largest chandelier in the United Kingdom measures 9.1 m (30 ft). Made in 1818, it weighs 1 tonne and hangs in the Chinese Room at the Royal Pavilion, Brighton.

Pottery
The tallest vase on record that was made on a potter's wheel is 5.66 m (18 ft 7 in) in height. It was completed on 10 Feb 1996 by Ray Sparks of The Creative Clay Company (Australia) Queensland.

The world's largest terracotta flowerpot is 1.95 m (6 ft 5 in) tall, with a circumference of 5.23 m (17 ft 1 in). It was hand-built by Peter Start and Albert Robinson at The Plant Pottery, Barby, Northants, UK, in May 1985.

Quilt
The world's largest quilt was made by The Saskatchewan Seniors' Association, Canada. Measuring 47.36 x 25.20 m (155 ft 4½ in x 82 ft 8 in), it was constructed in June 1994.

The largest patchwork quilt made in the United Kingdom measures 15.24 x 28.3 m (50 ft x 92 ft 10 in). It was completed on 14 Aug 1990 by Anchor Housing Association scheme residents across the country.

Silver
The world's largest single pieces of silver are a pair of water jugs weighing 242.7 kg (10,408 troy oz), made by Gorind Narain in 1902 for the Maharaja of Jaipur. They are 1.6 m (5 ft 3 in) tall and have an 8,182-litre (1,800-gal) capacity. They are in the City Palace, Jaipur, India.

Sofa
The world's longest sofa is made of red leather and is 7.32 m (24 ft) long. It seats 17 people and was made by Art Forma (Furniture) Ltd of Castle Donington, near Derby, UK, for the Swiss company Spühl AG, in May 1995.

Tablecloth
The largest tablecloth is 457.81 m (1,502 ft) long, 1.37 m (4 ft 6 in) wide and was made by the Sportex division of Artex International in Highland, Illinois, USA, on 17 Oct 1990.

The largest British tablecloth is 300.5 x 1.83 m (985 ft 9½ in x 6 ft) and was made by Tonrose Limited, Manchester, in June 1988.

Clothing

Wedding dresses
The world's longest wedding dress train measured 157 m (515 ft), and was made by the Hansel and Gretel bridal outfitters of Gunskirchen, Germany, in 1992.

The longest British wedding dress train was 29.8 m (97 ft 7¾ in) in length and was made by Margaret Riley of Thurnby Lodge, Leics, for the blessing of the marriage of Diane and Steven Reid on 6 May 1990.

Fan
A hand-painted chintz and wood fan that was 8 m (26 ft 3 in) in length when unfolded, and 4.5 m (14 ft 8 in) high was made by Victor Troyas Oses of Peralta, Spain, in Oct 1994.

Scarf
The longest scarf ever knitted is 32.19 km (20 miles 4 yd) in length. It was made by residents of Abbeyfield Houses for the Abbeyfield Society of Potters Bar, Herts, UK, and was completed on 29 May 1988.

Zip-fastener
The longest zip-fastener was laid around the centre of Sneek, Netherlands, on 5 Sept 1989. The brass zipper, made by Yoshida (Netherlands) Ltd, is 2,851 m (9,353 ft 6¾ in) long and has 2,565,900 teeth.

Games and toys

Christmas cracker
The largest functional cracker was 45.72 m (150 ft) long and 3.04 m (10 ft) in diameter. It was made by the international rugby league player Ray Price for Markson Sparks! of NSW, Australia, and was pulled in the car park at Westfield Shopping Town, Chatswood, Sydney, on 9 Nov 1991.

Fireworks
The largest firework was *Universe I Part II*, exploded for the Lake Toya Festival, Hokkaidō, Japan, on 15 July 1988. The 700-kg (1,543-lb) shell was 139 cm (54¾ in) in diameter and burst to a diameter of 1.2 km (¾ mile).

A self-propelled vertical firework wheel 19.3 m (63 ft 6 in) in diameter was designed by Tom Archer and built by Essex Pyrotechnics Ltd, UK. It was fired on 9 July 1994 and its eight revolutions had a mean speed in excess of 5 rpm.

Jigsaw puzzles
The largest jigsaw had 43,924 pieces and covered 4,783 m² (51,484 ft²). Assembled

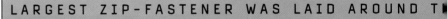

LARGEST ZIP-FASTENER WAS LAID AROUND T▶

LARGEST NEON SIGN IS SITUATED ON HONG KONG ISLAND AND CONTAI

on 8 July 1992, it was devised by the Centre Socio-Culturel d'Endoume, Marseille, France, on the theme of the environment.

A puzzle with 204,484 pieces was made by BCF Holland b.v., Almelo, Netherlands, and assembled by students of Gravenvoorde School between 25 May and 1 June 1991. It measured 96.25 m² (1,036 ft²).

Rope
A rope 172 m (564 ft 4 in) long, with a diameter of 1.54 m (5 ft ½ in), was made from rice straw for the annual Naha City Festival, Okinawa, Japan, in Oct 1995. It is the largest rope made from natural materials and weighs 26.73 tonnes (58,929 lb).

Yo-yo
A yo-yo 3.17 m (10 ft 4 in) in diameter and weighing 407 kg (897 lb) was devised by J. N. Nichols (Vimto) Ltd and made by engineering students at Stockport College, UK. It was launched by crane from a height of 57.5 m (187 ft) at Wythenshawe, Manchester, on 1 Aug 1993 and yo-yoed about four times.

Tools
Axe
A steel axe 18.28 m (60 ft) long, 7 m (23 ft) wide and weighing 7 tonnes was designed and built by BID Ltd of Woodstock, New Brunswick, Canada. It was presented to the town of Nackawi on 11 May 1991 to commemorate its selection as 1991 Forestry Capital of Canada. Calculations suggested that a 140-tonne lumberjack would be needed to swing the giant axe, but a crane was used to lift it into its concrete 'stump' instead.

Knife
The penknife with the most blades is the Year Knife, made by cutlers Joseph Rodgers &

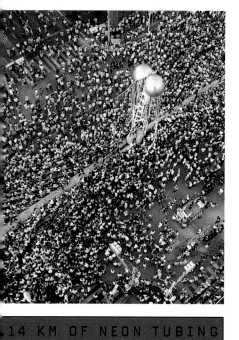

Sons of Sheffield, S Yorkshire, UK, who were granted a trademark in 1682. The knife was made in 1822, and a blade was added every year until space ran out in 1973. In 1970 it was acquired by the largest British hand tool manufacturers, Stanley Works (Great Britain) Ltd of Sheffield.

Pencil
Students at Huddersfield Technical College constructed a pencil weighing 24 kg (53 lb) for Cliffe Hill School, Lightcliffe, Halifax, W Yorkshire, UK, in 1995.

Advertising signs
Largest advertising sign
The two-sided sign at the Hilton Hotel and Casino in Las Vegas, Nevada, USA, had a total area of 7,648.5 m² (82,328 ft²) and was 110.3 m (362 ft) high when completed in Dec 1993. Part of it fell down in a storm on 18 July 1994, but it remains both the largest and the tallest sign, as well as the world's largest illuminated sign.

Most conspicuous sign
The electric Citroën sign on the Eiffel Tower, Paris, France, was switched on in July 1925 and could be seen 38 km (24 miles) away. It was in six colours and used 250,000 lamps and 90 km (56 miles) of electric cable. The letter 'N' was 20.8 m (68 ft 5 in) tall.

Largest advertisement on a building
In May and June 1995, a 4,402-m² (47,385-ft²) sign was displayed near Chiswick, London, UK, to promote Gulf Air.

Largest hoarding
The hoarding for the Bassat Ogilvy Ford España promotion is 145 m (475 ft 9 in) long and 15 m (49 ft 3 in) high. It is sited at Plaza de Toros Monumental de Barcelona, Spain, and was installed on 27 April 1989.

Longest illuminated sign
A 60-m-long (197-ft) sign at Ramat Gan, Israel, lit by 16,000-W metal-halide projectors, was erected by Abudi Signs Industry Ltd.

The longest illuminated sign in the United Kingdom is shared by P & O European Ferries, Stena Line and Sea France at Dover Eastern Docks, Kent. At 87.5 m (287 ft 1 in) in length and 65 cm (25½ in) in height, it was installed by Dover Sign Co. in Aug 1993.

Largest neon signs
The largest neon sign is 111.4 x 19.05 m (365 ft 6 in x 62 ft 6 in) and was built to promote 999, a traditional Chinese medicine from the Nanfang Pharmaceutical Factory. It was erected between Nov 1992 and April 1993 on Hong Kong Island and contains 13.14 km (8 miles 290 yd) of neon tubing.

The world's longest neon sign is the letter 'M' installed on the Great Mississippi River Bridge, Memphis, Tennessee, USA. The sign is 550 m (1,800 ft) in length and uses 200 high-intensity lamps.

Flags and banners
Longest banner
On 15 Nov 1995, a banner 7.99 km (4 miles 1,698 yd) long was created by Nestlé's Milo as part of the Palang Jai Thai Tum Dai campaign in Thailand. The campaign was a joint effort between the Ministry of Education, the Thailand Amateur Sports Associations Club and Nestlé's Milo, and was designed to gain support for the Thai national team participating in the South East Asian Games. The banner was covered in messages of encouragement from Thai students.

Reebok International Ltd of Massachusetts, USA, flew a banner reading 'Reebok Totally Beachin' from a single-seater plane from 13 to 16 and 20 to 23 March 1990 for four hours each day. The banner was 15 m (50 ft) high and 30 m (100 ft) long.

Largest flag
The largest flag flown from a flagstaff is a Brazilian national flag in Brasilia, measuring 20 x 14.3 m (65 ft 6 in x 46 ft 9 in).

Left
The Eiffel Tower, Paris, France, is one of the most recognizable sights in the world. From 1925 to 1936, it was illuminated by the Citroën sign advertising the French motor company. It could be seen from 38 km (24 miles) away, which is further than the distance from Dover, Kent, UK, to Calais, France.

Far left and left
The 1995 Naha Giant Tug-of-War held in Okinawa, Japan, included the joining of two ropes (Yin and Yang) to symbolize the prosperity of humankind. These make up the largest rope in the world. The tug-of-war festivities originated in religious observances, including prayers for a bountiful harvest, abundant rain and peace.

Collections

Above
Paul Høegh Poulsen, who owns the largest bottle cap collection in the world, started his hobby in 1956 with his twin brother, Jørgen. He now exchanges caps with more than 100 collectors from all over the world.

Right
Lotta Sjölin of Sweden could not afford to collect old cars, so instead began a parking meter collection. She has travelled the world by train to gather her 292 parking meters.

Food and drink

Salt and pepper shakers
Ruth Rasmussen of Traer, Iowa, USA, has collected a record 13,900 salt and pepper shakers since 1946. Her collection is stored in two buildings.

Refrigerator magnets
Louise J. Greenfarb of Spanaway, Washington, USA, had collected 17,000 refrigerator magnets by May 1996.

Beer cans
William B. Christensen of Madison, New Jersey, USA, has a collection of more than 75,000 different beer cans from some 125 countries, colonies and territories.

Beer labels (Labology)
Jan Solberg of Oslo, Norway, had collected 424,868 different beer labels from around the world by June 1995.

Beer mats (Tegestology)
To May 1996, Leo Pisker of Langenzersdorf, Austria, had collected a total of 148,230 different beer mats from 160 countries. Both the largest and the smallest mats in his collection, which measure 5,776 cm^2 (895 in^2) and 6.25 cm^2 (1 in^2) respectively, come from the United Kingdom.

The largest collection of British beer mats to date contains more than 74,200 examples and is owned by Timothy Stannard of Birmingham, W Midlands, UK. Stannard's collection includes an oval mat from Theakston Brewery measuring 102 x 79 cm (3 ft 4¼ in x 2 ft 7¼ in).

Bottle caps
Since 1956 Paul Høegh Poulsen of Rødovre, Denmark, has colllected 82,169 different bottle caps from 179 countries.

Bottle collections
Peter Broeker of Geesthacht, Germany, has a collection of 8,131 different full beer bottles from 110 countries.

David L. Maund's bottle collection contained a total of 11,476 miniature Scotch whisky bottles and 323 miniature Guinness bottles by May 1996.

Edoardo Giaccone of Gardone Riviera, Brescia, Italy, has 5,502 different full-sized whisky bottles in his collection, which is housed in his specially built *whiskyteca*.

Claive Vidiz, the president of the Brazilian Whisky Collector's Association, has a collection of 2,571 full original whisky bottles housed in a specially built museum in São Paulo, Brazil. The last bottle to enter his collection was a "Madam Speaker's Order",

presented by Anthony A. Greener and Philip Yea of Guinness plc on their visit to the museum on 21 April 1996.

Cigarettes

Cigarettes
Robert E. Kaufman of New York, USA, collected a total of 8,390 different brands of cigarette from 173 countries and territories. After his death in March 1992, his wife Naida took over the collection. The oldest brand is *Lone Jack*, dated to *c.* 1885, and both the longest and shortest cigarettes in the world are represented.

Cigarette cards
The largest known cigarette card collection in the world belonged to Edward Wharton-Tigar of London, UK, who had more than 1 million

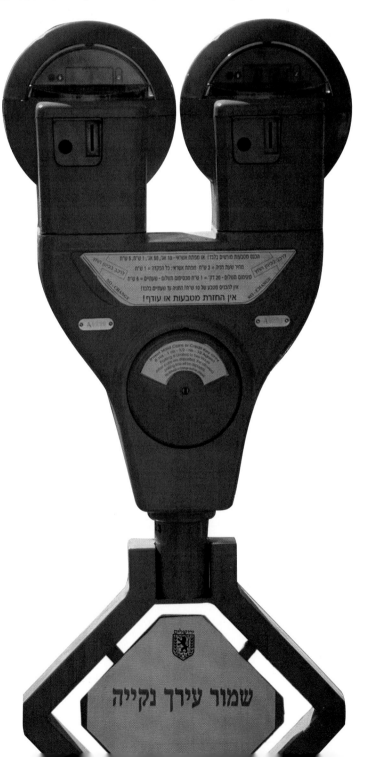

Most credit cards 1,397

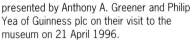

cigarette and trade cards in a total of 45,000 sets. Wharton-Tigar bequeathed his collection to the British Museum, who have agreed to make it available for public study.

Cigarette lighters
Francis Van Herle of Beringen, Belgium, has collected a total of 58,259 different cigarette lighters to June 1996.

Cigarette packets
The largest verified private collection in the world consists of a total of 130,620 cigarette packets from 268 different countries and territories, accumulated by Claudio Rebecchi of Modena, Italy, since 1962. The most represented country in the collection is Japan, with 14,080 packets.

Matches
Matchbox labels
Since 1925, Teiichi Yoshizawa of Chiba-Ken, Japan, has collected a record-breaking 743,512 different matchbox labels from more than 130 countries. His collection includes advertising labels.

Phillumenist Robert Jones of Indianapolis, Indiana, USA, has amassed approximately 280,000 matchbox labels, excluding advertising labels.

Matchbook covers
Ed Brassard of Seattle, Washington, USA, had a collection of 3,159,119 matchbook covers by March 1995.

Attire and accessories
Buttons
Students of Rolling Hills Primary School, Vernon, New Jersey, USA, along with their teacher Ellen Dambach, collected a record total of 1 million clothing buttons between Jan and June 1995.

Earrings
Carol McFadden of Oil City, Pennsylvania, USA, had collected 22,623 different pairs of earrings by April 1996. She had her ears pierced in 1992 and again in 1995.

Watches
Robert Walker of Yakima, Washington, USA, has acquired a record-breaking collection of more than 1,920 pocket and wrist watches over a period of 20 years. The most valuable watches amongst them are stored in a vault and were not counted as part of the collection in May 1987.

Writing
Books
John Benham of Avoca, Indiana, USA, owns more than 1.5 million books. Most of his collection is stored in a two-storey building, a six-car garage, and under tarpaulin outdoors.

Pens
By May 1996, Vilma Valma Turpeinen of Tampere, Finland, had collected 26,000 different pens.

Money
Credit cards
The largest collection of valid credit cards is 1,397 different cards belonging to Walter Cavanagh of Santa Clara, California, USA. The cost of acquisition to 'Mr Plastic Fantastic' was nil, but the cards are worth more than $1.65 million in credit. They are kept in the world's longest wallet, which is 76.2 m (250 ft) long and weighs 17.49 kg (38 lb 8 oz).

Piggy banks
Ove Nordström of Spånga, Sweden, has collected more than 3,075 piggy banks in the last 39 years.

Parking meters
Lotta Sjölin of Solna, Sweden, had collected 292 different parking meters by July 1996. She has obtained disused meters from local authorities all over the world since 1989.

Left
Louise Greenfarb, whose car licence plate reads MGNTLDY, started collecting magnets in the 1960s. She has more than 500 cookie sheets, each of which has 25–30 magnets stuck to them. With plans to collect magnets for the rest of her life, she jokes that her house may become the next magnetic pole.

Below
Edward Wharton-Tigar not only collected cigarette cards, but also wrote about them in the bi-monthly magazine for The Cardophilic Society, of which he was president and chairman.

Ties (Grabatology)
A record-breaking collection of 10,453 ties that had been accumulated by grabatologist Bill McDaniel of Santa Maria, California, USA, was purchased by a museum in St Augustine, Florida, in 1992.

In the United Kingdom, the champion tie collector is Tom Holmes from Walsall, W Midlands. By May 1996 Holmes had collected a record total of 9,598 different ties. The term 'grabatologist' was coined especially for him in 1993 by the Guild of British Tie Makers.

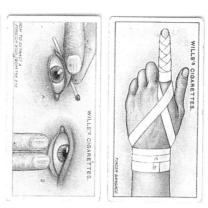

100
101
102
103
104
105
106
107
108
109
110
111
112
113
114
115
116
117
118

IN WORLD'S GREATEST WILDCAT, OIL GUSHED

Science and

WORLD'S SMALLEST BRILLIANT CUT DIAMOND HAS 57 FACETS AND WEIGHS 0.0000743 CARA

HOTTEST FLAME CAN REACH A TEMPERATURE OF 4,988°C

HEAVIEST KNOWN ELEMENT HAS A MASS OF 277 AND A LIFETIME

LARGEST SCIENTIFIC INSTRUMENT, THE L

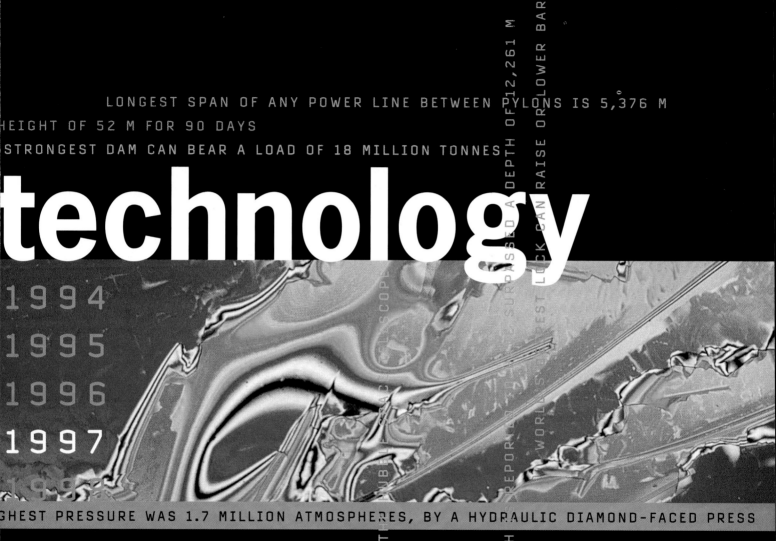

LONGEST SPAN OF ANY POWER LINE BETWEEN PYLONS IS 5,376 M

HEIGHT OF 52 M FOR 90 DAYS

STRONGEST DAM CAN BEAR A LOAD OF 18 MILLION TONNES

technology

1994

1995

1996

1997

GHEST PRESSURE WAS 1.7 MILLION ATMOSPHERES, BY A HYDRAULIC DIAMOND-FACED PRESS

FASTEST SUPERCOMPUTER ACHIEVED 328 GIGAFLOPS

MILLIONTHS OF A SECOND

The physical world

Right
Scientists check Princeton's Tokamak Fusion Test Reactor (TFTR), which is being used to research nuclear fusion as a power source. The reactor uses a super-hot plasma of deuterium (heavy hydrogen) confined by large magnets. Fusion reaction takes place at about 100 million°C.

Far right
A sample of aerogel, a new material consisting of microscopic fibres of silica, making it the least dense solid. It has been called 'frozen smoke'.

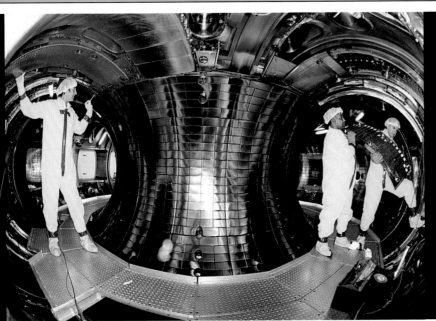

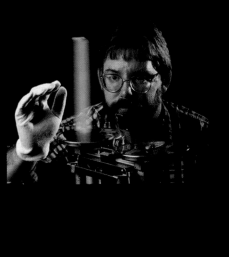

The sub-atomic world
Lightest and heaviest quarks
There are three families of sub-atomic particles, each of which contains two quarks and two leptons. The lightest quark is the up quark, with a mass of 6 MeV, and the heaviest is the top quark (discovered at Fermilab, Batavia, Illinois, USA, in 1995), with a mass of 170 GeV.

Lightest and heaviest leptons
The three neutrino leptons are all predicted to have zero mass, while the heaviest lepton is the tau (which was discovered in 1975), at 1.777 GeV.

Heaviest quanta
The heaviest gauge boson is the $Z°$ (discovered in 1983), at 91.19 GeV. It also has the shortest lifetime of any particle, at 2.64×10^{-25} seconds.

Lightest and heaviest hadrons
The lightest hadron is the neutral pion meson (discovered in 1949), at 134.976 MeV. The heaviest is the upsilon (11020) meson (discovered in 1984), at 11.02 GeV.

Isotopes
Most and fewest isotopes
There are at least 2,670 known isotopes. Tin (Sn) has the most, at 38. It also has the highest number of stable isotopes, at 10. Hydrogen (H) has the least number of accepted isotopes, at three.

Most and least stable isotopes
The most stable radioactive isotope is tellurium 128, with a half-life of 1.5×10^{24} years. The least stable isotope is lithium 5, which decays in 4.4×10^{-22} seconds.

The 112 elements
The most common elements
Hydrogen is the commonest element in both the Universe (over 90%) and the Solar System (70.68%). Iron is the commonest element in the Earth (36% of the mass), while molecular nitrogen (N_2) is the most common in the atmosphere (75.52% by mass).

Heaviest element
The heaviest known element is 112, provisionally named ununbium (Uub), literally 1-1-2. It was produced at Gesellschaft für Schwerionenforschung, Darmstadt, Germany, in Feb 1996. It has a mass of 277 and decays in a lifetime of 240 millionths of a second. It is situated in the same group in the periodic table as zinc, cadmium and mercury.

Hardest element
The diamond allotrope of carbon (C) has a Knoop value of 8,400. The Knoop value of one of the softest minerals, gypsum, is 40.

Highest tensile strength
The strongest element is boron (B), with a tensile strength of 5.7 GPa (5.7×10^9 Pa).

Most ductile element
One gram of gold (Au) can be drawn to 2.4 km (1 oz to 43 miles).

Most and least dense metals
At room temperature, the least dense metal is lithium (Li), at 0.5334 g/cm. The densest is osmium (Os), at 22.59 g/cm^3.

Lightest and densest gases
At NTP (normal temperature and pressure, 0°C and one atmosphere), the lightest gas is hydrogen (H) at 0.00008989 g/cm^3 (0.005612 lb/ft^3). The densest is radon (Rn), at 0.01005 g/cm^3 (0.6274 lb/ft^3).

Highest melting and boiling points
For metals, tungsten (W) has the highest melting point, at 3,414°C (6,177°F), and the highest boiling point, at 5,847°C (10,557°F). The graphite form of carbon sublimes directly from solid to vapour at 3,704°C (6,699°F).

Lowest melting and boiling points
Helium (He) cannot be solid at normal atmospheric pressure, the minimum pressure being 2.532 MPa (24.985 atmospheres) at a temperature of −272.375°C (−458.275°F). Helium also has the lowest boiling point, at −268.928°C (−452.070°F).

Chemical extremes
Smelliest substances
The most evil of the 17,000 or so smells to have been classified to date are considered to be ethyl mercaptan (C_2H_5SH) and butyl seleno-mercaptan (C_4H_9SeH). Both are said to smell of rotting cabbage, garlic, onions, burnt toast and sewer gas.

Sweetest substance
The sweetest known substance is Talin, obtained from the Katemfe plant in West Africa, which is 6,150 times sweeter than a 1% sucrose solution.

Highest melting point 3,704°C

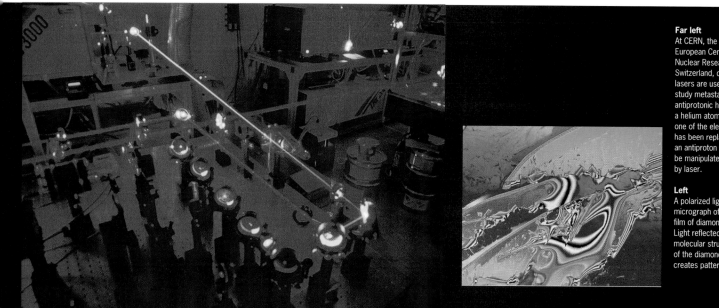

EMENT, 112, WAS ARTIFICIALLY PRODUCED IN GERMANY IN FEB 1996

Bitterest substance
The substances with the bitterest taste are based on the denatonium cation and have been produced commercially as both the benzoate and the saccharide.

Strongest acid
The strongest known acid is an 80% solution of antimony pentafluoride in hydrofluoric acid, which is estimated to be at least 10^{18} times stronger than concentrated sulphuric acid.

Least dense solid
So-called aerogels are the least dense solids. They consist of globules of silicon and oxygen atoms joined into long strands and separated by a honeycomb of air bubbles so that the substance is 99% air, weighing $0.005g/cm^3$ (5 oz per cubic foot).

Most absorbent substance
The most absorbent substance yet devised is a mixture of starch, acrylamide and acrylic acid. It can retain water at 1,300 times its own weight.

Physical extremes
Highest temperature
The highest man-made temperature ever achieved is 510 million°C (920 million°F), which is 30 times hotter than the centre of the Sun. This was attained on 27 May 1994 at the Tokomak Fusion Test Reactor at the Princeton Plasma Physics Laboratory in the USA as part of an experiment to collect atomic fusion energy.

Lowest temperature
The lowest possible temperature is −273.15°C (−459.67°F)—a point when all atomic and molecular thermal motion ceases. The lowest temperature ever obtained is 280 picoKelvin (2.8×10^{-10} K), which was achieved at the Low Temperature Laboratory of the Helsinki University of Technology, Finland, in 1993. The cooled material was the nuclear region of an atom. A picokelvin is a trillionth of a degree (one million millionths of a degree).

The record for the coldest temperature ever achieved for normal atoms was set in 1993, by scientists at the University of Lancaster, UK, when they cooled copper atoms to 12-millionths of a degree above absolute zero.

Highest pressure
A sustained laboratory pressure of 170 GPa (1.7 million atmospheres) was reported from the giant hydraulic diamond-faced press at the Carnegie Institution's Geophysical Laboratory, Washington DC, USA, in June 1978.

Best vacuum
Japanese scientists obtained a vacuum of 7×10^{-16} atmospheres inside a stainless steel chamber in Jan 1991.

Largest electrical current
The world record for the largest ever electrical current was achieved by scientists at Oak Ridge National Laboratory in the USA in April 1996. They sent a current of 2 million amperes per square centimetre down a superconducting wire. (Standard household wires carry a current of less than 1,000 ampere/cm^2).

Hottest flame
Carbon subnitride (C_4N_4) is capable, at one atmosphere pressure, of generating a flame calculated to reach 4,988°C (9,010°F).

Highest voltage
The highest ever potential difference obtained in a laboratory has been 32±1.5 MV, by the National Electrostatics Corporation at Oak Ridge, Tennessee, USA, on 17 May 1979.

Highest superconducting temperature
A superconductor is a substance that loses all electrical resistance below a critical temperature. The highest critical temperature yet attained is −140.7°C (−221.3°F), achieved at the Laboratorium für Festkörperphysik, Zürich, Switzerland, for a mixture of oxides of mercury, barium, calcium and copper.

Brightest light
The world record intensity for laser light was recently achieved by scientists at the University of Michigan, USA, with a pulse in an argon laser of 10–20 watts/cm^2. During this pulse of radiation, the microscopic pressure in the laser's plasma was the greatest to have ever been artificially produced, at 1,000 million atmospheres or 10^{14} Pascals.

Strongest and weakest magnetic fields
The strongest continuous magnetic field was 38.7 teslas, measured at the Massachusetts Institute of Technology, USA, in May 1994. The weakest magnetic field (8×10^{-15} teslas) is used for research into the weak magnetic fields generated in the heart and brain.

Power

Oil

Longest crude-oil pipeline
The Interprovincial Pipe Line Inc. installation spans North America from Edmonton, Alberta, to Montreal, Quebec, Canada, via Chicago, USA. Along its 3,787.2 km (2,353 miles), 82 pumping stations maintain a daily flow of 6 million litres (1.6 million gal).

Largest oil producer and consumer
Oil production in Saudi Arabia in 1995 was estimated at 7,867,000 barrels per day.

The USA consumed 17.7 million barrels of oil per day, or 26% of the world's total, in 1994.

Right
A wind farm in Alamont Pass, California, USA.

Largest oil field
Developed by Aramco, the Ghawar oil field in Saudi Arabia has an estimated ultimate recovery (EUR) of 82 billion barrels of oil and measures 240 x 35 km (150 x 22 miles).

Largest oil refinery
On 1 Jan 1996, the Amoco refinery in Texas City, USA, had a crude capacity of 433,000 barrels per day.

Heaviest oil platform
The *Pampo* platform off Rio de Janeiro, Brazil, built by the Petrobrás company, weighs 24,000 tonnes, covers 3,900 m^2 (41,979 ft^2) and produces 33,000 barrels per day.

Tallest oil platform
In April 1996, the 'Mars' tension leg platform was installed in the Gulf of Mexico. Designed and engineered by the Shell Oil Company, it set a new water-depth record for a production platform, extending 896 m (2,940 ft) from sea bed to surface.

Worst oil spill
A marine blow-out under the drilling rig Ixtoc I in the Gulf of Campeche, Gulf of Mexico, on 3 June 1979, caused a slick that spread 640 km (400 miles) by 5 Aug 1979. It was eventually capped on 24 March 1980 after an estimated loss of up to 500,000 tonnes.

The worst single assault on the ecosystem was by Iraqi president Saddam Hussein on 19 Jan 1991, when he ordered the pumping of Gulf crude from the Sea Island terminal, Kuwait, and from seven large tankers. Estimates put the loss at 816,000 tonnes.

Largest offshore oil disaster
The largest offshore oil disaster occurred on the Piper Alpha oil production platform in the North Sea on 6 July 1988, when 167 people were killed.

Largest oil tanks
The five Aramco 1.5-million-barrel storage tanks at Ju'aymah, Saudi Arabia, are 21.94 m (72 ft) tall and have a diameter of 117.6 m (386 ft). They were completed in 1980.

Largest oil gusher
The greatest wildcat ever recorded blew at Alborz No.5 well, near Qum, Iran, on 26 Aug 1956. The oil gushed to a height of 52 m (170 ft) at a rate of around 120,000 barrels per day and at a pressure of 62,055 kPa (9,000 lb/in^2). It was closed after 90 days by B. Mostofi and Myron Kinley of Texas, USA.

Gas

Largest natural gas producer
The Commonwealth of Independent States (CIS) produced 704 billion m^3 (24,893.3 billion ft^3) of natural gas in 1995.

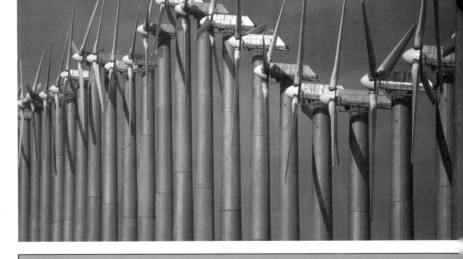

Largest natural gas deposit
A deposit at Urengoi, Russia, has an estimated ultimate recovery of 8 trillion m^3 (285 trillion ft^3).

Longest natural gas pipeline
In 1995, the TransCanada pipeline transported a total of 66.6 million m^3 (2,351.5 billion ft^3) of gas through 13,955 km (8,671 miles) of pipe.

Largest gas holder
A gas holder at the Ruhrkohle AG Prosper coking plant, Essen, Germany, has a working gas volume of 325,000 m^3 (11,480,000 ft^3) under standard conditions.

Largest gas flare
The greatest gas flare recorded burnt at Gassi Touil in the Algerian Sahara from 13 Nov 1961 to 28 April 1962. The flames rose to a height of 137 m (450 ft) and the smoke to 182 m (600 ft). It was eventually extinguished

by Paul Neal ('Red') Adair of Houston, Texas, USA, using 245 kg (540 lb) of dynamite, for a fee of $1 million plus expenses.

Water and steam

Deepest water bore
The Stensvad Water Well 11-W1 is 2,231 m (7,320 ft) deep. It was drilled by the Great Northern Drilling Co. Inc. in Rosebud County, Montana, USA, from Oct to Nov 1961.

The Thermal Power Co. geothermal steam well in Sonoma County, California, USA, construction of which began in 1955, has reached a depth of 2,752 m (9,029 ft).

Oldest steam engine
The oldest steam engine in working order is the Smethwick Engine. Designed by James Watt (1736–1819) and built by the

Birmingham Canal Company in 1779 at a cost of £2,000, the pump worked on the locks at Smethwick, W Midlands, UK, until 1891.

Oldest water mill
The oldest water mill in continuous commercial use is Priston Mill near Bath, Somerset, UK, first mentioned in AD 931 in a charter of King Athelstan. It is driven by the Conygre Brook.

Wind power

Tallest windmill
St Patrick's Distillery Mill in Dublin, now without sails, is 45.72 m (150 ft) tall.

The tallest working windmill in Europe is de Noord Molen at Schiedam, Netherlands, at 33.33 m (109 ft 4 in).

Largest wind generator
The $55-million Boeing Mod-5B wind generator in Oahu, Hawaii, USA, has 97.5-m (320-ft) rotors, and produces 3,200 kW when the wind reaches 51 km/h (32 mph).

Chimneys and towers
Tallest chimney
The coal power plant No. 2 stack at Ekibastuz, Kazakhstan, which was completed in 1987, is 420 m (1,378 ft) tall. The diameter tapers from 44 m (144 ft) at the base to 14.2 m (46 ft 7 in) at the top, and the chimney weighs 60,000 tonnes.

Chimney with greatest internal volume
A chimney constructed by M. W. Kellog Co. for Empresa Nacional de Electricidad S. A., Puentes de García Rodríguez, Spain, is 350 m (1,148 ft) in height, contains 15,750 m³ (20,600 yd³) of concrete and 1,315 tonnes of steel and has a total internal volume of 189,720 m³ (248,100 yd³).

Largest cooling tower
A cooling tower adjacent to the nuclear plant at Uentrop, Germany, completed in 1976, is 180 m (590 ft) tall.

Power plants
Largest solar electric power facility
In terms of nominal capacity, the largest solar electric power facility in the world is the Harper Lake Site (LSP 8 & 9) in the Mojave Desert, California, USA, operated by UC Operating Services. The two solar electric generating stations (SEGS) have a nominal capacity of 160 MW (80 MW each). The station site covers 518 ha (1,280 acres).

Largest generator
The largest operational generator is a turbo-generator of 1,450 MW (net) under installation at Ignalina atomic power station, Lithuania.

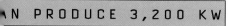

N PRODUCE 3,200 KW

Greatest capacity of a power plant
The Itaipu hydro-electric plant on the Paraná River near the Brazil–Paraguay border was opened in 1984 and has now attained its ultimate rated capacity of 13,320 MW.

Biggest blackout
The greatest power failure on record struck seven north-eastern US states and Ontario, Canada, on 9–10 Nov 1965. About 30 million people over an area of 207,200 km² (80,000 miles²) were plunged into darkness, but only two were killed.

Largest transformers
The largest single-phase transformers are rated at 1,500,000 kVA. Of the eight that are in service at the American Electric Power Service Corporation, five step down from 765 to 345 kV.

Largest turbines
The largest hydraulic turbines are rated at 815 MW, have a 407-tonne runner, a 317.5-tonne shaft and were installed by Allis-Chalmers (now Voith Hydro) at the Grand Coulee Third Powerplant, Washington, USA.

Largest nuclear power station
The six-reactor Zaporozhe power station in the Ukraine has a gross output of 6,000 MW.

Most nuclear reactors
The USA has 109 nuclear reactors, with a total capacity of 98,729 MW. As of Dec 1995, they were generating 673.402 million kilowatt hours, or 29.5% of the world total of nuclear power.

Power lines
Highest voltages
The highest voltages carried on a DC (direct current) line are 1,330 kV over 1,970 km (1,224 miles) on the DC Pacific Inter-Tie in the USA, which stretches from about 160 km (100 miles) east of Portland, Oregon, to a location east of Los Angeles, California.

The highest voltages that are carried on a three-phase AC (alternating current) line are 1,200 kV over a distance of more than 1,610 km (1,000 miles) in Russia. The first section carries the current from Siberia to northern Kazakhstan, while the second takes it from Siberia to the Urals.

Longest transmission lines
The longest span of any power line between pylons is 5,376 m (17,638 ft), across the Ameralik Fjord near Nuuk, Greenland. Built and erected by A. S. Betonmast of Oslo, Norway, in 1991–92 as part of the 132-kV line serving the 45-MW Buksefjorden Hydro Power Station, each of the four conductors weighs 38 tonnes.

Highest transmission lines
The world's highest power lines span 3,627 m (11,900 ft) across the Straits of Messina, Italy, from towers that are 205 m (675 ft) high on the Sicily side and 224 m (735 ft) on the Calabria side.

Batteries
Largest battery
The 10-MW lead-acid battery at Chino, California, USA, has a design capacity of 40 MWh. It is currently used at an electrical sub-station for levelling peak demand loads. The $13-million project is a cooperative effort by Southern California Edison Co. Electric Power Research Institutes and International Lead Zinc Research Organization Inc.

Most durable battery
The zinc-foil and sulfur dry-pile batteries made by Watlin and Hill, London, UK, have powered ceaseless tintinnabulation in a bell jar at the Clarendon Laboratory, Oxford, since 1840.

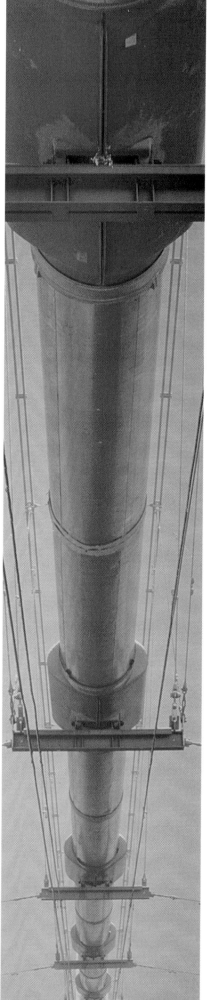

Left
The 3,787.2-km (2,353-mile) pipeline crossing North America is the world's most extensive crude-oil pipeline.

Mining and precious stones

Deepest mine 3,581 m

Right
The world's largest diamond on record, the *Cullinan*, was discovered in 1905 in the side wall of an open mine at the Premier Diamond Mine. It was named after Sir Thomas Major Cullinan, founder and chairman of the Premier Mining Company, and presented to Edward VII of the United Kingdom in 1907.

Fastest drilling
In June 1988, during the drilling of four wells, Harkins & Company Rig 13 achieved a depth of 10,538 m (34,574 ft) within one month—an average of 24 m (80 ft) per hour—in McMullen County, Texas, USA.

Largest mines
The world's largest gold mine covers a total area of 27,903 ha (68,948 acres). Owned by the Free State Cons Gold Miners Ltd, the mine is located in South Africa's Free State. In 1996, 90 tonnes of gold were mined there.

The world's largest platinum mine produces a total of 28 tonnes per year. It is owned by the Rustenburg Platinum Mines Group, Transvaal, South Africa.

The largest uranium mine in terms of world production is Cameco's Lake mine in Saskatchewan, Canada, which produces 5,380 tonnes of uranium per year, or 15.5% of total world production.

Worst mining disaster
In the world's most devastating mining disaster, 1,549 people were killed by a coal dust explosion at Honkeiko (Benxihu) Colliery, China, on 26 April 1942.

Precious stones
Largest diamonds
The largest diamond on record, the *Cullinan*, weighed 3,106 carats and was discovered on 26 Jan 1905 at the Premier Diamond Mine, near Pretoria, South Africa. It was cut into 106 polished diamonds and produced the largest cut fine-quality colourless diamond, which weighs 530.2 carats.

Mining
Deepest penetration into the Earth
A geological exploratory borehole near Zapolarny in the Kola peninsula of Arctic Russia was reported to have surpassed a depth of 12,261 m (40,236 ft) by 1983. When construction began on 24 May 1970, the target depth was 15,000 m (49,212 ft), but work had to be discontinued due to lack of funds. The temperature of the rocks at the bottom of the hole is about 210°C (378°F).

Deepest mines
The Western Deep Levels Mine at Carltonville, Transvaal, South Africa, is the deepest mine in the world. The gold mine reached a depth of 3,581 m (11,749 ft) on 12 July 1977.

The deepest open-pit copper mine in the world is at Bingham Canyon, near Salt Lake City, Utah, USA. It descends to a depth of 800 m (2,625 ft).

The deepest open-cast coal mine is situated near Bergheim, Germany. It reaches a depth of 325 m (1,066 ft).

Deepest ocean drilling
The deepest recorded drilling into the sea bed is 2,111 m (6,926 ft), by the Ocean Drilling Program vessel *JOIDES Resolution* in the eastern equatorial Pacific in 1993. The greatest amount of core to be recovered in a single leg of this program was 6,731 m (22,084 ft) in 1995. The sediment cores, which are composed of calcareous ooze and hemipelagic muds, were recovered from the North Atlantic and the Norwegian–Greenland seas on Leg 162.

Deepest ice-core drilling
In July 1993, after five years of drilling, American researchers reached the bottom of the Greenland ice sheet, striking bedrock at a depth of 3,053.51 m (10,019 ft).

Australia's opal mines have produced the world's largest opal.

At 0.16–0.17 mm in diameter and just 0.11 mm in height, it is smaller than the average grain of sand.

Largest star ruby
The *Eminent Star* ruby is an oval cabochon with a six-ray star. It measures 109 x 90.5 x 58 mm (4¼ x 3⅝ x 2¼ in) and weighs 6,465 carats. Believed to have been discovered in India, it is owned by Kailash Rawat of Eminent Gems Inc., New York, USA.

Largest cut emerald
A natural beryl weighing 86,136 carats was found in Carnaiba, Brazil, in Aug 1974. It was carved by Richard Chan in Hong Kong and was valued at £718,000 in 1982.

Largest single crystal
The largest single emerald crystal of gem quality on record was found in 1969 at the Cruces Mine near Gachala, Colombia. It

Largest rough black opal
The largest uncut black opal of gem quality weighed 1,982.5 carats and was found at Lightning Ridge, NSW, Australia, in Nov 1986. Named *Halley's Comet*, it measured 100 x 66 x 63 mm (4 x 2⅝ x 2½ in) after cleaning.

Largest piece of jade
A single lens of nephrite jade weighing 577 tonnes was found in the Yukon Territory of Canada by Max Rosequist in July 1992. It is owned by Yukon Jade Ltd.

Largest amber
The *Burma Amber*, which weighs 15.25 kg (33 lb 10 oz), is kept in the Natural History Museum, London, UK.

Largest mass of gold
The *Holtermann Nugget*, a slab of slate weighing 235.14 kg (7,560 troy oz), was found on 19 Oct 1872 in the Beyers &

Left
The painstaking task of panning for gold only occasionally yields nuggets. The largest gold nugget weighed 70.92 kg (2,280¼ troy oz).

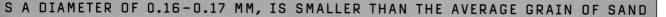

LARGEST MASS OF GOLD CONSISTED OF 82.11 KG OF GOLD IN A 235.14-KG SLAB OF SLATE

Several large pieces of low-quality diamonds have been found, including a carbonado of 3,167 carats discovered in Brazil in 1905.

The largest known single piece of rough diamond that is still in existence weighs 1,462 carats and is retained by De Beers in London, UK.

Largest cut diamond
The *Golden Jubilee Diamond*, purchased from De Beers by a syndicate of Thai businessmen and presented to the King of Thailand on his golden jubilee, weighs 545.67 carats. It is now mounted in the Thai royal sceptre.

Smallest brilliant cut diamond
A 57-facet stone weighing 0.0000743 carats was fashioned by hand by Pauline Willemse at Coster Diamonds B.V. in Amsterdam, Netherlands, between 1991 and 1994.

weighs 7,025 carats and is presently owned by a private mining concern.

Largest star sapphire
A stone weighing 9719.5 carats was cut in London, UK, in Nov 1989. It has been named the *Lone Star* and is owned by Harold Roper.

Largest opal
The largest single piece of white opal of gem quality weighs 26,350 carats and was found in July 1989 at the Jupiter Field at Coober Pedy in South Australia. It has been named *Jupiter-Five* and is privately owned.

Largest black opal
A piece of black opal found on 4 Feb 1972 at Lightning Ridge, NSW, Australia, produced a finished gem called the *Empress of Glengarry*, which weighs 1,520 carats and measures 121 x 80 x 15 mm (4¾ x 3⅛ x ⅝ in).

Holtermann Star of Hope mine, Hill End, NSW, Australia. It contained 82.11 kg (2,640 troy oz) of gold.

Largest pure gold nugget
The *Welcome Stranger*, a gold nugget weighing 70.92 kg (2,280¼ troy oz), was discovered at Moliagul, Victoria, Australia, in 1869. It yielded 69.92 kg (2,248 troy oz) of pure gold.

Largest platinum nugget
A nugget weighing 9,635 g (340 oz) was found in the Ural Mountains, Russia, in 1843 but was melted down shortly afterwards.

Largest existing nugget
The largest surviving platinum nugget is known as the *Ural Giant* and weighs 7,860.5 g (277¼ oz). It is in the custody of the Diamond Foundation in the Kremlin, Moscow, Russia.

S A DIAMETER OF 0.16–0.17 MM, IS SMALLER THAN THE AVERAGE GRAIN OF SAND

Left
The largest piece of amber in the world—reputed to be from Burma—was presented to the Natural History Museum, London, UK, by Major J. F. E. Bowring in 1940. His father had bought it from a Chinese dealer in Canton for £300.

Bridges and tunnels

Right
The main span of the Humber Estuary Bridge, E Yorkshire, UK, is the world's longest bridge span. The bridge was officially opened by HM the Queen on 17 July 1981.

Far right
Opened at 4:00 a.m. on 5 June 1996, the new Severn bridge links Monmouthshire to Gloucestershire.

Tallest bridge towers 227 m

Bridges

Longest bridge
The Second Lake Pontchartrain Causeway, which joins Mandeville and Metairie, Louisiana, USA, is 38.42 km (23 miles 1,538 yd) long. It was completed in 1969.

Longest cable-suspension bridges
The main span of the Humber Estuary Bridge linking E Yorkshire and Lincolnshire, UK, is 1,410 m (4,626 ft) long. It was constructed from 1972 to 1980. The towers are 162.5 m (533 ft 1⅝ in) tall from datum and are 3.6 cm (1⅜ in) out of parallel to allow for the curvature of the Earth. Including the Hessle and the Barton side spans, the bridge is 2.22 km (1 mile 670 yd) long.

The Seto-Ohashi double-deck bridge linking Kojima, Honshu, with Sakaide, Shikoku, Japan, is the longest road and rail bridge, at 12.3 km (7 miles 1,132 yd). Built at a cost of £4.9 billion, it was opened in 1988.

Longest cable-stayed bridge
The Pont de Normandie in Le Havre, France, has a cable-stayed main span of 856 m (2,808 ft). It was opened to traffic in 1995.

The United Kingdom's longest-span cable-stayed bridge is the second Severn Bridge, officially opened on 5 June 1996, with a main span of 456 m (1,496 ft). The length of the crossing structure is 5,168 m (16,955 ft), making it the longest British bridge.

Longest cantilever bridges
The Pont de Québec over the St Lawrence River in Canada has the longest cantilever truss span. It is 549 m (1,800 ft) between the piers and 987 m (3,239 ft) in total, and carries a rail track and two carriageways. Work began in 1899, and the bridge was opened to traffic in 1917, at a cost of $Can22.5 million and 87 lives.

The longest British cantilever bridge is the Forth Bridge, linking Fife and Edinburgh. Its two main spans are 521 m (1,710 ft) long, and it carries a double rail track over the Firth of Forth 47.5 m (156 ft) above the water level. Work began in Nov 1882, and the first test trains crossed on 22 Jan 1890 after an expenditure of £3 million.

Longest steel arch bridge
The world's longest steel-arch bridge is the New River Gorge bridge near Fayetteville, West Virginia, USA. It was completed in 1977 and has a span of 518 m (1,700 ft).

Longest stone arch bridges
Rockville Bridge north of Harrisburg, Pennsylvania, USA, was completed in 1901. It is 1,161 m (3,810 ft) long, and its 48 spans contain 196,000 tonnes of stone.

The world's longest stone arch span is the Wuchaohe Bridge at Fenghuang, Hunan Province, China, at 120 m (394 ft). It was completed in 1990.

Widest long-span bridge
Sydney Harbour Bridge, Australia, is 48.8 m (160 ft) wide. It carries two electric overhead railway tracks, eight road lanes, and a cycle track and footway.

Highest bridges
The suspension bridge over the Royal Gorge on the Arkansas River, Colorado, USA, is 321 m (1,053 ft) above the water level. It has a main span of 268 m (880 ft) and was constructed in six months in 1929.

The world's highest railway bridge is the Yugoslav Railways Mala Reka viaduct at Kolašin on the Belgrade–Bar line. It is 198 m (650 ft) high and was opened in 1976.

Bridge at the highest altitude
A 30-m-long (98-ft 5-in) Bailey bridge near Khardung-La, Ladakh, India—designed and constructed by Lt Col. S. G. Vombatkere and an Indian Army team in 1982—is 5,602 m (18,380 ft) above sea level.

Tallest bridge
The towers of the Golden Gate Bridge, which connects San Francisco and Marin County, California, USA, rise to a height of 227 m (745 ft) above the water. Completed in 1937, the suspension bridge has an overall length of 2,733 m (8,966 ft).

Tunnels

Longest water-supply tunnels

The world's longest tunnel of any kind is the New York City West Delaware water-supply tunnel, built between 1937 and 1944. It is 4.1 m (13 ft 6 in) in diameter and extends 169 km (105 miles).

The longest tunnel in the United Kingdom is the Thames Water Ring Main, which was completed in Dec 1994 to supply half of London's water needs. It is 80 km (50 miles) long and carries as much as 1,300 million litres (285 million gal) of drinking water a day to up to 6 million people.

Longest rail tunnels

The Seikan rail tunnel has an overall length of 53.85 km (33 miles 811 yd) and was bored to a depth of 240 m (787 ft) beneath sea level and 100 m (328 ft) below the seabed of the Tsugaru Strait between Tappi Saki, Honshū, and Fukushima in Hokkaidō, Japan. Tests on the 23.3-km (14½-mile) underwater section began in 1964 and construction was started in June 1972. It was holed through on 27 Jan 1983, after the loss of 66 lives, and the first test run took place in March 1988.

Construction of the longest undersea tunnel— the £10-billion Channel Tunnel beneath the English Channel between Folkestone, Kent, UK, and Calais, France—began on 1 Dec 1987. The service tunnel drives met on 1 Dec 1990 and the tunnel was officially opened on 6 May 1994. The length of each twin rail tunnel is 49.94 km (31 miles 55 yd) and each is 7.6 m (24 ft 11 in) in diameter. The submarine section is 14.7 km (9⅛ miles) longer than that of the Seikan tunnel, but the tunnel's total length is less.

The longest main-line rail tunnel in the United Kingdom is the 7-km (4-mile) Severn Tunnel linking Monmouthshire and Gloucestershire. It was constructed with more than 76 million bricks between 1873 and 1886.

Longest continuous subway

The Moscow metro Kaluzhskaya underground railway line from Medvedkovo to Bittsevsky Park is around 37.9 km (23½ miles) long and was completed early in 1990.

Longest road tunnels

The two-lane St Gotthard tunnel from Göschenen to Airolo, Switzerland, is 16.32 km (10 miles 248 yd) long and was opened to traffic in Sept 1980. Construction began in autumn 1969, and cost 19 lives and Sw.Fr.690 million (then £175 million).

The longest British road tunnel is the Mersey (Queensway) Tunnel joining Liverpool and Birkenhead, Merseyside, which is 3.43 km (2 miles 231 yd) long, or 4.62 km (2 miles 1,532 yd) including branch tunnels. Work began in Dec 1925, and the tunnel was opened on 18 July 1934. The four-lane roadway is 11 m (36 ft) wide and carries around 7.5 million vehicles a year.

Largest road tunnel

The road tunnel with the largest diameter is the Yerba Buena Island tunnel, San Francisco, California, USA. It is 24 m (77 ft 10 in) wide, 17 m (56 ft) high and 165 m (540 ft) long. Around 250,000 vehicles pass through on its two decks every day.

Lowest road tunnel

The Hitra Tunnel in Norway, linking the mainland to the island of Hitra, reaches a depth of 264 m (866 ft) below sea level. It is 5.6 km (3½ miles) long with three lanes, and was opened in Dec 1994.

Longest hydro-electric irrigation tunnels

The Orange–Fish Rivers tunnel, South Africa, was bored between 1967 and 1973 at an estimated cost of £60 million. It is 82.9 km (51½ miles) long, and the lining, at a minimum thickness of 23 cm (9 in), gives a completed diameter of 5.33 m (17 ft 6 in).

The Majes dam project in Peru involves 98 km (60⅞ miles) of tunnels for hydroelectric and water-supply purposes.

Oldest navigable tunnel

The Malpas tunnel on the Canal du Midi in south-west France was completed in 1681 and is 161 m (528 ft) long. It enables vessels to navigate from the Atlantic Ocean to the Mediterranean Sea via the River Garonne to Toulouse and the Canal du Midi to Sète.

Longest machine-bored tunnel

The longest unsupported machine-bored tunnel is the Three Rivers water tunnel, built in Atlanta, Georgia, USA, from 1980 to 1982. It is 9.37 km (5 miles 1,447 yd) long.

RRIES TWO RAILWAY LINES, EIGHT ROAD LANES, AND A CYCLE TRACK AND WALKWAY

Canals and dams

WORLD'S LONGEST DAM HAS A CREST LENGTH OF 41.2 KM

Canals

Earliest canals

Relics of the oldest canals in the world, dated by archaeologists at *c.* 4000 BC, were discovered near Mandali, Iraq, early in 1968.

The earliest canals in the United Kingdom were cut by the Romans. In the Midlands, the Fossdyke Canal, which runs for 17 km (11 miles) between Lincoln and the River Trent at Torksey, Lincs, was built *c.* AD 65 and scoured in 1122. It is still in use today.

Longest canals

The longest canal in the ancient world was the Grand Canal of China, which ran from Beijing to Hangzhou. It was begun in 540 BC and completed in 1327, by which time it extended for 1,781 km (1,107 miles). It was allowed to silt up and had a maximum depth of 1.8 m (6 ft) in 1950, but is now plied by vessels weighing up to 2,000 tonnes.

The Belomorsko-Baltiyskiy Canal from Belomorsk to Povenets, Russia, is 227 km (141 miles) long and has 19 locks. Completed

LONGEST BIG-SHIP CANAL IS THE SUEZ CANAL. IT TOOK 10 YEARS TO BUILD, WI

Longest canal 1,781 km

with the use of forced labour in 1933, it is unable to accommodate ships of more than 5 m (16 ft) in draught.

The longest big-ship canal is the Suez Canal, linking the Red and Mediterranean seas, opened on 17 Nov 1869. It took 10 years to build, with a workforce of 1.5 million people. It is 162.2 km (100⅘ miles) long from Port Said lighthouse to Suez Roads and has a minimum width of 300 m (984 ft) and a maximum width of 365 m (1,198 ft).

Busiest canal

The busiest ship canal in terms of number of transits is the Kiel Canal, linking the North Sea with the Baltic Sea in Germany. In 1995, there were 43,287 transits.

The busiest canal in terms of tonnage of shipping is the Suez Canal, with 417,852,000 grt in the fiscal year 1995.

Largest canal system

The sea-water cooling system associated with the Madinat Al-Jubail Al-Sinaiyah construction project in Saudi Arabia is believed to be the world's largest canal system. It currently brings 11 million m³ (388 million ft³) of sea-water a day to cool the industrial establishments and will bring 19.5 million m³ (689 million ft³) when industry consumption reaches its peak.

Longest artificial seaway

The St Lawrence Seaway stretches 304 km (189 miles) along the New York State–Ontario

border from Montreal to Lake Ontario. It enables ships up to 222 m (728 ft) long and 8 m (26 ft 3 in) draught (some of which weigh 26,400 tonnes) to sail a total of 3,769 km (2,342 miles) from the North Atlantic up the St Lawrence estuary and across the Great Lakes to Duluth, Minnesota, USA. The seaway was opened on 25 April 1959.

Longest irrigation

The Karakumsky Canal stretches about 1,200 km (745 miles) from Haun-Khan to Ashkhabad, Turkmenistan. The course length is 800 km (500 miles).

Locks

Largest lock

The Berendrecht lock, linking the River Scheldt with docks in Antwerp, Belgium, is the largest sea lock. First used in April 1989, it is 500 m (1,640 ft) long, 68 m (223 ft) wide and has a sill level of 13.5 m (44 ft). Each of its four sliding lock gates weighs 1,500 tonnes.

The largest and deepest British lock is the Royal Portbury Lock, Bristol. Opened in 1977, it measures 365.7 x 42.7 m (1,119 ft 10 in x 140 ft 1 in) and is 20.2 m (66 ft) deep.

Deepest lock

The world's deepest lock is the Zhaporozhe lock on the River Dniepr, Ukraine, which can raise or lower barges 37.4 m (123 ft).

BRATSKOYE RESERVOIR IN RUSSIA HAS A VOLU

Highest rise and longest flight

The highest lock elevator overcomes a head of 68.6 m (225 ft) at Ronquières on the Charleroi–Brussels Canal, Belgium. Two 236-wheeled caissons can each carry 1,370 tonnes, and take 22 minutes to cover the 1,432-m-long (4,698-ft) inclined plane.

The longest flight of locks in the United Kingdom is on the Worcester and Birmingham Canal at Tardebigge, Hereford & Worcester. Within a 4-km (2½-mile) stretch, the Tardebigge (30 locks) and Stoke (six locks) flights drop the canal 78.9 m (259 ft).

Largest cut

The Corinth Canal in Greece is 6.33 km (3.93 miles) long, 8 m (26 ft) deep and 24.6 m (81 ft) wide at the surface, and has an extreme depth of cutting of 79 m (259 ft). It was opened in 1893 and is still in use today.

The Gaillard Cut ('the Ditch') on the Panama Canal is 82 m (270 ft) deep between Gold Hill and Contractor's Hill, with a bottom width of 152 m (500 ft).

Dams

Largest dam

Measured by volume, the largest dam is New Cornelia Tailings on Ten Mile Wash in Arizona, USA, which has a volume of 209.5 million m³ (274.5 million yd³). It is an earth-fill dam.

The biggest dam in the United Kingdom is National Power's Gale Common Tailings Dam at Cridling Stubbs, N Yorkshire. Approximately 15 million m³ (20 million yd³) of compacted fill have so far been put into place.

Highest dam
The Nurek dam, at 300 m (984 ft) on the River Vakhsh, Tajikistan, is the world's highest.

The rock-fill Llyn Brianne dam, Ceredigion, is the highest dam in the United Kingdom, reaching 91 m (298 ft 7 in) in Nov 1971. It became operational on 20 July 1972.

Longest dam
The Kiev dam across the River Dniepr, Ukraine, completed in 1964, has a crest length of 41.2 km (25.6 miles).

Strongest dam
The Sayano-Shushenskaya dam on the River Yenisey, Russia, is designed to bear a load of 18 million tonnes from a fully-filled reservoir of 31,300 million m³ (41,000 million yd³) capacity. The dam was completed in 1987 and is 245 m (804 ft) high.

Largest concrete dam
The Grand Coulee dam on the Columbia River, Washington State, USA, built from 1933–42, has a crest length of 1,272 m (4,173 ft) and is 168 m (548 ft) high. Some 19,595,000 tonnes of concrete were poured to build it.

Highest concrete dam
Grande Dixence, on the River Dixence in Switzerland, was built between 1953 and 1961 to a height of 285 m (935 ft), with a crest length of 700 m (2,297 ft), using 5,960,000 m³ (7,800,000 yd³) of concrete.

Reservoirs
Largest reservoir
The largest fully man-made reservoir is the Bratskoye reservoir on the River Angara in Russia, which has a volume of 169.3 km³ (40.6 miles³) and an area of 5,470 km² (2,112 miles²). It was completed in 1967.

The largest artificial lake by surface area is Lake Volta, Ghana, formed by the Akosombo dam and completed in 1965. By 1969, it had filled to an area of 8,482 km² (3,275 miles²) and had 7,250 km (4,505 miles) of shoreline.

The completion of the Owen Falls Dam near Jinja, Uganda, in 1954 marginally raised the level of the natural lake by adding 204.8 km³ (49.1 miles³). This technically turned it into a reservoir with a surface area of 69,484 km² (26,828 miles²) and a capacity of 2.7 x 10¹² m³ (3.5 x 10¹² yd³).

The British lake with the greatest capacity is Loch Quoich, Highland, which was filled to 382 billion litres (84 billion gal) between Feb 1954 and Jan 1957 and acquired a surface area of 1,922 ha (4,750 acres) and a perimeter of 44.1 km (27⅖ miles).

Largest water tower
The Waterspheroid at Edmond, Oklahoma, USA, built in 1986, rises to a height of 66.5 m (218 ft) and has a capacity of 1,893,000 litres (416,000 gal). It was built by Chicago Bridge and Iron Na-Con, Inc.

Largest levees
The Mississippi levees were begun in 1717 and vastly augmented by the US Federal Government after the floods of 1927. They extended for 2,787 km (1,732 miles) along the main river from Cape Girardeau, Missouri, USA, to the Gulf of Mexico and comprised more than 765 million m³ (1,000 million yd³) of earthworks. Levees on the tributaries made up an additional 3,200 km (2,000 miles). Extensive flooding in summer 1993 resulted in widespread damage to the levees.

Largest tidal river barrier
The Oosterscheldedam, a storm-surge barrier in the Netherlands, has 65 concrete piers and 62 steel gates and is 9 km (5½ miles) long. It was opened in Oct 1986.

Below
The Corinth Canal in Greece has an extreme depth of cutting of 79 m (259 ft).

WORKFORCE OF 1.5 MILLION, OF WHOM 120,000 PERISHED DURING CONSTRUCTION

169.3 KM³ AND COVERS 5,470 KM²

Precision engineering

Heaviest magnet 36,000 tonnes

Scientific instruments

Largest scientific instrument
The Large Electron Positron (LEP) collider at CERN, Geneva, Switzerland is 3.8 m (12 ft 6 in) in diameter and 27 km (17 miles) in circumference, and is arguably the world's largest machine. More than 60,000 tonnes of technical equipment have been installed in the tunnel and its eight working zones.

Finest balance
The Sartorius Microbalance Model 4108, made in Germany, can weigh objects of up to 0.5 g ($\frac{9}{500}$ oz) to an accuracy of 0.01μg, or 1×10^{-8} g (3.5×10^{-10} oz)—little more than $\frac{1}{60}$ of the weight of the ink on this full stop.

Fastest centrifuge
The highest man-made rotary speed achieved is 7,250 km/h (4,500 mph), by a tapered 15.2-cm (6-in) carbon fibre rod rotating in a vacuum at Birmingham University, UK, in 1975.

Most powerful laser
The 'Nova' laser at the Lawrence Livermore National Laboratory, California, USA, has 10 arms producing laser pulses capable of generating 100×10^{12} W of power, much of which is delivered to a target the size of a grain of sand, in 1×10^{-9} seconds. For this brief instant, the power is 200 times greater than the combined output of all US electrical generating plants. The laser is 91 m (300 ft) long and as tall as a three-storey building.

Heaviest magnet
The 10-GeV synchrophasotron in the Joint Institute for Nuclear Research, Dubna, near

WORLD'S SLOWEST MACHINE CAN BE CONTROLLED

THINNEST GLASS IS 0.025–0.035 MM THICK

Moscow, Russia, weighs 36,000 tonnes and has a diameter of 60 m (196 ft).

Largest electromagnet
An octagonal magnet forming part of the L3 detector experiment at the LEP storage ring at CERN, has 6,400 tonnes of low carbon steel yoke and 1,100 tonnes of aluminium coil. A uniform magnet field of 5 kilogauss is created by 300 amperes of current flowing through the coil. The magnet is taller than a four-storey building, and has a volume of 1,728 m³ (59,320 ft³). It weighs 7,810 tonnes, with more metal than the Eiffel Tower.

Most powerful particle accelerator
In 1987, a centre of mass energy of 1.8 TeV (1.8×10^{12} eV) was achieved by colliding proton and antiproton beams in the proton synchrotron 'Tevatron' at the Fermi National Accelerator Laboratory, Illinois, USA.

Thinnest glass
The German firm Deutsche Spezialglas AG have developed a Type D263 glass for use in

electronic and medical equipment, which has a thickness that varies between 0.025 mm and 0.035 mm.

Smallest thermometer
Dr Frederich Sach of the State University of New York at Buffalo, USA, has developed an ultra-microthermometer to measure the temperature of single living cells. Its tip is 1μm in diameter—$\frac{1}{50}$ of the diameter of a human hair.

Smallest microphone
A microphone measuring 1.5 x 0.76 mm ($\frac{3}{50}$ x $\frac{3}{100}$ in) and with a frequency response of 10 Hz–10 kHz was developed in 1967 by Prof. Ibrahim Kavrak of Boğaziçi University, Istanbul, Turkey, in order to measure pressure in fluid flow.

Largest barometers
An oil-filled barometer 16.8 m (55 ft 1½ in) high was constructed at Stedelijk Lyceum Borgerhout, Belgium, in March 1994. It attained a standard height of 13.58 m

(44 ft 6 in), at which pressure mercury would stand at 0.76 m (2 ft 6 in).

A permanently installed barometer 13 m (42 ft) tall was built by Alan Mills and John Pritchard of the Dept. of Physics and Astronomy, Leicester University, UK, in 1991.

Slowest machine
A nuclear environmental machine for testing stress corrosion, developed by Nene Instruments of Wellingborough, Northants, UK, can be controlled at 1 million millionth of a millimetre per minute, or 1 m (3 ft 4 in) in 2,000 million years.

Smallest prism
In 1989, a prism with 0.13-mm sides was created at the National Institute of Standards and Technology, Colorado, USA.

Sharpest objects
The sharpest manufactured objects are glass micro-pipette tubes with bevelled tips, an outer diameter of 0.02μm and an inner diameter of 0.01μm. The latter are 6,500 times thinner than a human hair. They are used in intracellular work on living cells.

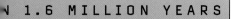

1.6 MILLION YEARS

Oldest working clock
The faceless clock at Salisbury Cathedral, UK, dates from c. 1386. It was restored in 1956, having struck the hours for 498 years and ticked more than 500 million times.

Largest clock
The astronomical clock in the Cathedral of St Pierre, Beauvais, France, was constructed in 1865–68. It has 90,000 parts and is 2.1 m (40 ft) high, 6.09 m (20 ft) wide and 2.7 m (9 ft) deep.

Heaviest watch
The 24.3-m (80-ft) Eta 'watch' on the Swiss pavilion at Expo '86 in Vancouver, British Columbia, Canada, weighed 35 tonnes.

Smallest watch
Watches just over 12 mm (½ in) long and 4.8 mm (³⁄₁₆ in) wide are produced by Jaeger le Coultre, Switzerland. They are equipped with a 15-jewelled movement, which together with the case weighs less than 7 g (¼ oz).

Cameras
Largest cameras
The largest and most expensive industrial camera is the 27-tonne Rolls-Royce camera commissioned in 1956 and owned by BDC Holdings Ltd., Derby, UK. It is 2.69 m (8 ft 10 in) high, 2.51 m (8 ft 3 in) wide and 14.02 m (46 ft) long. The f16 Cooke Apochromatic lens measures 160 cm (63 in).

A pinhole camera was created from a 10.4 x 2.9 x 2.64-m (34 x 9½ x 9-ft) Portakabin unit by John Kippen and Chris Wainwright at the National Museum of Photography, Film and Television, Bradford, W Yorkshire, UK, in

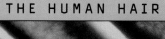

THE HUMAN HAIR

A hair's breadth
The smallest thermometer is used to measure the temperature of single living cells. Its tip is approximately ¹⁄₅₀ of the diameter of a human hair (above).

Glass micro-pipette tubes have bevelled tips with an inner diameter that is 6,500 times thinner than a human hair.

The Large Optics Diamond turning machine can sever a human hair lengthways 3,000 times.

MILLION MILLIONTH OF A MILLIMETRE PER MINUTE

Smallest man-made object
The tips of probes scanning tunnelling microscopes have been shaped to end in a single atom. In 1990, it was announced that Eigler and Schweizer of the IBM Almaden Research Center, California, USA, had used an STM to reposition single atoms of xenon on a nickel surface to spell out 'IBM'. Other laboratories have used similar techniques on single atoms of different elements.

Finest cut
In June 1983, it was reported that the $13-million Large Optics Diamond turning machine at the Lawrence Livermore National Laboratory, California, USA, could sever a human hair lengthways 3,000 times.

Timepieces
Most accurate timekeeping device
A commercially available atomic clock accurate to one second in 1.6 million years, manufactured by Hewlett-Packard of Palo Alto, California, USA, was unveiled in Dec 1991. Designated the HP 5071A primary frequency standard with caesium-2 technology, the device costs $54,000.

1990. The unit produced a direct positive image measuring 10.2 x 1.8 m (33 x 6 ft).

Fastest camera
A camera built for research into high-power lasers by The Blackett Laboratory of Imperial College of Science and Technology, London, UK, registers images at a rate of 33 billion frames per second.

The fastest production camera is the Imacon 675, made by Hadland Photonics Ltd, Herts, which can operate at 600 million frames/sec.

Smallest camera
The smallest marketed camera is the circular Japanese 'Petal' camera, which is 29 mm (1⁷⁄₅₀ in) in diameter, 16.5 mm (1³⁄₂₀ in) thick, and has a focal length of 12 mm (⁴⁷⁄₁₀₀ in).

Largest lens
The National Museum of Photography, Film and Television, UK, displays a 215-kg (474-lb) lens with a 1.372-m (54-in) diameter. Made by Pilkington Special Glass Ltd of St Asaph, Denbighshire, its focal length of 8.45 m (27 ft 9 in) enables observers to read writing on the museum's walls from 12.19 m (40 ft).

Space technology

Largest refractor 101.6 cm

Telescopes

Earliest telescopes

There is strong evidence to suggest that Leonard Digges (c. 1520–59) invented a refractor, and possibly also a reflector, in Elizabethan times.

In 1608, three Dutch spectacle-makers claimed to have invented telescopes and produced refracting telescopes. Of these, credit is usually given to Hans Lippershey, but it was Galileo who brought the invention to the notice of the scientific world, constructing and using telescopes in 1609.

The first successful reflector was built by Sir Isaac Newton (1642–1727), in 1668 or 1669. He presented what was probably a copy of it to the Royal Society in 1671.

Largest refractors

A 101.6-cm (40-in) refractor was completed in 1897. Situated at the Yerkes Observatory, Williams Bay, Wisconsin, USA, it is 18.9 m (62 ft) long and belongs to the University of Chicago, Illinois. Although the refractor is now almost 100 years old, it is still in full use on clear nights.

A refractor measuring 150 cm (59 in) was built in France and shown at the Paris Exhibition in 1900, but it was a failure and was never used for scientific work.

The largest refractor in the United Kingdom is the 71.1-cm (28-in) Great Equatorial Telescope of 1893, installed in the Old Royal Observatory, Greenwich, London.

Largest infra-red telescope

The UKIRT (United Kingdom Infrared Telescope), which is situated on Mauna Kea, Hawaii, USA, has a 374-cm (147-in) mirror, and is good enough to be used for visual as well as infra-red work.

Largest telescope

The Keck I telescope on Mauna Kea, Hawaii, USA, has a 1,000-cm (394-in) mirror made up of 36 segments fitted together to produce the correct curve. The first image of the spiral galaxy NGC1232 was obtained in Nov 1990, when nine of the segments were in place. When completed, Keck II will work with Keck I as an interferometer. Theoretically, they will be able to see a car's headlights separately from 25,000 km (15,500 miles) away.

Largest reflectors

The largest single-mirror telescope currently in use is the 6-m (19-ft 8-in) reflector on Mt Semirodriki near Zelenchukskaya in the Caucasus Mts., Russia, at an altitude of

Largest space telescope

The world's largest space telescope is the NASA Edwin P. Hubble Space Telescope, which weighs 11 tonnes and is 13.1 m (43 ft) in overall length, with a 240-cm (94½-in) reflector. It was placed in orbit at an altitude of 613 km (381 miles) aboard a US space shuttle on 24 April 1990. Construction of the telescope cost $2.1 billion (£1.4 billion).

Largest solar telescope

The McMath solar telescope at Kitt Peak, Arizona, USA, has a 2.1-m (6-ft 11-in) primary mirror. The light is sent to it via a 32° inclined tunnel from a coelostat (rotatable mirror) at the top end. Extensive modifications to it are now being planned.

Top
The largest space telescope in the world is the NASA Edwin P. Hubble Space Telescope, which was placed in orbit in 1990 and has made it possible to take photographs of an unprecedented quality.

Middle
A view of two galaxies from the Hubble telescope.

Bottom
Jupiter is the largest planet in the Solar System and has the fastest rotation of any planet. The ESA *Ulysses* spacecraft staged a fly-by of Jupiter after achieving the fastest escape velocity from Earth.

2,080 m (6,830 ft). Completed in 1976, it has never come up to expectations, partly because it is not set up on a good observation site.

The largest satisfactory single-mirror telescope is the 508-cm (200-in) Hale reflector at Mt Palomar, California, USA.

The largest British reflector is the 420-cm (165-in) William Herschel, completed in 1987. It is set up at the Los Muchachos Observatory on La Palma, Canary Islands.

A 183-cm (72-in) reflector was made by the third Earl of Rosse (1800–67), and set up at Birr Castle, Co. Offaly, Republic of Ireland, in 1845. The mirror was made of speculum metal (an alloy of copper and tin), and was used to discover the spiral forms of the galaxies. It was last used in 1909, but is now being restored and should be operational again in 1997.

Largest Schmidt telescope

A Schmidt telescope uses a spherical mirror with a correcting plate and can cover a very wide field with a single exposure. The largest such telescope is the 2-m (6-ft 6¾-in) instrument at the Karl Schwarzschild Observatory at Tautenberg, Germany. It has a clear aperture of 134 cm (52¾ in) with a 200-cm (78¾-in) mirror and a focal length of 4 m (13 ft). It was brought into use in 1960.

Largest planned telescope

The largest telescope ever should be the VLT (Very Large Telescope) at Cerro Paranal, northern Chile, which is being planned by the European Southern Observatory. It will comprise four 8.2-m (26-ft 8-in) telescopes, providing the light-grasp of a 16-m (52-ft 6-in) mirror. The first units may be working by 1997.

Observatories

The oldest building still standing is the 'Tower of the Winds', which was used by Andronichus of Cyrrhus in Athens, Greece, c. 100 BC. The observatory is equipped with sundials and clepsydras (water clocks).

The highest observatory in the world is situated on Mt Chacaltaya, Bolivia, at an altitude of 5,200 m (17,060 ft). Opened in 1962, it is equipped with gamma-ray sensors but no telescopes.

The lowest 'observatory' is at Homestake Mine, South Dakota, USA. The 'Telescope' is a tank of cleaning fluid (perchloroethylene), containing chlorine, which can trap neutrinos from the Sun. The installation is located 1.7 km (1 1/16 miles) below ground level in the shaft of a gold-mine.

Planetaria
The ancestor of the modern planetarium is the rotatable Gottorp Globe, built by Andreas Busch in Denmark c. 1660. It was 10.54 m (34 ft 7 in) in circumference, weighed nearly 3.5 tonnes and is preserved in St Petersburg, Russia. The stars were painted on the inside.

YSSES SPACECRAFT AFTER DEPLOYMENT FROM *DISCOVERY*

The first modern planetarium was opened in 1923 at Jena, Germany. It was designed by Walther Bauersfelt of the Carl Zeiss company.

The world's largest planetarium is in the Ehime Prefectural Science Museum, Niihama City, Japan. It has a dome with a diameter of 30 m (98 ft 5 in). Up to 25,000 stars can be displayed, and viewers can observe Space as it is seen from other planets.

Rockets
Earliest rockets
'Flying fireworks' propelled by gunpowder (charcoal-saltpetre-sulfur) were described by Zeng Gongliang of China in 1042.

War rockets originated in 1245 near the city of Hangzhou, the capital of China between 1127 and 1278.

The pioneer of military rocketry in the United Kingdom was Col. Sir William Congreve (1772–1828), Comptroller of the Royal Laboratory, Woolwich, London, and Inspector of Military Machines. His '6 lb-rocket' was developed to a range of 1,800 m (2,000 yd) by 1805. It was first used by the Royal Navy against Boulogne, France, on 8 Oct 1806.

The first launch of a liquid-fuelled rocket (patented in 1914) was by Dr Robert Hutchings Goddard (1882–1945) of the USA, at Auburn, Massachusetts, on 16 March 1926. It reached an altitude of 12.5 m (41 ft) and travelled a distance of 56 m (184 ft).

The earliest Soviet rocket was the semi-liquid-fuelled GIRD–R1 (object 09), begun in 1931 and tested on 17 Aug 1933.

The first Soviet fully liquid-fuelled rocket, GIRD–X, was launched on 25 Nov 1933.

Highest velocity
The first space vehicle to achieve the Third Cosmic velocity sufficient to break out of the Solar System was *Pioneer 10*. The Atlas SLV–3C launcher with a modified Centaur D second stage and a Thiokol TE–364–4 third stage left the Earth at 51,682 km/h (32,114 mph) on 2 March 1972.

The fastest escape velocity from Earth was 54,614 km/h (34,134 mph), by the ESA *Ulysses* spacecraft, powered by an IUS–PAM upper stage, after deployment from the space shuttle *Discovery* on 7 Oct 1990. It was en route to an orbit around the poles of the Sun via a fly-by of Jupiter.

The record speed of 252,800 km/h (158,000 mph) is recorded by the NASA–German *Helios A* and *B* solar probes each time they reach the perihelion (nearest point to the Sun) of their solar orbits.

Most powerful rocket
The NI booster of the former USSR (also known as the G–1 in the West), had a thrust of 4,620 tonnes when first launched from the Baikonur Cosmodrome at Tyuratam, Kazakhstan, on 21 Feb 1969. It exploded at takeoff +70 seconds, and three further launch attempts also failed.

Rocket engine
The most powerful rocket engine was built by the Scientific Industrial Corporation of Power Engineering of the former USSR in 1980. The RD–170 has a thrust of 806 tonnes in open space and 740 tonnes at the Earth's surface. It has a turbopump rated at 190 MW, burns liquid oxygen and kerosene, and powered the four strap-on boosters of the *Energiya* booster, launched in 1987 but now grounded by budget cuts.

Lunar records
The first direct hit on the Moon was achieved at 2 min 24 sec after midnight (Moscow time) on 14 Sept 1959 by the Soviet space probe *Luna II* near Mare Serenitatis.

The first photographic images of the hidden side of the Moon were collected by the Soviet *Luna III* from 6:30 a.m. on 7 Oct 1959, from a range of up to 70,400 km (43,750 miles). They were transmitted to the Earth from a distance of 470,000 km (292,000 miles).

Closest approach to the Sun
The research spacecraft *Helios B* came within 43.5 million km (27 million miles) of the Sun, carrying both US and West German instrumentation, on 16 April 1976.

Remotest man-made object
Pioneer 10 crossed the mean orbit of Pluto, 5.91 billion km (3.67 billion miles) away, on 17 Oct 1986, and is currently more than 9.6 billion km (6 billion miles) away. *Voyager 1*, which is travelling faster, will surpass *Pioneer 10* in remoteness from the Earth by the end of the century. *Pioneer 11* has left the Solar System and *Voyager 1* and *Voyager 2* are also leaving it.

Left
Pioneer 10 lifts off on 2 March 1972. It was the first probe to leave the Solar System, and is currently the remotest man-made object from Earth. It carries a plaque with messages from Earth to any distant civilization that may find it.

Communications

MOST UNUSUAL POSTAL DELIVERY SERVICE EMPLOYED 37 BELGIAN CATS IN 1879

Right
Astronaut Dale Gardner, a crew member of the space shuttle *Discovery*, approaches a Westar VI Satellite in a manned manoeuvering unit (MMU). The spent satellite was brought back to Earth on the *Discovery*. The world's first satellite, *Sputnik I*, was put into orbit in 1957 and reached an altitude of between 228.5 km (142 miles) and 946 km (588 miles), and a velocity of more than 28,565 km/h (17,750 mph). Its lifetime is believed to have been 92 days, ending on 4 Jan 1958.

Most phone calls 578 billion

anniversary of D-Day—when there were 1,502,415 calls.

The largest operational telephone was exhibited at a festival celebrating the 80th birthday of Centraal Beheer, an insurance company based in Apeldoorn, Netherlands, on 16 Sept 1988. It was 2.47 m (8 ft 1 in) high and weighed 3.5 tonnes. The handset was 7.14 m (23 ft 5 in) long and had to be lifted by crane in order to make a call.

The smallest operational telephone was created by Zbigniew Różanek of Pleszew, Poland, in Aug 1995. It measured just 3.97 x 1.6 x 3.3 cm (1 9/16 x 5/8 x 1 5/16 in).

The highest price paid for a phone card is believed to be for the first Japanese card, which sold for £28,000 in Jan 1992.

Fax machines
The largest facsimile machine in the world is made by WideCom Group Inc of Mississauga, Ontario, Canada. Called 'WIDEfax 36', it can transmit, print and copy documents up to 91 cm (36 in) wide.

Telecommunications
Satellite
The first artificial satellite, *Sputnik 1*, was put into orbit by an inter-continental ballistic missile from the Baikonur Cosmodrome at Tyuratam, Kazakhstan, on 4 Oct 1957.

Optical fibres and cables
The highest rate of transmission is 1.1 terabits per second, which is equivalent to 17 million simultaneous telephone calls. This was achieved by Fujitsu Laboratories at Kawasaki, Japan, in March 1996.

The longest transmission distance at a data rate of 20 gigabits/sec over a fibre path containing repeaters is 125,000 km (78,000 miles), achieved with a recirculating fibre loop at BT laboratories at Martlesham, Suffolk, UK, and reported in 1994.

The longest submarine telephone cable is FLAG (Fibre-optic Link Around the Globe), which runs for 27,000 km (16,800 miles) from Japan to the United Kingdom. It links three continents (Europe, Africa and Asia) and 11 countries, and can support 600,000 simultaneous telephone calls.

Telephones
The country with the most subscribers at the end of 1995 was the USA, with 165 million.

Monaco has the greatest number of telephone subscribers per head of population, with 96 per 100.

TALLEST STRUCTURE EVER CONSTRUCTED WAS TH

The country in which the most calls are made is the USA, with 578 billion in 1995.

The USA has the most cellular subscribers, at 34.9 million from a world total of 86.6 million at the end of 1995.

The country with the most cellular phone subscribers per head is Sweden, with 229 for every 1,000 people.

The busiest international telephone route is between the USA and Canada. In 1995, there were 4.5 billion minutes of two-way traffic between the two countries.

The country with which the United Kingdom has the most telephone contact is the USA— 1.5 billion minutes of two-way traffic in 1995.

The busiest telecommunications exchange— the Bellsouth network used at the International Broadcast Center in Atlanta, Georgia, USA, during the 1996 Olympic Games from 19 July to 4 August—could transmit 100 billion bits of information per second.

The largest switchboard in the world is in the Pentagon, Arlington, Virginia, USA, which has a total of 34,500 lines handling almost 1 million calls per day through 322,000 km (200,000 miles) of telephone cable. Its busiest ever day was 6 June 1994—the 50th

The world's smallest dedicated facsimile machine is the Real Time Strategies Inc. hand-held device Pagentry, which measures 7.6 x 12.7 x 1.9 cm (3 x 5 x 3/4 in).

Postal services
Cheapest post
The only country in the world to currently grant its citizens free postage is Andorra, where local, internal mail is transmitted without charge.

Most unusual postal services
The only undersea post office in the world was established in 1939 on the sea bed off the Bahamas, as part of the Williamson Photosphere (a glass-walled chamber for underwater observation), operated by the American Field Museum. The oval postmark was inscribed SEAFLOOR/BAHAMAS.

In 1879, a mail service in Belgium employed 37 cats to carry bundles of letters to villages within a 30-km (18 3/4-mile) radius of Liège, but the experiment was short-lived as the cats proved thoroughly undisciplined.

Slowest delivery of mail
In 1882, 1910, 1920, 1942, 1951 and 1954 the postal service in Paris, France, recovered letters that had lain on the bed of the Seine since the siege of 1870–71, when attempts

were made to float mail into the city in zinc-coated steel spheres known as *boules de moulins*, which were often sunk by German marksmen. The Parisian post office made every effort to deliver the letters to the addressees or their descendants.

Radio
Radio dishes
Radio waves from the Milky Way were first detected by Karl Jansky of Bell Telephone Laboratories, Holmdel, New Jersey, USA, in 1931, while he was investigating 'static' with an improvised 30.5-m (100-ft) aerial.

The only purpose-built radio telescope built before the outbreak of WWII was made by an amateur, Grote Reber, who detected radio emissions from the Sun.

The first large radio dish was the 76-m (250-ft) Lovell Telescope at Jodrell Bank, Cheshire, UK, which was completed in 1957. The dish is part of the MERLIN network, which includes other radio dishes in various parts of the United Kingdom.

The world's largest dish radio telescope is the partially steerable ionospheric assembly built over a natural bowl at Arecibo, Puerto Rico. Completed in Nov 1963, the dish covers 7.48 ha (18½ acres).

has links with tracking stations at Usuada and Kashima, Japan, and with the TDRS (Tracking and Data Relay Satellite), which is in a geosynchronous orbit. This is equivalent to a radio telescope with an effective diameter of 2.16 Earth diameters, or 27,523 km (17,102 miles).

The VLA (Very Large Array) of the US National Science Foundation is Y-shaped, with a total of 27 mobile antennae, each of which has a diameter of

ACTUAL SIZE 100%

FROM PAGENTRY

Left
The hand-held device Pagentry combines various functions, including the transmission of messages to fax machines. Weighing just 141.75 g (5 oz), it rates as the world's smallest fax machine.

...ARSZAWA RADIO MAST, AT 646.38 M IN HEIGHT

The largest fully-steerable dish is at the Max Planck Institute for Radio Astronomy of Bonn in the Effelsberger Valley, Germany. Completed in 1971, it is 100 m (328 ft) in diameter and weighs 3,048 tonnes.

Largest radio installation
The Australia Telescope includes dishes at Parkes, Siding Spring and Culgoora and also

25 m (82 ft). Each arm is 20.9 km (13 miles) long. The installation is near Socorro, New Mexico, USA, and was completed in Oct 1980.

Masts and towers
Tallest masts
The guyed Warszawa Radio mast at Konstantynow in Poland was the tallest

structure ever built. Prior to its fall during renovation work on 10 Aug 1991, it was 646.38 m (2,120 ft 8 in) tall. Designed by Jan Polak, it was completed on 18 July 1974 and weighed 550 tonnes.

A stayed 629-m-high (2,063-ft) television transmitting tower between Fargo and Blanchard, North Dakota, USA, is currently the world's tallest structure. It was built for KTHI-TV's Channel 11 in 1963 by a team from Hamilton Erection, Inc.

NTL's Belmont mast north of Horncastle, Lincs, is the tallest structure in the United Kingdom. It was completed in 1965 to a height of 385.5 m (1,265 ft), and a further 2.13 m (7 ft) was added when meteorological equipment was installed in Sept 1967. The mast serves Yorkshire Television and weighs 210 tonnes.

Tallest towers
The tallest free-standing structure in the world is the $63-million (£28-million) CN Tower in Toronto, Canada, which rises to a height of 553.34 m (1,815 ft 5 in). The tower was completed in 1975, and the 416-seat restaurant in the Sky Pod, which revolves at a height of 351 m (1,150 ft), often affords a view of hills 120 km (75 miles) away.

The tallest self-supported tower in the United Kingdom is the 330.5-m-tall (1,084-ft) NTL transmitter at Emley Moor, W Yorkshire, which was completed in Sept 1971. The structure cost £900,000, has an enclosed room 264 m (865 ft) up, and weighs more than 15,000 tonnes, including its foundations.

Left
Progress is constantly being made in the field of communications. BT's Office on the Arm—still in the prototype stage—can do all the things a standard computer can do, including sending e-mail and surfing the Internet.

Computers

Right
ENIAC (Electronic Numerical Integrator Analyzer and Computer) was held to be the first electronic computer until its patents were invalidated. In 1946, Eckert and Mauchly, the developers of ENIAC, set up the first US computer company, which led eventually to the evolution of the first popular commercial system, the Univac.

Below
The briefcase-sized Apple IIc, a portable version of the Apple II, set the pace for portable computers. It was first presented at the Moscone Centre in 1984, and by the end of the presentation 50,000 orders had been taken.

Earliest computers

First electronic computer

The first programmable electronic computer was the 1,500-valve Colossus, formulated by Prof. Max H. A. Newman and built by T. H. Flowers. It was run in Dec 1943 at Bletchley Park, Bucks, UK, to break the Polish coding machine Enigma, used by the Germans in WWII. It arose from a concept published in 1936 by Dr Alan Mathison Turing in his paper *On Computable Numbers with an Application to the Entscheidungsproblem*. Colossus was not declassified until 25 Oct 1975.

The world's first electronic computer is generally thought to be ENIAC, developed at the University of Pennsylvania by J. Presper Eckert and John W Mauchly. Based on about 18,000 vacuum tubes or valves, it ran its first program in Nov 1945 (an H-bomb simulation for scientists at Los Alamos), but was not officially unveiled until early the next year.

The Atanasoff–Berry Computer (ABC), which was developed at the University of Iowa, USA, in 1942 by John Atanasoff and Clifford Berry, was credited as being the first electronic computer when a US court invalidated the ENIAC patents.

First stored-programme computer

The Manchester University Mark I, which incorporated the Williams storage cathode ray tube (patented 11 Dec 1946), ran its first program, written by Prof. Tom Kilburn, for 52 minutes on 21 June 1948.

First microcomputer

The invention of the microcomputer was attributed to a team led by Marcian E. Hoff Jr of Intel Corporation with the production of the microprocessor chip '4004' from 1969 to 1971, but in 1990, with the award of US Patent No. 4942516, priority was accorded to Gilbert Hyatt, who devised a single-chip microcomputer at Micro Computer Inc. of Van Nuys, Los Angeles, USA, from 1968 to 1971.

First personal computer

The MITS Altair 8800 went on the market in 1975. For $395 (£180) it offered an Intel 8800 processor and 256 bytes of memory, toggle switches for data input and LEDs (light-emitting diodes) for output, but there was no keyboard or screen.

Fastest computers

Fastest general-purpose computer

The fastest general-purpose vector-parallel computer in the world is the Cray Y-MP C90 supercomputer, which has two gigabytes of central memory and a total of 16 CPUs (central processing units), giving a combined peak performance of 16 gigaflops (one gigaflop equals 1 billion floating point operations per second).

Fastest computer 16 gigaflops

Intel plans to install a faster supercomputer at Sandia, Texas, USA, in 1996. Using 9,072 Intel Pentium Pro processors, each running at about 200 MHz, and 608 gigabytes of memory, it will have a peak performance of about 1.8 teraflops (trillions of floating point operations per second).

World supercomputing speed record
In Dec 1994 a team of scientists from Sandia National Laboratories and Intel Corporation linked two of the largest Intel Paragon parallel-processing machines. The system achieved a performance of 281 gigaflops on the Linpack benchmark. The supercomputer also achieved 328 gigaflops running a program used for radar signature calculations. The two-Paragon system used 6,768 processors working in parallel.

Fastest chip
The world's fastest microprocessor is the Alpha 21164, developed by Digital Equipment Corporation of Maynard, Massachusetts, USA, and unveiled in Sept 1994. It can run at speeds of 300 MHz (compared to 66 MHz for a modern personal computer).

Most accurate calculation of π
The most decimal places to which π has been calculated is 6,442,450,000. Using computer programs written by Daisuke Takahasi, Prof.

CESS OF 5 MILLION COPIES

Yasumasa Kanada of the University of Tokyo, Japan, made two independent calculations by different methods and compared the results. The main program was run from 24 to 29 Sept 1995 (116 hr 38 min) and the verification program from 6 to 11 Oct on a HITAC S-3800/480 supercomputer.

The Internet
Largest computer network
The number of computers linked by the Internet has been doubling every year since 1987 and there were at least 9,472,000 computers on the 'Net' in Jan 1996. There may, however, be many more computers attached than this figure suggests, since many 'host', or server, computers are behind corporate 'firewalls' designed to exclude electronic visitors, including hackers.

Fastest-growing network
The fastest-growing part of the Internet is the World-Wide Web, a system that allows texts and pictures to be 'published' electronically. Although the Web was first implemented at the CERN physics research laboratory in 1990, it did not become popular until 1993, when the first 'Web browser', Mosaic, was released by America's National Center for Supercomputing Applications (NCSA). There were 623 Web sites by the end of 1993, 10,022 by the end of 1994, and at least 100,000 by Jan 1996.

Most popular host name
The most popular, non-functional name given to an Internet host computer is Venus, with 2,272 examples. The next most popular names are Pluto (2,052), Mars (2,023), Zeus (1,912), Jupiter (1,834), Mercury (1,705) and Saturn (1,638).

Biggest computer crash
The Internet Worm, a self-replicating program, was released onto the Internet on 2 Nov 1988 by Robert Morris Jr, a 23-year-old student at Cornell University, New York State, USA. The virus could penetrate security flaws in the software of many computers attached to the Internet and copy itself from machine to machine. It multiplied so rapidly that parts of the Internet were almost brought to a standstill, as an estimated 6,000 computers slowed down, crashed or were cut off from the 'Net'. Morris was convicted of violating the Computer Fraud and Abuse Act of 1986 and was sentenced to three years' probation, 400 hours of community service, a $10,050 (£5,600) fine and the cost of his supervision.

First Internet arrest
On 19 May 1996, Leslie Ibsen Rogge became the first man to be arrested as a result of his picture being posted on the FBI's web-site. Rogge, a convicted bankrobber and one of America's 10 Most Wanted, had escaped from federal custody in 1985.

Computer games
Best-selling computer game
The best-selling computer game in the world (counting all versions) is the city simulator Sim City, made by Maxis, which had sold more than 5 million copies by May 1996.

Most installed game
The most frequently installed game in the world is probably id Software's DOOM, which was released on 10 Dec 1993. The exact number installed is unknown because the game is distributed as 'shareware', enabling users to try it out before they purchase it. It is estimated that about 15 million shareware copies of DOOM have been downloaded from online networks or passed from player to player on floppy disks. The sequel, DOOM II, has sold more than 1.6 million copies since 10 Oct 1994.

Best-selling video game
The best-selling video game in the world is Super Mario Brothers, which is produced for the Nintendo Entertainment System. Nintendo, which is based in Kyōtō, Japan, has sold more than 65 million NES games consoles and in excess of 40 million copies of Super Mario Brothers for that system. The company has sold more than 125 million copies of games featuring the Mario character, and it manufactured its 1 billionth video game cartridge on 30 Oct 1995.

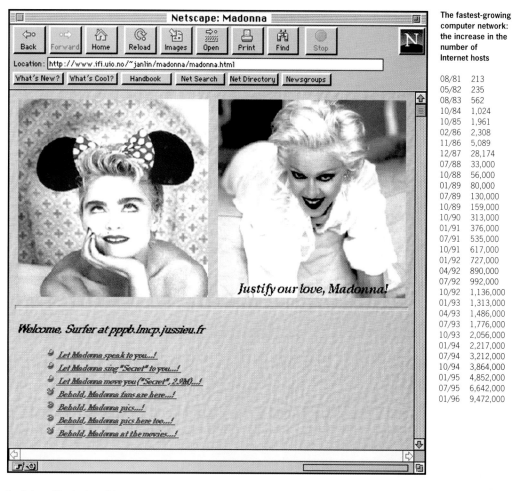

Justify our love, Madonna!

The fastest-growing computer network: the increase in the number of Internet hosts

Date	Hosts
08/81	213
05/82	235
08/83	562
10/84	1,024
10/85	1,961
02/86	2,308
11/86	5,089
12/87	28,174
07/88	33,000
10/88	56,000
01/89	80,000
07/89	130,000
10/89	159,000
10/90	313,000
01/91	376,000
07/91	535,000
10/91	617,000
01/92	727,000
04/92	890,000
07/92	992,000
10/92	1,136,000
01/93	1,313,000
04/93	1,486,000
07/93	1,776,000
10/93	2,056,000
01/94	2,217,000
07/94	3,212,000
10/94	3,864,000
01/95	4,852,000
07/95	6,642,000
01/96	9,472,000

Computer challenge

EXPLORE THE HAUNTED FOREST AND TREACHEROUS SWAMPS OF THE KREMLING'S ISLAND

Below
In Donkey Kong Country 2: Diddy Kong's Quest, Donkey Kong must be rescued by his friends from the Kremling's Island.

Would you like to be a Guinness record-holder? This year *The Guinness Book of Records* has got together with the three leading manufacturers of computer games, Sega, Nintendo and Sony. We have selected, from each manufacturer, two of the most up-to-date and challenging games.

All that you have to do is record your personal best score, following the individual rules that are set out on this page, and then send a photograph of the screen showing your score to Guinness.

The highest scoring competitors will be required to play the game under Guinness supervision, and the top scorers at this point will be invited to attend the final championship play-off.

Sega
Sega Rally Championship
Take the wheel of a Lancia Delta, a Toyota Celica or a Lancia Stratos with the choice of automatic or manual transmission as you hurtle around four extremely challenging circuits in your attempt to become the next Colin McRae.

Rules
Competitors must send in photographic evidence of their fastest time on the Lakeside course. This track can only be accessed once racers have come first on the Desert, Forest and Mountain courses. Competitors may choose any car but they must race using manual transmission.

Virtua Cop 2
Agents Michael 'Rage' Hardy and James 'Smarty' Cools are back once more to enforce the law on the streets of Virtua City. This time they have been joined by female partner Janet in their quest to finally rid the city of the EVL Corporation and they're sure to be taking no prisoners!

Rules
Competitors must send in photographic evidence of their highest score on "Ranking Mode". The Ranking Mode can only be accessed once all the stages of normal game play have been successfully completed.

Nintendo
Super Mario Kart
This is the first Go-Kart racing game to come out for the SNES. It features all of the Super Mario gang—Mario, Luigi, King Koopa, Toadstool, Princess Daisy and Donkey Kong Jr. Collect many different power-ups to speed you up; throw Koopa shells or banana peels at your opponents to slow them down. The Battle Mode is a two-player game; the split screen can be used to view both players battling it out.

Rules
A photograph must be provided to show that the Super Nintendo is switched on, with the TV in the same shot. No game enhancement devices, such as Action Replay or Game Genie, may be used. Challenge on Mario Kart will be run on Time

Become the next Colin McRae!

USE YOUR REFINED CONTROL SYSTEM TO RACE OV

VIRTUA COP 2

USE YOUR SKILLS TO FINALLY RID VIRTUA CITY OF THE EVL CORPORATION

Trial Mode, Mushroom Cup, Mario Circuit 1. Any of the eight characters can be used. Turbo starts are allowed, but no other cheats are permitted. Average times for this track are between 1:03:64 and 1:06:71.

To begin the challenge, select "one player time trial" and choose your character. Select Mushroom Cup, Mario Circuit 1 and begin the time trial. At the end of the race take a photograph of the screen displaying the lap and total course times.

Donkey Kong Country 2: Diddy Kong's Quest

In the sequel to Donkey Kong Country, Diddy Kong gets the spotlight, along with his girlfriend Dixie Kong—a great little monkey with a dangerous ponytail. The action starts on the wreck of the King K Rool's Gangplank Galleon, which has apparently broken up on a reef offshore of the Kremling's island. Diddy and his friends will have to work together to rescue Donkey Kong, exploring all the hidden

areas of the Kremling's island: a spooky haunted forest, treacherous swamps, a giant bee hive oozing with sticky honey and lava-filled caves.

Rules

On Donkey Kong Country 2, the challenge is to complete the game fully (102%) in the quickest time; this includes all Krem coins and all 40 DK coins. No cheats, such as 50 lives, are permitted. Average times for completing the game are between two and three hours.

To play, select "empty file" and choose "one player game". When you have finished, take a photograph of "save game screen" displaying the total percentage completed and the time it has taken.

Sony

Tekken 2 by Namco for Sony PlayStation

Tekken 2 reunites all the fighters from the first game, but ultimate boss Helhachi now

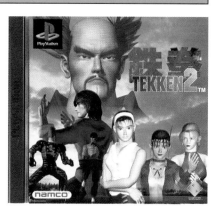

becomes a player character, while his son Kazuya steps into his shoes as the end-of-game boss. Two new player characters—Lei Fung (a Kung Fu fighting, street-wise cop) and Jun (a proud eco-warrior)—are introduced, as well as a whole host of hidden bosses and player characters, making a 24-strong gang in total. Be prepared for the plethora of gaming modes, whether playing in first perspective mode or traditional mode. For those players who want to be the best in terms of tactics, Tekken 2 also gives competitors the opportunity to perfect their skills in Practice mode.

Rules

Competitors should send photographic evidence of Total Time on Time Attack Mode, where all fighters must be fought in the quickest time possible.

Ridge Racer Revolution by Namco for Sony PlayStation

Using the 3D graphic engine that featured in the original Ridge Racer, the sequel provides more richly detailed cars and backgrounds for added realism. All new features include hidden new cars, a link-up option, a rear view mirror for blocking an opponent's way through, a total of six new courses, a refined control system, and remixed versions of some of the original's classic tunes plus an album's worth of new soundtracks.

Rules

Competitors must send in photographic evidence of their fastest Total Time lap times on Expert mode with the car of their choice.

LAP 1/3   TOTAL 00' 07"11   TIME 00' 07"11

7th

100 80 60 40 20 Km/h

X NEW COURSES IN THE RIDGE RACER REVOLUTION

WORLD'S LONGEST MOTORCYCLE WHEELIE WAS MAINTAINED F

HIGHEST SPEED RECORDED ON A NATIONAL RAIL SYSTEM IS 515.3 KM/H

Transport and

BUSIEST ROAD HAS A PEAK-HOUR VOLUME OF 25,500 VEHICLES ON A 1.5-KM STRET

1994
1995
1996
1997
1998

LONGEST EVER FLIGHT LASTED 64 DAYS 22 HR 19 MIN 5 SEC

TALLEST UNICYCLE WAS 31.01 M HIGH AND WAS RIDDEN FOR A DISTANCE OF 114.6

LARGEST EVER SHIP OF A

HIGHEST SPEED EVER ACHIEVED ON WATER IS AN ESTIMATED 555 KM/H

122
123
124
125
126
127
128
129
130
131
132
133
134
135
136
137
138

travel

...GHEST SPEED ACHIEVED BY A JET WAS 3,529.56 KM/H, BY A LOCKHEED SR-71A

...DISTANCE OF 331 KM

FASTEST ROAD CAR ATTAINED A SPEED OF 349.3 KM/H

...RGEST TRAFFIC JAM SAW 1.5 MILLION CARS CROSS THE EAST-WEST GERMAN BORDER IN 1990

LARGEST RAILWAY STATION HAS 67 TRACKS

...ND, THE CARGO VESSEL *JAHRE VIKING*, IS 458.45 M LONG

...IONAL HAD 00.20, AIRCRAFT MOVEMENTS IN 1995

BALLOON, GREATEST ALTITUDE OF REACHED, 51,800 M

AIRPORT, O'HARE INTERNATIONAL

Ships and boats

Right
The Stena HSS (High-speed Sea Service) is the world's fastest car ferry. At 126.6 x 40 m (415 x 131 ft), the £65-million craft is substantially larger than any other fast ferry, and its four gas turbines—developing a total of 100,000 horsepower—allow it to maintain a service speed of 40 knots.

Longest ship 458.45 m

Merchant shipping

Largest fleet
Panama has the world's largest merchant fleet, with a gross registered tonnage (grt) of 71.9 million tons at the end of 1995.

Largest cargo vessel
The largest ever ship of any kind is the oil tanker *Jahre Viking* (formerly known as the *Happy Giant* and the *Seawise Giant*), at 564,763 tonnes deadweight. It is 458.45 m (1,504 ft) long, and has a beam of 68.8 m (226 ft) and a draught of 24.61 m (80 ft 9 in). Disabled by bombardment in the Iran-Iraq war, it underwent a $60-million (£34-million) renovation in Singapore and in Dubai, United Arab Emirates, and was relaunched in 1991.

Largest container ship
The largest container vessel in service is *Regina Maersk*, built at Odense, Denmark, and completed in Jan 1996. It has a grt of 81,488 and a capacity of 6,000 TEU (Twenty-foot Equivalent Units—the standard container is 6.096 m or 20 ft long).

Largest barge
The largest RoRo (roll-on, roll-off) ships are four El Rey class barges with a weight of 16,700 tons and a length of 176.8 m (580 ft). Built by the FMC Corp of Portland, Oregon, USA, they are operated by Crowley Maritime Corp of San Francisco between Florida, USA, and Puerto Rico, and have tri-level lodging for up to 376 truck-trailers.

Largest liners
Cunard's RMS *Queen Elizabeth* was the largest passenger vessel ever built and had the largest displacement of any liner. She was 314 m (1,030 ft) long, 36 m (118 ft 7 in) wide, had a gross registered tonnage of

82,998 (formerly 83,673) and was powered by steam turbines that developed 168,000 hp. In 1970, she was moved to Hong Kong to be used for marine studies—as Seawise University—but was burnt out in three outbreaks of fire on 9 Jan 1972.

The longest passenger liner ever built is the *Norway*, which has a grt of 76,049, an overall length of 315.53 m (1,035 ft 7½ in) and a capacity of 2,022 passengers and 900 crew. Built as the SS *France* in 1960 and purchased in 1979 by Norwegian Knut Kloster, she is normally employed on cruises in the Caribbean and is based at Miami, USA. A refit in 1990 increased the number of passenger decks to 11. She draws 10.5 m (34 ft 6 in), has a beam of 33.5 m (110 ft) and cruises at 18 knots (33.3 km/h or 20.7 mph).

The largest cruise liner in service is the P&O Group's *Sun Princess*, which has a grt of 76,500 can carry 1,950 passengers. The ship was commissioned in Dec 1995 and built by the Fincantieri yard, Italy.

Largest existing British liner
Cunard's MV *Queen Elizabeth 2* has a grt of 69,053 and an overall length of 293 m (963 ft). She was built by John Brown & Co. (Clydebank) Ltd, Scotland, and refitted with diesel electric engines by Lloyd Werft, Bremerhaven, Germany, from 1986 to 1987, giving her a maximum speed of 32½ knots. She set a 'turn round' record of 3 hr 18 min at New York City, USA, on 14 Dec 1993.

Ferries

Largest car and passenger ferry
The largest car and passenger ferry in terms of tonnage is *Silja Europa*, which entered service in 1993 between Stockholm, Sweden, and Helsinki, Finland. Operated by the Silja Line, it has a grt of 59,914, is 201.8 m (662 ft) long and has a beam of 32.6 m (107 ft). It can carry 3,000 passengers, 350 cars and 60 lorries.

Fastest car ferries
Built in Finland, Stena Line's HSS *Explorer* is powered by quadruple gas turbines, giving a cruising speed of 40 knots and a top speed of 44 knots. It can carry 1,500 passengers and 375 cars. The largely aluminium catamaran hulls have a length of 126.6 m (415 ft) and a beam of 40 m (131 ft).

Largest international rail ferries
The *Klaipeda*, *Vilnius*, *Mukran* and *Greifswald*, operate in the Baltic Sea between Klaipeda, Lithuania, and Mukran, Germany. Each is 11,700 tons deadweight, has two 190.5-m (625-ft) decks and is 91.86 m (301 ft 5 in) wide. Built in Wismar, Germany, they can each lift 103 standard 14.83-m (48-ft 8-in), 84-ton railcars and can cover a distance of 506 km (273 nautical miles) in 17 hours.

Largest hovercraft
The SRN4 Mk III, a British-built civil hovercraft, weighs 305 tons and can accommodate 418 passengers and 60 cars. It is 56.38 m (185 ft) long, and its four Bristol Siddeley

Marine Proteus engines give it a maximum speed in excess of the scheduled permitted cross-Channel operating speed of 65 knots.

Largest hydrofoil
The 64.6-m (212-ft) long *Plainview* (314 tons full load) naval hydrofoil was launched by the Lockheed Shipbuilding and Construction Co. at Seattle, Washington, USA, in June 1965.

Sailing vessels and sails
Oldest active sailing ship
The oldest square-rigged sailing vessel that still goes to sea is the *India*, built in 1863 at Ramsey, Isle of Man, as the full-rigged, 1,197-ton ship *Euterpe*. It is preserved as a museum ship in San Diego, California, USA, and makes occasional day-trips under sail.

Largest sailing ship
The largest vessel to have been built in the era of sail was the *France II*, which had a grt of 5,806 and was launched at Bordeaux, France, in 1911. This steel-hulled, five-masted barque had a hull measuring 127.4 m (418 ft). Principally designed as a sailing vessel with a stump top gallant rig, she was fitted with two auxiliary engines, but these were removed in 1919 and she became a pure sailing vessel.

E WORLD'S LARGEST SHIP

France II was wrecked off New Caledonia in the South Pacific in 1922.

Largest sailing ship in service
The *Sedov*, built in 1921 in Kiel, Germany, and used for training by Russia is 109 m (357 ft) long and 14.6 m (48 ft) wide. It has a displacement of 6,300 tonnes, a grt of 3,556 and a sail area of 4,192 m^2 (45,123 ft^2).

Longest sailing ship
The 187-m (613-ft) French-built *Club Med 1* has five aluminium masts. Operated as a

Caribbean cruise vessel, it has powerful engines and is really a motor sailer.

Largest junks
The seagoing *Zheng He*, flagship of Admiral Zheng He's 62 treasure ships c. 1420, had a displacement of 3,150 tonnes and an estimated length of up to 164 m (538 ft).

In c. AD 280, a 183-m^2 (600-ft^2) floating fortress, built by Wang Jun on the Yangtze River, took part in the Jin-Wu river war.

Largest sails
The largest spars carried were those in HM battleship *Temeraire*, construction of which was completed at Chatham, Kent, UK, on 31 Aug 1877. The fore and main yards were 35 m (115 ft) in length. The foresail contained 1,555 m (5,100 ft) of canvas weighing 2.03 tonnes and the total sail area was 2,320 m^2 (25,000 ft^2). The ship was broken up in 1921.

Yachts
Largest yacht
The 147-m-long (482-ft) Saudi Arabian royal yacht *Abdul Aziz* was completed in 1984 at Vospers Yard, Southampton, Hants, UK. In 1987 it was estimated to be worth more than $100 million (£61 million).

Largest private yacht
The largest private (non-Royal) yacht is the 122-m (400-ft) former ferry *Alexander*, which was converted in 1986.

Tallest single-masted yacht
The American-built sloop *Zeus*, completed in 1994, has a 52.7-m-high (173-ft) high mast made from a single piece of carbon fibre.

Submarines
Smallest fully functional submarine
In 1991, William G. Smith of Bognor Regis, W Sussex, UK, built a submarine only 2.95 m

(9 ft 8 in) long, 1.15 m (3 ft 9 in) wide and 1.42 m (4 ft 8 in) high. It can remain underwater for at least four hours at depths of up to 30.5 m (100 ft).

Fastest manpowered underwater vehicles
The fastest speed attained by a man-powered propeller submarine is 6.696±0.06 knots (3.445 m/sec or 11.3 ft/sec). It was achieved by *SubStandard*, designed, built and crewed by William Nicoloff of Northridge, California, USA, on 30 March 1996.

The fastest man-powered non-propeller submarine, *SubDUDE*, reached 2.9±0.1 knots (1.49 m/sec or 4.88 ft/sec) on 21 Aug 1992. Designed by the Scripps Institution of Oceanography, University of California, USA, using a horizontal oscillating foil propulsion system, it was crewed by Kimball Millikan and Ed Trevino, with team leader Kevin Hardy.

Shipping disasters
Oldest shipwreck
The oldest known shipwreck is off Ulu Buren, near Kas, southern Turkey. It has been dated to the 14th century BC.

Largest shipwrecks
The 321,186-tonne deadweight VLCC (Very Large Crude Carrier) *Energy Determination* blew up in the Strait of Hormuz, Persian Gulf, on 12 Dec 1979.

The largest wreck removal was carried out in 1979 by Smit Tak International, who removed the remains of the 120,000-ton French tanker *Betelgeuse* from Bantry Bay, Ireland.

Biggest collision
The tanker *Venoil* (330,954 dwt) struck her sister ship *Venpet* (330,869 dwt) off the coast of southern Africa on 16 Dec 1977.

Worst single ship marine disaster
Some 7,700 people were killed and only 903 survived when the 25,484-ton German liner *Wilhelm Gustloff* was torpedoed off Danzig by the Soviet submarine S-13 on 30 Jan 1945.

Left
The largest cruise liner in current service, the *Sun Princess*, can carry almost 2,000 passengers and has a gross registered tonnage of 76,500.

Sailing and rowing

YOUNGEST PERSON TO CROSS THE ATLANTIC SOLO WAS 17 YEARS 176 DAYS OLD

Right
On 1 April 1994, on board the *Enza New Zealand*, Sir Peter Blake, with Sir Robin Knox-Johnston and a crew of six, won the Trophée Jules Verne in a time of 74 days 22 hr 17 min. The trophy is awarded to ships that complete a circumnavigation in less than 80 days. Blake's voyage was the world's fastest ever non-stop marine circumnavigation.

GREATEST DISTANCE EVER COVERED BY ANY SHIP IN A DAY'S RUN (24 HOURS)

Highest speed 300 knots

SAILING AND ROWING RECORDS
Smg=speed made good. All mileages are nautical.

TRANSATLANTIC
First east-west solo sailing
Vessel: 15-ton gaff sloop
Skipper: Josiah Shackford (USA)
Start: Bordeaux, France, 1786
Finish: Surinam (Guiana)
Duration: 35 days

First west-east solo sailing
Vessel: *Centennial*, 6.1 m (20 ft) long
Skipper: Alfred Johnson (USA)
Start: Shag Harbor, Maine, USA, 1876
Finish: Wales, UK
Duration: 46 days

First west-east solo sailing by a woman
Vessel: Lugger, 5.5 m (18 ft) long
Skipper: Gladys Gradeley (USA)
Start: Nova Scotia, Canada, 1903
Finish: Hope Cove, Devon, UK
Duration: 60 days

First east-west solo rowing
Vessel: *Britannia*, 6.7 m (22 ft) long
Skipper: John Fairfax (GB)
Start: Las Palmas, Canary Islands, 20 Jan 1969
Finish: Fort Lauderdale, Florida, USA, 19 July 1969
Duration: 180 days

Fastest east-west solo sailing
Vessel: *Fleury Michon* (IX) 18.3-m (60-ft) trimaran
Skipper: Philippe Poupon (France)
Start: Plymouth, Devon, UK, 5 June 1988
Finish: Newport, Rhode Island, USA, 15 June 1988
Duration: 10 days 9 hr (11.6 knots smg)

Fastest west-east solo sailing
Vessel: *Primagaz*, 18.3-m (60-ft) trimaran
Skipper: Laurent Bourgnon (France)
Start: Ambrose Light Tower, USA, 27 June 1994
Finish: Lizard Point, Cornwall, UK, 4 July 1994
Duration: 7 days 2 hr 34 min 42 sec (17.15 knots)

First west-east solo rowing
Vessel: *Super Silver*, 6.1 m (20 ft) long
Skipper: Tom McClean (Ireland)
Start: St John's, Newfoundland, Canada, 1969
Finish: Black Sod Bay, Republic of Ireland, 27 July 1969
Duration: 70.7 days

First row in both directions
Vessel: *QE III*, 6.05 m (19 ft 10 in) long
Skipper: Don Allum (GB)
Start: Canary Islands 1986 and St John's, Canada
Finish: Nevis, West Indies, and Ireland 1987
Duration: 114 days 77 days

Fastest east-west crewed sail
Vessel: *Primagaz*, 18.3-m (60-ft) trimaran
Skipper/crew: Laurent Bourgnon (France) and Cam Lewis (USA)
Start: Plymouth, Devon, UK, 5 June 1994
Finish: Newport, Rhode Island, USA, 14 June 1994
Duration: 9 days 8 hr 58 min 20 sec (12.49 knots)

Fastest west-east crewed sail
Vessel: *Jet Services 5*, 22.9-m (75-ft) catamaran sloop
Skipper: Serge Madec (France)
Start: Ambrose Light Tower, USA, 2 June 1990
Finish: Lizard Point, Cornwall, UK, 9 June 1990
Duration: 6 days 13 hr 3 min 32 sec (18.4 knots smg)

TRANSPACIFIC
First rowing
Vessel: *Britannia II*, 10.7 m (35 ft) long
Skippers: John Fairfax (GB) and Sylvia Cook (GB)
Start: San Francisco, USA, 26 April 1971
Finish: Hayman Island, Australia, 22 April 1972
Duration: 362 days

First east-west solo sailing
Vessel: *Pacific*, 5.48-m (18-ft) double-ender
Skipper: Bernard Gilboy (USA)
Start: 1882
Finish: Australia

First east-west solo rowing
Vessel: *Hele-on-Britannia*, 9.75 m (32 ft) long
Skipper: Peter Bird (GB)
Start: San Francisco, USA, 23 Aug 1982
Finish: Great Barrier Reef, Australia, 14 June 1983
Duration: 294 days over 14,480 km (9,000 miles)

First west-east solo sailings
Vessel: *Elaine*, 5.48 m (18 ft) long
Skipper: Fred Rebel (Latvia)
Start: Australia, 1932
and:
Vessel: *Sturdy II*, 11.2 m (36 ft) long
Skipper: Edward Miles (US)
Start: Japan, 1932 (via Hawaii)

First west-east solo rowing
Vessel: *Sector*, 8 m (26 ft) long
Skipper: Gérard d'Aboville (France)
Start: Choshi, Japan, 11 July 1991
Finish: Ilwaco, Washington, USA, 21 Nov 1991
Duration: 133 days over 10,150 km (6,300 miles)

Fastest sail
Vessel: *Lakota*, 18.29 m (60 ft) long
Skipper: Steve Fossett (USA), plus four crew
Start: Long Beach, California, USA, 5 July 1995
Finish: Honolulu, Hawaii, 11 July 1995
Duration: 6 days 16 hr 16 min (13.84 knots smg)

MARINE CIRCUMNAVIGATION
It is not possible to make a simple circumnavigation of the world by sea, which would be along the Equator. The World Sailing Speed Record Council gives the following rules: the vessel must start and return to the same point, must cross all meridians of longitude and must cross the Equator. It may cross some, but not all, meridians more than once. The vessel must cover at least 21,600 nautical miles in the course of the circumnavigation.

A non-stop circumnavigation is self-maintained; no water supplies, provisions, equipment or replacements of any sort may be taken aboard en route. Vessels may anchor but no physical help may be accepted apart from communications.

Ocean crossings
Fastest Atlantic crossings
The record for the fastest crossing is 2 days 10 hr 34 min 47 sec (45.7 knots smg), by the 68-m (222-ft) powerboat *Destriero*, from 6 to 8 Aug 1992.

The boat that makes the fastest regular commercial crossing (and therefore the winner of the Hales Trophy or 'Blue Riband') is the liner *United States* (formerly 51,988, now 38,216 gross tons), the former flagship of the United States Lines. From 3 to 7 July 1952, during her maiden voyage from New York, USA, to Le Havre, France, and Southampton, Hants, UK, she averaged 65.95 km/h (35.39 knots) for 3 days 10 hr 0 min on a route of 5,465 km (2,949 nautical miles) from the Ambrose light vessel to the Bishop Rock lighthouse, Isles of Scilly, Cornwall, UK. From 6 to 7 July, she steamed the greatest distance covered by any ship in 24 hours, at 1,609 km (868 nautical miles), averaging 67.02 km/h (36.17 knots). The maximum speed attained from her 240,000 shaft horsepower engines was 71.01 km/h (38.32 knots), in trials in June 1952.

Youngest solo transatlantic crossings
The youngest person to sail solo across the Atlantic was David Sandeman (GB), who was 17 years 176 days old when he made the crossing in a time of 43 days in 1976.

The youngest person to row solo across the Atlantic was Sean Crowley (GB), in 95 days 22 hr in 1988, aged 25 years 306 days.

Oldest solo transatlantic crossing
The oldest person to sail singlehandedly across the Atlantic was Stefan Szwarnowski (GB), in 72 days at the age of 76 years 165 days in 1989.

The oldest person to row solo across the Atlantic was Sidney Genders, at the age of 51 in 1970. His time was 160 days 8 hr.

Fastest Pacific crossing
The fastest crossing from Yokohama, Japan, to Long Beach, California, USA (8,960 km or 4,840 nautical miles) took 6 days 1 hr 27 min from 30 June to 6 July 1973, by the 50,315-ton container ship *Sea-Land Commerce*, at an average speed of 61.65 km/h (33.27 knots).

Fastest Channel crossing
The SeaCat catamaran ferry *Hoverspeed France* crossed the English Channel from Dover, Kent, UK, to Calais, France, in a record time of 34 min 23 sec on 15 Oct 1991 at an average speed of 70 km/h (37.87 knots).

Speed
Highest speed
The highest speed ever achieved on water is an estimated 555 km/h (300 knots), by Kenneth Peter Warby, on the Blowering Dam Lake, NSW, Australia, on 20 Nov 1977. This feat was achieved in Warby's unlimited hydroplane *Spirit of Australia*.

The official world water speed record is 511.11 km/h (275.8 knots), by Kenneth Warby on Blowering Dam Lake on 8 Oct 1978.

Highest women's speed
Mary Rife of Flint, Texas, USA, set a women's unofficial record of 332.6 km/h (206.72 mph) in her blown fuel hydro *Proud Mary* in Tulsa, Oklahoma, USA, on 23 July 1977. Her official record is 317 km/h (197 mph).

---

609 KM, BY THE LINER *UNITED STATES*, AT AN AVERAGE SPEED OF 67.02 KM/H

First
Vessel: *Vittoria Expedition of Ferdinand Magellan*
Skipper: Juan Sebastián de Elcano or del Cano and 17 crew
Start: Seville, Spain, 20 Sept 1519
Finish: San Lucar, Spain, 6 Sept 1522
Distance: 93,573.6 km (30,700 miles)
(Author Eduard Roditi advances the view that Magellan's slave, Enrique, who had been purchased in Malacca and understood the Filipino dialect Vizayan when he reached the Philippines from the east, was the first circumnavigator)

First solo
Vessel: *Spray*, 11.2-m (36-ft 9-in) gaff yawl
Skipper: Capt. Joshua Slocum (USA) (a non-swimmer)
Start: Newport, Rhode Island, USA, via Magellan Straits, Chile, 24 April 1895
Finish: 3 July 1898
Distance: 140,028 km (46,000 miles)

First east-west solo non-stop
Vessel: *British Steel*, 18-m (59-ft) ketch
Skipper: Chay Blyth, OBE, BEM (GB)
Start: Hamble River, Hants, UK, 18 Oct 1970
Finish: 6 Aug 1971, 292 days (3.08 knots)

First west-east solo non-stop
Vessel: *Suhaili*, 9.87-m (32-ft 4-in) Bermudan ketch
Skipper: Sir Robin Knox-Johnston, CBE, RD (GB)
Start: Falmouth, Cornwall, UK, 14 June 1968
Finish: 22 April 1969, 312 days (2.88 knots)

First west-east solo non-stop by a woman
Vessel: *Express Crusader*, 16.15 m (53 ft) long
Skipper: Dame Naomi Jones (New Zealand)
Start: Dartmouth, Devon, UK, 9 Sept 1977
Finish: Dartmouth, 8 June 1978
Duration: 265 sailing days + 7 days in port

Fastest non-stop
Vessel: *Enza*, 28-m (92-ft) catamaran
Skipper: Sir Peter Blake KBE (NZ), Sir Robin Knox-Johnston CBE, RD (GB) and six crew
Start: Ushant, France, 16 Jan 1994
Finish: Ushant, 1 April 1994
Duration: 74 days 22 hr 17 min (12.10 knots)

FASTEST SOLO NON-STOP
Vessel: *Ecureil d'Aquitaine II*, 18.3-m (60-ft) monohull
Skipper: Titouan Lamazou (France)
Start: Les Sables d'Olonne, France, Nov 1989
Finish: Les Sables d'Olonne, March 1990
Duration: 109 days 8 hr 48 m (8.23 knots)

Fastest east-west solo non-stop
Vessel: *Group 4*, 20.42-m (67-ft) sloop
Skipper: Mike Golding (GB)
Start: Southampton, Hants, UK, 21 Nov 1993
Finish: Southampton, 7 May 1994
Duration: 161 days 16 hr 32 m

Smallest
Vessel: *Acrohc Australis*, 3.6-m (11-ft 10-in) sloop
Skipper: Serge Testa (Australia)
Start: Brisbane, Australia, 1984
Finish: Brisbane, 1987
Duration: 500 days

BRITISH ISLES RECORDS
Around mainland, fastest
Vessel: *Drambuie Tantalus*, 15.3-m (50-ft) monohull
Skipper: Dag Pike (GB)
Start: Ramsgate, Kent, 9 July 1992
Finish: Ramsgate, 11 July 1992
Duration: 1 day 20 hr 3 min (36.6 knots smg)

Around mainland, fastest vessel under 50 ft
Vessel: *Rapier 29*, 8.8-m (29-ft)
Skipper: Steve Brownridge (GB)
Start: Southampton, Hants, 25 June 1993
Finish: Southampton, 27 June 1993
Duration: 2 days 15 hr 32 min (24.68 knots)

Around British Isles, fastest sailing vessel
(Taking in all the islands and rocks of Britain and Ireland including St Kildare, but not Rockall or the Channel Islands)
Vessel: *Lakota*, 18.29-m (60-ft) trimaran
Skipper: Steve Fossett (USA) and four crew
Start: Ventnor, Isle of Wight, 21 Oct 1994
Finish: Ventnor, 27 Oct 1994
Duration: 5 days 21 hr 5 min (12.67 knots)

ENGLISH CHANNEL
Both ways, fastest sailing multihull
Vessel: *Fleury Michon VIII*, 22.9-m (75-ft) trimaran
Skipper: Philippe Poupon (France)
Start: Calais, France, Dec 1986
Finish: Calais via Dover, Kent, UK, Dec 1986
Duration: 2 hr 21 min 57 sec (18.6 knots smg)

DURATION AND DISTANCE
Non-stop by sail three times around the world
Vessel: *Parry Endeavour*, 13.9-m (44-ft) Bermudan sloop
Skipper: Jon Sanders (Australia)
Start: Fremantle, W Australia, 25 May 1986
Finish: Fremantle, 13 March 1988
Duration: 71,000 miles in 658 days (4.5 knots)

Best day's run, under sail and solo
Vessel: *Primagaz*, 18.29-m (60-ft) trimaran
Skipper: Laurent Bourgnon (France)
Start: North Atlantic, 28 June 1994
Finish: North Atlantic, 29 June 1994
Duration: 540 miles in 24 hours (22.5 knots)

Best day's run, monohull fully crewed
Vessel: *Intrum Justitia*, 19.51-m (64-ft) monohull
Skipper: Lawrie Smith (GB)
Start: Southern Ocean, 20 Feb 1994
Finish: Southern Ocean, 21 Feb 1994
Duration: 428¹⁄₁₀ miles in 24 hours (17.8 knots)

Best day's run, sailboard
Vessel: *Fanatic board*, Gaastra sail
Skipper: Françoise Canetos (France)
Start: Sète, France, 13 July 1988
Finish: Sète, 14 July 1988
Duration: 227 miles in 24 hours (9.46 knots smg)

Fastest sea passage under sail
Vessel: *Pierre 1er*, 18.29 m (60 ft) long
Skipper: Florence Arthaud (France)
Start: Marseille, France, 26 Aug 1991
Finish: Carthage, Tunisia, 27 Aug 1991
Duration: 458 miles in 22 hr 9 min 56 sec (20.66 knots)

Motorcycles and cycles

Right and below
On 17 Jan 1985, Emilio Scotto set off on his Honda Gold Wing motorcycle, which he nicknamed 'The Black Princess', with just $300 and no previous travel experience. In the 3,728 days of his record-breaking motorcycle odyssey, Scotto visited 214 countries, learnt five languages, became a Muslim and married his girlfriend in India.

Motorcycles

Earliest motorcycles

The first motorized bicycle with an internal combustion engine was a wooden-framed machine built at Bad Cannstatt, Germany, in Oct and Nov 1885 by Gottlieb Daimler. First ridden by Wilhelm Maybach, it had a top speed of 19 km/h (12 mph) and developed half of one horsepower from its single-cylinder 264 cc four-stroke engine at 700 rpm. Known as the 'Einspur', it was lost in a fire in 1903.

The first motorcycles of entirely British production were the 1,046 cc Holden flat-four and the 2¾ hp Clyde single, both of which were produced in 1898.

Longest motorcycles

Gregg Reid of Atlanta, Georgia, USA, designed and built a 4.57-m-long (15-ft 6-in) 250 cc motorcycle weighing 235 kg (520 lb). The machine is street legal.

Les Nash of Coventry, W Midlands, UK, constructed a 'self made' 3,500 cc machine with a Rover V-8 engine. It measures 3.81 x 1.22 m (12 ft 6 in x 4 ft) and weighs more than 225 kg (500 lb).

Smallest motorcycles

Simon Timperley and Clive Williams of Progressive Engineering Ltd, Ashton-under-Lyne, Greater Manchester, UK, designed and constructed a motorcycle with a wheel-base of 108 mm (4¼ in), a seat height of 95 mm

(3¾ in) and a wheel diameter of 19 mm (¾ in) at the front and 24 mm (¹⁹⁄₂₀ in) at the back. It was ridden for 1 m (3 ft 3 in).

Magnor Mydland of Norway constructed a motorcycle with a wheel-base of 120 mm

(4¹⁸⁄₂₅ in), a seat height of 148 mm (5⅘ in) and a wheel diameter of 38 mm (1½ in) at the front and 49 mm (1⁹³⁄₁₀₀ in) at the back. He rode 570 m (1,870 ft) and reached a speed of 11.6 km/h (7.2 mph).

Highest motorcycle speeds

Dave Campos (USA) set AMA and FIM absolute records with an overall average of 518.450 km/h (322.150 mph) riding a 7-m-long (23-ft) streamliner named *Easyriders*, powered by two Ruxton Harley-Davidson engines. He completed the faster run at an average speed of 519.609 km/h (322.870 mph) at Bonneville Salt Flats, Utah, USA, on 14 July 1990.

The highest speed over two runs in the United Kingdom is 323.3 km/h (200.9 mph), by Michel Booys on a streamliner motorcycle built by Alexander Macfadzean and powered by a turbo-charged 588 cc Norton rotary engine, at Bruntingthorpe Proving Ground, Leics, on 24 Aug 1991.

The fastest ever time for a single run over 402 m (440 yd) from a standing start is 6.19 seconds, by Tony Lang of the USA on a supercharged Suzuki at Gainsville, Florida, USA, in 1994.

The highest terminal velocity at the end of a 402-m (440-yd) run from a standing start is 372.15 km/h (231.24 mph), by Elmer Trett of the USA at Virginia Motorsports Park in 1994.

Longest motorcycle rides

A Kinetic Honda DX 100 cc motor scooter was kept in motion for 1,001 hours, when

Fastest HPV 105.38 km/h

Har Parkash Rishi, Amarjeet Singh and Navjot Chadha covered 30,965 km (19,241 miles) at Traffic Park, Pune, Maharashtra, India, between 22 April and 3 June 1990.

Argentinian Emilio Scotto made the longest ever motorcycle journey, covering more than 735,000 km (456,729 miles). He left Buenos Aires on 17 Jan 1985 and returned on 2 April 1995, having used up 42,000 litres of fuel, 700 litres of oil, and 86 tyres.

The first woman to circumnavigate the world solo was Moniika Vega of Brazil, on her Honda 125 cc motorcycle. Her journey began at Milan, Italy, on 7 March 1990. She returned on 24 May 1991, having covered 83,500 km (51,885 miles) and visited 53 countries.

Jim Rogers and Tabitha Estabrook of New York, USA, travelled a total of 91,766 km (57,021 miles) across six continents between March 1990 and Nov 1991.

Motorcycle pyramid
The 'Shwet Ashwas' team from the Indian Military Police Corps constructed a 133-man

James Starley of Coventry, W Midlands, UK, constructed the first penny-farthing, or Ordinary bicycle, in 1870. It had wire-spoked wheels for lightness and was later available with an optional-speed gear.

Smallest bicycle
The smallest bicycle that can be ridden has wheels that are 19 mm (¾ in) in diameter. It was ridden for 4.1 m (13 ft 5½ in) by its constructor Neville Patten of Gladstone, Queensland, Australia, on 25 March 1988.

Jacques Puyoou of Pau, Pyrénées-Atlantiques, France, built a tandem 36 cm (14 in) long, which he has ridden with Madame Puyoou.

Largest bicycle
The largest bicycle by wheel diameter is 'Frankencycle', built by Dave Moore of Rosemead, California, and first ridden on 4 June 1989. The wheel diameter is 3.05 m (10 ft) and the bike is 3.40 m (11 ft 2 in) high.

Longest bicycle
The longest true bicycle (without a third stabilizing wheel) was designed and built by

11 May 1986; and 101.26 km/h (62.92 mph) for multiple riders, by Dave Grylls and Leigh Barczewski at the Ontario Speedway, California, on 4 May 1980.

The one-hour standing start record for a single rider is held by Pat Kinch, riding *Kingcycle Bean*, which averaged 75.57 km/h (46.96 mph) at Millbrook Proving Ground, Bedford, UK, on 8 Sept 1990.

Unicycles
Tallest unicycle
Steve McPeak rode a 31.01-m-tall (101-ft 9-in) unicycle (with a safety wire suspended from an overhead crane) for a distance of 114.6 m (376 ft) in Las Vegas, Nevada, USA, in Oct 1980.

Smallest unicycle
Peter Rosendahl of Sweden rode a 20-cm-high (8-in) unicycle with a wheel diameter of 20 mm (⁷⁸⁄₁₀₀ in), without attachments or extensions, for a distance of 2.2 m (7 ft 2½ in) at the Hansa Theater, Hamburg, Germany, on 14 Dec 1995.

pyramid on 11 motorcycles. They travelled 350 m (382 yd) at Bangalore, India, on 22 Sept 1995.

Motorcycle wheelie
Yasuyuki Kudō covered 331 km (205⁷⁄₁₀ miles) on the rear wheel of his Honda TLM220R at the Japan Automobile Research Institute Proving Ground on 5 May 1991.

The highest speed attained on the back wheel of a motorbike is 254.07 km/h (157.87 mph) by Jacky Vranken of Belgium on a Suzuki GSXR 1100 at St Truiden military airfield, Belgium, on 8 Nov 1992.

Most people on a motorcycle
The most people on one machine is 47, by the Army Corps of Brasília, Brazil, on a 1,200 cc Harley Davidson on 15 Dec 1995.

Oldest motorcyclist
Arthur Merrick Cook (b. 1895) of Exeter, Devon, UK, still rides his Suzuki 125 GS Special motorcycle every day.

Bicycles
Earliest bicycles
From 1839 to 1840, Kirkpatrick Macmillan of Dumfries, UK, built a machine that was propelled by cranks and pedals with connecting rods. It was the first such design to be actually constructed.

The history of cycling properly began with the *vélocipède*, built in March 1861 by Pierre Michaux and his son Ernest of rue de Verneuil, Paris, France.

Terry Thessman of Pahiatua, New Zealand. It is 22.24 m (72 ft 11½ in) long and weighs 340 kg (750 lb). It was ridden 246 m (807 ft) by four riders on 27 Feb 1988.

Bicycle wheelie
The longest bicycle wheelie, which lasted for 10 hr 40 min 8 sec, was achieved by Leandro Henrique Basseto at Madaguari, Paraná, Brazil, on 2 Dec 1990.

Human-powered vehicles (HPVs)
The world speed records for HPVs over a 200-m flying start are: 105.38 km/h (65.48 mph) for a single rider, by Fred Markham at Mono Lake, California, USA, on

Left
At the age of 15, Akira Matsushima, a junior high school student, cycled an average of 128 km (80 miles) per day for 44 days, with only three days' rest over the entire period.

Fastest sprint
Peter Rosendahl (Sweden) set a 100-m sprint record of 12.11 seconds from a standing start at Las Vegas, Nevada, USA, on 25 March 1994.

Endurance
Akira Matsushima of Japan unicycled a distance of 5,248 km (3,261 miles) from Newport, Oregon, to Washington DC, USA, from 10 July to 22 Aug 1992.

Backwards unicycling
Ashrita Furman of the USA rode 85.56 km (53 miles 300 yd) backwards, at Forest Park, Queens, New York, USA, on 16 Sept 1994.

Cars

HIGHEST ROAD-TESTED ACCELERATION IS 0-60 MPH IN 3.07 SEC

Production

Largest manufacturer

The largest manufacturer of motor vehicles and parts (and the largest manufacturing company) is General Motors Corporation, Detroit, Michigan, USA. Worldwide production by GM in 1994 was 5,543,012.

Longest production

The Morgan 4/4, built by the Morgan Motor Car Co. of Malvern, Hereford & Worcester, UK, had its 60th birthday in 1995.

Most cars produced

A total of 21,240,657 Volkswagen 'Beetles' had been produced to the end of 1995. The car is still produced in Puebla, Mexico, and São Paulo, Brazil.

The bestselling British car is the Mini. Since its launch in 1959, a total of 5.3 million have been produced.

Size

Largest private car

The Bugatti 'Royale' type 41 was assembled at Molsheim, France, by the Italian-born Ettore

thrust Rolls-Royce Avon 302 jet-powered *Thrust2*, designed by John Ackroyd.

Fastest rocket-engined cars

The highest speed attained in a rocket-powered car was an average of 1,016.086 km/h (631.367 mph) over the first kilometre, by 'The Blue Flame', a four-wheeled vehicle driven by Gary Gabelich on the Bonneville Salt Flats, Utah, USA, on 23 Oct 1970. For a short time, he exceeded 1,046 km/h (650 mph). The liquid natural gas/hydrogen peroxide rocket engine was capable of developing thrust up to 22,000 lb.

The highest land speed attained by a woman is 843.322 km/h (524.016 mph), by Kitty Hambleton in the three-wheeled SM1 Motivator over the Alvard Desert, Oregon, USA, on 6 Dec 1976. Her official two-way record was 825.126 km/h (512.710 mph).

Fastest piston-engined car

The highest recorded speed for a wheel-driven car is 696.350 km/h (432.692 mph), achieved by Al Teague in *Speed-O-Motive/ Spirit of 76* on Bonneville Salt Flats, Utah, USA, on 21 Aug 1991.

Most powerful current production car

The McLaren F1 6.1 develops in excess of 627 bhp.

Largest engine capacity

The greatest engine capacity of a production car is 13.5 litres, for the US Pierce-Arrow 6–66 Raceabout (1912–18), the US Peerless 6–60 (1912–14) and the Fageol (1918).

Fastest road cars

The highest speed attained by a standard production car is 349.3 km/h (217.1 mph) by a Jaguar XJ220 driven by Martin Brundle at the Nardo Circuit, Italy, on 21 June 1992.

The highest reported road-tested acceleration is 0–60 mph in 3.07 seconds, by a Ford

WORLD'S MOST EXPENSI

Bugatti and first built in 1927. It has an eight-cylinder engine with a capacity of 12.7 litres, and is more than 6.7 m (22 ft) long. The bonnet is more than 2.13 m (7 ft) long.

Longest car

A 30.5-m-long (100-ft), 26-wheeled limo was designed by Jay Ohrberg of Burbank, California, USA. Its features include a swimming pool with a diving board and a king-sized waterbed. It can be driven as a rigid vehicle or modified to bend in the middle.

Speed and power

Highest land speed

The official one-mile land speed record is 1,019.467 km/h (633.468 mph), set by Richard Noble on 4 Oct 1983 over the Black Rock Desert, Nevada, USA, in his 17,000-lb

Fastest diesel-engined car

The prototype 3-litre Mercedes C111/3 attained 327.3 km/h (203.3 mph) in tests on the Nardo Circuit, Italy, from 5 to 15 Oct 1978. In April 1978 it averaged 314.5 km/h (195.4 mph) for 12 hours and covered a world record 3,773.5 km (2,344¾ miles).

Fastest electric car

General Motors' *Impact*, driven by Clive Roberts (GB) at Fort Stockton Test Center, Texas, USA, on 11 March 1994, achieved 295.832 km/h (183.822 mph) over a two-way flying kilometre.

Fastest steam car

On 19 Aug 1985, *Steamin' Demon*, built by the Barber-Nichols Engineering Co., reached a speed of 234.331 km/h (145.607 mph) at Bonneville Salt Flats, Utah, USA.

RS200 Evolution driven by Graham Hathaway at the Millbrook Proving Ground, Beds, UK, on 25 May 1994.

The fastest lap by a production car on a British circuit was by Colin Goodwin at Millbrook, Beds, on 8 Dec 1995 in a Jaguar 220S. His average speed was 290.4 km/h (180.4 mph) and the peak speed over 0.8 km (½ mile) was 294.5 km/h (183 mph).

Longest skid marks

The longest recorded skid marks left on a public road were 290 m (950 ft) long. They were made by a Jaguar that was involved in an accident on the M1 near Luton, Beds, UK, on 30 June 1960.

The skid marks that were made when the jet-powered *Spirit of America*, driven by Norman

Craig Breedlove, went out of control at Bonneville Salt Flats, Utah, USA, on 15 Oct 1964, were almost 9.6 km (6 miles) long.

Cost

Most expensive British car
The most expensive list-price British standard car is the McLaren F1 6.1, which costs £634,500 including tax.

Most expensive second-hand car
The highest confirmed price to have been paid for a used car is $15 million, for the 1931 Bugatti Type 41 Royale Sports Coupé by Kellner. The vehicle was sold to the Meitec Corporation of Japan by Nicholas Harley on 12 April 1990.

The greatest distance that has been travelled on the contents of a standard fuel tank is 2,153.4 km (1,338 miles), by an Audi 100 TDI diesel car with a capacity of 80.1 litres (17⅗ gal). Stuart Bladon, with RAC observer Robert Proctor, drove from John O' Groats to Land's End, returning to Scotland between 26 and 28 July 1992.

Oldest drivers
Layne Hall (b. 1880 or 1884) of Silver Creek, New York, USA, was issued with a driving licence on 15 June 1989. It was valid until his 113th birthday in 1993 (according to the date on the licence), but he died on 20 Nov 1990.

Maude Tull of Inglewood, California, USA, took to driving at the age of 91, when her husband

between two rubber traffic cones was now required, but 'high cone attrition' soon led to the substitution of white lines.

Worst driver
It was reported that a 75-year-old male driver received 10 traffic tickets, drove on the wrong side of the road four times, committed four hit-and-run offences and caused six accidents, all within 20 minutes, in McKinney, Texas, USA, on 15 Oct 1966.

On 27 Nov 1975, British driver John Hogg, aged 28, was sentenced to 5¾ years in gaol and received his third, fourth and fifth life bans for drunken driving in a stolen car while disqualified. For his previous 40 offences, Hogg had received bans of 71½ years, plus two life bans.

Above
The Jaguar XJ220 is the fastest standard production car, achieving a speed of 349.3 km/h (217.1 mph) at the Nardo Circuit in 1992.

Far left
The higher specification Jaguar 220S set the record for the fastest lap on a British circuit.

RRENT PRODUCTION CAR IS THE McLAREN F1 6.1

Driving

Highest car mileage
A 1963 Volkswagen 'Beetle' owned by Albert Klein of Pasadena, California, USA, had a mileage of 2,583,810 km (1,605,505 miles) by 4 July 1996.

Lowest petrol consumption
A vehicle specially designed by students of Lycée St Joseph la Joliverie, St Sébastien sur Loire, France, achieved a performance of 7,591 mpg in the Shell Mileage Marathon at Silverstone, Northants, UK, on 17 July 1992.

The consumption record for a production car is 103.01 mpg, in a Daihatsu Charade 1.0 turbo diesel driven by Helen Horwood, Joanne Swift and John Taylor around the coast of mainland Britain—a distance of 5,827 km (3,621 miles)—from 7 to 14 Oct 1991.

On 9 Aug 1989, Stuart Bladon drove a Citroen AX 14DTR 180.26 km (112 miles 17 yd) on one gallon of fuel on the M11 motorway in a test run.

The greatest distance travelled without refuelling in a standard vehicle is 2,724 km (1,691½ miles), by a 1991 Toyota LandCruiser diesel station wagon with factory optional 174-litre (38⅕-gal) twin fuel tanks, driven by Ewan Kennedy from Nyngan, NSW, Australia, to Winton, Queensland, and back from 18 to 21 May 1992. The average speed was 60 km/h (37 mph).

died. She was issued with a renewal on 5 Feb 1976, at the age of 104.

The oldest British driver on record is Edward Newsom of Brighton, E Sussex, who was still driving on his 104th birthday on 22 July 1995. Newsom bought his first car, a Model T Ford, in 1914, and has never made an insurance claim.

The most advanced age at which an individual first passed the Department of Transport driving test is 90 years 229 days, by Gerty Edwards Land (b. 1897) on 27 April 1988 in Colne, Lancs, UK.

Youngest driver
Stephen Andrew Blackbourn of Lincoln, UK, passed both his driving test and the advanced driving test within five hours on his 17th birthday on 20 Feb 1989. Stephen's brother Mark was the previous recordholder.

Driving tests
Git Kaur Randhawa (b. 1937) from Hayes, Middx, UK, finally passed the Department of Transport driving test on her 48th attempt on 19 June 1987. She had had more than 330 driving lessons.

The easiest driving tests in the world are those in Egypt, where the ability to advance and reverse a distance of 6 m (19 ft 8 in) is often deemed sufficient. In 1979, it was reported that the ability to reverse accurately

Car antics

Amphibious circumnavigation
The only circumnavigation by an amphibious vehicle was undertaken by Ben Carlin of Australia in his jeep *Half-Safe*. Carlin arrived back in Montreal, Canada, on 8 May 1958, having completed a circumnavigation of 62,765 km (39,000 miles) over land and 15,450 km (9,600 miles) by sea and river.

Trans-Americas
Garry Sowerby of Canada, with American Tim Cahill as co-driver and navigator, drove a 1988 GMC Sierra K3500 from Ushuaia, Tierra del Fuego, Argentina, to Prudhoe Bay, Alaska, USA—a distance of 23,720 km (14,739 miles) in a total elapsed time of 23 days 22 hr 43 min from 29 Sept to 22 Oct 1987. They were surface freighted from Cartagena, Colombia, to Balboa, Panama, to bypass the Darién Gap.

Two-wheel driving
The Swede Bengt Norberg drove 310.391 km (192 miles 1,525 yd) on two wheels of a Mitsubishi Colt GTi-16V in 7 hr 15 min 50 sec. He also drove 44.808 km (27 miles 1,480 yd) in one hour at Rattvik Horse Track, Sweden. Both records were set on 24 May 1989.

Sven-Erik Söderman of Sweden achieved a speed of 164.38 km/h (102.14 mph) over a 100-m flying start on two wheels of an Opel Kadett at Mora Siljan airport, Sweden, on 2 Aug 1990. He also achieved a record speed of 152.96 km/h (95.04 mph) for the flying kilometre at the same venue on 24 Aug 1990.

Specialized vehicles

Right
The two Marion eight-caterpillar crawlers that are used to convey shuttles to their launch pads are the world's largest crawlers, with a loaded train weight of 8,165 tonnes.

Rocket-powered sled
The highest speed for a rocket-powered sled unrailed and on ice is 399 km/h (247.93 mph) by 'Oxygen', driven by Sammy Miller on Lake George, New York, USA, on 15 Feb 1981.

Solar-powered vehicles
The highest speed achieved by a solely solar-powered land vehicle is 78.39 km/h (48.71 mph), by Molly Brennan in the General Motors Sunraycer at Mesa, Arizona, USA, on 24 June 1988.

The highest speed using solar/battery power is 135 km/h (83.9 mph) by Star Micronics'

WORLD'S MOST POWERF

Solar Star, driven by Manfred Hermann on 5 Jan 1991 at Richmond RAAF Base, Richmond, NSW, Australia.

Most powerful vehicles
Wrecker
The Twin City Garage and Body Shop's 20.6-tonne International M6-23 'Hulk' 1969, which is stationed at Scott City, Missouri, USA, is 11 m (36 ft) long and can lift more than 295 tonnes on its short boom.

Fire engine
The 860-hp, eight-wheel Oshkosh firetruck manufactured by Oshkosh Truck Corporation, Wisconsin, USA, weighs 60 tonnes and is used for aircraft and runway fires. It can discharge 189,000 litres (41,600 gal) of foam through two turrets in 2 min 30 sec.

Largest vehicles
Largest land vehicle
'Big Muskie', built by Bucyrus Erie, is a walking dragline (a machine that removes dirt from coal) weighing 13,200 tonnes. It is too expensive to run, but can be found at Central Ohio Coal Co., Muskingham site, Ohio, USA.

Longest vehicle
The 174.3-m-long (572-ft) Arctic Snow Train was built by R.G. Le Tourneau Inc., Longview, Texas, USA, for the US Army, and driven by a crew of six. It has 54 wheels, a gross weight of 400 tonnes and a top speed of 32 km/h (20 mph). Now owned by Steve McPeak, who

and cost a total of $12.3 million to construct. The loaded train weight is 8,165 tonnes. Now used to take shuttles to their launch pads, they have the world's largest windscreen wiper blades, at 106 cm (42 in).

Largest dumper truck
The Terex Titan 33–19 manufactured by General Motors Corporation and now in operation at Westar Mine, British Columbia, Canada, has a loaded weight of 548.6 tonnes and a capacity of 317.5 tonnes. It is 17 m (56 ft) tall when tipping. The 16-cylinder engine delivers 3,300 hp, and the fuel tank holds 5,910 litres (1,300 gal).

Buses
Longest bus
The 32.2-m-long (105-ft-8-in) articulated DAF Super CityTrain buses of Zaïre have 110

carries out repairs in the often sub-zero temperatures of Alaska, it generates 4,680 shaft horsepower and has a fuel capacity of 29,648 litres (6,522 gal).

Largest ambulance
Articulated Alligator Jumbulances (marks VI, VII, VIII and IX) operated by the ACROSS Trust to convey sick and handicapped people across Europe are 18 m (59 ft) long. Built by Van Hool of Belgium at a cost of £200,000, they can carry 44 patients and staff.

Largest crawler
The two Marion eight-caterpillar crawlers built to convey Saturn V rockets to their launch pads at Cape Canaveral, Florida, USA, each measure 40 x 34.7 m (131 ft 4 in x 114 ft)

Largest fork lift truck
In 1991, Kalmar LMV of Lidhult, Sweden, manufactured three counterbalanced fork lift trucks, capable of lifting loads of up to 90 tonnes. They were built in order to assist in the construction of two pipelines from Sarir to the Gulf of Sirte and from Tszirbu to Benghazi, Libya.

Highest speeds
Pedal car
The record for the journey from John O' Groats, Highland, to Land's End, Cornwall, UK, in a pedal car is 59 hr 21 min. It was achieved by a team of five from Lea Manor High School and Community College, Luton, UK, from 30 May to 1 June 1993.

passenger seats and room for 140 'strap-hangers' in the first trailer and 60 seated and 40 'strap-hangers' in the second. Designed by the president of the Republic of Zaïre, Citoyen Mobutu Sese Seko Kuku Ngbendu wa za Banga, they weigh 28 tonnes unladen.

Largest fleet
The 11,282 single-decker buses in São Paulo, Brazil, make up the world's largest bus fleet.

Longest bus route
Expreso Internacional Ormeño S.A. of Lima, Peru, operates a regular service between Caracas, Venezuela, and Buenos Aires, Argentina. The 9,660-km (6,003-mile) route takes 214 hours but includes a 12-hour stop in Santiago, Chile, and 24-hour stop in Lima.

Caravans

Largest caravan
A two-wheeled five-storey caravan was built in 1990 for H. E Sheik Hamad Bin Hamdan Al Nahyan of Abu Dhabi, United Arab Emirates. It is 20 m (66 ft) long, 12 m (39 ft) wide and weighs 120 tonnes. There are eight bedrooms and bathrooms, four garages and water storage for 24,000 litres (5,275 gal).

Longest caravan journey
The 231,288-km (143,716-mile) journey in a Volkswagen Camper by Harry B. Coleman and Peggy Larson from 20 Aug 1976 to 20 April 1978 took them through 113 countries.

Fastest caravan
The world speed record for a caravan tow is 204.02 km/h (126.77 mph), for a Roadstar caravan towed by a 1990 Ford EA Falcon saloon and driven by 'Charlie' Kovacs, at

Snowmobiles

Greatest distance
John Outzen and Andre, Carl and Denis Boucher drove snowmobiles 16,499.5 km (10,252⅓ miles) from Anchorage, Alaska, USA, to Dartmouth, Nova Scotia, Canada, in 56 riding days from 2 Jan to 3 March 1992.

Tony Lenzini of Duluth, Minnesota, USA, drove his 1986 Arctic Cat Cougar snowmobile 11,604.9 km (7,211 miles) in 60 riding days between 28 Dec 1985 and 20 March 1986.

Taxis

Largest fleet
Mexico City has a fleet of 60,000 taxis.

Longest fare
Jeremy Levine, Mark Aylett and Carlos Aresse travelled from London, UK, to Cape Town,

South Africa and back from 3 June to 17 Oct 1994. Their 34,908-km (21,691-mile) trip cost £40,210.

Trams

Longest tram journey
The 105.5-km (65½-mile) trip from Krefeld St Tönis to Witten Annen Nord, Germany, can be achieved in 5 hr 30 min.

Largest tram system
St Petersburg, Russia, has the most extensive tramway system, with 2,402 cars on 64 routes and 690.6 km (429¹⁄₁₀ miles) of track.

Oldest trams
The oldest trams in revenue service are motorcars 1 and 2 of the Manx Electric Railway, running from Douglas and Ramsay, Isle of Man, British Isles, dating from 1893.

RE ENGINE CAN PUMP UP TO 189,000 LITRES OF FOAM IN 2 MIN 30 SEC

Mangalore Airfield, Seymour, Victoria, Australia, on 18 April 1991.

Go-karts

Outdoor mileage
The highest 24-hour mileage on an outdoor circuit by a four-man team is 1664.7 km (1,034⅖ miles) on a 1.3-km (⅘-mile) track at Brooklands, Weybridge, Surrey, UK, on 24–25 Feb 1995, by Stefan Dennis, David Brabham, and Russ and Steve Malkin.

Indoor mileage
The highest 24-hour mileage on an indoor track by a four-man team driving 160 cc karts is 1,422.6 km (883⁹⁄₁₀ miles) at the Welsh Karting Centre, Cardiff, UK, on 26 Nov 1993. The drivers were Ian O'Sullivan, Paul Marram, Richard Jenkins and Michael Watts.

Lawn mowers

Widest mower
The widest gang mower in the world is the 5-ton, 27-unit 'Big Green Machine' used by turf

ORAGE FOR 24,000 LITRES

farmer Jay Edgar Frick of Monroe, Ohio, USA. It is 18 m (60 ft) wide and can mow up to an acre a minute.

Greatest distance covered
A 12-hour run-behind record of 169.1 km (105¹⁄₁₀ miles) was set at Wisborough Green, W Sussex, UK, on 28–29 July 1990 by the 'Doctor's Flyers' team.

The greatest distance to have been covered in the annual 12-hour Lawn Mower Race (which operates under the rules of the British Lawn Mower Racing Association) is 468 km (291 miles), by John Gill, Robert Jones and Steve Richardson of Team Gilliams at Wisborough Green, W Sussex, UK, on 1 and 2 Aug 1992.

Left
The Terex Titan 33–19 is the world's largest dumper truck, with a capacity of 317.5 tonnes. The largest production tyres (not shown), designed for use by dumper trucks, measure 3.82 m (12 ft 6¼ in), and are made by the Bridgestone Corporation based in Tokyo, Japan.

Roads and services

LONGEST ROAD IS THE 24,140-KM PAN-AMERICAN HIGHWAY

Roads

Largest road system
The USA has the largest road system in terms of length, with a total of 6,284,500 km (3,905,000 miles) of graded roads.

Longest roads
The longest motorable road is the Pan-American Highway, which stretches from north-west Alaska, USA, to Santiago, Chile, then eastward to Buenos Aires, Argentina, before terminating in Brasilia, Brazil. It is more than 24,140 km (15,000 miles) long, with a small incomplete section in Panama and Colombia known as the Darién Gap.

The longest designated road in the United Kingdom is the 648-km-long (403-mile) A1 from London to Edinburgh.

Highest roads
The world's highest road is above the Changlung Valley in Aksai Chin (administered by China, but claimed by India) at an altitude of about 5,889 m (19,320 ft). This Chinese military road is not open to foreign traffic.

The highest unclassified road in the United Kingdom is a private lane leading to the summit of Great Dun Fell, Cumbria, which reaches an altitude of 847 m (2,780 ft). The road leads to a Ministry of Defence and Air Traffic Control installation, and a permit is required to use it.

The highest classified road in the United Kingdom is the A93 over the Grampians, which reaches an altitude of 665 m (2,182 ft) at the Cairnwell Pass.

Lowest roads
A road along the shores of the Dead Sea in Israel is 393 m (1,290 ft) below sea level.

The lowest surface road in the United Kingdom is north-east of Holme, Cambs. It is 1.62 m (5 ft 4 in) below sea level.

Widest roads
The widest road is the 2.4-km-long (1½-mile) Monumental Axis from the Municipal Plaza to the Plaza of the Three Powers in Brasilia, Brazil. The six-lane boulevard was opened in April 1960 and is 250 m (820 ft) wide.

The San Francisco–Oakland Bay Bridge Toll Plaza, California, USA, has 23 lanes to serve the bridge in Oakland.

There are 17 carriageway lanes side-by-side on the M61 at Linnyshaw Moss, Worsley, Greater Manchester, UK.

Busiest roads
Interstate 405 (the San Diego Freeway) in Orange County, California, USA, has a peak-hour volume of 25,500 vehicles on a 1.5-km

(⁹⁄₁₀-mile) stretch between Garden Grove Freeway and Seal Beach Boulevard.

The greatest traffic volume on a British motorway is 165,000 vehicles a day on the M25/M4 to M25/A3313 (Airport Way).

The busiest non-motorway road in the United Kingdom is the A3 Broadway/Kingston bypass/Kingston Road to Malden Road/Kingston bypass, with 125,000 vehicles per day.

Gibraltar has the highest traffic density in the world. In 1993, there were 767 vehicles per mile of serviceable road—a density of one vehicle per 2.09 m (6 ft 10½ in).

Traffic jams
The longest traffic jam on record extended 176 km (109 miles) from Lyon towards Paris, France, on 16 Feb 1980.

The worst traffic jams in the United Kingdom were each 64.3 km (40 miles) long. The first occurred on the M1 between Junction 16 (Milton Keynes) and Junction 18 (Rugby) on 5 April 1985. The second was on the M6 between Charnock Richard and Carnforth, Lancs, on 17 April 1987, and involved around 200,000 people and 50,000 vehicles.

The longest line of solid stationary traffic in the United Kingdom stretched 35.4 km (22 miles) from midway between Junction 9 (Leatherhead) and Junction 8 (Reigate) on the M25 on 17 Aug 1988.

Biggest traffic flow
An estimated total of 1.5 million cars crawled bumper-to-bumper over several crossings of the border between East and West Germany on 12 April 1990 (the start of the first Easter weekend after the fall of the Berlin Wall).

'SPAGHETTI JUNCTION' IS THE MOST COMPL

WORLD'S LOWE

Worst road accident
A petrol tanker exploded inside Salang Tunnel in Afghanistan on 3 Nov 1982, officially killing 176 people, although western estimates gave the number of deaths at around 1,100.

The worst road accident in the United Kingdom was a coach crash near Grassington, N Yorkshire, on 27 May 1975, in which 33 people died.

Most complex British interchange
The most complicated interchange is situated at Gravelly Hill north of Birmingham, on the Midland Link Motorway section of the M6. Popularly known as 'Spaghetti Junction', it has 18 routes on six levels, together with a diverted canal and river. It consists of 26,000 tonnes of steel, 250,000 tonnes of concrete

Longest street 1,896.3 km

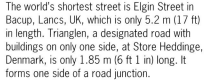

and 300,000 tonnes of earth, and cost £8.2 million to construct.

Junction intervals
A southbound driver who misses the exit at Junction 10 on the M11 in Herts, UK, has to drive 28.6 km (17¾ miles) to Junction 8. Junction 9 is only open to northbound drivers.

The shortest gap between motorway exits is less than 160 m (643 ft), between junctions 19 and 18 on the M8 in Glasgow, UK.

Longest ring-road
The M25 London Orbital Motorway is 195.5 km (121½ miles) long. Constructed from 1972 to 1986, it cost an estimated £909 million (£7.5 million per mile).

Streets
The world's longest street is Yonge Street, which extends 1,896.3 km (1,178³⁄₁₀ miles) north and west from Toronto, Canada, to Rainy River on the Ontario–Minnesota border.

The narrowest street in the world is Vicolo della Virilita (Virility Alley) in Ripatransone in Italy's Marche region. It averages 43 cm (1 ft 5 in) in width but is just 38 cm (1 ft 3 in) wide at the narrowest point.

The world's shortest street is Elgin Street in Bacup, Lancs, UK, which is only 5.2 m (17 ft) in length. Trianglen, a designated road with buildings on only one side, at Store Heddinge, Denmark, is only 1.85 m (6 ft 1 in) long. It forms one side of a road junction.

The steepest street in the world is Baldwin Street, Dunedin, New Zealand, which has a maximum gradient of 1 in 1.266.

The steepest motorable road in the British Isles is the unclassified Chimney Bank at Rosedale Abbey, N Yorkshire, which is signposted '1 in 3'. The county surveyor states that it is 'not quite' a 33% gradient.

An unclassified road at Ffordd Penllech, Harlech, UK, officially described as not suitable for motor vehicles, is 1 in 2.91 at its steepest point.

Services
Largest parking areas
The largest parking areas in the world are at the West Edmonton Mall, Alberta, Canada, and at the National Exhibition Centre, Birmingham, W Midlands, UK, which can both hold 20,000 vehicles.

Largest filling station
The world's largest concentration of petrol pumps is in Jeddah, Saudi Arabia. Of the 204 pumps, 96 are Tokheim Unistar (electronic) and 108 are Tokheim Explorer (mechanical).

Longest tow
The Automobile Association used a Land Rover to tow a replica Model T Ford van 8,038 km (4,995 miles) from Ascot, Berks, to Wimerpool, Notts, UK, on 4–12 May 1993.

Largest garage
The KMB Overhaul Centre, which is operated by the Kowloon Motor Bus Co. Ltd, Hong Kong, is the largest multi-storey service centre in the world. Built for double-decker buses, its four floors occupy more than 47,000 m² (506,000 ft²).

OAD INTERCHANGE IN THE UNITED KINGDOM, WITH 18 ROUTES ON SIX LEVELS

JAD IS 393 M BELOW SEA LEVEL ALONG THE SHORES OF THE DEAD SEA IN ISRAEL

Centre
The most complicated interchange on the British road network is 'Spaghetti Junction', situated on the M6 north of Birmingham.

Left
A record traffic flow of 1.5 million cars queued to cross the border from East Germany into West Germany on 12 April 1990.

Trains and railways

Trains

Below
Built between 1891 and 1905, the Trans-Siberian Railway connects the cities of European Russia with Vladivostok on the Pacific coast. The three main lines cross eight time zones.

Below right
France's high-speed TGVs (right of picture) allow it to operate the world's fastest rail service. The TGVs carry passengers at an average speed of 268 km/h (167mph) on three lines, the TGV Atlantique, the TGV Nord Europe and the TGV Sud Est.

Earliest trains

Wagons running on wooden rails were used for mining as early as 1550 at Leberthal, Alsace, France.

In the United Kingdom, trains were used to convey coal from Strelley to Wollaton near Nottingham from 1604 to 1615. They were also employed at Broseley Colliery, Shrops, in Oct 1605.

Richard Trevithick built his first steam locomotive for the 91.4-cm (3-ft) gauge iron plateway at Coalbrookdale, Shrops, UK, in 1803, but there is no evidence that it ran. His second locomotive drew wagons in a demonstration run at Penydarren, Merthyr Tydfil, UK, on 22 Feb 1804, but the vehicle broke the plate rails.

West rail system are also designed to run at 300 km/h (186 mph) in regular service.

The fastest point-to-point schedule is between Paris and St Pierre des Corps, near Tours. The 232-km (144-mile) trip takes 55 minutes at an average speed of 253 km/h (157 mph).

The highest ratified speed for a steam locomotive is 201 km/h (125 mph) over a distance of 402 m (440 yd). On 3 July 1938, the LNER 4-6-2 No. 4468 *Mallard* hauled seven coaches with a gross weight of 243 tonnes down Stoke Bank, near Essendine, between Grantham, Lincs, and Peterborough, Cambs, UK. The engine was damaged on the middle big-end bearing.

British Rail inaugurated their daily HST (High Speed Train) service between London, Bristol

It is powered by the fastest locomotives in service, the Class 91 25 kV electric type. On 2 June 1995, these locomotives powered the fastest train to carry fare-paying passengers, reaching a speed of 247.8 km/h (154 mph).

Most powerful locomotives

The most powerful steam locomotive in terms of tractive effort is No. 700, a triplex or triple-articulated six-cylinder 2-8-8-8-4 engine built in 1916 for the Virginian Railway, USA. Its tractive force was 75,433 kg (166,300 lb) when working compound and 90,519 kg (199,560 lb) when working simple.

The heaviest train hauled by a single engine is believed to be one of 15,545 tonnes, made up of 250 freight cars stretching 2.5 km (1.6 miles), pulled by the 2-8-8-8-2 *Matt H. Shay* (No. 5014). It ran on the Erie Railroad, USA, from 1914 until 1929.

Greatest load

The strongest rail carrier is the 336-tonne, 36-axle, 92-m-long (301-ft 10-in) 'Schnabel', which has a capacity of 807 tonnes and was

The first permanent public railway to use steam traction from its opening, on 27 Sept 1825, was the Stockton & Darlington Railway from Shildon to Stockton via Darlington, in Co. Durham, UK. The 7-tonne *Locomotion* could pull 48 tonnes at 24 km/h (15 mph). It was designed by George Stephenson.

Fastest speeds

The highest speed attained by a railed vehicle is 9,851 km/h (6,121 mph, or Mach 8), by an unmanned rocket sled over the 15.2-km (9½-mile) track at White Sands Missile Range, New Mexico, USA, on 5 Oct 1982.

The highest speed recorded on a national rail system is 515.3 km/h (320.2 mph), by the French SNCF high-speed TGV (Train à Grande Vitesse) Atlantique between Courtalain and Tours on 18 May 1990. TGV Atlantique and Nord services now run at up to 300 km/h (186 mph), as does the French portion of the Eurostar service between London and Paris. The New Series 500 trains for Japan's JR

and South Wales on 4 Oct 1976. One of the InterCity 125 trains used holds the world speed record for diesel trains, at 238 km/h (148 mph). This was set on a test run between Darlington and York on 1 Nov 1987.

The electric British Rail APT (Advanced Passenger Train) travelled at 262 km/h (163 mph) during technical trials on 20 Dec 1979. On its first revenue-earning run on 7 Dec 1981, it set a fastest Glasgow-to-London time of 4 hr 15 min but was later withdrawn from service because of technical problems.

The fastest trains in regular service in the United Kingdom run on the East Coast mainline between London (King's Cross) and Edinburgh. *The Scottish Pullman* is scheduled to cover the 633.2 km (393½ miles) in 4 hr 5 min, with two stops. Its average speed is 155.1 km/h (96.4 mph). The same train covers the 302.8 km (188⅛ miles) between London and York in 1 hr 45 min, reaching an average speed of 171.4 km/h (106.5 mph).

built for a US railway by Krupp, Germany, in March 1981.

The heaviest load to have been moved on rails is the 10,860-tonne Church of the Virgin Mary in Oct–Nov 1975. Built in 1548 in Most (now in the Czech Republic), the church was in the way of coal workings and was moved 730 m (800 yd) at 0.002 km/h (0.0013 mph) over four weeks, at a cost of £9 million.

Freight trains

The longest and heaviest freight train on record made a run on the 106.5-cm (3-ft 6-in) gauge Sishen–Saldanha railway in South Africa on 26–27 Aug 1989. It consisted of 660 wagons (each loaded to 105 tons gross), a tank car and a caboose, moved by nine 50 kV electric and seven diesel-electric locomotives distributed along the train. It was 7.3 km (4½ miles) long and weighed 69,393 tons (excluding locomotives), and travelled a distance of 861 km (535 miles) in 22 hr 40 min.

Longest passenger train
A 1,732.9-m-long (1,895-yd) passenger train had 70 coaches pulled by one electric locomotive, and weighed 2,786 tonnes. Owned by the National Belgian Railway Company, it took 1 hr 11 min 5 sec to cover the 62.5-km (38¾-mile) journey from Ghent to Ostend, Belgium, on 27 April 1991.

Tracks
Longest tracks
The longest rail journey that can be made without changing trains is 9,297 km (5,777 miles) on the Trans-Siberian line from Moscow to Vladivostok in Russia. There are 70 stops on the fastest regular journey, which is scheduled to take 6 days 12 hr 45 min.

Longest straight track
The Trans-Australian line over the Nullarbor Plain, run by Australian National Railways, is dead straight although not level for 478 km (297 miles) from Mile 496 between Nurina and Loongana, W Australia, to Mile 793, between Ooldea and Watson, S Australia.

bored tunnel and 32 km (20 miles) are 'cut and cover'. The 547-train system is operated by a staff of 14,000 serving 267 stations. Passengers made a total of 764 million journeys in 1994–95.

The underground system with the most stations is MTA New York City Transit, USA. There are 468 stations (277 underground) in a network covering 383 km (238 miles). The system carries an estimated 7.1 million passengers daily.

Underground tour
The record time for a tour of the London Underground, taking in every station, is 18 hr 18 min 9 sec, by Robert Robinson of Little Sandhurst, Surrey, and Tom McLaughlin of Finchampstead, Berks, UK, on 4 Oct 1994.

Busiest system
The Greater Moscow Metro, Russia, which was opened in 1935, has between 3.2 and 3.3 billion passengers a year. It has a total of 4,143 railcars, 158 stations and 255.7 km (158⅞ miles) of track.

Cornwall (southernmost) and Arisaig, Scotland (westernmost)—in 37 hr 14 min on 11–12 Sept 1995.

Most miles covered in one week
Andrew Kingsmell and Sean Andrews of Bromley, Kent, and Graham Bardouleau of Crawley, W Sussex, UK, travelled 21,090 km (13,105 miles) on the French national railway system in 6 days 22 hr 38 min, between 28 Nov and 5 Dec 1992.

Most miles covered in 24 hours
The greatest distance to have been travelled in the United Kingdom in 24 hours without duplicating any part of the journey is 2,842.5km (1,766¼ miles), by Norma and Jonathan Carter, aged 15, on 3–4 Sept 1992.

Longest journey
Ralph Ransome of Birchington, Kent, UK, commuted to London by British Rail for 73 years. The total distance that he covered during this time was estimated to be equivalent to travelling around the world 39 times. He retired on 5 Feb 1986, aged 93.

Highest and lowest lines
The standard gauge 143.5-cm (4-ft 8½-in) track on the Morococha branch of the Peruvian State Railways at La Cima is 4,818 m (15,806 ft) above sea level.

The Seikan Tunnel, which crosses the Tsugaro Strait between Honshū and Hokkaidō, Japan, descends to 240 m (787 ft) below sea level. It was opened in March 1988 and is 53.85 km (33 miles 811 yd) long.

Steepest railways
The Katoomba Scenic Railway in the Blue Mountains of NSW, Australia, is 311 m

Left
The London Underground is the world's largest underground railway system. It is 393 km (244 miles) long and has a fleet of 547 trains with a total of 3,985 carriages. Moorgate station has 10 platforms, a number not equalled by any other London Underground station except Baker Street.

(1,020 ft) long with a gradient of 1 in 0.82. A 220-hp electric winding machine hauls the car by twin cables 2.2 cm (⅞ in) in diameter.

The steepest gradient worked by adhesion is 1 in 11, between Chedde and Servoz on the metre-gauge SNCF Chamonix line, France.

Busiest rail system
In 1994, the East Japan Railway Co. carried 16,600,000 passengers daily and had a revenue of $19.5 billion.

Longest rail system
The USA has the longest rail network, with 271,619 km (168,776 miles) of track.

Underground railways
Most extensive systems
The most extensive underground or rapid transit railway system is the London Underground, UK. Its total length is 393 km (244 miles), of which 139 km (86 miles) are

Rail travel
Visits to all stations
Between 13 July and 28 Aug 1980, Alan M. Witton, of Chorlton, Manchester, UK, took 18 days 20 hr 16 min to visit 2,362 British Rail stations (every station that was open) in a continuous tour for charity that covered a total of 26,703 km (16,593 miles).

Colin M. Mulvany and Seth N. Vafiadis, of London, UK, visited 2,378 British Rail stations (every open station). They also travelled on the Tyne & Wear, Glasgow and London underground systems (a total of 333 stations) for charity. They travelled 24,990 km (15,528 miles) in 31 days 5 hr 8 min 58 sec, from 4 June to 5 July 1984, averaging a speed of 61.2 km/h (38.1 mph).

Visits to the remotest stations
Roger Elliott of Scunthorpe, Lincs, UK, visited the remotest stations of the United Kingdom—Thurso, Scotland (northernmost), Lowestoft, Suffolk (easternmost), Penzance,

Longest issued railway ticket
A 34.1-m-long (111-ft 10½-in) ticket was issued to Ronald, Norma and Jonathan Carter for a series of journeys throughout England between 15 and 23 Feb 1992.

Most countries visited in 24 hours
The record for the most countries to have been travelled through entirely by train within 24 hours is 11, by Alison Bailey, Ian Bailey, John English and David Kellie on 1–2 May 1993. Their journey began in Hungary and continued through Slovakia, the Czech Republic, Austria, Germany, back into Austria, Liechtenstein, Switzerland, France, Luxembourg, Belgium and the Netherlands and lasted 22 hr 10 min.

Longest stairway
The longest stairway in the world is the service staircase for the Niesenbahn funicular railway near Spiez, Switzerland, which is 1,669 m (5,476 ft) high. It has 11,674 steps and a bannister.

Aircraft

Right
The *Graf Zeppelin*—seen here housed in a naval hangar at Sumigaura aerodrome, Japan—was greeted by large crowds on its arrival in Tokyo in Sept 1929. It had achieved fame by setting airship distance records which still stand today.

Largest wingspan 97.51 m

The smallest monoplane ever flown is the *Baby Bird*, designed and built by Donald R. Stits. It is 3.35 m (11 ft) long, with a wingspan of 1.91 m (6 ft 3 in), and weighs 114.3 kg (252 lb) empty. It is powered by a 41.25-kW (55-hp) two-cylinder Hirth engine, giving a top speed of 177 km/h (110 mph). It was first flown by Harold Nemer on 4 Aug 1984 at Camarillo, California, USA.

Fastest airliners
The Tupolev Tu-144, first flown on 31 Dec 1968, was reported to have reached Mach 2.4, but normal cruising speed was Mach 2.2. It flew at Mach 1 for the first time on 5 June 1969 and exceeded Mach 2 on 26 May 1970, the first commercial transport to do so. Scheduled services began on 26 Dec 1975, flying freight and mail.

The BAC/Aérospatiale Concorde, first flown on 2 March 1969, cruises at up to Mach 2.2 and became the first supersonic airliner used on passenger services on 21 Jan 1976. The New York to London record is 2 hr 54 min 30 sec, set on 14 April 1990.

Airliners with the greatest capacity
The Airbus Super Transporter A300-600ST *Beluga* has a main cargo compartment volume of 1,400 m³ (49,441 ft³) and a maximum take-off weight of 150 tonnes. Its wingspan is 44.84 m (147 ft 1 in), its overall length is 56.16 m (184 ft 3 in) and the usable length of its cargo compartment is 37.7 m (123 ft 8 in). Altogether, four such aircraft are to be built.

The production airliner with the greatest capacity is the Ukrainian Antonov An-124 *Ruslan*, which has a cargo hold with a usable volume of 1,014 m³ (35,800 ft³) and a maximum take-off weight of 405 tonnes.

The Antonov An-225 *Mriya* (Dream), a modified version of the An-124, has been developed with a stretched fuselage providing as much as 1,190 m³ (42,000 ft³) of usable volume. Its cargo compartment has an unobstructed 43 m (141 ft) hold length, with a maximum width and height of 6.4 m (21 ft) and 4.4 m (14 ft 5 in) respectively.

The jet airliner with the highest capacity is the Boeing 747-400, which entered service with Northwest Airlines on 31 Jan 1989. It has a wingspan of 64.9 m (213 ft), a range of 13,340 km (8,290 miles) and can carry up to 566 passengers.

Most flights by a jet airliner
A McDonnell Douglas DC-9 Series 14, currently in service with Northwest Airlines, had made 100,746 flights by 1 Feb 1996. The aircraft was delivered new to Delta Air Lines in Sept 1966.

The most hours recorded by a jet airliner still in service is 99,825 hours, flown up to 1 March 1996 by a Boeing 747-200F in

Aircraft

Largest wingspan
The eight-engined, 193-tonne Hughes H4 Hercules flying-boat, usually dubbed the *Spruce Goose*, has a wingspan of 97.51 m (319 ft 11 in) and is 66.65 m (218 ft 8 in) long. It was raised 21.3 m (70 ft) into the air in a test run by Howard Hughes (1905–76), off Long Beach Harbor, California, USA, on 2 Nov 1947, but never flew again.

Among current aircraft, the Ukrainian Antonov An-124 has a 73.3-m (240-ft 5¾-in) wingspan.

A modified six-engine version of the An-124 known as Antonov An-225 *Mriya* (Dream), built to carry the former Soviet space shuttle *Buran*, has a wingspan of 88.4 m (290 ft).

Heaviest aircraft
The aircraft with the highest standard maximum take-off weight is the 600-tonne

Antonov An-225. One An-225—flown by Capt. Aleksandr Galunenko and a crew of seven pilots—lifted a payload of 156,300 kg (344,582 lb) to a height of 12,410 m (40,715 ft) on 22 March 1989. The flight covered a distance of 2,100 km (1,305 miles) in 3 hr 47 min.

Smallest aircraft
The smallest biplane ever flown was *Bumble Bee Two*, designed and built by Robert H. Starr of Tempe, Arizona, USA, and capable of carrying one person. It was 2.69 m (8 ft 10 in) long, with a wingspan of 1.68 m (5 ft 6 in), and weighed 179.6 kg (396 lb) empty. The highest speed attained was 306 km/h (190 mph). On 8 May 1988, after flying to a height of 120 m (400 ft), it crashed, and was totally destroyed.

service with Korean Air. The aircraft was delivered new to Lufthansa in March 1972.

Oldest jet airliner
The oldest jet airliner still in service is a Boeing 707-138 currently in operation with the Royal Saudi Arabian Air Force. It was rolled out after manufacture on 11 Feb 1959 and delivered to Qantas. It was acquired by Saudi Arabia in 1987.

Longest scheduled flights
The longest current non-stop scheduled flight is 12,823 km (7,968 miles), by South African Airways' New York–Johannesburg flight.

In terms of time taken, the longest flight is 15 hr 10 min, from Osaka to Istanbul with Turkish Airlines.

Longest non-service flights
The longest non-stop flight by a commercial airliner was 18,545 km (10,007 nautical miles), from Auckland, New Zealand, to Paris, France, in 21 hr 46 min on 17 and 18 June 1993 by the Airbus Industrie A340-200.

A Boeing 767-200ER Royal Brunei Airlines flight from Seattle, Washington, USA, to Nairobi, Kenya, from 8 to 9 June 1990 set a new speed and endurance record for the longest delivery flight by a twin-engined commercial jet. A great-circle distance of 14,856 km (8,016 nautical miles) was covered in 18 hr 29 min.

Speed
Fastest jet
The USAF Lockheed SR-71, a reconnaissance aircraft, is the fastest jet. First flown in its definitive form on 22 Dec 1964, it was reportedly capable of reaching almost 30,000 m (100,000 ft). It had a wingspan of 16.94 m (55 ft 7 in), a length of 32.73 m (107 ft 5 in) and weighed 77.1 tonnes at take-off. A speed of 3,529.56 km/h (2,193.17 mph) was achieved by a Lockheed SR-71A in July 1976.

Fastest combat jet
The fastest jet ever built for combat is the former Soviet Mikoyan MiG-25 fighter (NATO code name 'Foxbat'). The single-seat 'Foxbat-A' has a wingspan of 13.95 m (45 ft 9 in), is 23.82 m (78 ft 2 in) long, and has an estimated maximum take-off weight of 37.4 tonnes. The reconnaissance 'Foxbat-B' has been tracked by radar at approximately Mach 3.2.

Fastest piston-engined aircraft
On 21 Aug 1989, in Las Vegas, Nevada, USA, the *Rare Bear*, a modified Grumman F8F Bearcat piloted by Lyle Shelton, set the FAI approved world record for a 3-km (1⅞-mile) course with a speed of 850.24 km/h (528.33 mph).

Fastest propeller-driven aircraft
The former Soviet Tu-95/142 (NATO code-name *Bear*) has four 11,033 kW (14,795 hp) engines driving eight-blade contra-rotating propellers, with a maximum level speed of Mach 0.82.

The turboprop-powered Republic XF-84H experimental US fighter, which flew on 22 July 1955, had a top design speed of 1,078 km/h (670 mph), but was abandoned.

Airships
Earliest airship flight
Henri Giffard travelled the 27 km (17 miles) from Paris to Trappes, France, in his 43.8-m (144-ft) long steam-powered coal-gas airship on 24 Sept 1852.

Largest airships
The 213.9-tonne German *Hindenburg* (LZ 129) and the *Graf Zeppelin II* (LZ 130) each had a length of 245 m (803 ft 10 in) and a capacity of 200,000 m³ (7,062,100 ft³). The *Hindenburg* first flew in 1936, and the *Graf Zeppelin II* in 1938.

Greatest passenger load
The most people carried in an airship was 207, in the US Navy *Akron* in 1931.

G-BOAG

The transatlantic record is 117, by the German *Hindenburg* in 1937. It exploded at Lakehurst, New Jersey, USA, on 6 May 1937.

Greatest distance travelled
The FAI accredited straight-line record is 6,384.5 km (3,967¹⁄₁₀ miles), by the German *Graf Zeppelin*, captained by Dr Hugo Eckener, between 29 Oct and 1 Nov 1928.

From 21 to 25 Nov 1917, the German *Zeppelin* (L59) flew from Yambol, Bulgaria, to south of Khartoum, Sudan, and returned, covering at least 7,250 km (4,500 miles).

Longest flights
The longest recorded flight without refuelling by a non-rigid airship is 264 hr 12 min, by a US Navy Goodyear-built ZPG-2 class ship. Comdr. J. R. Hunt of the USN took off from South Weymouth Naval Air Station, Massachusetts, USA, on 4 March 1957, and flew 15,205 km (9,448 miles), landing back at Key West, Florida, USA, on 15 March.

Above
With a cruising speed of Mach 2.2, the Concorde is the fastest passenger airliner in the world. When the first passenger services began on 21 Jan 1976, there were simultaneous take-offs from London, UK, by the British Airways Concorde, and from Paris, France, by the Air France Concorde.

Left
American millionaire Howard Hughes' *Spruce Goose*—the plane with the world's largest wingspan—only flew once, for 914 m (1,000 yd).

Flying

Flights

Earliest flights

The first hop by a man-carrying aeroplane travelling entirely under its own power was made when Clément Ader flew in his *Eole* for about 50 m (164 ft) at Armainvilliers, France, on 9 Oct 1890. The machine was powered by a lightweight steam engine of his own design, which developed about 15 kW (20 hp).

The world's first controlled and sustained power-driven flight took place near the Kill Devil Hills, Kitty Hawk, North Carolina,

Below
The famous pointed nose of the Concorde is an eyecatching sight for plane spotters. The oldest Briton to fly celebrated her 110th birthday on the supersonic airliner.

USA, on 17 Dec 1903, when Orville Wright flew the 9 kW (12 hp) *Flyer I* 36.5 m (120 ft) at an airspeed of 48 km/h (30 mph), a ground speed of 10.9 km/h (6.8 mph) and an altitude of 2.5–3.5 m (8–12 ft) for about 12 seconds.

First jet-engined flight

The first ever flight by an aeroplane powered by a turbojet engine was made by the Heinkel He 178, piloted by Flugkapitän Erich Warsitz, at Marienehe, Germany, on 27 Aug 1939. The machine was powered by a Heinkel He S3b engine weighing 378 kg (834 lb) and designed by Dr Hans Pabst von Ohain.

First supersonic flight

On 14 Oct 1947, Capt. Charles Elwood Yeager flew over Lake Muroc, California, USA, in a Bell XS-1 rocket aircraft at an altitude of 12,800 m (42,000 ft), reaching Mach 1.015.

First transatlantic flights

The first crossing of the North Atlantic by air was by Lt. Comdr. Albert Cushion Read and his crew, who flew from Trepassey Harbor, Newfoundland, Canada, via the Azores, to Lisbon, Portugal, in the 155-km/h (84-knot)

US Navy/Curtiss flying-boat NC-4 from 16 to 27 May 1919. The whole 7,591-km (4,717-mile) flight, which originated at Rockaway Air Station, Long Island, New York, USA, on 8 May and ended at Plymouth, Devon, UK, on 31 May, took 53 hr 58 min.

The first non-stop transatlantic flight was achieved 18 days later, when Capt. John Williams Alcock and his navigator Lt. Arthur Whitton Brown left Lester's Field, St John's, Newfoundland, Canada, at 4:13 p.m. GMT on 14 June 1919, and landed at Derrygimla bog near Clifden, Co. Galway, Republic of Ireland, at 8:40 a.m. GMT on 15 June. They had covered 3,154 km (1,960 miles) in their Vickers Vimy, powered by two 270 kW (360 hp) Rolls-Royce Eagle VIII engines.

WORLD'S LONGEST EVER FLIGHT LASTED MORE THAN 64 DAYS AND COVERED

Top speed 3,529.56 km/h

Wilbur Wright photographs a test flight of his brother Orville in 1909. By then they had started to make exhibition flights in Europe as well as the United States.

First transpacific flight
The first non-stop transpacific flight was made by Major Clyde Pangborn and Hugh Herndon in the Bellanca cabin monoplane *Miss Veedol*. They took off from Sabishiro Beach, Japan, and covered the 7,335 km (4,558 miles) to Wenatchee, Washington State, USA, in 41 hr 13 min from 3 to 5 Oct 1931.

First circumnavigational flights
The earliest strict circumnavigation (whereby the craft must pass through two antipodal points and cover a minimum distance of 40,007.86 km or 24,859 miles 1,280 yd) was made by two US Army Douglas DWC seaplanes in 57 'hops' from 6 April to 28 Sept 1924, beginning and ending at Seattle, Washington State, USA. The *Chicago*, piloted by Lt. Lowell H. Smith and Lt. Leslie P. Arnold, and the *New Orleans*, piloted by Lt. Erik H. Nelson and Lt. John Harding, covered the 42,398 km (26,345 miles) in 371 hr 11 min.

The first circumnavigation without refuelling was by Richard G. Rutan and Jeana Yeager, in their specially constructed aircraft *Voyager* from Edwards Air Force Base, California, USA, from 14 to 23 Dec 1986. In 9 days 3 min 44 sec they covered 40,212 km (24,987 miles), averaging 186.11 km/h (115.65 mph).

Longest flight
Pilots Robert Timm and John Cook set the duration record when they took off from

Fastest transatlantic flight
Major James V. Sullivan and Major Noel F. Widdifield flew a Lockheed SR-71A 'Blackbird' eastwards on 1 Sept 1974 and crossed the Atlantic in 1 hr 54 min 56.4 sec. The average speed, reduced by refuelling from a Boeing KC-135 tanker aircraft, was 2,908.02 km/h (1,806.96 mph) on the 5,570.80-km (3,461½-mile) New York–London stage.

evacuation of Ethiopian Jews from Addis Ababa to Israel in Operation Solomon, which began on 24 May 1991. The figure included two babies born during the flight, which was made by an El Al Airlines Boeing 747.

Oldest pilots
Col. Clarence Cornish of Indianapolis, Indiana, USA, was still flying aircraft at the age of 96.

Left
At the age of 96, retired Army Col. Clarence Cornish prepares to take off on another flight. Since he had his pacemaker fitted, he always takes the precaution of having a fellow pilot with him, but he handles all the controls himself.

STANCE EQUAL TO SIX TIMES AROUND THE WORLD

McCarran Airfield, Las Vegas, Nevada, USA, in the Cessna 172 *Hacienda* just before 3:53 p.m. local time on 4 Dec 1958 and landed back at the same airfield just before 2:12 p.m. on 7 Feb 1959. In their record 64-day 22-hr 19-min 5-sec flight, they covered a distance equivalent to six times around the world and were refuelled without any landings.

Speed
Top speed
The official airspeed record is 3,529.56 km/h (2,193.17 mph), set by Capt. Eldon W. Joersz and Major George T. Morgan Jr in a Lockheed SR-71A 'Blackbird' over a 25-km (15½-mile) course near Beale Air Force Base, California, USA, on 28 July 1976.

Fastest circumnavigation
The fastest circumnavigation under FAI (Fédération Aéronautique Internationale) rules, which permit only flights exceeding the length of the Tropic of Cancer or the Tropic of Capricorn (36,787.6 km or 22,858¾ miles), was a flight lasting 31 hr 27 min 49 sec by an Air France Concorde from JFK airport in New York, USA, in an easterly direction via Toulouse, Dubai, Bangkok, Guam, Honolulu and Acapulco from 15 to 16 Aug 1995. There were 80 passengers and 18 crew on board flight AF1995.

Pilots and passengers
Oldest passengers
The oldest person ever to travel in an aeroplane is Jessica S. Swift, who flew from Vermont to Florida, USA, in Dec 1981, at the age of 110 years 3 months.

The oldest Briton to travel by aeroplane is Charlotte Hughes of Redcar, N Yorkshire, who was given a flight on Concorde from London, UK to New York, USA as a present for her 110th birthday present on 4 Aug 1987. In Feb 1992, Hughes became the oldest ever Briton.

Most experienced passenger
Edwin A. Shackleton of Bristol, UK, has been a passenger in 572 different types of aircraft. His first flight was in March 1943 in D. H. Dominie R9548. Other aircraft have included helicopters, gliders, microlights and gas and hot-air balloons.

Most hours as a supersonic passenger
Fred Finn has made 707 Atlantic crossings on Concorde. He commutes regularly between London, UK, and New Jersey, USA, and had flown 17,739,800 km (11,023,000 miles) by the end of March 1995.

Most passengers
The greatest ever passenger load on a commercial airliner was 1,088, during the

He made his first flight on 6 May 1918 and his first solo flight 21 days later. The last aircraft that he piloted was a Cessna 172, on 16 Aug 1995. His flying career has spanned more than four-fifths of the history of aviation.

Hilda Wallace of West Vancouver, British Columbia, Canada, became the oldest person to qualify as a pilot when she obtained her licence on 15 March 1989 at the age of 80 years 109 days.

Most flying hours
American pilot John Edward Long logged a total of 61,510 flying hours between May 1933 and April 1996 and has therefore spent more than seven years airborne.

Longest-serving military pilot
Squadron Leader Norman E. Rose, AFC and bar, AMN (RAF Retd) flew military aircraft without a break in service for 47 years from 1942 to 1989, achieving 11,539 hours of flying in 54 different categories of aircraft. He learnt to fly in a de Havilland Tiger Moth in Southern Rhodesia, and went on to fly Hawker Hurricanes in WWII.

Most aeroplanes flown
Capt. Eric Brown has flown 487 different basic types of aircraft as a command pilot. A WWII fighter pilot, he became chief naval test pilot at the Royal Aircraft Establishment at Farnborough, Hants, UK, and the foremost British test pilot of carrier-based aircraft.

FASTEST TRANSATLANTIC CROSSING LASTED 1 HR 54 MIN 56.4 SEC

Balloons and helicopters

TWO AMERICAN SCIENTIS

Ballooning

Earliest flight
A model hot-air balloon invented by Father Bartolomeu de Gusmão (1685–1724) was flown indoors at the Casa da India, Terreiro do Paço, Portugal, on 8 Aug 1709.

Longest flights
A Cameron R-150 helium-filled balloon flown by Steve Fossett covered 8,748.11 km (5,435 miles 1,443 yd) from the Olympic Stadium in Seoul, South Korea, to Mendham, Saskatchewan, Canada, on 17 to 21 Feb 1995. This was the first solo Pacific crossing in a balloon.

Richard Abruzzo and Troy Bradley set a duration record of 144 hr 16 min in *Team USA*, when they crossed the Atlantic Ocean from Bangor, Maine, USA, to Ben Slimane, Morocco, from 16 to 22 Sept 1992.

First solo Atlantic crossing
Col. Joe Kittinger (USAF) lifted off from Caribou, Maine, USA, on 14 Sept 1984, in the 2,850-m^3 (101,000-ft^3) helium-filled balloon *Rosie O'Grady*. He landed at Montenotte, near Savona, Italy, 86 hours later, after a journey covering 5,701 km (3,543 miles).

Greatest altitude
An 1.35-million-m^3 (47.8-million-ft^3) unmanned Winzen balloon launched at Chico, California, USA, on 27 Oct 1972, attained an altitude of 51,800 m (170,000 ft).

The greatest unofficial altitude reached in a manned balloon is 37,750 m (123,800 ft), by Nicholas Piantanida of the USA, in Feb 1996. He lifted off from Sioux Falls, South Dakota, and was killed upon landing in Iowa.

The official record in a closed gondola is 34,668 m (113,740 ft), by Comdr. Malcolm D. Ross (USNR) and Lt. Comdr. Victor A. Prother (USN), who ascended from USS *Antietam* over the Gulf of Mexico on 4 May 1961 in a 339,800-m^3 (12 million-ft^3) balloon.

On 26 Sept 1956, Keith Lang and Harold Froelich, scientists from Minneapolis, USA, accidentally ascended to an altitude of 12,840 m (42,126 ft) in an open gondola without pressure suits. During their 6½-hour flight, at maximum altitude and without goggles, they observed the Earth and recorded a temperature of –58°C (–72°F).

Largest balloon
An unmanned balloon made by Winzen Research, Inc. of South St Paul, Minnesota, USA, had an inflatable volume of 2 million m^3 (70 million ft^3) and was 300 m (1,000 ft) in height. It did not get off the ground and was destroyed at its launch on 8 July 1975.

Hot-air ballooning
Per Lindstrand (GB) reached a record altitude of 19,811 m (64,997 ft) in a Colt 600 hot-air balloon over Laredo, Texas, USA, on 6 June 1988.

Richard Branson (GB) and his pilot Per Lindstrand were the first people to cross the Atlantic Ocean in a hot-air balloon, on 2–3 July 1987. They ascended from Sugarloaf, Maine, USA, and completed the 4,947-km (3,075-mile) journey to Limavady, Co. Londonderry, UK, in 31 hr 41 min.

Richard Branson and Per Lindstrand flew across the Pacific Ocean in the *Virgin Otsuka Pacific Flyer* from the southern tip of Japan to Lac la Matre, Yukon, north-west Canada between 15 and 17 Jan 1991. Their 73,600-m^3 (2.6 million-ft^3) hot-air balloon was the largest ever flown. In making the journey, they set FAI records for both duration (46 hr 15 min) and distance (great-circle distance of 7,671.9 km or 4,768 miles).

The first overflight of the summit of Mt Everest was by *Star Flyer 1*, piloted by Chris Dewhirst (Australia) with cameraman Leo Dickinson and *Star Flyer 2*, piloted by Andy Elson and cameraman Eric Jones (GB), on 21 Oct 1991. The 6,800-m^3 (240,000-ft^3) balloons set records for the highest launch and touchdown, at 4,735 m (15,536 ft) and 4,940 m (16,200 ft) respectively.

The FAI endurance record for a gas and hot-air balloon is 144 hr 16 min, by Richard Abruzzo and Troy Bradley in Sept 1992.

The distance record for a gas and hot-air balloon is 8,748.11 km (5,435 miles 1,443 yd), by Steve Fossett, from Seoul, South Korea, to Mendham, Saskatchewan, Canada, on 17–21 Feb 1995.

Greatest number of passengers
Super Maine rose to a tethered height of 12.25 m (50 ft) on 19 Feb 1988 with 61 passengers on board. Built by Tom Handcock of Portland, Maine, USA, the balloon had a total capacity of 73,600 m^3 (2.6 million ft^3).

The Dutch balloonist Henk Brink carried 50 passengers and crew in an untethered flight in *Nashua Number One* on 17 Aug 1988. The flight set out from Lelystad airport in the Netherlands, and lasted 25 minutes, reaching an altitude of 100 m (328 ft). The balloon had a capacity of 24,000 m^3 (850,000 ft^3).

Most people to jump from a balloon
On 12 Sept 1992, 15 people (a group of Royal Marines plus friends) parachuted from a hot-air balloon over the Somerset/Devon county boundary, UK. The same group made a similar ascent on 1 Oct 1992, and 10 people jumped simultaneously from a height of 1,800 m (6,000 ft).

Right
American helicopter pilot Ron Bower circumnavigated the globe in a record time of 24 days 4 hr 36 min 24 sec in his Bell 206B-3 Jetranger III in 1994. In making this trip, he became the first person to fly a western helicopter across Russia.

was set by John Trevor Eggington with co-pilot Derek J. Clews, when they achieved an average speed of 400.87 km/h (249.09 mph) over Somerset, UK, in Aug 1986, in a Westland Lynx demonstrator.

Greatest load
A Mil Mi-26 heavy-lift helicopter lifted a mass of 56.77 tonnes to 2,000 m (6,560 ft) on 3 Feb 1982, near Moscow, Russia.

Longest flight
Under FAI rules, the longest unrefuelled non-stop flight was by Robert Ferry, who flew a Hughes YOH-6A a distance of 3,561.6 km (2,213 $\frac{1}{10}$ miles) from Culver City, California to Ormond Beach, Florida, USA, in April 1966.

Fastest circumnavigation
Ron Bower (USA) flew around the world in his Bell 206B-3 JetRanger III in 24 days 4 hr 36 min 24 sec. He flew eastwards from Fort Worth, Texas, USA, on 28 June 1994 and returned on 22 July, after 85 stops.

Highest altitude
An Aérospatiale SA315B Lama piloted by Jean Boulet flew at 12,442 m (40,820 ft) over Istres, France, on 21 June 1972.

Longest hover
Doug Daigle, Brian Watts and Dave Meyer of Tridair Helicopters, and Rod Anderson of Helistream, Inc., California, USA, hovered for 50 hr 50 sec in a 1947 Bell 47B in Dec 1989.

Worst helicopter disasters
A Russian military helicopter carrying 61 refugees was shot down near Lata, Georgia, on 14 Dec 1992.

In the British Isles, 45 passengers in a Chinook were killed in a crash off Sumburgh, Shetland Islands, on 6 Nov 1986.

CIDENTALLY ASCENDED TO AN ALTITUDE OF 12,840 M IN THE OPEN GONDOLA OF A BALLOON

Helicopters
Earliest helicopters
The Chinese are known to have built helicopter-like toys as early as the 4th century BC, and Leonardo da Vinci (1452–1519) designed a craft that resembled a helicopter.

A helicopter-like craft was built in France by Paul Cornu and flown for 20 seconds in 1907.

In 1935, the French Breguet-Dorand Laboratory Gyroplane was the first helicopter to fly successfully and be fully controllable.

Fastest helicopter
Under FAI rules, the record for the highest speed to have been reached in a helicopter

Largest helicopter
The world's largest helicopter was a Russian Mil Mi-12 powered by four 6,500-hp (4,847-kW) turboshaft engines. The craft had a rotor diameter of 67 m (219 ft 10 in), was 37 m (121 ft 4½ in) long and weighed 103.3 tonnes. A prototype was demonstrated at the Paris Air Show in 1971, but it never entered service.

Largest rotorcraft
The Piasecki Heli-Stat used four Sikorsky S-58 airframes attached to a surplus Goodyear ZPG-2 airship and was powered by four 1,525-hp piston engines. It was 104.5 m (343 ft) long, 33.8 m (111 ft) high, and 45.4 m (149 ft) wide. It was first flown in Oct 1985 at Lakehurst, New Jersey, USA, but was destroyed in a crash on 1 July 1986.

Smallest helicopter
A single-seat Seremet WS-8 ultra-light helicopter built in Denmark in 1976 is the world's smallest helicopter, with a 35-hp engine, an empty weight of 53 kg (117 lb) and a rotor diameter of 4.5 m (14 ft 9 in).

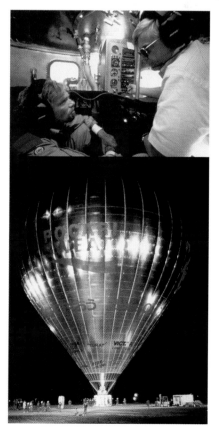

Centre
Still a popular sport, ballooning provided the first viable method of flying.

Left and below left
Setting off from Sugarloaf, Maine, USA, Richard Branson and Per Lindstrand became the first people to cross the Atlantic Ocean in a hot-air balloon.

Transport terminals

Longest rail platform 833 m

Right
The spectacular Port of New York and New Jersey is the largest in the world. It serves one of the world's busiest cities.

Ports

Largest ports
The Port of New York and New Jersey, USA, has a navigable waterfront of 1,215 km (755 miles) and covers 238 km² (92 miles²). A total of 261 general cargo berths and 130 other piers can take 391 ships at a time.

The largest British port by tonnage is London (including Tilbury), which handles 55 million tonnes each year.

The largest British container port is Felixstowe, Suffolk, which handled 1,923,936 TEUs (Twenty-foot Equivalent Units) in 1995.

Busiest ports
The busiest port is Rotterdam, Netherlands, which covers 100 km² (38 miles²) and has 122.3 km (76 miles) of quays. It handled 294.6 million tonnes of cargo in 1995.

Hong Kong port is the leading container port, handling 12,582,692 TEUs in 1995.

The busiest British port is Dover, Kent, which handled 24,209 ship movements (including hovercrafts) in 1995. It also handled 17,872,712 passengers, 2,893,835 accompanied vehicles, 158,167 coaches and 1,055,926 road haulage vehicles.

Largest dry docks
The Daewoo Okpo No. 1 Dry Dock, Koje Island, South Korea, is 530 m (1,740 ft) long

by 131 m (430 ft) wide, and has a maximum shipbuilding capacity of 1,200,000 tons dwt. The gates are the world's biggest, at 14 m (46 ft) high and 10 m (33 ft) thick at the base.

The largest British dry dock is the Harland & Wolff building dock, Queen's Island, Belfast. At 556 m (1,825 ft) in length and 93 m (305 ft) in width, the dock can accommodate tankers of 1 million tons dwt.

Longest breakwaters
The South Breakwater at Galveston, Texas, USA, is 10.85 km (6¾ miles) long.

The longest British breakwater is the North Breakwater at Holyhead, Anglesey, which is 2.39 km (1½ miles) long.

Longest deep-water jetty
The 1,520-m-long (5,000-ft) Quai Hermann du Pasquier at Le Havre, France, is part of an enclosed basin and has a constant water depth of 9.8 m (32 ft) on both sides.

Tallest lighthouses
The steel tower near Yamashita Park, Yokohama, Japan, is 106 m (348 ft) high and has a visibility range of 32 km (20 miles).

The tallest British lighthouse is Bishop Rock Lighthouse, Isles of Scilly, which stands 49 m

(160 ft 9 in) tall. Established in 1858, it was converted to automatic operation in 1992.

Most powerful lighthouses
The lights with the greatest range are 332 m (1,089 ft) above the ground on the Empire State Building, New York City, USA. Each

four-arc mercury bulb is visible 130 km (80 miles) away on the ground and 490 km (300 miles) away from aircraft.

The most powerful British lighthouse is Strumble Head on Ynysmeicl, Pembrokeshire. It has an intensity of 6,000,000 candelas and a 39-km (24-mile) range. Electrified in 1965, it became automatic in 1980.

Stations

Largest railway stations
Grand Central Terminal, New York City, USA, (built 1903–13), covers 19 ha (48 acres) on two levels, and has 67 tracks. More than 550 trains and 210,000 commuters use it daily.

The largest British station is Waterloo, London, covering 12.3 ha (30½ acres). In 1993, five new platforms were added for trains using the Channel Tunnel. Its 24 platforms have a total length of 6.19 km (3 miles 1,496 yd).

Oldest station
Liverpool Road Station, Manchester, UK, is the world's oldest station. First used on 15 Sept 1830, it was closed on 30 Sept 1975.

Highest station
Condor station in Bolivia is at an altitude of 4,786 m (15,705 ft) on the metre gauge Rio Mulato–Potosi line.

Longest platforms
The longest railway platform is at Kharagpur, India, at 833 m (2,733 ft) in length.

The largest airport in the United Kingdom is Heathrow, at 1,197 ha (2,958 acres). Some 92 companies from 83 countries run scheduled services into the airport, and in 1995 a staff of 56,700 handled 419,000 aircraft movements and 54,450,000 passengers (including transit).

Busiest airports
O'Hare International near Chicago, Illinois, USA, had 67,253,358 passengers and 900,207 aircraft movements in 1995, making it the world's busiest airport.

Heathrow, UK, handles more international traffic than any other airport, with

Petroleum Helicopter, Inc. for energy-related offshore operations in the Gulf of Mexico.

Highest heliport
Sonam heliport on the Siachen Glacier in Kashmir, India, is located at an altitude of 5,950 m (19,500 ft).

Longest runways
The runway at Edwards Air Force Base, Muroc, California, USA, is the world's longest, at 11.92 km (7 miles 715 yd).

The longest civil airport runway—4.89 km (3 miles 79 yd) in length—is at Pierre van Ryneveld airport, Upington, South Africa.

Left
O'Hare International, near Chicago, is the world's busiest airport, with an average of one take-off or landing every 35 seconds, around the clock. This has led to it being called 'the crossroads of the world'.

Far left
Grand Central Station in New York is the largest station in the world. It has 41 tracks on its upper level and 26 on its lower level.

E WORLD'S BUSIEST INTERNATIONAL AIRPORT, WAS 14,695 PEOPLE IN ONE HOUR

The State Street Center on 'The Loop' in Chicago, Illinois, USA, has the longest subway platform, at 1,066 m (3,500 ft) in length.

Largest goods yard
Bailey Yard at North Platte, Nebraska, USA, covers 1,153 ha (2,850 acres), has 418 km (260 miles) of track and handles an average of 108 trains and 8,500 wagons every day.

Airports

Largest airports
The £2.1-billion King Khalid international airport outside Riyadh, Saudi Arabia, covers 225 km² (55,040 acres). It opened in 1983.

The largest terminal is at Hartsfield International Airport, Atlanta, Georgia, USA. Opened in 1980, it has a floor area of 53 ha (131 acres) and is still expanding. It handled 57,734,755 passengers in 1995, but has the capacity for 70 million.

The Hajj Terminal at the £2.8-billion King Abdul-Aziz airport near Jeddah, Saudi Arabia, is the world's largest roofed structure. Designed to cater for the annual influx of pilgrims, it covers 1.5 km² (370 acres).

46,810,000 passengers in 1995. On 30 June 1995 a record 193,678 passengers passed through. The busiest hour ever was on 14 July 1995, when 14,695 passengers passed through the four terminals.

Busiest landing area
Bien Hoa Air Base, South Vietnam, handled 1,019,437 take-offs and landings in 1970.

Lowest international airport
Schiphol, Amsterdam, Netherlands, is 4.5 m (15 ft) below sea level.

Lowest landing field
El Lisan on the east shore of the Dead Sea is 360 m (1,180 ft) below sea level, making it the world's lowest landing field. BOAC Short C-class flying boats operated there at 394 m (1,292 ft) below sea level during WWII.

Largest heliports
The largest ever heliport was An Khe, South Vietnam. During the Vietnam War it covered an area of 2 x 3 km (1¼ x 1¾ miles) and could accommodate 434 helicopters.

The heliport at Morgan City, Louisiana, USA, has pads for 48 helicopters. It is operated by

The longest British runway normally available to civil aircraft is Heathrow's 3.9-km (2-mile 739-yd) long Northern Runway (09L/27R).

Northernmost and southernmost runways
The most northerly major runway is at Barrow, Alaska, USA. The strip has all-year scheduled flights to 10 other places in Alaska.

The southernmost major runway is at Ushuaia, Argentina. It has year-round scheduled flights to four other places in Argentina.

Largest hangars
Hangar 375 ('Big Texas') at Kelly Air Force Base, Texas, USA, is the largest free-standing hangar. The high bay covers 610 x 90 x 27.5 m (2,000 x 300 x 90 ft) and is enclosed by a 17.8-ha (44-acre) concrete apron.

Delta Air Lines' jet base at Hartsfield International Airport, Atlanta, Georgia, USA, covers 56.6 ha (175 acres).

Tallest control tower
The control tower at Denver International Airport, Colorado, USA, is 99.7 m (327 ft) tall. It is made of 5,000 tonnes of concrete and 650 tonnes of steel.

WATERLOO STATION HAS 24 PLATFORMS WITH A COMBINED LENGTH OF 6.19 KM

HIGHEST PRICE PA

MOST EXPENSIVE FILM COST AN ESTIMATED $160 MILLI

WORLD'S LONGEST EVER DANCE MARATHON LASTED 5,148 HR 28 MIN 30 S

LONGEST APPLAUSE LASTED 1 HR 20 MIN THROUGH 101 CURTAIN CALLS

LONGEST CLASSICAL PERFORMANCE WAS AN 18-HR 40-MIN RENDITION OF SATIE'S *VEXATIO*

1994
1995
1996
1997
1998

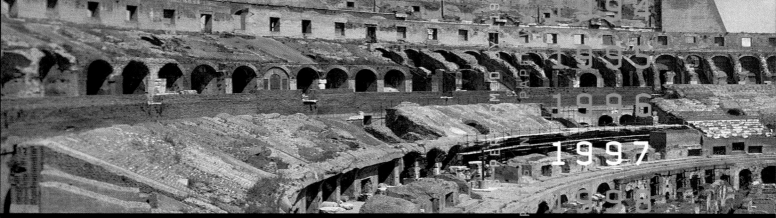

LONGEST CONGA PERFORMED BY 119,986 PEOPLE

SALE OF A DAILY BRITISH NEWSPAPER WAS 3,889,118 COPIES OF THE *SUN* IN NOV 1995

144
145
146
147
148
149
150
151
152
153
154
155
156
157
158
159

RLD'S TOP-SELLING LIVING AUTHOR IS DAME BARBARA CARTLAND

R A LIVING ARTIST'S WORK IS $20.68 MILLION

OM 29 AUG 1930 TO 1 APRIL 1931

THE MOUSETRAP FOR A RECORD 6,240 PERFORMANCES

The arts

ROLL OF PINK WOVEN POLYPROPYLENE

UNDERSTUDIED ROLE

STS OF 600,

ORLD'S LARGEST AMPHITHEATRE, THE COLOSSEUM, CAN ACCOMMODATE 87,000 SPECTATORS

EATEST DISTANCE EVER DANCED BY ONE PERSON WAS 21.1 KM

MOST COSTUME CHANGES IN ONE FILM WAS 65, BY LIZ TAYLOR IN *CLEOPATRA*

Buildings for the arts

Right
In ancient Rome, the world's largest amphitheatre, the Colosseum, was sometimes flooded for mock sea battles. Other spectacles included the martyrdom of early Christians to lions or gladiators.

LARGEST EVER AUDIENCE AT A THEATRICAL PRODUCTION WAS 10,000, AT T

Smallest theatre 30 seats

Galleries and museums

Largest art gallery
The Winter Palace and the neighbouring Hermitage Museum in St Petersburg, Russia, extend over 24 km (15 miles). The 322 galleries house 2.8–3 million works of art and objects of archaeological interest.

Largest museum
The Smithsonian Institution in Washington DC, USA, comprises 16 museums and the National Zoological Park. It contains more than 140 million items and has in excess of 6,000 employees.

The American Museum of Natural History in New York City, USA, was founded in 1869 and consists of 23 interconnected buildings. The buildings of the Museum and Planetarium together cover 111,484 m^2 (1.2 million ft^2) of floor space and accommodate more than 30 million artefacts and specimens. The museum attracts more than 3 million visitors each year.

Oldest museum
The Ashmolean Museum in Oxford, UK, was built between 1679 and 1683 and named after the collector Elias Ashmole (1617–92). Since 1924, it has housed an exhibition of historic scientific instruments.

Most popular museums
The Smithsonian's National Air and Space Museum, Washington DC, USA, had the highest recorded museum attendance on 14 April 1984. The doors had to be closed temporarily due to the 118,437 visitors.

The museum with the greatest attendance in the United Kingdom is the British Museum, which was founded in 1753 and opened to the public in 1759. Construction of the main building in Bloomsbury, London, began in 1823, and in 1995, 6,131,893 people passed through its doors. The museum is also the largest in the United Kingdom, with a total floor area of 8.7 ha (21.5 acres).

Richest museum
The J. Paul Getty Museum at Malibu, California, USA, was established with an initial budget of $1.4 billion (£700 million) in Jan 1974 and now has an annual budget well in excess of $100 million (£65 million) for acquisitions to stock its 38 galleries.

Opera houses and theatres

Largest opera house
The Metropolitan Opera House, New York City, USA, was completed in Sept 1966 at a cost of $45.7 million (£16.3 million). It has a seating and standing room capacity of 4,065, and the auditorium, which is 137 m (451 ft) deep, seats 3,800 people. The stage is 70 m (230 ft) wide and 45 m (148 ft) deep.

Largest theatres
The world's largest building that is used for theatrical purposes is the National People's Congress Building (*Ren min da hui tang*) on the west side of Tiananmen Square, Beijing, China. It was completed in 1959 and covers an area of 5.2 ha (12.9 acres). When used as a theatre, the building can seat up to 10,000 people, and did so in 1964 for the play *The East is Red*.

The largest purpose-built theatre is the Perth Entertainment Centre, Western Australia, with 8,500 seats and a main stage area of 21.3 x 13.7 m (70 x 45 ft). The building was opened on 26 Dec 1974.

Smallest theatre
The Piccolo in Juliusstrasse, Hamburg, Germany, is the smallest regularly operated professional theatre. It was founded in 1970 and has a maximum capacity of 30 people.

Largest stage
The world's largest stage is at the Hilton Theatre at the Reno Hilton, Nevada, USA. Measuring 53.3 x 73.4 m (175 x 241 ft), the stage has three main lifts, each of which can raise 1,200 performers weighing a total of 40 tonnes and two turntables with a circumference of 19.1 m (62 ft 6 in) each. The stage is lit by 800 spotlights.

UNITED STATES LIBRAR

Largest amphitheatre

The Flavian amphitheatre, or Colosseum, in Rome, Italy, was completed in AD 80, covers 2 ha (5 acres) and has a capacity of 87,000. It has a maximum length of 187 m (612 ft) and a maximum width of 175 m (515 ft).

Film studios and cinemas

Largest studios

The largest film studio complex in the world is at Universal City, Los Angeles, California, USA. The site, called the Back Lot, covers 170 ha (420 acres), and has 561 buildings and 34 sound stages.

The largest studio in the United Kingdom is Pinewood Studios in Iver, Bucks, which covers 37.2 ha (92 acres). Opened in 1936, it includes 18 stages.

Largest film set

The largest ever film set was the Roman Forum designed by Veniero Colosanti and John Moore for Samuel Bronston's production of *The Fall of the Roman Empire* (1964). It measures 400 x 230 m (1,312 x 755 ft) and

accommodated a total of 4.54 million litres (1.2 million gal) of water, a full-scale section of a 600,000-tonne supertanker and three scaled-down nuclear submarines.

Largest cinemas

The world's largest cinema is the Radio City Music Hall in New York City, USA, which opened on 27 Dec 1932 with 5,945 (now 5,910) seats.

Kinepolis, the first eight screens of which opened in Brussels, Belgium, in 1988, is the world's largest cinema complex. It has 26 theatres, each with seating for 160–700 people, and an IMAX theatre with a 20 x 30 m (65 ft 7 in x 98 ft 5 in) screen and seating for 450 people. The total seating capacity of the complex is around 6,000.

The Odeon, Leicester Square, London, is the biggest cinema in the United Kingdom, with 1,965 seats.

Biggest screen

The largest permanently installed cinema screen in the world is in the Ssangyong

collections, 23,934,708 other print materials, and 82,498,662 audio and visual materials. The library occupies about 265,000 m² (2.85 million ft²) in the Capitol Hill buildings, and has additional offices and branches worldwide. It has 856 km (532 miles) of shelving and approximately 4,600 employees.

The largest library in the United Kingdom is the British Library, which has 19 buildings in London, a 24.3-ha (60-acre) site at Boston Spa, W Yorkshire, and employs around 2,400 people. It contains over 18 million volumes, and stock increases necessitate more than 3.22 km (2 miles) of new shelving annually.

The largest public reference library in Europe is the Mitchell Library in Glasgow, UK, which has a floor area of 50,000 m² (528,200 ft²), and a total of 1,222,779 volumes on 64.3 km (40 miles) of shelving.

The Newspaper Library at Colindale, north London, UK, opened in 1932 and has 600,000 volumes and parcels comprising 70,000 different titles on 29 km (18 miles) of shelving.

TIONAL PEOPLE'S CONGRESS BUILDING IN BEIJING

was built on a 22.25-ha (55-acre) site outside Madrid, Spain. A total of 1,100 workmen spent seven months laying the surface of the forum with 170,000 cement blocks, erecting 6,700 m (22,000 ft) of concrete stairways, 601 columns and 350 statues, and constructing 27 full-size buildings.

Largest studio stage

The 007 silent stage at Pinewood Studios, UK, was designed by Michael Brown for producer Albert R. Broccoli and set creator Ken Adam and built in 1976 for the James Bond film *The Spy Who Loved Me*. The set measures 102 x 42 x 12 m (336 x 139 x 41 ft) and

Earthscape Pavilion in the Science Park, Taejon, South Korea, which measures 33.3 x 24.7 m (109 ft 3 in x 81 ft ½ in)

A temporary screen measuring 90.5 x 10 m (297 x 33 ft) was used at the 1937 Paris Exposition in Paris, France.

Libraries

Largest library

The United States Library of Congress (founded on 24 April 1800) in Washington DC contains 108,433,370 items, including 16,764,805 books in the classified

The Document Supply Centre in W Yorkshire, UK, has 157.7 km (98 miles) of shelving. It is the world's largest library inter-lending operation, handling more than 3 million requests from British and overseas libraries for items that they do not hold in stock.

The National Sound Archive in London, UK, holds a record 1 million discs and 62,000 hours of recorded tape.

Largest CD ROM library

MicroPatent of East Haven, Connecticut, USA, the commercial publisher of patent information, has a collection of 1,730 CD ROM discs with almost 20 million pages listing every US utility patent from 1976 to the present day.

Left to right
The Golden Room, the White Hall and the façade of the Winter Palace in St Petersburg (formerly Leningrad), Russia. Together with the adjoining Hermitage Museum, the Winter Palace constitutes the largest art gallery in the world. The permanent collection that is housed there includes more than 16,000 paintings and 12,000 sculptures.

Visual arts

THE LARGEST SCRAP-METAL SCULPTURE IN THE WORLD IS *POWERFUL*, WHICH IS 17 M TALL

Right
Since the early 1970s the Bulgarian-born sculptor Christo (b. 1935) has consistently held the record for producing the largest work of art through his explorations of the relationship between the visual arts and the natural world. Between 1972 and 1976 he worked on *Running Fence*, a single piece of 7.6-m-wide (25-ft) polypropylene that ran for 40 km (25 miles) through the desert of Sonoma and Marin counties, California, USA. He surpassed this with his *Wrapped Islands*, one of which is seen right.

Most sculptures 33 million

Largest works

Largest work of art
The largest work of art was created by the US conceptual artist Christo between 1980 and 1983. *Wrapped Islands* involved the encircling of 11 islands in Key Biscayne off the Florida Coast, USA, by 600,000 m^2 (6.5 million ft^2) of pink woven polypropylene.

Largest work of art made with flowers
The largest installation using flowers was *Puppy*, executed by the American artist Jeff Koons at the Documenta exhibition in Kassel, Germany, in 1992. It measured about 12.3 x 5.5 x 6 m (40 ft 5 in x 18 ft x 19 ft 6 in) and was made with live flowers and earth built up on a stainless steel frame.

Largest painting
A 7,127.8-m^2 (76,726-ft^2) painting of Elvis Presley was completed by students of Savannah College of Art and Design and members of the local community on Tybee Island, Georgia, USA, on 8 April 1995.

The largest British painting is the oval *Triumph of Peace and Liberty* by Sir James Thornhill on the ceiling of the Painted Hall in the Royal Naval College, Greenwich. It measures 32.3 x 15.4 m (106 x 51 ft) and took 20 years to complete (1707–27).

Largest mosaics
The world's largest mosaic is on the walls of the central library of the Universidad Nacional Autónoma de México in Mexico City. The scenes all represent the pre-Hispanic past. The two largest of the four walls measure 1,203 m^2 (12,949 ft^2).

The largest Roman mosaic in the United Kingdom is the Woodchester Pavement in Gloucester, which dates from c. AD 325. It measures 14.3 m^2 (47 ft^2) and comprises 1.6 million tesserae (tiles). It was excavated in 1793 and has now been re-covered with protective earth. A total reconstruction was carried out by Robert and John Woodward of Stroud, Glos, and completed in June 1987.

Sculptures and carvings

Largest sculptures
The mounted figures of Jefferson Davis, Gen. Robert Edward Lee and Gen. Thomas Jonathan (Stonewall) Jackson are 27.4 m (90 ft) high and cover 0.5 ha (1⅓ acres) on the face of Stone Mountain, near Atlanta, Georgia, USA. Roy Faulkner was on the mountain face for 8 years 174 days with a thermo-jet torch, working with the sculptor Walker Kirtland Hancock and other helpers, from 12 Sept 1963 to 3 March 1972.

The largest scrap-metal sculpture in the world was built by Sudhir Deshpande of Nashik, India, and unveiled in Feb 1990. Named

Powerful, the colossus weighs 27 tonnes and stands 17 m (55 ft 9 in) tall.

The longest sand sculpture ever made was *The GTE Directories Ultimate Sand Castle*, which was built by more than 10,000 volunteers at Myrtle Beach, South Carolina, USA, on 31 May 1991. It was 26,375.9 m (86,535 ft) long.

Most sculptures
The 15 buildings of the Meenakshi temple complex in Madurai, India, are decorated with an estimated 33 million sculptures—the greatest number at any one site.

Hill carvings
In Aug 1968, a hill figure with a record height of 100 m (330 ft) was found on a hill above Tarapacá, Chile.

The largest human hill carving in the United Kingdom is the 'Long Man' of Wilmington, E Sussex, which is 68 m (226 ft) in length.

The oldest of the 'White Horses' in the United Kingdom is the Uffington horse in Oxfordshire. It was originally thought to date from the late Iron Age (c. 150 BC), but more recent reports suggest that it could be up to 3,000 years old. It measures 114 m (374 ft) from nose to tail and is 36 m (120 ft) high.

Most valuable works
Most valuable painting
Leonardo da Vinci's *Mona Lisa* (*La Gioconda*) was assessed for insurance purposes at $100 million in 1962, but insurance was not concluded because the cost of the strictest security precautions was less than that of the premiums. In 1517 King Francis I of France bought the work, which was painted around 1503–07 and measures 77 x 53 cm (30½ x 20⁹/₁₀ in), for his bathroom for 4,000 gold florins, or 13.94 kg (37³⁵/₁₀₀ lb) troy of gold (about £124,000).

The highest price ever paid for a painting by a British artist is £11 million, for Turner's *Van Tromp Going About to Please His Master*, which was sold by the University of London, UK, in Feb 1993.

Highest priced work of a living artist
Willem de Kooning's *Interchange* sold for $20.68 million (£13 million) at Sotheby's, New York, USA, on 8 Nov 1989.

The highest price ever paid for a work by a British artist who was living at the time of the sale was $6.27 million (£3.71 million), for *Triptych May-June* by Francis Bacon (1909–92), which was sold at Sotheby's, New York, USA, on 2 May 1989.

The record price paid for a currently living British artist is $2 million (£1.2 million), for David Hockney's *Grand Procession of Dignitaries in the Semi-Egyptian Style*, sold at Sotheby's, New York, USA, on 2 May 1989.

MILLION FOR EIGHT WORKS

Royal Academy
Oldest RA
The oldest Royal Academician was (Thomas) Sidney Cooper, who died aged 98 on 8 Feb 1902, having exhibited 266 paintings in a record 69 consecutive years (1833–1902).

Youngest RA
Mary Moser (later Lloyd) was 24 years old when she was elected to the Royal Academy in 1768, on its foundation.

Youngest exhibitor
The youngest exhibitor at the Royal Academy of Arts Annual Summer Exhibition was Lewis Melville 'Gino' Lyons. His *Trees and Monkeys* was painted on 4 June 1965, submitted on 17 March 1967 and exhibited on 29 April 1967—the day before his fifth birthday.

Exhibitions and collections
Largest collections
The Hermitage Museum in St Petersburg, Russia, has more than 12,000 sculptures, 16,000 paintings, 600,000 drawings and works on paper and 266,000 examples of the applied arts on permanent display.

The largest private collection in the world is the Royal Collection of HM Queen Elizabeth II, which at a recent estimate contained about 250,000 works, including more than 7,000 paintings. This compares with just 2,300 paintings in the United Kingdom's national collection in the National Gallery.

The largest repository of one artist's works is the Musée National Picasso in Paris, France, which contains a total of 251 paintings, 160 sculptures, 29 collages, 16 papiers collés and more than 3,000 works on paper by the world's most prolific artist. Picasso produced an estimated 13,500 paintings or designs, 100,000 prints or engravings, 34,000 book illustrations and 300 sculptures or ceramics in his 78-year career. His oeuvre has been valued at £500 million.

Highest exhibition attendances
The Tutankhamun exhibition, which was held at the British Museum, London, UK, between 30 March and 10 Dec 1972, attracted a record-breaking 1,694,117 visitors.

The highest attendance for the exhibition of a living artist is 321,392, at the Willem de Kooning retrospective at the Metropolitan Museum of Art, New York, USA, between 11 Oct 1994 and 8 Jan 1995.

The highest attendance for an exhibition by a British artist is 300,709, at the Lucian Freud retrospective at the Metropolitan Museum of Art, New York, USA, between 16 Dec 1993 and 27 March 1994.

Vandalism and forgery
Worst vandalism
The most devastating act of vandalism against works of art is the car bomb attack on the Uffizi gallery, Florence, Italy, on 27 May 1993, when 33 works were mutilated and three paintings (Bartolomeo Manfredi's *Scenes of Life* and *Bona Ventura* and Gerrit von Honthorst's *Nativity*) were destroyed. The building itself suffered severe structural damage and the Italian Ministry of Culture estimated the total damage to be about 30 billion Italian lire (£13 million).

The single most destructive act of vandalism against a work of art in the United Kingdom occurred on 17 July 1987, when Robert Cambridge shot at the *Leonardo Cartoon*, valued at more than $35 million (£19 million), from a distance of 2 m (7 ft) in the National Gallery, London, UK. The work was severely damaged but has subsequently been restored.

Most successful forger
The Dutchman Hans van Meergeren earned about $4 million (£1 million) for producing six fake Vermeers and two fake Pieter de Hoochs between 1937 and 1943. One of the fakes, *Christ and the Woman Taken in Adultery*, was found in the collection of the Nazi Feldmarschal Herman Göring.

The written word

Books and writing

Oldest books and written records

The oldest handwritten book that is still intact is a Coptic Psalter dated to about 1,600 years ago, found in 1984 at Beni Suef, Egypt.

Fragments of Roman wooden tablets found at Vindolanda, Northumberland, are the earliest known substantial written records in British history. Containing letters and a quotation from Virgil, they have been dated to c. AD 100.

The earliest known British manuscript is a bifolium of Eusebius's *Historia Ecclesiastica* dated to c. AD 625.

First mechanically printed book

It is widely accepted that the world's first ever mechanically printed full-length book was the Gutenberg Bible, printed in Mainz, Germany, c. 1454 by Johann Henne zum Gensfleisch zur Laden, also known as 'zu Gutenberg'.

Largest publications

The *Yongle Dadian* (the great thesaurus of the Yongle reign) consisted of 22,937 manuscript chapters (370 of which still survive) in 11,095 volumes. It was written by 2,000 Chinese scholars from 1403 to 1408.

The entire Buddhist scriptures are inscribed on 729 marble slabs measuring 1.5 x 1 m (5 ft x 3 ft 6 in) housed in 729 stupas in the Kuthodaw Pagoda in Myanmar (Burma). They were incised between 1860 and 1868.

The largest British publication is the 1,112-volume *British Parliamentary Papers* published by the Irish University Press from 1968 to 1972. A set weighs 3.3 tonnes and would take six years to read at 10 hours per day. Its production involved £15,000 worth of gold ingots and the skins of 34,000 Indian goats.

The largest dictionary is the 33-volume, 34,519-page *Deutsches Wörterbuch*, begun by Jacob and Wilhelm Grimm in 1854 and completed in 1971.

The largest English-language dictionary is the 20-volume *Oxford English Dictionary*, which has 21,543 pages. The longest entry is for the verb 'set', with more than 60,000 words.

The world's largest encyclopedia in current use is *La Enciclopedia Universal Ilustrada*

Europeo-Americana, with 105,000 pages and a yearly supplement of 165.2 million words.

The largest English-language encyclopedia is *The New Encyclopaedia Britannica*. The current (15th) edition consists of more than 32,000 pages in 32 volumes, and has more than 44 million words.

The largest fictional publication is the novel *Tokugawa Ieyasu* by Sohachi Yamaoka, which has been serialized in Japanese daily newspapers since 1951. If published in its entirety, it would fill almost 40 volumes.

The ongoing biography of Sir Winston Churchill, co-authored by his son Randolph and by Martin Gilbert, is the longest ever biography. It currently comprises 22 volumes.

The longest poem ever published is the Kirghiz folk epic *Manas*. According to the *Dictionary of Oriental Literatures*, this three-part epic runs to about 500,000 lines.

Smallest bound book

The smallest book ever marketed is printed on 22-gsm paper and measures 1 mm^2 ($\frac{1}{25}$ in^2). Containing the children's story *Old King Cole!*, 85 copies were published in 1985 by The Gleniffer Press, UK. The pages can be only be turned with a needle.

Authors and sales

Best-selling fiction

The top-selling fiction writer is Dame Agatha Christie, whose 78 crime novels have sold an estimated 2 billion copies in 44 languages.

The top-selling living author is Dame Barbara Cartland, with global sales of more than 650 million for her 635 titles published.

Brazilian author Jorge Amado has had his 32 novels published in 48 different languages in 60 countries, from his first book *O País do Carnaval* in 1931 to his most recent *A Descoberta da América pelos Turcos* in 1994.

Alistair MacLean's 30 books have been translated into 28 languages, and 28 have sold more than 1 million copies each in the United Kingdom. It has been estimated that a MacLean novel is bought every 18 seconds.

Sales of around 30 million have been credited to: *Valley of the Dolls* (1966, now out of print) by Jacqueline Susann, which sold 6.8 million copies in the first six months; *To Kill a Mockingbird* (1960) by Harper Lee; and *Gone With the Wind* (1936) by Margaret Mitchell.

Most weeks on a best-seller list

The Road Less Traveled by M. Scott Peck had its 598th week on the *New York Times* list on

WARNING SIGNS *Mostly triangular*

14 April 1995. More than 5 million copies are currently in print.

In the United Kingdom, the hardback edition of *A Brief History of Time* by Prof. Stephen Hawking appeared in *The Sunday Times* best-seller list (which excludes books published yearly) for 237 weeks to May 1995.

The Country Diary of an Edwardian Lady by Edith Holden (1871–1920) was at number one in *The Sunday Times* list for 64 weeks.

Best-selling non-fiction book

The best-selling and most widely distributed book is the Bible, with an estimated 2.5 billion copies sold between 1815 and 1975. The whole Bible has been translated into 349 languages and parts of it have been translated into a further 2,123 languages.

Excluding non-copyright works such as the Bible and the Koran, the best-selling book is

The Guinness Book of Records, first published in Oct 1955 by Guinness Superlatives, a subsidiary of Arthur Guinness Son & Co. (Park Royal) Ltd. Global sales in some 37 languages passed 79 million by June 1996.

It is reported that 800 million copies of the booklet Quotations from the Works of Mao Zedong were sold or distributed from 1966, when possession became virtually mandatory in China, to 1971, when its promoter died.

Most prolific authors
A lifetime output of 72–75 million words has been calculated for Charles Harold St John Hamilton, alias Frank Richards, creator of Billy Bunter. From 1915 to 1926 he wrote up to 80,000 words a week for boys' weeklies.

Brazilian novelist José Carlos Ryoki de Alpoim Inoue had 1,036 novels published from 1 June 1986 to Aug 1995.

On 9 Feb 1989, American horror writer Stephen King was reported to have scooped a $46-million (£26-million) advance for his next four books.

The highest advance paid to a British author is £17 million (over about five years) for three novels, in a deal between Barbara Taylor Bradford and HarperCollins concluded on 6 May 1992.

Longest literary gestation
In 1629, the ecclesiastical historian Jean Bolland began Acta Sanctorum, a chronicle of saints' lives, and completed the first two parts before he died in 1665. The work was later taken up by a group of Belgian Jesuits known as Bollandists, and additions were made periodically over the next three centuries. An introduction for the final part was published in 1940, and there are now 67 folio volumes of the completed work.

In 1978, Oxford University Press celebrated the 500th anniversary of the printing of the first book in the city of Oxford, UK, in 1478. This was before OUP itself was in existence.

Most prolific British publisher
Oxford University Press was the most prolific British publishing imprint in 1995, with 1,784 new titles and 614 new editions published in the United Kingdom.

Largest print runs
It is believed that Van Antwerp Bragg and Co. printed about 60 million copies of the 1879 edition of The McGuffey Reader, compiled by Henry Vail, for distribution to public schools in the USA in the pre-copyright era.

The initial print order for the postcode directory produced by Deutsche Bundespost for United Germany in 1993 was a record 42,300,000 copies.

In the United Kingdom, the total print run of The Highway Code since 1931 is 117 million.

OK IS $14 MILLION, FOR CLANCY'S *WITHOUT REMORSE*

In the world of fiction, Penguin Books Ltd, UK, ordered a run of 3 million for the 1960 paperback version of Lady Chatterley's Lover.

The highest order for an initial print run of a work of fiction is 2.8 million, by US publisher Doubleday for John Grisham's The Rainmaker.

Fastest printing
On 5 Aug 1993, a total of 2,000 bound copies of The Book Fair Book, printed by Print Holdings (Pvt) Ltd, were produced in a time of 5 hr 23 min at the Zimbabwe International Book Fair.

PYRIGHT BOOK OF ALL TIME

The most prolific British author is currently Dame Barbara Cartland, who has averaged 23 novels per year for the last 19 years. She has been translated into 36 languages.

British author Enid Mary Blyton (1897–1968) is believed to have written at least 600 books and has been translated into 30 languages.

The most successful British textbook writer is Ronald Ridout, with 515 titles published since 1958 and sales of 91.35 million.

Most translated author
The world's most translated novelist is Sidney Sheldon, whose books have been distributed to more than 180 countries, in 51 languages.

Greatest advance
In Aug 1992 it was reported that Berkeley Putnam paid $14 million (£7.3 million) for the North American rights to Without Remorse by Tom Clancy.

In Dec 1984, Oxford University Press received back proofs of Constable's Presentments from the Dugdale Society. They had been sent out for correction in Dec 1949.

Oldest author
Sarah Louise Delany's second book, The Delany Sisters' Book of Everyday Wisdom, was published by Kodansha America in 1994, when she was 105 years old. Her sister and co-author, A. Elizabeth Delany, was 103.

Author with the most pseudonyms
The 325 pen names of the minor Russian humorist Konstantin Arsenievich Mikhailov (b. 1868), are listed in the Dictionary of Pseudonyms (1960). Ranging from Ab. to Z, they are mostly abbreviations of his real name.

Publishing and printing
Oldest publishers
Cambridge University Press, UK, has printed and published since 1584. The University received Royal Letters Patent 'to print and sell all manner of books' on 20 July 1534.

Bookshops and libraries
Largest bookshops
W. & G. Foyle Ltd of London, UK, stocks the most titles and has the longest shelving, at 48 km (30 miles), of any bookshop. Its premises cover 7,044 m² (75,825 ft²).

The world's biggest bookstore in terms of square footage is Barnes & Noble at 105 Fifth Ave at 18th Street, New York City, USA. It covers 14,330 m² (154,250 ft²) and has 20.71 km (12 miles 1,530 yd) of shelving.

Most overdue library book
A book borrowed from Sidney Sussex College, Cambridge, UK, by Col. Robert Walpole in 1667 or 1668 was found by Prof. Sir John Plumb in the Marquess of Cholmondeley's library 288 years later. No fine was exacted.

Largest library catalogue
In 1990, the British Library published its General Catalogue of Printed Books to 1975 on three CD-ROMs, priced at £9,000. The printed version is in 360 volumes with a total of 178,000 pages.

Newspapers and periodicals

Heaviest newspaper 5.4 kg

Newspapers
Oldest newspapers
There is a surviving copy of a news pamphlet published in Cologne, Germany, in 1470.

The oldest existing newspaper in the world is the Swedish official journal *Post och Inrikes Tidningar*, founded in 1645 and published by the Royal Swedish Academy of Letters.

Oldest British newspapers
The *London Gazette* (originally the *Oxford Gazette*) was first published on 16 Nov 1665.

The current newspaper with the earliest origins is *Berrow's Worcester Journal* (originally the *Worcester Post Man*), which is published in Worcester. According to tradition, it was founded in 1690 and has appeared weekly since June 1709, although no complete file exists.

The earliest foundation date for any British newspaper still published under the same title is 1712, for the *Stamford Mercury*.

The oldest Sunday newspaper in the United Kingdom is *The Observer*, which was first issued on 4 Dec 1791.

Largest newspaper
The 14 June 1993 edition of the daily newspaper *Het Volk*, published in Ghent, Belgium, had a page size of 142 x 99.5 cm (55⁹⁄₁₀ x 39⅕ in). It sold 50,000 copies.

Largest British newspaper
The *Worcestershire Chronicle* was the largest British newspaper. A surviving issue of 16 Feb 1859 measures 82 x 57 cm (32¼ x 22½ in).

Heaviest newspaper
The heaviest single issue of a newspaper was the 14 Sept 1987 edition of the *Sunday New York Times*, which weighed more than 5.4 kg (12 lb) and contained 1,612 pages.

Smallest newspaper
A newspaper entitled *Tit Bits from all the Most Interesting Books, Periodicals and Newspapers in the World*, dated 5 Sept 1885 and owned by Mark Sundquist of Shoreline, Washington, USA, is the world's smallest newspaper, with an original page size of 5.4 cm x 6.9 cm (2⅛ x 2¾ in).

Highest circulations
Komsomolskaya Pravda, the youth paper of the former Soviet Communist Party, was founded in 1925 and attained its peak daily circulation of 21,975,000 copies in May 1990.

The eight-page weekly newspaper *Argumenty i Fakty* of Moscow, USSR (now Russia), was founded in 1978 and sold 33,431,100 copies in May 1990, when it had an estimated readership of more than 100 million people.

Yomiuri Shimbun, which was founded in 1874 and publishes morning and evening editions in Tokyo, Japan, has the highest circulation of any currently published newspaper. In Jan 1996 it had a combined daily circulation of 14.565,474.

Highest British circulations
The *News of the World*, founded in 1843, had peak sales of 8,480,878 copies in April 1951, with an estimated readership of more than 19 million. Average sales in Feb 1996 were 4,656,716, with an estimated daily readership of 12 million.

Right
The world's oldest periodical, *Philosophical Transactions of the Royal Society*, was first published in 1665. Founders and early members of the Royal Society included philosopher Joseph Glanvill and inventor Robert Hooke.

Far right
The medical journal *The Lancet* is the oldest weekly periodical in the United Kingdom. Its first editor was Thomas Wakely, and its reports played an important part in medical and hospital reform movements.

The highest net sale of any daily newspaper is that of the *Sun*, with a sale of 4,889,118 on 18 Nov 1995, at a reduced price of 10 pence.

Most misprints
A passage concerning 'Pop' Paul VI on page 19 of *The Times* of 22 Aug 1978 contained 97 misprints in 5½ single column inches.

Editors and contributors
Longest editorship
Sir Etienne Dupuch of Nassau, Bahamas, was editor-in-chief of the *Tribune* from 1 April 1919 to 1972 and continued as a contributing editor until his death on 23 Aug 1991, making a total of 72 years as editor.

The longest editorship of a British national paper was 57 years, by C. P. Scott of the *Manchester Guardian* (*The Guardian* from 1959), who occupied the post from the age of 26 in 1872 until his retirement in 1929.

Longest-running feature
Mary MacArthur of Port Appin, Argyll and Bute, UK, has contributed a regular feature as district correspondent to the *Oban Times* and the *West Highland Times* since 1926, a period of some 70 years.

Most syndicated columnist
Ann Landers (née Esther Pauline Friedman) appears in more than 1,200 newspapers and has a readership estimated at some 90 million people. Her only serious rival is Abigail Van Buren, known as 'Dear Abby' (née Pauline Esther Friedman), Lander's identical twin sister, who is based in Beverly Hills, California, USA.

Cartoon strips
Longest-running cartoon strip
The longest-running newspaper comic strip in the world is the 'Katzenjammer Kids' (Hans and Fritz), which was created by Rudolph Dirks and first published in the *New York Journal* on 12 Dec 1897. The strip is now drawn by cartoonist Hy Eisman. It is currently

The longest-running annual in the United Kingdom is *Old Moore's Almanack*, which has been published since 1697, when it appeared as a broadsheet produced by Dr Francis Moore of Southwark, London, UK, to advertise his 'physiks'. Published by W. Foulsham & Co. Ltd of Cippenham, Berks, total sales to date are more than 113 million.

Largest periodical
The bulkiest consumer magazine ever to have been published was the 10 Jan 1990 issue of *Shukan Jutaku Joho (Weekly Housing Information)*, which ran to a total of 1,940 pages. Published in Japan by the Recruit Company Ltd, the magazine retailed for the sum of 350 yen (£1.50).

Largest circulations
By May 1996, total sales of *The Truth that Leads to Eternal Life* through non-commercial channels reached 107,686,489 in 117 languages. Sold by Jehovah's Witnesses, it was published by the Watch Tower Bible and Tract Society of New York City, USA, on 8 May 1968.

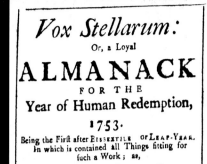

Vox Stellarum:
Or, a Loyal
ALMANACK
FOR THE
Year of Human Redemption,
1753.
Being the First after BISSEXTILE or LEAP-YEAR. In which is contained all Things fitting for such a Work; as,

A TABLE of Terms and their Returns; the Fulls, Changes, and Quarters of the Moon; the Rising, Southing, and Setting of the Seven Stars, and other Fix'd Stars of Note; the Moon's Age, and A Tide Table fitted to the same; the Rising and Setting of the Sun; the Rising, Southing and Setting of the Moon; Mutual Aspects, Monthly Observations, and many other Things useful and pleasant.
Unto which are added,
Astrological Observations on the Four Quarters of the Year; an HIEROGLYPHICK alluding to these present Times. A remarkable Chronology; the Eclipses, and other Matters both curious and profitable.

By FRANCIS MOORE, Physician.

LONDON: Printed by J. BETTENHAM, for the Company of STATIONERS.

Left
Astrological almanacs were pioneered by Scottish observers more than four centuries ago. The Stationer's Company published the first English almanacs, one of the oldest and most famous of which is Francis Moore's *Vox Stellarum*, which now appears as *Old Moore's Almanack*.

NGLE COLUMN INCHES IN *THE TIMES* OF 22 AUG 1978

EVERYTHING ELSE WAS TAKEN.. 8-28

VAL—HER TWIN SISTER

syndicated by King Features Syndicate to approximately 50 newspapers.

Most syndicated cartoon strip
'Peanuts', which is drawn by Charles Schultz, was first published in Oct 1950 and currently appears in a total of 2,620 newspapers in 75 countries and 26 languages.

Periodicals
Oldest periodical
The world's oldest periodical that remains in publication is *Philosophical Transactions of the Royal Society*, which is published in London, UK, and first appeared on 6 March 1665. The Royal Society is the oldest and most prominent British scientific society.

Oldest British periodicals
The oldest weekly periodical to be published in the United Kingdom is the medical journal *The Lancet*, which first appeared in 1823.

In 1974, the US weekly *TV Guide* became the first magazine to sell a billion copies in a year. It has the highest paid circulation of any weekly periodical, at 13,175,549 to 31 Dec 1995.

In its 47 basic international editions, *Reader's Digest*, which was established in Feb 1922, circulates in excess of 27 million copies monthly in a total of 18 different languages. The US edition alone has a run of more than 15 million copies, while the British edition, which was established in 1939, has a run of almost 1.7 million copies. Between Jan and Dec 1995, its readership in the United Kingdom was estimated to have reached about 5.7 million.

Parade, the US syndicated colour magazine, is distributed with a total of 340 newspapers every Sunday. As of April 1996 it had a circulation of 37.166 million, which is the highest in the world for any magazine. At the rate of $629,600 (£409,000) for a four-colour page, it is also the most expensive magazine in which to advertise.

Largest British circulation
Before deregulation of the listings market in March 1991, the highest circulation of any periodical in the United Kingdom was that of the *Radio Times* (instituted in 1923). Average weekly sales for July to Dec 1989 were 3,037,129 copies, with a readership of 9,031,000. The highest sales figure for any issue was 11,037,139 copies, for the 1989 Christmas edition.

Advertising
Longest advertising campaign
The Jos Neel Co., a clothing store in Macon, Georgia, USA, ran an advertisement in the upper left corner of page 2A of *The Macon*

Telegraph every day from 22 Feb 1889 to 16 Aug 1987. This amounted to a total of 35,291 'ads'.

Most advertising pages
The most pages of advertisements sold in a single issue of a periodical is 829.54, in the Oct 1989 edition of *Business Week*.

Letters to editor
Longest letter to an editor
The *Upper Dauphin Sentinel* of Pennsylvania, USA, published an epistle on the American Civil War containing 25,513 words over eight issues from Aug to Nov 1979. It was written by John Sultzbaugh of Lykens, Pennsylvania.

Most letters to an editor
David Green, an author and solicitor from Castle Morris, Pembrokeshire, UK, had his 138th letter published in the main correspondence columns of *The Times* on 11 March 1996. Green's most prolific year was 1972, with 12 letters published. His shortest letter was 'Sir, "Yes" ', on 31 May 1993.

Shortest letter to *The Times*
A letter comprising the single abbreviated symbol 'Dr²?' was written by R. S. Cookson of north London on 30 July 1984. It concerned the correct form of recording a plurality of academic doctorates.

On 8 Jan 1986, a letter was sent to *The Times* by a seven-year-old girl from the Isle of Man. The brief epistle read 'Sir, Yours faithfully Caroline Sophia Kerenhappuch Parkes', and was intended to inform readers of her unusual name, Kerenhappuch, which had been mentioned in a letter the previous week from Rev. John Ticehurst, on the subject of uncommon 19th-century names.

Far left
With more than 16,000 strips to date and more than 355 million readers a day, Charles M. Schultz's 'Peanuts' is translated into Chinese, Serbo-Croat and even Latin (where Snoopy becomes Snupius and Charlie Brown is Carolius Niger).

Music and instruments

LONGEST EVER ENCORE WAS OF THE ENTIRE OPERA *IL MATRIMONIO SEGRETO* IN 1792

Far right
Opera singer Placido Domingo (b. 1941) was applauded through 101 curtain calls for a record 1 hr 20 min for his performance in *Otello* in Vienna, Austria, on 30 July 1991.

Below right
The Tsar Kolokol, cast by Russian brothers I. F. and M. I. Motorin on 25 Nov 1735, is the heaviest bell in the world. It stands 6.14 m (20 ft) high and measures 60 cm (24 in) at its thickest point. Cracked in a fire in 1737, the bell has stood, unrung, on a platform in the Kremlin in Moscow, Russia, since 1836, with the broken section alongside it.

Largest choir 60,000 singers

Classical music
Most prolific composer
Georg Philipp Telemann (1681–1767) of Germany wrote 12 complete sets of services (one cantata every Sunday) for a year, 78 services for special occasions, 40 operas, 600–700 orchestral suites, 44 passions, and concertos, sonatas and other chamber music.

Johann Melchior Molter (c. 1695–1765) of Germany wrote more than 170 symphonies.

Longest symphony
The Symphony No. 2 (the *Gothic*) by Havergal Brian, composed between 1919 and 1927, lasted 1 hr 39 min in a recording broadcast by the BBC. A performance calls for an orchestra of 160 players, an organ, four small brass bands, four large mixed choirs, a children's choir and four vocal soloists, making it also the largest symphony. Brian wrote an even larger work, *Prometheus Unbound*, lasting 4 hr 11 min, but the full score is missing.

Longest performance
Satie's *Vexations*, put on at the Pocket Theatre, New York City, USA, in 1963, lasted 18 hr 40 min, when John Cage directed it to be played 840 times.

Quietest piece
John Cage's *4'33"*, written in 1952, consists of 4 min 33 sec of silence.

Classical concert attendance
An estimated 800,000 people attended a free concert by the New York Philharmonic in Central Park, New York, USA, on 5 July 1986.

Opera
Longest opera
The longest commonly performed opera is *Die Meistersinger von Nürnberg* by Wagner. An uncut version presented by the Sadler's Wells company between 24 Aug and 19 Sept 1968 entailed 5 hr 15 min of music.

Shortest opera
The shortest published opera is *The Sands of Time* by Simon Rees and Peter Reynolds, first performed on 27 March 1993 at The Hayes, Cardiff, UK, when it lasted 4 min 9 sec.

Youngest singer
The youngest singer ever to take an adult role in an opera was Ginetta Gloria La Bianca, who sang the part of Gilda in Verdi's *Rigoletto* at the age of 15 years 316 days at Velletri, Italy, on 24 March 1950.

Oldest singer
Mark Reizen sang the part of Prince Gremin in *Eugene Onegin* at the Bolshoi Theatre, Moscow, Russia, on his 90th birthday on 13 July 1985.

Longest career
Danshi Toyotake of Hyogo, Japan, performed in *Musume Gidayu* for a total of 91 years from the age of seven in 1898.

Most applause
In July 1991 Placido Domingo received applause for a record 1 hr 20 min at the Vienna Staatsoper in Austria.

On 24 Feb 1988, Luciano Pavarotti received 165 curtain calls and was applauded for 1 hr 7 min after singing the part of Nemorino in Gaetano Donizetti's *L'elisir d'amore* at the Deutsche Oper in Berlin, Germany.

The most curtain calls at a ballet is 89, by Dame Margot Fonteyn and Rudolf Nureyev for *Swan Lake* at the Vienna Staatsoper in 1964.

Longest encore
The only opera known to have been encored in its entirety is *Il Matrimonio Segreto* by Domenico Cimarosa. The Austro-Hungarian Emperor Leopold II is reputed to have so

QUIETEST PIECE OF MUSI

enjoyed the work in 1792 that he invited all the participants to supper, and then had them perform it all again.

Musicians
Longest musical careers
The Romanian pianist Cella Delavrancea (1887–1991) gave her last public recital, receiving six encores, when she was 103 years old.

Yiannis Pipis (b. 1889) of Cyprus has been a professional folkloric violinist since 1912.

Jennie Newhouse from High Bentham, N Yorkshire, UK, was the regular organist at St Boniface church from 1920 to 1994.

Highest price paid to hear a singer
Up to $653 (£150)—equivalent to £6,600 in 1996—was paid for seats at the 1850 US concerts of Johanna Maria Lind, who had a vocal range from g to e^{111}, the middle register of which is still regarded as unrivalled.

Orchestras and bands

Most prolific conductor
Austrian conductor Herbert von Karajan (1908–89) made more than 800 recordings encompassing all the major works. During his career he conducted the London Philharmonic Orchestra, the Vienna Staatsoper and La Scala Opera of Milan, and founded the Salzburg Festival in 1967. He was principal conductor of the Berlin Philharmonic Orchestra for 35 years.

Largest orchestra
Johann Strauss the younger conducted a 987-strong orchestra supported by a choir of 20,000 at the World Peace Jubilee, Boston, Massachusetts, USA, in 1872.

In Dec 1991, the 2,000-piece 'Young People's Orchestra and Chorus of Mexico', consisting of 53 Mexican youth orchestras and of

Largest guitar band
In 1994, 1,322 guitarists played *Taking Care of Business* for 68 min 40 sec in an event organized by Music West, Vancouver, Canada.

Largest marching band
A band with 6,017 players marched for 940 m (3,084 ft) at Stafsberg Airport, Hamar, Norway, on 27 June 1993.

Largest one-man band
Rory Blackwell, aided by his double left-footed perpendicular percussion-pounder, his three-tier right-footed horizontal 22-pronged differential beater and his 12-outlet bellows-powered horn-blower, played 108 instruments simultaneously in Devon, UK, in May 1989.

Fastest rendition of *Sailor's Hornpipe*
On 26 Oct 1995, Nicholas Hudson, Paul Taylor and Peter Younghusband from the trombone section of the BNFL band, played the *Sailor's Hornpipe* in 13.99 seconds at the Children's BBC Big Bash exhibition at the Birmingham NEC, UK.

Musical instruments

Grandest grand piano
In 1935 a 3.55-m-long (11-ft 8-in) piano was made by Chas H. Challen & Son Ltd, UK. It weighed 1.25 tonnes.

Heaviest bells
The Tsar Kolokol in Moscow, Russia, weighs 202 tonnes and is 6.6 m (22 ft) in diameter.

The heaviest bell still in use is the Mingun bell in Mandalay, Myanmar (Burma), at 92 tonnes.

Largest organ
The largest, loudest instrument ever made is the now only partially functional Auditorium Organ in Atlantic City, New Jersey, USA.

Completed in 1930, it had two consoles, 1,477 stop controls and 33,112 pipes. Its volume was equal to that of 25 brass bands.

The largest fully functional organ is the six-manual Grand Court Organ in the Wanamaker Store, Philadelphia, Pennsylvania, USA, which has 30,067 pipes.

Largest brass instrument
The contrabass tuba stands 2.28 m (7 ft 6 in) tall, with 11.8 m (39 ft) of tubing and a bell 1 m (3 ft 4 in) across. It was constructed c. 1896–98 for a world tour by the band of US composer John Philip Sousa.

Largest double bass
A double bass 4.26 m (14 ft) tall was built in 1924 in Ironia, New Jersey, USA, by Arthur K. Ferris. It weighed 590 kg (1,300 lb) and had leather strings totalling 31.7 m (104 ft).

Largest guitar
The largest playable guitar is 11.63 m (38 ft 2 in) tall and 4.87 m (16 ft) wide. Modelled on the Gibson 'Flying V', it was made by students of Shakamak High School, Jasonville, Indiana, USA, in 1991.

A fully functional acoustic guitar 8.66 m (28 ft 5 in) long can be seen at the Stradivarium exhibition in The Exploratory, Bristol, UK.

Largest drum
A drum 3.96 m (13 ft) in diameter was built by the Supreme Drum Co., London, UK, and played at the Royal Festival Hall in 1987.

Largest drum set
A drum set consisting of 308 pieces—153 drums, 77 cymbals, 33 cowbells, 12 hi-hats, eight tambourines, six wood blocks, three gongs, three bell trees, two maracas, two triangles, two rain sticks, two bells, one ratchet, one set of chimes, one xylophone, one afuche and one doorbell—was built by Dan McCourt of Michigan, USA, in 1994.

Left
Opera, in the form in which we recognize it today, began in Italy in the 16th century, where a Florence-based group of intellectuals called the Camerata developed it as an attempt to recapture the spirit of Greek drama. The first opera is generally considered to be *Dafne*, produced c. 1597 with music mainly by Jacopo Peri, and words by Ottavio Rinuccini. It was performed privately for a group of Florentine noblemen.

'33", CONSISTS OF 4 MIN 33 SEC OF SILENCE

musicians from Venezuela and the former USSR, gave a concert in Mexico City.

Largest bottle orchestra
The Brighton Bottle Orchestra performed a musical medley on 444 miniature Gordon's gin bottles on 21 May 1991.

Largest choir
A choir of some 60,000 singers sang in unison as the finale to a contest in Breslau, Germany, in 1937.

Largest band
In 1964, a 20,100-strong band was made up of players from Norges Musikkorps Forbund bands at Ullevaal Stadium, Oslo, Norway.

The BT Massed Pipes and Drums of the World Event for Marie Curie Cancer Care on 20 Aug 1995 involved a record 2,739 registered pipers and drummers.

Left
At the 1991 Brighton International Festival, E Sussex, UK, Terry Garoghan and Peter Miller, who make up the Brighton Bottle Orchestra, gave a record-breaking performance on 444 miniature gin bottles. It took 18 hours to tune the bottles, which were filled with water, and about 10 times the normal rate of puff (90 breaths per minute) to play them. Here they show their skills on bottles of Guinness and on miniature bottles of Gordon's gin.

WORLD'S LARGEST DRUM SET HAS 308 PIECES, INCLUDING 33 COWBELLS

Cinema

Right
The city of Bombay (or Mumbai) is the heart of the Indian film industry, which celebrates its centenary this year. Some of 'Bollywood's' actors—such as Dilip Kumar, Raj Kapoor and Annitabh Buchchan—have achieved legendary status, and classic blockbusters such as *Mother India* and *Kughal-e-Azan* have provided entertainment for millions of viewers.

Output and expenditure

Greatest output
India produces more feature length films than any other country. In 1995, 750 films in 19 languages were produced in Bombay, Madras and Calcutta.

Most expensive films
The most expensive film ever produced is *Waterworld* (USA, 1995), which cost an estimated $160 million (£104 million).

In terms of real costs adjusted for inflation, the most expensive film ever made was *Cleopatra* (USA, 1963), which cost $44 million (£16 million)—equivalent to more than $175 million (£130 million) in 1996.

Least expensive full-length feature film
The total production cost for the Australian film *The Shattered Illusion* (1927) was £300. It took 12 months to make and included spectacular scenes of a ship in a storm.

Most expensive film rights
In 1978, Columbia paid a record sum of $9.5 million (£5 million) for the film rights to the Broadway musical *Annie*.

A contract worth $4 million (£2,750,000) plus profit-sharing was signed by New Line on 20 July 1993 for the American psycho-thriller *The Long Kiss Goodnight* by Shane Black.

Box office records

Highest grossing film
Universal's *Jurassic Park* (USA, 1993) had earned a record $913 million (£568 million) by June 1996, of which $357 million (£222 million) was taken in North America.

Greatest loss
MGM's *Cutthroat Island* (USA, 1995), starring Geena Davis and directed by Renny Harlin, cost more than $100 million (£65 million) to produce, promote and distribute. In its first weekend it grossed $2.3 million (£1.5 million) and by May 1996 it had reportedly earned back just $11 million (£7.3 million).

Highest cinema attendance
Mainland China had peak cinema attendance figures of 21.8 billion people in 1988.

The peak year for cinema attendance in the United Kingdom was 1946, which saw a weekly average of 31.4 million viewers.

Longest films and series

Longest film
The longest film to have been commercially released in its entirety was Edgar Reitz's *Die Zweite Heimat* (Germany, 1992), which lasted 25 hr 32 min. It was premièred in Munich from 5 to 9 Sept 1992.

Longest series of films
In Hong Kong, 103 features have been made about 19th-century martial-arts hero Huang Fei-Hong, starting with *The True Story of Huang Fei-Hong* (1949). The latest production is *Once Upon a Time in China 5* (1995).

The longest-running series with the same star is the 46 *Tora-San* comedy films made by Shockiku Studios, Japan, between Aug 1969 and Dec 1995, featuring Kiyoshi Atsumi in a 'Chaplinesque' role.

PRINTER SYNCH:

FILM FORWARD

Most extras in one film 300,000

The British 'Carry On' film series began in 1958 with *Carry On Sergeant* and ended with *Carry On Columbus* in 1992. Kenneth Williams appeared in 25 of the 30 films.

Directors

Longest directorial career
King Vidor made his directorial debut in 1913, with *Hurricane in Galveston*, and ended his record-breaking 67-year career in 1980 with the documentary *The Metaphor*.

Oldest directors
The Dutch director Joris Ivens directed the Franco-Italian co-production *Une Histoire de Vent* in 1988 at the record age of 89. He had made his directorial debut with the Dutch film *De Brug* in 1928.

Hollywood's oldest ever director was George Cukor, who was 81 years old when he made his 50th and final film, MGM's *Rich and Famous*, in 1981.

Youngest director
Lex the Wonderdog, a thriller of canine detection, was written, produced and directed by the 13-year-old Sydney Ling (b. 1959), the youngest-ever director of a professionally made, feature length film.

Oldest performers
The oldest screen performer ever to have appeared in a speaking role in a film was Jeanne Louise Calment (b. 1875), who was 114 years of age when she portrayed herself in the 1990 Canadian film *Vincent and Me*, a modern-day fantasy about a young girl who travels through time to the 19th century to meet Vincent van Gogh. Ms Calment, who is currently the oldest living person in the world, is the last person alive to have met the artist.

The record for the oldest ever British film performer was set by Dame Gwen Ffrancon-Davies when she appeared in the Sherlock Holmes TV movie *The Master Blackmailer* (1991) at the age of 100. She died a month after the screening.

Longest film careers
German actor Curt Bois made his debut in *Der Fidele Bauer* (1908) at the age of eight and his final appearance in *Wings of Desire* (1988) at the age of 80.

The most enduring star of the big screen was Lillian Gish (1893–1993), who first appeared in *An Unseen Enemy* in 1912 and ended her career with *The Whales of August* in 1987.

Left
Elizabeth Taylor (b. 1932) won her first Oscar for *Butterfield 8* (1960). In 1963, she set the record for the most costume changes in one film, when she sported a total of 65 outfits in the film *Cleopatra*. In 1966, Taylor won a further Oscar for her role in *Who's Afraid of Virginia Woolf?*, in which she starred with her then husband, Richard Burton.

Below left
Using computer animation to create the most realistic prehistoric animals ever shown on screen, Stephen Spielberg adapted Michael Crichton's novel *Jurassic Park* to make the highest grossing film of all time.

OSCARS

Most Oscars
20 statuettes and 12 other plaques and certificates, including posthumous awards, to Walt Disney (1901–66).

Most Oscars for a starring role
Four (from 12 nominations), to Katharine Hepburn (b. 1907), for *Morning Glory* (1932–33), *Guess Who's Coming to Dinner* (1967), *The Lion in Winter* (1968) and *On Golden Pond* (1981).

Most Oscars for one film
11, to *Ben-Hur* (1959).

Most Oscars in 1996
Five (from 10 nominations), to *Braveheart* (Paramount): best picture, best director (Mel Gibson), best cinematography (John Toll), best sound effects editing (Lon Bender and Per Halberg) and best make-up (Peter Frampton, Paul Pattison and Lois Burwell). In winning his award, Mel Gibson became the latest well-known actor to receive an Oscar for directing, following in the footsteps of Woody Allen, Robert Redford, Kevin Costner and Clint Eastwood.

Most nominations for one film
14, to *All About Eve* (1950).

HAVE BEEN PAID £8 MILLION FOR A SINGLE FILM

Performers
Highest earning performer
Through a percentage of the film's receipts in lieu of his salary, Jack Nicholson stood to receive as much as $60 million (£40 million) for his role as 'The Joker' in Warner Brothers' $50-million (£33-million) film *Batman*.

Highest earning child performer
Macaulay Culkin (b. 1980) was paid the sum of $1 million (£550,000) for the film *My Girl* (1991) at the age of 11. This was followed by a contract for $5 million (£3.3 million) plus 5% of gross for *Home Alone II: Lost in New York* (1992), the sequel to his 1990 box office hit. Culkin's fee for *Richie Rich* (USA, 1994) is reputed to have been $8 million (£5 million).

Most performers
More than 300,000 extras are believed to have appeared in the funeral scene in *Gandhi*, the 1982 epic directed by Sir Richard Attenborough.

Costumes
Most costumes
The largest number of costumes to have been used in one film was 32,000, in *Quo Vadis* in 1951.

Most costume changes
Actress Elizabeth Taylor wore a record 65 costumes costing a total of about $130,000 (£56,500) in *Cleopatra* (1963).

Oscar statuette ©A.M.P.A.S.®

Theatre and dance

Right
The world's oldest indoor theatre, the Teatro Olimpico in Vicenza, Italy, was constructed over four centuries ago.

Theatre

Oldest indoor theatres
The Teatro Olimpico in Vicenza, Italy, was designed by Andrea di Pietro, alias Palladio. Begun three months before his death in 1580, and finished by his pupil Vicenzo Scamozzi in 1583, it is preserved in its original form.

The oldest British theatre still in use is the Theatre Royal in Bristol, which opened on 30 May 1766 with a *Concert of Musick and a Specimen of Rhetorick*. The City Varieties Music Hall in Leeds, W Yorkshire, was a singing room in 1762, and claims to outdate the Theatre Royal.

Longest runs
The longest continuous run of a show is that of *The Mousetrap*, written by Dame Agatha Christie, which opened on 25 Nov 1952 at the Ambassadors Theatre, London, UK, and moved to the St Martin's Theatre next door on 25 March 1974, after 8,862 performances. Its run continued there, and by 28 May 1996, it had reached its 18,110th performance.

The most performances of any theatrical presentation is 47,250 (to April 1986), by *The Golden Horseshoe Revue*, at Disneyland Park, California, USA, from 16 July 1955 to 12 Oct 1986, seen by 16 million people.

The longest-running musical is *The Fantasticks,* an off-Broadway musical that opened on 3 May 1960 and had been performed 14,934 times at the Sullivan Street Playhouse, Greenwich Village, New York, USA, by 23 May 1996.

Cats is the longest-running ← musical on both the West End and Broadway. It opened on 12 May 1981 at the New London Theatre, Drury Lane, London, UK, where the 6,278th show was performed on 28 May 1996.

The longest-running musical in the United Kingdom was *The Black and White Minstrel Show*, later *Magic of the Minstrels*. The total (but discontinuous) number of performances was 6,464, to 7,794,552 people. It opened at the Victoria Palace, London, on 25 May 1962 and closed on 4 Nov 1972, reopening for a season at the New Victoria in 1973.

The longest-running comedy in the United Kingdom was *No Sex Please We're British*, which opened at the Strand Theatre, London, on 3 June 1971 and transferred to the Duchess Theatre on 2 Aug 1986, ending on 5 Sept 1987 after 6,761 performances. It was directed by Allan Davis throughout its run.

Shortest run
The shortest theatrical run on record was that of *The Intimate Review* at the Duchess Theatre, London, on 11 March 1930. With scene changes taking up to 20 minutes each, the management scrapped seven scenes to get the finale on before midnight. The run was described as 'half a performance'.

Lowest attendance
On 24 Nov 1983, the comedy *Bag* opened to an attendance of nil at Grantham Leisure Centre, Lincs, UK.

Greatest theatrical loss
The American producers of the Royal Shakespeare Company's musical *Carrie* had lost $7 million when it closed on 17 May 1988 after five performances on Broadway.

Highest advance sales
The musical *Miss Saigon* opened on Broadway in April 1991 after generating record advance sales of $36 million.

Most prolific performers
The greatest number of theatrical, film and television roles played by one performer is 3,389 since 1951, by Jan Leighton of New York City, USA.

Kanzaburo Nakamura performed in 806 Kabuki titles from 1926 to 1987. As each title in this classical Japanese theatrical form lasts 25 days, he has given 20,150 performances.

Most durable performers
Kanmi Fujiyama (b. 1929) played the lead in 10,288 performances by the comedy company Sochiku Shikigeki from Nov 1966 to June 1983.

David Raven played Major Metcalfe in *The Mousetrap* on 4,575 occasions between 22 July 1957 and 23 Nov 1968.

Dame Anna Neagle played the lead role in *Charlie Girl* at the Adelphi Theatre, London, UK, for 2,062 of 2,202 performances between 15 Dec 1965 and 27 March 1971, and in all 327 performances in Australasia.

Longest-serving understudy
On 12 March 1994, Nancy Seabrooke retired from *The Mousetrap* aged 79, after understudying the part of Mrs Boyle for 15 years and 6,240 performances, and performing it 72 times. If the cast was healthy, she could leave after the first interval and be home for the Nine O'Clock News.

Most ardent theatre-goers
Dr H. Howard Hughes, Prof. Emeritus of Texas Wesleyan College, USA, attended 6,136 shows between 1956 and 1987.

Briton Edward Sutro saw 3,000 first-night productions between 1916 and 1956, and may have seen more than 5,000 shows in his 60 years of theatre-going.

Dance

Largest cast
The most ballet dancers in a British production is 2,000, in the London Coster Ballet of 1962, directed by Lillian Rowley, at the Royal Albert Hall, London.

Most turns
Delia Gray (b. 1975) of Bishop's Stortford, Herts, UK, achieved 166 *fouettés rond de jambe en tournant* during the Harlow Ballet School's 1991 summer workshop at The Playhouse, Harlow, Essex, UK.

Entrechat douze
Wayne Sleep (b. 1948) performed the fastest *entrechat douze* on 7 Jan 1973 for the BBC *Record Breakers* programme in the United Kingdom. He was in the air for 0.71 seconds.

Grands jetés
On 28 Nov 1988, Wayne Sleep performed 158 *grands jetés* along Dunston Staiths, Gateshead, Tyne & Wear, UK, in two minutes.

Longest chorus line
On 28 March 1992, at the Swan Centre, Eastleigh, Hants, UK, 543 members of the

...TIRED FROM PROFESSIONAL BALLROOM DANCING

cast of *Showtime News*, a production by Hampshire West Guides, performed a routine choreographed by the professional dancer Sally Horsley.

Largest dance
An estimated 48,000 people took part in a Birdie Dance during the 1994 Oktoberfest-Zinzinnati in Cincinnati, Ohio, USA.

Longest dances
Mike Ritof and Edith Boudreaux danced for 5,148 hr 28 min 30 sec to win $2,000 at the Merry Garden Ballroom, Chicago, Illinois, USA, from 29 Aug 1930 to 1 April 1931. Rest periods were cut from 20, to 10, to 5, to 0 minutes per hour, with steps needing to be at least 25.4 cm (10 in), and a maximum of 15 seconds allowed for closure of eyes.

The greatest distance danced by one person is 21.1 km (13 miles 176 yd), by Elizabeth Ursic, who tap-danced her way along the Arizona Half Marathon at Tempe, Arizona, USA, on 10 Jan 1993.

Rosie Radiator led 12 tap dancers through the streets of San Francisco, California, USA, in a routine covering 15.47 km (9 miles 1,074 yd) in July 1994.

Ballroom dancing
The most successful professional ballroom dancing champions are Bill and Bobbie Irvine, who won 13 world titles from 1960 to 1968.

Roy Castle performed 1 million taps in a record 23 hr 44 min.

The oldest competitive ballroom dancer was Albert J. Sylvester (1889–1989) of Corsham, Wilts, UK, who was also personal secretary to British prime minister David Lloyd-George. He retired from dancing at the age of 94.

Conga
The longest recorded conga was the Miami Super Conga, held in conjunction with *Calle Ocho*—a party where Cuban-Americans invite the rest of Miami to join them in a celebration of life. Held on 13 March 1988, it was performed by 119,986 people.

The longest conga in the United Kingdom was performed by 8,659 people from the South-Eastern Region of the Camping and Caravanning Club of Great Britain and Ireland, at Brands Hatch, Kent, on 4 Sept 1982.

Country dancing
The largest genuine Scottish country dance staged was a 512-some reel, organized by the Toronto branch of the Royal Scottish Country Dance Society and held in Toronto, Canada, on 17 Aug 1991.

Flamenco
The fastest flamenco dancer on record is Solero de Jérez, who attained 16 heel taps per second in Brisbane, Australia, in 1967.

Hokey-cokey
The most participants in a hokey-cokey was 6,748, at Bangor, Co. Down, UK, during VE day celebrations on 6 May 1995.

Limbo
The lowest flaming bar under which a limbo dancer has passed is 15.25 cm (6 in) above the floor, by Dennis Walston ('King Limbo') at Kent, Washington State, USA, in March 1991.

On 10 May 1993, Syamala Gowri passed under a bar 11.94 cm (4 7/10 in) off the floor on roller skates at Hyderabad, Andhra Pradesh State, India.

Tap
The fastest rate measured is 32 taps per second, by Stephen Gare of Sutton Coldfield, W Midlands, UK, at the Grand Hotel in Birmingham, on 28 March 1990.

Roy Castle (1932–94), host of the BBC *Record Breakers* programme from 1972 to 1993, performed 1 million taps in 23 hr 44 min at the Guinness World of Records exhibition, Piccadilly, London, UK, from 31 Oct to 1 Nov 1985.

The greatest number of tap dancers to participate in a single routine was 6,553, outside Macy's department store in New York City, USA, on 20 Aug 1995.

Worst case of dancing mania
The worst outbreak of the pathological condition tarantism was in Aachen, Germany, in 1374, when hordes of people broke into frenzied and compulsive choreomania in the streets. It lasted for hours, until injury or complete exhaustion occurred.

Left
A girl is supported by her partner as she collapses with exhaustion at a dance-hall marathon. The most taxing public marathon lasted for a total of 5,148 hr 28 min 30 sec between 29 Aug 1930 and 1 April 1931.

Below
'King Limbo', Dennis Walston, limbo-danced his way into the record books by easing himself under a flaming bar 15.25 cm (6 in) off the ground.

LIMBO

15 14 13 12 11 10 9 8 7 6 5 4 3 2 1

LARGEST THEME PARK, DISNEY WORLD, COVERS 12,140 HA

Leisure and

[illegible] DISTANCE THAT A HUMAN BEING HAS BEEN FIRED FROM A CANNON IS 54.94

1994

1995

1996

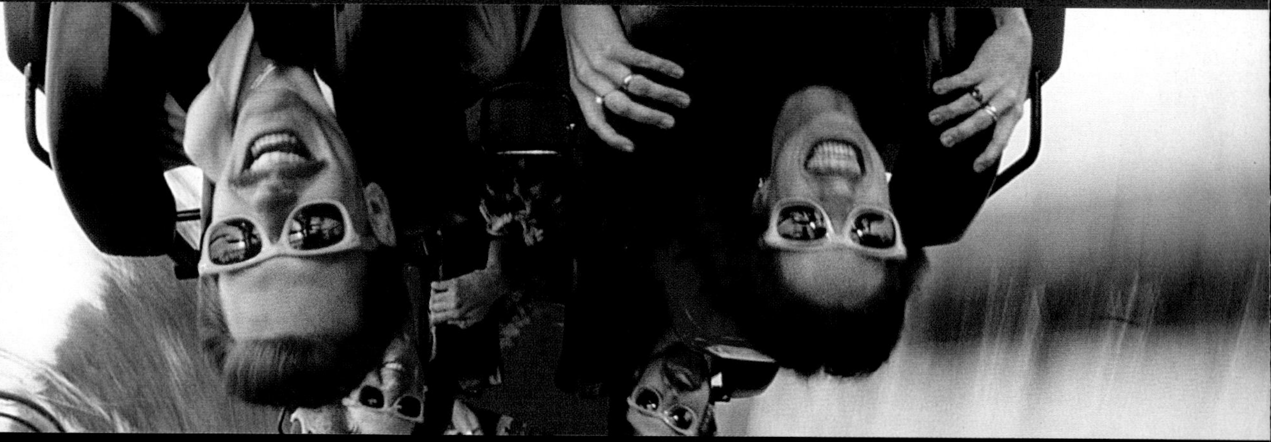

1998

160
161
162
163
164
165
166
167
168
169
170
171
172
173
174
175
176
177
178
179

entertainment

...RGEST SHOPPING MALL WAS VISITED BY MORE THAN 20 MILLION SHOPPERS IN 1995

...FISH AND 356 TONNES OF POTATOES EVERY YEAR

MOST EXPENSIVE HOTEL ROOM COSTS $25,000

...ASTEST ROLLER COASTER, *SUPERMAN THE ESCAPE*, HAS A DESIGN SPEED OF 161 KM/H

LARGEST MAZE HAS 3.27 KM OF PATHS

SLOWEST CHESS MOVE LASTED 2 HR 20 MIN

...EST-SELLING SINGLES ARTISTS ON THE 1990S UK SINGLES CHART ARE TAKE THAT

...,200 ELECTRIC UNITS AND 8,300 DIESEL UNITS IN 40 YEARS

...A BRITISH COMPETITION IS £22,590,829, IN THE NATIONAL LOTTERY

...AUDIENCE OF MORE THAN 1.1 BILLION

...BY BABYLON ZOO

...SPACEMAN, BY BABYLON ZOO

...UNITED KINGDOM IS

...THE WORLD TRADE CENTER TOWERS

...TOOK PLACE AT 11 M BETWEEN THE WORLD TRADE CENTER TOWERS

...CHARITY SINGLE

...FASTEST-SELLING NON-CHARITY SINGLE

...HIGHEST HIGH-WIRE FEAT

...BAYWATCH HAS A SECRET

Buildings for leisure

Nightclubs and restaurants

Largest nightclub
The world's largest nightclub is 'Gilley's Club' (formerly 'Shelly's') on Spencer Highway, Houston, Texas, USA. Built in 1955, it was extended in 1971 to provide seating for 6,000 people. Its roof covers 1.6 ha (4 acres).

Largest restaurants
The Royal Dragon (Mang Gorn Luang) restaurant in Bangkok, Thailand, opened in Oct 1991 and can seat 5,000 people. The service area covers 1.6 ha (4 acres), and the 541 waiters wear roller skates to ensure speedy service of up to 3,000 dishes an hour.

The world's largest fish-and-chip restaurant is Harry Ramsden's at White Cross, Guiseley, W Yorkshire, UK. Its 140 staff serve 213 tonnes of fish and 356 tonnes of potatoes to 1 million customers each year.

Bars and public houses

Tallest bar
The bar at Humperdink's Seafood and Steakhouse in the Las Colinas business development in Irving, Texas, USA, is 7.69 m (25 ft 3 in) high and has two levels of shelving containing more than 1,000 bottles. If an order has to be met from the upper level, it is reached by climbing a ladder.

Longest bar
The longest permanent bar in the world is the 123.7-m-long (405-ft 10-in) counter in the Beer Barrel Saloon, which opened at Put-in-Bay, South Bass Island, Ohio, USA, in 1989. The bar is fitted with 56 beer taps and surrounded by 160 bar stools.

Oldest pubs
'The Fighting Cocks' pub at St Albans, Herts, UK, is an 11th-century structure on an 8th-century site.

The timber frame of the Royalist Hotel, Digbeth Street, Stow-on-the-Wold, Glos, UK, is known to have existed as early as AD 947 and was called 'The Eagle and the Child' in the 13th century.

'Ye Olde Ferry Boat Inn' at Holywell, Cambs, UK, is reputed to have existed in AD 560, but no documentation is available before AD 1100.

According to local church records dating back to AD 905, the 'Bingley Arms' in Bardsey, W Yorkshire, UK, which was restored and extended in 1738, existed as the 'Priest's Inn' at that time.

Longest pub name
'The Old Thirteenth Cheshire Astley Volunteer Rifleman Corps Inn' in Stalybridge, Manchester, UK, has 55 letters in its name.

Commonest pub name
There are approximately 630 pubs called the 'Red Lion' in the United Kingdom.

Hotels

Oldest hotel
The Hōshi Ryokan at the village of Awazu in Japan dates back to AD 717, when Garyo Hōshi built an inn close to a hot-water spring said to have miraculous healing powers. The nearby waters are still celebrated for their recuperative effects, and the hotel now has 100 bedrooms.

Tallest hotels
Measured from the street level of its main entrance, the 73-storey Westin Stamford in Raffles City, Singapore, completed in March 1985, is 226.1 m (742 ft) high.

The Westin Stamford Detroit Plaza, USA, is 227.9 m (748 ft) tall (measured from its rear entrance level).

The Ryujyong Hotel, North Korea, which has been under construction for 20 years, is reported to be 105 storeys high.

The tallest British hotel, the London Forum, has 27 storeys and is 132 m (380 ft) tall.

Largest hotel lobby
The lobby at the Hyatt Regency in San Francisco, California, USA, is 107 m (350 ft) long, 49 m (160 ft) wide, and 52 m (170 ft) high—the height of a 17-storey building.

Most expensive hotel room
The Galactic Fantasy Suite at the Crystal Palace Resort and Casino, Nassau, Bahamas, costs $25,000 (£17,360) a night, but the casino's big spenders are likely to be accommodated on a complimentary basis. Facilities include a personal robot servant called 'Ursula', a rotating sofa and bed, a thunder-and-lightning sound-and-light show and pulsating light columns activated by body heat.

Stadia

Largest exhibition centres
The International Exposition Center in Cleveland, Ohio, USA, is situated on a 76-ha (188-acre) site adjacent to Cleveland Hopkins

Largest beer-selling establishment
The 'Mathäser' in Munich, Germany, seats 5,500 and sells up to 48,000 litres (84,470 pints) of beer daily.

Smallest pub
The ground floor of 'The Nutshell' in Bury St Edmunds, Suffolk, UK, is 4.82 x 2.28 m (15 ft 10 in x 7 ft 6 in). It was personally granted a licence by a thirsty King Charles II (1630–85).

The 'Lakeside Inn', The Promenade, Southport, Merseyside, UK, has a floor area of 6.7 x 4.87 m (22 x 16 ft) and is 4.57 m (15 ft) high.

'The Smiths Arms' pub in Godmanstone, Dorset, UK, has external dimensions of 12.04 x 3.5 m (39 ft 6 in x 11 ft 6 in) and is 3.65 m (12 ft) in height.

The smallest bar room in a pub measures 1.27 x 2.39 m (4 ft 2 in x 7 ft 10 in). It is in the 'Dove Inn', Chiswick, London, UK.

Largest hotels
The largest hotel in the world is the MGM Grand Hotel/Casino in Las Vegas, Nevada, USA, which consists of four 30-storey towers on a site covering a total area of 45.3 ha (112 acres). The hotel has 5,005 rooms, with suites of up to 560 m^2 (6,000 ft^2) in size, a 15,200-seat arena, and a 13.3-ha (33-acre) theme park.

The largest hotel in the United Kingdom is the Grosvenor House Hotel in Park Lane, London. It is eight storeys high, covers an area of 1 ha (2½ acres) and caters for more than 100,000 visitors a year in 470 rooms and 140 fully-serviced apartments.

The London Forum Hotel in Cromwell Road has the greatest capacity of any hotel in the United Kingdom, providing accommodation for up to 1,856 guests in a total of 910 bedrooms. Opened in 1973, the hotel employs 281 full-time staff.

International Airport, in a building covering 232,250 m^2 (2.5 million ft^2). The Center accommodates 200 events each year.

The largest British exhibition centre is the National Exhibition Centre, Birmingham, W Midlands, which opened in 1976. It has 15 halls covering 158,000 m^2 (1.7 million ft^2), a 12,300-seat arena, two hotels, parking for 21,000 cars, numerous restaurants and a lake on a 250-ha (618-acre) site.

Largest air-supported buildings
The octagonal Pontiac Silverdome Stadium in Detroit, Michigan, USA, is 235 m (770 ft) long and 183 m (600 ft) wide, and can accommodate 80,311 people. The air pressure supporting the 4-ha (10-acre) translucent 'Fiberglas' roofing is 34.4 kPa (5 lb/ft^2). The main floor covers 123 x 71 m (402 x 232 ft), and the roof is 62 m (202 ft) high. The structural engineers were Geiger-Berger Associates of New York City, USA.

Longest bar counter 123.7 m

The largest standard-size airhall is 262 m (860 ft) long, 42.6 m (140 ft) wide and 19.8 m (65 ft) high. First sited at Lima, Ohio, USA, it was manufactured by Irvin Industries of Stamford, Connecticut, USA.

Largest stadia
The open Strahov Stadium in Prague, Czech Republic, completed in 1934, could accommodate 240,000 spectators for mass displays of up to 40,000 Sokol gymnasts.

The largest covered stadium in the world is the Aztec Stadium in Mexico City, Mexico, opened in 1968. It has a capacity of 107,000 for football, although there was a record attendance of 132,274 people for a boxing match on 20 Feb 1993. Almost all its seats are under cover.

JST EXPENSIVE HOTEL ROOM, THE GALACTIC FANTASY SUITE, COSTS $25,000 PER NIGHT

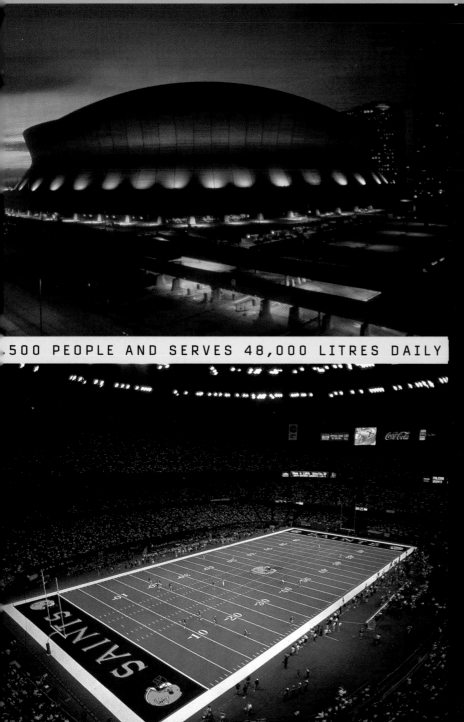

500 PEOPLE AND SERVES 48,000 LITRES DAILY

The world's largest indoor stadium is the $173-million (£109-million) Superdome in New Orleans, Louisiana, USA. Completed in May 1975, it is 83.2 m (273 ft) tall and covers 5.26 ha (13 acres). It has a seating capacity of 97,365 for conventions and 76,791 for American football matches.

Largest domes
The world's largest dome is the Louisiana Superdome in New Orleans, USA, which has a diameter of 207.26 m (680 ft).

The largest British dome is the Bell Sports Centre, Perth, Tayside, which has a diameter of 67 m (222 ft). It was designed by D. B. Cockburn and constructed by Muirhead & Sons Ltd of Grangemouth, Falkirk.

Largest roofs
The transparent acrylic glass 'tent' roof over the Munich Olympic Stadium, Germany, has an area of 85,000 m^2 (915,000 ft^2) and rests on a steel net supported by masts.

The longest span is 240 m (787 ft 4 in), for the major axis of the elliptical Texas Stadium, at Irving, Texas, USA, completed in 1971.

Tallest floodlights
The tallest lighting columns are the six towers of the Melbourne Cricket Ground, Victoria, Australia. Built in 1985, they are each 75 m (246 ft) high and weigh 120 tonnes.

Largest football stadia
The Maracanã Municipal Stadium in Rio de Janeiro, Brazil, has a normal capacity of 205,000 people, of whom 155,000 can be seated. A dry moat 2.13 m (7 ft) wide and more than 1.5 m (5 ft) deep protects players from spectators—and vice versa.

The British football stadium with the greatest volume is Hampden Park, Glasgow, the home of Queen's Park Football Club, which was opened on 31 Oct 1903. Its record attendance was 149,547 on 17 April 1937, but the current Ground Safety Certificate limits the seated capacity to 38,335.

Top
The 26.8-m (88-ft) MGM lion welcomes visitors to the largest hotel in the world, the MGM Grand. Themed rooms are decorated as 'The Wizard of Oz', 'Hollywood' and 'Casablanca', and 1.6 ha (4 acres) of gaming area include 3,500 machines ranging from nickel to $500 slots.

Middle and bottom
Up to 76,791 spectators can attend each American football match held at the Louisiana Superdome. They are provided with instant replays, produced on a gondola with six 8-m (26-ft) TV screens.

Recreation

FASTEST ROLLER COASTER IN THE WORLD HAS A DESIGN SPEED OF 161 KM/H

Right
Although maximum speeds and dimensions claimed for gravity-based rides have long been exaggerated for commercial reasons, passengers on the latest roller coasters can attest to their ability to provide the thrills promised by advertisements. The first of a new generation of linear-powered lines is *Superman The Escape*, a ride that outstrips all others in terms of height and speed.

Largest naturist site 340 ha

Resorts

Pleasure piers

The longest pleasure pier in the world is Southend Pier in Southend-on-Sea, Essex, UK. The original wooden pier was opened in 1830 and extended in 1846. The present iron pier is 2.15 km (1 mile 598 yd) long and was opened in 1889. Between 1949 and 1950 the pier had a peak 5.75 million visitors. It has been breached by 14 vessels since 1830, and there have been three major fires.

The resort with the greatest number of piers was Atlantic City, New Jersey, USA, which had a total of eight, built from 1883 to 1912. Only five of them remain.

Blackpool in Lancashire has three piers (the North, Central and South piers)—the most of any British resort.

Largest pleasure beach

Virginia Beach, Virginia, USA, has 45 km (28 miles) of beach front on the Atlantic and 16 km (10 miles) of estuary frontage on Chesapeake Bay. The city of Virginia Beach covers 803 km^2 (310 miles^2) and has a total of 147 hotels and 2,323 campsites.

Largest naturist resorts

The largest naturist site is Domaine de Lambeyran in southern France, which covers 340 ha (840 acres).

LARGEST FERRIS WHEEL IS 100 M IN DIAMETE

The Centre Helio Marin at Cap d'Agde in southern France is visited by approximately 250,000 people per annum.

The largest naturist site in the United Kingdom is the Naturist Foundation in Orpington, Kent, which has an area of 20 ha (50 acres).

Spas

The largest spa in terms of accommodation is Vichy, Allier, France, with 14,000 hotel rooms.

The highest French spa is Barèges in the Hautes-Pyrénées, which is 1,240 m (4,068 ft) above sea level.

Largest amusement resorts

The US theme park Disney World covers 12,140 ha (30,000 acres) and is located 32 km (20 miles) south-west of Orlando, Florida, USA. It was opened in Oct 1971 after an investment of $400 million (£160 million).

The largest amusement park within the United Kingdom—and the most frequently visited tourist attraction in the country—is Blackpool Pleasure Beach, Lancs, which received a total of 7.4 million visitors during 1995. In 1996 the Pleasure Beach celebrated the 100th anniversary of its opening.

WORLD'S LARGEST MAZ

Alton Towers, Staffs, has the highest paid attendance of any British attraction, with more than 27 million visitors in 1995.

Big wheels
The original Ferris wheel, named after its constructor George W. Ferris, was erected in 1893 at the Midway, Chicago, Illinois, USA, at a cost of $385,000 (£79,200). At 76 m (250 ft) in diameter and 240 m (790 ft) in circumference, it weighed 1,087 tonnes and had 36 cars each carrying 40 seated and 20 standing passengers, giving a record capacity of 2,160. It was moved to St Louis, Missouri, USA, in 1904 and eventually sold as scrap for $1,800 (£370).

The largest diameter of a currently operating wheel is 100 m (328 ft), for the Cosmoclock 21 at Yokohama City, Japan. It is 105 m (344 ft 6 in) high, with 60 gondolas each with eight seats. Each of the 60 arms holding the gondolas serves as a second hand for the 13-m-long (42-ft 7¾-in) electric clock. Other features include illumination by laser beams and acoustic effects by sound synthesizers.

The greatest ever diameter of any British ferris wheel was 86.5 m (284 ft), for a wheel erected for the Earl's Court Exhibition in London in 1897. The largest diameter of a British wheel currently in operation is 61 m (200 ft) diameter, for a wheel with a capacity of 240 people at Margate, Kent.

Swing
A glider swing with a height of 9.1 m (30 ft) was constructed by Kenneth R. Mack of Langenburg, Saskatchewan, Canada, for

was designed by Intamin AG of Switzerland and features a 126.5-m (415-ft) steel support structure and a design speed of 161 km/h (100 mph).

The tallest traditional complete-circuit roller coaster is *Fujiyama* at the Fujikyu Highland amusement park, Japan. It is 79 m (259 ft) tall, and has a lift height of 71.5 m (235 ft), a vertical drop of 70 m (230 ft) and a design speed of 130 km/h (81 mph).

The tallest roller coaster in the United Kingdom is the non-inversion Pepsi-Max Big One at Blackpool Pleasure Beach, Lancs, UK, which has an actual lift height of 61.3 m (201 ft) and a first drop of 62.5 m (205 ft).

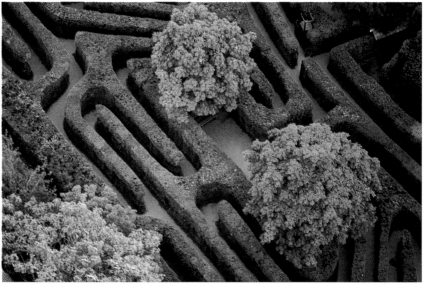

Made from beech hedges, the maze was created in 1891.

The maze with the greatest path length is at Longleat, near Warminster, Wilts, UK. It has 2.72 km (1 mile 1,214 yd) of paths flanked by 16,180 yew trees and was opened in 1978.

Promenade
The longest covered promenade is the Long Corridor in the Summer Palace in Beijing, China, which extends for 728 m (2,388 ft). Built entirely of wood, it is divided into 273 sections by crossbeams which, together with the ceiling and side pillars, have more than 10,000 paintings of Chinese landscapes, episodes from folk tales, flowers and birds.

Left
The maze at Hampton Court Palace—the former Royal residence built by Cardinal Wolsey in 1515 and presented to King Henry VIII a decade later—measures 68 x 25 m (222 x 82 ft). Created in the 17th century, it is the oldest surviving hedge maze in the United Kingdom.

ID HAS 60 GONDOLAS WITH EIGHT SEATS EACH

Uncle Herb's Amusements in 1986. The swing is capable of taking its four riders to a height of 7.6 m (25 ft) off the ground.

Roller coasters
The world's oldest operating roller coaster is the *Rutschebahnen* (Scenic Railway) Mk. 2, which was constructed at the Tivoli Gardens, Copenhagen, Denmark, in 1913. It has remained open ever since.

The oldest operating roller coaster in the United Kingdom is the *Scenic Railway* at Dreamland, Margate, Kent, which is a traditional wooden coaster that has continued to operate since it first opened to the public on 3 July 1920.

The world's longest roller coaster is *The Ultimate* at Lightwater Valley Theme Park in Ripon, N Yorkshire, UK. The tubular-steel track is 2.29 km (1 mile 740 yd) in length.

The tallest and fastest roller coaster in the world is *Superman The Escape* at Six Flags Magic Mountain, Valencia, California, USA. This linear-powered reverse-free-fall coaster

The complete-circuit multi-element roller coaster with the greatest number of loops or inversions is the Dragon Khan at Port Aventura, Salou, Spain, which was designed by Bolliger & Mabillard of Switzerland. Riders are turned upside-down eight times over the steel track, which extends for a distance of 1,269.8 m (4,166 ft).

Mazes and promenades
Mazes
The oldest surviving British hedge maze is at Hampton Court Palace, Greater London. It was designed by George London and Henry Wise in 1690.

The largest maze ever constructed was in a cornfield at Shippensburg, Pennsylvania, USA. Its total path length was 3.27 km (2 miles 53 yd) and it covered an area of 16,000 m² (172,225 ft²). It stood for two months, in Aug and Sept 1995.

The largest permanent maze in the world is the hedge maze at Ruurlo, Netherlands, which covers a total area of 8,740 m² (94,080 ft²).

Shopping
Longest shopping centres
The $1.1-billion West Edmonton Mall, Alberta, Canada, was opened in 1981 and completed four years later. It covers 483,080 m² (5.2 million ft²) on a 49-ha (121-acre) site and has 11 major department stores and more than 800 stores and services. Parking is provided for 20,000 vehicles and more than 20 million shoppers visited in 1995.

The largest shopping complex in the United Kingdom is the MetroCentre, Gateshead, Tyne and Wear, which has a 54.63-ha (135-acre) site housing 350 retail units that give a gross selling area of 145,000 m² (1.56 million ft²). The complex also includes a leisure centre, an 11-screen cinema, parking for 12,000 cars, a coach park and a purpose-built British Rail station and bus station.

The largest wholesale merchandise mart is the Dallas Market Center, Texas, USA, the five buildings of which cover nearly 641,000 m² (6.9 million ft²) in five buildings. The whole complex has an area of 70 ha (175 acres) and houses 2,580 showrooms displaying the wares of more than 50,000 manufacturers.

Longest mall
The longest shopping mall is 720 m (2,360 ft) in length and is part of the £40-million shopping centre at Milton Keynes, Bucks, UK.

Far left
The largest ever ferris wheel in the United Kingdom was built for the Earl's Court Exhibition of 1897. It had 10 first-class and 30 second-class cars, with each car carrying 30 people.

AD 3.27 KM OF PATHS AND COVERED 16,000 M²

Hobbies and pastimes

Right
The crossword shown here was written for *The Guinness Book of Records* by Roger Squires, the world's most prolific crossword compiler. The clues are related to facts found on this page and elsewhere in the book.

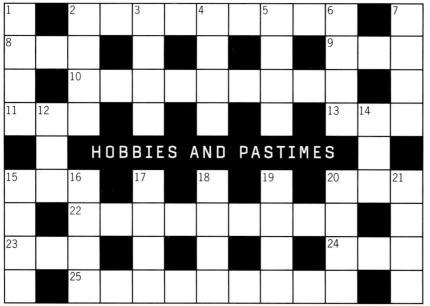

HOBBIES AND PASTIMES

ACROSS
2 Children's game (9)
8 Cricketers often take a ___ break (3)
9 Skaters need it! (3)
10 Word puzzle (9)
11 Birdspotters will know this diving bird (3)
13 Hard wood used by modellers (3)
15 Used for many water sports (3)
20 Scull used by rowers (3)
22 Cultivating one's own plot (9)
23 Single spot domino (3)
24 Series of winning cards in bridge (3)
25 Solo game (9)

DOWN
1 Skiers use this volcano (4)
2 Horse kept for riding (4)
3 Billiard game (4)
4 Angler's throw (4)
5 Implement used in DIY (4)
6 Concealment used in birdwatching (4)
7 Sporting side (4)
12 Employment (3)
14 Measure of silk (3)
15 Children's card game (4)
16 A long time (4)
17 There is an ____ tradition in children's games (4)
18 Worn to indicate a grade in judo (4)
19 Type of equipment for music buffs (2–2)
20 Part in pantomime for amateur actors (4)
21 Skating area (4)

Leisure pursuits
Films
Gwilym Hughes saw his first film in 1953 while in hospital, and on 12 Jan 1996 had logged a total of 22,447 films in his film diary.

Pub visits
Bruce Masters of Flitwick, Beds, UK, has visited a record 28,461 pubs and 1,466 other drinking establishments since 1960.

Snail racing
In July 1995 a garden snail named 'Archie', owned by six-year-old Carl Bramham of Pott Row, Norfolk, UK, covered a 33-cm (13-in) course in two minutes.

Worm charming
In 1980, at the first World Worm Charming Championship at Willaston, Cheshire, UK, Tom Shufflebotham charmed a record 511 worms out of a 3-m^2 (9$\frac{7}{8}$-ft^2) plot in 30 minutes.

Crosswords and games
Most prolific compiler
Roger F. Squires of Ironbridge, Shrops, UK, compiles 38 puzzles singlehandedly each week, and is one of only three compilers to have had puzzles published in all five British broadsheet newspapers. His output to May 1996 was more than 48,000 crosswords (two thirds of them cryptic and one third quick). His millionth clue was published in *The Daily Telegraph* on 6 Sept 1989.

Largest published crossword
In July 1982, Robert Turcot of Quebec, Canada, compiled a crossword with 82,951 squares. Containing 12,489 clues across and 13,125 down, it covered 3.55 m^2 (38$\frac{1}{4}$ ft^2).

Fastest crossword solutions
The fastest time taken to complete *The Times* crossword under test conditions is 3 min 45 sec, by Roy Dean of Bromley, Kent, UK, in the BBC *Today* radio studio on 19 Dec 1970.

Dr John Sykes won *The Times*/Collins Dictionaries championship 10 times from 1972 to 1990, solving the four puzzles in an average time of eight minutes each. He won by a record margin of 9 min 30 sec at the Hilton Hotel, London, UK, in 1991, and set a championship best of 4 min 28 sec in 1989.

Hopscotch
The record for the most games of hopscotch completed in 24 hours is 390, by Ashrita Furman of Jamaica, New York, USA, from 2 to 3 April 1995.

Solitaire
The shortest ever time taken to complete a game of solitaire is 10 seconds, by Stephen Twigge at Scissett Baths, Huddersfield, W Yorkshire, UK, on 2 Aug 1991.

'Spotting'
Birdspotting
The world's leading birdspotter or 'twitcher' is Phoebe Snetsinger of Webster Groves, Missouri, USA, who has seen 8,040 of the 9,700 known species (82%) since 1965. She has seen all of the world's families on the official list and well over 90% of the genera.

The most species spotted in a 24-hour period is 342, by Terry Stevenson, John Fanshawe and Andy Roberts of Kenya on the second day of the Birdwatch Kenya '86 event.

Trainspotting
Bill Curtis of Clacton-on-Sea, Essex, UK, is acknowledged as the world champion trainspotter or 'gricer' (after Richard Grice, the first champion, who held the title from 1896 to 1931). He has spotted 60,000 locomotives, 11,200 electric units and 8,300 diesel units in various countries over 40 years.

WORLD'S TOP TRAINSPOTT

Fastest-flying kite 193 km/h

SOLUTION
ACROSS: 2 Hopscotch. 8 Tea. 9 Ice. 10 Crossword. 11 Auk. 13 Elm. 15 Sea. 20 Oar. 22 Gardening. 23 Ace. 24 Run. 25 Solitaire.
DOWN: 1 Etna. 2 Hack. 3 Pool. 4 Cast. 5 Tool. 6 Hide. 7 Team. 12 Use. 14 Lea. 15 Snap. 16 Ages. 17 Oral. 18 Belt. 19 Hi-Fi. 20 Ogre. 21 Rink.

Kite flying

Highest kites
A record height of 9,740 m (31,955 ft) was reached by a train of eight kites over Lindenberg, Germany, on 1 Aug 1919.

A kite flown by Henry Helm Clayton and A. E. Sweetland at the Blue Hill Weather Station, Milton, Massachusetts, USA, on 28 Feb 1898 attained a record height for a single kite of 3,801 m (12,471 ft).

Longest kite
A 1,034.45-m-long (3,394-ft) kite was made and flown by Michel Trouillet and a team of helpers at Nîmes, France, on 18 Nov 1990.

Largest kite
A 553-m^2 (5,952-ft^2) kite was first flown at Scheveningen, Netherlands, on 8 Aug 1981.

Fastest kite
A record 193 km/h (120 mph) was achieved by a kite flown by Pete DiGiacomo at Ocean City, Maryland, USA, on 22 Sept 1989.

Most figure-of-eights
The greatest number of figure-of-eights to have been achieved in an hour is 2,911, by

Models

Largest matchstick model
Joseph Sciberras made a scale replica of St Publius Parish Church, Floriana, Malta, from more than 3 million matchsticks. It measures 2 x 2 x 1.5 m (6 ft 7 in x 6 ft 7 in x 5 ft).

Smallest model car
Nippondenso of Japan created a motorized model of Toyota's first passenger car, the 1936 AA Sedan, in 1993. It is 4.785 mm ($19/100$ in) long, 1.730 mm ($7/100$ in) wide and 1.736 mm ($7/100$ in) high.

Top distances (24 hour) by model cars
In Sept 1994, a 1:64 scale car made by H. O. Racing and Hobbies of San Diego, California, USA, went 603.631 km (375 miles 139 yd).

Under BSCRA rules, the record for a 1:64 scale car is 320.029 km (198 miles 1,508 yd), at the Rolls Royce Sports Hall, Derby, UK, on 1 and 2 Oct 1994.

Under BSCRA rules, a 1:32 scale car owned by the North London Society of Model Engineers team at the ARRA club, Southport, Merseyside, UK, covered a record-breaking 492.364 km (305 miles 1,670 yd) in 1986.

8 hr 43 min, by Maynard Hill and Robert Rosenthal from Bealeton, Virginia, USA, to Ridgeland, South Carolina, on 29 Aug 1995.

Fastest speeds by model planes
The overall speed record is 395.64 km/h (245.84 mph), by a model flown on control lines by Leonid Lipinski (USSR) in Dec 1971.

The top speed by a radio-controlled model is 390.92 km/h (242.91 mph), by Walter Sitar (Austria) on 10 June 1977.

Longest flights by model aircraft
Maynard Hill (USA) flew a powered model for 33 hr 39 min 15 sec from 1 to 2 Oct 1992.

Jean-Pierre Schiltknecht flew a solar-driven model airplane for a record 10 hr 43 min 51 sec at Wetzlar, Germany, on 10 July 1991.

Top distances (24 hour) by model boats
Lowestoft Model Boat Club members crewed a radio-controlled scale model for 178.93 km (111 miles 317 yd) at Dome Leisure Park, Doncaster, UK, from 17 to 18 Aug 1991.

David and Peter Holland of Doncaster, S Yorkshire, UK, members of the Conisbrough

GHEST ALTITUDE EVER ATTAINED BY A RADIO-CONTROLLED MODEL AIRCRAFT IS 8,205 M

Left
The world's largest radio-controlled model aircraft is a replica of the Antonov An-225 *Mriya*. Made by Simon Cocker of Congleton, Cheshire, UK, it was first flown in July 1995.

Far left
The smallest model car in the world is a replica of a Toyota. Its bumper is 50 microns thick (hair is 80 microns thick) and its motor, the coil of which is 1 mm ($4/100$ in) in diameter, powers the car to a top speed of 0.018 km/h (0.011 mph).

S SEEN ABOUT 60,000 LOCOMOTIVES OVER 40 YEARS

Stu Cohen at Ocean City, Maryland, USA, on 25 Sept 1988.

Most kites flown on a single line
The greatest number of kites ever flown on a single line is 11,284, by Sadao Harada and a team of helpers at Sakurajima, Kagoshima, Japan, on 18 Oct 1990.

Longest flight
The longest recorded flight ever made by a kite lasted a total of 180 hr 17 min. It was flown by the team from Edmonds Community College at Long Beach, Washington State, USA, between 21 and 29 Aug 1982. Managing the flight of this J-25 parafoil was Harry N. Osborne.

Largest model aircraft
The largest radio-controlled model aircraft was a glider weighing 20.4 kg (45 lb), with a wingspan of 5.64 m (18 ft 6 in).

Highest altitude by a model plane
A radio-controlled model owned by Maynard L. Hill (USA) reached a height of 8,205 m (26,919 ft) on 6 Sept 1970.

Greatest distances by models
On 26 June 1995, Maynard Hill and Robert Rosenthal (USA) set a closed-circuit record of 1,250 km (776 miles 1,256 yd).

The longest straight flight to a named landing point was 737.9 km (458 miles 897 yd) in

and District Modelling Association, crewed a scale model of the Bridlington trawler *Margaret H* on a single battery for 24 hours for a record 53.83 km (33 miles 792 yd) at the Dome Leisure Complex, Doncaster, from 15 to 16 Aug 1992.

Greatest distance by a model train
A standard 'Life-Like' BL2 HO scale electric train pulled six eight-wheel coaches for a total of 1,207 hr 30 min from 4 Aug to 23 Sept 1990, covering a distance of 1,463.65 km (909½ miles). The event was organized by Ike Cottingham and Mark Hamrick of Mainline Modelers of Akron, Ohio, USA.

Smallest model railway
A miniature model railway 1:1,400 in scale was constructed by Bob Henderson of Gravenhurst, Ontario, Canada.

Board games

Right
A giant outdoor chess set in Sydney, Australia, provides recreation for anyone who wishes to play. The World Championship for chess was officially instituted in 1886 and the rating system used is the Elo System, which was devised by Arpad E. Elo (1903–92)

Below right
Chess may have developed as early as AD 200, although the oldest pieces found so far (in Nashipur, India) have been dated to c. AD 900. First played in India, the game spread to Russia, the Middle East—the origin of the stone board and metal pieces shown here—and parts of the Far East, before reaching British shores via the Mediterranean in the 12th century.

Slowest timed move 2 hr 20 min

GREATEST NUMBER OF DRAUGHT MATCHES PLAYED WITHOUT A DEFEAT OR A DR

From its introduction in 1957, the women's World Championship title was won by the USSR 11 times.

Youngest world champions
Gary Kimovich Kasparov (USSR, now Russia) was the youngest to win the men's title on 9 Nov 1985, at the age of 22 years 210 days.

Maya Grigoryevna Chiburdanidze (USSR, now Georgia) won the 1978 women's title at the age of 17.

Oldest world champion
The oldest male titleholder was Wilhelm Steinitz (Austria, later USA), who was 58 years

Chess
Longest World Championship titleholders
The longest undisputed tenure was 26 years 337 days, by Dr Emanuel Lasker of Germany from 1894 to 1921.

The women's World Championship title was held by the Czech (later British) player Vera Francevna Stevenson-Menchik from 1927 until her death in 1944. She successfully defended it a record seven times.

Most World Championship wins
The USSR won the biennial men's team title (Olympiad) a record 18 times between 1952 and 1990.

10 days when he lost to Dr Emanuel Lasker on 26 May 1894.

Most British titles
Dr Jonathan Penrose won 10 titles from 1958 to 1963 and from 1966 to 1969.

Rowena Mary Bruce won 11 women's titles between 1937 and 1969.

Youngest grand masters
The youngest individual to qualify as an International Grand Master is Peter Leko of

BEST SINGLE-TURN SCRABB

Hungary, at the age of 14 years 144 days on 30 Jan 1994.

In 1989, Michael Adams, aged 17 years 216 days, became the youngest Briton to qualify.

Highest rating
The highest rating ever attained on the officially adopted Elo System is 2,815, by Gary Kasparov (USSR) in 1993.

The highest rating by a woman player is 2,675, by Judit Polgar (Hungary) in 1996.

The highest Elo rating by a British player is 2,685, by Nigel David Short in 1991.

The Russian chess player Gary Kasparov (b. 1963) beat Anatoly Karpov in 1985 to become the youngest ever world chess champion.

172, OVER FOUR HOURS

The top rating by a British woman is 2,355, by Susan Kathryn Arkell on 1 July 1988.

Most games played
The greatest number of consecutive games ever played is 663, by the Czech (later German) Vlastimil Hort over a period of 32½ hours at Porz, Germany, from 5 to 6 Oct 1984. Hort played 60–120 opponents at a time, winning over 80% of games and averaging 30 moves per game.

The most games played simultaneously is 311, by Ulf Andersson at Alvsjo, Sweden, on 6 Jan 1996. He was defeated only twice.

Anatoly Yevgenyevich Karpov (USSR, now Russia) averaged 45.2 competitive games per year and played in a total of 32 tournaments (winning 26) during his tenure as world champion from 1975 to 1985.

Slowest moves
The slowest moves made in an official event (before time clocks) are reputed to have been those of Louis Charles Paulsen (Germany) v. Paul Charles Morphy (USA) at the first American Chess Congress, New York, in 1857. The game ended in a draw on move 56 after 15 hours. Paulsen had used about 11 of them.

ORE IS 392 FOR 'CAZIQUES'

Grand Master Friedrich Sämisch of Germany ran out of the allotted time (2 hr 30 min for 45 moves) after only 12 moves, in Prague, Czechoslovakia, in 1938.

The record for the slowest recorded move played since the introduction of time clocks was set at Vigo, Spain, in 1980, when Francisco R. Torres Trois took a total of 2 hr 20 min over his seventh move against Luis M. C. P. Santos.

The Master game involving the greatest number of moves was the draw between Ivan Nikolić and Goran Arsović in a tournament in Belgrade (then in Yugoslavia) on 17 Feb 1989. A total of 269 moves were made in a time of 20 hr 15 min.

Draughts
World champions
Walter Hellman of the USA won a record eight world titles during his World Championship tenure from 1948 to 1975.

The youngest winner is Patricia Breen of Co. Carlow, Republic of Ireland, who was 16 when she achieved victory in the Women's World Draughts Championship held at Weston-super-Mare, Somerset, UK, on 1 April 1993.

British titles
The biennial British Championship has been won a record six times by Samuel Cohen, in 1924, 1927, 1929, 1933, 1937 and 1939.

John McGill won a record six Scottish titles between 1959 and 1974.

Greatest number of opponents
Charles Walker played a record 306 games simultaneously at Dollywood, Pigeon Force, Tennessee, USA, on 22 Oct 1994. He won 300 matches, drew five and lost one.

The most consecutive opponents played without a defeat or draw is 172 over four hours, by Nate Cohen of Portland, Maine, USA, at Portland on 26 July 1981.

Scrabble
Greatest number of titles
Philip Nelkon has won the British National title four times (1978, 1981, 1990 and 1992).

Youngest winner
Allan Saldanha was victorious in the British National Championships in 1993, at the age of 15 years 239 days.

World Championship winners
The first World Championship was held in London, UK, in 1991 and was played in English. The winner was American player Peter Morris (USA), who collected a first prize of $10,000 (£5,600).

The youngest World Championship winner is British player Mark Hyman, who won the title in 1993, at the age of 26 years 320 days.

Highest scores
The highest ever competitive game score is 1,049, by Phil Appleby in June 1989. His margin of victory, 796 points, is also a record. The total included a single-turn score of 374 for the word 'OXIDIZERS'.

The highest competitive single-turn score on record is 392, by Dr Saladin Karl Khoshnaw in Manchester, UK, in April 1982. Khoshnaw laid down the word 'CAZIQUES', which means 'native chiefs of West Indian aborigines'.

Below
Scrabble was developed by Alfred Butts (USA) in 1931, although it did not go on sale until 1946, when it was known as Lexico. The trademark name of Scrabble was first used in 1948.

Games and gambling

Right
In a deck of 52 cards there are 635,013,559,600 bridge hands, while the number of possible bridge deals among four players is truly astronomic— 53,644,737,765, 488,792,839,237, 400,000. The odds against a player holding the hand shown here—or any other hand—are 635,013,559,599 to 1.

Below right
The first gambling slot machine with a variable payout was manufactured in San Francisco, USA, in 1905. The highest prize available was 50 cents for three bells— somewhat less than the highest ever payout on a machine, which was more than $9.3 million (£5 million).

Card games
Contract Bridge championships
The biggest bridge tournament was Epson World Bridge Championship from 20 to 21 June 1992. It was contested by more than 102,000 players playing the same hands at more than 2,000 centres worldwide.

The holder of the most world titles is the USA, which has won the World Championship (Bermuda Bowl) a record 14 times (1950–51, 1953–54, 1970–71, 1976–77, 1979, 1981, 1983, 1985, 1987 and 1995).

Italy's Squadra Azzura won 13 world titles and three team Olympiads from 1957 to 1975. Giorgio Belladonna was in all winning teams.

The USA have had a record six wins in the women's World Championship for the Venice Trophy (1974, 1976, 1978, 1987, 1989 and 1991), and three women's wins at the World Team Olympiad (1976, 1980 and 1984).

Cribbage
Five maximum 29-point hands were achieved by Sean Daniels of Astoria, Oregon, USA, from 1989 to 1992. Paul Nault of Athol, Massachusetts, USA, had two such hands in eight games in a tournament in March 1977.

The most points scored in 24 hours by a team of four, playing singles in two pairs, is 139,454, by Colin Cooper, John Dunk, Peter Hyam and John Wilson at HMP Doncaster from 16 to 17 Sept 1995.

Marbles
Most titles
The most frequent winners of the British Championship are the Toucan Terribles, who won 20 consecutive titles from 1956 to 1975. Three founder members, Len Smith, and Jack and Charlie Dempsey, played in every title win. They were finally beaten in 1976 by the Pernod Rams, captained by Len Smith's son, Paul. Len Smith won the individual title a total of 15 times (1957–64, 1966 and 1968–73), but lost to his son Alan in 1974.

Fastest time
The record for clearing the ring, with a diameter of 1.75–1.9 m (5 ft 9 in–6 ft 3 in), of 49 marbles is 2 min 56 sec, by the 'Black Dog Boozers' of Crawley, W Sussex, UK, at BBC Television Centre, London, for *Record Breakers* on 14 Sept 1987.

Tiddlywinks
World Championships
Larry Kahn (USA) has won the tiddlywinks singles title 14 times from 1983 to 1995.

Geoff Meyers and Andy Purvis have won a record seven pairs titles from 1991 to 1995.

National Championships
Alan Dean won the singles title six times (1971–73, 1976, 1978 and 1986), and the pairs title six times. Jonathan Mapley won the pairs title seven times (1972, 1975, 1977, 1980, 1983–84 and 1987).

Potting records
The record for potting 24 winks from 45 cm (18 in) is 21.8 seconds, by Stephen Williams of Altrincham Grammar School in May 1966.

In 1966, Allen R. Astles potted 10,000 winks in 3 hr 51 min 46 sec at Aberystwyth, UK.

The most winks potted in relay is 41 in three minutes, by Patrick Barrie, Nick Inglis, Geoff Myers and Andy Purvis of Cambridge University Tiddlywinks Club, UK, in 1989 and 1995.

The high-jump record is 3.49 m (11 ft 5 in), by Adrian Jones, David Smith and Ed Wynn of Cambridge University Tiddlywinks Club, UK, on 21 Oct 1989.

The long-jump record is 9.52 m (31 ft 3 in), by Ben Soares of St Andrews Tiddlywinks Society on 14 Jan 1995.

Skittles

Highest score at West Country skittles
The highest score by a team of eight is 99,051, by the 'Alkies' team at Courtlands Holiday Inn, Torquay, Devon, UK, in April 1987. They reset the skittles after every ball.

Highest hood skittle score
In June 1992, 12 players from the Semilong Working Mens Club, Northampton, UK, scored a record 144,648 pins in 24 hours.

Highest long alley score
A team from the Carpenters Arms, Leigh, Dorset, UK, scored 94,151 in March 1995.

Highest table skittle score
In April 1990, 12 players at the Castle Mona, Newcastle, Staffs, UK, attained the highest 24-hour score of 116,047 skittles.

Gambling

Biggest win
The largest individual win is $111,240,463.10 (£74,353,689), by Leslie Robbins and Colleen DeVries of Fond du Lac, Wisconsin, USA, in the Powerball lottery of 7 July 1993.

Horse racing
The highest secured odds were 3,072,887 to 1, by a woman from Nottingham, UK. For a five-pence accumulator on five horses in May 1995, she won £153,644.40 for the accumulator and £208,098.79 in total.

Edward Hodson from Wolverhampton, W Midlands, UK, landed a 3,956,748 to 1 bet for a 55-pence stake on 11 Feb 1984, but his bookmaker had a £3,000 payout limit.

Odds of 31,793 to 1 on a 'double' were paid by the New Zealand Totalisator Agency Board on a five-shilling tote ticket at Addington, Christchurch, in 1951.

A payout of $1,627,084.40 (£988,211)— after income tax of $406,768 (£249,550)— was paid to Britons Anthony Speelman and Nicholas Cowan on a $64 (£39.25) nine-horse accumulator at Santa Anita racecourse, California, USA, on 19 April 1987. Their first seven selections won and the payout was for a jackpot, accumulated over 24 days.

The largest ever payout by a bookmaker in the United Kingdom was £567,066.25, by

Ladbrokes to Dick Mussell of Havant, Hants, for the combination of an accumulator, trebles, doubles and singles on five horses at Cheltenham on 12 March 1992.

The biggest recorded tote win was £341 2s 6d to 2s, representing odds of 3,410¼ to 1, by Catharine Unsworth of Blundellsands, Liverpool, Merseyside, UK, on a race won by *Coole* at Haydock Park on 30 Nov 1929.

The highest odds in Irish tote history was £289.64 for a 10-pence unit on *Gene's Rogue* at Limerick on 28 Dec 1981.

The only recorded instance of a racing correspondent forecasting 10 out of 10 winners on a race card occurred on 28 July 1974. It was by Charles Lamb of the *Baltimore News American* at Delaware Park, Wilmington, Delaware, USA.

The record for a British correspondent is seven out of seven winners, for a meeting at Wolverhampton on 22 March 1982 by Bob Butchers of the *Daily Mirror*. This feat was repeated by Fred Shawcross of the *Today* newspaper at York on 12 May 1988.

BE CALLED IN BINGO WAS ON THE 86TH NUMBER. THERE WERE 32 WINNERS

The top prize won in any British competition is £22,590,829, by Mark Gardiner and Paul Maddison of Hastings, E Sussex, UK, in the National Lottery draw of 10 June 1995.

Slot machines
The biggest win on a 'one-armed bandit' is $9,357,489.41 (£5,167,314), by Delores Adams at Harrah's Reno Casino-Hotel, Nevada, USA, on 30 May 1992.

Bingo
The largest 'house' in bingo sessions was 15,756, at the Canadian National Exhibition, Toronto, on 19 Aug 1983. There was a record one-game payout of $Can100,000 (£58,000) at the same event.

The earliest 'Full House' calls were on the 15th number, by: Norman A. Wilson at Guide Post Working Men's Club, Bedlington, UK, on 22 June 1978; Anne Wintle of Bryncethin, Mid Glamorgan, UK, on a coach trip on 17 Aug 1982; and Shirley Lord at Kahibah Bowling Club, NSW, Australia, on 24 Oct 1983.

The latest 'Full House' call was on the 86th number, at Hillsborough Working Men's Club, Sheffield, S Yorkshire, UK, on 11 Jan 1982. There were 32 winners.

Football pools
The record individual payout in the United Kingdom is £2,924,622.60, by Littlewoods Pools to a syndicate at the Yew Tree Inn, Worlsey, Greater Manchester, for matches played on 19 Nov 1994.

The record total payout in one week is £4,457,671, by Littlewoods for matches played on 12 March 1994.

Left
Edna de Paolo of Boontown, New Jersey, USA, shows the card that helped her to victory in her state's first legal game of bingo at the Mt Virgin Catholic Church in Garfield in 1954. The origins of bingo can be traced back to keno, a lottery game developed in the 1880s but thought to have evolved from the 17th-century Italian game *tumbule*.

The circus

Right
Performing elephants poke their trunks out of a circus tent during Sanger's Circus Tour of 1937. Circus shows traditionally consist of a combination of acrobats, clowns and performing animals, but animals acts have declined in popularity in recent times.

Below right
One of the most daring circus feats is the human cannonball, which was first performed in 1871. When David Smith broke the record for the greatest distance that a human cannonball had been fired, in 1995, he beat a record that had stood for more than 50 years.

Flexible pole
The world's first quadruple back somersault on the flexible pole to be performed in public was achieved by Maxim Dobrovitsky (USSR) and the Egorov Troupe at the International Circus Festival of Monte Carlo, Monaco, on 4 Feb 1989.

Corina Colonelu Mosoianu of Romania is the world's only circus performer to have completed a triple full twisting somersault on the flexible pole. She performed this on 17 April 1984 at Madison Square Garden, New York City, USA.

High wire
A record-breaking seven-person pyramid (three layers) was achieved on the high wire by the Great Wallendas of Germany at Wallenda Circus, USA, in 1947.

PHILIPPE PETIT WALKED T

The world's highest ever high-wire feat (ground-supported) took place at a height of 411 m (1,350 ft) between the towers of the World Trade Center in New York City, USA, on 7 Aug 1974. It was performed by Philippe Petit (France).

Skipping
Walfer Guerrero of Colombia achieved a record-breaking 521 consecutive turns skipping on a tightrope at Circus Carré in Haarlem, Netherlands, on 1 June 1995.

Aerial acts
Trapeze acts
The highest trapeze act was performed by Mike Howard (GB), who was suspended from a hot-air balloon between Glastonbury and Street, Somerset, UK, on 10 Aug 1995, reaching an altitude of 6,000–6,200 m (19,600–20,300 ft).

Janet May Klemke (USA) performed a record 305 one-arm planges at Medina Shrine Circus, Chicago, Illinois, USA, on 21 Jan 1938.

A single-heel hang on a swinging bar was first performed by Angela Revelle in Australia in 1977.

Flying return trapeze acts
A flying return trapeze act was first performed by Jules Léotard at Cirque Napoléon, Paris, France, on 12 Nov 1859.

In April 1897, Lena Jordan from Latvia performed the first triple back somersault on the flying trapeze, to Lewis Jordan of the USA in Sydney, Australia.

The world record for the greatest ever number of back somersaults is a quadruple back, achieved by Miguel Vásquez to Juan Vásquez (Mexico), at Ringling Bros. and Barnum & Bailey Circus, Tucson, Arizona, USA, on 10 July 1982.

The greatest number of consecutive triple back somersaults is 135, by Jamie Ibarra to Alejandro Ibarra (Mexico), from 23 July to 12 Oct 1989, at various locations in the USA.

Stunts
Human cannonball
The world's first human cannonball was Eddie Rivers ('Lulu') of the USA, who was fired from a Farini cannon at Royal Cremorne Music Hall, London, UK, in 1871.

The record for the greatest distance that a human being has ever been fired from a cannon is 54.94 m (180 ft). It was set by David Smith at Manville, New Jersey, USA, on 13 Aug 1995.

Human arrow
The first human arrow in the world was Tony Zedoras, at Barnum & Bailey Circus, USA, in 1896. For his record-breaking performance Zedoras was billed as 'Alar'.

The record for the greatest distance that a human being has been fired from a bow is 22.9 m (75 ft), by the Bulgarian performer Vesta Gueschkova ('Airiana'), who was launched from a crossbow at Ringling Bros. and Barnum & Bailey Circus, Tampa, Florida, USA, on 27 Dec 1995.

Highest trapeze 6,000–6,200 m

Human pyramid

The heaviest ever pyramid made up of human beings weighed a total of 771 kg (1,700 lb). The record-breaking feat was performed by Tahar Douis supporting 12 members of the Hassani Troupe in three levels at the BBC TV studios, Birmingham, W Midlands, UK, on 17 Dec 1979.

The highest human pyramid in the world was 12 m (39 ft) tall. It was achieved when Josep-Joan Martínez Lozano of the Colla Vella dels Xiquets mounted a nine-high pyramid at Valls, Spain, on 25 Oct 1981.

Plate spinning

The world record for the greatest number of plates to have been spun simultaneously is 108, by Dave Spathaky of London, UK, on 23 Nov 1992, for the *Tarm Pai Du* television programme in Thailand.

Risley

The first back somersault feet-to-feet in the world was performed by Richard Risley Carlisle (USA), after whom the feat was

only one person on each level) in Shanghai, China, in 1993.

Trampoline

Marco Canestrelli of the USA performed a septuple twisting back somersault to bed at Ringling Bros. and Barnum & Bailey Circus, St Petersburg, Florida, USA, on 5 Jan 1979. On 28 March 1979, he went on to achieve a quintuple twisting back somersault to a two-high column, to Belmonte Canestrelli, at Ringling Bros. and Barnum & Bailey Circus, New York City, USA.

On 30 June 1981, French trampolinist Richard Tisson achieved a triple twisting triple back somersault at Berchtesgaden, Germany.

Animal acts
Horseback riding

The world record for the greatest number of consecutive somersaults on horseback is 23, by James Robinson of the USA at Spalding & Rogers Circus, Pittsburgh, Pennsylvania, USA, in 1856.

Left
In 1947 the Great Wallendas set a record for the largest pyramid of human beings ever achieved on the high wire. One of the most famous names in the world of the circus, their record remains intact half a century later.

unaided lion-tamer is 40, by 'Captain' Alfred Schneider in 1925.

Clyde Raymond Beatty (USA) handled 43 'mixed cats' (lions and tigers) simultaneously in 1938. He was the featured attraction at every show he appeared in for more than 40 years and insisted on being called a lion-trainer rather than a lion-tamer.

Performers and audiences
Most performers

The most performers in a circus act was 263, plus about 175 animals, in the Barnum & Bailey Circus cast during its 1890 US tour.

The most performers in an animal-free circus was 61, for Cirque du Soleil's production of *Fascination* on their 1992 tour of Japan.

Largest audiences

An audience of 52,385 saw Ringling Bros. and Barnum & Bailey at the Superdome, New Orleans, Louisiana, USA, on 14 Sept 1975.

The largest circus audience in a tent was 16,702 (15,686 paid), for Ringling Bros. and Barnum & Bailey, at Concordia, Kansas, USA, on 13 Sept 1924.

Worst circus disaster

In 1944, 168 people were killed in a fire in the Ringling Bros. and Barnum & Bailey Circus main tent at Hartford, Connecticut, USA.

Circus edifices
Oldest permanent circus building

The Cirque d'Hiver (originally the Cirque Napoléon), opened in Paris, France, on 11 Dec 1852.

Largest travelling circus tent

A Ringling Bros. and Barnum & Bailey tent used on US tours from 1921 to 1924 covered 8,492 m² (2.10 acres). It consisted of a round top 61 m (200 ft) in diameter with five middle sections, each 18 m (60 ft) wide.

Left
Horseback riding played a major role in the origin and subsequent evolution of the circus, especially in the USA, with two of the most significant records in this area set there. Although the Fredianis first performed a record-breaking three-high column on a horse in France, they soon introduced their feat to US audiences during a tour with Barnum & Bailey's Greatest Show on Earth.

named, and his son at the Theatre Royal, Edinburgh, UK, in 1844.

Stilt-walking

The tallest stilts ever mastered measured 12.43 m (40 ft 9½ in) from ground to ankle. On 3 Aug 1988, Eddy Wolf ('Steady Eddy') of Loyal, Wisconsin, USA, used aluminium stilts of this length to walk 25 steps without touching his safety handrail wires. The stilts, which weighed 25.9 kg (57 lb) each, were also the heaviest ever mastered.

Teeter board

The Shanghai Acrobats achieved a record-breaking six-person-high unaided column (with

Willy, Beby and Rene Fredianis of Italy performed a three-high column at Nouveau Cirque, Paris, France, in 1908.

'Poodles' Hanneford of Ireland holds the record for the greatest number of running leaps on and off a horse, with 26 at Barnum & Bailey Circus, New York, USA, in 1915.

Animal handling

In 1904, Willy Hagenbeck worked with a record 70 polar bears in a presentation at the Paul Busch Circus, Berlin, Germany.

The greatest number of lions ever to have been mastered and fed in a cage by an

Radio and recorded sound

Right
The Radio 4 drama *The Archers* was created by Godfrey Baseley. First broadcast in 1951, it is currently the longest running radio serial.

Middle right
Bob Geldof, together with Midge Ure, wrote and produced *Do They Know It's Christmas*, the best-selling single in the United Kingdom, which sold 1.6 million copies in its first week on sale in Dec 1984 and a worldwide total of more than 8 million copies.

Far right
Do They Know It's Christmas was performed by Band Aid at the Live Aid concert on 13 July 1985. Profits went to the Ethiopian Famine Relief Fund.

Radio

First broadcasts
The world's first advertised broadcast was made on 24 Dec 1906 by Canadian-born Prof. Reginald Aubrey Fessenden from the mast of the National Electric Signalling Company at Brant Rock, Massachusetts, USA. The transmission included Handel's *Largo*. Fessenden had broadcast speech as early as Nov 1900, but it was highly distorted.

The earliest experimental broadcasting transmitter in the United Kingdom was set up at the Marconi Works in Chelmsford, Essex, in Dec 1919. It broadcast a news service in Feb 1920. The earliest regular broadcast was made from the Marconi transmitter '2MT' at Writtle, Essex, on 14 Feb 1922.

Largest audience
The global estimated audience for the BBC World Service, which is broadcast in 41 languages, was 140 million regular listeners in 1995. (This is a conservative estimate, as figures for several countries are not available due to restrictions on audience research.)

The known peak listenership on BBC Radio was 30 million, for the boxing match between Lee Savold (US) and Bruce Woodcock (GB) on 6 June 1950.

Longest-running radio programmes
Rambling with Gambling, aired six days a week on WOR radio in New York City, USA, was first broadcast in March 1925 and has been continued by three generations of the Gambling family. The 21,881st show was broadcast on 30 April 1995.

The longest-running BBC series is *The Week's Good Cause*, which began on 24 Jan 1926.

The longest-running record programme is *Desert Island Discs*, which began on 29 Jan 1942. It was originally presented by its creator Roy Plomley, who died on 28 May 1985 after having presented 1,791 editions. It is now hosted by Sue Lawley. The most appearances on the show is four, by Arthur Askey. The most popular piece of music chosen by the guests is Beethoven's 'An die Freude' (Ode to Joy), which has been requested 60 times.

The longest-running solo radio feature is *Letter from America* by (Alfred) Alistair Cooke, which was first broadcast on 24 March 1946 by Raymond Gram Swing.

The longest-running serial is *The Archers*, first broadcast on 1 Jan 1951. The only role played without interruption from the start is that of Philip Archer, by Norman Painting.

Most radio stations
The USA had a total of 12,069 authorized radio stations on 31 April 1996—more than any other country.

Highest response to a radio show
From 21 to 27 June 1993, *FM Osaka 85.1* in Osaka, Japan, received a total of 8,091,309 calls in response to a phone-in lottery. The prize was 100,000 yen (then around £920), and the lines were open for 20 minutes at a time, 10 times a day. The maximum call-count in one day of phone-ins (3 hr 20 min) was 1,540,793, on 23 June.

Brain of Britain quiz
The youngest person to become 'Brain of Britain' on BBC radio was Anthony Carr of Anglesey, Gwynedd, in 1956, aged 16.

The oldest contestant was the author and translator Hugh Merrick, who competed in his 80th year in Aug 1977.

The record score in the quiz is 35, by both the 1981 winner, Peter Barlow of Richmond, Surrey, and the 1984 winner, Peter Bates of Taunton, Somerset.

Recorded sound

Most successful solo recording artists
Bing Crosby (1904–77) began his solo recording career in 1931 and had accumulated 156 hits by 1940. He recorded an estimated 2,600 songs in his lifetime and had 317 hits in the USA before the rock era.

Elvis Aron Presley (1935–77) holds the record for the most No. 1 hits by a solo artist since the beginning of the rock era in 1955, with a total of 18 in the USA and 17 in the United Kingdom.

Most successful group
The Beatles hold the record for the greatest sales by any group: all-time sales have been estimated by EMI at more than 1 billion discs and tapes.

Most successful UK debuts
Kylie Minogue, whose debut album *Kylie* topped the UK chart in July 1988, had her first 10 singles reach the Top 5.

In Sept 1994, *Saturday Night* entered the UK chart at No. 1, making Whigfield the first solo artist to debut in that position.

Sales awards
Since the Recording Industry Association of America (RIAA) introduced its awards on 14 March 1958, The Beatles have won the most platinum certifications, at 76.

Grammy Awards
The all-time record for awards to an individual is 31, to the Hungarian-born British conductor Sir Georg Solti since 1958.

The most Grammy awards won by a solo pop performer is 17, by Stevie Wonder.

The most Grammy Awards won by a pop group is eight, by the 5th Dimension.

The greatest number of people ever to share a Grammy Award is 46, by the Chicago Symphony Orchestra.

The most Grammy Awards won in one year is eight, by Michael Jackson in 1984.

Biggest-selling singles
The biggest-selling record to date is *White Christmas*, written by Irving Berlin and recorded by Bing Crosby on 29 May 1942. It is estimated that sales exceed 30 million.

The highest sales claimed for a 'pop' record is an unaudited 25 million, for *Rock Around the Clock* (copyright in 1953 by James E. Myers, under the name Jimmy DeKnight, and the late Max C. Freedman), which was recorded on 12 April 1954 by Bill Haley and his Comets.

The top-selling single by a British act worldwide is *I Want to Hold Your Hand* by The Beatles, released in 1963, with sales of more than 13 million.

The record for the biggest ever sales of a single in the United Kingdom is held by *Do They Know It's Christmas*, which was recorded by Band Aid in 1984. British sales have exceeded 3.6 million.

Biggest-selling albums
The best-selling album of all time is *Thriller* by Michael Jackson, with global sales of more than 47 million copies to date.

The best-selling album by a group is *Dark Side of the Moon* by Pink Floyd, sales of which are estimated at 22 million.

The album to have sold the greatest number of copies in the United Kingdom is *Sgt Pepper's Lonely Hearts Club Band* by The Beatles, sales of which have surpassed 4.25 million since its release in June 1967.

Happy Nation, released in some territories as *The Sign*, by the Swedish quartet Ace of Base, has sold more than 19 million copies worldwide, making it the best-selling debut album of all time.

The fastest selling non-charity single in the United Kingdom is Babylon Zoo's *Spaceman*. Released on 15 Jan 1996, it entered the singles chart at No. 1 after selling 420,000 copies in six days—28.8% of all singles sold that week.

Fastest-selling albums
The fastest-selling non-pop record of all time is *John Fitzgerald Kennedy—A Memorial Album*. Recorded on 22 Nov 1963, the day of President Kennedy's assassination, it sold 4 million copies at 99 cents each in six days from 7 to 12 Dec 1963.

The fastest-selling album in the United Kingdom is *Robson & Jerome*, which sold 483,000 copies from 18 to 23 Dec 1995.

Greatest advance sales
The record for the greatest advance sales for a single worldwide is 2.1 million copies, for *Can't Buy Me Love* by The Beatles, released on 21 March 1964.

The record for the highest ever advance sales of an album in the United Kingdom is 1.1 million copies, for *Welcome to the Pleasure Dome*, the debut album by the group Frankie Goes To Hollywood, which was released in 1984.

CHART IS 50, BY EVERYTHING BUT THE GIRL'S *MISSING*

The best-selling debut album in the United Kingdom is *Robson & Jerome* by Robson Green and Jerome Flynn, with sales of almost 2.5 million by 1996.

The best-selling movie soundtrack of all time is *Saturday Night Fever* (1977), with sales of more than 26.5 million.

The best-selling classical album is *In Concert*, which has had global sales of 5 million copies. It was recorded by José Carreras, Placido Domingo and Luciano Pavarotti in 1990.

Fastest-selling singles
In the USA, *We are the World*, by USA for Africa, is reported to have sold 800,000 copies in just three days in March 1985.

In the United Kingdom, *Do They Know It's Christmas* sold 1.6 million in its first week on sale in Dec 1984.

Longest gap between UK hits
The record for the longest gap between UK hits is 36 years, by Cuban orchestra leader Perez 'Prez' Prado, between *Patricia* in 1958 and *Guaglione* in 1994. The latter title was actually recorded in 1958, but it only became a hit after it was used in an advert for Guinness.

Most charted song in United Kingdom
In the United Kingdom, *Unchained Melody*, which was written by Alex North and Hy Zaret, has been a hit in a total of eight different versions, five of which have made the Top 10. It is also the only song to have been a No. 1 hit by three separate acts: Jimmy Young in 1955, the Righteous Brothers in 1990 and Robson Green and Jerome Flynn in 1995.

Oldest recording to enter UK chart
Winifred Shaw's song *Lullaby of Broadway* entered the UK singles chart in 1976, 41 years after it was recorded.

Oldest performer
The oldest artist to have had a hit with newly recorded material is the comedian George Burns, whose ironic *I Wish I Was 18 Again* entered the US singles chart on 19 Jan 1980—the day before his 84th birthday.

Phonographic identification
Dr Arthur B. Lintgen (b. 1932) of Rydal, Pennsylvania, USA, has a proven and as yet unique ability to identify the music on phonograph records purely by visual inspection and without hearing a note.

BRITISH CHARTS
The UK singles chart was introduced by the *New Musical Express* on 14 Nov 1952, as a Top 12. Since then the chart has become a Top 75 and is now compiled by CIN. Nearly 20,000 singles have charted for 5,000 different artists. The UK albums chart began on 8 Nov 1958 and has featured 14,000 albums by some 3,500 performers.

Most weeks on singles chart
The longest time that a single has spent on the chart is 165 weeks, for *My Way* by Frank Sinatra, in four separate runs, 1969–1995.

The record for the most consecutive weeks on the chart is 56, for Engelbert Humperdinck's *Release Me*, from 26 Jan 1967.

Most hit singles
Cliff Richard had a record 118 hit singles to May 1996.

Most No. 1 singles
The Beatles and Elvis Presley hold the record for the most No. 1 hit singles, with 17 each.

The most consecutive No. 1s is 11, by The Beatles between 1963 and 1966 (from *From Me to You* through to *Yellow Submarine*).

Most weeks on album chart
The first No. 1 album was the film soundtrack *South Pacific*, which held the position for a record 70 consecutive weeks and eventually spent a record total of 115 weeks at No. 1.

The album to spend the most weeks on the chart is *Bat Out of Hell* by Meat Loaf, with 472 weeks by Dec 1993.

The most weeks on the chart by a classical album is 81 weeks to Dec 1993, for Vivaldi's *Four Seasons* by Nigel Kennedy and the English Chamber Orchestra.

Most hit albums
The Beatles have had the most No. 1 albums, with 14, and Elvis Presley the most hit albums, with a total of 97 by May 1995.

Most weeks at No. 1
I Believe by Frankie Laine held the No. 1 position for 18 weeks (non-consecutive) from April 1953.

Bryan Adams spent a record 16 consecutive weeks at No. 1 from July to Oct 1991 with *(Everything I Do) I Do It For You*.

US CHARTS
Most weeks on singles chart
Bing Crosby's *White Christmas* spent a record total of 86 weeks on the chart between 1942 and 1962.

Missing by Everything But The Girl had been on the chart for a record-breaking 50 consecutive weeks to 20 July 1996.

Most hit singles
Elvis Presley has had a record 149 hit singles on the *Billboard* Hot 100 from 1956 to 1996.

Most No. 1 singles
The Beatles have had the most No. 1 hits, with 20.

Most weeks on album chart
Dark Side of the Moon by Pink Floyd enjoyed a total of 741 weeks on the *Billboard* charts, after which it was placed in the separate catalog chart, where it remains after five years.

Most No. 1 albums
The most No. 1 albums by a group is 17, by The Beatles.

Elvis Presley had a record nine No. 1 solo albums.

Most weeks at No. 1
Near You by Francis Craig topped the chart for 17 weeks in 1947.

Elvis Presley's 18 No. 1 records have occupied the top of the charts for a total of 80 weeks.

The most weeks at No. 1 by an album is 69 (non-consecutive), by the soundtrack *South Pacific* from May 1949.

Music of the 90s

TOP-SELLING OASIS SINGLE, *WONDERWALL*, SOLD 700,000 COPIES

Right
The huge popularity of Mancunian band Oasis looks set to make their second album, *(What's the Story) Morning Glory?*, the best-selling British album ever.

Far right
The best-selling singles artists of the 90s, from top to bottom:
Take That
Michael Jackson
Oasis
Madonna
Wet Wet Wet
Mariah Carey
Robson and Jerome
East 17
Bryan Adams
Whitney Houston

Hits of the 90s
Best-selling singles
Romantic ballads have made a massive impression in the nineties, constituting the top five singles of the decade to date. Leading the way with a total of 1.84 million sales (enough to make it one of the 10 biggest-sellers of all time in the United Kingdom) is *Unchained Melody/White Cliffs Of Dover*, the debut single by television stars Robson Green and Jerome Flynn. The former song dates back to 1955, and the latter back to 1942. The runner-up, *Love Is All Around* by Wet Wet Wet, is also an old song, having first been recorded by The Troggs in 1967.

Whitney Houston's revival of Dolly Parton's *I Will Always Love You*, placed fourth, is the biggest-selling single ever by a female soloist, while Whigfield's *Saturday Night* was the first ever debut single to enter the chart at No. 1. In 1995, the first UK rap No. 1 came with Coolio's *Gangsta's Paradise*.

Best-selling singles artists
Five international artists and five British superstars share the honours in a Top 10 that reflects the fact that almost half of all records brought in the United Kingdom are by indigenous talent. Although the decade was almost two years old before their first minor hits, Take That have sold almost 1 million singles more than any other act in the 90s. In third place are their fellow Mancunians Oasis, who have released far fewer singles and did not get their first break until well into 1994. Michael Jackson and Madonna, in second and fourth place, are perennially popular. The latter has had 21 consecutive Top 20 hits in the 90s—the lengthiest string of hits of this magnitude by any artist in the survey period.

Best-selling albums
Simply Red's *Stars* has spent longer at No. 1 (12 weeks) and sold more copies (3.24 million) than any other album. Released in Oct 1991, its success is all the more remarkable because it yielded only five hit singles, none of which climbed higher than No. 8. Oasis' second album *(What's The Story) Morning Glory?* established the group as the sales phenomenon of the mid 90s, selling 3 million copies in less than a year. It lingered longer in the Top 3 than any album since Simon & Garfunkel's *Bridge Over Troubled Water* and spent 39 weeks in a row in the Top 10. In third place, *Robson & Jerome* replaced Kylie Minogue's album *Kylie* as the biggest-selling debut album of all time.

Best-selling albums artists
Since establishing themselves in 1974, Queen have been hugely popular and remarkably consistent. Their tally of 46 hit singles is superior to any group except for Status Quo, while their total of 24 Top 10 hits is just three fewer than The Beatles' 27. They have proved equally successful as an album act, with nine No. 1s—a total beaten only by The Beatles and the Rolling Stones. Their total of 6 million album sales in the 90s is due partly to the release of a second volume of *Greatest Hits* in 1991, strong sales of their catalogue of 22 albums, and the poignant *Made In Heaven*, a 1995 release widely recognized as the group's last official album. They are the only act to have had two completely different and separate *Greatest Hits* albums sell more than 2 million copies each. Trailing Queen by nearly half a million sales, Simply Red have released a comparatively modest five albums, just two in the nineties. Madonna is the only other artist to sell 5 million albums in the 90s.

Record-breaking city
Overshadowed by Liverpool in the 1960s, Manchester has proved a more lasting and fertile breeding ground for musical talent than any city of comparable size.

Take That
Before disbanding in 1996, Take That, with 16 consecutive British hit singles, had sold a total of 4.5 million copies and were the most successful teen act since The Beatles. Of the last nine hits, all but one (*Love Ain't Here Anymore*) reached No. 1. Their best single in terms of sales was *Back for Good*, followed by *How Deep is Your Love*, *Babe*, *Everything Changes* and *Never Forget*.

Oasis
After just two albums of songs written by Noel Gallagher and sung by his brother Liam, Oasis have sold more than 4 million albums, including 3 million of their latest *(What's the Story) Morning Glory?*, which became one of the 10 best-selling albums of all time in the United Kingdom within six months of its release, and looks set to overtake The Beatles' *Sgt Pepper's Lonely Hearts Club Band* as the best-selling British album ever. Oasis have also sold upwards of 3 million singles, including 700,000 copies of their most successful, *Wonderwall*, which shares with Everything But the Girl's *Missing* the honour of being the best-selling single of the last 10 years not to reach No. 1.

Simply Red
Simply Red are the only British act to have had two albums sell more than 2 million copies in the United Kingdom. *Stars* is the No. 3 album of all time, with more than 3,600,000 copies sold, while *A New Flame* has sold more than 2,100,000 copies. Their five albums to date have sold approximately 9 million copies since 1985—more than any other act in the same time frame.

Most album sales 3.24 million

TAKE THAT SOLD ABOUT 1 MILLION SINGLES MORE THAN ANY OTHER 90S ACT

BEST-SELLING RECORDS (UK)
JAN 1990–JULY 1996

Best-selling singles
1 *Unchained Melody/White Cliffs of Dover*
  Robson Green and Jerome Flynn
2 *Love is all Around*
  Wet Wet Wet
3 *(Everything I Do) I Do It For You*
  Bryan Adams
4 *I Will Always Love You*
  Whitney Houston
5 *Think Twice*
  Celine Dion
6 *Gangsta's Paradise*
  Coolio featuring LV
7 *Killing Me Softly*
  The Fugees
8 *Saturday Night*
  Whigfield
9 *I Believe/Up on the Roof*
  Robson Green and Jerome Flynn
10 *Spaceman*
  Babylon Zoo

Best-selling artists (singles)
1 Take That
2 Michael Jackson
3 Oasis
4 Madonna
5 Wet Wet Wet
6 Mariah Carey
7 Robson Green and Jerome Flynn
8 East 17
9 Bryan Adams
10 Whitney Houston

Best-selling albums
1 *Stars*
  Simply Red
2 *(What's the Story) Morning Glory?*
  Oasis
3 *Robson & Jerome*
  Robson Green and Jerome Flynn
4 *The Immaculate Collection*
  Madonna
5 *Greatest Hits Volume II*
  Queen
6 *The Very Best of Elton John*
  Elton John
7 *The Bodyguard*
  Whitney Houston/Various
8 *Dangerous*
  Michael Jackson
9 *Simply the Best*
  Tina Turner
10 *Automatic for the People*
  REM

Best-selling artists (albums)
1 Queen
2 Simply Red
3 Madonna
4 REM
5 Elton John
6 Oasis
7 Luciano Pavarotti (including collaborations
  with José Carreras and Placido Domingo)
8 Michael Bolton
9 Michael Jackson
10 Take That

EUROVISION
The first Eurovision Song contest took place in May 1956 and was born out of the already popular San Remo music festival in Italy. In the first year, seven countries took part, each submitting two entries. Switzerland, the hosts of the event, were declared the winners. They were not to triumph again until 1988, when the Canadian chanteuse Celine Dion pipped the United Kingdom into second place by a mere point. The United Kingdom has been runner-up 14 times and has a better overall record than even Ireland, who won the contest for a record seventh time in 1996.

In spite of widespread criticism, the festival has continued to evolve over the years and the number of countries competing has grown steadily. Its popularity has proved something of a problem for its organizers, the European Broadcasting Union; in 1996 no fewer than 30 countries wished to take part, but programming constraints could only allow for 23 entrants. The decision to hold a 'mini-Eurovision' qualifier prior to the main contest added to the logistical headache of holding such a major international event, and this, combined with the financial burden placed on the host nation's television company, has meant that much press coverage has centred not on who will win, but on who can afford to win.

1956	*Refrains* by Lys Assia (Switzerland)
1957	*Net Als Toen* by Corry Brokken (Netherlands)
1958	*Dors, Mon Amour* by André Claveau (France)
1959	*Een Beetje* by Teddy Scholten (Netherlands)
1960	*Tom Pillibi* by Jacqueline Boyer (France)
1961	*Nous, Les Amoureux* by Jean Claude Pascal (Luxembourg)
1962	*Un Premier Amour* by Isabelle Aubret (France)
1963	*Dansevise* by Goethe and Jorgen Ingmann (Denmark)
1964	*Non Ho L'eta Per Amarti* by Gigliola Cinquetti (Italy)
1965	*Poupée De Cire, Poupée De Son* by France Gall (Luxembourg)
1966	*Merci Chérie* by Udo Jurgens (Austria)
1967	*Puppet On A String* by Sandie Shaw (UK)
1968	*La La La* by Massiel (Spain)
1969	*Boom Bang-A-Bang* by Lulu (UK)
(Tie)	*Un Jour, Un Enfant* by Frida Boccara (France)
(Tie)	*Vivo Cantando* by Salome (Spain)
(Tie)	*De Troubador* by Lennie Kuhr (Netherlands)
1970	*All Kinds Of Everything* by Dana (Ireland)
1971	*Un Banc, Un Arbre, Une Rue* by Severine (Monaco)
1972	*Après Toi (Come What May)* by Vicky Leandros (Luxembourg)
1973	*Tu Te Reconnaîtras (Wonderful Dream)* by Anne-Marie David (Luxembourg)
1974	*Waterloo* by Abba (Sweden)
1975	*Ding-A-Dong* by Teach-In (Holland)
1976	*Save Your Kisses For Me* by Brotherhood Of Man (UK)
1977	*L'Oiseau Et L'Enfant* by Marie Myriam (France)
1978	*A Ba Ni Bi* by Izhar Cohen & Alphabeta (Israel)
1979	*Hallelujah* by Milk & Honey (Israel)
1980	*What's Another Year* by Johnny Logan (Ireland)
1981	*Making Your Mind Up* by Bucks Fizz (UK)
1982	*Ein Bißchen Frieden (A Little Peace)* by Nicole (Germany)
1983	*Si La Vie Est Cadeau* by Corinna Hermes (Luxembourg)
1984	*Diggy-Loo Diggi-Ley* by Herreys (Sweden)
1985	*La Det Swinge (Let It Swing)* by Bobbysocks (Norway)
1986	*J'aime La Vie* by Sandra Kim (Belgium)
1987	*Hold Me Now* by Johnny Logan (Ireland)
1988	*Ne Partez Sans Moi* by Celine Dion (Switzerland)
1989	*Rock Me* by Riva (Yugoslavia)
1990	*Insieme; 1992* by Toto Cotugno (Italy)
1991	*Fangad Av En Stormvind* by Carola (Sweden)
1992	*Why Me?* by Linda Martin (Ireland)
1993	*In Your Eyes* by Niamh Kavanagh (Ireland)
1994	*Rock 'n' Roll Kids* by Paul Harrington and Charlie McGettigan (Ireland)
1995	*Nocturne* by Secret Garden (Norway)
1996	*The Voice* by Eimear Quinn (Ireland)

Television

Below right
The largest television contract in the world will reputedly earn Oprah Winfrey's company Harpo $300 million by the end of the year 2000.

Television sets

Largest set
The Sony Jumbo Tron colour TV screen at the Tsukuba International Exposition '85, which took place near Tokyo, Japan, measured 24.3 x 45.7 m (80 x 150 ft).

The largest cathode ray tubes for colour sets are 94-cm (37-in) models manufactured by Mitsubishi Electric of Japan.

Smallest sets
The Seiko TV-Wrist Watch, launched in Japan on 23 Dec 1982, has a 30.5-mm-wide (1⅕-in) screen and weighs 320 g (11¼ oz).

The smallest single-piece set is the Casio-Keisanki TV-10, which weighs 338 g (12 oz) and has a 6.85-cm-wide (2⁷⁄₁₀-in) screen. It was launched in Tokyo, Japan, in July 1983.

The smallest and lightest colour set is the Casio CV-1. Launched by the Casio Computer Co. Ltd of Japan in July 1992, it measures 60 x 24 x 91 mm (2⅖ x ⁹⁄₁₀ x 3³⁄₁₀ in) and weighs 168.5 g (6 oz) with a battery. It has a screen width of 35 mm (1⅜ in) and retails for 40,000 yen (about £200).

Television shows

World's longest-running show
NBC's *Meet the Press* was first transmitted on 6 Nov 1947 and was shown weekly from 12 Sept 1948. It was originally conceived by Lawrence E. Spivak, who appeared on each show as either moderator or panel member until 1975. By July 1996, more than 2,400 shows had been aired.

Longest-running British show
The longest-running programme in the United Kingdom is the seasonal ballroom dancing show *Come Dancing*, which was first transmitted on 29 Sept 1950.

Longest-running children's programme
Sooty was first presented on the BBC by its deviser Harry Corbett (1918–89) in 1952. In 1968, the show moved to Thames Television and when Harry retired in 1975 it was continued by his son Matthew (b. 1948), who still handles the puppets today.

Longest-running news programme
The *BBC News and Newsreel* was inaugurated on 5 July 1954, and Richard Baker read the news for a record 28 years, from 1954 until Christmas 1982.

Longest-running current affairs show
The longest running current affairs show in the United Kingdom is BBC's *Panorama*, which was first transmitted on 11 Nov 1953 and was broadcast weekly thereafter, with summer breaks.

Longest-running domestic drama
The longest-running domestic drama serial is Granada's *Coronation Street,* which ran twice weekly from 9 Dec 1960 until 20 Oct 1989, and has subsequently run three times weekly. William Roache has played Ken Barlow in every episode since the outset.

Longest-running comedy series
The longest-running British comedy series is *Last of the Summer Wine.* The first series started on 5 Nov 1973 and had run for 160 episodes by the end of 1996. It starred Bill Owen, Peter Sallis and Michael Bates.

Longest-running pop music show
The longest-running British pop music show is *Top of the Pops*. The first edition was presented by Jimmy Savile on 1 Jan 1964. Artists appearing were Dusty Springfield, the Rolling Stones, the Dave Clark Five, Swinging Blue Jeans and the Hollies. The Beatles and Cliff Richard and the Shadows were shown on

film. The programme celebrated its 1,000th edition on 5 May 1983.

Longest-serving presenter
The monthly *Sky at Night* show has been presented by Patrick Moore CBE without a break or a miss since 24 April 1957. The 500th edition was broadcast on 3 April 1995.

Videos

Fastest production
Tapes of the Royal Wedding of HRH Prince Andrew and Miss Sarah Ferguson on 23 July 1986 were produced by Thames Video Collection. Live filming ended with the departure of the honeymoon couple from Chelsea Hospital by helicopter at 4:42 p.m., and the first fully edited and packaged VHS tapes were purchased at 10:23 p.m.—5 hr 41 min later—from the Virgin Megastore in Oxford Street, London, UK.

Best-selling video
Walt Disney's *The Lion King* had sold 54 million copies worldwide by July 1996.

Writers and viewers

Most prolific scriptwriter
The world's most prolific TV writer was the Rt Hon. Lord Willis, whose total output since 1942 is estimated to be 20 million words. From 1949 until his death in 1992 he wrote 41 series, including the first seven years and 2.25 million words of *Dixon of Dock Green*, which ran on BBC TV from 1955 to 1976.

Largest audience
The highest audience for a single programme was 138.5 million, for the NBC transmission of Super Bowl XXX on 28 Jan 1996.

Baywatch is the most widely viewed programme in the world, with an estimated weekly audience of more than 1.1 billion in more than 103 countries, and on every continent, as of June 1996.

The largest audience for a single broadcast on British television is 30.15 million, for the 1986 Christmas edition of *East Enders*.

An audience of 39 million was estimated to have watched the wedding of TRH the Prince and Princess of Wales on 29 July 1981.

Most sets
The number of homes with TV sets surpassed 500 million worldwide in 1987. A total of 95.4 million US households had sets by May 1996 and 62.9 million of them had cable TV.

Advertisements

Highest rates
The highest ever TV advertising rate was $2.2 million (£1,430,000) per minute, for ABC network prime-time during the transmission of Super Bowl XXX on 28 Jan 1996.

In May 1996, the maximum cost of a peak (8:00 p.m. to 11:30 p.m.) weekday 60-second advertising slot on Thames Television was £130,000+VAT.

Fastest advertisement

An advert for Reebok's InstaPUMP shoes was created, filmed and aired during Super Bowl XXVII at the Atlanta Georgia Dome, USA, on 31 Jan 1993. Filming continued until the beginning of the fourth quarter of play, editing began in the middle of the third quarter and the finished product was aired during the break at the two-minute warning of the fourth quarter. It starred Emmitt Smith of the Dallas Cowboys and lasted 30 seconds.

Longest advertisement

The longest advert on British television was a 7-min 10-sec slot, by Great Universal Stores on TV-AM's *Good Morning Britain* on 20 Jan 1985. The broadcast cost £100,000.

Shortest advertisement

An advertisement lasting only four frames (there are 30 frames in a second) was aired on KING-TV's *Evening Magazine* on 29 Nov 1993. It was for Bon Marche's Frango candies, and cost $3,780 (£2,500).

The shortest advert on British television was for the 1993 *Guinness Book of Records* in 1992; it lasted just three seconds.

IS $2.2 MILLION A MINUTE DURING SUPER BOWL XXX

Finances

Most expensive TV rights

In Nov 1991, it was reported that a group of US and European investors, led by CBS, had paid $8 million (£4.5 million) for the TV rights to *Scarlett* by Alexandra Ripley, the sequel to Margaret Mitchell's *Gone With the Wind*. The eight-hour mini-series was screened in 1994.

Most expensive production

The mini-series *War and Remembrance* cost $110 million (£61 million), and took three

Left
The shortest advertisement ever shown on TV in the United Kingdom was devised by the agency Leo Burnett and broadcast on British satellite stations up to Christmas 1992. The three-second commercial was for the 1993 edition of *The Guinness Book of Records*, the world's highest-selling copyright book.

LARGEST CONTRACT IS REPUTED TO BE $300 MILLION OVER 6½ YEARS, BY OPRAH WINFREY

years to shoot. It was aired in the USA by ABC in two parts in 1988 and 1989.

Largest contracts

Oprah Winfrey reportedly earned $146 million (£94 million) between 1994 and 1995. She is said to have signed a contract in March 1994 which will reputedly earn her company Harpo $300 million by 31 Dec 2000.

The largest British TV contract was reported to be worth £9 million, inclusive of production expenses. It was signed in 1968 by Tom Jones, with ABC-TV in the USA and ATV in London, UK, for 17 one-hour shows a year from 1969 to 1974.

Biggest sale

The biggest ever sale of a TV programme was 1,144 episodes of *Coronation Street*, by Granada Television to CBKST Saskatoon, Saskatchewan, Canada, on 31 May 1971.

HIGHEST PRICE PAID AT AUCTION FOR ANY INSTRUMENT IS £902,000 FOR A VIOL

MORE THAN 1.5 MILLION STAFF

1994
1995
1996
1997
1998

LARGEST EMPLOYER IS INDI

LARGEST EV

LARGEST TRADING VOLUME ON A STOCK EXCHANGE W

LARGEST MANUFACTURING COMPANY IN THE WORLD IN TERMS OF REVENUE AN

180 181 182 183 184 185 186 187 188 189 190 191 192 193 194 195 196 197 198 199

RGEST RETAILING FIRM, WAL-MART, HAS 3,032 OUTLETS WORLDWIDE

WORLD'S MOST EXPENSIVE PIG, 'BUD', FETCHED $56,000

Commerce

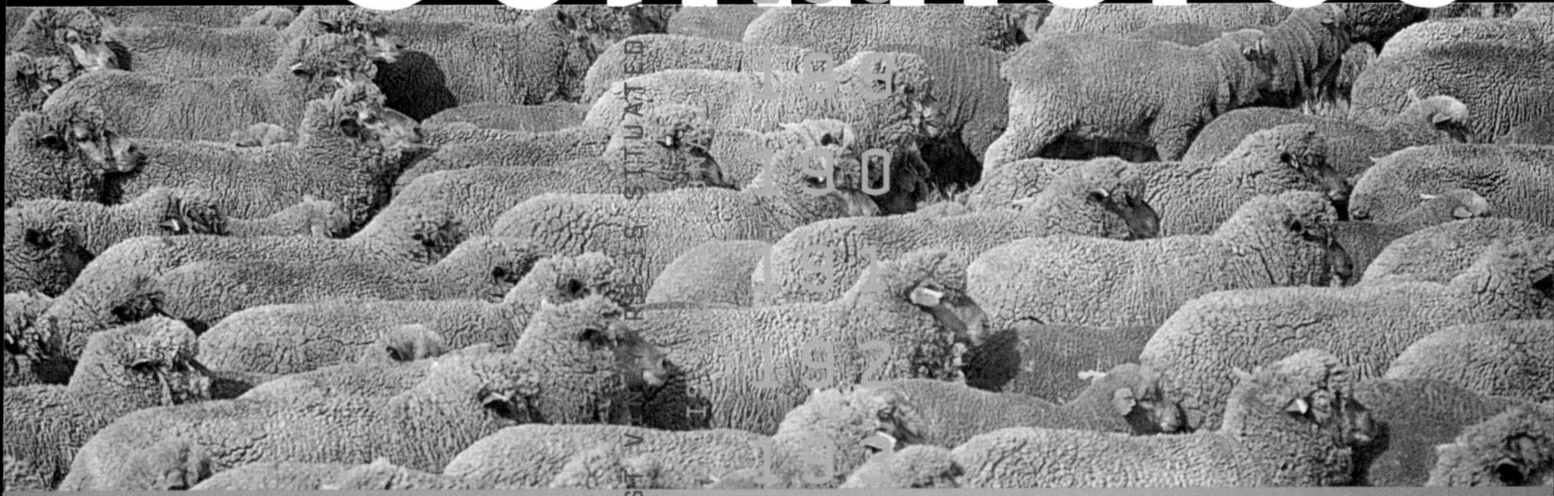

ARGEST SHEEP STATION IN THE WORLD GRAZES BETWEEN 50,000 AND 70,000 SHEEP

NORTHERNMOST V ... IS SITUATED AT 57°00' IN LATVIA

WORLD'S TALLEST BUI ... RS IN MALAYSIA, AT 451.9 M

HIGHEST RENT FOR PRIME OFFICES IS £99.77/FT² IN BOMBAY, INDIA

HEQUE WAS FOR THE SUM OF £2,474,655,000

ICHEST PERSON, THE SULTAN OF BRUNEI, HAS AN ESTIMATED FORTUNE OF $37 BILLION

.1 TRILLION ON THE NEW YORK EXCHANGE

PLOYEES IS GENERAL MOTORS CORPORATION OF DETROIT, USA

Commercial buildings

WORLD'S TALLEST BUILDING IS THE PETRONAS TOWERS OFFICE BLOCK, AT 451.9

Below right
The World Trade Center's twin towers represent the largest rentable office complex in the world. Below them is a six-storey basement, which includes a 1,800-car garage, loading docks, rail stations, a police station and a commissary supplying the restaurants.

Largest commercial spaces

Largest commercial buildings

In terms of floor area, the largest commercial building under one roof is the flower-auction building Bloemenveiling Aalsmeer (VBA) in Aalsmeer, Netherlands, which covers 710,000 m^2 (7.6 million ft^2).

In the United Kingdom, the Ford Parts Centre at Daventry, Northants, covers 142,674 m^2 (1.5 million ft^2). It was opened on 6 Sept 1972 at a cost of nearly £8 million, and 1,300 people are employed there.

Largest commercial development

The London Docklands Canary Wharf project is part of the world's largest urban regeneration project. More than 2.28 million m^2 (24.6 million ft^2) of commercial-development space and 19,844 new homes have been completed or are under construction over an area of 22 km^2 (8½ miles^2) in the London Docklands. With the completion of the Jubilee Line Underground extension in 1998, more than £4 billion will have been invested in new public transport. By March 1996 £6.3 billion had been invested by the private sector, and £1.7 billion by the London Docklands Development Corporation.

Largest public-works project

The largest construction project of modern times is the Madinat Al-Jubail Al-Sinaiyah project in Saudi Arabia, which was begun in 1976 to

LARGEST INDUSTRIAL BUILDING HAS 26.84 KM C

Highest office rent £108.57/ft^2

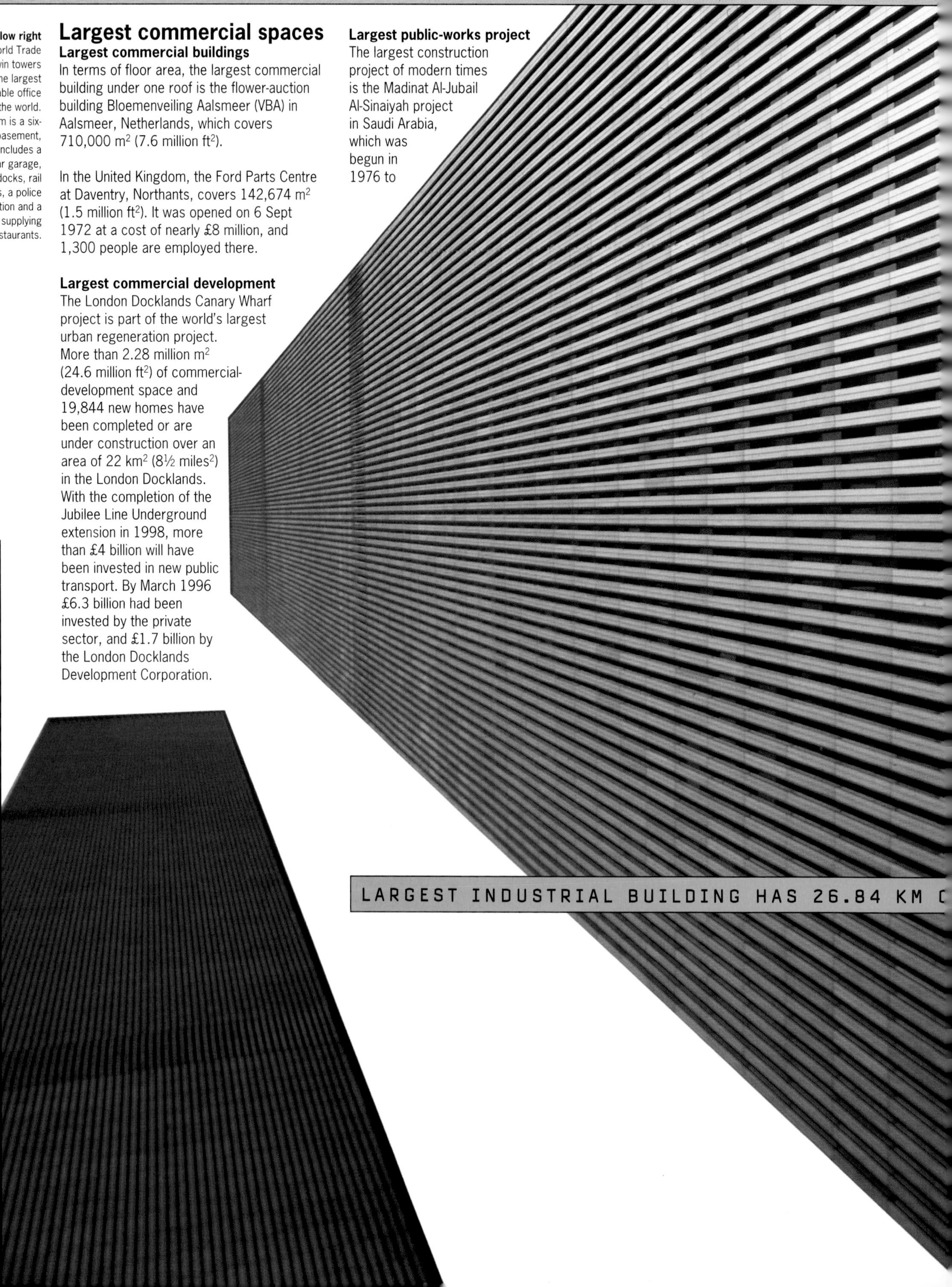

construct an industrial city and covers an area of 1,014,600,000 m² (250,705 acres). At the peak of construction, almost 52,000 workers were employed, representing 62 nationalities. A total of 270 million m³ (9,535 million ft³) of earth has been dredged and moved—enough to construct a 1-m-high (3-ft 3-in) belt around the Equator seven times over.

Tallest office block
In March 1996 the Petronas Twin Towers in Malaysia overtook the Sears Tower as the world's tallest building. The 73.6-m (241-ft) stainless steel pinnacles placed on the 88-storey towers increased their height to 451.9 m (1,482 ft 8 in).

Largest offices
The largest rentable office complex is the World Trade Center in New York City, USA, with 1,114,800 m² (12 million ft²) of rentable space in the seven buildings, including 406,000 m² (4.37 million ft²) in each of the twin towers. There are 99 lifts in each tower and 43,600 windows containing 182,900 m² (600,000 ft²) of glass. There are about 50,000 people working in 500 firms and organizations in the centre.

The largest single open-plan office in the United Kingdom is owned by British Gas West Midlands at Solihull, Warks, and was built by

Left
The Canary Wharf Tower is the tallest office building in the United Kingdom at 243.8 m (800 ft), and is part of the world's largest commercial development. The 50-storey building, resembling an obelisk and consisting of more than 16,000 pieces of steel, was designed by US architect Cesar Pelli, who later designed the Petronas Towers in Malaysia, the tallest building in the world.

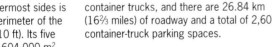
LARGEST RENTABLE OFFICE COMPLEX HAS 99 LIFTS IN EACH TOWER

Spooners (Hull) Ltd in 1962. It currently measures 230 x 49 m (753 x 160 ft) and can accommodate 2,125 staff.

Largest administrative building
The Pentagon, in Arlington, Virginia, USA, covers the largest ground area of any office building, and 23,000 military and civilian staff work there. Built to house the US Defense Department's offices, it was completed on 15 Jan 1943 and cost an estimated $83 million (£29.7 million). Each of the outermost sides is 281 m (921 ft) long, and the perimeter of the building is about 1,405 m (4,610 ft). Its five storeys enclose a floor area of 604,000 m² (149⅕ acres), and the total length of the corridors is 28 km (17½ miles).

OADWAY ON 15 LEVELS

Largest industrial building
The largest multi-level industrial building forming one discrete structure is the container freight station of Asia Terminals Ltd at Hong Kong's Kwai Chung container port. The 15-level building was completed in 1994 and has a total area of 865,937 m² (9,320,867 ft²). It measures 276 x 292 m (906 x 958 ft) and is 109.5 m (359 ft 3 in) tall. The entire area on each floor of the building is accessible by 14-m-long (46-ft) container trucks, and there are 26.84 km (16⅔ miles) of roadway and a total of 2,609 container-truck parking spaces.

Building with the greatest capacity
The Boeing Company's main assembly plant in Everett, Washington, USA, had a capacity of 5,564,200 m³ (196,476,000 ft³) on completion in 1968. Subsequent expansion

programmmes have increased the volume to 13.4 million m³ (472 million ft³). The site covers an area of 410 ha (1,025 acres).

Most expensive properties
Highest rents
In March 1994, Russia agreed to pay $115 million (£77 million) a year for 20 years to hire Kazakhstan's Baikonur space centre. The switch from landlord to tenant was a result of the break-up of the USSR.

The highest rents in the world for prime offices are in Bombay, India. They cost £99.77 per square foot per annum in Dec 1995. Added service charges and rates raise the price for the same period to £108.57 per square foot. The British equivalent in Dec 1995 was £42.50 per square foot per annum for offices in London's West End, rising to £70.57 with service charges included.

The highest office rents ever were those in the centre of Tokyo, Japan, in 1991. They reached £127.20 per square foot per annum in June of that year.

Highest purchase price
The most expensive piece of property on record is the land around the Meijiya Building, the retail food store in the Ginza district of central Tokyo, Japan, which was quoted in Oct 1988 by the Japanese National Land Agency to have reached a peak cost of 33.3 million yen per square metre (then equivalent to £142,680).

Left
Tokyo, as the largest city in Japan and one of the most populous cities in the world, had the highest ever office rents in June 1991. Prime spaces cost £127.20 per square foot per annum.

Architecture

FASTEST ELEVATORS CAN ASCEND 94 STOREYS IN 39 SECONDS

Right
Kansai Airport was initially to be built on a floating island but prohibitive costs and extreme weather conditions caused the idea to be rejected in favour of an artificial island. It was nonetheless the most expensive building project to date.

Below right
The Petronas Towers, seen here being built, are clad in a total of 85,000 m² (915,000 ft²) of stainless steel.

Centre
A model of the Petronas Towers, due for completion in early 1997. The complex forms part of Prime Minister Datuk Seri Dr Mohathir Mohamad's VISION 2020 project to achieve industrialized nation status for Malaysia by the year 2020.

Building projects
Most expensive building project

The total reported cost of constructing Kansai International Airport, Japan, which opened in 1994, was £10 billion. The project involved the construction of a 1.75-km-long (1$\frac{1}{10}$-mile) internal structure and an artificial island 5 km (3 miles) from the shore in Osaka Bay. The 4.27 x 1.25-km (2$\frac{13}{20}$ x $\frac{39}{50}$-mile) island was stabilized with 1 million sand piles, and took five years to complete. The terminal building was designed by Italian architect Renzo Piano with British structural engineer Peter Rice.

Biggest building sites

Federal investment of £8.5 billion in a new Chancellery, embassies and government buildings is transforming the derelict city centre of Berlin, Germany, into a showcase new capital. The city will also acquire two new mainline rail stations and a new underground line, while a new airport will be built to the south. The world's first Maglev (magnetic levitation) train will run between Hamburg and Berlin at up to 400 km/h (250 mph).

Building programmes in the Lujiazui district of Pudong, which is to become the new financial zone of Shanghai, China, include 50 new skyscrapers, a 95-storey tower that will rise above all other buildings, a new subway line and tunnel and a new airport.

Tallest buildings
Tallest building

Due for completion in early 1997, the twin Petronas Towers in Kuala Lumpur, Malaysia, have replaced the Sears Tower in Chicago, USA, as the tallest buildings in the world. Their 88 storeys, plus decorative spires, are 451.9 m (1,482 ft 8 in) in height. This compares with 443 m (1,453 ft 6 in) for the Sears Tower, which has 110 storeys. Designed by American architect Cesar Pelli, each stainless steel-clad tower has a circular plan, with set-backs producing a tapering look

as the building rises. The visual drama is enhanced by a 'skybridge' half-way up, which connects double-height 'skylobbies' in each tower. At the base is a six-storey shopping centre, an underground car park for 5,000 vehicles and a tunnel to serve it.

Tallest residential building

The 100-storey John Hancock Center soars 343.5 m (1,127 ft) above Chicago, USA. On a clear day, four states—Illinois, Indiana, Michigan and Wisconsin—can be seen from the 94th floor. The residential section has 703 condominium units covering 104,040 m² (1,119,910 ft²)—almost half the total area—over 48 floors. The world's fastest elevators, travelling at 549 m/min (1,800 ft/min), can carry passengers to the 94th floor in just 39 seconds. Enough steel to make 33,000 cars was used to construct the building's frame.

Costliest project £10 billion

British buildings
First underground house
In 1972 Arthur Quarmby began digging his house, Underhill, in Holme, W Yorkshire. With an internal area of 325 m² (3,500 ft²), the house has a 6-m (20-ft) diameter roof light, a figure-of-eight swimming pool, a music room and a cave with a peat fire.

Most energy-efficient house
The Autonomous House, Southwell, Notts, was an experiment by Robert and Brenda Vale to find out if it were possible to build a house that produces more energy than it consumes and has a minimal impact on the environment. Built with local and recycled materials where possible, the house contains high levels of insulation, which ensure that it is heated by the family that occupies it, and by solar and incidental gains. Rainwater from the roof runs to drums made from fruit juice containers in the basement and is used for drinking purposes, while grey water is discharged to the garden to maintain the water balance. A composting WC replaces the sewage connection, and electricity is provided by photovoltane panels. The 1,450 kWh produced each year is sold back to the national grid.

Left
The Chicago skyline is dominated by the Sears Tower (centre), until 1996 the world's tallest building, and by the John Hancock Center (right), the world's tallest residential building. Opened in 1970 at a cost of $100 million (£42 million), the Hancock Center's 2,012.5 km (1,250 miles) of wiring carries sufficient power to supply a city of 30,000 people.

AUTONOMOUS HOUSE PRODUCES MORE ENERGY THAN IT CONSUMES

Left
The Shri Swaminarayan Mandir is the first stone Hindu temple to be built outside India, where Hinduism originated approximately 4,000 years ago.

Largest post-war museum
The Royal Armouries Museum at Clarence Dock, Leeds, was opened on 17 March 1996. The combined area of the building and its ancillary structures is about 19,620 m² (211,195 ft²), and the total cost of the project was £42 million. The building houses the historic collection of arms and armour that was previously stored and kept on display at the Tower of London. In addition to the main museum buildings there is also a menagerie and tilt yard.

Largest stone Hindu temple outside India
The first stone Hindu temple constructed outside India is the Shri Swaminarayan Mandir, opened in Neasden, north London, in June 1995. The centrepiece is the 22-m-high (72-ft) central dome, which is a replica of the marble dome of the Delwara Jain Mandir at Abu, Rajasthan, India. At one point in its construction, the temple complex employed 1,546 artisans, 100 full-time volunteers and more than 1,000 part-time volunteers. Some materials—2,828 tonnes of limestone imported from Bulgaria and 2,000 tonnes of Carrara marble from Italy—were shipped to India, where sculptors worked on the traditional carvings for the ceilings and pillars. A year later the massive pieces were shipped back to London and reassembled on site. Built primarily from 226 English oak trees, supplemented by Burmese teak for the pillars, the complex includes a prayer hall with a capacity of up to 3,000 worshippers, a marriage hall and registry office, a sports hall, vegetarian kitchens, offices, gardens and residential accommodation for five monks. The funding for the project was more than £5 million and came from donations.

World of commerce

Businesses

Largest companies
The largest manufacturing company in the world in terms of revenue and employees is General Motors Corporation of Detroit, Michigan, USA, which has worldwide operations and a workforce of about 745,000. Assets in 1995 totalled $217,123 million (£135,000 million). The company announced a profit of $6.88 billion (£4.28 billion) for the year.

In the United Kingdom, the total assets less current liabilities of Shell Transport and Trading Co. plc in Dec 1995 were £55.58 billion. Most of this was its 40% share in the net assets of the Royal Dutch Shell Group of companies. Group companies employ approximately 106,000 staff.

Largest building contractor
The largest British construction group is Tarmac, which had sales of £2.4 billion in 1995 and employed a total of 19,980 staff. Peak sales turnover was £3.7 billion in 1990.

Largest restaurant chain
Brothers Dick and Mac McDonald pioneered the fast-food industry concept, and later sold their business to Ray A. Kroc, their national franchising agent, creating McDonald's Corporation in 1955. By the end of 1995, McDonald's licensed and owned more than 18,380 restaurants in a total of 89 countries. Worldwide sales in 1995 were nearly $30 billion (£19 billion).

Largest surveyors
The world's largest firm of surveyors and real-estate consultants is Jones Lang Wootton of London, UK, with 70 offices in 28 countries and 3,800 staff. Valuations completed in 1995 amounted to $154 billion (£99 billion), and capital transactions to $13.6 billion (£8.7 billion), resulting in a fee income of more than $365 million (£234 million).

Largest auctioneers
The largest firm of art auctioneers is the Sotheby Group of London and New York, founded in 1744. Sotheby's turnover in 1989 was a record $2.9 billion (£1.7 billion), and New York sales set a single-series record of $360.4 million (£215 million) in May 1990.

Largest chemists
The largest chain of chemist stores is Rite Aid Corporation of Camp Hill, Pennsylvania, USA, which had 2,771 US branches in July 1996.

The Walgreen Co. of Deerfield, Illinois, USA, has the largest volume of sales of any chemists, at $10.4 billion (£6.5 billion) in 1995.

The largest chain of pharmacies in the United Kingdom is Boots The Chemists, which had 1,221 retail stores at March 1996.

Largest British department store
The largest department store in the United Kingdom is Harrods Ltd of Knightsbridge, London, which was named after Henry Charles Harrod, who opened a grocery in Knightsbridge in 1849. It now has a total selling floor space of 10.5 ha (25 acres), with 40 elevators and 36 flights of stairs and escalators. It employs 3,500–4,000 people depending on the time of year, and achieved record sales of more than £459 million in the

year ending 27 Jan 1996. The record for one day of business is almost £14 million in the 1996 January Sale, with more than £26 million taken in the first four days and more than £64 million taken during the month.

Largest toyshop chain
The world's largest toyshop chain is Toys'R'Us, with 1,000 stores and 4 million m^2 (43 million ft^2) of retail space worldwide. Its head office is in Paramus, New Jersey, USA, and the largest single store is in Birmingham, UK, at 6,038.5 m^2 (65,000 ft^2).

Largest retailers
The world's largest retailing firm is Wal-Mart Stores, Inc. of Bentonville, Arkansas, USA, which was founded by Sam Walton in 1962 and had sales of $93.6 billion (£61 billion) and a net income of $2.74 billion (£1.8 billion) at 31 Jan 1996. At 1 May 1996, Wal-Mart had a total of 3,032 retail locations internationally and employed 658,200 people.

At Jan 1996, Woolworth Corporation of New York City, USA, was the retailer with the greatest number of outlets, operating 8,178 retail stores worldwide. Frank Winfield Woolworth opened his first store, 'The Great Five Cent Store', in Utica, New York, USA, on 22 Feb 1879.

Largest food company
The leading food company in the world is Nestlé, based in Switzerland, which had sales totalling Sw.fr.56.5 billion (£31.4 billion) in 1995. They are famous for a wide range of confectionery products, the best seller of which is KitKat, 13.2 billion fingers of which were sold worldwide during the year. Every second 418 KitKat fingers are consumed throughout the world.

Most profitable spirits producer
United Distillers, the spirits company owned by Guinness PLC, made a record profit of £673 million in 1995. The largest blender and bottler of Scotch whisky, its Shieldhall plant in Glasgow, UK, has the capacity to fill an estimated 210 million bottles of Scotch a year. This is equivalent to approximately 160 million litres (35 million gal), most of

which is exported. The world's best-selling brands of Scotch and gin—Johnnie Walker Red Label and Gordon's respectively—are both products of United Distillers.

Largest airline
Delta Air Lines of Atlanta, Georgia, USA, carries the greatest number of passengers on its planes. In 1995, their 4,800 daily flights flew 86,992,109 travellers to 48 US states and 31 countries.

Largest law firm
Baker & McKenzie, a law firm founded in Chicago, Illinois, USA, in 1949, employed 1,893 lawyers, 517 of whom are partners, in a total of 34 countries in April 1996. It also has the highest revenues, at $594 million (£382 million) in 1995.

Largest insurance companies
The Blue Cross and Blue Shield Association of Chicago, Illinois, USA, has more than 65 million members, and contracts with about 80% of all hospitals and 75% of physicians in the US.

The company with the highest volume of insurance in force is the Metropolitan Life Insurance Co. of New York City, USA, with $1.386 trillion (£90 billion) at year-end 1995.

The Prudential Insurance Company of America, which has headquarters at Newark, New Jersey, has the greatest volume of consolidated assets, with a total of $219 billion (£140 billion) in 1995.

In the United Kingdom, the Prudential Corporation plc had assets of £82 billion on 1 Jan 1995.

Smallest company equity
The smallest ever company in the United Kingdom was Frank Davies Ltd, which was incorporated on 22 Aug 1924 with a ½d share capital divided into two ¼d shares. Converting to decimal coinage (£0.002 divided into two shares of £0.001), it was finally dissolved in 1978 without ever having increased its share capital.

Most company directorships
Hugh T. Nicholson, formerly senior partner of Harmood Banner & Sons of London, UK, was director of all 451 companies of the Jasper group in 1961 and as a liquidating chartered accountant had seven other directorships.

The director with the most listings in the 1995 *Directory of Directors* is Reginald Frank, with 252.

ORLD'S LARGEST FOOD COMPANY NESTLE, ARE EATEN

RECORD TAKINGS IN A SINGLE DAY AT HARRODS WERE ALMOST £14 MILLION

N A SINGLE LIFE WAS REPUTEDLY $18 MILLION IN 1970

Profit and loss
Greatest sales
The *Fortune* 500 list of the world's leading industrial corporations of April 1996 is headed by General Motors Corporation of Detroit, Michigan, USA, with sales totalling $168.8 billion (£105 billion) in 1995.

Greatest losses
The world's worst annual net trading loss is $23.5 billion (£15.5 billion), by General Motors in 1992. The bulk of this figure was due to a single charge of $21 billion (£14 billion) for employees' health costs and pensions, which was disclosed because of new accountancy regulations in the USA.

In the United Kingdom, the greatest annual loss by a company is £3.91 billion, by the National Coal Board (now British Coal) in the year ending 31 March 1984.

Take-overs
Highest bid
The highest bid in a corporate take-over was $21 billion (£12 billion), for RJR Nabisco Inc., the tobacco, food and beverage company. It was made by the Wall Street leveraged-buyout firm Kohlberg Kravis Roberts, which offered

$90 (£50) a share on 24 Oct 1988. By 1 Dec 1988 the bid, led by Henry Kravis, had reached $109 (£60) per share to aggregate $25 billion (£14 billion).

Highest British bids
The largest successful takeover bid in British history was the offer of almost £9 billion by Glaxo plc for Wellcome, the rival drugs company, on 23 Jan 1995.

The largest ever bid for a British company was £13 billion, for BAT Industries on 11 July 1989. The bid was made by Hoylake, and led by Sir James Goldsmith, Jacob Rothschild and Kerry Packer.

Insurance
Largest policy
The largest ever life-assurance policy was for the sum of $100 million (£55.5 million) and was bought by an American entertainment corporation on the life of a leading US entertainment-industry figure. The policy was sold in 1990 by Peter Rosengard of London, UK, and placed by Shel Bachrach of Albert G. Ruben & Co. Inc. of Beverly Hills, California, USA, and Richard Feldman of the Feldman Agency, East Liverpool, Ohio, USA, with nine insurance companies to spread the risk.

Biggest payout
The highest ever payout on a single life was reported in Nov 1970 to be approximately $18 million (£7.5 million), to Linda Mullendore, the widow of a rancher from Oklahoma, USA. Her murdered husband had paid $300,000 (£126,000) in premiums in 1969.

Economics and employment

Below right
In 1995, Indian Railways, the largest employer in the world, had more than 1.6 million staff. In 1994/5, Indian passenger trains travelled a total of 394.8 million km (245.3 million miles) and freight trains travelled a distance of 241 million km (150 million miles) over a route with a total length of 62,660 km (38,936 miles).

National economies

Largest national debt
The US national debt stood at a record $5.129 trillion (£3.385 trillion) in fiscal year 1996. The gross interest was $332.414 billion (£216 billion) on the debt and the net interest was $202.957 billion (£132 billion).

Largest GNP
The US gross national product was a record $7.238 trillion (£4.7 trillion) for the year ending 31 Dec 1995.

Largest overseas debt
The USA was in overseas debt to the tune of more than $654 billion (£419.4 billion) at fiscal year-end 1994.

Among non-G7 countries, Mexico has the highest foreign debt, with $147.5 billion (£95 billion) at the end of 1994.

Most foreign aid given
The largest foreign aid donor by volume in 1995 was Japan, with aid given totalling $14.5 billion (£9.4 billion).

The highest 1995 ratio of official development assistance to GNP was 0.97%, in Denmark.

Balance of payments
The record deficit for a calendar year is the $166.3 billion (£91 billion) reported by the USA in 1987.

Japan had a record surplus of $131.5 billion (£87.9 billion) in 1993.

The highest ever British surplus was £6,748 million in 1981.

The worst British deficit was £21,726 million in 1989.

Highest inflation
The world's worst ever inflation occurred in Hungary in June 1946, when the 1931 gold pengö was valued at 130 million trillion (1.3×10^{20}) paper pengö. Notes were issued for 'Egymillárd billió' or 1,000 trillion (10^{21}) pengö on 3 June and withdrawn on 11 July 1946. Vouchers for 1 billion trillion pengö were issued for taxation payment only.

The best-known and most frequently analysed hyperinflationary episode was in Germany in 1923. The circulation of the Reichsbank mark reached 400,338,326,350,700,000,000 on 6 Nov and inflation was 755,700-millionfold on 1913 levels.

Belarus experienced the highest inflation rate in 1995, at 243.96%.

The worst rate of inflation in the United Kingdom in a year was 26.9%, from Aug 1974 to Aug 1975.

Lowest inflation
The lowest inflation rate in 1995 was in Seychelles, where the CPI fell by 1.28%.

Largest budget
The highest ever government expenditure was $1.519 trillion (£950 billion), by the US government for the fiscal year 1995.

The USA also had the highest ever revenue in 1995, at $1.355 trillion (£847 billion).

The largest ever general government expenditure in the United Kingdom was £289 billion, which was projected for the fiscal year 1994/5.

The highest ever general receipts by a British government are the £250 billion for the fiscal year 1994/5.

Largest fiscal surplus
The USA had a record surplus of $11.796 billion (£3,000 billion) in 1947/8.

Largest fiscal deficit
The worst fiscal deficit was $290 billion (£190 billion) in the USA in the fiscal year 1992.

Highest and lowest taxation
The highest rate of income tax in Denmark is 68%, but in extreme situations a net wealth tax of 1% can result in tax of more than 100%.

The sovereign countries with the least income tax are Bahrain and Qatar, at nil.

Highest and lowest British taxation
Until 1979, the former top earned and unearned rates in the United Kingdom were 83% and 98% respectively. The standard rate of tax was reduced to 24% and the higher rate remains at 40% in the 1996/7 budget.

In 1967/8, a 'special charge' of up to 9s (45 pence) in the pound additional to surtax brought the top British rate to 27s 3d in the pound (or 136%) on investment income.

No tax is levied on the Sarkese (inhabitants of Sark) in the Channel Islands, UK.

Income tax in the United Kingdom was at its lowest at 2d (0.83 pence) in the pound in 1875. It gradually climbed to 1s 3d (6.25 pence) by 1913.

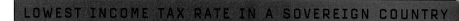

From April 1941 to 1946 the record peak of 10s (50 pence) in the pound was maintained to assist in the financing of the war effort.

Minimum lending rate
The highest ever figure for the British bank rate (which has been known as the minimum lending rate since 13 Oct 1972) was 17% from 15 Nov 1979 to 3 July 1980.

The longest period without a change was 12 years 13 days, from 26 Oct 1939 to 7 Nov 1951. During this time the rate stayed at 2%. This lowest ever rate was first attained on 22 April 1852.

Gold reserves
The world's greatest monetary gold reserves are those of the US Treasury, which stood at approximately 262 million fine oz during

1996, which is equivalent to $100 billion (£64 billion) at the June 1996 price of $382 (£245) per fine oz. The US Bullion Depository situated at Fort Knox, Kentucky, USA, has been the principal federal depository of US gold since Dec 1936: 147 million fine oz are stored there.

Employment
Largest employers
The world's largest commercial or utility employer is Indian Railways, with a total of 1,602,000 staff in 1994/5.

The largest employer in the United Kingdom is the National Health Service, with 763,000 directly-employed staff in Sept 1995.

Longest working lives
Mr Izumi began his working life goading draught animals at a sugar mill at Isen,

Theodore C. Taylor (1850–1952) served for a total of 86 years with J. T. & J. Taylor of Batley, W Yorkshire, UK. This included 56 years as chairman.

Edward William Beard (1878–1982), a builder from Swindon, Wilts, UK, retired in Oct 1981 after a total of 85 years with the firm that he had founded in 1896.

Longest pension
Miss Millicent Barclay was born on 10 July 1872, three months after the death of her father, Col. William Barclay, and became immediately eligible for a Madras Military Fund pension to continue until her marriage. She died unmarried on 26 Oct 1969, having drawn the pension every day of her life, for 97 years 3 months.

Lowest unemployment
The lowest unemployment figure occurred in Switzerland in Dec 1973, when the total number of jobless people there was reported to be only 81 from a population of 6.6 million.

Strikes
Most disruptive strikes
The strike at the plumbing-fixtures factory of the Kohler Co. in Sheboygan, Wisconsin, USA, between April 1954 and Oct 1962, is alleged to have cost the United Automobile Workers' Union about $12 million to sustain.

The most serious single labour dispute in the United Kingdom was the General Strike of 4 to 12 May 1926, called by the Trades Union Congress in support of the Miners' Federation. It lasted nine days, and the 1,580,000 people involved lost 14,220,000 working days.

In 1926, a total of 2,750,000 people were involved in 323 different labour disputes in the United Kingdom. The working days lost during the year amounted to 162,300,000—the highest figure ever recorded.

Longest strikes
The world's longest recorded strike ended on 4 Jan 1961, after 33 years. It concerned the employment of barbers' assistants in Copenhagen, Denmark.

The longest industrial dispute in the United Kingdom lasted a total of 8½ years. It began in July 1986, when 38 men were sacked by Sheffield engineering works Keeton Sons and Co., and ended on 31 Dec 1994. In the course of the dispute, several strikers reached retirement age, others found new employment, and one died.

The most protracted national strike in the United Kingdom was called by the National Union of Mineworkers on 8 March 1984 and lasted until 5 March 1985. HM Treasury estimated the cost to be £2,625 million, or £118.93 per household.

Trade unions
Largest
The largest trade union in the world is the Professionalnyi Soyuz Rabotnikov Agro-Promyshlennogo Kompleksa (Agro-Industrial

L, IN BAHRAIN AND QATAR

JRKING LIFE IN 1872 AND CONTINUED FOR A RECORD-BREAKING 98 YEARS

Far left
The public in New York City is kept constantly up-to-date on the state of the US national debt—the largest in the world—by the national debt clock on Manhattan Island.

Left
A group of children play with virtually worthless banknotes in Germany in the 1920s, when the country experienced rapid and uncontrolled inflation as a result of post-war political and social instability. One dollar was worth 50 marks in 1922 and 2.5 trillion marks in 1924. This economic crisis, which almost caused a revolution, was 'solved' by the Nazi's rearmament programme, put into action when they acceded to power in 1933, with Hitler as chancellor.

Tokunoshima, Japan, in 1872, and retired as a sugar-cane farmer 98 years later in 1970, aged 105.

The record for the longest working career in the United Kingdom is 97 years, by Susan O'Hagan (1802–1909). She was in domestic service with three generations of the Hall family of Lisburn, near Belfast, Co. Antrim, from the age of 10 to the age of 107, when she was still carrying out light duties.

Longest period in one job
The longest recorded period spent in an industrial job in the United Kingdom is 86 years, by Miss Polly Gadsby, who began factory work with Archibald Turner & Co. of Leicester in 1846, when she was just nine years old. In 1932 she was still at her bench wrapping elastic, aged 95.

The lowest recorded peacetime level of unemployment in the United Kingdom was 0.9% on 11 July 1955, when 184,929 persons were registered.

The highest employment figure reported in the United Kingdom is 26,093,000—94.3% of the workforce—in Dec 1989.

Highest unemployment
The highest level of unemployment in the United Kingdom was recorded on 23 Jan 1933, when the total number of unemployed people on the Employment Exchange registers was 2,979,400, or 23% of the insured working population.

The highest level of post-war unemployment in the United Kingdom is 12.2% of the workforce (3,407,729 unemployed) on 9 Jan 1986.

Complex Workers' Union) in Russia, which had 15.2 million members in Jan 1993.

The largest union in the United Kingdom is UNISON, formed on 1 July 1993 from the NALGO/NUPE/COHSE merger. It has 1.37 million members, compared with a peak membership of 2,086,281 for the Transport and General Workers' Union in 1979.

Smallest
The smallest trade union was the Jewelcase and Jewellery Display Makers' Union (JJDMU), founded in 1894. It was dissolved on 31 Dec 1986 by its general secretary, Charles Evans. The motion was seconded by Fergus McCormack, its only surviving member.

The smallest current British union is the 13-member Sheffield Wool Shear Workers, UK.

Money and finance

Right
The New York Stock Exchange had a record day's trading of 652,829,000 shares on 15 Dec 1995, compared with the 16,410,030 traded on 29 Oct 1929, the 'Black Tuesday' of the Wall Street Crash. The market value of stocks listed on the NYSE reached an all-time high of $6.4 trillion (£4.2 trillion) on 30 April 1996, and the largest stock trade in its history involved a 48,788,800-share block of Navistar International Corporation stock sold at $10 (£6.70) per share on 10 April 1986. The highest price paid for a seat on the exchange was $1.25 million (£800,000) in 1996, while the lowest 20th-century price was $17,000 (£4,000), in 1942.

Largest cheque £2,474,655,000

Paper money

Earliest notes
Paper money was invented by the Chinese in AD 812 and was prevalent by AD 970.

The earliest banknotes (*banco-sedlar*) were issued in Stockholm, Sweden, in July 1661. The oldest surviving notes are five dalers dated 6 Dec 1662.

The oldest surviving printed Bank of England note is a £555 note to bearer dated 1699.

Largest and smallest notes
The largest paper money was the one-guan note of the 1368–99 Chinese Ming Dynasty issue, at 22.8 x 33 cm (9 x 13 in).

The smallest national note was the 10-bani note issued in Romania in 1917. Its printed area measured 27.5 x 38 mm (1 1/16 x 1 1/2 in).

The smallest German *Notgeld* (emergency money) were the 1/3-pfennig notes of Passau (1920–21), at 18 x 18.5 mm (11/16 x 3/4 in).

Highest-value notes
The highest-value notes in circulation are US Federal Reserve $10,000 notes, 345 of which remain in circulation or unretired.

The highest value of any note issued by the US Federal Reserve System is $100,000, used for transactions between the Federal Reserve and the Treasury Department.

The highest value of notes ever issued in the United Kingdom is £1,000. First printed in 1725, they were discontinued on 22 April 1943 and withdrawn on 30 April 1945.

Lowest-value notes
The lowest value and lowest denomination of a legal tender banknote is one-sen (or 1/100th of a rupiah) Indonesian note. Its exchange value in June 1996 was 358,624 to £1.

The lowest denomination of Bank of England notes was half-crown (now 12 1/2 pence) in 1941. Very few examples survive, and they are valued at not less than £1,500.

Highest circulation of British notes
A record £21,720 million worth of Bank of England notes was circulated on 27 Dec 1995—equivalent to a pile more than 400 km (250 miles) high in new £5 notes.

Most expensive banknotes
The highest price paid at auction for a single lot of banknotes was £240,350 (including buyer's premium), by Richard Lobel on behalf of a consortium, at Phillips, London, UK, on 14 Feb 1991. It consisted of a cache of more

than 17 million British military notes found in a vault in Berlin, Germany.

Largest banknote collection
Israel Gerber of Israel has acquired notes from 215 different countries since 1962.

Cheques and coins
Largest cheques
A cheque for £2,474,655,000 was issued on 30 March 1995 and signed by Nicholas Morris, company secretary of Glaxo plc, UK.

An internal US Treasury cheque for the sum of $4,176,969,623.57 (approximately £1.5 billion) was drawn on 30 June 1954.

Largest and smallest mints
The US Treasury covers 4.7 ha (11½ acres) in Philadelphia, Pennsylvania. It has an annual production capacity of 12 billion coins but produced a record 19,519,253,440 coins in fiscal year 1995.

The smallest issuing mint is a single-press mint housed in a small room. It belongs to the Sovereign Military Order of Malta, Rome, Italy.

Largest hoards
About 80,000 Roman aurei (now worth about £640 million) were found near Modena, Italy, in 1714. The hoard is believed to have been deposited c. 37 BC.

The largest deliberately buried hoard found is the 150,000-coin Brussels hoard of 1908.

Largest trading volume
The largest trading volume in 1995 was $3.1 trillion (£2 trillion), on the New York Stock Exchange, USA.

London Stock Exchange records
The busiest ever session on the London market was on 28 Jan 1993, when 1.3 billion shares were traded.

The highest number of equity bargains in one day on the London Stock Exchange was 114,973, on 22 Oct 1987.

The highest number of equity bargains in one year is 13,557,455, in 1987.

£10 billion in 1996. It has 1,091 branches and more than 20 million British households have a Halifax account.

Largest flotation
The flotation of British Gas plc in 1986 had an equity offer that produced £7.75 billion to 4.5 million shareholders.

The most investors for one issue is 5.9 million in the Mastergain '92 equity fund floated by the Unit Trust of India in April and May 1992.

Biggest rights issue
The largest British rights issue on record is £1,350 million, by Zeneca in 1993.

BANKNOTES IN THE UNITED KINGDOM WAS £21,720 MILLION ON 27 DEC 1995

The largest British hoard consisted of more than 20,000 silver coins, the majority of them pence of Edward I (1272–1307), found in Tutbury, Staffs, in 1831.

The largest known accidental hoard is an estimated 60 million coins from the Spanish Plate Fleet, which sank off the coast of Florida, USA, in 1715. About half were recovered by Spanish authorities shortly after the event and an estimated 500,000 have been recovered by modern salvors.

The largest ever hoard in terms of weight is 43 tonnes of gold, from the White Star Liner HMS *Laurentic*, mined in 40.2-m-deep (132-ft) water off Fanad Head, Donegal, Ireland, in 1917. Of the 3,211 ingots, 3,191 have been recovered by the Royal Navy, Cossum Diving Syndicate and Consortium Recovery Ltd.

Stock exchanges
Oldest exchange
The oldest stock exchange is in Amsterdam in the Netherlands and was founded in 1602 with dealings in printed shares of the United East India Company of the Netherlands in the Oude Zijds Kapel.

FT-SE 100 share index records
The FT-SE 100 index reached a closing high of 3,748.7 on 18 Jan 1996.

On 16 Feb 1996, the intraday peak reached an all-time high of 3,791.6.

The lowest ever closing figure was 986.9, on 23 July 1984.

The greatest rise in a day is 142.2 points to 1,943.8, on 21 Oct 1987.

The greatest fall in a day's trading was 250.7 points to 1,801.6, on 20 Oct 1987.

Largest banks and building societies
The largest multilateral development bank is the International Bank for Reconstruction and Development (World Bank). Based in Washington DC, USA, it had assets of $169 billion (£109 billion) for the 1995 fiscal year.

The world's biggest lender is the government-controlled House Loan Corporation in Japan.

The largest building society is the Halifax Building Society of W Yorkshire, UK, which had assets of £98.7 billion and lending of

Highest share value
The highest denomination of any share quoted in the world was a single share in Moeara Enim Petroleum Corporation, Netherlands. It was worth 165,000 Dutch florins (£50,600) on 22 April 1992.

Highest AGM attendance
A world record total of 20,109 shareholders attended the AGM of American Telephone and Telegraph Company (now called AT&T Corp) in April 1961.

Greatest personal loss
The highest recorded personal paper losses on stock values were incurred by Ray A. Kroc (1902–84), former chairman of McDonald's Corporation. They amounted to $65 million (£28 million) on 8 July 1974.

Biggest bankruptcy
The world's biggest corporate bankruptcy in terms of assets amounted to $35.9 billion (£22.4 billion). It was filed by Texaco in 1987 as a result of Judge Solomon Casseb Jr's Dec 1985 ruling that Texaco make financial reparation to Pennzoil for having used unethical practices to break up a proposed merger between Pennzoil and Getty Oil.

HIGHEST EVER SHARE DENOMINATION WAS £50,600 FOR A SINGLE SHARE

Wealth

Right
The invention of the TetraPak container allowed the Rausing brothers, who left their home in Sweden in the 1980s, to become two of the richest men in the world. Hans Rausing retired in Aug 1995, handing over control of the Tetra Laval company to his brother Gad, who now lives in Switzerland.

World's wealthiest people

First millionaires
The earliest dollar millionaire was Cornelius Vanderbilt, who left $100 million (£20.7 million) on his death in 1877.

The cosmetician Madame C. J. Walker (1857–1919) of Delta, Louisiana, USA, was reputedly the first self-made female millionaire. An uneducated black orphan, her fortune was founded on a hair straightener.

First billionaires
The first people to leave $1 billion on their deaths were John Davison Rockefeller (1839–1937), the American founder of Standard Oil, and Andrew William Mellon (1855–1937), a US financier. Rockefeller is believed to have been the first to accumulate $1 billion.

Richest people
The richest person in the world is HM Sir Muda Hassanal Bolkiah Mu'izzaddin Waddaulah (b. 1946), the sultan, self-appointed prime minister and finance and home affairs minister of Brunei. His fortune is estimated at $37 billion (£25 billion).

HM Queen Elizabeth II is generally said to be the world's wealthiest woman, although the exact extent of her fortune has always been

the subject of controversy. *The Sunday Times* estimated her personal fortune at £450 million in April 1996. This excludes her art collection, worth at least £4 billion, which is now controlled by the Royal Collection Trust, a charitable trust. It also takes into account the fact that she is paying tax to the tune of at least £1 million a year.

The richest man in the United Kingdom according to *The Sunday Times* in April 1996 is Hans Rausing, former controller of Tetra Laval, the manufacturer of TetraPak containers for milk and fruit juices. He is believed to be worth £2.88 billion.

Richest families
It was tentatively estimated in 1974 that the combined value of the assets nominally controlled by the 1,600-member Du Pont family may be of the order of $150 billion (£64 billion). The capital of Pierre Du Pont (1730–1817) enabled his son Eleuthère Irénée Du Pont to start his explosives company in the USA after the family emigrated there from France on 1 Jan 1800.

The Walton retailing family in the USA is worth an estimated $24 billion (£14 billion).

In the United Kingdom, the Sainsbury family of retailing giants is worth an estimated

£2.52 billion. The largest British supermarket chain grew from a single dairy shop in London in 1869 to more than 260 stores in 1990.

Youngest millionaires
The youngest person ever to accumulate $1 million was the American child film actor Jackie Coogan (1914–84), who co-starred with Sir Charles Chaplin in *The Kid* (1921). In 1923 and 1924 he was earning $22,000 (£5,000) a week, and 60% of his films' profits.

The youngest female millionaire was the American child actor Shirley Temple (b. 1928), who had accumulated wealth exceeding $1 million before she reached the age of 10.

Youngest billionaire
William ('Bill') Gates was 20 years old when he set up the software company Microsoft of Seattle, Washington, USA, in 1976. He became a billionaire within 11 years, and is reportedly worth $18 billion (£11.6 billion).

Shortest period as 'millionaire'
In May 1994 Howard Jenkins of Tampa, Florida, USA, a 31-year-old roofing-company employee, discovered that the sum of $88 million (£58.6 million) had been mistakenly transferred into his bank account. He initially withdrew $4 million (£2.7 million), but his conscience got the better of him and he returned the sum in full.

Greatest miser
If meanness is measurable as a ratio between expendable assets and expenditure, then Henrietta 'Hetty' Howland Green (1835–1916), who kept a balance of more than $31,400,000 (£6.6 million) in one bank alone, is the all-time world champion miser. Her son had to have his leg amputated because of her delays in finding a free medical clinic, and she ate cold porridge because she was too thrifty to heat it. On her death, her estate proved to be worth $95 million (£20 million), which is equivalent to £816 million in 1996.

Income

Highest incomes
The world's greatest incomes derive from the collection of royalties per barrel of oil by the rulers of oil-rich sheikhdoms who have not formally revoked personal entitlement. Shaikh Zayid ibn Sultan an-Nuhayan, head of state of the United Arab Emirates, arguably has title to approximately $9 billion (£6 billion) of the country's annual gross national product.

Highest salary
US fund manager George Soros earned at least $1.1 billion (£735 million) in 1993, according to *Financial World's* list of the most highly paid individuals on Wall Street.

Highest fees
The most highly paid investment consultant in the world is Harry D. Schultz, who has homes in Monte Carlo, Monaco, and in Zürich,

Switzerland. His standard fee for a one-hour consultation is $2,400 (£1,600) on weekdays, increasing to $3,400 (£2,200) at weekends. Most popular are the five-minute phone consultations, for which he charges $200 (£130). His 'International Harry Schultz Letter' sells at $50 (£30) per copy, and a life subscription to it costs $2,400 (£1,600).

Highest lecture fees
Dr Ronald Dante was paid $3,080,000 (£2,040,000) for lecturing students on hypnotherapy at a two-day course held in Chicago, Illinois, USA, from 1 to 2 June 1986. Teaching for eight hours each day, he earned $192,500 (£127,600) per hour.

Legacies and bequests
Largest British wills
The will with the largest value ever proved in the United Kingdom was that of the 6th Marquess of Bute, who left an estate worth £130,062,015 at his death in 1994.

FORD FOUNDATION LEFT A RECORD SINGLE CASH BEQUEST OF $500 MILLION

On 29 April 1985, the estate of Sir Charles Clore (1904–79) was agreed by a court hearing to be worth £123 million. The Inland Revenue initially wanted to claim the sum of £84 million in duties but eventually settled for £67 million.

The largest fortune ever to be proved in the will of a woman in the United Kingdom is £92,814,057 net, the sum left by Dorothy de Rothschild (1895–1988) of the European financial family.

Largest dowry
The largest dowry on record was bestowed by Elena Patiño, the daughter of the Bolivian tin millionaire Don Simón Iturbi Patiño (1861–1947). In 1929, she created a dowry worth £8 million—equivalent to £205 million in 1996—from a fortune that was at one time estimated to be worth about £125 million.

Greatest bequests
The largest single bequest in the history of philanthropy was the $1-billion (£550-million) art collection that belonged to the American publisher Walter Annenberg. On 12 March 1991, Annenberg announced his intention to leave the collection to the Metropolitan Museum of Art in New York City, USA.

The largest ever single cash bequest was worth $500 million (£180 million), equivalent to £2.5 billion in 1996. The sum was left to 4,157 educational and other institutions by the Ford Foundation (established 1936) of New York City, USA. It was announced on 12 Dec 1955.

The greatest bequests to have been made by a British millionaire were those of William Richard Morris, later Viscount Nuffield (1877–1963), which totalled more than £30 million between 1926 and his death on 22 Aug 1963.

Top
The precise extent of the fortune of Queen Elizabeth II is open to debate, but her assets are reputed to be the greatest of any woman in the world. Estimates and comparisons of extreme personal wealth are beset with intractable difficulties, caused mainly by reticence and the element of approximation in the valuation of assets. As US oil billionaire Jean Paul Getty once remarked, "If you can count your millions, you are not a billionaire." A further complication is that much of the wealth of the world's monarchs represents national rather than personal assets.

Middle
The childhood acting career of Shirley Temple, now Mrs Charles Black, lasted from 1934 to 1939 and made her the world's youngest ever female millionaire.

Bottom
Bill Gates, whose mansion is seen here in the process of being built, was the youngest dollar billionaire in the USA in 1992. Gates founded his first computer companies at the age of 14 and dropped out of Harvard at 19 to write a version of Basic, a powerful computer language. Situated on a hillside, his home overlooks Lake Washington towards Seattle and the Olympic Mountains, and includes a small movie theatre, a pool and a reception hall large enough to entertain 100 guests for dinner.

Most valuable items

Collections

Stamps

Mauritius 'Bordeaux Cover', a letter sent to wine merchants in Bordeaux in 1847 and franked with the one-penny and 2d first issues of Mauritius was bought for Sw.Fr.5,750,000 (£2,590,090) by an anonymous buyer in less than a minute at a sale at the Hotel International, Zurich, Switzerland, in Nov 1993.

A collection comprising 183 pages of the classic issues of Mauritius was bought by Japanese engineer-industrialist Hıroyukı Kanaı for Sw.Fr.15,000,000 (£6,756,756) at the Mauritius auction of 3 Nov 1993.

Coins

The highest price for a collection is $25,235,360 (£11,560,000), for the Garrett family collection of US and colonial coins collected between 1860 and 1942, which had been donated to Johns Hopkins University, Baltimore, Maryland, USA. Four auctions were held from 28 to 29 Nov 1979 and from 25 to 26 March 1981 at the Bowers & Ruddy Galleries, Wolfeboro, New Hampshire, USA.

Antiques

Clock

The highest price paid for a clock is £905,882, by a private bidder at Christie's, New York, USA, on 24 April 1991, for a rare 1927 Cartier 'Egyptian Revival' clock.

Furniture

Barbara Piasecka Johnson of Princeton, New Jersey, USA, paid £8.58 million ($15.1 million) at Christie's, London, UK, on 5 July 1990 for the 18th-century Italian 'Badminton Cabinet', owned by the Duke of Beaufort.

Jewellery

The Duchess of Windsor's collection raised £31,380,197 when it was sold at Sotheby's, Geneva, Switzerland, on 3 April 1987.

The most valuable individual items are two diamond drop earrings of 58.6 and 61 carats, bought and sold anonymously for £3.1 million at Sotheby's, Geneva, on 14 Nov 1980.

Playing cards

The highest price paid for a deck of playing cards is $143,352 (£99,000), by the Metropolitan Museum of Art, New York City, USA, at Sotheby's, London, UK, on 6 Dec 1983. Dating from c.1470–85, it was the oldest known complete hand-painted set.

Teddy bear

A Steiff bear named 'Teddy Girl' was sold for £110,000, more than 18 times the estimate, by Christie's, London, UK, on 5 Dec 1994 to Japanese businessman Yoshihiro Sekiguchi. It was made in 1904, only a year after Steiff made the first jointed plush teddy bear.

Toys

A hand-painted replica of the 'Charles' hose reel—a piece of fire-fighting equipment—built c. 1870 was sold to a telephone bidder for $231,000 (£128,333) at Christie's, New York City, USA, on 14 Dec 1991.

Art

Painting

Portrait of Dr Gachet, by Vincent van Gogh, which was completed only weeks before the artist's suicide in 1890, was sold within three minutes at Christie's, New York, USA, on 15 May 1990, for $82.5 million (£49.1 million).

Print

Christ Presented to the People, a 1655 etching by Rembrandt, was sold at Christie's, London, UK, in Dec 1985, for £561,600.

Drawing

Jardin de Fleurs (1888), by Vincent Van Gogh, was sold by Christie's, New York, USA, on 14 Nov 1990, for $8.36 million (£4.27 million).

Poster

A poster by Charles Rennie Mackintosh (1868–1928) was sold by Christie's, London, UK, on 4 Feb 1993, for £68,200.

Sculpture

An unnamed couple from Brighton, W Sussex, UK, paid £100 for *The Dancing Faun* by sculptor Adrien de Vries (1545/6–1626) in the 1950s, and the figure stood unremarked upon in their garden for the next 40 years. It was bought for the sum of £6.82 million by London dealer Cyril Humpris at Sotheby's, London, on 7 Dec 1989.

Photograph

Georgia O'Keeffe: A Portrait—Hands with Thimble, a photograph of Georgia O'Keeffe's hands by her husband Alfred Stieglitz, was sold at Christie's, New York, USA, on 8 Oct 1993 for a record $398,500 (£260,458).

Books and writing

Book

On 6 Dec 1983, Hans Kraus, acting for the Hermann Abs consortium, paid £8.14 million for the 226-leaf manuscript *The Gospel Book of Henry the Lion, Duke of Saxony*, at Sotheby's, London, UK. The book, which measures 34.3 x 25.4 cm (13½ x 10 in), was illuminated c.1170 by the monk Herimann at Helmershausen Abbey, Germany, and has 41 full-page illustrations.

Manuscript

The 'Codex Hammer', an illustrated manuscript in which Leonardo da Vinci predicted the invention of the submarine and the steam engine, was sold for the record sum of $30.8 million (£19,388,141) at Christie's, New York, USA, on 11 Nov 1994. The buyer was Bill Gates, co-founder and chairman of Microsoft.

Most expensive atlas

A version of Ptolemy's *Cosmographia* dating from 1492 was sold for the sum of $1,925,000 (£1,666,666) at Sotheby's, New York City, USA, on 31 Jan 1990.

Most expensive letter

The highest price paid on the open market for a single letter was $748,000 (£409,683), for

a letter written by Abraham Lincoln, on 8 Jan 1863, defending the Emancipation Proclamation against criticism. It was sold at Christie's, New York, to Profiles in History of Beverly Hills, California, USA, on 5 Dec 1991.

Pens

The most expensive writing pen, Montblanc's Meisterstück Solitaire Royal fountain pen, is made of solid gold and encased with 4,810 diamonds—the height in metres of the Mont Blanc mountain. It can be made to order for £75,000, in six months.

Musical instruments

Piano

The sum of $390,000 (£177,272) was paid for a Steinway grand of c. 1888 sold by the Martin Beck Theater at Sotheby Parke Bernet, New York, USA, on 26 March 1980.

Clothes and accessories

Dress

A wedding dress created by Hélène Gainville with jewels by Alexander Reza was unveiled in Paris, France, on 23 March 1989. Embroidered with diamonds mounted on platinum, the bridal outfit was sold for $7,301,587.20 (£4,269,934).

Shoes

The red slippers worn by Judy Garland in the film *The Wizard of Oz* were sold at Christie's, New York, USA, on 2 June 1988 for the sum of $165,000 (£90,000).

Emperor Field Marshal Jean-Bédel Bokassa of the Central African Empire (now Republic) commissioned pearl-studded shoes at a cost of $85,000 (£48,571) from the House of Berluti, Paris, France, for his self-coronation at Bangui on 4 Dec 1977.

purchased for $16,548,750 (£10,507,143) by Sheikh Ahmed Fitaihi, who obtained it for his chain of jewellery shops in Saudi Arabia.

The highest price on record for a rough diamond is £5.8 million, for a 255.10-carat stone found in Guinea and purchased by the William Goldberg Diamond Corporation in partnership with the Chow Tai Fook Jewellery Co. Ltd of Hong Kong in March 1989.

Pearl

La Régente, an egg-shaped pearl weighing 15.13 g (302.68 grains) was sold for $864,280 (£457,533) at Christie's, Geneva, Switzerland, on 12 May 1988. The gem used to form part of the French Crown Jewels.

Sapphire

A step-cut 62.02-carat stone was sold as a sapphire and diamond ring at Sotheby's,

THE WIZARD OF OZ SOLD FOR A RECORD-BREAKING $165,000 IN 1988

Guitar

A Fender Stratocaster guitar that used to belong to US rock legend Jimi Hendrix was sold by his former drummer 'Mitch' Mitchell for £198,000 at Sotheby's, London, UK, on 25 April 1990.

Violoncello

The highest price paid at auction for a violoncello is £682,000, at Sotheby's, London, UK, on 22 June 1988. The instrument, a Stradivarius known as 'The Cholmondeley', was made in Cremona, Italy, c. 1698.

Violin

The highest price ever paid at an auction for a violin is £902,000, for the 'Mendelssohn' Stradivarius of 1720, which was named after descendants of the composer, a German banking family. The instrument was sold to a mystery buyer at Christie's, London, UK, on 21 Nov 1990. The sum was also the highest price ever to have been paid at auction for a musical instrument.

Most expensive watch

The highest price ever paid for a watch is Sw.Fr.4.95 million (£1,864,300), at Habsburg Feldman, Geneva, Switzerland, on 9 April 1989 for a Patek Philippe 'Calibre '89' with 1,728 separate parts.

Wallet

The most expensive wallet is a platinum-cornered, diamond-studded crocodile creation made by Louis Quatorze of Paris and Mikimoto of Tokyo which sold in Sept 1984 for £56,000.

Gems

Diamonds

Many sales of polished diamonds are often considered private transactions, and the prices paid are not disclosed.

A 100.10-carat pear-shaped 'D' Flawless diamond was sold at Sotheby's, Geneva, Switzerland, on 17 May 1995. It was

St Moritz, Switzerland, on 20 Feb 1988, for the sum of $2,791,723 (£1,581,713).

Emerald

The highest price ever paid for a single lot of emeralds is $3,080,000 (£1,951,219), for an emerald and diamond necklace made by Cartier, London, UK, in 1937. Consisting of 12 stones weighing a total of 108.74 carats, the necklace was sold at Sotheby's, New York, USA, on 26 Oct 1989.

The highest price paid for a single emerald is $2,126,646 (£1,320,488), for a 19.77-carat emerald and diamond ring made by Cartier in 1958, and sold at Sotheby's, Geneva, Switzerland, on 2 April 1987.

Ruby

On 26 Oct 1989, a ruby and diamond ring weighing a total of 32.08 carats and made by Chaumet of Paris, France, was sold at Sotheby's, New York, USA, for the sum of $4,620,000 (£2,926,829).

Left to right
'Teddy Girl', the world's most expensive teddy bear, was made in 1904 and has a particularly well-documented history. Teddy bears are named after Theodore Roosevelt, the US president who had a fondness for bear hunting.

Made of solid gold and encrusted with diamonds, the Meisterstück Solitaire Royal by Montblanc is the most expensive pen in the world.

A Fender Stratocaster that once belonged to experimental electric guitarist Jimi Hendrix (1942–70) became the most expensive guitar ever when sold at auction in 1990. Fender, a US firm, first produced the groundbreaking Stratocaster in 1954.

$2,126,646, FOR A 19.77-CARAT CARTIER EMERALD AND DIAMOND RING

Farming and viticulture

Farms

Largest farms

The largest farms in the world are *kolkhozy* (collective farms) in the former USSR. These were reduced in number from 235,500 in 1940 to 26,900 in 1988 and represented a total cultivated area of 169.2 million ha (417.6 million acres). Units covering an area of more than 25,000 ha (60,000 acres) each were not uncommon.

The pioneer farm owned by Laucídio Coelho near Campo Grande, Mato Grosso, Brazil, from *c.* 1901 covered an area of 8,700 km² (3,358 miles²) and supported about 250,000 head of cattle at the owner's death in 1975.

The largest holdings in the United Kingdom are the Scottish hill farms in the Moray and Aberdeenshire region.

The largest arable holding is farmed by Elveden Farms Ltd at Elveden, Suffolk, where 4,081 ha (10,084 acres) are farmed on an estate covering 9,148 ha (22,603 acres). Production in 1995 included 8,661 tonnes of combinable crops and 33,375 tonnes of sugar beet. The other crops, which include potatoes, onions, carrots and parsnips, yielded 30,272 tonnes, and the livestock includes 1,127 lambs and 17,041 pigs.

Largest cattle stations and cow sheds

The world's largest ever cattle station was the Victoria River Downs Station in Northern Territory, Australia, which covered an area of 90,650 km² (35,000 miles²) until 1915— nearly three times the size of Belgium.

The largest cattle station in the world at present is the Anna Creek station in South Australia, which is owned by the Kidman family. It covers an area of 30,000 km² (11,600 miles²), or 23% the size of England. The biggest part of it is Strangway, which covers 14,000 km² (5,500 miles²).

Within the United Kingdom, the National Agricultural Centre at Kenilworth, Warks, was completed in 1967 and can house up to 1,480 cows.

The longest cowshed in the United Kingdom belongs to the Yorkshire Agricultural Society at Harrogate, N Yorkshire. It is 139 m (456 ft) long and has 753 cattle stalls.

Largest piggery

The largest piggery in the world is the COMTIM unit near Timişoara in Romania. It houses 70,000 sows that produce around 1,200,000 pigs per year.

Largest sheep stations

The sheep station that covers the greatest area is Commonwealth Hill in north-west South Australia, which grazes between 50,000 and 70,000 sheep, along with some 24,000 uninvited kangaroos, in an area of 10,567 km² (4,080 miles²). It is enclosed by 221 km (138 miles) of dog-proof fencing.

The sheep station that houses the greatest head count in the world is Sir William Stevenson's 16,579-ha (40,970-acre) Lochinver station in New Zealand, which had 127,406 sheep on 1 Jan 1993.

Largest sheep drive

The greatest sheep drive on record involved the movement of a total of 43,000 sheep a distance of 64 km (40 miles) from Barcaldine to Beaconsfield station, Queensland, Australia, by 27 horsemen in 1886.

Longest farm fence

The dingo-proof wire fence enclosing the main sheep-farming areas of Australia is 1.8 m (6 ft) high, with an additional 30 cm (1 ft) underground, and stretches for a distance of 5,531 km (3,437 miles). The Queensland state government discontinued its full maintenance of the fence in 1982.

Longest line of tractors

On 6 Aug 1995, a record 322 Ferguson tractors gathered in a line when they worked together for 1½ hours at Cooley, Co. Louth, Republic of Ireland.

Crops

Highest potato yield

Roger Southwell harvested a record 205.65 tonnes of potatoes in a period of four hours from an area of 2.46 ha (6 acres) at Watermill Farm, Northwold, Norfolk, UK, on 1 Nov 1989. The machinery that was used by Southwell was made by Standen Engineering Ltd of Ely, Cambs.

Highest barley yield

A record yield of 12.2 tonnes/ha of winter barley from 21.29 ha (52½ acres) was achieved at Stockton Park (Leisure) Ltd's Edington Mains, Chirnside, Scottish Borders, UK, on 2 Aug 1989.

Largest wheat field

The largest single fenced field sown with wheat measured 14,160 ha (35,000 acres) and was sown in 1951 south-west of Lethbridge, Alberta, Canada.

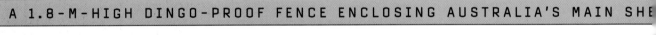

A 1.8-M-HIGH DINGO-PROOF FENCE ENCLOSING AUSTRALIA'S MAIN SHE

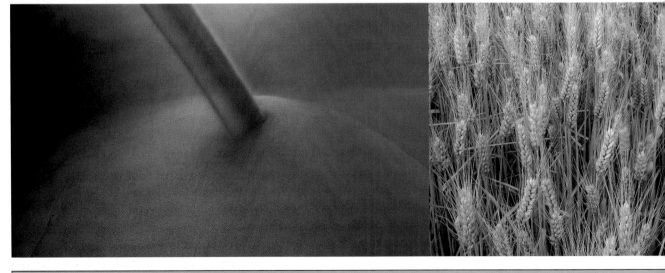

LARGEST VINEYARD IN THE WORLD LIES BETWEEN THE PYRENEES AND T

The record wheat yield in the United Kingdom is 13.99 tonnes/ha (111.4 cwt/acre) from an area of 17.49 ha (43¼ acres), by Gordon Rennie of Clifton Mains, Newbridge, West Lothian, in 1981.

Biggest hop farm
The world's leading private hop growers are John I. Haas, Inc., who have farms in Oregon and Washington, USA, and in Tasmania and Victoria, Australia, that cover a net area of 2,403 ha (5,940 acres).

Largest grain elevator
The largest grain elevator in the world is a single-unit elevator operated by the C-G-F Grain Co. at Wichita, Kansas, USA. It consists of a triple row of storage tanks, 123 on each side of the central loading tower or 'head house'. The entire unit is 828 m (2,717 ft) in length and 30.5 m (100 ft) wide. Each tank reaches a height of 37 m (120 ft) and has an internal diameter of 9.1 m (30 ft), which gives a total storage capacity of 7.3 million hl (20 million bushels) of wheat.

Viticulture
Oldest vat
The world's oldest known vat is still in use at Hugel et Fils (founded 1639) in Riquewihr, Haut-Rhin, France. Twelve generations of the family have used it since 1715.

Largest vats
The world's largest wooden wine cask is the Heidelberg Tun, which is found in the cellar of the Friedrichsbau, Heidelberg, Germany. Completed in 1751, it has a total capacity of 221,726 litres (48,773 gal).

The largest British vat is named 'Strongbow' and is used by H. P. Bulmer Ltd, the English cider-makers of Hereford. It is 19.65 m (64 ft 6 in) in height and 23 m (75 ft 6 in) in diameter, and it has a capacity of 7.41 million litres (1.63 million gal).

Largest vineyards
The largest vineyard in the world is in France and extends over the Mediterranean slopes that lie between the Pyrenees and the Rhône in the *départements* of Gard, Hérault, Aude and Pyrénées-Orientales. It covers an area of 840,000 ha (2,075,685 acres), 52.3% of which is *monoculture viticole* (given over to grapes alone).

The largest vineyard in the United Kingdom is Denbies Wine Estate in Dorking, Surrey, which covers a total area of 107 ha (265 acres). Planting began in 1986, and the 276,000 vines that have been planted have an annual production capacity of approximately 500,000 bottles.

Most northerly vineyard
The most northerly vineyard in the world to grow grapes for wine is in Sabile, Latvia. Latvia's only vineyard, it is situated at 57°00'N, and has been producing wine since at least the Middle Ages.

Most southerly vineyard
The most southerly commercial vineyards are found south of latitude 45°S in central Otago, South Island, New Zealand.

Largest vines
This world's largest vine was planted in 1842 at Carpinteria, California, USA. By 1900 it was yielding more than 9 tonnes of grapes in some years, and averaged 7 tonnes per year until it died in 1920.

The largest British vine is the Great Vine at Hampton Court, Greater London, planted in 1768. It has a circumference of 2.16 m (7 ft 1 in) and branches up to 34.7 m (114 ft) long, and its average yield is 318.8 kg (703 lb).

In 1990 Leslie Stringer of Dartford, Kent, UK, obtained a yield of more than 2,300 kg (5,071 lb) from the Dartford Wondervine, which had been planted in 1979. It was grown from a cutting that was taken from a vine planted in Banstead, Surrey, in 1962.

Left
The largest agricultural showground in the United Kingdom is the National Agricultural Centre at Kenilworth, where up to 1,480 cows can be housed. The Royal Show, which takes place there in midsummer, is the annual highlight for the British farming industry. More than 7,000 animals are gathered for the occasion, and agricultural machinery, dairy equipment and livestock products are put on display for the more than 180,000 people who visit the four-day event.

From left to right
The United States had the highest coarse-grain production in 1995, with 209.6 million tonnes—26% of the world's total.

Wheat is a cereal plant derived from *Triticum*, a wild grass that grows in the Middle East. The world's leading producer in 1995 was China, with 102.2 million tonnes of a world total of 541.1 million tonnes.

Potatoes were grown by the Andean Indians for at least 2,000 years before they were introduced to Europe. In 1995 China was the leading producer, with 45.8 million tonnes.

Domestic sheep are descended from wild sheep that were once found in the Middle East. Today, dozens of different breeds are reared all over the world for their wool, meat and milk, and they have become the basis of major industries in Australia and New Zealand, where the world's largest sheep stations are to be found.

EAS IS THE LONGEST FENCE IN THE WORLD, EXTENDING OVER 5,531 KM

ONE IN SOUTHERN FRANCE AND COVERS A TOTAL AREA OF 840,000 HA

Livestock

Far right
The smallest breed of cattle in the United Kingdom is the miniature Dexter. Average bulls are approximately 1.1 m (3 ft 7 in) in height.

Below
The middle white pig is the rarest breed of British pedigree pig, with only 103 breeding sows in the world. More than 90% of the breed are in the United Kingdom, and the rest are in Japan, imported there at the specific request of the Emperor, who was very partial to the tender meat that they provide.

Cattle

Leading cattle producer
In 1995, the USA produced 11.5 million tons of cattle.

Most expensive cattle
The Beefalo Cattle Co. of Calgary, Alberta, Canada, paid $2.5 million (£1.1 million) for the 'beefalo' (⅜ bison, ⅜ Charolais, ¼ Hereford) *Joe's Pride*, on 9 Sept 1974.

The highest price in the United Kingdom was £233,000, for a 14-month-old Canadian Holstein bull, *Pickland Elevation B. ET*, by Premier Breeders of Northumberland in 1982.

The top price paid for a cow is $1.3 million (£1 million), for a Friesian at auction in East Montpelier, Vermont, USA, in 1985.

In the United Kingdom, Brian Draper of Shrewsbury, Shrops, paid 65,000 guineas (£68,250) for *Grantchester Heather VIII*, a Friesian cow, on 12 Aug 1992.

Largest cattle
Val di Chianini cattle, found in Arezzo and Siena, Italy, have bulls that average 1.73 m (5 ft 8 in) at the shoulder and weigh 1,300 kg (2,870 lb). Chianini oxen have been known to attain heights of 1.9 m (6 ft 2¾ in).

The heaviest cow on record was *Mount Katahdin*, a Holstein–Durham cross that reached a weight of 2,270 kg (5,000 lb) several times between 1906 and 1910. He stood 1.88 m (6 ft 2 in) at the shoulder and had a 3.96-m (13-ft) girth.

The largest British breed is the South Devon. Bulls stand up to 1.55 m (5 ft 1 in) at the shoulder and weigh about 1,250 kg (2,755 lb). The heaviest specimen on record weighed 1,680 kg (3,700 lb).

The British record for any breed is 2,032 kg (4,480 lb), for the Bradwell Ox, owned by William Spurgin. In 1830, when six years old, it measured 4.57 m (15 ft) from nose to tail and had a maximum girth of 3.35 m (11 ft).

Smallest cattle
The smallest domestic breed of cattle is the Ovambo of Namibia. Bulls average 225 kg (496 lb) and cows just 160 kg (353 lb).

The smallest British breed is the miniature Dexter. Bulls weigh 450 kg (990 lb) and stand 1.1 m (3 ft 7 in) at the shoulder. In May 1984, a height of 86.3 cm (2 ft 10 in) was reported for 'Mayberry', an adult Dexter cow owned by R. Hillier of South Littleton, Evesham, Worcs.

Most prolific cows
In 1964, it was reported that a cow called 'Lyubik' had given birth to seven calves in Mogilev, Belarus.

In 1928, T. G. Yarwood of Manchester, UK, reported a case of five live calves at one birth.

The lifetime record for the greatest number of calves to one cow is 39, by 'Big Bertha', a Dremon owned by Jerome O'Leary of Co. Kerry, Republic of Ireland. She also holds the record for the oldest ever cow, having died just short of her 49th birthday in 1993.

Nordjydens Hubert, a Danish Holstein–Friesian bull that died at the age of 12 in Jan 1996,

left a total of 220,000 surviving progeny by artificial insemination.

Highest milk yields
The highest recorded lifetime yield is 211,025 kg (465,224 lb) to 1 May 1984, from cow No. 289, owned by M. G. Maciel & Son of Hanford, California, USA.

The greatest recorded yield for a single lactation is 26,963 kg (59,443 lb) in 1995 from a Friesian cow, *Acme Goldy 2*, owned by Bryce Miller of Northants, UK. It also achieved a world record protein yield for 365 days, with 966 kg (2,129 lb).

The highest reported yield in a day is 109.3 kg (241 lb) by *Urbe Blanca* in Cuba in June 1982.

Biggest cheese producer
The USA produced an estimated 2.95 billion kg (6.5 billion lb) of cheese in 1995.

Pigs

Leading pig producer
China produced 420 million head, or 42% of the world total, in 1994.

Most expensive pigs
On 5 March 1983, E. A. Bud Olson and Phil Bonzio paid $56,000 (£37,300) for a crossbred barrow named 'Bud', owned by Jeffrey Roemisch of Texas, USA.

In the United Kingdom, an anonymous buyer paid a record 4,000 guineas (£4,200) in April 1994 for a Gloucestershire Old Spot boar,

Heaviest cow 2,270 kg

CHINA, WITH 10,060 BILLION TONNES IN 1994

rooster named 'Weirdo', killed two cats and maimed a dog.

The largest known chicken is *Big Snow*, a rooster that weighed 10.51 kg (23 lb 3 oz) in 1992. Bred by Ronald Alldridge, it had a chest girth of 84 cm (2 ft 9 in).

Hens' eggs
The highest authenticated rate of laying is 371 in 364 days, by a White Leghorn in a test at the College of Agriculture, University of Missouri, USA, from 1978 to 1979.

The British record is 353 eggs in 365 days in a test at Milford, Surrey, in 1957. The chicken was a Rhode Island Red named *Wonderful Lady*.

The heaviest egg weighed 454 g (16 oz) and had a double yolk and shell. It was laid by a White Leghorn in the USA in 1956.

The largest egg had five yolks and was 31 cm (12¼ in) around the long axis. It was laid by a Black Minorca at Damsteads Farm, Lancs, UK, in 1896.

Foston Sambo 21, bred and sold by F. L. Robinson and Co. of Foston, Derbys.

Largest and smallest pigs
'Big Bill', a Poland–China hog weighed 1,157.5 kg (2,552 lb) in 1933 and stood 1.52 m (5 ft) tall at the shoulder.

The heaviest known British pig was a 639.5-kg (1,410-lb) Old Spot boar bred by Joseph Lawton of Cheshire, which was 1.43 m (4 ft 8¼ in) tall.

The Mini Maialino, bred by Stefano Morini of Italy, is the smallest breed, with a typical weight of 9 kg (20 lb).

Largest pig litter
Sow 570, a Meishan cross Large White–Duroc, produced a record litter of 37 piglets at Mr and Mrs M. P. Ford's Eastfield House Farm in Melbourne, York, UK, on 21 Sept 1993. Of the 36 that were born alive, 33 survived.

Goats
Leading goat producer
In 1994, China produced 58 million head, or 24% of the world total.

Largest and smallest goats
Mostyn Moorcock, a British Saanen owned by Pat Robinson, weighed 181 kg (400 lb) and had a shoulder height of 111.7 cm (44 in).

The smallest goats are certain pygmy goat species that weigh 15–20 kg (33–44 lb).

Highest goat milk yield
The highest recorded yield is 3,499 kg (7,714 lb) in 365 days in 1977, by *Osory Snow-Goose* owned by Mr and Mrs Jameson of Leppington, NSW, Australia.

Cynthia-Jean ('Baba'), owned by Carolyn Freund-Nelson of Northport, New York, USA, has lactated continuously since June 1980.

Sheep
Leading mutton producer
In 1994, China produced 67 million head of a worldwide total of 461 million head.

Most expensive sheep
The highest price is $A450,000 (then £205,000), for the Collinsville stud JC&S43 at the 1989 Adelaide Ram Sales, South Australia.

In the United Kingdom, Michael Scott sold a Scottish Blackface ram lamb named *Old Sandy* for £32,000 on 14 Oct 1988.

Largest sheep
Stratford Whisper 23H, a Suffolk ram owned by Joseph and Susan Schallberger of Boring, Oregon, USA, weighed 247.2 kg (545 lb) and stood 1.09 m (43 in) tall in March 1991.

Smallest sheep
Ouessant sheep of Brittany, France, have an average weight of 13–16 kg (29–35 lb).

Poultry
Leading poultry producer
The USA produced 13.4 million tonnes in 1994—27% of the world total.

Leading egg producer
In 1994, about 25% of the world's eggs—10,060 billion tonnes— were produced in China.

Largest chicken
The heaviest breed is the White Sully. The largest, a 10-kg (22-lb)

LARGEST RELIGION IN THE WORLD, CHRISTIANIT

MOST DENSELY POPULATED COUNTRY, BANGLADESH, H

GREATEST NUMBER OF FATALITIES IN A TERRORIST ATTACK WAS THE 329 PEOP

The

LONGEST TIME EVER SPENT ON DEATH ROW IS 39 YEARS, BY POISONER SADAMICHI HIRASA

LARGEST DECLARED DIVOR

COSTLIEST WAR IN TERMS OF HUMAN LIFE WAS WWI

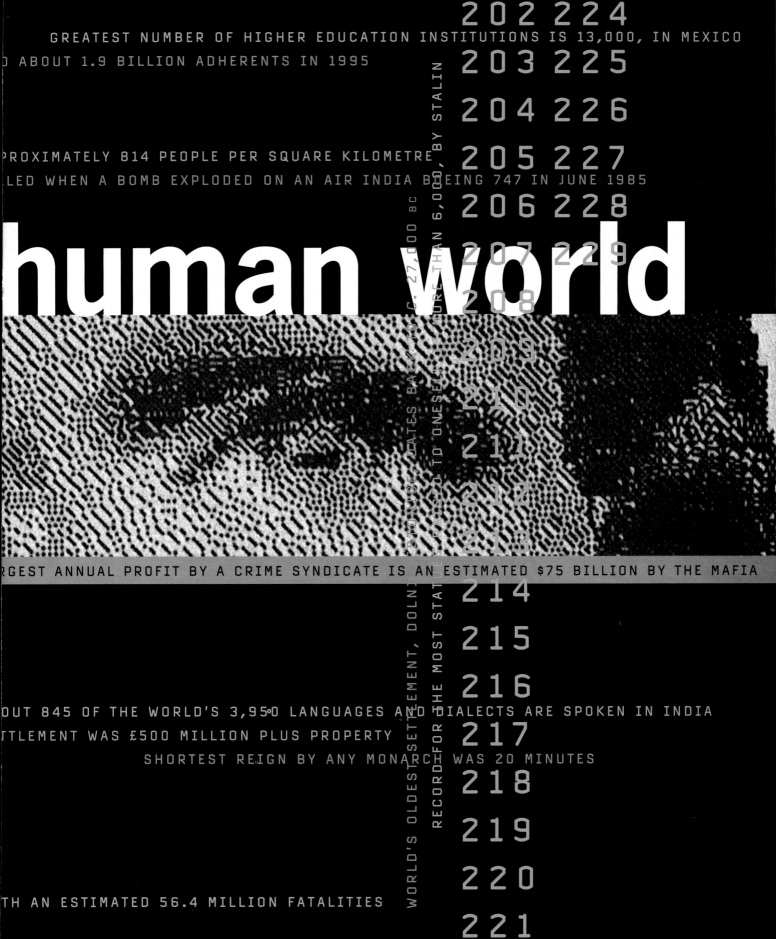

GREATEST NUMBER OF HIGHER EDUCATION INSTITUTIONS IS 13,000, IN MEXICO

ABOUT 1.9 BILLION ADHERENTS IN 1995

PROXIMATELY 814 PEOPLE PER SQUARE KILOMETRE

LED WHEN A BOMB EXPLODED ON AN AIR INDIA BOEING 747 IN JUNE 1985

BY STALIN

c. 27,000 BC

MORE THAN 6,000, TO ONESELF

human world

GEST ANNUAL PROFIT BY A CRIME SYNDICATE IS AN ESTIMATED $75 BILLION BY THE MAFIA

WHICH DATES BACK

OUT 845 OF THE WORLD'S 3,950 LANGUAGES AND DIALECTS ARE SPOKEN IN INDIA

TLEMENT WAS £500 MILLION PLUS PROPERTY

SHORTEST REIGN BY ANY MONARCH WAS 20 MINUTES

WORLD'S OLDEST SETTLEMENT, DOLNI

RECORD FOR THE MOST STATUES

TH AN ESTIMATED 56.4 MILLION FATALITIES

World geography

Right
The longest boundary in the world is between the USA and Canada. This photograph shows part of the border between Maine in the far north-west of the USA and Quebec in Canada.

Territories
Largest country
Russia has a total area of 17,075,400 km² (6,592,800 miles²)—11.5% of the world's total land area. It is 70 times as big as the United Kingdom but its population is only 2.51 times greater, at 147,168,000 in 1995.

Smallest country
The smallest independent country is the State of the Vatican City or Holy See (Stato della Città del Vaticano), which was made an enclave within the city of Rome, Italy, on 11 Feb 1929. It covers 44 ha (108¾ acres).

Smallest republic
Nauru in the Pacific Ocean covers 2,129 ha (5,261 acres).

Smallest colony
The City of Gibraltar has a total area of 5.8 km² (2¼ miles²).

Pitcairn Island is the only inhabited island of a group of four forming a British colony in Polynesia. The island covers an area of 388 ha (1½ miles²), although the whole colony covers 48 km² (18½ miles²).

Smallest state
The seat of the Sovereign Military Order of Malta and the official residence of the Grand Master in Rome, Italy, has an area of 1.2 ha (3 acres). It maintains diplomatic relations with a number of foreign governments and its legal status is the same as other states. It is thus sometimes called the 'smallest state in the world'.

Largest political division
The Commonwealth, a free association of 53 independent states and their dependencies, covers an area of 31,793,193 km² (12,275,351 miles²) and has a population of about 1.7 billion. Almost all member countries once belonged to the former British Empire.

Boundaries and coastlines
Most boundaries
The continent of Africa has 112 of the world's 306 national land boundaries. (Only 145 of the estimated 420 maritime boundaries have so far been agreed.)

The ratio of boundaries to area of land is greatest in Europe.

The country that has the greatest number of land boundaries is China, at 16 (with Mongolia, Russia, North Korea, Hong Kong, Macau, Vietnam, Laos, Myanmar [Burma], India, Bhutan, Nepal, Pakistan, Afghanistan, Tajikistan, Kyrgyzstan and Kazakhstan) that extend for 24,000 km (14,900 miles).

The country with the largest number of maritime boundaries is Indonesia, with 19.

Longest boundaries
Including the Great Lakes boundaries but excluding the 2,547-km (1,538-mile) frontier with Alaska, the boundary between Canada and the USA extends for a total distance of 6,416 km (3,987 miles).

The longest maritime boundary extends for 2,697 km (1,676 miles) between Greenland and Canada.

Shortest boundary
The shortest boundary of any country is the 4.07-km (2-mile 931-yd) 'frontier' separating the Vatican City from Rome, Italy.

Zambia, Zimbabwe, Botswana and Namibia almost meet at a single point on the Zambezi River in Africa.

Most traversed frontier
There are nearly 500 million crossings of the 3,110-km (1,933-mile) border between the USA and Mexico every year.

Longest coastline
Canada has 243,798 km (151,489 miles) of coastline, including islands.

Shortest coastline
The sovereign country with the shortest coastline is Monaco, with 5.61 km (3½ miles), excluding piers and breakwaters.

Lowest and highest
The country with the lowest 'high point' is Maldives, which rises to a maximum altitude of 2.4 m (8 ft).

The country with the highest 'low point' is Lesotho. The bed of the Senqu (Orange) River is 1,381 m (4,530 ft) above sea level where it flows out of the country.

Settlements
Oldest settlement
The settlement of Dolní Vvstonice in the Czech Republic has been dated to the Gravettian culture c. 27,000 BC.

Oldest town
The oldest known walled town is Arīḥā (Jericho). The radiocarbon dating on specimens from the lowest levels reached by archaeologists indicates habitation there by more than 2,000 people as early as 7800 BC.

Oldest capital city
The oldest capital city in the world is Dimishq (Damascus), Syria. It has been continuously inhabited since c. 2500 BC.

Highest capital cities
The highest capital in the world (before the annexation of Tibet by China), was Lhasa, at 3,684 m (12,087 ft) above sea level.

HABITED SINCE C. 2500 BC

La Paz de Ayacucho, the administrative and de facto capital of Bolivia, is at an altitude of 3,631 m (11,913 ft). Its airport, El Alto, is 4,080 m (13,385 ft) above sea level.

Highest town
The town of Wenchuan, which was founded on the Qinghai–Tibet road north of the Tangla range in China in 1955, is 5,100 m (16,730 ft) above sea level.

Highest settlement
A settlement on the T'e-li-mo trail in southern Tibet is at an altitude of 6,020 m (19,750 ft).

Lowest settlement
The Israeli settlement of Ein Bokek on the shores of the Dead Sea is 393.5 m (1,291 ft) below sea level.

Northernmost village
Ny-Alesund, a coal-mining settlement on King's Bay, Vest-Spitsbergen, in the Norwegian territory of Svalbard, is situated at 78°55'N.

Northernmost town
Dikson in Russia, which has a population of 1,400, is situated at 73°32'N.

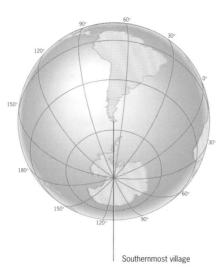

Southernmost village

Northernmost village

Northernmost capital
Reykjavík in Iceland, which had a population of 103,036 in 1994, is at 64°08'N.

Southernmost village
Puerto Williams on the north coast of Isla Navarino in Tierra del Fuego, Chile, is situated at 54°57'S.

Southernmost capital city
Wellington in New Zealand, with a population of 331,100, is situated at 41°17'S.

Furthest large town from the sea
Urumqi (Wulumuqi), capital of China's Xinjiang Uygur autonomous region, is about 2,500 km (1,500 miles) from the nearest coastline.

Closest capitals
The nearest capitals of two neighbouring countries are the Vatican City and Rome, Italy, as the Vatican is surrounded by Rome.

Furthest capitals
The greatest distance between the capitals of countries sharing a common border is 4,200 km (2,600 miles), between Moscow (Russia) and Pyongyang (Democratic People's Republic of Korea).

British settlements
Oldest settlements
The name of the tin trading post Salakee on St Mary's, Isles of Scilly, has pre-Celtic roots, which indicates a settlement there prior to 550 BC.

Smallest town
The smallest place with a town council is Fordwich, Kent, which has 249 inhabitants.

Largest village
The village of Lancing, W Sussex, has an estimated population of 18,100.

Largest new town
Milton Keynes, Bucks, has 161,000 inhabitants and a projected population of 175,000 by the year 2000.

Most remote village (mainland)
Inverie, Highland, is a 43.5-km (27-mile) walk from the nearest village, Arnisdale.

Left
The smallest sovereign country is the State of the Vatican City, which is an enclave within Rome and the seat of the Roman Catholic Church. Its most famous building is St Peter's Basilica, with the imposing St Peter's Square before it.

MOST NORTHERLY TOWN IN THE WORLD IS DIKSON IN RUSSIA, AT 73°32'N

World population

WORLD POPULATION IS NOW MORE THAN THAT OF THE WHOLE WORLD 150 YEARS AGO

Population and settlement

World population

The world population is currently an estimated 5,804 million. At the beginning of the century it was 1,633 million, and it is expected to be 6,158 million in 2000. Matej Gaspar, who was born on 11 July 1987 in Zagreb, Croatia (then Yugoslavia), was symbolically named the world's 5 billionth inhabitant by the United Nations Secretary-General.

The peak annual increase of 2.04% from 1965 to 1970 had declined to 1.57% by 1990 to 1995, but the world population is still growing by more than 87 million people every year. The average daily increase is about 240,000, or 167 people per minute.

Most populous country

China had an estimated population of 1,206,600,000 in mid 1995 and has a rate of natural increase of more than 14.3 million people per year. Its population is more than that of the whole world 150 years ago.

Most densely populated countries

Of countries covering an area of more than 2,500 km^2 (1,000 miles^2), the most densely populated is Bangladesh, which has a population of 120,093,000 (1995) living in an area of 147,570 km^2 (56,977 miles^2), giving a density of 814/km^2 (2,108/mile^2).

Most densely populated territories

The Portuguese province of Macau on the southern coast of China has an estimated population of 428,000 (1995) in an area of 19.3 km^2 (7½ miles^2), giving a density of 22,176/km^2 (57,067/mile^2).

Of territories covering more than 1,000 km^2, Hong Kong, which has a total area of 1,075 km^2 (415 miles^2), contains an estimated 6,205,000 people (1995), giving a density of 5,772/km^2 (14,952/mile^2).

Most populous city

The most populous urban agglomeration as listed in the UN's *World Urbanization Prospects, The 1994 Revision*, is Tokyo, Japan, with 26,500,000 people in 1994.

Least populous country

The independent state with the smallest population is the Vatican City, which had 1,000 inhabitants in 1995.

Most sparsely populated territories

Antarctica has been occupied by relays of scientists since 1943. The population varies seasonally and can reach 4,000, a density of one person every 3,550 km^2 (1,325 miles^2).

In 1995, Greenland had a population of 55,800 over an area of 2,175,600 km^2 (840,000 miles^2), giving a density of one person to every 39 km^2 (15^1/$_{10}$ miles^2).

GLOBAL POPULATION INCREASES BY 167 PER MINUT

Migration

Emigration

A greater number of people emigrate from Mexico than any other country, mainly to the USA. In the fiscal year to Sept 1986, a record 1,615,854 illegal immigrants were arrested by US patrols on the Mexican border. The number of legal immigrants in the same period was 68,500.

The Soviet invasion of Afghanistan in Dec 1979 caused an influx of 2.9 million Afghanis into Pakistan and 2.2 million into Iran.

A total of 124,000 British citizens emigrated from the United Kingdom in 1993. The most emigrants in a year was 360,000 in 1852, when the United Kingdom comprised Great Britain and all of Ireland. Most of the emigrants were fleeing Ireland for the USA in the wake of the potato famine.

Immigration

Records show that between 1820 and 1994 the USA received 61,503,866 official immigrants. One in 76 of the US population, however, is an illegal immigrant.

The peak period of immigration into the United Kingdom was from 1 July 1961 to 30 June 1962, when approximately 430,000 Commonwealth citizens entered the country.

Peak population increase 2.04%

Social trends

Highest birth rate
The worldwide crude birth rate (number of births per 1,000 people) was estimated at 25 in 1990–95.

D IS ESTIMATED TO REACH 6,158 MILLION IN 2000

The lowest rate of natural increase to have been recorded in an independent country in recent times was –2.9 per 1,000 (11.7 births and 14.6 deaths), in Hungary between 1990 and 1995.

Suicides
Every day there are an estimated 2,700 suicides worldwide. The highest annual rate is 47 per 100,000 people, in Sri Lanka in 1991. The lowest recorded rate is 0.04 per 100,000 people in Jordan (one case in 1970).

Marriage rate
Vanuatu in the Pacific Ocean has a record annual marriage rate of 34 per 1,000 members of the population.

Divorce rate
The USA has the highest number of divorces, with a total of 1,191,000 divorces in 1994, or 4.6 per 1,000 population. The peak rate was 5.4 per 1,000, in 1979.

Infant mortality rates
The world infant mortality rate (deaths at the age of under one year per 1,000 live births) was 64 for 1990–95.

The lowest recorded infant mortality rate for 1990–95 is four, in Japan.

The highest estimated infant mortality rate in 1990–95 was 166, in Sierra Leone.

The worst infant mortality rate of recent times was in Ethiopia in 1969, when it was unofficially estimated at almost 550.

In 1994, there was a record low British infant mortality rate of 6.2.

Life expectancy
World life expectancy has risen from 46.4 years in 1950–55 to 64.4 years in 1990–95.

The country with the highest average life expectancy at birth is Japan, with 83 years for women and 76.3 years for men in 1992.

The lowest estimated rates for 1985–90 are 39.4 years for males in Sierra Leone and 42.0 years for females in Afghanistan.

In 1890–1900, life expectancy in India was at a record low of 23.7 years.

Life expectancy in the United Kingdom in 1994 was 79.4 years for females and 74.2 for males. In 1901, it was 45.5 years for males and 49.0 years for females. There is some evidence that life expectancy in Britain in the 5th century AD was 33 years for males and 27 years for females.

Gender ratio
There are an estimated 1,015 males in the world for every 1,000 females.

The largest recorded shortage of women is in the United Arab Emirates, which has an estimated 566 females to every 1,000 males.

The largest recorded shortage of males is in Latvia, which has an estimated 1,167 females to every 1,000 males.

The highest crude birth rate estimated by the United Nations in 1990–95 was 52.5, in Niger. Excluding the Vatican City, the lowest rate was 9.7, in Spain.

Natural increase
The global rate of natural increase was estimated at 15.7 (25 births less 9.3 deaths) per 1,000 in 1990–95, compared with a peak of 20.4 per 1,000 in 1965–70.

The highest available recorded rate in 1990–95 is 38.8 (43.6 less 4.8), in Oman.

Death rate
The crude death rate (the number of deaths per 1,000 people of all ages) for the whole world in 1990–95 was estimated at 9.3.

East Timor had a peak death rate of 45 per 1,000 in 1975–80. However, this had fallen to 17.4 by 1990–95. The highest estimated rate in the world in 1990–95 was 25.2, in Sierra Leone.

The lowest estimated rate for 1990–95 was 2.7, in the United Arab Emirates.

HIGHEST AVERAGE LIFE EXPECTANCY IS 83 YEARS, FOR JAPANESE WOMEN

Worst disasters

MOST DEATHS IN A BOMBING RAID WAS APPROXIMATELY 83,000, IN TOKYO IN 1945

Right
The *Exxon Valdez* oil spillage in 1989 is believed to have been directly responsible for the deaths of an estimated 580,000 birds and 5,500 otters. One of the costliest disasters in real terms, with an eventual clean-up expenditure of about $20 billion (£12.5 billion), it had one positive result—the Valdez principles that were subsequently drawn up by an alliance of environmental groups, bankers and investment fund managers provide guidelines for corporate conduct in terms of the protection of the environment.

Most terrorist fatalities 329

Wartime and terrorist
Greatest bomb fatalities
The atomic bomb dropped on Hiroshima, Japan, on 6 Aug 1945, killed more than 100,000 people on that day. A further 55,000 died from radiation within a year.

In WWII, a bombing raid on Tokyo, Japan, on 10 March 1945, killed about 83,000 people and injured 41,000.

Worst submarine disaster
The American freighter SS *Thompson Lykes* rammed and sank the Free French submarine *Surcouf*, which was carrying 130 officers and men, in the Caribbean on 18 Feb 1942. There were no survivors.

Worst deliberate dam burst
Guomindang forces fighting the Japanese dynamited the Yangtze Jiang dam at Huayuan Kou, China, in April 1938, killing 890,000.

Worst case of genocide
Between 1311 and 1340 the invading Mongol army exterminated approximately 35 million Chinese peasants.

Greatest mass suicides in wartime
Rather than subject themselves to defeat and humiliation by the Romans, 960 Jewish zealots committed suicide after a prolonged siege of Massada, their fortress stronghold, during the Roman–Jewish war of AD 66–73.

MOST EXTREME CASE OF MASS PANIC SAW A TOTAL ▶

Some 7,000 Japanese committed suicide, many by jumping off cliffs to their deaths, in July 1944 during the US Marines' assault of the island of Saipan in WWII.

Worst case of mass panic
On 2 July 1991, 1,426 Muslim pilgrims were trampled to death in a stampede along a tunnel from Mecca to Mina, a pilgrim tent city, in Saudi Arabia.

Most fatalities in a terrorist attack
On 23 June 1985, 329 people were killed when a bomb exploded on an Air India Boeing 747 over the Atlantic Ocean south-west of Ireland. Sikh extremists were suspected.

The capsizing of the *Herald of Free Enterprise* in 1987, which killed 193, was the worst British maritime disaster of recent times.

Industrial and poisonings

Worst industrial waste disaster
On 3 Dec 1984, the methylisocyanate gas leak at a Union Carbide pesticide plant in Bhopal, India, killed approximately 3,350 people and left a further 20,000 with serious medical conditions.

Worst nuclear disasters
The overheating of a nuclear waste container caused the 1957 explosion at a complex at Kyshtym in Russia, which released radioactive compounds that dispersed over an area of 23,000 km^2 (8,900 miles^2). More than 30 small communities within a 1,200-km^2 (460-mile^2) radius were eliminated from maps of the USSR in the years following the accident, and about 17,000 people were evacuated. A 1992 report indicates that 8,015 people died over a 32-year period of observation as a direct result of discharges.

The worst disaster involving a nuclear reactor took place at Chernobyl No. 4 in the USSR (now the Ukraine). Although the official Soviet total of immediate deaths on 26 April 1986 was 31, it is not known how many of the 200,000 people involved in the clean-up operation died in the five-year period following the disaster due to radiation exposure, since no systematic records were kept.

Greatest mass poisoning
In May 1981, an eight-year-old boy was the first of more than 600 victims of the Spanish cooking-oil scandal. In June it was discovered that the cause of his death was the use of 'denatured' industrial colza from rapeseed.

Although not ranking among the 20 largest oil spills, because of its environmentally sensitive location the 38,000-tonne *Exxon Valdez* spillage off Alaska, USA, on 24 March 1989 was an ecological disaster. Pollution eventually covered 2,590 km^2 (1,000 miles^2) of land.

Worst Space disasters
On 24 Oct 1960, 91 people were killed when an R-16 rocket exploded at the Baikonur Space Center in the USSR (now Kazakhstan).

Excluding accidents on the ground, the most deaths to occur in a Space accident is seven, when US space shuttle *Challenger* exploded 73 seconds after take-off on 28 Jan 1986.

Worst train disaster
On 6 June 1981, more than 800 passengers died when their train plunged off a bridge into the Bagmati River at Bihar, India.

Worst underground train disaster
On 28 Oct 1995, approximately 300 people in an underground train were killed in a fire at Baku, Azerbaijan.

Worst lift disaster
In May 1995, a lift at Vaal Reefs Mine, South Africa, fell 490 m (1,600 ft), killing 105.

Worst accidental explosion
On 7 Dec 1917, the French freighter *Mont Blanc*, packed with 5,000 tons of explosives and combustibles, collided with another ship in Halifax harbour, Nova Scotia, Canada, creating a blast that was felt more than 95 km (60 miles) away and killed 1,635.

Left
The aftermath of the Jonestown disaster, in which members of the People's Temple sect killed themselves by drinking cyanide-adulterated punch after bizarre rehearsals of mass suicide staged by cult leader Jim Jones, who had fled San Francisco, USA, with 900 followers after accusations of financial irregularities. Jones himself was found to have died of a gunshot.

426 PILGRIMS DIE IN A STAMPEDE ALONG A TUNNEL FROM MECCA TO MINA

Greatest mass suicide by poisoning
The greatest mass suicide in peacetime occurred on 18 Nov 1978, when 913 members of the People's Temple cult died of mass cyanide poisoning at Jonestown near Port Kaituma, Guyana.

Most lethal smog
From 4 to 9 Dec 1952, between 3,500 and 4,000 people—mainly the elderly and children—died in London, UK, from acute bronchitis caused by smog carrying a high concentration of dirt from industrial areas.

Transport

Worst air accident
The worst air crash occurred on 27 March 1977, when two Boeing 747s (Pan-Am and KLM) collided on the runway at Tenerife, Canary Islands, killing 583 people.

Worst maritime disasters
The worst British maritime disaster in recent times occurred when the Townsend Thoresen *Herald of Free Enterprise* capsized off Zeebrugge, Belgium, on 6 March 1987, with the loss of 193 lives, all British.

Famine, fire and water

Worst famines
The worst famine killed about 40 million people in northern China from 1959 to 1961.

The worst British famine (when Ireland was part of the United Kingdom) was the 1846–51 Irish potato famine. About 1 million died.

Worst fires in single buildings
The most people killed in a fire in a single building is 1,670, in the theatre in Guangdong (Canton), China, in May 1845.

The highest death toll in a single building in the United Kingdom was 188, in the Theatre Royal in Exeter, Devon, in Sept 1887.

Most disastrous flood
The world's most disastrous flood occurred when the Huang He River in China burst its banks in Oct 1887, resulting in the death of 900,000 people.

Worst accidental dam disaster
In 1975 the Banqiao and Shimantan dams in Henan Province, China, burst almost simultaneously, killing about 230,000 people.

Left
The space shuttle *Challenger* was the first flight to take off but not reach Space. Among the casualties was schoolteacher Sharon Christa McAuliffe, who had won a national contest to become the first ordinary citizen in Space.

WORST EVER AIR ACCIDENT KILLED 583 PEOPLE ON A RUNWAY IN TENERIFE

Buildings for living

Right
The Imperial Palace in the centre of Beijing, China, is the world's largest palace, covering a total area of 960 x 750 m (3,150 x 2,460 ft).

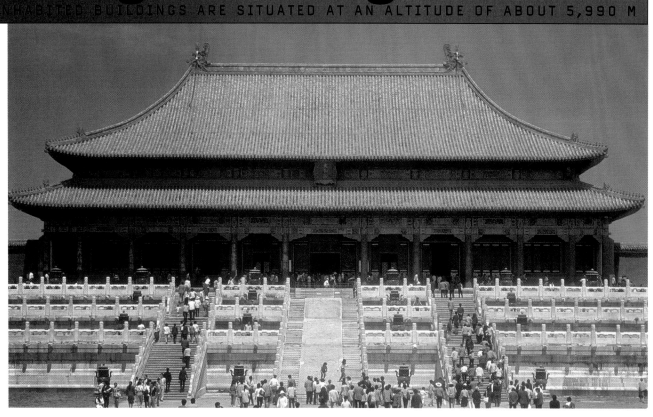

Remote dwellings

Highest altitude
The highest inhabited buildings in the world are in the Indo-Tibetan border fort of Bāsisi, which is located close to the Māna Pass (31° 04' N, 79° 24' E) at an altitude of around 5,990 m (19,650 ft).

In April 1961, a three-room dwelling believed to date from c. 1480 (the late pre-Columbian period) was discovered at an altitude of 6,600 m (21,650 ft) on the mountain of Cerro Llullaillaco on the border between Argentina and Chile.

Northernmost habitation
The Danish scientific station that was established in Pearyland, northern Greenland, in 1952, is situated more than 1,450 km (900 miles) north of the Arctic Circle. It is manned every summer.

The drifting Soviet research station 'North Pole 15' passed within 2.8 km (1¼ miles) of the North Pole in Dec 1967.

The northernmost continuously inhabited place is the Canadian Department of National Defence outpost at Alert on Ellesmere Island, Northwest Territories (82° 30' N, 62° W), which was set up in 1950.

Southernmost habitation
The most southerly permanent human habitation in the world is the Amundsen–Scott South Polar Station, which belongs to the USA and was completed in 1957. It was replaced by a new station in 1975.

Palaces

Largest palaces
The Imperial Palace in Beijing, China, covers 960 x 750 m (3,150 x 2,460 ft). The outline dates from its initial construction under the third Ming Emperor, Yongle (1402–24), but most of the intra-mural buildings (five halls and 17 palaces) date from the 18th century.

The Palace of Versailles, which is located 23 km (14 miles) to the south-west of Paris, France, is 580 m (1,903 ft) in length and has a total of 375 windows in its façade. Construction, which was completed in 1682 for Louis XIV, occupied more than 30,000 workmen under Jules Hardouin-Mansart (1646–1708).

The world's most southerly habitation is the Amundsen–Scott South Polar Station.

Istana Nurul Iman, the palace of HM the Sultan of Brunei in the capital Bandar Seri Begawan, was completed in Jan 1984 at a reported cost of £300 million. With 1,788 rooms and 257 lavatories, it is the world's largest residence. An underground garage accommodates the sultan's 153 cars.

The largest royal palace in the United Kingdom is Hampton Court, Greater London. Acquired from Cardinal Wolsey by Henry VIII in 1525, it was greatly enlarged by the latter and by William III, Queen Anne and George I and now covers an area of 1.6 ha (4 acres) within 271 ha (670 acres) of grounds. The last resident monarch was George II.

The largest palace in royal use in the United Kingdom is Buckingham Palace, London, which stands in 15.8 ha (39 acres) of gardens and has 600 rooms, including a 34-m-long (112-ft) ballroom used for investitures. The site after which it is named was bought by John Sheffield, the first Duke of Buckingham and Normanby (1648–1721), in 1703, and the palace was reconstructed in the Palladian style from 1825 to 1836, according to a design by John Nash (1752–1835). The 186-m-long (610-ft) East Front was built in 1846 and refaced in 1912.

Castles and forts
Oldest castle
The oldest stone castle in the United Kingdom is Chepstow Castle, Monmouthshire, UK, which was built c. 1067 on the west bank of the River Wye by William fitz Osbern.

Largest castle
The largest ancient castle in the world is Hradčany Castle in Prague, Czech Republic, which was originally constructed in the 9th

floor area of 21,460 m² (231,000 ft²). It was owned by the late Prince Johannes von Thurn und Taxis, whose family use only 95 of the rooms. The castle is valued at more than 336 million DM (£122 million).

Largest fort
Fort George in Ardersier, Highland, UK, which was constructed between 1748 and 1769, is 640 m (2,100 ft) in length and has an average width of 189 m (620 ft). The fort is located on a site that covers a total area of 17.2 ha (42½ acres).

Houses
Most rooms
The British house with the greatest number of rooms is Knole, situated near Sevenoaks, Kent, UK, which is believed to have had 365 rooms, one for every day of the year. Constructed around seven courtyards, its total depth from front to back is approximately 120 m (400 ft). Building was begun in 1456 by Thomas Bourchier, Archbishop of Canterbury (1454–86), and the house was extended by Thomas Sackville, the first Earl of Dorset, in around 1603–08.

Smallest house
The smallest British house is a 19th-century fisherman's cottage at The Quay, Conwy, UK, which consists of two tiny rooms and a staircase. It has a frontage of 1.82 m (6 ft), is 3.09 m (10 ft 2 in) high and measures 2.54 m (8 ft 4 in) from front to back.

Narrowest house
The narrowest house frontage on record in the United Kingdom is one of just 1.19 m (3 ft 11 in). This is on the house at 50 Stuart Street, Millport, on the island of Great Cumbrae, N Ayrshire, UK.

Above
The 19th-century fisherman's cottage at The Quay, Conwy, UK, is the smallest house in the United Kingdom.

century. The building is an oblong irregular polygon with an axis of 570 m (1,870 ft) and an average transverse diameter of 128 m (420 ft), giving a total surface area of 7.28 ha (18 acres).

Largest inhabited castle
The world's largest inhabited castle is the royal residence of Windsor Castle at Windsor, Berks, UK. Originally constructed in the 12th century, the building is in the form of a waisted parallelogram and measures 576 x 164 m (1,890 x 540 ft).

Largest moat
The moats surrounding the Imperial Palace in Beijing, China, are 49 m (161 ft) wide and have a total length of 3,290 m (10,793 ft).

Largest residence
The largest non-palatial residence in the world is St Emmeram Castle in Regensburg, Germany, which has 517 rooms and a total

Largest estate
The largest housing estate to be found in the United Kingdom is the Becontree Estate, which is situated in Barking and Redbridge, London. It covers an area of 676 ha (1,670 acres) and is located on a site that extends over a total area of 1,214 ha (3,000 acres). Constructed between 1921 and 1929, the estate contains a total of 26,822 homes, and has an estimated population of almost 90,000 people.

Oldest inhabited house
The oldest house in the United Kingdom is Barton Manor in Pagham, W Sussex, UK, which includes structures dating from Saxon times (c. AD 800).

Longest resident in one house
Virginia Hopkins Phillips, a resident of Onancock, Virginia, USA, lived in the same house from her birth in 1891 until shortly after her 102nd birthday in 1993.

Flats
Tallest block of flats
The John Hancock Center in Chicago, Illinois, USA, is 343.5 m (1,127 ft) and 100 storeys high. Floors 44–92 are residential.

The tallest purely residential block of flats is the 70-storey Lake Point Tower in Chicago, Illinois, USA, which is 195 m (640 ft) high and has 879 apartments.

The tallest residential block in the United Kingdom is Shakespeare Tower, Barbican, City of London. The 44-storey block, completed on 24 March 1969, is 127.77 m (419 ft 2½ in) high and contains 116 flats.

Largest complex
The largest complex of private blocks is the Barbican Estate, in the City of London, UK, designed by Chamberlin, Bon & Powell. It occupies 16 ha (40 acres) and includes 2,014 flats and parking for 1,710 cars.

Royalty and government

SHORTEST EVER REIGN WAS 20 MINUTES, BY LUIS FILIPE OF PORTUGAL IN 1908

Right
The most expensive coronation per head of population was that of Jean-Bédel Bokassa, who had himself crowned emperor of the Central African Republic in 1977.

Monarchs
Longest reigns
Minhti, King of Arakan, which is now part of Myanmar (Burma), is reputed to have reigned for 95 years, between 1279 and 1374.

The longest well documented reign of any monarch is that of Phiops II (also known as Pepi II or Neferkare), a pharaoh of the 6th Dynasty in ancient Egypt. He began his reign c. 2281 BC, aged six, and is believed to have reigned for about 94 years.

The King of Thailand, Bhumibol Adulyadej (Rama IX), is the longest-reigning living monarch. Born in 1927, he ascended the throne on 9 June 1946.

The longest-reigning queen is HM Queen Elizabeth II. She succeeded to the British throne on 6 Feb 1952, on her father's death.

Shortest reign
The Crown Prince Luís Filipe of Portugal was technically King of Portugal (Dom Luís III) for about 20 minutes on 1 Feb 1908, when his father was fatally shot in Lisbon. The Crown Prince was also mortally wounded.

Oldest and heaviest monarch
King Taufa'ahau Tupou IV of Tonga was born in 1918. In Sept 1976, he had grown to 1.90 m (6 ft 3 in) in height and weighed 209.5 kg (33 st), but by 1993 he had slimmed to 127 kg (20 st).

Heads of state
Longest service
Musoma Kanijo is reputed to have been chief of the Nzega district of western Tanganyika (now part of Tanzania) for more than 98 years, from 1864, when he was eight years old, until his death in 1963.

Oldest head of state
The oldest living head of state is Nouhak Phoumsavanh (b. 9 April 1914), who is president of Laos.

Youngest head of state
Mswati III, the current king of Swaziland, was born in 1968.

Largest meeting of world leaders
For the 50th Anniversary of the United Nations, a Special Commemorative Meeting of the General Assembly was held in New York City, USA, from 22 to 24 Oct 1995. It was addressed by 200 speakers, including 128 heads of state and government.

Legislatures
Largest elections
In the 1991 elections for the Indian Lok Sabha (Lower House), 315,439,908 people out of an electorate of 488,678,993 cast their votes in 511 constituenices. Equivalent details for the 1996 elections were not available at the time of going to press.

Closest elections
In general elections in Zanzibar (now part of Tanzania) on 18 Jan 1961, the Afro-Shirazi Party won by a single seat, when Chake-Chake seat on Pemba Island was gained by just one vote.

The narrowest recorded percentage win in an election was for the office of Southern District Highway Commissioner in Mississippi, USA, on 7 Aug 1979. Robert E. Joiner was declared the winner over W. H. Pyron, by 133,587 votes to 133,582. The loser obtained more than 49.999% of the votes.

Most decisive elections
North Korea recorded a 100% turnout of electors and a 100% vote for the Workers' Party of Korea in the general election that took place on 8 Oct 1962.

Most corrupt elections
In the Liberian presidential election of 1927, President Charles D. B. King was returned with an official majority of 234,000 over his opponent, Thomas J. R. Faulkner of the People's Party. He thereby claimed a 'majority' more than 15½ times greater than the entire electorate.

Most elections contested
Since 1979, independent candidate John C. Turmel ('The Engineer') of Nepean, Ontario, Canada, has contested 41 elections at municipal, provincial and federal level. In 1993 he founded the federal Abolitionist Party of Canada.

Highest personal majority
Boris Yeltsin gained 4,726,112 votes in the parliamentary elections in the Soviet Union on 26 March 1989. He received 5,118,745 of the 5,722,937 votes cast in the Moscow constituency. His closest rival obtained 392,633 votes.

Benazir Bhutto achieved 98.48% of votes in the Larkana-III constituency at the 1990

YOUNGEST CURRENTLY SERVING PRIME MINISTE

general election in Pakistan, with a total of 94,462 votes. The next candidate obtained just 718 votes.

Largest ballot paper
For the municipal elections of 18–19 Nov 1994 in Prague, Czech Republic, there were 1,187 candidates for the one constituency covering the city. The ballot paper, measuring 101.5 x 71.5 cm (3 ft 4 in x 2 ft 4 in), was delivered to all 1,018,527 registered voters, who could nominate up to 55 candidates for the 55 available seats.

Prime ministers
Oldest prime minister
El Hadji Muhammad el Mokri, Grand Vizier of Morocco, is said to have been 116 Muslim years (112½ Gregorian years) old when he died in Sept 1957.

The greatest age at which a prime minister has been first appointed is 81, for Morarji Ranchhodji Desai of India in March 1977.

Youngest prime minister
The youngest currently living prime minister is Dr Mario Frick of Liechtenstein, who assumed the role in Dec 1993, at the age of 28.

1818 (11 June–4 Aug), 1820 (1 March–21 April) and 1826 (3 June–23 July).

The most ministries held is five, by Stanley Baldwin from 22 May 1923 to 28 May 1937.

Shortest British ministry
The Duke of Wellington was in office for 22 days from 17 Nov to 9 Dec 1834.

Youngest in office in the United Kingdom
William Pitt declined office at the age of 23 years 275 days but assumed the role of prime minister at the age of 24 years 205 days on 19 Dec 1783.

Oldest in office in the United Kingdom
William Gladstone was 82 years 171 days old when he was elected and 84 years 64 days old upon leaving office on 3 March 1894.

Members of Parliament
Youngest MPs
Henry Long (1420–90) was returned for an Old Sarum seat at the age of 15. Minors were debarred in law in 1695, and in fact in 1832.

The youngest current MP is Matthew Taylor (b. 1963), Liberal Democrat MP for Truro, UK.

British elections
Most votes
The most votes to have been cast in one election is 33,610,399, in the general election of 9 April 1992.

The greatest number of votes to have been cast for one party is 14,094,116, for the

Left
Screaming Lord Sutch is the longest-serving political leader in the United Kingdom, and has been a familiar face on the political scene since 1963. He has contested 39 elections or by-elections, and lost his deposit every time. Bookmakers William Hill offer shorter odds for Elvis Presley crashing a UFO into the Loch Ness Monster (14 million to one) than for Lord Sutch becoming prime minister (15 million to one).

.NG TAUFA'AHAU OF TONGA IS THE OLDEST AND HEAVIEST MONARCH IN THE WORLD

Longest term of office
The longest-serving prime minister of a sovereign state is Khalifa bin Sulman al-Khalifa of Bahrain, who had already been in office for 1½ years when Bahrain gained independence in Aug 1971.

The longest-serving—and first—British prime minister was Sir Robert Walpole, who held the post from 3 April 1721 to 11 Feb 1742.

The only British prime minister to retain power for four successive general elections was Lord Liverpool, in 1812 (30 Sept–24 Nov),

Oldest MPs
Sir Francis Knollys, 'the ancientest Parliament man in England', seems to have been 90 when he was re-elected for Reading in 1640 and was probably 97 or 98 when he died.

The oldest 'Father of the House' (MP with the longest unbroken service) was the Rt Hon. Charles Pelham Villiers (Wolverhampton South), who died on 16 Jan 1898, aged 96.

The current 'Father' is the Rt Hon. Sir Edward Heath (Old Bexley and Sidcup), who took the oath as MP on 2 March 1950.

Longest service
The longest continuous service was by C. P. Villiers, who was a member for 63 years.

Sir Francis Knollys was elected for Oxford in 1575 and died a sitting member for Reading in 1648, but his service was not continuous.

Shortest service
Capt. the Hon. Edward Legge, RN, was returned unopposed for Portsmouth on 15 Dec 1747. News later came that he had died in the West Indies 87 days before polling.

In 1780, John Kirkman, standing for the City of London, died before polling had ended but was still returned.

A. J. Dobbs (Labour, Smethwick) was elected on 5 July 1945, but died in a car crash on the way to take his seat.

Conservatives in the general election of 9 April 1992.

The greatest number of votes to have been cast for an individual is 75,205, for Sir Cooper Rawson (Conservative) in Brighton, Sussex, in 1931.

The highest general election turnout was 93.42% in Fermanagh and S Tyrone in 1951.

Fewest votes
F. R. Lees (Temperance Chartist) of Ripon, Yorks, received no votes in Dec 1860.

The lowest general election turnout was 29.7%, in Kennington, London, in 1918.

Narrowest majority
Matthew Fowler (Liberal) of Durham and H. E. Duke (Unionist) of Exeter, Devon, both won by a majority of one vote in 1895 and in 1910 respectively.

Most recounts
There were seven recounts in the constituencies of Brighton and Kemptown, in 1964, and in Peterborough, in 1966.

Most elections contested
Screaming Lord Sutch of the Official Monster Raving Loony Party has contested 39 elections or by-elections, and has lost his deposit on each occasion.

Lowest election expenses
Alan Hope stood as an Official Monster Raving Loony Party candidate for Teignbridge in the 1992 general election. His expenses were nil.

Left
King Taufa'ahau Tupou IV of Tonga, the world's oldest serving monarch, was born in 1918 and acceded to the throne in 1965 upon the death of Queen Salote, his mother. The king went on to lead the nation to independence in 1970.

Legal matters

Right
Former US district attorney Vic Feazell claimed that his reputation had been ruined by a libellous Dallas TV station in 1985, and in 1991 was awarded world record damages of $58 million (£34.3 million) for defamation.

election of President Ranasinghe Premadasa as head of state in 1988 by opposition leader Sirimavo Bandaranaike. A total of 977 witnesses gave evidence between 19 June 1989 and 30 June 1992. The challenge was rejected by the court on 1 Sept 1992.

The longest criminal trial, which took place in Hong Kong, lasted from 30 Nov 1992 to 29 Nov 1994. The High Court sat for 398 days to hear charges against 14 South Vietnamese boat people accused of murdering 24 North Vietnamese adults and children, who died in a blazing hut during a riot at a refugee camp in Feb 1992. The defendants were acquitted, but some were convicted of lesser charges.

The longest British trial was the Tichborne personation case. The civil trial began on 11 May 1871 and collapsed after 103 days, on 6 March 1872. The criminal trial went on for 188 days. On 28 Feb 1874 Arthur Orton, alias Thomas Castro, who claimed to be Roger Charles Tichborne, the elder brother of Sir Alfred Joseph Doughty-Tichborne, 11th Bt, was sentenced for two counts of perjury. The

Law

Oldest judicial code
The code of King Ur-Nammu dates back to the third dynasty of Ur, Iraq, c. 2250 BC.

Oldest British statutes
Some statutes enacted by Henry II (1133–89) and earlier kings have been assimilated into the Common Law.

The oldest English statute in the Statute Book is a section of the Statute of Marlborough of 18 Nov 1267, re-entitled 'The Distress Act 1267' in 1948. It was most recently cited in the High Court in 1986.

Shortest British statute
The shortest statute is the Parliament (Qualification of Women) Act 1918, which runs to 27 operative words: 'A woman shall not be disqualified by sex or marriage from being elected to or sitting or voting as a Member of the Commons House of Parliament.' Section 2 has a further 14 words giving the short title.

Longest British statute
The Income and Corporation Taxes Act 1988 is more than 1,000 pages long and weighs 2.5 kg (5 lb 8 oz). Lord Houghton of Sowerby appealed to fellow peers in Nov 1987 'not to walk about with it' for fear of ruptures.

Litigation and trials

Most protracted litigation
A controversy over the claim of the Prior and Convent of Durham Cathedral to administer the spiritualities of the diocese during a vacancy in the See grew fierce in 1283. The dispute flared up again in 1672 and 1890,

and an attempt in Nov 1975 to settle the 692-year-old issue was unsuccessful. Neither side admits the legitimacy of writs of appointment issued by the other even though identical persons are named.

From April 1945 to Jan 1990, Gaddam Hanumantha Reddy brought a series of legal actions against the Hyderabad state government and the Indian government over a period of 44 years 9 months and 8 days, after complaining that his results in the entrance examination for the Hyderabad Civil Service entitled him to greater seniority and higher pay. He won the battle and received his promotion, but the litigation outlasted the entire period of his employment in the Indian Administrative Service.

Longest hearings
The longest civil case heard before a jury is *Kemner* v. *Monsanto Co.* at St Clair County Court House, Belleville, Illinois, USA, from 6 Feb 1984 to 22 Oct 1987. The testimony, concerning an alleged toxic chemical spill in Sturgeon, Missouri, in 1979, lasted 657 days, after which the jury deliberated for two months. Residents of Sturgeon were awarded $1 million (£609,000) nominal compensatory damages and $16,280,000 (£9,915,000) punitive damages. This was overturned by the Illinois Appellate Court on 11 June 1991 because the jury in the first trial had not found that any damage had resulted from the spill.

The Supreme Court of Sri Lanka spent a record 527 days hearing a challenge to the

whole case spanned 1,025 days, but the jury were out for only 30 minutes.

The longest civil case in British history is the 'McLibel' trial, which began on 28 June 1994 and was continuing in summer 1996. McDonald's Corporation are suing Helen Steel and Dave Morris for libel over a factsheet entitled 'What's wrong with McDonald's?'.

The longest retirement by a British jury was in Jan 1996, at the end of the trial of Kevin and Ian Maxwell on fraud charges. The jury was out for 12 days before acquitting both men.

Highest bail
The highest bail by a British court was set on 24 March 1994, when Leonard Bartlett and Iain Mackintosh of London were bailed on fraud charges by Bow Street Magistrates' Court subject to the condition that they should each provide sureties worth £10 million (later reduced to £1 million). In Feb 1996, they were jailed for 5 and 3½ years respectively.

The highest bail on which a defendant was released by a British court is £3.5 million, set on 17 Dec 1990 for Asil Nadir, who faced 18 charges of theft and false accounting amounting to £25 million after the collapse of Polly Peck International, the company of which he was chairman, in Sept 1990. He jumped bail and fled to Cyprus on 4 May 1993.

Highest attendance at a trial
At one point in the 12½-hour trial of Major Jesús Sosa Blanco from 22 to 23 Jan 1959

for an alleged 108 murders, 17,000 people were at the Havana Sports Palace, Cuba.

Highest viewing figures for a trial
A daily average of 5.5 million Americans watched live coverage of the O. J. Simpson murder trial on three major cable TV networks from 24 Jan to 3 Oct 1995. The jury reached a verdict of not guilty on 3 Oct.

Awards and costs
Greatest damages
The largest civil damages are $11.12 billion (£7.69 billion), to Pennzoil Co. against Texaco Inc. for the latter's allegedly unethical tactics in breaking up a merger in Jan 1984. The verdict was delivered on 10 Dec 1985, and an out-of-court settlement of $5.5 billion (£3 billion) was reached on 19 Dec 1987.

The record for the largest damages against an individual was set on 10 July 1992, when Charles H. Keating Jr, former owner of Lincoln Savings and Loan of Los Angeles, California, USA, was ordered by a federal jury to pay $2.1 billion (£1.1 billion) to 23,000 small investors defrauded by his company. The figure was subject to approval by the judge.

The greatest personal-injury damages awarded to an individual were $163,882,660

attorney Vic Feazell on 20 April 1991 at Waco, Texas, USA. He claimed he had been libelled by a Dallas-based TV station and one of its reporters in 1985. The parties reached an undisclosed settlement on 29 June 1991.

The record damages for libel in the United Kingdom was £1.5 million, to Lord Aldington against historian Count Nikolai Tolstoy and property developer Nigel Watts. The award was made by a High Court jury on 30 Nov 1989 following accusations that Lord Aldington had been a war criminal, but he did not receive any of the damages.

Compensation for wrongful imprisonment
Robert McLaughlin was awarded $1,935,000 (£1,225,000) in Oct 1989 for wrongful imprisonment for a murder in New York City, USA, in 1979. Sentenced to 15 years in prison, he had served six years (1980–86) when his foster father proved his innocence.

Highest costs
The Blue Arrow trial, involving the illegal support of the company's shares during a rights issue in 1987, is estimated to have cost approximately £35 million. The trial, at the Old Bailey, London, UK, lasted a year, ending on 14 Feb 1992. Four of the defendants received suspended prison sentences but were later cleared on appeal.

The shortest will in English law was contested in *Thorne* v. *Dickens* in 1906 but later admitted to probate. It consisted of the words 'All for mother', in which 'mother' was his wife.

The longest will on record consisted of four bound volumes containing 95,940 words, primarily concerning $100,000 (£21,000) worth of property belonging to Frederica Evelyn Stilwell Cook. It was proved in 1925.

The smallest will preserved by the Record Keeper is an identity disc 3.8 cm (1½ in) in diameter and engraved with 40 words, including the signatures of two witnesses. Belonging to A. B. William Skinner, who was killed aboard HMS *Indefatigable* in 1916, it was proved on 24 June 1922.

Largest divorce settlement
The largest declared settlement was £500 million plus property, to S. Khashóggi in 1982.

In the mid 1980s Anne Bass of Texas, USA, is said to have rejected $535 million (£365 million) as inadequate to live in the style to which she had been made accustomed.

The highest award made by a British court was £9 million, to Maya Flick. On 25 Oct 1995 her former husband failed in an attempt to stop her seeking a higher award.

(£109,109,627), awarded in the Supreme Court of the State of New York, USA, on 27 July 1993, to Shiyamala Thirunayagam, who was almost completely paralysed after the car in which she was travelling hit a broken-down truck in the fast lane of the New Jersey Turnpike on 4 Oct 1987. As the defendants would have challenged the jury's verdict in a higher court, Thirunayagam agreed to accept a lump sum of $8,230,000 (£5,479,000) for suffering and a guarantee that the defendants would pay up to $55 million (£36,600,000) for future medical expenses.

Compensation following the 1984 Union Carbide Corporation plant disaster in Bhopal, India, was agreed at $470 million (£267 million) on 14 Feb 1989, after a settlement between Union Carbide and the Indian government, which was representing more than 500,000 people.

The record award in a sexual harassment case was $50 million (£32 million) in punitive damages, to Peggy Kimzey, a former employee of Wal-Mart, on 28 June 1995. The jury at Jefferson City, Missouri, also awarded her $35,000 (£22,000) for humiliation and mental anguish and $1 (63 pence) in lost wages. Wal-Mart said it would appeal.

Defamation
The highest award by a jury in a libel case is $58 million (£34.3 million), to former district

Wills and settlements
Wills
The shortest valid will in the world is that of Bimla Rishi of Delhi, India. It consists of four characters in Hindi, meaning 'All to son', and is dated 9 Feb 1995.

Judges and lawyers
Longest-serving judges
The oldest recorded active judge was Judge Albert R. Alexander of Missouri, USA, who was enrolled as a member of the Clinton County Bar in 1926 and was later the magistrate and probate judge of Clinton County until his retirement in 1965, at the age of 105.

The greatest recorded age at which a British judge has sat on a bench is 93 years 9 months, by Sir William Francis Kyffin Taylor (later Lord Maenan), who retired as presiding judge of the Liverpool Court of Passage in 1948, having held that position since 1903.

Sir Salathiel Lovell was still sitting when he died on 3 May 1713 in his 94th or 95th year.

Youngest judges
John Payton was elected Justice of the Peace in Plano, Texas, USA, and took office at the age of 18 years 11 months in Jan 1991.

Most successful lawyer
Sir Lionel Luckhoo of Georgetown, Guyana, obtained 245 successive murder acquittals between 1940 and 1985.

Longest-serving solicitors
William George, brother of David Lloyd George, passed his preliminary examination in 1880 and practised until he was 101, in 1966.

The oldest law firm is Pickering Kenyon of London, UK, founded in 1561.

Left
In 1982, the lawyers of Soraya Khashóggi secured a record divorce settlement from her husband Adnan, a millionaire Saudi entrepreneur, property-owner and arms dealer.

Crime

Right
The greatest drugs haul in terms of value took place on 28 Sept 1989, when 20 tonnes of cocaine with an estimated street value of $6–7 billion (£3.7-4.4 billion) was seized in a raid on a warehouse in Los Angeles, California, USA. The amount of cocaine seized was said by the Los Angeles drug squad to be enough to give all of the city's 3 million residents a 'fix' every day for three months.

Criminal organizations
Most profitable crime syndicate
The Mafia's annual turnover in vice, gambling, protection rackets, narcotics, prostitution and other fields was estimated at $200 billion (£114.4 billion) by *US News & World Report* in Dec 1982. In March 1986, Rudolph Giuliani, US Attorney for the southern district of New York, estimated that the Mafia has an annual profit of $75 billion (£51 billion).

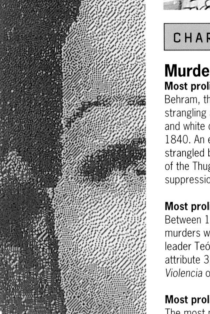

Largest crime syndicate
Japan's Yamaguchi-gumi gang has about 30,000 members, making it the largest group of *Yakuza* or gangsters.

Assassinations
Earliest attempt
An unsuccessful attempt was made on the life of Amonemhat I, the pharaoh of the Middle Kingdom of Egypt, *c.* 2000 BC.

Most attempts
The French president, Charles de Gaulle, is said to have survived 31 plots from 1944 to 1966, although some were foiled before attacks occurred.

Murderers
Most prolific murderer
Behram, the Indian Thug, was found guilty of strangling at least 931 victims with his yellow and white cloth strip, or *ruhmal*, from 1790 to 1840. An estimated 2 million Indians were strangled by Thugs (*burtotes*) during the reign of the Thuggee cult from 1550 until its suppression by the British Raj in 1853.

Most prolific 20th-century murderer
Between 1948 and his death in 1963, 592 murders were attributed to Colombian bandit leader Teófilo ('Sparks') Rojas. Some sources attribute 3,500 slayings to him during *La Violencia* of 1945–62.

Most prolific British murderers
The most prolific substantiated serial killers in the United Kingdom were William Burke and William Hare, who murdered 16 people in Edinburgh from 1827 to 1828 in order to sell their bodies to the anatomist Dr Robert Knox.

Mary Ann Cotton is believed to have poisoned between 14 and 20 people with arsenic, including her husbands and children. She was convicted of only one murder and hanged in Durham Jail on 24 March 1873.

Dominic 'Mad Dog' McGlinchey admitted to at least 30 killings in Northern Ireland in a press interview in Nov 1983. In March 1986 he was jailed for 10 years for shooting with intent to resist arrest on 17 March 1984, but was released on 5 March 1993.

At the Old Bailey on 7 May 1981, Londoner John Thompson was jailed for life for the 'specimen' murder by arson of Archibald Campbell. There were 36 other victims at the Spanish Club, Denmark Street, London.

The biggest murder in the United Kingdom this century was committed by the unknown person(s) who planted a bomb on Pan Am flight PA103. The aircraft crashed over Lockerbie, Dumfries and Galloway, on 21 Dec 1988, killing 270 people (including 11 people on the ground).

Robberies
Biggest robberies
From April to May 1945, the Reichsbank was robbed following Germany's collapse. In *Nazi Gold* (1984), authors Ian Sayer and Douglas Botting estimate that the total haul was equivalent to £2.5 billion at 1984 values.

On 23 April 1986, the Filipino government announced that it had identified $860.8 million (£569.5 million) that had been 'salted' by the former president Ferdinand Marcos and his wife Imelda.

On 2 May 1990 a mugger stole treasury bills and certificates of deposit worth £292 million from a moneybroker's messenger in the City of London, UK. Details were given to central banks worldwide, and the chances of the thief benefiting were very remote.

Biggest art robberies
The *Mona Lisa* may be the most valuable object ever stolen (it has never been valued). The painting disappeared from the Louvre, Paris, France, on 21 Aug 1911, and was recovered in Italy in 1913.

On 14 April 1991, 20 paintings worth about $500 million (£279 million) were stolen from

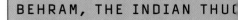

Highest ransom £1 billion

the Van Gogh Museum, Amsterdam, Netherlands, but were found in an abandoned car near the museum 35 minutes later.

On 18 March 1990, 11 paintings (by Degas Rembrandt, Vermeer, Manet and Flinck), a Chinese bronze beaker from c. 1200 BC and a finial in the form of an eagle, worth a total of about $200 million (£124 million) were stolen

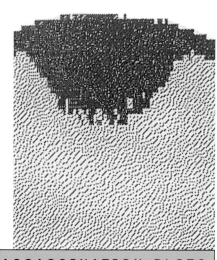

ASSASSINATION PLOTS

from the Isabella Stewart Gardner Museum in Boston, Massachusetts, USA.

On 24 Dec 1985, 140 'priceless' gold, jade and obsidian artefacts were stolen from the National Museum of Anthropology, Mexico City. Most were recovered in June 1989.

Biggest bank robbery
In Jan 1976, during the civil disorder in Beirut, Lebanon, guerrillas broke into the British Bank of the Middle East in Bab Idriss and cleared out safe-deposit boxes with contents valued at $9–22 million (£10–25 million).

Biggest train robbery
A mail train from Glasgow was ambushed and robbed near Mentmore, Bucks, UK, on 8 Aug 1963. The gang escaped with 120 mailbags containing £2,631,784 in banknotes, which were being taken to London for destruction. Only £343,448 was recovered.

Biggest jewel theft
On 11 Aug 1994, gems with an estimated value of FF 250 million (£30 million) were stolen from the jewellery shop at the Carlton Hotel in Cannes, France, by a three-man gang.

Most burglaries
Christine and Vic Kelly, who owned the village shop in Kimberworth, S Yorkshire, UK, are reported to have suffered 72 burglaries at their premises over the 10 years to 1994.

Largest object stolen by one person
On 5 June 1966, armed only with a sharp axe, N. William Kennedy slashed the mooring lines of the 10,639-dwt SS *Orient Trader* at Wolfe's Cove, St Lawrence Seaway, Canada. The vessel drifted to a waiting blacked-out tug, thus evading a ban on any shipping movements during a violent wildcat waterfront strike. It then sailed for Spain.

Fraud and forgery
Biggest bank fraud
In Sept 1989, the *Banca Nazionale del Lavoro*, Italy, admitted that it had been defrauded of a huge amount of funds, subsequently estimated at around $5 billion (£3 billion). Its branch in Atlanta, Georgia, USA, had made unauthorized loan commitments to Iraq.

Biggest tax fraud
The biggest British tax fraud occurred when almost £140 million of Nissan UK's profits were siphoned off into a Swiss bank account, costing the Inland Revenue £97 million in lost corporation tax.

Greatest banknote forgery
'Operation Bernhard', run by Major Bernhard Krüger of the German Third Reich during WWII, involved more than £130 million in counterfeit £5, £10, £20 and £50 British banknotes. The notes had been produced by 140 Jewish prisoners at Sachsenhausen concentration camp.

Kidnapping
Biggest ever ransom
From 1532 to 1533, a hall full of gold and silver (£1 billion in modern money) was paid to the Spanish conquistador Francisco Pizarro for the release of Atahualpa, the last emperor of the Incas of Peru.

Biggest modern ransom
On 20 June 1975, the sum of 1,500 million pesos (£26 million) was paid to the left-wing urban guerrilla group *Montoneros* for the release of brothers Jorge and Juan Born of the family firm Bunge and Born in Buenos Aires, Argentina.

Narcotics
Largest haul
The largest drugs haul in terms of weight was made by authorities in Bilo, Pakistan, on 23 Oct 1991. The seizure comprised 38.9 tonnes of hashish and 3.23 tonnes of heroin.

Largest operation
In the 14-month 'Operation Tiburon' carried out by the Drug Enforcement Administration and the Colombian authorities, 2,903 tonnes of Colombian marijuana were seized. The arrest of 495 people and the capture of 95 vessels was announced on 5 Feb 1982.

S CONVICTED OF STRANGLING AT LEAST 931 VICTIMS

Punishment

Capital punishment

Largest hangings
The most people hanged from one gallows is 38 Sioux Indians, executed by William J. Duly outside Mankato, Minnesota, USA, on 26 Dec 1862 for the murder of unarmed citizens.

A Nazi Feldkommandant hanged 50 Greek resistance men in Athens on 22 July 1944.

Last executions
The last public execution in England took place outside Newgate Prison, London, at 8 a.m. on 26 May 1868, when Michael Barrett was hanged for his part in the Fenian bomb outrage of 13 Dec 1867.

The last people executed in the United Kingdom were Peter Anthony Allen, hanged at Walton Prison, Liverpool, and John Robson Walby (Gwynne Owen Evans), hanged at Strangeways Gaol, Manchester, on 13 Aug 1964. They had both been found guilty of the capital murder of John Alan West.

The last person legally executed for witchcraft was Anna Göldi at Glarus, Switzerland, on 18 June 1782.

The last person executed for witchcraft in the United Kingdom was Jenny Horn, who was burned alive at Dornoch, Highland, in 1722.

The last execution by burning in the United Kingdom was in March 1789, when a woman named Murphy was 'burnt with fire until she was dead' outside Newgate Prison, London.

The last person sentenced to death in the British Isles was Tony Teare, 22, convicted at Douglas, Isle of Man, of murdering Corinne Bentley, 22, and condemned to hang on 10 July 1992. The sentence was commuted to life imprisonment, and later that year the Manx parliament became the last part of the British Isles to abolish the death penalty.

The last person publicly guillotined in France was murderer Eugen Weidmann, at Versailles on 17 June 1939.

The last man to be executed by beheading in the United Kingdom was Simon Fraser, Lord Lovat, who was beheaded on Tower Hill, London, on 7 April 1747.

The last person guillotined was torturer and murderer Hamida Djandoubi, 28, on 10 Sept 1977 at Baumettes Prison, Marseille, France.

Longest time on Death Row
Sadamichi Hirasawa (1893–1987) spent 39 years in Sendai Prison, Japan, until his death at the age of 94. He was convicted of poisoning 12 bank employees with potassium cyanide to carry out a theft of £100 in 1948.

Executioners
The Sanson family supplied France with executioners from 1688 to 1847. During the

Largest fine $650 million

Sadamichi Hirasawa spent a record 39 years on Death Row for theft and poisoning.

Reign of Terror, Charles-Henri Sanson executed almost 3,000 victims from 1793 to 1794, including the king, Louis XVI.

From 1901 to 1956, the Pierrepoint family largely monopolized the execution of murderers in the United Kingdom. Albert Pierrepoint hanged some 450 people in several countries, including 27 war criminals in one day in Germany.

The longest period of office held by a public executioner was 45 years, by William Calcraft (1800–79). Between 1829 and 1874 he officiated at almost every hanging outside, and later inside, Newgate Prison, London.

The oldest active executioner in British history is John Murdoch, who was 64 when he was retained as an assistant hangman in Scotland in 1831. He carried out his last execution in Glasgow 20 years later.

Prison sentences
Longest sentences
Chamoy Thipyaso and seven associates were each jailed for 141,078 years by the Bangkok Criminal Court, Thailand, on 27 July 1989 for

THAILAND, FOR FRAUD

swindling the public through a multi-million dollar deposit-taking business.

A sentence of 384,912 years (9 years for each of the 42,768 letters that he had failed to deliver) was demanded at the prosecution of Gabriel March Grandos, 22, at Palma de Mallorca, Spain, on 11 March 1972.

The longest sentence imposed on a mass murderer was 21 consecutive life sentences and 12 death sentences. John Gacy killed 33 boys and young men between 1972 and 1978 in Illinois, USA, and was eventually executed on 10 May 1994.

Longest time served
Paul Geidel (1894–1987), a 17-year-old porter in a New York hotel, was convicted of

second-degree murder on 5 Sept 1911. He was released from the Fishkill Correctional Facility, Beacon, New York, on 7 May 1980, having served 68 years 245 days.

Oldest prisoner
Bill Wallace (1881–1989) spent the last 63 years of his life in Aradale Psychiatric Hospital, Ararat, Victoria, Australia, after shooting a man to death in Dec 1925.

Prisons
Highest prison population
Some human rights organizations estimate that there are 20 million prisoners in China, or 1,658 people in every 100,000.

The USA has the highest officially acknowledged prison population per capita, with 565 prisoners per 100,000 people.

Prison fatalities
The most prison fatalities in a single incident occurred at Fort William, Calcutta, India, on 20 June 1756. Under the order of the Nawab of Bengal, 145 men and one woman were locked in a military prison cell measuring only 5.5 x 4.25 m (18 x 14 ft)—the 'Black Hole of Calcutta'. When it was opened at 6 a.m. the next morning 123 men had suffocated or been crushed to death.

Most expensive prison
Spandau Prison, in Berlin, Germany, built in 1887 for 600 prisoners, was used solely for Nazi war criminal Rudolf Hess (1894–1987) for the last 20 years of his life. The cost of maintaining a staff of 105 was estimated in 1976 to be $415,000 a year. The prison was demolished after Hess committed suicide.

Jailbreaks
On 11 Feb 1979, an Iranian employee of the Electronic Data Systems Corporation led a mob into Gasr prison, Teheran, Iran, to rescue two American colleagues (the mob were not looking for the Americans). Some 11,000 other prisoners took advantage of their arrival and the Islamic Revolution to escape. The plan to free the Americans was developed by their employer H. Ross Perot.

The most successful jailbreak by a prisoner who was eventually recaptured was by Leonard T. Fristoe, who was jailed for killing two sheriff's deputies in 1920 and escaped from the Nevada State Prison, Carson City, Nevada, USA, on 15 Dec 1923. He was turned in by his son—following an argument—on 15 Nov 1969 at Compton, California, after nearly 46 years of freedom under the name Claude R. Willis.

Most arrests
On 9 Sept 1982, Tommy Johns of Brisbane, Queensland, Australia, faced his 2,000th conviction for drunkenness since 1957. He had been arrested almost 3,000 times at the time of his last drink on 30 April 1988.

Mass arrests
In the biggest mass arrest reported in a democratic country, 15,617 demonstrators were rounded up by South Korean police on 11 July 1988 to ensure security in advance of the 1988 Olympic Games in Seoul.

The largest mass arrest in the United Kingdom occurred on 17 Sept 1961, when 1,314 demonstrators supporting unilateral nuclear disarmament were arrested for staging a sit-down and obstructing highways leading to Parliament Square, London.

Fines
Heaviest fine
The world's largest ever fine was imposed on the US securities house Drexel Burnham Lambert in Dec 1988 for insider trading. The total figure was $650 million, of which $300 million was direct fines. The balance was to be placed in an account to pay parties defrauded by Drexel's actions.

Heaviest fine imposed on an individual
Michael Milken agreed to pay a fine of $200 million on 24 April 1990 and to settle civil charges that had been filed by the Securities and Exchange Commission. The payments were in settlement of a criminal racketeering and securities fraud suit brought by the US government. Milken was released from a 10-year prison sentence in Jan 1993.

Left
Eugen Weidmann, the last person to be publicly guillotined in France, was executed in front of a large crowd at Versailles on 17 June 1939.

Left
In the most successful jailbreak by a prisoner who was eventually recaptured, Leonard T. Fristoe escaped from prison in 1923 and enjoyed almost 46 years of freedom before being caught.

MOST PROLIFIC EXECUTIONER DESPATCHED 3,000 VICTIMS IN TWO YEARS

Honours

Victoria Cross

Double awards

The only men awarded a bar to the Victoria Cross are: Surg.-Capt. (later Lt-Col.) Arthur Martin-Leake VC*, VD, RAMC (1902 and bar 1914); Capt. Noel Godfrey Chavasse VC*, MC, RAMC (1916 and posthumous bar 1917); Second-Lt. (later Capt.) Charles Hazlitt Upham VC*, NZMF (1941 and bar 1942).

Most VCs awarded in a war

A total of 634 VCs were awarded in WWI.

Most VCs awarded for a single action

A total of 11 VCs were awarded for the action at Rorke's Drift in the Zulu War in Jan 1879.

Youngest recipient

Hospital apprentice Andrew Fitzgibbon of the Indian Medical Services was 15 years old

Life saving

The most awards to a member of the Royal Life Saving Society is 227 since 1960, by Eric Deakin of Hightown, Lancs, UK.

The greatest rescue was of 2,735 people from the aircraft carrier *Lexington*, sunk in the Battle of the Coral Sea on 8 May 1942.

The greatest rescue without loss of life was from the *Susan B. Anthony*. All 2,689 passengers survived when it was sunk off Normandy, France, on 7 June 1944.

Most awards for civilian gallantry

Reginald H. Blanchford of Guernsey received the MBE for gallantry in 1950; the Queen's

Highest price paid for a George Cross

The sum of £20,250 was paid at Christie's on 14 March 1985 for the George Cross awarded to Sgt. Michael Willets (3rd Battalion Parachute Regiment), who was killed by an IRA bomb in Ulster, Northern Ireland, in 1971.

Orders

Oldest orders

The earliest known official honour is the 'Gold of Honour', awarded during the 18th Dynasty in Egypt—c. 1440–1400 BC—for extraordinary valour.

The oldest true order was the Order of St John of Jerusalem, which was legitimized in 1113. The Sovereign Military Order of Malta is its direct descendant.

Youngest recipient of knighthood

A knighthood was conferred on HRH the Prince George (1762–1830), later George IV,

when he was awarded a VC for bravery at the Taku Forts in northern China on 21 Aug 1860.

Oldest recipient

Capt. William Raynor was awarded the VC when he was 62, for his part in blowing up an arms store besieged by insurgents on 11 May 1857, the second day of the Indian Mutiny.

Highest price paid for a VC

The posthumous VC and other medals awarded to Major Edward Mannock in 1919 for bravery of the first order in aerial combat was sold to a private collector at Billingshurst, W Sussex, UK, in 1992, for £132,000.

Courage and public service

Most lifeboat medals

Sir William Hillary (1771–1847), founder of the Royal National Lifeboat Institution in 1824, was awarded four RNLI Gold Medals, in 1825, 1828 and 1830 (twice).

Commendation in 1957; the Life Saving Medal of The Order of St John in Gold in 1957, with gold bar in 1963; the George Medal in 1958; the Carnegie Hero Fund's Bronze Medallion in 1959; and the OBE in 1961. He was made a Knight of Grace of The Order of St John in 1970 and received the American Biographical Institute's Silver Shield of Valor in 1992.

Youngest recipients of awards

Kristina Stragauskaitė of Lithuania was awarded a medal 'For Courage in Fire' when she was 4 years 252 days old, after saving the lives of her younger brother and sister in a fire at the family home in April 1989.

The youngest person to receive an official gallantry award is Julius Rosenberg of Winnipeg, Canada, who was awarded the Medal of Bravery in March 1994. In Sept 1992, the then five-year-old had saved his three-year-old sister from a black bear by growling at the creature.

when he was 29 days old, by virtue of his ex-officio membership in the Order of the Garter consequent upon his creation as Prince of Wales in Aug 1762.

Oldest recipient of knighthood

Sir Robert Mayer (1879–1985) became a Knight Bachelor on his 100th birthday.

Order of Merit

The oldest recipient of the Order of Merit was Dame Ninette de Valois, at the age of 94 on 2 Dec 1992.

The youngest is HRH the Duke of Edinburgh, on his 47th birthday, 10 June 1968.

Peerage

Oldest peers

The Rt Hon. Emanuel Shinwell was created a life baron in 1970 and died in 1986, aged 101 years 202 days.

The Countess Desmond was said to be 140 when she died in 1604 but was probably 104.

The oldest living peer is the Rt Hon. Jeffery Amherst, fifth Earl Amherst (b. 1896).

Youngest peers
As the eldest sons of a sovereign, 12 dukes of Cornwall became peers at birth. The ninth Earl of Chichester inherited his title at his birth in April 1944, 54 days after his father's death.

Longest and shortest peerage
The longest tenure of a peerage is 87 years 10 days, by Charles St Clair, Lord Sinclair, (1768–1863). He succeeded to the title at the age of seven, and died at 94.

The law assumes that the Hon. Wilfrid Carlyl Stamp survived his father, Josiah Charles Stamp, the first Baron Stamp, by a 'split second' when both were killed in the German bombing of London on 16 April 1941.

Most titles
The most titled person in the world is the 18th Duchess of Alba, Doña María del Rosario Cayetana Fitz-James Stuart y Silva (b. 1926). She is 14 times a Spanish grandee, five times a duchess, once a countess-duchess, 18 times a marchioness, 18 times a countess and once a viscountess.

Nobel prizes
Most Nobel prizes by country
The USA has won a total of 227 prizes, either outright or shared. This grand total includes record totals of 74 for physiology or medicine, 60 for physics, 41 for chemistry, 18 for peace, and 23 for economics. The only category for which the USA has not been awarded the most prizes is literature.

The country that has been awarded the most Nobel prizes for literature is France, with a total of 12.

Bragg's award was for work done when he was 23, as was the chemistry prize won by Theodore W. Richards (1868–1928) of the USA in 1914.

Science and academia
Most honorary degrees
Since 1954, 131 honorary degrees have been awarded to the Rev. Father Theodore M. Hesburgh (b. 1917), president of the University of Notre Dame, South Bend, Indiana, USA.

The Royal Society
The longest term as a Fellow of the Royal Society is 68 years, by Sir Hans Sloane (1660–1753), who was elected in 1685.

The longest-lived Fellow was Sir Rickard Christophers (1873–1978).

Left
Other than Buddha, to whom more statues have been raised by his followers than to any other person, the most common human subjects of statues have been totalitarian leaders—such as Stalin, Lenin and Mao Tse-tung—who were seeking to raise their public profiles.

TION WAS 11, FOR THE DEFENCE OF RORKE'S DRIFT

The shortest definite peerage is one of 30 minutes, in the case of Charles Brandon, the third Duke of Suffolk, who died at the age of 13 or 14 at Buckden, Cambs, UK, on 14 July 1551, shortly after succeeding his brother, Henry. Both of them were suffering from a fatal illness.

Titles
Most post-nominal letters
HRH the Duke of Windsor (1894–1972) had 10 sets of post-nominal letters when he was Prince of Wales. These letters were KG, KT, KP, GCB, GCSI, GCMG, GCIE, GCVO, GBE, MC. As a privy cousellor, he also included PC after his name, and later appended the ISO but omitted OM, CH and DSO—orders of which he had also been sovereign.

Lord Roberts, also a privy counsellor, was the only non-royal to hold eight sets of official post-nominal letters.

OTHER HENRY IN 1551

Most prizes won by an organization
The International Committee of the Red Cross won the Nobel Peace Prize outright in 1917 and 1944 and shared it in 1963.

Most prizes won by an individual
The greatest number of Nobel prizes won by one person is two: Mme Marja Skłodowska Curie (1867–1934) won prizes for physics in 1903 (shared) and chemistry in 1911; Prof. John Bardeen (1908–91) won the prize for physics in 1956 (shared) and 1972 (shared); Prof. Frederick Sanger won chemistry prizes in 1958 and 1980 (shared); and the Office of the United Nations' High Commissioner for Refugees, Geneva, Switzerland, won the Peace Prize in 1954 and 1981.

Oldest laureate
Prof. Francis Peyton Rous (1879–1970) of the USA shared the prize for physiology or medicine at the age of 87, in 1966.

Youngest laureates
Prof. Sir Lawrence Bragg (1890–1971) won the 1915 physics prize at 25.

The youngest Fellow of the Royal Society is believed to have been Sir Joseph Hodges, who was elected on 5 April 1716, when he was about 12 years old.

The oldest person to have been elected a Fellow was Sir Rupert Edward Cecil Lee Guinness, the second Earl of Iveagh, who was elected in 1964 at the age of 90.

Most valuable annual prize
In 1996, the Louis Jeantet Prize for Medicine was worth SFr 2,100,000 (about £1,130,000).

Statues
Most statues
More statues have been raised to Buddha than to any other person.

The record for raising statues to oneself was set by Stalin (1879–1953), who was leader of the Soviet Union from 1924 to his death, when there were an estimated 6,000 statues to him in the USSR and eastern Europe. The last one was demolished in 1992 in Mongolia.

Military and defence

War

Longest wars
The longest continuous war was the Thirty Years' War between various European countries from 1618 to 1648. (The Hundred Years' War between England and France was an irregular succession of wars.)

The *Reconquista*, a series of campaigns to recover the Iberian Peninsula from the Islamic Moors, began in 718 and continued intermittently for 774 years until 1492, when the last Moorish stronghold was conquered.

Shortest war
The shortest war was between the United Kingdom and Zanzibar (now part of Tanzania), and lasted from 9:00 to 9:45 a.m. on 27 Aug 1896. A Royal Navy Squadron delivered an ultimatum to the self-appointed sultan to evacuate his palace and surrender. The response demanded was only forthcoming after 45 minutes of bombardment.

Bloodiest wars
By far the most costly war in terms of human life was WWII (1939–45), in which the number of fatalities, including battle deaths and civilians of all countries, is estimated to have been 56.4 million. Poland lost 6,028,000, or 17.2% of its total population of 35,100,000.

In its war of 1864–70 against Brazil, Argentina and Uruguay, Paraguay's population was reduced from 407,000 to 221,000, of whom fewer than 30,000 were adult males.

Bloodiest battles
The 142-day battle of the Somme in France in 1916 resulted in an estimated 1.22 million dead and wounded, of whom 398,671 were British (57,470 on the first day) and more than 600,000 were German.

The losses of the German Army Group Centre on the Eastern Front in 17 days from 22 June to 8 July 1944 totalled 350,000.

The greatest death toll in a battle is an estimated 1,109,000 in the Battle of Stalingrad, USSR (now Volgograd, Russia), which ended with the German surrender on 31 Jan 1943. A further 650,800 Soviet soldiers disappeared and only 1,515 Soviet civilians from a pre-war population of more than 500,000 were found alive after the battle.

The final drive on Berlin, Germany, by the Soviet Army and the ensuing battle for the city from 16 April to 2 May 1945 involved a total of 3.5 million men, 52,000 guns and mortars, 7,750 tanks and 11,000 aircraft.

British battles
The bloodiest battle on British soil was the battle of Towton, near Tadcaster, N Yorkshire, on 29 March 1461, when 36,000 Yorkists defeated 40,000 Lancastrians. The total loss is estimated at between 28,000 and 38,000.

The last invasion of Great Britain took place on 22 Feb 1797, when Irish-American adventurer General Tate landed at Carreg Wastad Point, Pembrokeshire, accompanied by 1,400 French troops. They surrendered outside Fishguard to Lord Cawdor's force of the Castlemartin Yeomanry and some local inhabitants armed with pitchforks.

The last pitched land battle in Great Britain was at Culloden Field, Drummossie Moor, near Inverness, Highland, on 16 April 1746.

Largest evacuations
The greatest evacuation in military history was carried out by 1,200 Allied naval and civil craft from the beachhead at Dunkerque (Dunkirk), France, between 26 May and 4 June 1940. A total of 338,226 British and French troops were evacuated.

The largest ever civilian evacuation followed the Iraqi invasion of Kuwait in Aug 1990, when Air India evacuated 111,711 Indian nationals who were working in Kuwait.

Worst siege
The worst siege in history was the 880-day siege of Leningrad, USSR (now St Petersburg, Russia), by the German Army from 30 Aug 1941 until 27 Jan 1944. It is estimated that between 1.3 and 1.5 million defenders and citizens died, including 641,000 people who starved to death in the city and 17,000 civilians killed by shelling.

Armies and equipment

Largest armed force
In 1995, the land, sea and air forces of the People's Liberation Army in China had an estimated total personnel of 2,930,000. Around 1.2 million reserves, plus many more for local militia duty, can be mobilized. China also has the largest army numerically, at 2.2 million in mid 1995.

Bombs
The heaviest conventional bomb used operationally was the RAF's 7.74-m-long (25-ft 5-in) Grand Slam, which weighed 9,980 kg (22,000 lb). The device was dropped on Bielefeld railway viaduct, Germany, on 14 March 1945. In all, 41 Grand Slam bombs were dropped by 617 Sqn RAF in 1945.

In 1949 the United States Air Force tested a bomb weighing 19,050 kg (42,000 lb) at Muroc Dry Lake, California, USA.

The heaviest known nuclear bomb was the MK 17, carried by US B-36 bombers in the mid 1950s. It weighed 19,050 kg (42,000 lb) and was 7.47 m (24 ft 6 in) long.

The first atomic bomb was dropped on Hiroshima, Japan, by the USA at 8:16 a.m. on 6 Aug 1945. It had an explosive power equivalent to 15 kilotons of TNT. Codenamed *Little Boy*, the bomb was 3.05 m (10 ft) long and weighed 4,080 kg (9,000 lb).

The most powerful thermonuclear device ever tested had the power of about 57 megatons of TNT. It was detonated by the former USSR in the Novaya Zemlya area at 8:33 a.m. GMT on 30 Oct 1961. The shockwave circled the world three times, taking 36 hr 27 min for the first circuit. The device was the prototype 100-megaton bomb.

Bombers
The Soviet four-jet Tupolev Tu-160 was the heaviest bomber, with a maximum take-off weight of 275 tonnes (606,270 lb).

The 10-engined Convair B-36J, which weighed 185 tonnes, had the greatest wingspan at 70.1 m (230 ft), but it is no longer in service. Its top speed was 700 km/h (435 mph).

The fastest bombers are the US variable-geometry or 'swing-wing' General Dynamics FB-111A, which has a maximum speed of Mach 2.5, and the Soviet swing-wing Tupolev Tu-22M, which has an estimated over-target speed of Mach 2.0 but could be as fast as Mach 2.5.

Tanks
The heaviest ever tank was the German Panzer Kampfwagen Maus II, which weighed 192 tonnes. By 1945 it had reached only the experimental stage and was abandoned.

The heaviest operational tank was the 75.2-tonne French Char de Rupture 2C bis of 1922. It carried a 15.5-cm (6⅛-in) howitzer and was powered by two 250-hp engines giving it a top speed of 12 km/h (7.5 mph).

The fastest tracked armoured reconnaissance vehicle is the British *Scorpion*, which can touch 80 km/h (50 mph) with a 75% payload.

The US experimental tank M1936 was clocked at 103.4 km/h (64.3 mph) during official trials in the United Kingdom in 1938.

The greatest production of a tank was that of the Soviet T-54/55 series. More than 50,000 were built between 1954 and 1980 in the USSR alone, with further production in the one-time Warsaw Pact countries and China.

Guns
The largest gun was the *Schwerer Gustav*, a gun of a calibre of 80 cm (31½ in) with a barrel 28.87 m (94 ft 8½ in) long, used by

RE A 4.8-TONNE PROJECTILE A DISTANCE OF 46.7 KM

Germany in the siege of Sevastopol, USSR, in July 1942. Built by Krupp, its remains were discovered near Metzenhof, Bavaria, Germany, in Aug 1945. The whole assembly of the gun was 42.9 m (141 ft) long and weighed 1,344 tonnes, with a crew of 1,500. The range for an 8.1-tonne projectile was 20.9 km (13 miles), and for the 4.8-tonne projectile, 46.7 km (29 miles).

The greatest altitude attained by a projectile fired from a gun was achieved by the HARP (High Altitude Research Project) gun, which consisted of two barrels with a calibre of 42 cm (16½ in) fused in tandem into a single barrel 36.4 m (119 ft 5 in) long and weighing 150 tonnes. On 19 Nov 1966, an 84-kg (185-lb) projectile was fired to an altitude of 180 km (112 miles) at Yuma, Arizona, USA.

The *Paris-Geschütz*, the long-range gun that the Germans used to shell Paris, France, in WWI, had a calibre of 21 cm (8¼ in), a designed range of 127.9 km (79½ miles) and an achieved range of 122 km (76 miles) from the Forest of Crépy in March 1918.

Largest battleships
The Japanese vessels the *Yamato* and the *Musashi* had a full-load displacement of 69,988 tons, an overall length of 263 m (863 ft), a beam of 38.7 m (127 ft) and a full load draught of 10.8 m (35 ft 5 in). They were armed with nine 460-mm (18⅛-in) guns in three triple turrets. Each gun weighed 164.6 tonnes, was 22.8 m (75 ft) long and fired 1,451-kg (3,200-lb) projectiles.

Largest aircraft carriers
The warships with the largest full-load displacement are the aircraft carriers USS *Nimitz*, *Dwight D. Eisenhower*, *Carl Vinson*, *Theodore Roosevelt*, *Abraham Lincoln*, *George Washington* and *John C. Stennis*. The last three displace 102,000 tons. The ships are 332.9 m (1,092 ft) long, have 1.82 ha (4½ acres) of flight deck and can reach speeds of well over 56 km/h (30 knots).

Top
In the incredibly hard-fought first Battle of the Somme during WWI, Allied forces progressed slowly, losing some 600,000 men in an advance of only 11 km (7 miles). The Germans sustained a similar number of casualties. This was the first battle in which tanks were employed.

Middle
More people died in WWII than in any other war. One of the key moments of the war, and the greatest seaborne invasion in military history, was the Normandy Invasion of 6 June 1944. Although a huge success for the Allies, they suffered more casualties than the Germans—15,000 against 10,000.

OCKWAVE OF THE MOST POWERFUL THERMONUCLEAR DEVICE CIRCLED THE GLOBE THREE TIMES

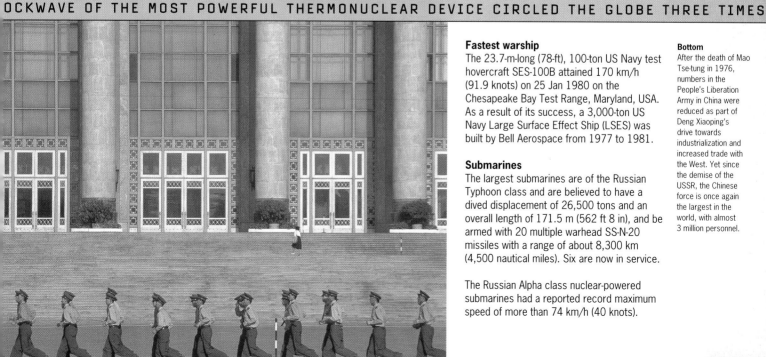

Fastest warship
The 23.7-m-long (78-ft), 100-ton US Navy test hovercraft SES-100B attained 170 km/h (91.9 knots) on 25 Jan 1980 on the Chesapeake Bay Test Range, Maryland, USA. As a result of its success, a 3,000-ton US Navy Large Surface Effect Ship (LSES) was built by Bell Aerospace from 1977 to 1981.

Submarines
The largest submarines are of the Russian Typhoon class and are believed to have a dived displacement of 26,500 tons and an overall length of 171.5 m (562 ft 8 in), and be armed with 20 multiple warhead SS-N-20 missiles with a range of about 8,300 km (4,500 nautical miles). Six are now in service.

The Russian Alpha class nuclear-powered submarines had a reported record maximum speed of more than 74 km/h (40 knots).

Bottom
After the death of Mao Tse-tung in 1976, numbers in the People's Liberation Army in China were reduced as part of Deng Xiaoping's drive towards industrialization and increased trade with the West. Yet since the demise of the USSR, the Chinese force is once again the largest in the world, with almost 3 million personnel.

Education

Right
Mr and Mrs Harold Erickson of Naples, Florida, USA, hold the joint record for the most graduates in one family; their 14 children obtained degrees between 1962 and 1978.

Education systems

Primary schools
The country with the most primary schools is China, which had 861,878 in 1993.

Secondary schools
At general secondary level, India has the most schools, with 241,129 in 1994.

The lowest pupil-to-teacher ratio at secondary school level is in San Marino, which has 5.8 pupils per teacher.

Higher education
Mexico has the greatest number of higher education institutions, with 13,000.

The USA has the greatest number of tertiary-level students, with 14,600,000.

Canada has the highest student ratio, with 6,980 tertiary-level students per 100,000 of the population.

Universities

Oldest universities
The Sumerians had scribal schools, or E-Dubba, soon after 3500 BC.

The oldest existing educational institution is the University of Karueein, founded in AD 859 in Fez, Morocco.

The oldest university in Europe, the University of Bologna, in Italy, was founded in 1088.

The oldest British university is the University of Oxford, founded c. 1167.

Largest universities
The university with the highest enrolment is the State University of New York, USA, which had 381,568 students at 64 campuses throughout the state in late 1995.

The greatest enrolment for a university in one city is at the City University of New York, USA, which had 206,500 students in late 1995 and has 21 campuses throughout the city.

The largest British universities are the University of London, which had 92,660 students (69,560 internal, 23,100 external) in 1994/5; and the Open University, near Milton Keynes, Bucks, which had 135,300 registered students (123,800 undergraduates and 11,500 postgraduates) in 1995.

The world's largest university building is the M.V. Lomonosov State University on the Lenin Hills south of Moscow, Russia. Built between 1949 and 1953, it is 240 m (787 ft 5 in) tall, and has 32 storeys and 40,000 rooms.

Professorships

Youngest professors
Colin Maclaurin was 19 years old when he was elected to Marischal College, Aberdeen, UK, as Professor of Mathematics in Sept 1717. In 1725 he was made Professor of Mathematics at Edinburgh University on the recommendation of Sir Isaac Newton, who had become a professor at the University of Cambridge at the age of 26.

Henry Phillpotts became a don at Magdalen College, University of Oxford, UK, on 25 July 1795, aged 17 years 80 days.

Longest professorships
Dr Joel Hildebrand, Professor Emeritus of Physical Chemistry at the University of California, Berkeley, USA, became an assistant professor in 1913 and published his 275th research paper 68 years later in 1981.

The longest British professorship lasted 63 years. It was held by Thomas Martyn, who was Professor of Botany at the University of Cambridge from 1762 until his death in 1825.

The last professor-for-life was pathologist Henry Roy Dean (1879–1961), who held the position for his last 39 years at the University of Cambridge.

Graduates

Most graduates in one family
The world record for the most graduates in a single family is 14, and is held by two families. Mr and Mrs Harold Erickson of Naples, Florida, USA, saw all of their 11 sons and three daughters obtain university or college degrees between 1962 and 1978, while the 10 sons and four daughters of Mr and Mrs Robert Johnson of Edwards, Mississippi, USA, all obtained their degrees between 1959 and 1983.

RIZAL HIGH SCHOOL I

Youngest undergraduates and graduates
Michael Kearney became the world's youngest graduate in June 1994, at the age of 10 years 4 months, when he obtained his BA in anthropology from the University of South Alabama, USA.

In the United Kingdom, the record for the youngest undergraduate is 10 years 4 months, by Alexander Hill, who entered St Andrews University in Nov 1795, and by William Thomson (later Lord Kelvin), who entered Glasgow University in Oct 1834.

Matthew Trout of Upholland, Lancs, is the youngest British undergraduate this century. In Feb 1994, aged 10 years 10 months, he began an Open University course leading to a degree in mathematics.

Ganesh Sittampalam of Surbiton, Surrey, is the youngest British graduate this century. In July 1992 he obtained a mathematics degree from the University of Surrey at the age of 13 years 5 months.

Youngest doctorate
On 13 April 1814, the mathematician Carl Witte of Lochau was made a Doctor of Philosophy of the University of Giessen, Germany. He was just 12 years old.

Youngest doctorate at age 12

THE EXAMINATION RECORD OF NICHOLAS BARBERIS

'O' Modern Greek

'O' French

'O' Maths SMP

'O' Logic

'O' English

'O' Physics

'O' German

'O' Religious Studies

'O' Geography

'O' History

'O' Chemistry

'O' Computing Studies

'O' Latin

'O' English Literature

'O' Russian

E PHILIPPINES HAD 19,783 PUPILS IN 1995/6

'AO' Electricity + Electronics

'AO' Pure Maths and
       Theoretical Mechanics

'AO' Pure Maths and
       Probability

'AO' Pure Mathematics

'AO' Russian Studies

'A' Physics

'A' German

'A' Modern Greek

'A' Further Maths

'A' Chemistry

'A' French

'A' Maths

All grades obtained are
A grades

Schools

Oldest British schools

King's School in Canterbury, Kent, is said to have been founded by St Augustine between his arrival in Kent in AD 597 and his death in about AD 604. Cor Tewdws (College of Theodosius) at Llantwit Major, Vale of Glamorgan, reputedly burnt down in AD 446, was refounded by St Illtyd in 508 and flourished into the 13th century. Winchester College, Hants, was founded in 1382. Lanark Grammar School, S Lanarkshire, claims to have been referred to in a papal bull drawn up by Lucius III in 1183.

Largest schools

Rizal High School in Pasig, Manila, Philippines, had 19,738 pupils in 1995/6.

The highest ever enrolment in a British school was 2,767, at Banbury Comprehensive, Oxon, in the 1975 summer term.

The highest enrolment in the United Kingdom for 1995/6 was 2,306, at St Louise's Comprehensive College, Belfast.

Pupils and teachers

Most schools attended

The greatest documented number of schools attended by one pupil is 265, by Wilma Williams (now Mrs R. J. Horton) from 1933 to 1943, when her parents were in showbusiness in the USA.

Most O and A levels

Since 1965, Dr Francis L. Thomason of Hammersmith, London, UK, has passed 70 O and A/O levels, 16 A levels and one S level. Of the 87, 36 have been at the top grade.

Terry Tyacke of Trowbridge, Wilts, UK, has passed a total of 21 A levels since 1973.

The most top-grade A levels attained at one sitting is seven, by Matthew James of Mortimer Wilson School, Alfreton, Derbys, UK, in June 1993; by Stephen Murrell (who also obtained an eighth pass at grade B) of Crown

Woods School, Eltham, London, in June 1978; and by Ben Woolley of Lancing College, W Sussex, in June 1994.

Robert Pidgeon of St Peter's School, Bournemouth, Dorset, secured 13 O-level passes at grade A in one sitting in summer 1975. He subsequently passed three A levels at grade A and two S levels with firsts.

Nicholas Barberis achieved 27 top grades while at Eltham College, London, passing 20 O and A/O levels and seven A levels, all at grade A, between 1984 and 1988.

Oldest and youngest GCSE and A level

Ganesh Sittampalam of Surbiton, Surrey, UK, is the youngest person to have passed an A level, achieving grade A in both Mathematics and Further Mathematics in June 1988, at the age of nine years four months

George Lush of Hatfield, Herts, UK, obtained grade D in A level Italian in 1969, just a few months before his 89th birthday.

Sonali Pandya of Edgware, London, UK, obtained a GCSE grade E pass in Computer Studies in June 1993, at the age of eight years two months.

Longest teaching careers

Medarda de Jesús León de Uzcátegui, alias La Maestra Chucha, has taught in Caracas, Venezuela, for a total of 85 years. In 1911, at the age of 12, she set up a school called Modelo de Aplicación together with her two sisters. Since getting married in 1942, she has run her own school, the Escuela Uzcátegui, from her home.

David Rhys Davies (1835–1928) taught as a pupil-teacher and subsequently a teacher and headmaster for 76 years. Most of his career was spent at Talybont-on-Usk School, near Brecon, Powys, UK, and Dame Anna Child's School, Whitton, Powys.

Elsie Marguerite Touzel of Jersey, Channel Islands, began her career in 1905, aged 16. She taught at various Jersey schools until her retirement on 30 Sept 1980.

Left
Michael Kearney of Mobile, Alabama, USA, was the youngest person to receive his high-school diploma (equivalent to British A levels), at the age of six years five months. He subsequently began studying towards an Associate of Science Degree at the age of six years seven months, and went on to become the world's youngest graduate, at the age of 10 years and 4 months.

Languages

GREATEST LIVING LINGUIST SPEAKS AND WRITES 58 LANGUAGES

Languages

Commonest language
Chinese, which is spoken by more than 1 billion people, is the commonest first language. 'Common speech' (*putōnghuà*) is the standard form of Chinese, with a pronunciation based on that of Beijing.

The most widespread and second most commonly spoken language is English, with an estimated 800 million–1.5 billion speakers. Of these, approximately 310 million are native speakers and live mainly in the USA (about 216 million), the United Kingdom (53 million), Canada (17 million) and Australia (15 million).

Greatest number of languages
About 845 of the world's 3,950 languages and dialects are spoken in India.

Rarest sounds
The rarest speech sound is probably 'ř', termed a 'rolled post-alveolar fricative', which occurs in very few languages and is the last sound mastered by Czech children.

The southern Bushman language !xo has a click which is articulated with both lips and written as ☉ . This character is usually referred to as a 'bull's-eye', and the sound, essentially a kiss, is termed a 'velaric ingressive bilabial stop'.

Commonest sound
No language is known to be without the vowel 'a' (as in the English 'father').

Linguists

Greatest linguist
Dr Harold Williams (1876–1928) of New Zealand, a journalist and foreign editor of *The Times*, spoke 58 languages and many dialects (including Latin, Greek, Hebrew and many European and Pacific languages) fluently, and was the only person able to converse with every delegate at the League of Nations in their own language.

Greatest living linguist
Ziad Fazah (b. 1954), originally from Liberia but now a naturalized Brazilian citizen, speaks and writes 58 languages.

Words

Longest words
Lengthy concatenations and some compound, agglutinative and nonce words can be written in the closed-up style of a single word. The

OF THE 3,950 LANGUAGES AND DIALECTS IN T

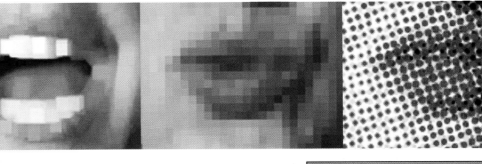

Longest alphabet 74 letters

Longest alphabet 74 letters

Papua New Guinea has the greatest concentration of separate languages due to its many isolated valleys. There are an estimated 869 languages, each with an average of 4,000 speakers.

Most complex languages
The Amele language of Papua New Guinea has the most verb forms, with more than 69,000 finite forms and 860 infinitive forms.

Haida, a North American Indian language, has the greatest number of prefixes, at 70.

Tabassaran, a language of south-east Daghestan, uses a record 48 noun cases.

The language used by the Inuit people has 63 forms of the present tense, and simple nouns have as many as 252 inflections.

Fewest irregular verbs
The artificial language Esperanto has no irregular verbs. More than 1 million of the textbooks published in 1887 by its inventor, Dr Ludwig Zamenhof of Warsaw, Poland, have been bought by potential speakers.

Volapük, an earlier interlanguage invented by Johann Martin Schleyer (1831–1912), also has completely regular configuration.

Most irregular verbs
English has 283 irregular verbs, 30 of which are formed simply by adding a prefix.

Most synonyms
The condition of being inebriated has more synonyms in English than any other noun: American Paul Dickson has published 2,660 words and phrases in his *Word Treasury*.

Longest alphabet
The language containing the most characters is Khmer (Cambodian), with 74. (Some are not currently used.)

Shortest alphabet
Rotokas of central Bougainville Island, Papua New Guinea, has 11 letters in its alphabet: a, b, e, g, i, k, o, p, ř, t and u.

Most and fewest consonants
The language with the largest number of distinct consonantal sounds is that of the Ubykhs in the Caucasus, with between 80 and 85. Ubykh speakers migrated from the Caucasus to Turkey in the 19th century, and the last fully competent speaker, Tevfik Esenç, died in Oct 1992.

The language with the fewest consonants is Rotokas, with just six.

Most and fewest vowels
The language with the most vowels is Sedang, a central Vietnamese language with 55 distinguishable vowel sounds.

The language with the fewest vowels is the Caucasian language Abkhazian, with two.

LONGEST EVER SURNAME W

longest known example is a compound 'word' of 195 Sanskrit characters (transliterating to 428 letters in the Roman alphabet). It describes the region near Kanci, Tamil Nadu, India, and appears in a 16th-century work by Tirumalāmbā, Queen of Vijayanagara.

The longest word in the *Oxford English Dictionary* is 'pneumonoultramicroscopicsilico-volcanoconiosis' (-koniosis), a 45-letter word meaning 'a lung disease caused by the inhalation of very fine silica dust'. It is described as 'factitious' by the editors.

Most succinct word
A Fuegian (southernmost Argentina and Chile) word, *mamihlapinatapai*, is the most difficult word to define briefly. It means 'looking at each other hoping that either will offer to do something which both parties desire but are unwilling to do'.

Longest scientific name
The systematic name for the deoxyribonucleic acid (DNA) of the human mitochondria contains 16,569 nucleotide residues and is around 207,000 letters long. It was published in key form in *Nature* on 9 April 1981.

Longest palindromes
Saippuakivikauppias, Finnish for 'a dealer in lye', is the longest known palindromic word.

The longest palindrome in the *Oxford English Dictionary* is tattarrattat, a nonce word meaning rat-a-tat.

Certain baptismal fonts found in Greece and Turkey bear the circular inscription NIΨON ANOMHMATA MH MONAN OΨIN ('wash [my] sins, not only [my] face'). It also appears in other churches.

Longest anagrams
The longest scientific transposals are hydroxydesoxycorticosterone and hydroxydeoxycorticosterones (27 letters).

The longest non-scientific English words that can form anagrams are representationism and misrepresentation (17 letters).

Longest abbreviation
The 14 initials of the Syarikat Kerjasama Orang-orang Melayu Kerajaan Hilir Perak

the construction of the Academy of Building and Architecture of the USSR.

Commonest words and letters
The most frequently used words in written English are, in descending order of frequency: the, of, and, to, a, in, that, is, I, it, for and as.

The most commonly used word in English conversation is 'I'.

The commonest letter is 'e'. More words begin with the letter 's' than any other, but the most commonly used initial letter is 't', as in 'the', 'to', 'that' or 'there'.

Most meanings
The most overworked word in the English language is 'set', for which Dr Charles Onions (1873–1965) of Oxford University Press gave a total of 58 noun uses, 126 verbal uses and 10 uses as a participial adjective.

Texas, USA, on 12 Sept 1984. Within a month, Mr Williams had filed an amendment extending his daughter's first name to 1,019 letters and her middle name to 36 letters.

Shortest forename
The forename A has been used for five generations in the Lincoln Taber family of Fingringhoe, Essex, UK.

Most forenames
Mr A. Lindup-Badarou from Truro, Cornwall, UK, who was formerly known as A. Hicks, had a record-breaking total of 3,530 forenames in March 1995.

Longest surnames
A six-barrelled surname was borne by Major L. S. D. O. F. (Leone Sextus Denys Oswolf Fraudatifilius) Tollemache-Tollemache de Orellana-Plantagenet-Tollemache-Tollemache (1884–1917), known at school as Tolly.

The last recorded example of a non-repetitious five-part name is that of Lady

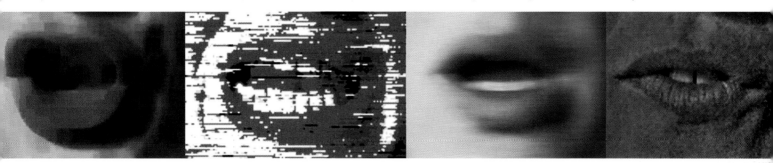

Kerana Jimat Cermat Dan Pinjam-meminjam Wang Berhad (the Malay name for the Cooperative Company of the Lower State of Perak Government's Malay People for Money Savings and Loans Ltd) situated in Teluk Anson, Perak, West Malaysia, combine to make the world's longest abbreviation, S.K.O.M.K.H.P.K.J.C.D.P.W.B. This abbreviation is in turn abbreviated to Skomk.

Shortest abbreviation
The 55-letter full name of the city of Los Angeles—El Pueblo de Nuestra Señora la Reina de los Angeles de Porciúncula—in California, USA, is abbreviated to L.A., which is 3.63% of its full length.

Longest acronym
NIIOMTPLABOPARMBETZHELBETRABSBOMO NIMONKONOTDTEKHSTROMONT, which has a total of 56 letters (or 54 letters in Cyrillic), is found in the *Concise Dictionary of Soviet Terminology, Institutions and Abbreviations* (1969) and is the longest acronym in the world. It is used to refer to the laboratory for reinforcement, concrete and ferroconcrete operations for composite-monolithic and monolithic constructions, of the Department of the Technology of Building-assembly operations of the Scientific Research Institute of the Organization for Mechanization and Technical Aid—the organization employed in

Names
Shortest place names
Single-letter place names can be found in various countries around the world. Examples include the villages of Y in France, Å in Denmark, Norway and Sweden, and the River E in Highland, UK.

Most spellings
The spelling of the Dutch town of Leeuwarden has been recorded in 225 different versions since AD 1046.

In the United Kingdom, Bromsberrow in Gloucestershire has been spelt 161 different ways since the 10th century, as reported by local historian Lester Steynor.

Commonest British place name
The name Newton, which means 'new settlement', occurs 467 times in Great Britain—151 times in its simple form and 316 times as part of a compound place name. Of those towns with the name in its simple form, 90 are in Scotland.

Longest forename
The longest personal name that has ever appeared on a birth certificate is Rhoshandiatellyneshiaunneveshenk Koyaanisquatsiuth Williams, for a girl born to Mr and Mrs James Williams of Beaumont,

Caroline Jemima Temple-Nugent-Chandos-Brydges-Grenville (1858–1946).

The longest single-word English surname is Featherstonehaugh, variously pronounced Featherstonehaw, Festonhaw, Fessonhay, Freestonhugh, Feerstonhaw or Fanshaw.

In Scotland, the surname Nin (feminine of Mac) Achinmacdholicachinskerray (29 letters) is recorded in an 18th-century parish register.

Shortest surnames
The most common single-letter surname in the world is O, which is prevalent in Korea.

Among the 47 million names that feature on the Department of Social Security index for the United Kingdom, there are six examples of surnames that are only one letter long—A, B, J, N, O and X.

Commonest English surname
In the English-speaking world, the commonest surname is Smith. The most recent count showed that 659,050 Smiths were registered for national insurance in the United Kingdom, of whom 10,102 were John Smith and another 19,502 were John (plus one or more names) Smith. Including uninsured persons, there were more than 800,000 Smiths in England and Wales alone.

Religion

Longest cathedral nave 183.2 m

Religions

Earliest religion
Human burial, which has religious connotations, is known from c. 60,000 BC among *Homo sapiens neanderthalensis* in the Shanidar cave, northern Iraq.

Largest religions
Christianity is the predominant religion, with 1.9 billion adherents in 1995 (33.2% of the world's population). There were 970 million Roman Catholics in the same year.

The largest non-Christian religion is Islam. There were 1.1 billion Muslims in 1995.

Religious figures

Saints
The shortest interval between the death of a saint and his or her canonization was 337 days in the case of St Peter of Verona, Italy, who was canonized on 9 March 1253.

The longest interval between death and canonization is 857 years in the case of St Leo III, who was canonized in 1673.

Bishops
Louis François de la Baume de Suze (1603–90) was a bishop for a record 76 years 273 days from 6 Dec 1613.

The oldest Roman Catholic bishop on record was Edward Howard (1877–1983), Archbishop of Portland-in-Oregon, USA, who celebrated mass about 27,800 times.

Herbert Welch of the United Methodist Church, who was elected a bishop for Japan and Korea in 1916, died in 1969 aged 106.

The youngest bishop was HRH the Duke of York and Albany, second son of George III, who was elected Bishop of Osnabrück at the age of 196 days on 27 Feb 1764. He resigned 39 years later.

Longest church career
The Rev. K. M. Jacob was made a deacon in the Marthoma Syrian Church of Malabar in Kerala, southern India, in 1897. He served his church until his death in 1984.

Longest-serving chorister
John Love Vokins (1890–1989) joined the choir of Christ Church, Heeley, Sheffield, S Yorkshire, UK, in 1895 and was still singing in 1987.

Right
Soaring Gothic arches over an 11,240-m² (121,000-ft²) floor give the cathedral of St John the Divine, New York, USA, a volume of 476,350 m³ (16,822,000 ft³).

Popes
The longest papal reign was 31 years 236 days from 1846, by Pius IX (Giovanni Maria Mastai-Ferretti).

The shortest papal reign was two days by Stephen II, who died in AD 752.

The longest-lived popes were St Agatho, who is said to have been 106 when he died in 681, and Leo XIII (Gioacchino Pecci) who was 93 years 140 days old at his death in 1903.

The youngest elected pope was John XII (Ottaviano), who was 18 years old when he took on the role in AD 955.

The last British pope was Adrian IV (Nicholas Breakspear) of Abbots Langley, Herts, who was elected on 4 Dec 1154.

Places of worship

Earliest places of worship
Decorated Upper Palaeolithic caves in Europe (c. 30,000–10,000 BC) may have been used as places of worship or religious ritual.

The oldest surviving Christian church is a converted house in Qal'at es Salihiye (formerly Douro-Europos) in Syria, dating from AD 232.

The oldest places of worship in the United Kingdom are the stone circles or henges of the Neolithic period, such as Avebury, Wilts, dating from c. 3000–2800 BC.

The oldest surviving ecclesiastical building in the United Kingdom is a 6th-century cell built by St Brendan in AD 542 on Eileach an Naoimh, Garvellachs, Argyll and Bute.

Temples
The largest religious structure is Angkor Wat ('City Temple'), Cambodia, covering 162.6 ha (402 acres). Built to the Hindu god Vishnu by Khmer king Suryavarman II between 1113 and 1150, its curtain wall measures 1.64 km² (⅝ miles²), and its population, before it was abandoned in 1432, was 80,000. The whole complex of 72 major monuments extends over 24 x 8 km (15 x 5 miles).

The largest Buddhist temple is Borobudur, near Jogjakarta, Indonesia, built in the 8th century. It is 31.4 m (103 ft) tall and measures 123 m² (162,847 ft²).

The largest Mormon temple is the Salt Lake City Temple, Utah, USA, dedicated in 1893. It has a floor area of 23,505 m² (253,015 ft²).

The Rongbu temple, located at an altitude of c. 5,100 m (16,750 ft), is the highest temple. Situated 40 km (25 miles) from Mt Everest between Tingri and Shigatse in Tibet and containing nine chapels, it is home to a number of lamas and nuns.

Cathedrals
The largest cathedral is the Gothic cathedral church of St John the Divine of the Diocese of New York, USA, which has a floor area of 11,240 m² (121,000 ft²) and a volume of 476,350 m³ (16,822,000 ft³). The cornerstone was laid on 27 Dec 1892, but work was stopped in 1941 and only resumed in earnest in July 1979. The nave is the world's longest at 183.2 m (601 ft) in length, with a vaulting 37.8 m (124 ft) high.

The cathedral covering the largest area is Santa María de la Sede, Seville, Spain. Built between 1402 and 1519, it is 126.2 m (414 ft) long, 82.6 m (271 ft) wide and 30.5 m (100 ft) high to the vault of the nave.

The largest British cathedral is the Cathedral Church of Christ in Liverpool. Finally consecrated on 25 Oct 1978 after 74 years, the building encloses 9,687 m² (104,275 ft²) and has an overall length of 193.9 m (636 ft). The Vestey Tower is 100.9 m (331 ft) high

and contains both the highest vaulting in the world—53.3 m (175 ft) maximum at undertower—and the highest Gothic arches ever built, with 32.6-m (107-ft) apexes.

The smallest church designated as a cathedral is the Christ Catholic Church, Highlandville, Missouri, USA, consecrated in 1983. It measures 4.3 x 5.2 m (14 x 17 ft) and has seating for 18 people.

The smallest cathedral in use in the United Kingdom is the Cathedral of the diocese of The Isles at Millport, Cumbrae, N Ayrshire, built in 1849–51. The nave measures 12.2 x 6.1 m (40 x 20 ft) and the total floor area is 197.3 m² (236 yd²).

Stained glass
Pieces of stained glass excavated by Prof. Rosemary Cramp at Monkwearmouth and Jarrow and dated at before AD 850 were set into a window of that date in St Paul's Church, Jarrow, Co. Durham, UK.

The largest stained-glass window covers 2,079 m² (2,487 yd²). It is in Resurrection Mausoleum, Justice, Illinois, USA.

Synagogues
The largest synagogue is Temple Emanu-El on Fifth Avenue at 65th Street, New York City,

Above and left
The temple at Angkor Wat, Cambodia, is the largest religious structure in the world. It extends over an area of 24 x 8 km (15 x 5 miles).

TALLEST CATHEDRAL SPIRE IS 160.9 M HIGH

ACCOMMODATE A TOTAL OF 300,000 WORSHIPPERS

Churches
The largest church is the Basilica of Our Lady of Peace (Notre Dame de la Paix) at Yamoussoukro, Ivory Coast. Completed in 1989, it covers 30,000 m² (323,000 ft²) and has seating for 7,000 people. Including its golden cross, it is 158 m (518 ft) high.

The elliptical basilica of St Pius (Saint-Pie) X at Lourdes, France, completed in 1957 at a cost of £2 million, has a capacity of 20,000 under its span arches and is 200 m (660 ft) long.

The smallest church is the chapel of Santa Isabel de Hungría in Colomares, a monument to Christopher Columbus at Benalmádena, Málaga, Spain. It is irregular in shape and has a total floor area of 1.96 m² (21⅛ ft²).

The largest parish is Christ Church Cathedral on the Falkland Islands, South Georgia and South Sandwich Islands and the British Antarctic Territory. The Rev. Canon Stephen Palmer is responsible for churches that are 1,575 km (980 miles) apart.

USA. Completed in Sept 1929, it has a frontage of 45.7 m (150 ft) on Fifth Avenue and 77.1 m (253 ft) on 65th Street. The main sanctuary can accommodate 2,500 people, and the Beth-El Chapel seats 350. When the temple's other three sanctuaries are also in use, 5,500 people can be accommodated.

The largest synagogue in the United Kingdom is the Edgware Synagogue, Greater London, completed in 1959, with seating for 1,630.

The British synagogue with the highest registered membership is Stanmore and Canons Park Synagogue in Greater London, which has 2,474 members.

Mosques
The largest mosque is Shah Faisal Mosque near Islamabad, Pakistan, which has a total area of 18.97 ha (46.87 acres). The covered part of the prayer hall has an area of 0.48 ha (1.19 acres). The complex can accommodate 100,000 worshippers in the prayer hall and courtyard and 200,000 in the grounds.

The tallest minaret in the world is at the Great Hassan II Mosque, Casablanca, Morocco, and is 200 m (656 ft) in height. It was completed in 1993 at a cost of 5 billion dirhams (£360 million).

Spires
The Protestant Cathedral of Ulm in Germany has the world's tallest cathedral spire. The building is early Gothic and was begun in 1377, but the 160.9-m (528-ft) tower in the centre of the west façade was not completed until 1890.

The Chicago Temple/First United Methodist Church in Chicago, Illinois, USA, has the tallest church spire. It consists of a 22-storey skyscraper (erected in 1924) surmounted by a parsonage at 100.5 m (330 ft), a 'Sky Chapel' at 121.9 m (400 ft) and a steeple cross at 173.1 m (568 ft) above street level.

The church of St Mary (Salisbury Cathedral), Wilts, has the highest spire in the United Kingdom. The Lady Chapel was built between 1220 and 1225, and the spire was added before 1305. It reaches a height of 123.1 m (404 ft).

Stupas
The Shwedagon pagoda in Yangon (Rangoon), Myanmar (Burma), is 99.3 m (326 ft) high and was built on the site of an 8.2-m (27-ft) pagoda dating from 585 BC.

The Jetavanarama dagoba in the ancient city of Anuradhapura, Sri Lanka, is 120 m (400 ft) high.

Monuments and edifices

Monuments

Tallest monument
The stainless steel Gateway to the West arch in St Louis, Missouri, USA, was completed on 28 Oct 1965 to commemorate westward expansion after the 1803 Louisiana Purchase. It is a sweeping arch spanning 192 m (630 ft) and rising to the same height. It was designed in 1947 by the Finnish-American architect Eero Saarinen.

Tallest monumental column
The tapering column on the bank of the San Jacinto River near Houston, Texas, USA, was built from 1936 to 1939 to commemorate the Battle of San Jacinto (1836). It is 173 m (570 ft) tall, 14 m (47 ft) square at the base and 9 m (30 ft) square at the observation tower, which is topped by a 199.6-tonne star.

Largest obelisks (monolithic)
The largest obelisk is the 'skewer' or 'spit' (obeliskos in Greek) of Tuthmosis III, which was brought from Aswan, Egypt, by Emperor Constantius in the spring of AD 357 and repositioned in the Piazza San Giovanni in Laterano, Rome, Italy, on 3 Aug 1588. Once 36 m (118 ft 1 in) tall, it now stands 32.81 m (107 ft 7 in) and weighs 455 tonnes.

The unfinished obelisk at Aswan, Egypt, probably commissioned by Queen Hatshepsut c.1490 BC, is 41.75 m (136 ft 10 in) long and weighs 1,168 tonnes.

The largest obelisk in the United Kingdom is Cleopatra's Needle on the Embankment, London, which is the world's 11th tallest, at 20.88 m (68 ft 5 in). Weighing 189.35 tonnes, it was towed up the River Thames from Egypt on 21 Jan 1878 and positioned on 13 Sept.

Longest an obelisk has remained in situ
The record time for a raised obelisk to remain in position is held by the edifice at Heliopolis, Egypt, erected by Senusret I c. 1750 BC.

Largest henges
The largest British megalithic prehistoric monument and the largest henge is the 11.5-ha (28½-acre) earthworks and stone circles of Avebury, Wilts, 'rediscovered' in 1646. The earliest calibrated date in the area of this Neolithic site is c. 4200 BC. The work is 365 m (1,200 ft) in diameter with a ditch 12 m (40 ft) wide around the perimeter.

The henge of Durrington Walls, Wilts, UK, obliterated by road-building, had a diameter of 472 m (1,550 ft). It was built c. 2500 BC and required about 900,000 man-hours.

Tallest menhir
The Grand Menhir Brisé at Locmariaquer, Brittany, France, was originally 18 m (59 ft) high and weighed about 300 tonnes, but is now in four pieces.

Largest trilithons
The largest trilithons are at Stonehenge, Wilts, UK, with single sarsen blocks that weigh more than 45 tonnes and required more than 550 people to drag them up a 9° gradient. The earliest stage of the building of the ditch has been dated to 2950 BC.

Oldest scheduled British monument
Kent's Cavern, near Torquay, Devon, is a cave site containing deposits more than 300,000 years old, from the Lower Palaeolithic period.

LARGEST OBELISK IN THE WORLD, THE 'SKEWER'

Youngest scheduled British monument
A hexagonal pillbox and 48 concrete tank-traps near Christchurch, Dorset, were built in WWII and have been protected since 1973.

Earthworks and mounds

Largest earthworks
The longest, most extensive pre-mechanical era earthworks were the Linear Earth Boundaries, dated to c. 1300 in the Benin Empire and earlier in the Edo state (formerly Bendel) of Nigeria. In 1993 it was estimated that their total length was around 16,000 km (10,000 miles), and that the volume of earth moved was 75 million m³ (100 million yd³).

The greatest prehistoric earthwork in the United Kingdom is Wansdyke (originally Wodensdic), which ran 138 km (86 miles) from Portishead, Somerset, to Inkpen Beacon and Ludgershall, Berks. It was built by the Belgae (c. 150 BC) as their northern boundary.

Largest mounds
The largest artificial mound is a gravel memorial to the Seleucid King Antiochus I (who reigned from 69 to 34 BC) on the summit of Nemrud Dağ, Turkey. It is 59.8 m (197 ft) tall and covers 3 ha (7½ acres).

The largest British mound is Silbury Hill, a 39-m-high (130-ft) cone with a 2-ha (5½-acre) base near Marlborough, Wilts. Its construction, dated to 2745±185 BC, involved the moving of 680,000 tonnes of chalk over 18 million working hours. It has been shown to be based on an innermost central mound, similar to contemporary round barrows.

Columns and walls

Tallest columns
The tallest load-bearing stone columns in the world are 21 m (69 ft) high and are situated in the Hall of Columns of the Temple of Amun at Karnak, the ancient capital of Upper Egypt.

Longest walls
The Great Wall of China is the longest wall in the world, with a main-line length of 3,460 km (2,150 miles)—nearly three times the length of the British mainland.

The longest Roman wall in the United Kingdom was Hadrian's Wall, built from AD 122 to 126 and abandoned in AD 383. It extended for 118 km (73½ miles) from Bowness-on-Solway, Cumbria, to Wallsend-on-Tyne, Tyne and Wear.

Thickest walls
Ur-nammu's mud brick city walls at Ur (now Muqayyar, Iraq) were 27 m (88 ft) thick.

The thickest walls in the United Kingdom are at the Great Tower or Donjon of Flint Castle, Flintshire. They were built between 1277 and 1280 and are 7 m (23 ft) thick.

Statues and shrines

Longest statues
At 'about 305 m' (1,000 ft) in length, the recumbent Sakya Buddha near Bamiyan, Afghanistan, was the world's longest ever statue. Now in ruins, the plastered rubble statue is believed to date from the 3rd or 4th century AD.

Tallest statues
The world's tallest statue is a bronze effigy of Buddha which was completed in Tokyo, Japan, in Jan 1993. It is 120 m (394 ft) high, 35 m (115 ft) wide and weighs 1,000 tonnes. A joint Japanese–Taiwanese project, it took seven years to construct.

The statue of Maitreya at the Lama Temple (Yonghegong) in north-east Beijing, China, stands 26 m (85 ft) high and is carved out of

WORLD'S TALLEST STAT

a single piece of white sandalwood tree. The Imperial Court allowed two years for the carving of the statue, completed in 1750.

Largest ziggurats
The largest ziggurat ever built was the Ziggurat of Choga Zambil of the Elamite King Untas (c. 1250 BC), which was situated 30 km (18½ miles) from Haft Tepe, Iran. The outer base measured 105 x 105 m (344 x 344 ft) and the fifth 'box', almost 50 m (164 ft) above it, measured 28 x 28 m (92 x 92 ft).

The world's largest partially surviving ziggurat is the Ziggurat of Ur (now Muqayyar, Iraq), which has a base measuring 61 x 45.7 m (200 x 150 ft). It was built to three storeys in the reign of Ur-nammu (c. 2250–2232 BC) and is surmounted by a summit temple. The first storey and part of the second storey survive to a height of 18 m (60 ft).

Longest wall 3,460 km

Burial places

Largest cemeteries
Ohlsdorf Cemetery in Hamburg, Germany, is the largest cemetery in the world, covering an area of 400 ha (990 acres). It has been in continuous use since 1877 and a total of 972,020 burials and 408,471 cremations had taken place there by 31 Dec 1995.

The largest cemetery in the United Kingdom is Brookwood Cemetery, Surrey, owned by Ramadan Güney. It covers 200 ha (500 acres) and more than 231,000 interments have been held there to date.

Tallest cemetery
The permanently illuminated Memorial Necrópole Ecumênica in Santos, near São Paulo, Brazil, has 10 storeys and covers an area of 1.8 ha (4½ acres). Construction began in March 1983 and the first burial was held on 28 July 1984.

Largest crematorium
The largest crematorium in the world is the Nikolo-Arkhangelskiy Crematorium in east Moscow, Russia, which has seven twin cremators of British design. Completed in March 1972, it covers 210 ha (519 acres) and has six Halls of Farewell for atheists.

Oldest crematorium
The oldest crematorium in the United Kingdom was built in 1879 at Woking, Surrey. The first cremation there took place on 26 March 1885.

Largest pyramids
The largest pyramid in the world, and the largest monument constructed, is the pyramid to Quetzalcóatl at Cholula de Rivadabia, 101 km (63 miles) south-east of Mexico City. The edifice is 54 m (177 ft) tall and its base covers an area of almost 18.2 ha (45 acres). Its total volume is estimated at 3.3 million m^3 (4.3 million yd^3), compared with that of the Pyramid of Khufu at Giza, Egypt, which is currently 2.4 million m^3 (3.1 million yd^3).

Top
The pyramids of Giza are the only one of the Seven Wonders of the World, first designated by Antipater of Sidon in the 2nd century BC, to still substantially exist. Located south-west of Cairo, Egypt, they were built by three 4th Dynasty pharaohs: Khwfw (Khufu or Cheops), Kha-f-Ra (Khafre, Khefren or Chepren) and Menkaure (Mycerinus). The largest pyramid, the 'Horizon of Khufu', was built to an original height of 146.6 m (481 ft) c. 2250 BC but has been reduced to 137.5 m (451 ft 1 in) by the loss of its topmost stones and pyramidion. With a baseline of 230.4 m (755 ft 10 in), it covers slightly more than 5 ha (13 acres). It has been estimated that 100,000 workers took 30 years to manoeuvre the 2,300,000 limestone blocks, which weighed an average of 2.5 tonnes each, into position. The other six wonders were the Hanging Gardens of Babylon, the Statue of Zeus at Olympia, the Temple of Artemis, the Tomb of King Mausolus, the Colossus of Rhodes and the Pharos of Alexandria. Of these, fragments of the Temple of Artemis at Ephesus in Turkey, built c. 350 BC, and of the Tomb of Mausolus of Caria, built at Halicarnassus (now Bodrum) in Turkey c. 325 BC, have been found. No trace remains of the others.

PIT' OF TUTHMOSIS III, WAS ONCE 36 M IN HEIGHT

S A BRONZE BUDDHA IN TOKYO, WHICH IS 120 M HIGH AND WEIGHS 1,000 TONNES

Oldest pyramid
The Djoser Step Pyramid at Saqqâra, Egypt, was built to a height of 62 m (204 ft) by Imhotep (Djoser's royal architect) c. 2630 BC.

Largest tombs
The Mount Li tomb, the burial place of Qin Shi Huangdi, first Emperor of Qin, was built during his reign from 221 to 210 BC and is situated 40 km (25 miles) east of Xianyang, China. The two walls surrounding the grave measure 2,173 x 974 m (7,129 x 3,195 ft) and 685 x 578 m (2,247 x 1,896 ft). Several pits in the tomb contained a vast army consisting of an estimated 8,000 terracotta soldiers and horses (life-size and larger).

A tomb on Okinawa, Japan, for 180,000 people who died in WWII was enlarged in 1985 to accommodate a further 9,000 bodies thought to be buried on the island.

Middle
The Great Wall of China was built by 300,000 workmen and an unknown number of political prisoners between 214 and 204 BC. Built to repel Mongol invaders, it comprised 3,460 km (2,150 miles) of mainline wall and 3,530 km (2,195 miles) of branches and spurs once it was finished.

Bottom
The Temple of Amun at Karnak, opposite Thebes on the Nile in Egypt, contains the tallest load-bearing stone columns. They were built in the 19th dynasty in the reign of Rameses II, c. 1270 BC.

230 252 274 296 318
231 253 275 297 319
232 254 276 298 320
233 255 277 299 321
234 256 278 300 322
235 257 279 301 323

236 258 280 302 324
237 259 281 303 325 **Sports**
238 260 282 304 326

GREG LOUGANIS (USA) HOLDS THE RECORD FOR THE MOST WORLD DIVING TITLES, AT FI

239 261 283 305 327   1992
240 262 284 306 328   199
241 263 285 307   199
242 264 286 308   1997
243 265 287 309 331   1998

244 266 288 310 332
245 267 289 311 333
246 268 290 312 334
247 269 291 313 335

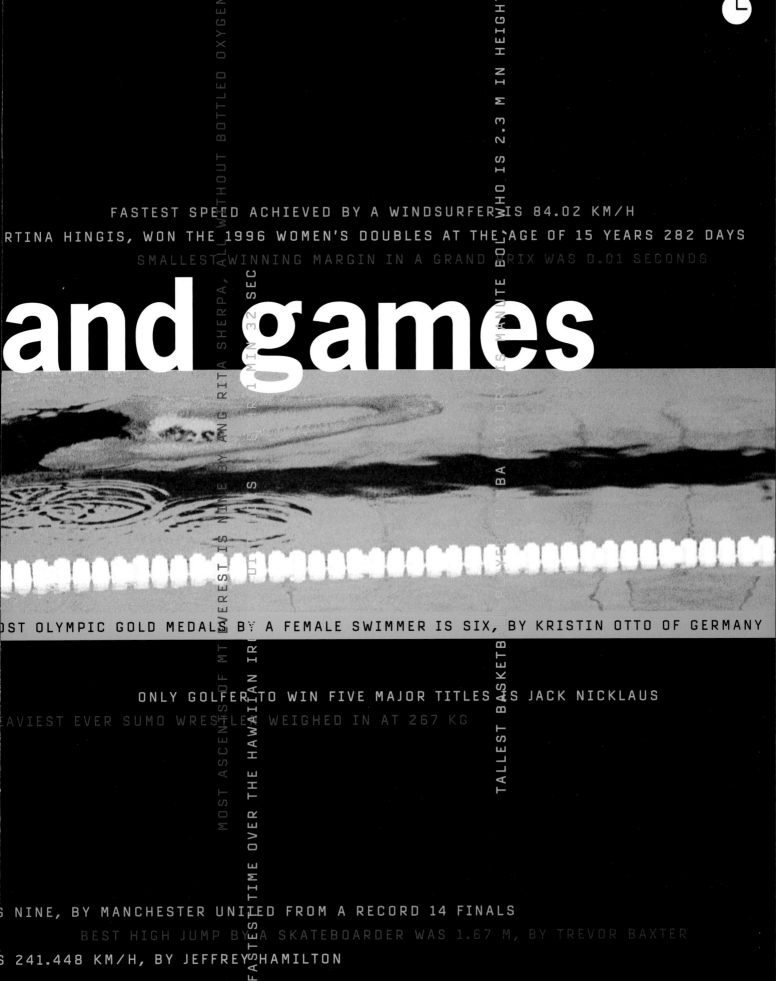

FASTEST SPEED ACHIEVED BY A WINDSURFER IS 84.02 KM/H

RTINA HINGIS, WON THE 1996 WOMEN'S DOUBLES AT THE AGE OF 15 YEARS 282 DAYS

SMALLEST WINNING MARGIN IN A GRAND PRIX WAS 0.01 SECONDS

and games

ST OLYMPIC GOLD MEDALS BY A FEMALE SWIMMER IS SIX, BY KRISTIN OTTO OF GERMANY

ONLY GOLFER TO WIN FIVE MAJOR TITLES S JACK NICKLAUS

AVIEST EVER SUMO WRESTLER WEIGHED IN AT 267 KG

NINE, BY MANCHESTER UNITED FROM A RECORD 14 FINALS

BEST HIGH JUMP BY A SKATEBOARDER WAS 1.67 M, BY TREVOR BAXTER

S 241.448 KM/H, BY JEFFREY HAMILTON

Athletics

Fastest speed 43.37 km/h

Right
US track and field athlete Jesse Owens (1913–80) held the world long-jump record for 25 years (1935–60). His finest hour was on 25 May 1935, when he set six world records in just 45 minutes at Ann Arbor, Michigan, USA: a 9.4-second 100 yd at 3:15 p.m., an 8.13-m (26-ft 8¼-in) long jump at 3.25 p.m., a 20.3-second 220 yd (and 200 m) at 3:45 p.m. and a 22.6-second 220-yd (and 200-m) low hurdles at 4:00 p.m.

Olympics
Most Olympic medals

The most Olympic gold medals is 10 (an absolute Olympic record), by Raymond Clarence Ewry (USA) in the standing high, long and triple jumps (1900, 1904, 1906, 1908).

The most women's gold medals is four, by: Francina 'Fanny' Elsje Blankers-Koen (Netherlands), 100 m, 200 m, 80-m hurdles and 4 x 100-m relay in 1948; Elizabeth 'Betty' Cuthbert (Australia), 100 m, 200 m and 4 x 100-m relay in 1956 and 400 m in 1964; Bärbel Wöckel (GDR), 200 m and 4 x 100-m relay in 1976 and 1980; and Evelyn Ashford (USA), 100 m and 4 x 100-m relay in 1984, 1988 and 1992.

The most gold medals won by a British athlete (excluding tug of war and walking) is two, by: Charles Bennett (1,500 m and 5,000-m team in 1900); Alfred Edward Tysoe (800 m and 5,000-m team in 1900); John Thomas Rimmer (4,000-m steeplechase and 5,000-m team in 1900); Albert George Hill (800 m and 1,500 m in 1920); Douglas Gordon Arthur Lowe (800 m in 1924 and 1928); Sebastian Newbold Coe (1,500 m in 1980 and 1984) and Francis Morgan 'Daley' Thompson (decathlon 1980 and 1984). Thompson was also decathlon World Champion in 1983.

The record for the most gold medals at one celebration is five, by Paavo Johannes Nurmi (Finland) in 1924 (1,500 m, 5,000 m, 10,000-m cross-country and 3,000-m team and cross-country team).

The most gold medals for individual events at one celebration is four, by Alvin Christian Kraenzlein (USA) in 1900 (60 m, 110-m hurdles, 200-m hurdles and long jump).

The record for the greatest number of medals won is 12 (nine gold and three silver), by Paavo Nurmi (Finland), 1920, 1924 and 1928.

The most medals won by a woman athlete is seven, by Shirley Barbara de la Hunty (Australia) with three gold, one silver and three bronze in the 1948, 1952 and 1956 Games. A recently discovered photo-finish of the 1948 200 m indicates that she finished third, and not fourth as officially listed.

Irena Szewinska (Poland) is the only woman athlete to win a medal in four successive Games (three gold, two silver and two bronze in 1964, 1968, 1972 and 1976).

The most medals by a British athlete is four, by Guy Montagu Butler (gold for the 4 x 400-m relay and silver for the 400 m in 1920, and bronze for each in 1924) and by Sebastian

Coe (gold in the 1,500 m in 1980 and 1984 and silver at 800 m in 1980 and 1984).

The record for British women is three, by: Dorothy Hyman (silver in the 100 m in 1960 and bronze in the 1960 200 m and the 1964 4 x 100-m relay; Mary Denise Rand (gold in the long jump, silver in the pentathlon and bronze in the 4 x 100-m relay in 1964) and Kathryn Jane Cook (bronze at the 1980 and 1984 4 x 100-m relay and in the 1984 400 m).

Oldest champions

Irish-born Patrick Joseph 'Babe' McDonald (USA) was 42 years 26 days old when he won the 25.4-kg (56-lb) weight throw at Antwerp, Belgium, on 21 Aug 1920.

Lia Manoliu (Romania) was 36 years 176 days old when she won the discus in 1968.

Oldest medallists

Tebbs Lloyd Johnson (GB) was 48 years 115 days old when he won the bronze in the 1948 50,000-m walk.

The oldest woman medallist, Dana Zátopková (Czechoslovakia), was 37 years 348 days old when she won the silver in the javelin in 1960.

Youngest champions

The youngest gold medallist, Barbara Pearl Jones (USA), was 15 years 123 days old when she was in the winning 4 x 100-m relay team at Helsinki, Finland, on 27 July 1952.

The youngest male champion was Robert Bruce Mathias (USA), who won the decathlon at the London Games on 5 and 6 Aug 1948 at the age of 17 years 263 days.

World championships
Most medals

Frederick 'Carl' Lewis has won a record 10 medals: a record eight gold (100 m, long jump and 4 x 100-m relay, 1983; 100 m, long jump and 4 x 100-m relay, 1987; 100 m and 4 x 100-m relay, 1991) plus silver at long jump, 1991, and bronze at 200 m, 1993. He also won eight Olympic golds, 1984–92.

The most medals won by a woman is 13, by Merlene Ottey (Jamaica), with three gold, four silver and six bronze from 1983 to 1995.

The most gold medals by a woman is four, by Jackie Joyner-Kersee (USA): long jump in 1987 and 1991 and heptathlon in 1987 and 1993.

World Indoor Championships
The most individual titles is four, by: Stefka Kostadinova (Bulgaria) for the high jump in 1985, 1987, 1989 and 1993; Mikhail Shchennikov (Russia) for the 5,000-m walk in 1987, 1989, 1991 and 1993; and Sergey Bubka (Ukraine) for the pole vault in 1985, 1987, 1991 and 1995.

Most international appearances
The greatest number of internationals to have been contested for any nation is 89, by shot-putter Bjørn Bang Andersen for Norway between 1960 and 1981.

The record for the most WAAA outdoor titles is 14, by Suzanne Allday (seven each at shot and discus between 1952 and 1962) and Judy Oakes.

The most full Great Britain international appearances by one athlete is 76, by Judy Oakes between 1976 and 1996.

Oldest internationals
The oldest full Great Britain international was Donald James Thompson, who took part in the 200-km walk at Bazencourt, France, on 20 and 21 April 1991, aged 58 years 89 days. In the same race, Edmund Harold Shillabeer became the oldest international debutant, aged 51 years 260 days.

The oldest woman international was Ann Sayer, who was 57 years 169 days old when she took part in the 200-km walk at Bazencourt, France, on 2 and 3 April 1994.

Highest jump above own head
Franklin Jacobs (USA) cleared 59 cm (23¼ in) above his head when he jumped 2.32 m (7 ft 7¼ in) at New York, USA, on 27 Jan 1978.

The women's record for the highest jump above one's own head is 32 cm (12¾ in), by Yolanda Henry (USA) when she jumped 2.00 m (6 ft 6¾ in) at Seville, Spain, on 30 May 1990.

Oldest world record-breaker
Gerhard Wiedner (West Germany) was 41 years 71 days old when he set a record of 2 hr 30 min 38.6 sec for the 20-mile walk at Hamburg, Germany, on 25 May 1974.

Youngest world record-breaker
Wang Yan (China) set a record for the women's 5,000-m walk at the age of 14 years 334 days at Jian, China, on 9 March 1986. Her time was 21 min 33.8 sec.

BEST WINNING SEQUENCE IS 150 CONSECUTIVE HIGH-JUMP COMPETITIONS

Most participants
The greatest number of participants at a world championships is 11,475 (9,328 men, 2,147 women), for the 1993 World Veterans' Athletic Championships at Miyazaki, Japan.

British athletics
Most titles
The record for the most national senior titles by one athlete is 37, by Judith Miriam Oakes at the shot: 14 WAAA or AAA outdoor, 14 indoor (WAAA/AAA) and nine UK titles between 1977 and 1996.

The record for the greatest number of men's senior AAA titles (excluding tug-of-war events) by one athlete is 14 individual and one relay, by Emmanuel McDonald Bailey (Trinidad) between 1946 and 1953.

The most outdoors appearances is 61, by hammer thrower Andrew Howard Payne (South Africa, then GB) from 1960 to 1974.

The most outdoors titles in one event is 13, by Denis Horgan (Ireland) in the shot put between 1893 and 1912.

Youngest internationals
The youngest man was high jumper Ross Hepburn, who jumped against the USSR on 26 Aug 1977, aged 15 years 316 days.

The youngest woman was Janis Walsh, who was 14 years 324 days old when she competed against Belgium at the 60 m and the 4 x 200-m relay (indoor) on 15 Feb 1975.

General records
Fastest speed
An analysis of the times taken by Ben Johnson (Canada) and Carl Lewis (USA) to cover each 10 m of the 100-m final in the 1988 Olympic Games in Seoul on 24 Sept 1988 shows that both reached a peak speed (at 40–50 m and 80–90 m respectively) of 0.83 seconds for 10 m, i.e. 43.37 km/h (26.95 mph). Johnson won the race in a time of 9.79 seconds (with an average speed of 36.77 km/h or 22.85 mph) but was later disqualified.

In the women's 1988 100-m final, Florence Griffith Joyner (USA) was timed at 0.91 seconds for each 10 m between 60 m and 90 m (i.e. 39.56 km/h or 24.58 mph).

Longest winning sequence
Iolanda Balas (Romania) won a record 150 consecutive high-jump events (1956–67).

The record at a track event is 122, at the 400-m hurdles by Edwin Corley Moses (USA) between 1977 and 1987.

Most versatile athletes
Mildred 'Babe' Zaharias (USA) won two Olympic golds (80-m hurdles and javelin) and a silver (high jump) in 1932, and set world records in these events, 1930–32. She was an All-American basketball player for three years and set the world record for throwing the baseball: 90.22 m (296 ft). She also won the US Women's Amateur golf title (1946) and the US Women's Open (1948, 1950, 1954), and excelled in several other sports.

Charles Burgess Fry (GB) equalled the world long-jump record of 7.17 m (23 ft 6½ in) in 1893, represented England in a soccer match against Ireland in 1901 and played first-class rugby for the Barbarians. At cricket he headed the English batting averages for six seasons and captained England in 1912. He was also an excellent angler and tennis player.

Far left
The photo-finish of the men's 100 m at the 1948 Olympic Games shows Harrison Dillard (USA) taking first place in a time of 10.3 seconds, equalling the then Olympic record of Americans Eddie Tolan and Jesse Owens.

Left
Although he had to settle for silver in the 5,000 m at the 1920 Olympic Games, shown here, Finnish athlete Paavo Nurmi (1897–1973), seen on the right, set records for both the most Olympic medals and the most gold medals at one celebration, with five in 1924.

Athletics: world records

Right
Leroy Burrell, the 100-m world record-holder, was also a member of the Santa Monica Track Club relay team— whose colours he sports in this picture—that set the world 4 x 200-m record in 1994.

Far right
Mike Powell set the long-jump world record during an epic contest against Carl Lewis at the 1991 World Championships.

World outdoor records are scheduled by the IAAF. Fully automatic electric timing is mandatory for events up to 400 m.

MEN

RUNNING
100 m: 9.85*
Leroy Russell Burrell (USA)
Lausanne, Switzerland, 6 July 1994
200 m: 19.66
Michael Duane Johnson (USA)
Atlanta, Georgia, USA, 23 June 1996
400 m: 43.29
Harry Lee 'Butch' Reynolds Jr (USA)
Zürich, Switzerland, 17 Aug 1988
800 m: 1:41.73
Sebastian Newbold Coe (GB)
Florence, Italy, 10 June 1981

30,000 m: 1:29:18.8
Toshihiko Seko (Japan)
Christchurch, New Zealand,
22 March 1981
1 hour: 21,101 m
Arturo Barrios (Mexico, now USA)
La Flèche, France, 30 March 1991
110-m hurdles: 12.91
Colin Ray Jackson (GB)
Stuttgart, Germany, 20 Aug 1993
400-m hurdles: 46.78
Kevin Curtis Young (USA)
Barcelona, Spain, 6 Aug 1992
3,000-m steeplechase: 7:59.18
Moses Kiptanui (Kenya)
Zürich, Switzerland, 16 Aug 1995
4 x 100-m: 37.40
USA (Michael Marsh, Leroy Burrell, Dennis A Mitchell, Frederick Carleton 'Carl' Lewis)

having taken drugs for years, invalidating his 9.83 seconds at Rome in 1987.

FIELD EVENTS
High jump: 2.45 m (8 ft ½ in)
Javier Sotomayor (Cuba)
Salamanca, Spain, 27 July 1993
Pole vault (high alt.): 6.14 m (20 ft 1¾ in)
Sergey Nazarovich Bubka (Ukraine)
Sestriere, Italy, 31 July 1994
Pole vault (low alt.): 6.13 m (20 ft 1¼ in)
Sergey Bubka (Ukraine)
Tokyo, Japan, 19 Sept 1992.
Long jump: 8.95 m (29 ft 4½ in)
Michael Anthony 'Mike' Powell (USA)
Tokyo, Japan, 30 Aug 1991
Triple jump: 18.29 m (60 ft ¼ in)
Jonathan David Edwards (GB)
Gothenburg, Sweden, 7 Aug 1995

1,000 m: 2:12.18
Sebastian Coe (GB)
Oslo, Norway, 11 July 1981
1,500 m: 3:27.37
Noureddine Morceli (Algeria)
Nice, France, 12 July 1995
1 mile: 3:44.39
Noureddine Morceli (Algeria)
Rieti, Italy, 5 Sept 1993
2,000 m: 4:47.88
Noureddine Morceli (Algeria)
Paris, France, 3 July 1995
3,000 m: 7:25.11
Noureddine Morceli (Algeria)
Monte Carlo, Monaco, 2 Aug 1994
5,000 m: 12:44.39
Haile Gebrselassie (Ethiopia)
Zürich, Switzerland, 16 Aug 1995
10,000 m: 26:43.53
Haile Gebrselassie (Ethiopia)
Hengelo, Netherlands, 5 June 1995
20,000 m: 56:55.6
Arturo Barrios (Mexico, now USA)
La Flèche, France, 30 March 1991
25,000 m: 1:13:55.8
Toshihiko Seko (Japan)
Christchurch, New Zealand, 22 March 1981

IN 1993 CUBAN ATHLETE JAVIER SOTOMAYOR S

Barcelona, Spain, 8 Aug 1992
and: USA (John A Drummond Jr, Andre Cason, Dennis A Mitchell, Leroy Burrell)
Stuttgart, Germany, 21 Aug 1993
4 x 200-m: 1:18.68
Santa Monica Track Club, USA
(Michael Marsh, Leroy Burrell,
Floyd Wayne Heard, Carl Lewis)
Walnut, California, USA, 17 April 1994
4 x 400-m: 2:54.29
USA (Andrew Valmon, Quincy Watts,
Butch Reynolds, Michael Johnson)
Stuttgart, Germany, 21 Aug 1993
4 x 800-m: 7:03.89
Great Britain (Peter Elliott, Garry Peter Cook, Stephen Cram, Sebastian Coe)
Crystal Palace, London, UK, 30 Aug 1982
4 x 1,500-m: 14:38.8
West Germany (Thomas Wessinghage, Harald Hudak, Michael Lederer, Karl Fleschen)
Cologne, Germany, 17 Aug 1977

* Ben Johnson (Canada) ran 9.78 seconds at Seoul in 1988, but was disqualified after a positive drugs test. He later admitted to

Shot: 23.12 m (75 ft 10¼ in)
Eric Randolph 'Randy' Barnes (USA)
Los Angeles, USA, 20 May 1990
Discus: 74.08 m (243 ft)
Jürgen Schult (GDR)
Neubrandenburg, Germany, 6 June 1986
Hammer: 86.74 m (284 ft 7 in)
Yuriy Georgiyevich Sedykh (USSR, now Russia)
Stuttgart, Germany, 30 Aug 1986
Javelin: 98.48 m (323 ft 1 in)
Jan Zelezny (Czech Republic)
Jena, Germany, 25 May 1996
Decathlon: 8,891 points
Dan Dion O'Brien (USA)
Talence, France, 4–5 Sept 1992:
100-m: 10.43
Long jump: 8.08 m (26 ft 6¼ in)
Shot: 16.69 m (54 ft 9¼ in)
High jump: 2.07 m (6 ft 9½ in)
400 m: 48.51
110-m hurdles: 13.98
Discus: 48.56 m (159 ft 4 in)
Pole vault: 5.00 m (16 ft 4¼ in)
Javelin: 62.58 m (205 ft 4 in)
1,500 m: 4:42.10

WOMEN

RUNNING
100 m: 10.49
Delorez Florence Griffith Joyner (USA)
Indianapolis, Indiana, USA, 16 July 1988
200 m: 21.34
Delorez Florence Griffith Joyner (USA)
Seoul, South Korea, 29 Sept 1988
400 m: 47.60
Marita Koch (GDR)
Canberra, Australia, 6 Oct 1985
800 m: 1:53.28
Jarmila Kratochvílová (Czechoslovakia)
Munich, Germany, 26 July 1983
1,000 m: 2:29.34
Maria Lurdes Mutola (Mozambique)
Brussels, Belgium, 25 Aug 1995
1,500 m: 3:50.46
Qu Yunxia (China)
Beijing, China, 11 Sept 1993
1 mile: 4:15.61
Paula Ivan (Romania)
Nice, France, 10 July 1989

100-m hurdles: 12.21
Yordanka Donkova (Bulgaria)
Stara Zagora, Bulgaria, 20 Aug 1988
400-m hurdles: 52.61
Kim Batten (USA)
Gothenburg, Sweden, 11 Aug 1995
4 x 100-m: 41.37
GDR (Silke Gladisch, Sabine Rieger, Ingrid
Auerswald, Marlies Göhr)
Canberra, Australia, 6 Oct 1985
4 x 200-m: 1:28.15
GDR (Marlies Göhr, Romy
Müller, Bärbel Wöckel,
Marita Koch)
Jena, Germany,
9 Aug 1980

WORLD RECORD FOR THE HIGH JUMP OF 2.45 M, IN SALAMANCA, SPAIN

2,000 m: 5:25.36
Sonia O'Sullivan (Ireland)
Edinburgh, UK, 8 July 1994
3,000 m: 8:06.11
Wang Junxia (China)
Beijing, China, 13 Sept 1993
5,000 m: 14:36.45
Fernanda Ribeiro (Portugal)
Hechtel, Belgium, 22 July 1995
10,000 m: 29:31.78
Wang Junxia (China)
Beijing, China, 8 Sept 1993
20,000 m: 1:06:48.8
Isumi Maki (Japan)
Amagasaki, Japan, 20 Sept 1993
25,000 m: 1:29:29.2
Karolina Szabo (Hungary)
Budapest, Hungary, 23 April 1988
30,000 m: 1:47:05.6
Karolina Szabo (Hungary)
Budapest, Hungary, 23 April 1988
1 hour: 18,084 m
Silvana Cruciata (Italy)
Rome, Italy, 4 May 1981

4 x 400-m: 3:15.17
USSR (Tatyana Ledovskaya, Olga Nazarova,
Maria Pinigina, Olga Bryzgina)
Seoul, South Korea, 1 Oct 1988
4 x 800-m: 7:50.17
USSR (Nadezhda Olizarenko, Lyubov Gurina,
Lyudmila Borisova, Irina Podyalovskaya)
Moscow, USSR, 5 Aug 1984

FIELD EVENTS
High jump: 2.09 m (6 ft 10¼ in)
Stefka Kostadinova (Bulgaria)
Rome, Italy, 30 Aug 1987
Pole vault: 4.45 m (14 ft 7 in)
Emma George (Australia)
Sapporo, Japan, 14 July 1996
Long jump: 7.52 m (24 ft 8¼ in)
Galina Chistyakova (USSR)
Leningrad, USSR, 11 June 1988
Triple jump: 15.50 m (50 ft 10¼ in)
Inessa Kravets (Ukraine)
Gothenburg, Sweden, 10 Aug 1995
Shot: 22.63 m (74 ft 3 in)
Natalya Venedictovna Lisovskaya (USSR)
Moscow, USSR, 7 June 1987

Discus: 76.80 m (252 ft)
Gabriele Reinsch (GDR)
Neubrandenburg, Germany, 9 July 1988
Hammer: 69.44 m (227 ft 10 in)
Olga Kuzenkova (Russia)
Sydney, Australia, 17 Feb 1996
Javelin: 80.00 m (262 ft 5 in)
Petra Felke (GDR)
Potsdam, Germany, 9 Sept 1988
Heptathlon: 7,291 points
Jacqueline Joyner-Kersee (USA)
Seoul, South Korea, 23–24 Sept 1988:
100-m hurdles: 12.69
High jump: 1.86 m (6 ft 1¼ in)
Shot: 15.8 m (51 ft 10 in)
200 m: 22.56
Long jump: 7.27 m (23 ft 10¼ in)
Javelin: 45.66 m (149 ft 10 in)
800 m: 2:08.51

Far left
At one time, Sebastian
Coe held the world
records for 800 m,
1,000 m, 1,500 m,
and the mile. The first
two still stand, 15
years after being set.

Left
Stefka Kostadinova
set the world high-
jump record of 2.09 m
when she won the
1987 world title.

Athletics: British records

FASTEST EVER MILE BY A BRITISH ATHLETE IS 3:46.32, BY STEVE CRAM IN 1985

Right
Steve Smith equalled his own British high-jump record of 2.37 m when winning bronze at the 1993 World Championships. Earlier in the year he had won bronze at the Indoor World Championships, again clearing 2.37 m. His current record, 2.38 m, was set in Feb 1994.

Far right
Kriss Akabusi broke the previous 400-m hurdles record, which had stood for 22 years, by a huge one-fifth of a second in 1990. He improved on the mark a further three times, winning Olympic Bronze on the final occasion.

MEN

RUNNING
100 m: 9.87
Linford Christie
Stuttgart, Germany, 15 Aug 1993
200 m (high altitude): 19.87
John Paul Lyndon Regis
Sestriere, Italy, 31 July 1994
200 m (low altitude): 19.94
John Regis
Stuttgart, Germany, 20 Aug 1993
400 m: 44.37
Roger Anthony Black
Lausanne, Switzerland
3 July 1996
800 m: 1:41.73
Sebastian Newbold Coe
Florence, Italy, 10 June 1981

30,000 m: 1:31:30.4
James Noel Carroll Alder
Crystal Palace, London, UK, 5 Sept 1970
1 hour: 20,855 m
Carl Thackery
La Flèche, France, 31 March 1990
110-m hurdles: 12.91
Colin Ray Jackson
Stuttgart, Germany, 20 Aug 1993
400-m hurdles: 47.82
Kriss Kezie Uche Chukwu Duru Akabusi
Barcelona, Spain, 6 Aug 1992
3,000-m steeplechase: 8:07.96
Mark Robert Rowland
Seoul, South Korea, 30 Sept 1988
4 x 100-m: 37.77
National team (Colin Jackson, Anthony Alexander Jarrett, John Regis, Linford Christie)
Stuttgart, Germany, 22 Aug 1993

High jump (indoors): 2.38 m (7 ft 9¾ in)
Stephen James Smith
Wuppertal, Germany, 4 Feb 1994
Pole vault: 5.71 m (18 ft 8¾ in)
Nick Buckfield
Birmingham, W Midlands, UK
16 June 1996
Long jump: 8.23 m (27 ft)
Lynn Davies
Berne, Switzerland, 30 June 1968
Triple jump: 18.29 m (60 ft ¼ in)
Jonathan David Edwards
Gothenburg, Sweden, 7 Aug 1995
Shot: 21.68 m (71 ft 1½ in)
Geoffrey Lewis Capes
Cwmbran, Gwent, UK, 18 May 1980
Discus: 64.32* m (211 ft)
William Raymond Tancred
Woodford, Essex, UK, 10 Aug 1974

BEST 100 M WAS 9.87 SECONDS, BY LINFORD CHRIST[

1,000 m: 2:12.18
Sebastian Coe
Oslo, Norway, 11 July 1981
1,500 m: 3:29.67
Stephen Cram
Nice, France, 16 July 1985
1 mile: 3:46.32
Stephen Cram
Oslo, Norway, 27 July 1985
2,000 m: 4:51.39
Stephen Cram
Budapest, Hungary, 4 Aug 1985
3,000 m: 7:32.79
David Robert Moorcroft
Crystal Palace, London, UK, 17 July 1982
5,000 m: 13:00.41
David Moorcroft
Oslo, Norway, 7 July 1982
10,000 m: 27:23.06
Eamonn Thomas Martin
Oslo, Norway, 2 July 1988
20,000 m: 57:28.7
Carl Edward Thackery
La Flèche, France, 31 March 1990
25,000 m: 1:15:22.6
Ronald Hill
Bolton, Lancashire, UK, 21 July 1965

4 x 200-m: 1:21.29
National team (Marcus Adam, Adeoye Mafe, Linford Christie, John Regis)
Birmingham, W Midlands, UK, 23 June 1989
4 x 400-m: 2:57.53
National team (Roger Black, Derek Redmond, John Regis, Kriss Akabusi)
Tokyo, Japan, 1 Sept 1991
4 x 800-m: 7:03.89
National team (Peter Elliott, Garry Peter Cook, Stephen Cram, Sebastian Coe)
Crystal Palace, London, UK, 30 Aug 1982
4 x 1,500-m: 14:56.8
National team (Alan David Mottershead, Geoffrey Michael Cooper, Stephen John Emson, Roy Wood)
Bourges, France, 24 June 1979

FIELD EVENTS
High jump: 2.37 m (7 ft 9¼ in)
Stephen James Smith
Seoul, South Korea, 20 Sept 1992
and Stuttgart, Germany, 22 Aug 1993

Hammer: 77.54 m (254 ft 5 in)
Martin Girvan
Wolverhampton, W Midlands, UK, 12 May 1984
Javelin: 91.46 m (300 ft 1 in)
Stephen James Backley
Auckland, New Zealand, 25 Jan 1992
Decathlon: 8,847 points
'Daley' Thompson
Los Angeles, USA, 8–9 Aug 1984:
100 m: 10.44
Long jump: 8.01 m (26 ft 3½ in)
Shot: 15.72 m (51 ft 7 in)
High jump: 2.03 m (6 ft 8 in)
400 m: 46.97
110-m hurdles: 14.33
Discus: 46.56 m (152 ft 9 in)
Pole vault: 5.00 m (16 ft 4¾ in)
Javelin: 65.24 m (214 ft)
1,500 m: 4:35.00

* William Tancred threw 64.94 m (213 ft 1 in) at Loughborough, Leics, UK, on 21 July 1974 and Richard Charles Slaney threw 65.16 m (213 ft 9 in) at Eugene, Oregon, USA, on 1 July 1985, but these were not ratified.

Longest triple jump 18.29 m

4 x 200-m: 1:31.57
National team (Donna-Marie Louise Hartley, Verona Marolin Elder, Sharon Colyear, Sonia Lannaman)
Crystal Palace, London, UK, 20 Aug 1977
4 x 400-m: 3:22.01
National team (Phyllis Smith, Lorraine I Hanson, Linda Keough, Sally Gunnell)
Tokyo, Japan, 1 Sept 1991
4 x 800-m: 8:19.9
National team (Ann Margaret Williams, Paula Tracy Fryer, Yvonne Murray, Diane Delores Edwards)
Sheffield, S Yorkshire, UK, 5 June 1992

FIELD EVENTS
High jump: 1.95 m (6 ft 4¾ in)
Diana Clare Elliot
Oslo, Norway, 26 June 1982
Pole vault: 3.90 m (12 ft 9½ in)
Katherine 'Kate' Staples
Ljubljana, Slovenia, 26 May 1996
Long jump: 6.90 m (22 ft 7¾ in)
Beverly Kinch
Helsinki, Finland, 14 Aug 1983

Far left
At the 1995 World Championships, Jonathan Edwards completed back-to-back world record leaps. In doing so he became the first athlete to legally clear the 18-m and 60-ft triple-jump barriers.

Left
Sally Gunnell has broken the British 400-m hurdles eight times, winning the world title on the last occasion, in a then world record time of 52.74 seconds.

WOMEN

RUNNING
100 m: 11.10
Kathryn Jane Smallwood (later Cook)
Rome, Italy, 5 Sept 1981
200 m: 22.10
Kathryn Cook
Los Angeles, California, USA, 9 Aug 1984
400 m: 49.43
Kathryn Cook
Los Angeles, California, USA, 6 Aug 1984
800 m: 1:57.42
Kirsty Margaret McDermott
Belfast, UK, 24 June 1985
1,000 m: 2:32.82
Kelly Holmes
Sheffield, S Yorkshire, UK, 23 July 1995
1,500 m: 3:59.96
Zola Budd
Brussels, Belgium, 30 Aug 1985
1 mile: 4:17.57
Zola Budd
Zürich, Switzerland, 21 Aug 1985

2,000 m: 5:26.93
Yvonne Carol Grace Murray
Edinburgh, UK, 8 July 1994
3,000 m: 8:28.83
Zola Budd
Rome, Italy, 7 Sept 1985
5,000 m: 14:48.07
Zola Budd
Crystal Palace, London, UK
26 Aug 1985
10,000 m: 30:57.07
Elizabeth McColgan
Hengelo, Netherlands, 25 June 1991
100-m hurdles: 12.82
Sally Jane Janet Gunnell
Zürich, Switzerland, 17 Aug 1988
400-m hurdles: 52.74
Sally Gunnell
Stuttgart, Germany, 19 Aug 1993
4 x 100-m: 42.43
National team (Regina Hunte, Kathryn Smallwood, Beverley Lanita Goddard, Sonia May Lannaman)
Moscow, USSR, 1 Aug 1980

Triple jump: 14.66 m (48 ft 1 in)
Ashia Hansen
Gateshead, Tyne and Wear, UK, 21 Aug 1995
Shot: 19.36 m (63 ft 6¼ in)
Judith Miriam Oakes
Gateshead, Tyne and Wear, UK, 14 Aug 1988
Hammer: 64.90 m (212 ft 11 in)
Lorraine Anne Shaw
Bedford, UK, 10 June 1995
Discus: 67.48 m (221 ft 5 in)
Margaret Elizabeth Ritchie
Walnut, California, USA, 26 April 1981
Javelin: 77.44 m (254 ft 1 in)
Fatima Whitbread
Stuttgart, Germany, 28 Aug 1986
Heptathlon: 6,645 points
Denise Lewis
Götzis, Austria, 25–26 May 1996:
100-m hurdles: 13.18
High jump: 1.84 m (6 ft ¼ in)
Shot: 14.36 m (47 ft 1¼ in)
200 m: 24.06
Long jump: 6.60 m (21 ft 7¾ in)
Javelin: 47.86 m (157 ft)
800 m: 2:16.84

WOMEN'S JAVELIN RECORD IS A THROW OF 77.44 M, BY FATIMA WHITBREAD

Indoor athletics

WORLD INDOOR LONG-JUMP RECORD IS 8.79 M, BY CARL LEWIS IN NEW YORK IN 1984

Right
Frank Fredericks, Namibia's finest athlete, celebrates his world 200-m indoor record at Liévin.

Far right
Colin Jackson, the holder of world records for indoor and outdoor hurdling, is also an accomplished long jumper.

To be eligible for records, indoor track performances around a turn must take place on an athletics track with a circumference of not more than 200 m.

MEN

RUNNING
50 m (high altitude): 5.56*
Donovan Bailey (Canada)
Reno, Nevada, USA, 9 Feb 1996
50 m (low altitude): 5.61
Manfred Kokot (GDR)
Berlin, Germany, 4 Feb 1973
and: James Sanford (USA)
San Diego, California, USA, 20 Feb 1981
60 m: 6.41*
Andre Cason (USA)
Madrid, Spain, 14 Feb 1992

50-m hurdles: 6.25
Mark McKoy (Canada)
Kobe, Japan, 5 March 1986
60-m hurdles: 7.30
Colin Jackson (GB)
Sindelfingen, Germany, 6 March 1994
4 x 200-m: 1:22.11
United Kingdom (Linford Christie, Darren Braithwaite, Ade Mafe, John Regis)
Glasgow, UK
3 March 1991
4 x 400-m: 3:03.05
Germany (Rico Lieder, Jens Carlowitz, Karsten Just, Thomas Schönlebe)
Seville, Spain
10 March 1991
5,000-m walk: 18:07.08
Mikhail Shchennikov (Russia)
Moscow, Russia, 14 Feb 1995

Heptathlon: 6,476 points
Dan Dion O'Brien (USA),
Toronto, Canada, 13–14 March 1993:
60 m: 6.67
long jump: 7.84 m (25 ft 8½ in)
shot: 16.02 m (52 ft 6½ in)
high jump: 2.13 m (6 ft 11¾ in)
60-m hurdles: 7.85
pole vault: 5.20 m (17 ft ¾ in)
1,000 m: 2:57.96

ANDRE CASON COVERED 6C

FASTEST-EVER WOMAN OVER THE INDOOR 5,000 M IS LIZ MCCOLGAN, W

200 m: 19.92
Frank Fredericks (Namibia)
Liévin, France, 18 Feb 1996
400 m: 44.63
Michael Johnson (USA)
Atlanta, Georgia, USA, 4 March 1995
800 m: 1:44.84
Paul Ereng (Kenya)
Budapest, Hungary, 4 March 1989
1,000 m: 2:15.26
Noureddine Morceli (Algeria)
Birmingham, W Midlands, UK, 22 Feb 1992
1,500 m: 3:34.16
Noureddine Morceli (Algeria)
Seville, Spain, 28 Feb 1991
1 mile: 3:49.78
Eamonn Coghlan (Ireland)
East Rutherford, New Jersey, USA
27 Feb 1983
3,000 m: 7:30.72
Haile Gebrselassie (Ethiopia)
Stuttgart, Germany, 4 Feb 1996
5,000 m: 13:10.98
Haile Gebrselassie (Ethiopia)
Sindelfingen, Germany, 27 Jan 1996

* Ben Johnson (Canada) set a world record for 50 m of 5.55 seconds at Ottawa, Canada, on 31 Jan 1987 and a 60-m world record of 6.41 seconds at Indianapolis, USA, on 7 March 1987, but these were invalidated when he admitted to having taken drugs following his disqualification after the 100-m final at the 1988 Olympics.

FIELD EVENTS
High jump: 2.43 m (7 ft 11½ in)
Javier Sotomayor (Cuba)
Budapest, Hungary, 4 March 1989
Pole vault: 6.15 m (20 ft 2¼ in)
Sergey Nazarovich Bubka (Ukraine)
Donetsk, Ukraine, 21 Feb 1993
Long jump: 8.79 m (28 ft 10¼ in)
Frederick Carleton 'Carl' Lewis (USA)
New York, USA, 27 Jan 1984
Triple jump: 17.77 m (58 ft 3½ in)
Leonid Voloshin (Russia)
Grenoble, France, 6 Feb 1994
Shot: 22.66 m (74 ft 4¼ in)
Eric Randolph 'Randy' Barnes (USA)
Los Angeles, California, USA, 20 Jan 1989

WOMEN

RUNNING
50 m: 5.96
Irina Privalova (Russia)
Madrid, Spain, 9 Feb 1995
60 m: 6.92
Irina Privalova (Russia)
Madrid, Spain, 11 Feb 1993 and 9 Feb 1995
200 m: 21.87
Merlene Ottey (Jamaica)
Liévin, France, 13 Feb 1993
400 m: 49.59
Jarmila Kratochvílová (Czechoslovakia)
Milan, Italy, 7 March 1982
800 m: 1:56.40
Christine Wachtel (GDR)
Vienna, Austria, 13 Feb 1988
1,000 m: 2:31.23
Maria Lurdes Mutola (Mozambique)
Stockholm, Sweden, 25 Feb 1996
1,500 m: 4:00.27
Doina Melinte (Romania)
East Rutherford, New Jersey, USA
9 Feb 1990

Fastest 5,000-m walk 18:07.08

A RECORD 6.41 SECONDS

T A WORLD RECORD TIME OF 15:03.17 IN BIRMINGHAM ON 22 FEB 1992

1 mile: 4:17.14
Doina Melinte (Romania)
East Rutherford, New Jersey, USA, 9 Feb 1990
3,000 m: 8:33.82
Elly van Hulst (Netherlands)
Budapest, Hungary, 4 March 1989
5,000 m: 15:03.17
Elizabeth McColgan (GB)
Birmingham, W Midlands, UK, 22 Feb 1992
50-m hurdles: 6.58
Cornelia Oschkenat (GDR)
Berlin, Germany, 20 Feb 1988
60-m hurdles: 7.69*
Lyudmila Narozhilenko (Russia)
Chelyabinsk, Russia, 4 Feb 1993
4 x 200 m: 1:32.55
S. C. Eintracht Hamm, West Germany
(Helga Arendt, Silke-Beate Knoll, Mechthild Kluth, Gisela Kinzel)
Dortmund, Germany, 19 Feb 1988
4 x 400-m: 3:27.22
Germany (Sandra Seuser, Katrin Schreiter,

Annett Hesselbarth, Grit Breuer)
Seville, Spain, 10 March 1991
3,000-m walk: 11:44.00
Alina Ivanova (Ukraine)
Moscow, Russia, 7 Feb 1992

FIELD EVENTS
High jump: 2.07 m (6 ft 9½ in)
Heike Henkel (Germany)
Karlsruhe, Germany, 9 Feb 1992
Pole vault: 4.28 m (14 ft ¼ in)
Sun Caiyun (China)
Tianjin, China, 27 Feb 1996
Long jump: 7.37 m (24 ft 2¼ in)
Heike Drechsler (GDR)
Vienna, Austria, 13 Feb 1988
Triple jump: 15.03 m (49 ft 3½ in)
Iolanda Chen (Russia)
Barcelona, Spain, 11 March 1995
Shot: 22.50 m (73 ft 10 in)
Helena Fibingerová (Czechoslovakia)
Jablonec, Czechoslovakia, 19 Feb 1977

Pentathlon: 4,991 points
Irina Belova (Russia),
Berlin, Germany, 14–15 Feb 1992:
60-m hurdles: 8.22
high jump: 1.93 m (6 ft 3¾ in)
shot: 13.25 m (50 ft 5½ in)
long jump: 6.67 m (21 ft 10½ in)
800 m: 2:10.26

* Narozhilenko recorded a time of 7.63 seconds at Seville, Spain, on 4 Nov 1993, but was disqualified on a positive drugs test.

FASTEST WOMEN'S 400 M IS 49.59 SECONDS, BY JARMILA KRATOCHVILOVA

Long-distance running

Right
The New York Marathon is one of the largest annual marathons, with more than 20,000 finishers. Here the mass of runners cross the Verrazano-Narrows Bridge which links Brooklyn with Staten Island.

Below right
At the end of the 1908 Olympic Games at White City, Italian runner Dorando Pietri was helped over the finish line by Sir Arthur Conan Doyle (the creator of the famous fictional detective Sherlock Holmes) after collapsing five times on the last part lap of the track. Pietri was disqualified, but such was the public sympathy for him that Queen Alexandra presented a special gold cup to him the following day.

Long-distance running

'End to end'

The fastest confirmed run from John O' Groats to Land's End is 10 days 2 hr 25 min, by Richard Brown (GB) in 1995.

The women's record is 13 days 10 hr 1 min, by Sandra Brown from 5 to 18 May 1995.

A relay team of 10 from Vauxhall Motors A. C. covered the distance in 76 hr 58 min 29 sec from 31 May to 3 June 1990.

Longest running race

The 1929 trans-continental race from New York City to Los Angeles, California, USA, covered 5,898 km (3,665 miles). The Finnish-born Johnny Salo was the winner, in a time of 79 days. His elapsed time of 525 hr 57 min 20 sec (giving a mean speed of 11.21 km/h or 6.97 mph) left him only 2 min 47 sec ahead of Englishman Pietro 'Peter' Gavuzzi.

The longest annual race is the New York 1,300 Mile race, held at Ward Island Park, New York, USA, since 1987. The fastest race time is 16 days 14 hr 29 min 19 sec, by Georg Jermolajevs (Latvia) from 11 to 28 Sept 1996.

Longest runs

Robert J. Sweetgall (USA) ran 17,071 km (10,608 miles) around the perimeter of the USA, starting and finishing in Washington DC, from 9 Oct 1982 to 15 July 1983.

In 1983 Ron Grant (Australia) ran around Australia, covering 13,383 km (8,316 miles) in 217 days 3 hr 45 min.

Max Telford (New Zealand) ran 8,224 km (5,110 miles) from Anchorage, Alaska, USA, to Halifax, Nova Scotia, Canada, in 106 days 18 hr 45 min from 25 July to 9 Nov 1977.

Al Howie (GB) ran 7,295.5 km (4,533 miles 352 yd) across Canada, from St Johns to Victoria, in 72 days 10 hr 23 min in 1991.

The fastest time across the USA is 46 days 8 hr 36 min by Frank Giannino Jr (USA), for the 4,989 km (3,100 miles) from San Francisco, California, to New York in 1980.

The women's trans-America record is 69 days 2 hr 40 min, by Mavis Hutchinson (South Africa) from 12 March to 21 May 1978.

Greatest mileage

Douglas Alistair Gordon Pirie (GB), who set a total of five world records in the 1950s, estimated that he had run a total distance of 347,600 km (216,000 miles) in the 40 years to 1981.

Dr Ron Hill (b. 1938), the 1969 European and 1970 Commonwealth marathon champion, has not missed a day's training since 20 Dec 1964. His meticulously compiled training log shows a total of 211,765 km (131,585 miles) from 3 Sept 1956 to 20 May 1996. He has finished 115 marathons, all sub 2:52 (except his last one) and has raced in 57 nations.

Mass relay records

The record for 100 miles (161 km) by 100 runners from one club is 7 hr 53 min 52.1 sec by Baltimore Road Runners Club, Towson, Maryland, USA, on 17 May 1981.

The women's record is 10 hr 15 min 29.5 sec, by the Dolphin South End Runners, Los Altos Hills, California, USA, on 29 July 1995.

The 100 x 100-m record is 19 min 14.19 sec, by a team from Antwerp, Belgium, in 1989.

The longest ever relay was 17,391 km (10,806 miles) on Highway No. 1 around Australia, by 23 runners of the Melbourne Fire Brigade in 50 days 43 min in 1991.

The greatest distance covered in 24 hours by a team of 10 is 487.343 km (302.281 miles), by Puma Tyneside RC at Monkton Stadium, Jarrow, UK, from 10 to 11 Sept 1994.

Consecutive hours

Every hour for 1,000 consecutive hours Craig Rowe (Australia) ran 3.307 km within a hour, at Manly Beach, Australia, in 1993.

Marathon

Oldest

The Boston marathon, the oldest major marathon, was first held in 1897, when it was run over 39 km (24 miles 1,232 yd).

Longest ever race 5,898 km

Fastest
It should be noted that courses may vary in severity. The following are the best times on courses with verified distances.

The men's world record is 2 hr 6 min 50 sec, by Belayneh Dinsamo (Ethiopia) at Rotterdam, Netherlands, on 17 April 1988.

The women's world record is 2 hr 21 min 6 sec, by Ingrid Kristiansen (Norway) at London, UK, on 21 April 1985.

The British men's record is 2 hr 7 min 13 sec, by Stephen Henry Jones at Chicago, Illinois, USA, on 20 Oct 1985.

The British women's record is 2 hr 25 min 56 sec, by Véronique Marot at London, UK, on 23 April 1989.

Most competitors
The most confirmed finishers in a marathon is 38,706, at Boston on 15 April 1996.

Most marathons run
Horst Preisler (Germany) ran 631 marathons between 1974 and 29 May 1996.

Henri Girault (France) ran 330 races at 100 km from 1979 to July 1995 and competed on every continent but Antarctica.

John A. Kelley (USA) finished the Boston Marathon 61 times between 1928 and 1992. He won in 1933 and 1945.

Oldest finishers
The oldest man was Dimitrion Yordanidis (Greece), who ran in Athens, Greece, on 10 Oct 1976, aged 98, finishing in 7 hr 33 min.

The oldest woman was Thelma Pitt-Turner, who ran the 1985 Hastings (New Zealand) marathon in 7 hr 58 min at the age of 82.

Half marathon
The world record time for a half marathon on a properly measured course is 58 min 31 sec, by Paul Tergat (Kenya) at Milan, Italy, on 30 March 1996.

The best British time is 60 min 59 sec, by Steve Jones from Newcastle to South Shields, Tyneside, UK, on 8 June 1986.

Paul Evans ran a half marathon in a time of 60 min 9 sec at Marrakech, Morocco, on 15 Jan 1995, and Ingrid Kristiansen (Norway) ran a half marathon in a time of 66 min 40 sec at Sandnes, Norway, on 5 April 1987, but there is uncertainty over the measurement of both courses.

Liz McColgan ran a half marathon in 67 min 11 sec at Tokyo, Japan, on 26 Jan 1992, but the course was 33 m downhill—slightly more than the allowable 1 in 1,000 drop. She also ran a British best time of 68 min 42 sec at Dundee, UK, on 11 Oct 1992.

Backwards running
Timothy 'Bud' Badyna (USA) ran the fastest backwards marathon in 3 hr 53 min 17 sec at Toledo, Ohio, USA, on 24 April 1994. He also ran 10 km in 45 min 37 sec at Toledo on 13 July 1991.

Donald Davis (USA) ran 1 mile (1.6 km) in a time of 6 min 7.1 sec at the University of Hawaii on 21 Feb 1983.

Ferdie Ato Adoboe (Ghana) ran 100 yd in 12.7 sec (100 m in 13.6 seconds) at Smith College, Northampton, Massachusetts, USA, on 25 July 1991.

Arvind Pandya (India) ran backwards across America, from Los Angeles, California, to New York, in a time of 107 days from 18 Aug to 3 Dec 1984. He also ran backwards from John O' Groats to Land's End (1,512 km or 940 miles) in 26 days 7 hr from 6 April to 2 May 1990.

OK 10 DAYS 2 HR 25 MIN

ULTRA LONG-DISTANCE WORLD RECORDS (TRACK)
MEN
50 km: 2:48:06
Jeff Norman (GB)
Timperley, Manchester, UK, 7 June 1980
50 miles: 4:51:49
Don Ritchie (GB)
Hendon, London, UK, 12 March 1983
100 km: 6:10:20
Don Ritchie (GB)
Crystal Palace, London, UK, 28 Oct 1978
100 miles: 11:30:51
Don Ritchie (GB)
Crystal Palace, London, UK, 15 Oct 1977
200 km: 15:11:10*
Yiannis Kouros (Greece)
Montauban, France, 15–16 March 1985
200 miles: 27:48:35
Yiannis Kouros (Greece)
Montauban, France, 15–16 March 1985
500 km: 60:23:00
Yiannis Kouros (Greece)
Colac, Australia, 26–29 Nov 1984
500 miles: 105:42:09
Yiannis Kouros (Greece)
Colac, Australia, 26–30 Nov 1984
1,000 km: 136:17:00
Yiannis Kouros (Greece)
Colac, Australia, 26 Nov–1 Dec 1984
24 hours 293.704 km
Yiannis Kouros (Australia)
Coburg, Australia, 13–14 April 1996
48 hours: 473.496 km
Yiannis Kouros (Australia)
Surgères, France, 3–5 May 1996
Six days: 1,022.068 km
Yiannis Kouros (Greece)
New York, USA, 2–8 July 1984
Six days (indoors): 1,030 km
Jean-Gilles Bossiquet (France)
La Rochelle, France, 16–23 Nov 1992

WOMEN
50 km: 3:18:52
Carolyn Hunter-Rowe (GB)
Barry, Vale of Glamorgan, UK, 3 March 1996
50 miles: 6:07:58
Linda Meadows (Australia)
Burwood, Australia, 18 June 1994
100 km: 7:50:09
Ann Trason (USA)
Hayward, California, USA, 3–4 Aug 1991
100 miles: 14:29:44
Ann Trason (USA)
Santa Rosa, California, USA, 18–19 March 1989
200 km: 19:28:48*
Eleanor Adams (GB)
Melbourne, Australia, 19–20 Aug 1989
200 miles: 39:09:03
Hilary Walker (GB)
Blackpool, Lancashire, UK, 5–6 Nov 1988
500 km: 77:53:46
Eleanor Adams (GB)
Colac, Australia, 13–15 Nov 1989
500 miles: 130:59:58
Sandra Barwick (New Zealand)
Campbelltown, Australia, 18–23 Nov 1990
One hour: 18.084 km
Silvana Cruciata (Italy)
Rome, Italy, 4 May 1981
24 hours: 240.169 km
Eleanor Adams (GB)
Melbourne, Australia, 19–20 Aug 1989
48 hours: 366.512 km
Hilary Walker (GB)
Blackpool, Lancashire, UK, 5–7 Nov 1988
Six days: 883.631 km
Sandra Barwick (New Zealand)
Campbelltown, Australia, 18–24 Nov 1990

* No stopped time known.

Walking and cross country

Right
Runners put their fitness to the test in the Lake District, UK, during the fell-running World Cup in 1988. The inaugural international Cross-Country Championships took place at the Hamilton Park Racecourse, UK, on 28 March 1903. Since 1973, the events have been official World Championships under the auspices of the International Amateur Athletic Federation.

Below far right
Andrey Perlov, the holder of the 30-km and 50-km road-walking world records, is also the current Olympic 50-km road-walking champion.

Best backwards walk 12,875 km

Walking
Most Olympic medals
The only walker to have won three gold medals in the Olympics is Ugo Frigerio (Italy), with the 3,000 m in 1920 and the 10,000 m in 1920 and 1924.

Ugo Frigerio's bronze medal in the 50,000 m in 1932 brought his total number of Olympic medals to a record four. He shares this record with Vladimir Stepanovich Golubnichiy (USSR), who won gold medals in 1960 and 1968, a silver medal in 1972 and a bronze in 1964, all for the 20 km.

The record for the most gold medals won in the Olympic Games by a British walker is two, by George Edward Larner for the 3,500 m and the 10 miles in 1908.

The greatest number of Olympic medals won by a British walker is three, by Ernest James, who was twice 'walker up' to Larner and finished second in the 10,000 m in 1912.

Most titles
Four-time Olympian Ronald Owen Laird of the New York AC won a total of 65 US national titles between 1958 and 1976, plus four Canadian Championships.

The record for the greatest number of British national titles to have been won by a British

walker is 27, by Vincent Paul Nihill between 1963 and 1975.

'End to end'
The fastest ever walk over the 1,426.4 km (886 miles 525 yd) of the British mainland from Land's End to John O' Groats took a time of 12 days 3 hr 45 min, by WO2 Malcolm Barnish of the 19th Regiment, Royal Artillery, from 9 to 21 June 1986.

The fastest ever time by a woman walker from Land's End to John O' Groats is 13 days 17 hr 42 min, by Ann Sayer from 20 Sept to 3 Oct 1980.

The Irish 'end to end' record over the 644 km (400 miles 350 yd) from Malin Head, Donegal, to Mizen Head, Cork, is 5 days 22 hr 30 min, by John 'Paddy' Dowling between 18 and 24 March 1982.

Greatest distance in 24 hours
The greatest distance walked in 24 hours is 228.93 km (142 miles 440 yd), by Jesse Castenda (USA) at Albuquerque, New Mexico, USA, from 18 to 19 Sept 1976.

The greatest distance ever covered by a woman walker in 24 hours is 211.25 km

(131 miles 465 yd), by Annie van der Meer-Timmermann (Netherlands) at Rouen, France, from 10 April to 11 May 1986.

Backwards walking
Plennie L. Wingo, then of Abilene, Texas, USA, completed his record-breaking 12,875-km (8,000-mile) trans-continental walk from Santa Monica, California, USA, to Istanbul, Turkey, from 15 April 1931 to 24 Oct 1932.

The greatest distance that is known to have been covered in a time of 24 hours by a walker moving backwards is 153.52 km (95 miles 704 yd), by Anthony Thornton (USA) in Minneapolis, Minnesota, USA, from 31 Dec 1988 to 1 Jan 1989.

Cross-country running
World Championships
The greatest ever margin of victory in a World Championship race is 56 seconds or 356 m (390 yd), by John 'Jack' Thomas Holden (England) at Ayr Racecourse, S Ayrshire, UK, on 24 March 1934.

The record for the most team victories is held by England, with 45 for men, 11 for junior men and seven for women.

The USA and USSR each has a record eight women's team victories.

The greatest number of men's individual victories is five, by John Ngugi (Kenya) from 1986 to 1989 and in 1992.

The women's race has been won a record five times by Doris Brown-Heritage (USA) from 1967 to 1971, and by Grete Waitz (Norway) from 1978 to 1981 and in 1983.

Marcel van de Wattyne (Belgium) ran in a record 20 races, from 1946 to 1965.

The women's record for the greatest number of appearances is 16, by Jean Lochhead (Wales), 1967–79, 1981 and 1983–84.

English Championship
The most individual titles won is four, by Percy Haines Stenning (Thames Hare and Hounds), 1877–80, and Alfred E. Shrubb (South London Harriers), 1901–04.

The most successful club in the team race has been Birchfield Harriers from Birmingham, UK, with a total of 28 wins and one tie from 1880 to 1988.

The greatest number of individual wins in the English women's championships is six, by Lillian Styles, 1928–30, 1933–34 and 1937.

The most successful team is Birchfield Harriers, with a record total of 13 titles.

OK 12 DAYS 3 HR 45 MIN

Largest field
The largest recorded field in any cross-country race in the world was 11,763 starters (10,810 of whom finished) in the 30-km (18-mile 1,125-yd) Lidingöloppet race near Stockholm, Sweden, on 3 Oct 1982.

Orienteering
Most titles
The men's world relay title has been won a record seven times by Norway, in 1970, 1978, 1981, 1983, 1985, 1987 and 1989.

Sweden have won the women's world relay title a record-breaking 10 times, in 1966, 1970, 1974, 1976, 1981, 1983, 1985, 1989, 1991 and 1993.

The record for the greatest number of women's world orienteering titles won is three, by Annichen Kringstad (Sweden), in 1981, 1983 and 1985.

The greatest number of men's world titles won by one person is two by Åge Hadler (Norway), in 1966 and 1972, Egil Johansen (Norway), in 1976 and 1978, and Øyvin Thon (Norway), in 1979 and 1981.

Sweden have won the men's skiing relay title a record five times, in 1977, 1980, 1982, 1984 and 1990.

Finland have won the women's skiing relay a record five times, in 1975, 1977, 1980, 1988 and 1990.

The record for the greatest number of individual skiing titles won is four, by Ragnhild Bratberg (Norway), with victories in the Classic in 1986 and 1990 and the Sprint in 1988 and 1990.

The men's record for the most individual skiing titles is three, by Anssi Juutilainen (Finland), who won the Classic in 1984 and 1988 and the Sprint in 1992.

Carol McNeill won the women's British title a record six times, in 1967 and 1969 and from 1972 to 1976.

Geoffrey Peck won the men's British individual title a record five times (1971, 1973, 1976–77 and 1979).

Terry Dooris of Southern Navigators has competed in all 30 British individual championships, from 1967 to 1996.

Most competitors
The record for the greatest number of competitors at an orienteering event in one day is 38,000, for the Ruf des Herbstes held at Sibiu, Romania, in 1982.

The largest event is the five-day O-Ringen at Småland, Sweden, which attracted a total of 120,000 competitors in July 1983.

TRACK-WALKING WORLD RECORDS
The International Amateur Athletic Federation recognises men's records at 20 km, 30 km, 50 km and two hours, and women's at 5 km and 10 km.

MEN
10 km: 38:02.60
Jozef Pribilinec (Czechoslovakia)
Banská Bystrica, Czechoslovakia, 30 Aug 1985
20 km: 1:17:25.6
Bernardo Segura (Mexico)
Fana, Norway, 7 May 1994
30 km: 2:01:44.1
Maurizio Damilano (Italy)
Cuneo, Italy, 4 Oct 1992
50 km: 3:41:28.2
René Piller (France)
Fana, Norway, 7 May 1994
One hour: 15,577 m
Bernardo Segura (Mexico)
Fana, Norway, 7 May 1994
Two hours: 29,572 m
Maurizio Damilano (Italy)
Cuneo, Italy, 4 Oct 1992

WOMEN
3 km: 11:48.24
Ileana Salvador (Italy)
Padua, Italy, 19 Aug 1993
5 km: 20:07.52 (unratified)
Beate Anders (GDR)
Rostock, Germany, 23 June 1990
10 km: 41:56.23
Nadezhda Ryashkina (USSR)
Seattle, Washington, USA, 24 July 1990

WALKING
It should be noted that severity of road race courses and the accuracy of their measurement may vary. This sometimes makes comparisons of times unreliable.

WORLD BESTS
MEN
30 km: 2:02:41
Andrey Perlov (USSR)
Sochi, USSR, 19 Feb 1989
50 km: 3:37:41
Andrey Perlov (USSR)
Leningrad, USSR, 5 Aug 1989

WOMEN
10 km: 41:04
Yelena Nikolayeva (Russia)
Sochi, Russia, 20 April 1996
20 km: 1:27:30
Liu Hongyu (China)
Beijing, China, 1 May 1995
50 km: 4:41:57
Kora Boufflert (France)
Ay-Champagne, France, 17 Sept 1995

BRITISH BESTS
MEN
20 km: 1:22:03
Ian Peter McCombie
Seoul, South Korea, 23 Sept 1988
30 km: 2:07:56
Ian Peter McCombie
Edinburgh, UK, 27 April 1986
50 km: 3:51:37
Christopher Lloyd Maddocks
Burrator, Devon, UK, 28 Oct 1990

WOMEN
10 km: 45:28
Victoria Anne Lupton
Livorno, Italy, 10 July 1993
20 km: 1:40:45
Irene Bateman
Basildon, Essex, UK, 9 April 1983

Weightlifting

MOST WORLD TITLE WINS IS NINE, BY NAIM SULEYMANOGLU

Right
In international weightlifting competitions, results are determined on the aggregate weight of two lifts—the snatch and the jerk. In the former, the bar and weights are raised from the ground to above the head in a single movement, and the arms must be locked for a successful lift. In the latter, two movements are involved. The Fédération Internationaliste Haltérophile et Culturiste, now the International Weightlifting Federation, was established in 1905.

Weightlifting

Most titles and medals

The weightlifter to have won the most world titles, including Olympic Games, is Naim Suleymanoğlü of Turkey (previously Neum Shalamanov of Bulgaria), who claimed nine, 1985–86, 1988–89 and 1991–95.

Norbert Schemansky (USA) won a record four Olympic medals (1952 middle-heavyweight gold, 1948 heavyweight silver, and 1960 and 1964 heavyweight bronze).

Heaviest lifts to bodyweight

The first man to clean and jerk more than three times his bodyweight was Stefan Topurov (Bulgaria) on 24 Oct 1983, when he lifted 180 kg (396¾ lb) at Moscow, USSR.

The first to snatch 2½ times his bodyweight was Naim Suleymanoğlü, who lifted 150 kg (330½ lb) at Cardiff, UK, on 27 April 1988.

The first woman to clean and jerk more than twice her own bodyweight was Cheng Jinling (China), who lifted 90 kg (198 lb) in the 44-kg class of the 1988 World Championships.

FIRST MAN TO CLEAN AND JERK MORE THAN THREE TIMES HIS OWN BODYWEIGHT W

Best team deadlift 3,041,450 kg

WORLD WEIGHTLIFTING RECORDS
From 1 Jan 1993, the International Weightlifting Federation (IWF) introduced modified weight categories, making the existing records redundant. This is the current list for the new weight categories.

Bodyweight 54 kg (119 lb)
Snatch: 130.5 kg (287½ lb) by Halil Mutlu (Turkey)
Warsaw, Poland, 3 May 1995
Jerk: 160 kg (352¾ lb) by Halil Mutlu (Turkey)
Istanbul, Turkey, 18 Nov 1994
Total: 290 kg (639¼ lb) by Halil Mutlu (Turkey)
Istanbul, Turkey, 18 Nov 1994

Bodyweight 59 kg (130 lb)
Snatch: 140 kg (308½ lb) by Hafiz Suleymanoğlü (Turkey)
Warsaw, Poland, 3 May 1995
Jerk: 170 kg (374¼ lb) by Nikolai Pershalov (Bulgaria)
Warsaw, Poland, 3 May 1995
Total: 305 kg (672¼ lb) by Nikolai Pershalov (Bulgaria)
Melbourne, Australia, 13 Nov 1993

Bodyweight 64 kg (141 lb)
Snatch: 148.5 kg (327¼ lb) by Wang Guohua (China)
Yachiyo, Japan, 5 April 1996
Jerk: 183 kg (403¼ lb) by Valerios Leonidis (Greece)
Warsaw, Poland, 4 May 1995
Total: 330 kg (727½ lb) by Naim Suleymanoğlü (Turkey)*
Istanbul, Turkey, 20 Nov 1994
*Formerly Naim Suleimanov or Neum Shalamanov of Bulgaria

Bodyweight 70 kg (154¼ lb)
Snatch: 161 kg (354¾ lb) by Kim Myong-nam (North Korea)
Yachiyo, Japan, 6 April 1996
Jerk: 193.5 kg (426½ lb) by Kim Myong-nam (North Korea)
Yachiyo, Japan, 6 April 1996
Total: 352.5 kg (777 lb) by Kim Myong-nam (North Korea)
Yachiyo, Japan, 6 April 1996

Bodyweight 76 kg (167½ lb)
Snatch: 170 kg (374¾ lb) by Ruslan Savchenko (Ukraine)
Melbourne, Australia, 16 Nov 1993
Jerk: 208 kg (458½ lb) by Pablo Lara (Cuba)
Szekszárd, Hungary, 20 April 1996
Total: 372.5 kg (821 lb) by Pablo Lara (Cuba)
Szekszárd, Hungary, 20 April 1996

Bodyweight 83 kg (183 lb)
Snatch: 177.5 kg (391¼ lb), by Pyrros Dimas (Greece)
Warsaw, Poland, 5 May 1995
Jerk: 212.5 kg (468¼ lb) by Pyrros Dimas (Greece)
Guangzhou, China, 22 Nov 1995
Total: 387.5 kg (854¼ lb) by Pyrros Dimas (Greece)
Warsaw, Poland, 5 May 1995

Bodyweight 91 kg (200½ lb)
Snatch: 186 kg (410 lb) by Aleksey Petrov (Russia)
Istanbul, Turkey, 24 Nov 1994
Jerk: 228.5 kg (503¾ lb) by Kakhi Kakhiasvilis (Greece)
Warsaw, Poland, 6 May 1995
Total: 412.5 kg (909 lb) by Aleksey Petrov (Russia)
Sokolov, Czech Republic, 7 May 1994

Bodyweight 99 kg (218½ lb)
Snatch: 192.5 kg (424¼ lb) by Sergey Syrtsov (Russia)
Istanbul, Turkey, 25 Nov 1994
Jerk: 228 kg (502½ lb) by Anatoliy Khrapaty (Kazakhstan)
Yachiyo, Japan, 8 April 1996
Total: 417.5 kg (920¼ lb) by Sergey Syrtsov (Russia)
Istanbul, Turkey, 25 Nov 1994

Bodyweight 108 kg (238 lb)
Snatch: 200 kg (441 lb) by Timur Taimazov (Ukraine)
Istanbul, Turkey, 26 Nov 1994
Jerk: 235.5 kg (519 lb) by Timur Taimazov (Ukraine)
Sokolov, Czech Republic, 8 May 1994
Total: 435 kg (959 lb) by Timur Taimazov (Ukraine)
Istanbul, Turkey, 26 Nov 1994

Bodyweight over 108 kg (238 lb)
Snatch: 205 kg (452 lb) by Aleksandr Kurlovich (Belarus)
Istanbul, Turkey, 27 Nov 1994
Jerk: 253.5 kg (558¾ lb) by Andrey Chemerkin (Russia)
Warsaw, Poland, 7 May 1995
Total: 457.5 kg (1,008½ lb) by Aleksandr Kurlovich (Belarus)
Istanbul, Turkey, 27 Nov 1994

WOMEN'S WEIGHTLIFTING RECORDS

Bodyweight 46 kg (101¼ lb)
Snatch: 81 kg (178½ lb) by Guang Hong (China)
Guangzhou, China, 17 Nov 1995
Jerk: 105 kg (231½ lb) by Guang Hong (China)
Yachiyo, Japan, 4 April 1996
Total: 185 kg (407¾ lb) by Guang Hong (China)
Yachiyo, Japan, 4 April 1996

Bodyweight 50 kg (110¼ lb)
Snatch: 88 kg (194 lb) by Jiang Baoyu (China)
Pusan, South Korea, 3 July 1995
Jerk: 110.5 kg (243½ lb) by Liu Xiuhia (China)
Hiroshima, Japan, 3 Oct 1994
Total: 197.5 kg (435¼ lb) by Liu Xiuhia (China)
Hiroshima, Japan, 3 Oct 1994

Bodyweight 54 kg (119 lb)
Snatch: 92.5 kg (204 lb) by Zhang Juhua (China)
Hiroshima, Japan, 3 Oct 1994
Jerk: 113.5 kg (250 lb) by Zhang Xixiang (China)
Yachiyo, Japan, 5 April 1996
Total: 202.5 kg (446¼ lb) by Zhang Juhua (China)
Hiroshima, Japan, 3 Oct 1994

Bodyweight 59 kg (130 lb)
Snatch: 99 kg (218¼ lb) by Chen Xiaomin (China)
Warsaw, Poland, 6 May 1996
Jerk: 124 kg (273¼ lb) by Xiu Xiongying (China)
Warsaw, Poland, 6 May 1996
Total: 220 kg (485 lb) by Chen Xiaomin (China)
Hiroshima, Japan, 4 Oct 1994

Bodyweight 64 kg (141 lb)
Snatch: 106 kg (233½ lb) by Li Hongyun (China)
Warsaw, Poland, 7 May 1996
Jerk: 130 kg (286½ lb) by Li Hongyun (China)
Istanbul, Turkey, 22 Nov 1994
Total: 235 kg (518lb) by Li Hongyun (China)
Istanbul, Turkey, 22 Nov 1994

Bodyweight 70 kg (154¼ lb)
Snatch: 102.5 kg (226 lb) by Tang Weifang (China)
Hiroshima, Japan, 4 Oct 1994
Jerk: 129 kg (284¼ lb) by Tang Weifang (China)
Guangzhou, China, 22 Nov 1995
Total: 230 kg (507 lb) by Tang Weifang (China)
Hiroshima, Japan, 4 Oct 1994

Bodyweight 76 kg (167¼ lb)
Snatch: 106 kg (233½ lb) by Dai Yanan (China)
Warsaw, Poland, 10 May 1996
Jerk: 140 kg (308½ lb) by Zhang Guimei (China)
Shilong, China, 18 Dec 1993
Total: 235 kg (518 lb) by Zhang Guimei (China)
Shilong, China, 18 Dec 1993

Bodyweight 83 kg (183 lb)
Snatch: 110 kg (242½ lb) by Wei Xiangying (China)
Warsaw, Poland, 11 May 1996
Jerk: 135 kg (297½ lb) by Chen Shu-Chih (Taiwan)
Guangzhou, China, 24 Nov 1995
Total: 242.5 kg (534½ lb) by Wei Xiangying (China)
Warsaw, Poland, 11 May 1996

Bodyweight over 83 kg (183 lb)
Snatch: 108.5 kg (239 lb) by Wang Yanmei (China)
Warsaw, Poland, 12 May 1996
Jerk: 155 kg (341½ lb) by Li Yajuan (China)
Melbourne, Australia, 20 Nov 1993
Total: 260 kg (573 lb) by Li Yajuan (China)
Melbourne, Australia, 20 Nov 1993

Women's World Championships

The most gold medals won at the Women's World Championships is 12, by Peng Liping (China) in the 52-kg class (1988–89 and 1991–92), and Milena Trendafilova (Bulgaria) in the 67.5-kg/70-kg/75-kg class (1989–93).

Powerlifting
Most titles

The greatest number of powerlifting world titles won by an individual is 17, by Hideaki Inaba (Japan) at 52 kg, from 1974 to 1983, and from 1985 to 1991.

The most women's world titles is six, by Beverley Francis (Australia) at 75 kg (1980 and 1982) and 82.5 kg (1981 and 1983–85); and by Sisi Dolman (Netherlands) at 52 kg (1985–86 and 1988–91).

The most world titles by a British lifter is seven, by Ron Collins at 75 kg (1972–74), and at 82 kg (1975–77 and 1979).

British lifter Edward John Pengelly won a record 14 consecutive national titles, at 60 kg (1976–79) and 67.5 kg (1980–89). He also won four world titles, at 60 kg (1976–77 and 1979) and 67.5 kg (1985), and a record 10 European titles, at 60 kg (1978–79) and 67.5 kg (1981 and 1983–89).

Powerlifting feats

Lamar Gant (USA) was the first man to deadlift five times his own bodyweight, lifting 299.5 kg (661 lb) in 1985.

Cammie Lynn Lusko (USA) was the first woman to lift more than her bodyweight with one arm, with 59.5 kg (131 lb) at Milwaukee, Wisconsin, USA, on 21 May 1983.

Cathy Millen (New Zealand) holds eight world records in two bodyweight categories, as well as 16 British Commonwealth and 20 New Zealand records in five categories. She has also won five World Championship titles and her 1994 total (682.5 kg or 1,505 lb) is the highest ever by a woman.

Timed lifts

A 24-hour deadlifting record of 3,041,450 kg (6,705,241 lb) was set by a team of 10 at the Forum Health Club, Birmingham, UK, on 30 and 31 March 1996.

The 24-hour deadlift record by an individual is 371,094 kg (818,121 lb), by Anthony Wright at HM Prison Featherstone, Wolverhampton, W Midlands, UK, from 31 Aug to 1 Sept 1990.

A nine-man team from the Forum Health Club, Chelmsleywood, W Midlands, UK, set a 24-hour bench press record of 4,025,120 kg (8,873,860 lb) from 19 to 20 March 1994. An individual 12-hour record of 535,835 kg (1,181,312 lb) was set by Chris Lawton at the Waterside Wine Bar, Solihull, W Midlands, UK, on 3 June 1994.

A 10-man team from St Albans Weightlifting Club and Ware Boys Club, Herts, UK, set a squat record of 2,168,625 kg (4,780,994 lb) from 20 to 21 July 1986.

A record of 137,531 arm-curling repetitions using three 22-kg (48½-lb) weightlifting bars and dumb-bells was set by a team of nine from Pontefract Squash Club, W Yorkshire, UK, from 15 to 16 April 1995.

E BULGARIAN STEFAN TOPUROV, WHO LIFTED 180 KG IN MOSCOW IN OCT 1983

WORLD POWERLIFTING RECORDS
(All weights in kilograms)

MEN

52 kg
Squat: 270.5, Andrzej Stanaszek (Poland), 1995
Bench press: 177.5, Andrzej Stanaszek, 1994
Deadlift: 256, E. S. Bhaskaran (India), 1993
Total: 590, Andrzej Stanaszek (Poland), 1995

56 kg
Squat: 277.5, Magnus Karlsson (Sweden), 1995
Bench press: 175.5, Magnus Karlsson, 1995
Deadlift: 289.5, Lamar Gant (USA), 1982
Total: 625, Lamar Gant, 1982

60 kg
Squat: 295.5, Magnus Karlsson, 1994
Bench press: 180.5, Magnus Karlsson, 1993
Deadlift: 310, Lamar Gant, 1988
Total: 707.5, Joe Bradley (USA), 1982

67.5 kg
Squat: 300, Jessie Jackson (USA), 1987
Bench press: 200, Kristoffer Hulecki (Sweden), 1985
Deadlift: 316, Daniel Austin (USA), 1991
Total: 765, Aleksy Sivokon (Kazakhstan), 1995

75 kg
Squat: 328, Ausby Alexander (USA), 1989
Bench press: 217.5, James Rouse (USA), 1980
Deadlift: 337.5, Daniel Austin (USA), 1994
Total: 850, Rick Gaugler (USA), 1982

82.5 kg
Squat: 379.5, Mike Bridges (USA), 1982
Bench press: 240, Mike Bridges, 1981
Deadlift: 357.5, Veli Kumpuniemi (Finland), 1980
Total: 952.5, Mike Bridges, 1982

90 kg
Squat: 375, Fred Hatfield (USA), 1980
Bench press: 255, Mike MacDonald (USA), 1980
Deadlift: 372.5, Walter Thomas (USA), 1982
Total: 937.5, Mike Bridges, 1980

100 kg
Squat: 423, Ed Coan (USA), 1994
Bench press: 261.5, Mike MacDonald (USA), 1977
Deadlift: 390, Ed Coan, 1993
Total: 1,035, Ed Coan, 1994

110 kg
Squat: 415, Kirk Karwoski (USA), 1994
Bench press: 270, Jeffrey Magruder (USA), 1982
Deadlift: 395, John Kuc (USA), 1980
Total: 1,000, John Kuc, 1980

125 kg
Squat: 455, Kirk Karwoski, 1995
Bench press: 278.5, Tom Hardman (USA), 1982
Deadlift: 387.5, Lars Norén (Sweden), 1987
Total: 1,045, Kirk Karwoski, 1995

125+ kg
Squat: 447.5, Shane Hamman (USA), 1994
Bench press: 310, Antony Clark (USA), 1994
Deadlift: 406, Lars Norén, 1988
Total: 1,100, Bill Kazmaier (USA), 1981

WOMEN

44 kg
Squat: 156, Raija Koskinen (Finland), 1995
Bench press: 82.5, Irina Krylova (Russia), 1993
Deadlift: 165, Nancy Belliveau (USA), 1985
Total: 372.5, Svetlana Tesleva (Russia), 1995

48 kg
Squat: 167.5, Raija Koskinen, 1995
Bench press: 96, Irina Krylova, 1995
Deadlift: 182.5, Majik Jones (USA), 1984
Total: 402.5, Yelena Yamkich (Russia), 1995

52 kg
Squat: 175.5, Mary Jeffrey (USA), 1991
Bench press: 105, Mary Jeffrey, 1991
Deadlift: 197.5, Diana Rowell (USA), 1984
Total: 452.5, Mary Jeffrey, 1991

56 kg
Squat: 191.5, Carrie Boudreau (USA), 1989
Bench press: 115, Mary Jeffrey, 1988
Deadlift: 222.5, Carrie Boudreau, 1995
Total: 522.5, Carrie Boudreau, 1995

60 kg
Squat: 210, Beate Amdahl (Norway), 1993
Bench press: 115.5, Eriko Himeno (Japan), 1995
Deadlift: 213, Ruthi Shafer (USA), 1983
Total: 502.5, Vicki Steenrod (USA), 1985

67.5 kg
Squat: 230, Ruthi Shafer, 1984
Bench press: 120, Vicki Steenrod, 1990
Deadlift: 244, Ruthi Shafer, 1984
Total: 565, Ruthi Shafer, 1984

75 kg
Squat: 240.5, Yelena Sukhoruk (Ukraine), 1995
Bench press: 143, Tammy Diande (USA), 1994
Deadlift: 252.5, Yelena Sukhoruk, 1995
Total: 605, Yelena Sukhoruk, 1995

82.5 kg
Squat: 240, Cathy Millen (New Zealand), 1991
Bench press: 150.5, Cathy Millen, 1993
Deadlift: 257.5, Cathy Millen, 1993
Total: 637.5, Cathy Millen, 1993

90 kg
Squat: 260, Cathy Millen, 1994
Bench press: 160, Cathy Millen, 1994
Deadlift: 260, Cathy Millen, 1994
Total: 682.5, Cathy Millen, 1994

90+ kg
Squat: 277.5, Juanita Trujillo (USA), 1993
Bench press: 157.5, Ulrike Herchenhein (Germany), 1994
Deadlift: 240, Ulrike Herchenhein, 1994
Total: 640, Juanita Trujillo, 1994

BRITISH POWERLIFTING RECORDS
(All weights in kilograms)

MEN

52 kg
Squat: 223.5, Peter Kemp, 1995
Bench press: 130, Phil Stringer, 1981
Deadlift: 225, John Maxwell, 1988
Total: 530, Phil Stringer, 1982

56 kg
Squat: 235, Phil Stringer, 1982
Bench press: 137.5, Phil Stringer, 1983
Deadlift: 229, Precious McKenzie, 1973
Total: 577.5, Gary Simes, 1991

60 kg
Squat: 250, Phil Richard, 1995
Bench press: 145, Phil Richard, 1995
Deadlift: 275, Eddy Pengelly, 1977
Total: 645, Eddy Pengelly, 1979

67.5 kg
Squat: 290, Rodney Hypolite, 1994
Bench press: 165.5, Mick McCrohon, 1994
Deadlift: 295, Eddy Pengelly, 1982
Total: 722.5, Rodney Hypolite, 1994

75 kg
Squat: 302.5, John Howells, 1979
Bench press: 185, Peter Fiore, 1981
Deadlift: 310, Robert Limerick, 1984
Total: 760, Steve Alexander, 1983

82.5 kg
Squat: 337.5, Mike Duffy, 1984
Bench press: 210, Mike Duffy, 1981
Deadlift: 355, Ron Collins, 1980
Total: 855, Ron Collins, 1980

90 kg
Squat: 347.5, David Caldwell, 1985
Bench press: 227.5, Jeff Chandler, 1985
Deadlift: 350.5, Ron Collins, 1980
Total: 870, David Caldwell, 1985

100 kg
Squat: 380, Tony Stevens, 1984
Bench press: 225.5, Brian Reynolds, 1992
Deadlift: 362.5, Tony Stevens, 1984
Total: 955, Tony Stevens, 1984

110 kg
Squat: 372.5, Tony Stevens, 1984
Bench press: 250, John Neighbour, 1990
Deadlift: 380, Arthur White, 1982
Total: 940, John Neighbour, 1987

125 kg
Squat: 390, John Neighbour, 1990
Bench press: 250, John Neighbour, 1990
Deadlift: 373, David Cullen, 1992
Total: 957.5, Steven Zetolofsky, 1984

125+ kg
Squat: 380, Steven Zetolofsky, 1979
Bench press: 258, Terry Purdoe, 1971
Deadlift: 377.5, Andy Kerr, 1982
Total: 982.5, Andy Kerr, 1983

WOMEN

44 kg
Squat: 130, Helen Wolsey, 1991
Bench press: 68, Helen Wolsey, 1991
Deadlift: 152.5, Helen Wolsey, 1990
Total: 350, Helen Wolsey, 1991

48 kg
Squat: 132.5, Helen Wolsey, 1990
Bench press: 75, Suzanne Smith, 1985
Deadlift: 155, Helen Wolsey, 1990
Total: 355, Helen Wolsey, 1990

52 kg
Squat: 143, Jenny Hunter, 1988
Bench press: 82, Jenny Hunter, 1988
Deadlift: 173.5, Jenny Hunter, 1988
Total: 395, Jenny Hunter, 1988

56 kg
Squat: 160, Tony Hollis, 1995
Bench press: 88.5, Tony Hollis, 1995
Deadlift: 182.5, Jenny Hunter, 1988
Total: 420, Jenny Hunter, 1988

60 kg
Squat: 163.5, Jessica Kattan, 1995
Bench press: 92.5, Mandy Wadsworth, 1992
Deadlift: 192.5, Jackie Blasbery, 1994
Total: 425, Jessica Kattan, 1994

67.5 kg
Squat: 175, Debbie Thomas, 1988
Bench press: 102.5, Sandra Berry, 1992
Deadlift: 198, Sandra Berry, 1992
Total: 460, Sandra Berry, 1992

75 kg
Squat: 202.5, Judith Oakes, 1989
Bench press: 115, Judith Oakes, 1989
Deadlift: 215, Judith Oakes, 1989
Total: 532.5, Judith Oakes, 1989

82.5 kg
Squat: 215, Judith Oakes, 1988
Bench press: 122.5, Joanne Williams, 1990
Deadlift: 217.5, Judith Oakes, 1989
Total: 542.5, Judith Oakes, 1988

90 kg
Squat: 200, Beverley Martin, 1989
Bench press: 115, Joanne Williams, 1989
Deadlift: 215, Beverley Martin, 1990
Total: 495, Beverley Martin, 1989

90+ kg
Squat: 221, Beverley Martin, 1995
Bench press: 137.5, Myrtle Augee, 1989
Deadlift: 230, Myrtle Augee, 1989
Total: 587.5, Myrtle Augee, 1989

Mountaineering

Right
Special equipment is needed to tackle the icy peaks of the Himalayas, the world's highest mountain range. The highest peak is Mt Everest.

Mountaineering

Mt Everest

The summit of Mt Everest—at 8,848 m (29,029 ft)—was first reached at 11:30 a.m. on 29 May 1953, by Edmund Percival Hillary (b. 1919) of New Zealand and Sherpa Tenzing Norgay (1914–86) of Nepal. The successful expedition was led by Col. (later Hon. Brigadier) Henry Cecil John Hunt (b. 1910).

The first woman to climb Everest was Junko Tabei (b. 1939) of Japan, who reached the summit on 16 May 1975.

Ang Rita Sherpa (b. 1947) of Nepal holds the record for the most conquests of Everest, with 10 ascents in 1983, 1984, 1985, 1987, 1988, 1990, 1992, 1993, 1995 and 1996, all without the use of bottled oxygen.

Reinhold Messner (b. 1944) of Italy was the first person to make the entire climb solo on 20 Aug 1980.

Reinhold Messner, with Peter Habeler (b. 1942) of Austria, made the first ascent without bottled oxygen on 8 May 1978.

The first Britons to successfully complete the climb were Douglas Scott (b. 1941) and Dougal Haston (1940–77), on 24 Sept 1975.

The first British woman to climb Everest was Rebecca Stephens (b. 1961), who reached the summit on 17 May 1993.

The oldest person to climb Everest was Ramon Blanco (b. 1933) of Spain, who was 60 years 160 days old when he reached the summit on 7 Oct 1993.

The most people to reach the summit in one expedition was 20, from 7 to 10 May 1990. The American, Soviet and Chinese climbers were participating in the Mt Everest International Peace Climb, led by James W. Whittaker.

The most people to reach the summit on one day was 40 climbers (32 men and eight women) from nine separate expeditions, on 10 May 1993. They were from the USA, Canada, Australia, Great Britain, Russia, New Zealand, Finland, Lithuania, India and Nepal.

Most successful mountaineer

Reinhold Messner was the first person to scale all 14 of the world's mountains that are over 8,000 m (26,250 ft)—all without bottled oxygen. With his ascent of Kangchenjunga in 1982, he became the first person to climb the three highest mountains, having earlier reached the summits of Everest and K2.

Highest bivouac

Mark Whetu (b. 1959) of New Zealand and Michael Anthony Rheinberger (1940–94) of Australia reached the summit of Everest on

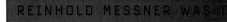

REINHOLD MESSNER WAS T

The highest mountain is Mt Everest, at 8,848 m (29,029 ft).

26 May 1994 and bivouacked 20 m (65 ft) below the summit. Rheinberger died the next day during the descent.

Greatest walls

The most demanding free climbs in the world are rated at 5.13. The main location for such climbs is the Yosemite Valley, California, USA.

Worst mountaineering disasters

On 13 July 1990, 43 people were killed in a mountaineering accident that occurred on Lenin Peak in the USSR (now on the Tajikistan/Kyrgyzstan border).

RST PERSON TO SCALE EVERY MOUNTAIN OVER 8,000 M

Left
Abseiling, a controlled rope descent, is a technique generally used by mountaineers on cliff faces. Abseilers in search of records, however, more often make their attempts down the sides of buildings.

Mountain racing

Mt Cameroon
Reginald Esuke of Cameroon descended from the summit of Mt Cameroon at 4,095 m (13,435 ft) to Buea Stadium at 915 m (3,002 ft) in 1 hr 2 min 15 sec on 24 Jan 1988. He achieved a vertical rate of 51 m (167 ft 6 in) per minute.

Timothy Leku Lekunze of Cameroon set a record of 3 hr 46 min 34 sec for the race to the summit of Mt Cameroon and back. He achieved this on 25 Jan 1987, when the temperature varied from 35°C (95°F) at the start to 0°C (32°F) at the summit.

The record time for the ascent of Mt Cameroon is 2 hr 25 min 20 sec, by Jack Maitland of Great Britain in 1988.

The women's record for the Mt Cameroon race is 4 hr 42 min 31 sec by Fabiola Rueda (b. 1963) of Colombia in 1989.

Ben Nevis
The record time for the race from Fort William Town park in Scotland, UK, to the summit of Ben Nevis, at an altitude of 1,343 m (4,406 ft), and back is 1 hr 25 min 34 sec, by Kenneth Stuart, on 1 Sept 1984.

The women's record for the Ben Nevis race is 1 hr 43 min 25 sec, by Pauline Haworth, on 1 Sept 1984.

Snowdon
The record for the race from Llanberis in Wales, UK, to the summit of Snowdon at 1,085 m (3,560 ft) is 1 hr 2 min 29 sec, set by Kenneth Stuart in 1985.

The women's record for the race from Llanberis to Snowdon is 1 hr 12 min 48 sec by Carol Greenwood in 1993.

Abseiling

Overall distance record
A team of four Royal Marines set an overall abseiling distance record of 1,105.5 m (3,627 ft) when each descended the Boulby Potash Mine, Cleveland, UK, from 7.6 m (25 ft) below ground level to the shaft bottom on 2 Nov 1993.

Longest descent on a building
On 1 July 1992, two teams of 12, representing the Royal Marines of Great Britain and the Canadian School of Rescue Training, abseiled 446.5 m (1,465 ft) from the Space Deck of the CN Tower in Toronto, Canada. Two ropes were used, and the first member of each team reached the ground at exactly the same time.

The greatest distance abseiled by 10 people in an eight-hour period is 108.92 km (67 miles 1,197 yd), by a team from the 10th (Volunteer) Batallion of the Parachute Regiment. They achieved this by abseiling 1,427 times down the side of the Barclays Bank branch in Fenchurch Street, London, UK, on 6 May 1995.

Human fly
The longest climb on the vertical face of a building occurred on 25 May 1981, when Daniel Goodwin, aged 25, of California, USA, climbed 443.2 m (1,454 ft) up the Sears Tower in Chicago, USA, using suction cups and metal clips for support.

MOUNTAIN ENDURANCE RUNNING AND WALKING

Lakeland 24-hour
The record is 76 peaks, by Mark McDermott of Macclesfield Harriers, who started from Braithwaite, Cumbria, UK, on 19–20 June 1988 and covered 140 km (87 miles) and 11,900 m (39,000 ft) of ascents and descents.

Scottish 24-hour
The Scottish 24-hour record is 28 Munros (mountains over 914 m or 3,000 ft) from Cluanie Inn, with 10,668 m (35,000 ft) of ascents and descents, by Jon Broxap on 30–31 July 1988.

Bob Graham Round
The record for the round of 42 lakeland peaks covering a total distance of 99 km (62 miles) and 7,900 m (26,000 ft) of ascents and descents is 13 hr 54 min, by William Bland, aged 34, on 19 June 1982.

Ernest Roger Baumeister (b. 1941) of the Dark Peak Fell Runners Club ran the double Bob Graham Round in 46 hr 34 min 30 sec on 30 June–1 July 1979.

The women's single round record is 18 hr 49 min, by Anne Stentiford of the Macclesfield Harriers on 21 Sept 1991.

Scottish 4,000-ft peaks
The record for traversing all eight 1,219-m (4,000-ft) peaks, a 136-km (85-mile) cross-country route from Glen Nevis to Glen More, is 21 hr 39 min, by Martin Stone on 4 July 1987.

Scottish 3,000-ft peaks
The Munros record for climbing and linking the 277 peaks over 914 m (3,000 ft) on foot is 66 days 22 hr by Hugh Symonds (b. 1953). He covered 2,211 km (1,374 miles) and climbed 128,600 m (422,000 ft) between Ben Hope and Ben Lomond from 19 April to 25 June 1990. He rowed to Skye, sailed to Mull, and ran between all the other peaks.

Welsh 3,000-ft peaks
The record for traversing the 15 Welsh peaks from Snowdon to Foel Fras is 4 hr 19 min 56 sec, by Colin Donnelly on 11 June 1988.

The women's record is 5 hr 28 min 41 sec, set by Angela Carson on 5 Aug 1989.

English 3,000-ft peaks
The record for a circuit of the four English peaks from Keswick, Cumbria, is 7 hr 35 min, by William Bland on 15 June 1979.

British Three Peaks record
The Three Peaks route from sea level at Fort William, Highland, to sea level at Caernarvon, via the summits of Ben Nevis, Scafell Pike and Snowdon, was walked by Arthur Eddleston (1939–84) of Cambridge H in five days 23 hr 37 min from 11 to 17 May 1980.

The women's walking record is 7 days 31 min by Ann Sayer from 8 to 15 Sept 1979.

Gymnastics and stamina

USSR HAS WON A RECORD 14 WORLD AND FOUR OLYMPIC MODERN PENTATHLON TEAM TITLES

Left
Vitaliy Scherbo (Belarus) has won more individual gymnastics titles than anyone else (13).

RECORD FOR THE MOST MEN'S WORLD CHAMPIONSHIP GYMNASTICS TITLES IS 13

Most team gymnastics titles is 21

Gymnastics
World Championships

The most women's titles (including Olympic Games) is 12 individual wins and six team wins by Larisa Semyonovna Latynina (USSR), 1954–64. The USSR won the team title on 21 occasions (11 World and 10 Olympics).

The winner of the most individual men's titles is 13, by Vitaliy Scherbo (Belarus) from 1992 to 1995. He also won a team gold in 1992. The USSR won the men's team title a record 13 times (eight World Championships, five Olympics) between 1952 and 1992.

Aurelia Dobre (Romania) was the youngest to win the women's overall world title, at the age of 14 years 352 days at Rotterdam, Netherlands, on 23 Oct 1987.

Daniela Silivas (Romania) was aged 14 years 185 days when she won the gold medal for balance beam on 10 Nov 1985.

The youngest male world champion was Dmitriy Bilozerchev (USSR), who was 16 years 315 days old when he won at Budapest, Hungary, on 28 Oct 1983.

Olympics

The men's team title has been won a record five times by Japan (1960, 1964, 1968, 1972 and 1976) and the USSR (1952, 1956, 1980, 1988 and 1992). The USSR won the women's title 10 times (1952–80, 1988 and 1992). The 1992 successes were by the Unified team from the republics of the former USSR.

The most men's individual gold medals is six, by Boris Shakhlin of the USSR (one in 1956, four in 1960 and one in 1964) and by Nikolay Yefimovich Andrianov of the USSR (one in 1972, four in 1976 and one in 1980).

Vera Caslavska-Odlozil (Czechoslovakia) has won seven women's individual gold medals (three in 1964 and four in 1968).

Larisa Latynina won nine gold (six individual), five silver and four bronze medals, 1956–64. Her total of 18 medals is an Olympic record.

The most medals won by a male gymnast is 15 (seven gold, five silver, three bronze) by Nikolay Andrianov (USSR), 1972–80.

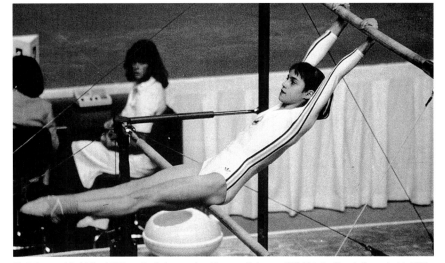

Nadia Comaneci (b. 12 Nov 1961) was the first person to achieve a perfect score of 10.00 in the Olympic Games, in July 1976.

Aleksandr Nikolayevich Dityatin (USSR) is the only man to win a medal in all eight categories in the same Games, at Moscow in 1980.

Perfect scores (10.00)
Hans Eugster (Switzerland) scored 10.00 in the compulsory parallel bars at the 1950 World Championships.

Nadia Comaneci (Romania) was the first to achieve a perfect score at the Olympic Games, scoring 10.00 seven times at Montreal, Canada, in July 1976.

World Cup
Two men's World Cup titles have been won by Nikolay Andrianov (USSR), Aleksandr Dityatin (USSR) and Li Ning (China), and two women's titles by Maria Yevgenyevna Filatova (USSR).

Rhythmic Sportive Gymnastics
The most overall individual world titles is three, by Maria Gigova (Bulgaria) in 1969, 1971 and 1973, and Maria Petrova (Bulgaria), 1993–95.

Bulgaria has won a record nine team titles, in 1969, 1971, 1981, 1983, 1985, 1987, 1989 (shared), 1993 and 1995.

Bianka Panova (Bulgaria) won all four apparatus gold medals, all with maximum scores, and won a team gold in 1987.

At the 1988 Olympics, Marina Lobach (USSR) won the Rhythmic Gymnastic title with perfect scores in all six disciplines.

Trampolining
Most titles
The most World Championship titles is nine by Judy Wills (USA), with a record five individual wins from 1964 to 1968, two pairs (1966–67) and two tumbling (1965–66).

Aleksandr Moskalenko (Russia) has won five World Championship titles: three individual (1990–94) and two pairs (1992–94).

A record nine British titles have been won by Sue Challis (1980–82, 1984–85, 1987, 1990 and 1992–93).

Left
Competitors battle it out during the strenuous 1.5-km swimming leg of the 1995 World Championship triathlon, won for the second time by British participant Simon Lessing.

Eva Fjellerup (Denmark) has won the women's individual title three times (1990–91, 1993).

András Balczo has won three Olympic golds, as a member of the winning team in 1960 and 1968 and as the 1972 individual champion.

Lars Hall (Sweden) is alone in having won two individual Olympic titles (1952 and 1956).

Pavel Serafimovich Lednyev (USSR) won a record seven Olympics medals (two team gold, one team silver, one individual silver, three individual bronze) from 1968 to 1980.

Biathlon
Most titles
Two men's Olympic individual titles have been won by Magnar Solberg of Norway (1968 and 1972) and Frank-Peter Rötsch (GDR) at both 10 km and 20 km in 1988.

Aleksandr Ivanovich Tikhonov (USSR) won four relay golds from 1968 to 1980 and silver in the 20 km in 1968.

The most women's titles is two, by Anfissa Restzova of Russia (7.5 km in 1992 and 4 x 7.5 km in 1994) and Myriam Bédard of Canada (7.5 km and 15 km in 1994).

7.5 km from 1989 to 1990). Kaya Parve (USSR) has won six titles: two individual and four relay from 1984 to 1986 and in 1988.

Triathlon
Hawaiian Ironman
Record times for the Hawaii Ironman, in which competitors swim 3.8 km (2⅖ miles), cycle 180 km (112 miles), and run a full marathon of 42.195 km (26 miles 385 yd) are: (men) 8 hr 7 min 45 sec, by Mark Allen (USA) in 1993; (women) 8 hr 55 min 28 sec by Paula Newby-Fraser (Zimbabwe) in 1992.

Paula Newby-Fraser (Zimbabwe) has won a record seven times (1986, 1988–89 and 1991–94).

The most men's wins is six, by Dave Scott (USA), 1980, 1982–84 and 1986–87, and Mark Allen (USA), 1989–93 and 1995.

The fastest time recorded over the Ironman distances is 8 hr 1 min 32 sec, by Dave Scott (USA), at Lake Biwa, Japan, on 30 July 1989.

World Championships
The annual race (1.5-km swim, 40-km cycle and 10-km run) has been won twice by Spencer Smith (GB) (1993–94) and Simon

HAWAII IRONMAN COMPETITORS SWIM 3.8 KM, CYCLE 180 KM AND RUN 42.195 KM

The most British titles by a man is five, by Stewart Matthews from 1976 to 1980.

Modern pentathlon
Most titles
András Balczo (Hungary) won six individual (five world, 1963, 1965–67 and 1969, and one Olympic, 1972) and seven team titles (five world and two Olympic, 1960–70).

The USSR has won 14 world and four Olympic team titles.

Poland have won a record seven women's World Championship team titles (1985, 1988–92 and 1995).

Frank Ullrich (GDR) has won a record six individual world titles, four at 10 km from 1978 to 1981 (including the 1980 Olympics) and two at 20 km from 1982 to 1983.

Aleksandr Tikhonov (USSR) was in 10 winning Soviet relay teams from 1968 to 1980, and won four individual titles.

Two men have won the Biathlon World Cup four times: Frank Ullrich (GDR) in 1978 and from 1980 to 1982, and Franz Peter Rötsch (GDR), 1984–85 and 1987–88.

The most women's individual World Championship titles is three, by Anne-Elinor Elvebakk of Norway (10 km in 1988 and

Lessing (GB) (1992 and 1995) in the men's event, and Michelle Jones (Australia) (1992–93) and Karen Smyers (USA) (1990 and 1995) in the women's.

Mark Allen (USA) has won a 'World Championship' race—3.2-km swim (4 km since 1988), 120-km cycle, and 32-km run) in Nice, France—10 times, 1982–86, 1989–93.

Paula Newby-Fraser has a record four World Championship women's wins, 1989–92.

The record times are 5 hr 46 min 10 sec by Mark Allen (USA) in 1986 (men's), and 6 hr 27 min 6 sec by Erin Baker (New Zealand) in 1988 (women's).

American football

Right
Emmitt Smith scored a record 25 touchdowns in one season for the Dallas Cowboys in 1995.

MOST GAMES PLAYED BY ONE PERSON IS 340, IN A RECORD 26 SEASONS

National Football League

Most NFL titles
The Green Bay Packers won a record 11 NFL titles, in 1929–31, 1936, 1939, 1944, 1961–62 and 1965–67.

Most consecutive wins
The greatest number of consecutive wins is 18, achieved twice by the Chicago Bears, in 1933–34 and 1941–42; by the Miami Dolphins in 1972–73; and by the San Francisco 49ers in 1988–89.

The most consecutive games without defeat is 25 (22 wins, three ties), by Canton in 1921–23.

Most games played
George Blanda (b. 1927) played in a record 340 games in a record 26 seasons in the NFL (Chicago Bears 1949–58, Baltimore Colts 1950, Houston Oilers 1960–66 and Oakland Raiders 1967–75).

The greatest number of consecutive games is 282, by Jim Marshall (Cleveland Browns 1960 and Minnesota Vikings 1961–79).

Longest run from scrimmage
Tony Dorsett (b. 1954) scored on a touchdown run of 99 yards for the Dallas Cowboys when they played the Minnesota Vikings on 3 Jan 1983.

Longest pass completion
A pass completion of 99 yards has been achieved eight times, and always resulted in a touchdown. The most recent was a pass from Brett Favre to Robert Brooks of the Green Bay Packers against the Chicago Bears on 11 Sept 1995.

Super Bowl

Most wins
The greatest number of Super Bowl wins is five, by the San Francisco 49ers (1982, 1985, 1989–90 and 1995) and the Dallas Cowboys (1972, 1978, 1993–94 and 1996).

Highest scores
The records for both the highest team score and the greatest victory margin were set on 28 Jan 1990, when the San Francisco 49ers beat the Denver Broncos 55–10 in New Orleans, Louisiana.

The highest aggregate score was achieved in 1995, when the San Francisco 49ers beat the San Diego Chargers 49–26.

Highest attendance
The highest ever attendance is 103,985, for Super Bowl XIV between the Pittsburgh Steelers and the LA Rams at the Rose Bowl, Pasadena, California, on 20 Jan 1980.

Dan Marino is one of the most successful quarterbacks in the history of the NFL. He holds numerous records: most notably, career records for most passes completed, most yards gained passing and most touchdown passes thrown.

Longest pass completion 99 yards

NATIONAL FOOTBALL LEAGUE RECORDS

MOST POINTS
Career 2,002
George Blanda
(Chicago Bears, Baltimore Colts, Houston Oilers,
Oakland Raiders), 1949–75
Season 176
Paul Hornung
(Green Bay Packers), 1960
Game 40
Ernie Nevers
(Chicago Cardinals v. Chicago Bears),
28 Nov 1929

MOST TOUCHDOWNS
Career 156
Jerry Rice
(San Francisco 49ers), 1985–95
Season 25
Emmitt Smith
(Dallas Cowboys), 1995
Game 6
Ernie Nevers
(Chicago Cardinals v. Chicago Bears),
28 Nov 1929
William Jones
(Cleveland Browns v. Chicago Bears),
25 Nov 1951
Gale Sayers
(Chicago Bears v. San Francisco 49ers),
12 Dec 1965

MOST YARDS GAINED RUSHING
Career 16,726
Walter Payton
(Chicago Bears), 1975–87
Season 2,105
Eric Dickerson
(Los Angeles Rams), 1984
Game 275
Walter Payton
(Chicago Bears v. Minnesota Vikings),
20 Nov 1977

MOST YARDS GAINED RECEIVING
Career 14,004
15,123
Jerry Rice
(San Francisco 49ers), 1985-95
Season 1,848
Jerry Rice
(San Francisco 49ers), 1995
Game 336
Willie Anderson
(Los Angeles Rams v. New Orleans Saints),
26 Nov 1989

MOST NET YARDS GAINED
Career 21,803
Walter Payton
(Chicago Bears), 1975–87
Season 2,535
Lionel James
(San Diego Chargers), 1985
Game 373
Billy Cannon
(Houston Oilers v. New York Titans), 10 Dec 1961

MOST YARDS GAINED PASSING
Career 48,841
Dan Marino
(Miami Dolphins), 1983–95
Season 5,084
Dan Marino
(Miami Dolphins), 1984
Game 554
Norm Van Brocklin
(Los Angeles Rams v. New York Yanks),
28 Sept 1951

MOST PASSES COMPLETED
Career 3,910
Dan Marino
(Miami Dolphins), 1983-95
Season 404
Warren Moon
(Houston Oilers), 1991
Game 45
Drew Bledsoe
(New England Patriots v. Minnesota Vikings),
13 Nov 1994

PASS RECEPTIONS
Career 942
Jerry Rice
(San Francisco 49ers), 1985–95
Season 123
Herman Moore
(Detroit Lions), 1995
Game 18
Tom Fears
(Los Angeles Rams v. Green Bay Packers),
3 Dec 1950

FIELD GOALS
Career 373
Jan Stenerud
(Kansas City Chiefs, Green Bay Packers,
Minnesota Vikings), 1967–85
Season 35
Ali Haji-Sheikh
(New York Giants), 1983
Game 7
Jim Bakken
(St Louis Cardinals v. Pittsburgh Steelers),
24 Sept 1967
Rich Karlis
(Minnesota Vikings v. Los Angeles Rams),
5 Nov 1989
Longest 63 yd
Tom Dempsey
(New Orleans Saints v. Detroit Lions), 8 Nov 1970

SUPER BOWL GAME AND CAREER RECORDS

POINTS
Game 18
Roger Craig (San Francisco 49ers), 1985
Jerry Rice (San Francisco 49ers), 1990 and
1995
Ricky Watters (San Francisco 49ers), 1995
Career 42
Jerry Rice, 1989–90, 1995

TOUCHDOWNS
Game 3
Roger Craig, 1985
Jerry Rice, 1990 & 1995
Ricky Watters, 1990
Career 7
Jerry Rice, 1989–90, 1995

TOUCHDOWN PASSES
Game 6
Steve Young (San Francisco 49ers), 1995
Career 11
Joe Montana (San Francisco 49ers), 1982,
1985, 1989–90

YARDS GAINED PASSING
Game 357
Joe Montana, 1989
Career 1,142
Joe Montana, 1982, 1985, 1989–90

YARDS GAINED RECEIVING
Game 215
Jerry Rice 1989
Career 512
Jerry Rice 1989–90, 1995

YARDS GAINED RUSHING
Game 204
Timmy Smith (Washington Redskins), 1988
Career 354
Franco Harris, 1975–6, 1979–80

PASSES COMPLETED
Game 31
Jim Kelly (Buffalo Bills), 1994
Career 33
Joe Montana, 1982, 1985, 1989–90

PASS RECEPTIONS
Game 11
Dan Ross (Cincinnati Bengals), 1982
Jerry Rice, 1989
Career 28
Jerry Rice, 1989–90, 1995

FIELD GOALS
Game 4
Don Chandler (Green Bay Packers), 1968
Ray Wersching (San Francisco 49ers), 1982
Career 5
Ray Wersching, 1982, 1985

MOST VALUABLE PLAYER AWARD
3 times
Joe Montana, 1982, 1985, 1990

Baseball

Right
Baseball was first played in the USA in the 19th century and is derived from the English game of rounders. The World Series started in 1903 as an end-of-season game between the winners of the two professional leagues in the USA—the National League and the American League.

Far right
Still regarded by many as the greatest baseball player of all time, 'Babe' Ruth hit 714 home runs from 8,399 times to bat during the 1920s and 1930s.

World Series

Most wins
The New York Yankees won a record 22 times between 1923 and 1978, in a record 33 series appearances between 1921 and 1981.

Most valuable player
The only men to have won this award twice are: Sanford 'Sandy' Koufax (Los Angeles NL, 1963 and 1965), Robert 'Bob' Gibson (St Louis NL, 1964 and 1967) and Reginald Martinez 'Reggie' Jackson (Oakland AL 1973 and New York AL 1977).

Best attendance
The highest ever attendance for a World Series is 420,784, for the six games in which the Los Angeles Dodgers beat the Chicago White Sox 4–2 from 1 to 8 Oct 1959.

The record attendance for a single World Series game is 92,706, for the fifth game of the same series at the Memorial Coliseum, Los Angeles, on 6 Oct 1959.

Major League

Most National League titles
The record for NL titles is 19, by the Dodgers (Brooklyn 1890–1957 and Los Angeles 1958–88).

Most American League titles
A record 33 titles were won by the New York Yankees between 1921 and 1981.

Most games played
Peter Edward 'Pete' Rose played in a record 3,562 games with a record 14,053 at bats for Cincinnati NL from 1963 to 1978 and from 1984 to 1986, Philadelphia NL from 1979 to 1983 and Montreal NL in 1984.

Calvin Edwin Ripken Jr played in a record 2,200 successive games for the Baltimore Orioles AL between 30 May 1982 and the end of May 1996.

Batting

Most home runs
Henry Louis 'Hank' Aaron holds the career record for the greatest number of home runs, at 755: 733 for the Milwaukee Braves from 1954 to 1965 and the Atlanta Braves from 1966 to 1974 (NL) and 22 for the Milwaukee Brewers from 1975 to 1976 (AL).

George Herman 'Babe' Ruth (New York AL) hit 714 home runs from 8,399 times at bat, giving him the highest home-run percentage of all time at 8.5%.

Joshua Gibson of Homestead Grays and Pittsburgh Crawfords (Negro League clubs) achieved a career total of nearly 800 home runs, including an unofficial record for a season's total of 75 in 1931.

The US major league record for home runs in a season is 61, by Roger Eugene Maris for the New York Yankees in 162 games in 1961.

The record for the greatest number of official home runs in a minor league season is 72, by Joe Bauman of Roswell Rockets, New Mexico, in 1954.

'BABE' RUTH (1895-194

The most home runs in a major league game is four, first achieved by Robert Lincoln 'Bobby' Lowe for Boston v. Cincinnati on 30 May 1894. The feat has been achieved a further 10 times since then.

The most consecutive games hitting home runs is eight, by Richard Dale Long for Pittsburgh NL from 19 to 28 May 1956 and by Donald Arthur Mattingly for New York AL in July 1987.

Longest home run
The longest measured home run in a major league game is 634 ft (193 m), by Mickey Mantle for the New York Yankees against the Detroit Tigers at Briggs Stadium, Detroit, on 10 Sept 1960.

Most consecutive hits
Michael Franklin 'Pinky' Higgins had 12 consecutive hits for Boston AL from 19 to 21 June 1938. This record was later equalled by Walter 'Moose' Droppo for Detroit AL, from 14 to 15 July 1952.

Joseph Paul DiMaggio hit in a record 56 consecutive games for New York in 1941. He was 223 times at bat, and had 91 hits, scoring a total of 16 doubles, four triples and 15 home runs.

Pitching

Most games won by a pitcher
Denton True 'Cy' Young had a record 511 wins and a record 749 complete games from a total of 906 games and 815 starts in his

career for Cleveland NL 1890–98, St Louis NL 1899–1900, Boston AL 1901–08, Cleveland AL 1909–11 and Boston NL 1911. He pitched a record total of 7,357 innings.

The career record for the most games pitching is 1,070, by James Hoyt Wilhelm for nine teams between 1952 and 1972. He set the record with 143 wins by a relief pitcher.

The season record is 106 games, by Michael Grant Marshall for Los Angeles NL in 1974.

Most consecutive games won by a pitcher
Carl Owen Hubbell pitched the New York Giants to a record 24 consecutive wins: 16 in 1936 and eight in 1937.

Most consecutive scoreless games
Orel Leonard Hershiser IV pitched a record 59 consecutive shutout innings from 30 Aug to 28 Sept 1988.

Perfect game
The first person to pitch a perfect nine innings game was John Lee Richmond for Worcester against Cleveland in the NL on 12 June 1880. This record has been equalled on 13 subsequent occasions, but no pitcher has pitched a perfect game more than once. On 26 May 1959 Harvey Haddix Jr pitched a perfect game for 12 innings for Pittsburgh against against Milwaukee in the NL, but lost in the 13th.

Cy Young award
The most wins is four, by Stephen Norman Carlton (Philadelphia NL) in 1972, 1977, 1980 and 1982, and by Greg Maddux (Chicago, Atlanta NL) from 1992 to 1995.

Fastest pitcher
Lynn Nolan Ryan, then of the California Angels, pitched at 162.3 km/h (100.9 mph) at Anaheim Stadium, California, on 20 Aug 1974.

Throws and base runs
Longest throw
Glen Edward Gorbous threw a record 135.88 m (445 ft 10 in) on 1 Aug 1957.

The record throw by a woman was 90.2 m (296 ft), by Mildred Ella 'Babe' Didrikson, at Jersey City, New Jersey, on 25 July 1931.

Fastest base runner
The fastest ever time for circling bases is 13.3 seconds, by Ernest Evar Swanson at Columbus, Ohio, in 1932, at an average speed of 29.70 km/h (18.45 mph).

Players and spectators
Youngest and oldest players
Frederick Joseph Chapman pitched for Philadelphia in the American Association at the age of 14 years 239 days on 22 July 1887, but did not play again.

The youngest major league player was Cincinnati pitcher Joseph Henry Nuxhal, who played one game in June 1944 at the age of 15 years 314 days. He did not play again in the NL until 1952.

The youngest player in a minor league game was Joe Louis Reliford, for the Fitzgerald Pioneers against Statesboro Pilots in the Georgia State League, at the age of 12 years 234 days on 19 July 1952.

Leroy Robert 'Satchel' Paige pitched for Kansas City As AL at the age of 59 years 80 days on 25 Sept 1965.

Record attendances
The all-time season record for attendances for both leagues is 70,257,938, in 1993.

The record season attendance for one league is 36,912,502, for the NL in 1991.

The record for one team is 4,483,350, for the home games of the Colorado Rockies at Mile High Stadium, Denver, in 1993.

An estimated 114,000 spectators attended a demonstration game between Australia and an American Services team in the 1956 Olympics in Melbourne, Australia.

US MAJOR LEAGUE

BATTING RECORDS
Batting
Career average: .366, Tyrus Raymond 'Ty' Cobb (Detroit AL, Philadelphia AL) 1905–28.
Season average: .440, Hugh Duffy (Boston NL) 1894.
Runs
Career: 2,245, Tyrus Raymond Cobb 1905–28.
Season: 192, William Robert Hamilton (Philadelphia NL) 1894.
Runs batted in
Career: 2,297, Henry 'Hank' Aaron 1954–76.
Season: 190, Lewis Rober 'Hack' Wilson (Chicago NL) 1930.
Game: 12, James LeRoy Bottomley (St Louis NL) 16 Sept 1924; Mark Whiten (St Louis NL) 7 Sept 1993. Innings: 7, Edward Cartwright (St Louis AL) 23 Sept 1890.
Base hits
Career: 4,256 Peter Edward Rose (Cincinnati NL, Philadelphia NL, Montreal NL, Cincinnati NL) 1963–86.
Season: 257, George Harold Sisler (St Louis AL) 1920.
Total bases
Career: 6,856, Henry 'Hank' Aaron 1954–76.
Season: 457, George Herman 'Babe' Ruth (New York AL) 1921.
Stolen bases
Career: 1,149, Rickey Henley Henderson (Oakland AL, New York AL, Oakland AL, Toronto AL, Oakland AL) 1979–95.
Season: 130, Rickey Henderson (Oakland AL) 1982.

PITCHING RECORDS
Games won
Career: 511, Denton True 'Cy' Young (Cleveland NL, St Louis NL, Boston AL, Cleveland AL, Boston NL) 1890–1911.
Season: 60, Charles Gardner Radbourn (Providence NL) 1884.
Shutouts
Career: 113, Walter Perry Johnson (Washington AL) 1907–27.
Season: 16, George Washington Bradley (St Louis NL) 1876; Grover Cleveland Alexander (Philadelphia NL) 1916.
Strikeouts
Career: 5,714, Lynn Nolan Ryan (New York NL, California AL, Houston NL, Texas AL) 1966–93.
Season: 383, Lynn Nolan Ryan (California AL) 1973.
Game (9 innings): 20, Roger Clemens (Boston AL) 29 April 1986.
No hit games
Career: 7, Lynn Nolan Ryan 1973–91.
Earned run average
Season: .90 Ferdinand Schupp (140 inns) (New York NL) 1916; .96 Hubert 'Dutch' Leonard (222 inns) (Boston AL) 1914; 1.12 Robert Gibson (305 inns) (St Louis NL) 1968.

WORLD SERIES

Most series played: 14
Lawrence Peter 'Yogi' Berra (New York AL) 1947–63.
Most series played by pitcher: 11
Edward Charles 'Whitey' Ford (New York AL) 1950–64.
Most home runs in a game: 3
George Herman 'Babe' Ruth (New York AL) 6 Oct 1926 and 9 Oct 1928; and Reginald Martinez Jackson (New York, AL) 18 Oct 1977.
Most runs batted in: 6
Robert C. Richardson (New York AL) 8 Oct 1960
Most strikeouts: 17
Robert Gibson (St Louis NL) 2 Oct 1968
Perfect game (9 innings)
Donald James Larson (New York AL) 8 Oct 1956

Basketball

Right
Dennis Rodman of the Chicago Bulls, who hold the record for the most NBA wins in a single season.

Titles and scores

Most Olympic titles

The USA has won 10 men's Olympic titles and won 63 consecutive matches from the introduction of the sport to the Games in 1936 until 1972, when they lost 50–51 to the USSR in the disputed final in Munich. Since then they have won a further 29 matches and lost once more to the USSR, in 1988.

The women's title has been won a record three times by the USSR in 1976, 1980 and 1992 (the last time by the Unified team from the republics of the ex-USSR).

Most World Championship titles

The USSR has won most titles at both the men's World Championships, with three (1967, 1974 and 1982), and the women's, with six (1959, 1964, 1967, 1971, 1975 and 1983). Yugoslavia have also won three men's world titles (1970, 1978 and 1990).

Most English titles

The most English National Championship titles is eight, by London Central YMCA (1957–58, 1960, 1962–64, 1967 and 1969).

The English National League title has been won seven times by Crystal Palace (1974, 1976–78, 1980 and 1982–83). In the 1989/90 season, Kingston won all five domestic trophies: the National League and Championship play-offs, the National Cup, the League Cup and the WIBC.

The English Women's Cup has been won a record eight times by the Tigers (1972–73, 1976–80 and 1982).

Highest international score

In a senior international match, Iraq beat Yemen 251–3 at the Asian Games at New Delhi, India, in Nov 1982.

Highest individual scores

The highest score by a woman is 156 points, by Marie Boyd (now Eichler) of Central HS,

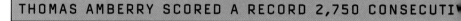

Lonaconing, Maryland, USA, in a 163–3 victory over Ursaline Academy, Cumbria, on 25 Feb 1924.

The 13-year-old Mats Wermelin scored all the points in a 272–0 win in a regional tournament at Stockholm, Sweden, on 5 Feb 1974.

Highest British scores

The highest score in a British championship was when England beat Wales by 125–54 on 1 Sept 1978.

The highest score recorded in a match in the United Kingdom is 250, by the Nottingham YMCA Falcons v. Mansfield Pirates at Nottingham, on 18 June 1974.

The highest score in a senior National League match is 174–40, by Chiltern Fast Break v. Swindon Rakers on 13 Oct 1990.

The highest score in the National Cup is 157, by Solent Stars v. Corby (57) on 6 Jan 1991.

Michael Jordan, seen with Magic Johnson, holds the record for the highest career average for players exceeding 10,000 points.

Longest goal 27.49 m

The highest score by a British player is 124, by Paul Ogden for St Albans School, Oldham, when they beat South Chadderton 226–82 on 9 March 1982.

The highest individual score in a league match in the United Kingdom is 108 by Lewis Young for Forth Steel in his team's 154–74 win over Stirling in the Scottish League Division One at Stirling on 2 March 1985.

The record in an English National League (Division One) or Cup match is 73 points by: Terry Crosby (USA) for Bolton v. Manchester Giants on 26 Jan 1985; Billy Hungrecker for Worthing v. Plymouth on 20 March 1988; and Renaldo Lawrence for Stevenage v. Gateshead on 30 Dec 1989.

NBA

Most titles
Boston Celtics have won a record 16 National Basketball Association titles (1957, 1959–66, 1968–69, 1974, 1976, 1981, 1984, 1986).

Highest score
The highest aggregate score in an NBA match was 370 when the Detroit Pistons beat the

for a record 3,882 minutes. Chamberlain went through his entire 1,045-game career without fouling out.

Most points
Kareem Abdul-Jabbar set NBA career records with 38,387 points (an average of 24.6 points per game), including 15,837 field goals in regular season games, and 5,762 points, including 2,356 field goals in play-off games.

The previous recordholder, Wilt Chamberlain, had a superior average of 30.1 points per game for his total of 31,419 for Philadelphia (1959–62), San Francisco (1962–65), Philadelphia (1964–68) and Los Angeles (1968–73). He scored 50 or more points in 118 games, including 45 in 1961/2 and 30 in 1962/3 to the next best career total of 17. He also set season's records for points and scoring average, with 4,029 at 50.4 per game, and for field goals, with 1,597 for Philadelphia in 1961/2.

The highest career average for players exceeding 10,000 points is 31.9, by Michael Jordan, with 24,489 points in 766 games for the Chicago Bulls from 1984 to 1996. Jordan also holds the career scoring average record

In one minute, from seven scoring positions, Jeff Liles scored 25 out of 29 attempts at Bethany, Oklahoma, USA, on 18 Sept 1994.

In 24 hours, Fred Newman scored 20,371 free throws from a total of 22,049 taken (92.39%) at Caltech, Pasadena, California, USA, from 29 to 30 Sept 1990.

Longest goal
Christopher Eddy scored a field goal from 27.49 m (90 ft 2¼ in) for Fairview High School v. Iroquois High School at Erie, Pennsylvania, USA, on 25 Feb 1989. The shot was made as time expired in overtime and won the game for Fairview, 51–50.

Spinning
Bruce Crevier (USA) spun 18 basketballs at the same time, at the ABC-TV studios in New York City, USA, on 18 July 1994.

Highest attendance
The largest ever crowd for a basketball match was 80,000, for the final of the European Cup Winners' Cup between AEK Athens and Slavia Prague at the Olympic stadium, Athens, Greece, on 4 April 1968. AEK Athens won the match 89–82.

Denver Nuggets 186–184 at Denver, on 13 Dec 1983. Overtime was played after a 145–145 tie in regulation time.

The highest score in regulation time is 320, when the Golden State Warriors beat Denver 162–158 at Denver on 2 Nov 1990.

Individual scoring
Wilton Norman 'Wilt' Chamberlain set an NBA record of 100 points for Philadelphia v. New York at Hershey, Pennsylvania, on 2 March

1962. This included a record 36 field goals and 28 free throws (from 32 attempts), and a record 59 points in a half (the second). The free throws record was equalled by Adrian Dantley for Utah v. Houston at Las Vegas, Nevada, on 5 Jan 1984.

Most games
Kareem Abdul-Jabbar (formerly Ferdinand Lewis Alcindor) took part in a record 1,560 NBA regular season games over 20 seasons, for the Milwaukee Bucks, 1969–75, and the Los Angeles Lakers, 1975–89, totalling 57,446 minutes played. He also played a record 237 play-off games.

The record for the most successive games is 906, by Randy Smith for Buffalo, San Diego, Cleveland and New York from 18 Feb 1972 to 13 March 1983.

The record for the most complete games in one season is 79, by Wilt Chamberlain for Philadelphia in 1962, when he was on court

for play-offs, at 33.9 for 4,717 points in 139 games from 1984 to 1996.

Most wins
Los Angeles Lakers won a record 33 successive NBA games from 5 Nov 1971 to 7 Jan 1972.

The most wins in one season is 72, by the Chicago Bulls in 1995/6.

Youngest and oldest players
The youngest NBA player is Bill Willoughby, who made his début for Atlanta Hawks on 23 Oct 1975 at the age of 18 years 156 days.

The oldest NBA regular player was Kareem Abdul-Jabbar, who made his last appearance for the Los Angeles Lakers at the age of 42 years 59 days in 1989.

Tallest player
The tallest player in NBA history is Manute Bol (Sudan) of the Washington Bullets, Golden State Warriors, Miami Heat and Phildelphia 76ers. The 2.3-m (7-ft 6¾-in) player made his professional début in 1985.

Other records

Tallest player
Suleiman 'Ali' Nashnush (1943–91) was reputed to be 2.45 m (8 ft ¼ in) tall when he played for the Libyan team in 1962.

Shooting speed
The greatest goal-shooting demonstration was by Thomas Amberry of the USA, when he scored 2,750 consecutive free throws at Seal Beach, California, USA, on 15 Nov 1994.

Left
At 2.3 m (7 ft 6¾ in), Manute Bol (b. 16 Oct 1962), a Sudanese who made his NBA debut in 1985, is the tallest player to have played in the NBA.

Cricketers

Right
Brian Lara, regarded by many as the best batsman of the present day, holds the record for the highest score in both Tests (375) and first-class matches (501).

Below right
Possibly the world's finest ever all-rounder, Gary Sobers was the first man ever to hit six sixes in an over. He also held the record for the highest innings in a test (365 not out) until it was broken by Brian Lara.

Batting records (team)
Highest innings
Victoria scored a record 1,107 runs in a time of 10 hr 30 min against New South Wales in an Australian Sheffield Shield match at Melbourne on 27–28 Dec 1926.

England scored 903 runs for seven declared in 15 hr 17 min, against Australia at The Oval, London, UK, on 20, 22 and 23 Aug 1938.

Lowest innings
The first-class record is 12, by Oxford University (who batted a man short) against the Marylebone Cricket Club (MCC) at Cowley Marsh, Oxford, UK, on 24 May 1877, and by Northamptonshire v. Gloucestershire at Gloucester, UK, on 11 June 1907.

The lowest Test innings is 26 by New Zealand in their match against England at Auckland, New Zealand, on 28 March 1955.

The lowest score for both innings is 34 (16 and 18) by Border v. Natal in a Currie Cup match at East London, South Africa, on 19 and 21 Dec 1959.

Batting records (individual)
Highest innings
Brian Charles Lara scored 501 not out in 7 hr 54 min for Warwickshire against Durham at Edgbaston, UK, on 3 and 6 June 1994.

The highest Test innings is 375 in 12 hr 46 min, by Brian Lara for England against the West Indies at Recreation Ground, St John's, Antigua, from 16 to 18 April 1994.

The most runs ever scored in a Test by an English player is 364, by Sir Leonard Hutton against Australia at The Oval, London, UK, on 20, 22 and 23 Aug 1938.

Most runs off an over
The first batsman to score 36 runs off a six-ball over was Sir Garfield 'Gary' St Auburn Sobers, off Malcolm Andrew Nash for Nottinghamshire against Glamorgan at Swansea, UK, on 31 Aug 1968.

In a Shell Trophy match for Wellington v. Canterbury at Christchurch, New Zealand, on 20 Feb 1990, Robert Howard Vance, who was deliberately trying to give away runs, bowled an over containing 17 no-balls and conceded 77 runs.

Most runs off a ball
The most runs ever scored off a single ball is 10, scored by Samuel Hill Wood off Cuthbert Burnup for Derbyshire v. MCC at Lord's, London, UK, on 26 May 1900.

Fastest scoring
Cedric Ivan James 'Jim' Smith scored 50 in 11 minutes for Middlesex v. Gloucestershire at Bristol, UK, on 16 June 1938.

Clive Clay Inman scored 50 runs off a record 13 balls in just eight minutes in his innings of 57 not out for Leicestershire against Nottinghamshire at Trent Bridge, Nottingham, UK, on 20 Aug 1965,

but full tosses were bowled to him in order to expedite a declaration.

The fastest century against genuine bowling was completed in 35 minutes off 40–46 balls by Percy George Herbert Fender, in his 113 not out for Surrey v. Northamptonshire at Northampton, UK, on 26 Aug 1920.

Glen Chapple struck a century in an estimated 21 minutes off 27 balls for Lancashire v. Glamorgan at Old Trafford, Manchester, UK, on 19 July 1993, but the bowlers were bowling to expedite a declaration.

The fastest limited-overs hundred in a major competition was by Graham David Rose off 36 balls for Somerset v. Devon at Torquay, UK, on 27 June 1990.

The fastest international limited-overs hundred was in 48 balls by Sanath Jayasuriya for Sri Lanka v. Pakistan at Singapore on 2 April 1996.

The fastest Test hundred took 70 minutes, by Jack Morrison Gregory off 67 balls for Australia v. South Africa at Johannesburg, South Africa, on 12 Nov 1921.

Isaac Vivian Alexander Richards scored 100 runs in 56 balls for the West Indies v. England at St John's, Antigua, on 15 April 1986.

Slowest scoring
Thomas Godfrey Evans took a record 1 hr 37 min to score his first run, before going on to score 10 not out for England in their match against Australia at Adelaide, Australia, from 5 to 6 Feb 1947.

Longest innings without scoring
Vincent Hogg played for a record 1 hr 27 min without scoring for Zimbabwe–Rhodesia 'B' in their match against Natal 'B' at Pietermaritzburg, South Africa, on 20 Jan 1980.

Bowling
Most wickets
Alfred 'Tich' Freeman, who played for Kent, UK, from 1929 to 1931, is the only bowler to have taken all 10 wickets in an innings on three occasions.

The fewest runs to have been scored off a bowler taking all 10 wickets is 10, off Hedley Verity for Yorkshire against Nottinghamshire

Highest team innings 1,107

INDIVIDUAL RECORDS

FIRST-CLASS (FC), TEST CAREER AND ENGLISH SEASON

BATTING
Most runs, FC
61,237 (av. 50.65), by Sir John Berry 'Jack' Hobbs, Surrey/England, 1905–34
Most runs, Test
11,174 (av. 50.56), by Allan Robert Border Australia (156 tests), 1978–94
Most runs, season
3,816, by Denis Charles Scott Compton Middlesex/England, 1947
Highest average, FC
95.14, by Sir Donald Bradman NSW/South Australia/Australia, 1927–49
Highest average, Test
99.94, by Sir Donald Bradman Australia (52 tests), 1928–48

BOWLING
Most wickets, FC
4,187 (av. 16.71), by Wilfred Rhodes Yorkshire/England, 1898–1930
Most wickets, Test
434 (av. 29.62), by Kapil Dev Nikhanj India (131 tests), 1978–94
Most wickets, season
304, by Alfred Percy 'Tich' Freeman Kent/England, 1928

WICKETKEEPING
Most dismissals, FC
1,649, by Robert William Taylor Derbyshire/England, 1960–88

---

1 NOT OUT IN 7 HR 54 MIN

Most dismissals, Test
355, by Rodney William Marsh Australia (96 tests), 1970–84
Most dismissals, season
128 (79 caught, 49 stumped), by Leslie Ethelbert George Ames Kent/England, 1929
Most catches, FC
1,473, by Robert Taylor Derbyshire/England, 1960–88
Most catches, Test
343, by Rodney Marsh Australia, 1970–84
Most catches, season
96, by James Graham Binks Yorkshire, 1960
Most stumpings, FC
418, by Leslie Ames Kent/England, 1926–51
Most stumpings, Test
52, by William Albert Stanley Oldfield Australia (54 tests), 1920–37
Most stumpings, season
64, by Leslie Ames Kent, 1932

FIELDING
Most catches, FC
1,018, by Frank Edward Woolley Kent/England, 1906–38
Most catches, Test
156, by Allan Robert Border Australia (156 tests), 1978–94
Most catches, season
78, Walter Reginald Hammond Gloucestershire/England, 1928

at Leeds, UK, on 12 July 1932 (the full analyses for some early performances of the feat are unknown).

James Charles 'Jim' Laker took 19 wickets for 90 runs (9–37 and 10–53) for England v. Australia at Old Trafford, Manchester, UK, from 27 to 31 July 1956.

Most consecutive wickets
The only cricketer to have taken four wickets with consecutive balls more than once is Robert James Crisp, for Western Province in their match against Griqualand West at Johannesburg, South Africa, on 24 Dec 1931 and against Natal at Durban, South Africa, on 3 March 1934.

Patrick Ian Pocock took five wickets in six balls, six wickets in nine balls, and seven wickets in eleven balls for Surrey v. Sussex at Eastbourne, E Sussex, UK, on 15 Aug 1972.

Most consecutive maidens
Hugh Joseph Tayfield bowled a record 16 consecutive eight-ball maiden overs (137 balls without conceding a run) for South Africa against England at Durban, South Africa, from 25 to 26 Jan 1957.

Most balls
The most balls ever bowled by one bowler in a match is 917, by Cottari Nayudu for Holkar v. Bombay at Bombay, India, from 4 to 9 March 1945.

The most balls bowled by one bowler in a test match is 774, by Sonny Ramadhin (7–49 and 2–179), for the West Indies v. England at Edgbaston, UK, from 29 May to 4 June 1957. In the second innings he bowled a record 588 balls (98 overs).

Most expensive bowling
The most runs ever conceded by a bowler in a match is 428, by Cottari Nayudu in the Holkar v. Bombay match in March 1945.

The most runs conceded in an innings is 362, by Arthur Alfred Mailey of New South Wales, playing against Victoria at Melbourne, Australia, from 24 to 28 Dec 1926.

The most runs conceded in a Test innings is 298, by Leslie O'Brien 'Chuck' Fleetwood-Smith for Australia v. England at The Oval, London, UK, from 20 to 23 Aug 1938.

Fastest bowling
The highest electronically measured speed of a ball is 160.45 km/h (99.7 mph), bowled by Jeffrey Robert Thomson (Australia) against the West Indies in Dec 1975.

Wicketkeeping
Most dismissals in an innings
The innings record is nine, by Tahir Rashid (eight catches and a stumping) for Habib Bank v. Pakistan Automobile Corporation at Gujranwala, Pakistan, on 29 Nov 1992; and Wayne James (seven catches and two stumpings) for Matabeleland v. Mashonaland Country Districts at Bulawayo, Zimbabwe, on 19 April 1996.

Most dismissals in a match
The match record is 13 by Wayne James (11 catches and two stumpings) for Matabeleland v. Mashonaland Country Districts at Bulawayo, Zimbabwe, from 19 to 21 April 1996.

Fielding
Most catches in a innings
The innings record is seven, by Michael Stewart for Surrey v. Northamptonshire at Northampton, UK, on 7 June 1957; and by Anthony Stephen Brown for Gloucestershire v. Nottinghamshire at Trent Bridge, Nottingham, UK, on 26 July 1966.

Most match catches
Walter Hammond held ten catches (four and six) for Gloucestershire v. Surrey at Cheltenham, UK, on 16 and 17 Aug 1928.

The most catches in a Test match is seven, by Greg Chappell for Australia v. England at Perth, Australia, from 13 to 17 Dec 1974; by Yajurvindra Singh for India v. England at Bangalore, India, from 28 Jan to 2 Feb 1977; and by Hashan Prasantha Tillekeratne for Sri Lanka v. New Zealand at Colombo, Sri Lanka, from 7 to 9 Dec 1992.

Far left
Percy Fender took just 35 minutes to complete a century for Surrey v. Northamptonshire in Aug 1920.

Left
Sanath Jayasuriya scored a limited-overs century in just 48 balls for Sri Lanka v. Pakistan at Singapore. He eventually scored 134 runs and hit a record 11 sixes during his innings.

Cricket

Right
In 1980 Ian Botham took 10 wickets and scored a century in a match against India. He has the best English all-round Test record.

Limited-overs internationals
Highest innings
The highest team innings score is 398–5, by Sri Lanka against Kenya in a World Cup match at Kandy, Sri Lanka, on 6 March 1996.

The highest score between Test-playing nations is 363–7 (55 overs), by England v. Pakistan at Trent Bridge, Nottingham, UK, on 20 Aug 1992.

Lowest innings
The lowest completed innings total is 43, by Pakistan v. the West Indies at Newlands, Cape Town, South Africa, on 25 Feb 1993.

Highest individual score
Isaac Vivian Alexander Richards scored 189 not out for the West Indies v. England at Old Trafford, Manchester, UK, on 31 May 1984.

Best bowling
The best bowling analysis is 7–37, by Aqib Javed for Pakistan v. India at Sharjah, United Arab Emirates, on 25 Oct 1991.

Career records
The most matches played in one career is 273, by Allan Border (Australia) between 1979 and 1994.

The most runs in a career is 8,648 (an average of 41.37), by Desmond Haynes (West Indies) in 238 matches, 1977–94.

The most wickets in a career is 285 (an average of 22.59), by Wasim Akram (Pakistan) in 198 matches between 1985 and 1996.

The most dismissals in a career is 209 (177 caught and 32 stumped), by Ian Healy (Australia), in 146 matches between 1988 and 1996.

The most catches by a fielder is 127, by Allan Border (Australia).

World Cup
The West Indies are the only side to have won the World Cup twice, in 1975 and 1989

Players
Oldest and youngest first-class cricketers
The Governor of Bombay, Raja Maharaj Singh, was 72 years 192 days old when he went out to bat for his XI v. Commonwealth XI at Bombay, India, on the opening day of a match played from 25 to 27 Nov 1950.

Esmail Ahmed Baporia (India) is reputed to have played for Gujarat against Baroda at Ahmadabad, India, on 10 Jan 1951, at the age of 11 years 261 days.

Oldest and youngest British players
Benjamin Aislabie played for MCC v. Cambridge University at Lord's on 1 and 2 July 1841, at the age of 67 years 169 days.

The youngest English first-class player was Charles Robertson Young, who played for Hampshire v. Kent at Gravesend on 13 June 1867 at the age of 15 years 131 days.

Oldest and youngest Test players
Wilfred Rhodes was 52 years 165 days old when he played for England v. West Indies at Kingston, Jamaica, on 12 April 1930.

Mushtaq Mohammad became the youngest ever Test cricketer when he played for Pakistan v. West Indies at Lahore, Pakistan, on 26 March 1959, aged 15 years 124 days.

The youngest ever English Test cricketer, Brian Close, was 18 years 149 days old when he played against New Zealand at Old Trafford, Manchester, UK, on 23 July 1949.

All-rounders
Wilfred Rhodes achieved the 'double' of 1,000 runs and 100 wickets a record 16 times, from 1903 to 1926.

George Herbert Hirst (Yorkshire and England) is the only player to have scored more than 2,000 runs (2,385) and taken more than 200 wickets (208) in the same season (1906).

The best all-round Test career was that of Kapil Dev Nikhanj (India), who scored 5,248 runs (an average of 31.05), took 434 wickets (an average of 29.64) and held 64 catches in 131 matches, between 1978 and 1994.

The best English all-round Test record is held by Ian Terence Botham, with 5,200 runs (an average of 33.54), 383 wickets (an average of 28.40) and 120 catches in 102 matches, between 1977 and 1992.

Two people have scored a century and taken 10 wickets in a Test match: Ian Botham (114, 6–58, 7–48) for England v. India in the Golden Jubilee Test at Bombay, India, from 15 to 19 Feb 1980; and Imran Khan Niazi (117, 6–98, 5–82) for Pakistan v. India at Faisalabad, Pakistan, from 3 to 8 Jan 1983.

County Championship
Most titles
The most wins is 30, by Yorkshire: 29 outright (the last in 1968) and one shared (in 1949).

Most consecutive titles
The most consecutive title wins is seven, by Surrey from 1952 to 1958.

'BETTY' WILSON WAS TH[

Women's cricket
Batting
The highest individual innings on record is 224 not out, by Mabel Bryant for Visitors v. Residents at Eastbourne, E Sussex, UK, in Aug 1901.

The record for the highest ever innings in a women's Test match is 204, scored by Kirsty Flavell in 555 minutes, playing for New Zealand v. England at Scarborough, N Yorkshire, UK, on 26 and 27 June 1996 in a four-day Test.

The greatest number of runs scored in an international career in women's cricket is 1,594, by Rachel Flint (England) in 22 Test matches (an average of 45.54) from Dec 1960 to July 1979. She scored a further 220 runs in three unofficial tests.

The greatest number of runs scored in one innings by a team in women's cricket is 567, by Tarana v. Rockley at Rockley, NSW, Australia, in 1896.

The highest team Test innings is 525, by Australia v. India at Ahmadabad, India, on 4 Feb 1984.

The lowest ever score by a team in a Test match is 35, by England v. Australia at St Kilda, Melbourne, Australia, on 22 Feb 1958.

Bowling
Mary Beatrice Duggan (England) took a record 77 wickets (an average of 13.49) in 17 Tests from 1949 to 1963. She also recorded the best Test analysis, taking 7–6 for England v. Australia at St Kilda, Melbourne, Australia, on 22 Feb 1958.

Rubina Winifred Humphries took 10–0 and scored all the runs for Dalton Ladies v. Woodfield SC, at Huddersfield, W Yorkshire, UK, on 26 June 1931. This feat was equalled by Rosemary White for Wallington LCC v. Beaconsfield LCC in July 1962.

All-rounder
Elizabeth 'Betty' Wilson (Australia) was the first ever player to score a century and take ten wickets in a Test match. She took 7–7 and 4–9, and went on to score exactly 100 runs in the second innings, playing against England at St Kilda, Melbourne, Australia, from 21 to 24 Feb 1958.

Enid Bakewell was the first English player to score a century and take 10 wickets in a Test match, against the West Indies at Edgbaston, UK, from 1 to 3 July 1979. She scored 112 not out and had match figures of 10–75.

Wicketkeeping
Lisa Nye claimed eight dismissals (six caught and two stumped) in an innings for England

throughout an innings of 836, in a Junior House match between Clarke's House (now Poole's) and North Town, at Clifton College, Bristol, UK, on 22 and 23 and from 26 to 28 June 1899. The scorer, E. W. Pegler, gave the score as '628—plus or minus 20, shall we say'.

Highest partnership
The highest ever recorded partnership was between Vinod Kambli (349 not out) and Sachin Tendulkar (326 not out) from 23 to 25 Feb 1988. They put on an unbeaten partnership of 664 runs for the third wicket, for Sharadashram Vidyamandir against St Xavier's High School during a Harris Shield match at Sassanian Ground, Bombay, India.

Fastest individual scoring
The fastest ever 50 was scored by Stanley Keppel 'Shunter' Coen (South Africa) in a record seven minutes, playing for Gezira v. the RAF in 1942.

Lindsay Martin scored a century off 20 deliveries (13 sixes, five fours and two singles) for Rosewater v. Warradale on 19 Dec 1987.

Most runs off a ball
Garry Chapman (partnered by Chris Veal) scored 17 (all run, with no overthrows) off a single delivery for Banyule against Macleod at Windsor Reserve, Victoria, Australia, on 13 Oct 1990. Chapman had pulled the ball to mid-wicket, where it disappeared into 25-cm-high (10-in) grass.

Successive sixes
Cedric Ivan James Smith hit a record nine successive sixes for a Middlesex XI v. Harrow and District at Rayner's Lane, Harrow, UK, in 1935. This was repeated by Arthur Dudley Nourse playing for a South African XI v. Military Police at Cairo, Egypt, in 1942/3. Nourse's innings included six sixes in an over.

Bowling
Nine wickets with nine consecutive balls were taken by Paul Hugo for Smithfield School v. Aliwal North, South Africa, in Feb 1931, and by Stephen Fleming, for Marlborough College 'A' XI v. Bohally Intermediate at Blenheim, New Zealand, in Dec 1967.

In the Inter-Divisional Ships Shield at Purfleet, Essex, UK, on 17 May 1924, Joseph William Brockley took all 10 wickets, clean bowled, for two runs in 11 balls. This included a triple hat-trick.

Bowling figures of 10 for 0 have been achieved by Jennings Tune (all bowled, in five overs) for Cliffe v. Eastrington in the Howden and District League at Cliffe, Yorkshire, UK, on 6 May 1922; by Wynton Edwards of Queen's College (10 overs) against Selborne College at Queenstown, South Africa, on 25 March 1950; by Errol Hall (27 balls) for Australian v. Tannymorel at Warwick, Queensland, Australia, on 2 Nov 1986; and by Alex Kelly (27 balls) for Bishop Auckland v. Newton Aycliffe in the Milburngate Durham County Junior League at Bishop Auckland, Durham, UK, in June 1994.

RST PLAYER TO SCORE A CENTURY AND TAKE TEN WICKETS IN A TEST MATCH

against New Zealand at New Plymouth, New Zealand, from 12 to 15 Feb 1992.

Most international appearances
Deborah Hockley (New Zealand) has made 89 appearances (18 Tests and 71 one-day internationals) between 1976 and 1996.

Janette Brittin earned 76 English caps (a record 24 Tests and a total of 52 one-day internationals) between 1976 and 1996.

World Cup
Australia have won the women's World Cup three times, in 1978, 1982 and 1988.

Lindsay Reeler scored 143 not out, for Australia v. Netherlands at Perth, Australia, on 29 Nov 1988.

Janette Brittin (England) has scored a record 1,007 runs in all World Cup matches.

The most wickets taken in World Cup matches is 39, by Lyn Fullston (Australia).

Minor cricket records
Highest individual innings
Arthur Edward Jeanne Collins scored an unprecedented 628 not out in 6 hr 50 min, over five afternoons' batting, carrying his bat

In 1881 Frederick Robert Spofforth clean bowled all ten wickets in both innings (for final figures of 20 for 48) at Bendemeer, NSW, Australia. This was repeated by J. Bryant for Erskine v. Deaf Mutes in Melbourne, Australia, on 15 and 22 Oct 1887, and by Albert Rimmer for Linwood School v. Cathedral GS at Canterbury, New Zealand, in Dec 1925.

In the 1910 season, H. Hopkinson of Mildmay Cricket Club, London, UK, took 99 wickets for 147 runs.

Longest throw
A 155-g (5½-oz) cricket ball is reputed to have been thrown 128.6 m (140 yd 2 ft) by left-hander Robert Percival on Durham Sands racecourse on 18 April 1882.

Wicketkeeping
Welihinda Badalge Bennett caught four and stumped six batsmen in one innings on 1 March 1953, for Mahinda College v. Galle CC at the Galle Esplanade, Sri Lanka.

Fielding
In a secondary schools' 11-a-side match in Wellington, New Zealand, on 16 March 1974, 13-year-old Stephen Lane held 14 catches in the field (seven in each innings) for St Patrick's College, Silverstream v. St Bernard's College, Lower Hutt.

Left
Rachel Flint, the leading run scorer in women's Test cricket, has scored 1,594 runs in 22 matches.

Football

World Cup (team)

Most wins
Brazil have won the World Cup a record four times, in 1958, 1962, 1970 and 1994.

Most appearances
Brazil are the only team to have taken part in all 15 finals tournaments. France and the USA are the only two other nations to have entered all World Cup competitions, although the latter withdrew in 1938 without playing.

The most winning teams played for is three, by Pelé (Brazil), in 1958, 1962 and 1970.

Youngest and oldest players in finals
Norman Whiteside was 17 years 41 days old when he played for Northern Ireland against Yugoslavia on 17 June 1982.

Albert Roger Milla was 42 years 39 days old when he played for Cameroon v. Russia on 28 June 1994.

The highest margin in the British Isles occurred when England beat Ireland 13–0 at Belfast on 18 Feb 1882.

The highest score between English clubs in a major competition was Preston North End's 26–0 win over Hyde in an FA Cup tie at Deepdale, Lancs, on 15 Oct 1887.

The highest score by one side in a Football League (First Division) match is 12, by: West Bromwich Albion, who beat Darwen 12–0 on 4 April 1892; Nottingham Forest, who beat Leicester Fosse 12–0 on 21 April 1909; and Aston Villa, who had a 12–2 victory over Accrington at Perry Barr, W Midlands, on 12 March 1892.

Right and far right
Brazil, shown here winning the World Cup in 1962 and in 1994, have won the competition a record four times. The Fédération Internationale de Football Association (FIFA), which was founded on 21 May 1904, instituted the first World Cup in Montevideo, Uruguay, on 13 July 1930. It is held quadrennially.

Most goals in one game 13

Most goals
The record for the most goals in one game was set in a qualifying match in Auckland, New Zealand, on 15 Aug 1981, when the home team beat Fiji 13–0.

The highest score during the final stages was achieved by Hungary in a 10–1 win over El Salvador at Elche, Spain, on 15 June 1982.

The highest ever match aggregate in the finals tournament was 12, when Austria beat Switzerland 7–5 at Lausanne, Switzerland, on 26 June 1954.

The most goals in a single finals tournament is 27 (five games), by Hungary in 1954.

Brazil have scored the most goals overall, with a total of 159 in 73 matches.

World Cup (individual)
Most appearances
Antonio Carbajal is the only player to have appeared in five World Cup finals tournaments, as goalkeeper for Mexico in 11 games in 1950, 1954, 1958, 1962 and 1966.

The most games in finals tournaments is 21, by: Uwe Seeler (West Germany), 1958–70; Wladyslaw Zmuda (Poland), 1974–86; Diego Armando Maradona (Argentina), 1982–94; and Lothar Matthäus (Germany), 1982–94.

Most goals
The most goals in one game is five, by Oleg Salenko in Russia's 6–1 win over Cameroon at Palo Alto, California, USA, on 28 June 1994.

The most goals in one tournament is 13, by Just Fontaine in six matches in 1958.

Fontaine Jairzinho (Brazil) and Alcide Ghiggia (Uruguay) are the only players to score in every match stage of a final series. Jairzinho scored seven in six games in 1970 and Ghiggia scored four in four games in 1950.

Gerd Müller scored 10 goals in 1970 and four in 1974, for the record aggregate of 14.

The most goals scored in a final is three, by Geoffrey Charles Hurst for England v. West Germany on 30 July 1966.

First-class team records
Highest scores
The highest score in a first-class match was Arbroath's 36–0 Scottish Cup win over Bon Accord on 5 Sept 1885. The score would have been higher but for the lack of nets and the consequent waste of retrieval time.

The highest known margin in an international was achieved in England's 17–0 victory over Australia at Sydney on 30 June 1951. England do not list the match as a full international.

The highest aggregate in League Football was 17 goals, in Tranmere Rovers' 13–4 win over Oldham Athletic in a Third Division (North) match at Prenton Park, Merseyside, on 26 Dec 1935.

The record margin in a League match was 13, in Newcastle United's 13–0 defeat of Newport County in a (Second Division) match on 5 Oct 1946, and in Stockport County's 13–0 defeat of Halifax Town in Third Division (North) on 6 Jan 1934.

Most goals in a season
In a professional league, the most goals by a British team is 142 in 34 matches, by Raith Rovers (Scottish Second Division) in 1937/8.

The English League record is 134 goals in 46 matches, by Peterborough United (Fourth Division) in 1960/1.

League championships
Most national league championships
The most successive championships is nine, by: Celtic (Scotland), from 1966 to 1974; CSKA, Sofia (Bulgaria), from 1954 to 1962; and MTK Budapest (Hungary), from 1917 to 1925. The Sofia club hold a European post-war record of 27 league titles.

English
The most League Championships (First Division) is 18, by Liverpool (1901, 1906, 1922–23, 1947, 1964, 1966, 1973, 1976–77, 1979–80, 1982–84, 1986, 1988 and 1990).

The record for the most wins in a season is 33 from 42 matches, by Doncaster Rovers in Third Division (North) in 1946/7.

The First Division record is 31 wins from 42 matches, by Tottenham Hotspur in 1960/1.

The most points in a season under the current scoring system is 102 from 46 matches, by Swindon in the Fourth Division in 1985/6. Under the new system the First Division record is Liverpool's 98 in 1978/9.

The only FA Cup and League Championship 'doubles' were by Preston North End in 1889, Aston Villa in 1897, Tottenham Hotspur in 1961, Arsenal in 1971, Liverpool in 1986 and Manchester United in 1994 and 1996.

Scottish
Rangers of Glasgow have won the Scottish League Championship 46 times between 1891 and 1996. Their 76 points (from a possible 84) in the 1920/1 Scottish First Division is a record for any division. A better percentage was achieved by Rangers in 1898/9 when they gained the maximum 36 by winning all their 18 matches.

Youngest players
The youngest FA Cup player, Andrew Awford, was 15 years 88 days old when he played in a qualifier for Worcester City on 10 Oct 1987.

The youngest player in a final was James Prinsep, for Clapham Rovers v. Old Etonians on 29 March 1879, aged 17 years 245 days.

Most medals
The most FA Cup-winners' medals is five, by: James Henry Forrest (1884–86, 1890–91); Sir Arthur Fitzgerald Kinnaird (1873, 1877–78, 1879, 1882); and Charles Harold Reynolds Wollaston (1872–73, 1876–78).

The most Scottish Cup-winners' medals won is eight by Charles Campbell (Queen's Park), 1874–76, 1880–82, 1884 and 1886.

Scottish FA Cup
The greatest number of wins is 30, by Celtic (1892, 1899, 1900, 1904, 1907–08, 1911–12, 1914, 1923, 1925, 1927, 1931, 1933, 1937, 1951, 1954, 1965, 1967, 1969, 1971–72, 1974–75, 1977, 1980, 1985, 1988–89, 1995).

Scottish League Cup
The most wins is 19, by Rangers between 1947 and 1993.

Derek Johnstone (Rangers) was 16 years 11 months old when he played in the final against Celtic on 24 Oct 1970.

Left
Paul Gascoigne or 'Gazza', a key player in Rangers' record 46th Scottish League Championship victory in 1996, is seen here moments after scoring England's second goal against Scotland in Euro '96 at Wembley.

The record for the highest paid attendance in the United Kingdom was the 149,547 spectators present at the Scotland v. England international at Hampden Park, Glasgow, on 17 April 1937. This total was probably exceeded at the FA Cup final between Bolton Wanderers and West Ham United at Wembley Stadium on 28 April 1923, when the crowd spilled onto the pitch and the start was delayed by 40 minutes. The counted admissions were 126,047 but there were an estimated 160,000 spectators.

The record attendance at a League match in the United Kingdom is 118,567, for Rangers v. Celtic at Ibrox Park, Glasgow, in Jan 1939.

Smallest crowds
The smallest ever crowd at a full home international was 2,315, at the game between Wales and Northern Ireland on 27 May 1982 at the Racecourse Ground, Wrexham, UK.

The smallest paying attendance at a Football League fixture was for the Stockport County v. Leicester City match at Old Trafford, Manchester, UK, on 7 May 1921. Stockport's ground was under suspension and the 'crowd' numbered 13, but an estimated 2,000 people gained free admission.

Due to disciplinary action by the European Football Union, there were no paying spectators when West Ham beat Castilla (Spain) 5–1 in the European Cup Winners' Cup at Upton Park, London, UK, on 1 Oct 1980, or when Aston Villa beat Besiktas (Turkey) 3–1 in the European Cup at Villa Park, Birmingham, UK, on 15 Sept 1982.

Most peripatetic fan
Ken Ferris of Redbridge, Essex, UK, watched a League match at all the League grounds in England and Wales (including Berwick Rangers) in 237 days from 1994 to 1995.

Left
Manchester United team and fans celebrate winning the double for an unprecedented second time, in 1996.

OTBALL MATCH WAS 199,854, IN BRAZIL IN 1950

Cup competitions
FA Cup
The most wins is nine (from a record 14 finals) by Manchester United (1909, 1948, 1963, 1977, 1983, 1985, 1990, 1994 and 1996).

The most goals in a final was in Blackburn Rovers' 6–1 defeat of Sheffield Wednesday in 1890 and Blackpool's 4–3 win over Bolton Wanderers in 1953.

The biggest margin of victory occurred in Bury's 6–0 defeat of Derby County in 1903.

Football League Cup
The most wins is five by Liverpool (1981–84, 1995) and Aston Villa (1961, 1975, 1977, 1994 and 1996).

Spectators
Largest crowds
The biggest recorded crowd at a football match was the 199,854 spectators at the Brazil v. Uruguay World Cup match in the Maracanã Municipal Stadium, Rio de Janeiro, Brazil, in July 1950.

Footballers

Top
The top scorer in Euro 96 with a total of five goals, Briton Alan Shearer commanded a world record transfer fee of £15 million in July 1996.

Middle
Pelé and Bobby Moore exchange shirts at the end of the 1970 World Cup match. Brazil went on to win the World Cup for a third time, and Pelé was awarded a record third winner's medal.

Bottom
Between 20 Sept 1972 and 15 June 1974—for a record 13 international matches—goalkeeper Dino Zoff prevented any goals being scored against Italy.

Goal scoring

Match
The most goals scored by one player in a first-class match is 16, by Stephan Stanis for Racing Club de Lens v. Aubry-Asturies in Lens, France, in a wartime French Cup game on 13 Dec 1942.

The most goals scored by one player in an international match is 10, by Sofus Nielsen for Denmark in their 17–1 victory over France in the 1908 Olympics, and by Gottfried Fuchs for Germany in their 16–0 victory over Russia in the 1912 Olympic tournament (consolation event) in Sweden.

The most goals scored in a match in the United Kingdom is 13, by John Petrie for Arbroath v. Bon Accord in a Scottish Cup match on 5 Sept 1885.

The most goals scored in an English league match is 10, by Joe Payne for Luton Town v. Bristol Rovers at Luton on 13 April 1936.

Season
The most goals in a league season is 60 in 39 games, by William Ralph 'Dixie' Dean for Everton (First Division) in 1927/8, and 66 in 38 games by James Smith for Ayr United (Scottish Second Division) in the same season. With three more in Cup ties and 19 in representative matches, Dean's total was 82.

Career
Artur Friedenreich (Brazil) scored 1,329 goals (undocumented) during a 26-year first-class football career from 1909 to 1935.

The most goals in a specified period is 1,279, by Edson Arantes do Nascimento or Pelé

Fastest goals
The fastest British league goals on record were six seconds, by: Albert E. Mundy for Aldershot v. Hartlepool United at Victoria Ground, Hartlepool, Co. Durham, on 25 Oct 1958; Barrie Jones for Notts County v. Torquay United on 31 March 1962; and Keith Smith for Crystal Palace v. Derby County at the Baseball Ground, Derby, on 12 Dec 1964.

Torquay United's Pat Kruse equalled the fastest goal on record when he headed the ball into his own net only six seconds after kick-off v. Cambridge United on 3 Jan 1977.

The record for the fastest confirmed hat-trick is 2½ minutes, by Ephraim 'Jock' Dodds for Blackpool v. Tranmere Rovers on 28 Feb 1942, and by Jimmy Scarth for Gillingham v. Leyton Orient on 1 Nov 1952.

Tommy Bryce scored for Queen of the South in the 9th, 10th and 11th minutes of their game against Arbroath on 18 Dec 1993.

A hat-trick in 1 min 50 sec is claimed for Maglioni of Independiente v. Gimnasia y Esgrima de La Plata in Argentina in 1973.

The international record is three goals in 3½ minutes, by George William Hall for England against Ireland on 16 Nov 1938 at Old Trafford, Manchester, UK.

International caps

Oldest
William Henry 'Billy' Meredith played outside right for Wales v. England at Highbury, London, UK, on 15 March 1920, at the age of 45 years 229 days. He played internationally

(Brazil) in 1,363 games from 7 Sept 1956 to 1 Oct 1977. His best year was 1959, with 126 goals, and his 1,000th goal was a penalty for his club Santos at the Maracanã Stadium, Rio de Janeiro, on 19 Nov 1969 when playing his 909th first-class match. He later added two goals in special appearances.

The international career record by an England player is 49 goals, by Robert 'Bobby' Charlton from April 1958 to May 1970.

The most goals scored in British first-class football is 550 (410 in Scottish League matches), by James McGrory of Celtic from 1922 to 1938.

The most goals in English league matches is 434, by George Arthur Rowley for West Bromwich Albion, Fulham, Leicester City and Shrewsbury Town, 1946–65. He scored 32 goals in the FA Cup and one for England 'B'.

for a record span of 26 years, between 1895 and 1920.

Youngest
The youngest British international was Norman Whiteside, who played for Northern Ireland v. Yugoslavia at the age of 17 years 41 days on 17 June 1982.

England's youngest international was James Frederick McLeod Prinsep, who played against Scotland at Kennington Oval, London, UK, on 5 April 1879, aged 17 years 252 days.

The youngest Welsh cap was Ryan Giggs, who was 17 years 321 days old when he played against Germany at Nüremberg, Germany, on 16 Oct 1991.

Scotland's youngest international was John Alexander Lambie, who was 17 years 92 days old when he played Ireland on 20 March 1886.

Most international appearances
The most appearances for a national team is 147, by Majed Abdullah Mohammed (Saudi Arabia) from 1978 to 1994.

The British record for the most appearances is 125, by Peter Shilton (England).

Longest careers
Peter Shilton made a record 1,380 senior British appearances, including a record 996 League appearances (286 for Leicester City, 110 for Stoke City, 202 for Nottingham Forest, 188 for Southampton, 175 for Derby County, 34 for Plymouth Argyle and one for Bolton Wanderers, one League play-off, 86 FA Cup, 102 League Cup, 125 internationals, 13 Under-23, four Football League XI and 53 European and other club competitions).

over Milton Keynes Reserves at Norwich, UK, on 25 Sept 1983.

The most goals in a season by one player in junior professional league football is 96, by Tom Duffy for Ardeer Thistle FC, Strathclyde, UK, in 1960/1.

Paul Anthony Moulden scored 289 goals in 40 games for Bolton Lads Club in Bolton Boys Federation intermediate league and cup matches in 1981/2. An additional 51 goals scored in other tournaments brought his total to 340—the highest season figure for one player in any class of competitive football.

Goalkeeping
Thomas McKenna, the goalkeeper for Folkestone Invicta under-13s, played for a

Best ball control
In July 1994 Ricardinho Neves (Brazil) juggled a regulation soccer ball non-stop with his feet, legs and head, without the ball touching the ground, for a record-breaking 19 hr 5 min 31 sec at Los Angeles Convention Center, California, USA.

The heading record is 7 hr 17 min 5 sec, by Tomas Lundman (Sweden) at Thorpe Park, Chertsey, Surrey, UK, on 27 June 1995.

Jan Skorkovsky of Czechoslovakia kept a football up for 7 hr 18 min 55 sec when he covered 42.195 km (26 miles 385 yd) for the Prague City Marathon on 8 July 1990.

Left
In 1991 Ryan Giggs became the youngest ever Welsh international. He had played for England under-15s just three years before.

TCH, ALL 22 PLAYERS AND ONE LINESMAN WERE BOOKED

Norman John Trollope made 770 League appearances for Swindon Town, 1960–80.

Highest transfer fee
The top transfer fee quoted for a player is £15 million, for British player Alan Shearer when he transferred from Blackburn Rovers to Newcastle United on 29 July 1996. Shearer is the first player since WWII to score 30 or more goals in three consecutive seasons and the first to score 100 Premiership goals.

Goalkeeping
The longest that a goalkeeper has prevented a goal being scored in top-class competition is 1,275 minutes, by Abel Resino of Athletico Madrid to 17 March 1991.

The goalkeeping record in international matches is 1,142 minutes, by Dino Zoff (Italy), from Sept 1972 to June 1974.

The British club record in competitive matches is 1,196 minutes, by Chris Woods for Rangers of Glasgow from 26 Nov 1986 to 31 Jan 1987.

Non first-class games
Highest scores
The highest team score is 49–0, by Drayton Grange Colts v. Eldon Sports Reserves in a Daventry and District Sunday League match at Grange Estate, Northants, UK, on 13 Nov 1988. Every member of the side scored at least one goal, including the goalkeeper.

The full-time score in an Under-14 League match between Midas FC and Courage Colts in Kent, UK, on 11 April 1976, was 59–1 after 70 minutes' play.

Dean Goodliff scored a record 26 individual goals for Deleford Colts in their 33–0 win over Iver Minors in the Slough Boys Soccer Combination Under-14 League at Iver, Bucks, UK, on 22 Dec 1985.

The greatest number of goals to have been scored by a female player is 22, by Linda Curl of Norwich Ladies in a 40–0 league victory

total of 1,417 minutes without conceding a single goal, between 24 Sept 1995 and 5 May 1996.

Most and least successful teams
Winlaton West End FC played 95 consecutive league games without defeat, 1976–80.

Penlake Junior Football Club remained unbeaten for a record 153 games in the Warrington Hilden Friendly League between 1981 and 1986.

The most consecutive losses is 39 league and cup games, by Stockport United FC from Sept 1976 to 18 Feb 1978, and by Poole Town in 1995/6.

Most undisciplined
In the local cup match between Tongham Youth Club, Surrey, and Hawley, Hants, UK, on 3 Nov 1969, the referee booked all 22 players, including one player who went to hospital, and a linesman.

In a Gancia Cup match at Waltham Abbey, Essex, UK, on 23 Dec 1973, the referee sent off the entire Juventus-Cross team and some club officials.

Glencraig United had all 11 team members and two substitutes for their 2–2 draw against Goldenhill Boys' Club on 2 Feb 1975 booked in the dressing room before a ball was kicked, when the referee took exception to the chant that greeted his arrival.

In June 1993, it was reported that 20 players were sent off in a league match between Sportivo Ameliano and General Caballero in Paraguay. When two Sportivo players were sent off, a 10-minute fight ensued and the referee dismissed a further 18 players. The match was abandoned.

Rugby League

Right
Wigan are the most successful club side in British Rugby League. Their dominance of the Challenge Cup in the late 1980s (a run of 43 games undefeated) was ended on 11 Feb 1996, when Salford beat them 26–16.

Records are based on the scoring system in use at the time.

HIGHEST EVER ATTENDANCE AT A RUGBY LEAG

Competitions

World Cup wins
Australia have won the World Cup a record seven times, in 1957, 1968, 1970, 1977, 1988, 1992 and 1995, and also won the International Championship in 1975.

Most titles
Wigan have won 17 League Championships, 1909, 1922, 1926, 1934, 1946–47, 1950, 1952, 1960, 1987 and 1990–96.

Wigan have won the Rugby League Challenge Cup 16 times, 1924, 1929, 1948, 1951, 1958–59, 1965, 1985 and 1988–95.

Four clubs have won all the major Rugby League trophies in one season: Hunslet in 1907/8, Huddersfield in 1914/5, and Swinton in 1927/8, all won the Challenge Cup, League Championship, County Cup and County League—the last two of which are now defunct. Wigan won the Challenge Cup, League Championship, Premiership and Regal Trophy (now defunct) in 1994/5.

Most successful teams
Wigan won a record 31 consecutive league games from Feb 1970 to Feb 1971.

Huddersfield were undefeated for 40 league and cup games in 1913/14.

Hull is the only club to win all league games in a season, with 26 in Division II in 1978/9.

Least successful teams
Runcorn Highfield lost a record 55 consecutive league games between 29 Jan 1989 and 27 Jan 1991.

Highest team scores

Highest scores in senior matches
The highest aggregate score in a game involving a senior club is 146 points, when Huddersfield beat Blackpool Gladiators 142–4 at Huddersfield, W Yorkshire, UK, in the first round of the Regal Trophy on 26 Nov 1994.

The highest score in league football is 104–4, by Keighley Cougars v. Highfield on 23 April 1995.

On 14 Sept 1986, St Helens beat Carlisle 112–0 in the Lancashire Cup.

The highest score ever achieved in a First Division game is 90–0, by Leeds v. Barrow on 11 Feb 1990.

The highest scoring draw is 46–46 between Sheffield Eagles and Leeds on 10 April 1994.

Challenge Cup Final
The highest score ever achieved in a Challenge Cup final is 40–32 by St Helens (eight tries and four goals) against Bradford Bulls, at Wembley, London, UK, on 27 April 1996. The match aggregate of 72 points is also a record.

International matches
Australia scored a record 86 points against South Africa (6), at Gateshead, Tyne and Wear, UK, on 10 Oct 1995.

England's highest score was its 73–6 defeat of France in a European Championship match at Gateshead, UK, on 12 June 1996.

Most points
During the 1994/5 season, Wigan scored a record 1,735 points in league and cup games, and Highfield conceded a record 1,687.

Highest individual scores

Most points, goals and tries in a game
George Henry 'Tich' West scored 53 points (10 goals and a record 11 tries) for Hull Kingston Rovers in their 73–5 Challenge Cup defeat of Brookland Rovers on 4 March 1905.

Most points in a league match
Dean John Marwood twice scored 42 points for Workington Town: in a 78–0 win over Highfield on 1 Nov 1992 and in a 92–4 defeat of the same team on 26 Feb 1995.

Most goals in a match
James 'Jim' Sullivan kicked 22 for Wigan against Flimby and Fothergill on 14 Feb 1925.

Most points in a season and career
Benjamin Lewis Jones (Leeds) scored 496 (194 goals, 36 tries) in 1956/7.

COSTLIEST CASH-ONLY TRANSFER WAS £440,000, FOR MARTIN OFFIA

Neil Fox scored 6,220 points (2,575 goals, including four drop goals, and 358 tries) in a senior Rugby League career lasting from 10 April 1956 to 19 Aug 1979.

Most tries in a season
Albert Aaron Rosenfeld (Huddersfield), an Australian-born wing-threequarter, scored 80 tries in 42 matches in the 1913/4 season.

Most tries in a career
Brian Bevan (Australia), a wing-threequarter, scored 796 tries in 18 seasons (16 with Warrington, two with Blackpool Borough) from 1945 to 1964. He scored 740 tries for Warrington, 17 for Blackpool and 39 in representative matches.

Most goals in a season
David Watkins (Salford) scored 221 goals in 47 matches in the 1972/3 season.

Most goals in a career
Jim Sullivan (Wigan) kicked 2,867 goals in his career from 1921 to 1946.

Greatest consecutive scores
David Watkins (Salford) played and scored in every club game in 1972/3 and 1973/4, contributing 41 tries and 403 goals—a total of 929 points in 92 games.

Papua New Guinea at Wagga Wagga, Australia, on 20 July 1988; and Andrew Johns (Australia) against South Africa at Gateshead, Tyne and Wear, UK, on 10 Oct 1995.

Record kicks and tries
Longest kicks
Arthur Atkinson (Castleford) kicked a 75-yd (68-m) penalty from his own 25-yd line in a league game at St Helens on 26 Oct 1929.

The longest drop goal is 61 yd (56 m), by Joseph 'Joe' Lydon for Wigan v. Warrington in a Challenge Cup semi-final at Maine Road, Manchester, UK, on 25 March 1989.

Fastest tries
Lee Jackson scored after nine seconds for Hull against Sheffield Eagles in a Yorkshire Cup semi-final at Don Valley Stadium, Sheffield, S Yorkshire, UK, on 6 Oct 1992.

The fastest try in an international match is 15 seconds, by Bobby Fulton for Australia against France at Odsal Stadium, Bradford, W Yorkshire, UK, on 1 Nov 1970.

Most Challenge Cup finals
The greatest number of appearances is 10, by Shaun Edwards, for Wigan from 1984 to

Left
Joe Lydon, record holder for the longest drop goal, began his career at Widnes and was transferred to Wigan in 1985 for the then world-record fee of £100,000.

The youngest representative player was Harold Wagstaff, who played for Yorkshire at the age of 17 years 141 days in Sept 1908, and for England against Australia at the age of 17 years 228 days in Jan 1909.

The youngest player ever to feature in a Cup final was Francis Cummins, who was 17 years 200 days old when he played for Leeds in their 16–26 defeat by Wigan at Wembley on 30 April 1994.

Left
Australian player Andrew Johns, seen here being collared by Bobby Goulding (England) during the 1995 World Cup final, holds the record for the most points scored by one player in a match at 30.

The youngest Great Britain international player ever is Paul Newlove, who played in the first test against New Zealand on 21 Oct 1989 at Old Trafford, Greater Manchester, UK, aged 18 years 72 days.

Oldest player
The oldest person ever to play for Great Britain was Jeffrey Grayshon, who was 36 years 250 days old when he played in a test match against New Zealand at Elland Road, Leeds, UK, on 9 Nov 1985.

Highest transfer fees
Paul Newlove moved from Bradford Bulls to St Helens for a deal valued at £500,000 (players plus cash) on 29 Nov 1995.

The costliest cash-only transfer was £440,000, for Martin Offiah from Widnes to Wigan on 3 Jan 1992.

TCH IS 102,569, AT ODSAL STADIUM IN 1954

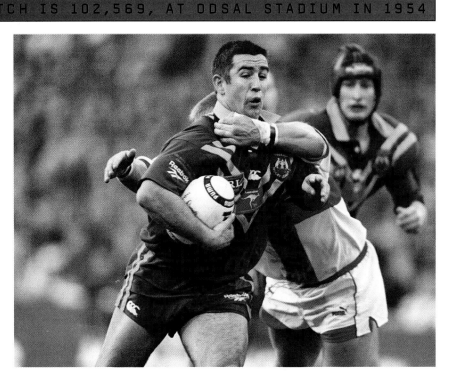

Individual international records
Jim Sullivan (Wigan) has played in the most internationals (60 for Wales and Great Britain from 1921 to 1939), kicked the most goals (160) and scored the most points (329).

Michael Sullivan played in 51 international games for England and Great Britain and scored a record 45 tries from 1954 to 1963.

The most points by an individual in a game is 30, by Michael O'Connor (Australia) against

1985 and from 1988 to 1995. He was on the winning side nine times (all but 1984), and during his career at Wigan, from 1983 to 1996, he has received 39 medals as winner or runner-up in major competitions.

Players and spectators
Youngest players
Harold Spencer Edmondson played his first league game for Bramley at the age of 15 years 81 days on 1 Feb 1919.

Greatest crowds
The greatest attendance at any Rugby League match is 102,569, for the Warrington v. Halifax Challenge Cup final replay at Odsal Stadium, Bradford, UK, on 5 May 1954.

The highest ever attendance at any international match is 73,631 spectators, for the World Cup Final between Australia and Great Britain at Wembley Stadium, London, UK, on 24 Oct 1992.

Rugby Union

Records are based on the scoring system in use at the time.

Team wins and scores

World Cup
No team has won more than once. The largest margin of victory in a final was 29–9, by New Zealand v. France in 1987.

The largest margin of victory in a Women's World Cup final was 38–23 by England v. USA.

International Championship
Wales has won a record 22 times outright and tied for first a further 11 times to 1994.

The greatest number of grand slams (winning all four matches) is 11, by England (1913–14, 1921, 1923–24, 1928, 1957, 1980, 1991–92 and 1995).

The highest score in an International Championship match was at Swansea, UK, on

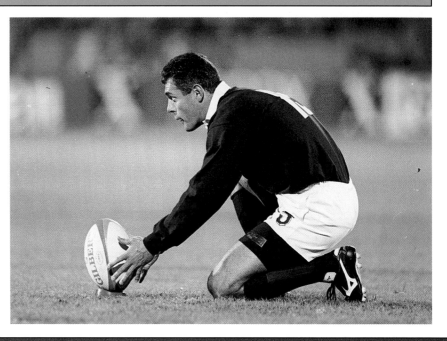

1 Jan 1910, when Wales beat France 49–14 (eight goals, one penalty goal, two tries, to one goal, two penalty goals, one try).

The highest individual score in a season is 67 points (three tries, 11 penalty goals and 11 conversions), by Jonathan Mark Webb in the four games of an International Championship series in 1992. England scored a record 118 points in their four games.

Internationals
The highest score in any full international is when Hong Kong beat Singapore 164–13 in a

Mark Wyatt was the first player to kick eight penalties in an international match. He scored all 24 of Canada's points in their victory over Scotland.

World Cup qualifying match at Kuala Lumpur, Malaysia, on 27 Oct 1994.

The highest aggregate score for any international match between the Four Home Unions is when England beat Wales by 82–0 (seven goals, one drop goal and six tries) at Blackheath, London, UK, on 19 Feb 1881.

Highest match scores
Scores of more than 200 points have been recorded in school matches.

In Denmark, Comet beat Lindo by 194–0 on 17 Nov 1973.

The highest British score is 174–0, by 7th Signal Regiment v. 4th Armoured Workshop, REME, on 5 Nov 1980 at Herford, Germany.

The highest match score in the Courage Clubs Championship is 146–0, by Billingham against Hartlepool Athletic at Billingham, Co. Durham, UK, on 3 Oct 1987.

Highest score in one season
Neath in South Wales, UK, scored 1,917 points (including a record 345 tries) in 47 games in the 1988/9 season.

Individual scores
Internationals
In the World Cup qualifying match between Hong Kong and Singapore at Kuala Lumpur, Malaysia, on 27 Oct 1994, Hong Kong's Ashley Billington scored 50 points (10 tries).

The most points scored by a British player in an international match is 44 (four tries, nine conversions and two penalty goals), by Gavin Hastings for Scotland v. Ivory Coast at Rustenberg, South Africa, on 26 May 1995.

The highest individual points score in a match between the major nations is 27 (one try, two conversions, five penalty goals and a drop goal), by Rob Andrew for England against South Africa at Pretoria on 4 June 1994.

The most tries in an international match between the major nations is five, by George Campbell Lindsay for Scotland v. Wales on 26 Feb 1887, and by Douglas 'Daniel' Lambert for England v. France on 5 Jan 1907.

The most penalty goals in a match is eight, by: Mark Andrew Wyatt, for Canada v. Scotland at St John, New Brunswick, Canada, on 25 May 1991; Neil Roger Jenkins for Wales v. Canada at Cardiff, Wales, on 10 Nov 1993; Santiago Meson for Argentina v. Canada at Buenos Aries, Argentina, on 12 March 1995; Gavin Hastings for Scotland v. Tonga at Pretoria, South Africa, on 30 May 1995; and Thierry Lacroix for France v. Ireland at Durban, South Africa, on 10 June 1995.

The record for the most points in a career is 911, by Michael Patrick Lynagh in 72 matches for Australia from 1984 to 1995.

The most career points by a British player is 755, by Gavin Hastings (689 for Scotland and 66 for the British Isles) from 1986 to 1995.

The most tries in one career is 63, by David Campese in 93 internationals for Australia between 1982 and 1996.

The record for the most career tries by a British player is 50, by Rory Underwood in 91 internationals for England and the British Isles between 1984 and 1996.

Most points in a career
William Henry 'Dusty' Hare scored a career record of 7,337 points in first-class games between 1971 and 1989 (1,800 for Nottingham, 4,427 for Leicester, 240 for England, 88 for the British Isles and 782 in other representative matches).

Most tries in a career
Alan John Morley scored a record 473 tries in senior rugby from 1968 to 1986, including a record of 378 for one club (Bristol).

Most points in one match
Jannie van der Westhuizen scored a record 80 points (14 tries, nine conversions, one dropped goal and one penalty goal) in one match, in Carnarvon's 88–12 defeat of Williston at Carnarvon, North West Cape, South Africa, on 11 March 1972.

AINST WILLISTON IN 1972

Best all-rounder
Barrie Burnham scored all possible ways (try, conversion, penalty goal, drop goal, goal from mark) when Meralomas beat Georgians 20–11 at Vancouver, Canada, on 26 Feb 1966.

Kicks, tries and goal posts
Longest kicks
The longest successful drop goal on record is 82 m (90 yd), by Gerald Hamilton 'Gerry' Brand for South Africa v. England at Twickenham, Greater London, UK, on 2 Jan 1932. It was taken 6 m (7 yd) inside the England 'half', 50 m (55 yd) from the posts, and dropped over the dead ball line.

The place kick record is reputed to be 91 m (100 yd), at Richmond Athletic Ground, London, UK, by Douglas Francis Theodore Morkel in an unsuccessful penalty for South Africa against Surrey on 19 Dec 1906. It was not measured until 1932.

Ernie Cooper landed a penalty from 74 m (81 yd) from the post with a kick that carried over the dead ball line at the Bridlington School 1st XV match against an Army XV at Bridlington, E Yorkshire, UK, on 29 Jan 1944.

The record in an international is 64.22 m (70 yd 8½ in), by Paul Huw Thorburn for Wales v. Scotland on 1 Feb 1986.

Fastest tries
The record for the fastest try in an international game was set by Herbert Leo

'Bart' Price, who scored for England v. Wales at Twickenham on 20 Jan 1923 less than 10 seconds after kick-off.

The fastest try in any game was scored in eight seconds, by Andrew Brown for Widden Old Boys v. Old Ashtonians at Gloucester, UK, on 22 Nov 1990.

Highest posts
The world's highest Rugby Union goal posts are 33.54 m (110 ft ½ in) high, and are situated at the Roan Antelope Rugby Union Club, Luanshya, Zambia.

The highest Rugby Union goal posts in the United Kingdom are those at Old Halesonines RFC, Stourbridge, W Midlands, which are 22.16 m (72 ft 8½ in) tall.

Club championship wins
RFU Club Competition
Bath have had a record 10 outright wins (1984–87, 1989–90, 1992, 1994–96).

Courage Clubs Championship
Bath has won seven times, in 1987, 1989, 1991–94 and 1996.

Welsh Rugby Union Challenge/Swalec Cup
The most victories is nine, by Llanelli (1973–76, 1985, 1988 and 1991–93).

Scottish League Division One
Hawick has won the Scottish League Division One on a record 10 occasions, between 1973 and 1986.

Hong Kong Sevens
The record number of wins in the Hong Kong Sevens competition is seven, by Fiji (1977–78, 1980, 1984 and 1990–92).

Middlesex Seven-a-sides
Harlequins have won the title a record 13 times (1926–9, 1933, 1935, 1967, 1978 and 1986–90).

Players and spectators
Most international appearances
Philippe Sella (France) has played 111 games for France, between 1982 and 1995.

The greatest number of international appearances by a British player is 91, by Rory Underwood (85 for England and six for the British Isles), between 1984 and 1995.

William James 'Willie John' McBride made a record 17 appearances for the British Isles.

The greatest number of consecutive international appearances is 63, by Sean Brian Thomas Fitzpatrick (New Zealand) between 1986 and 1995.

The most consecutive appearances by a British player is 53, by Willie John McBride for Ireland from 1964 to 1975, and by Gareth Edwards, who never missed a match during his career for Wales from 1967 to 1978.

Left
In his career for England and the British Isles, Rob Andrew scored 407 points, including 27 points in one match against South Africa.

Youngest internationals
Ninian Jamieson Finlay and Charles Reid were both 17 years 36 days old when they played for Scotland in 1875 and 1881 respectively.

Semi Hekasilau Spec Taupeaafe was 16 years of age when he played in a Test for Tonga against Western Samoa in 1989.

Greatest crowd
The greatest paying attendance is 104,000, when Scotland played Wales at Murrayfield, Edinburgh, UK, on 1 March 1975.

Stick-and-ball sports

LARGEST CROWD FOR A HURLING MATCH WAS 84,865, AT CROKE PARK IN 1954

Right
The origins of stick-and-ball games can be traced back 4,000 years, but modern hockey became established as a team sport only in the late 19th century.

Hockey

Most Olympic medals
India held the men's Olympic title from the re-introduction of Olympic hockey in 1928 until 1960, when Pakistan beat them 1–0 at Rome, Italy. They had their eighth win in 1980.

Of the six Indians to have won three men's team gold medals, two have also won a silver medal: Leslie Walter Claudius, in 1948, 1952, 1956 and 1960 (silver), and Udham Singh, in 1952, 1956, 1964 and 1960 (silver).

World Cup
The most men's FIH World Cup wins is four, by Pakistan in 1971, 1978, 1982 and 1994.

The record for the most women's titles is five, by the Netherlands in 1974, 1978, 1983, 1986 and 1990.

Champions' Trophy
The most men's titles is six, by Australia, 1983–85, 1989–90 and 1993.

Australia has also won the women's title a record three times, in 1991, 1993 and 1995.

International matches, men's
The highest score in an international was India's 24–1 defeat of the USA at Los Angeles, California, USA, in the 1932 Olympic Games.

The most goals scored in an international in the United Kingdom was England's 16–0 defeat of France at Beckenham, Kent, UK, on 25 March 1922.

The most international appearances is 286, by Heiner Dopp for West Germany (indoors and out) between 1975 and 1989.

The most international appearances by a player from the United Kingdom is 234, by Jonathan Nicholas Mark Potter, with 106 games for England and 128 for Great Britain between 1983 and 1994.

The most international appearances by an Irish player is 135, by William David Robert McConnell from 1979 to 1993, and Stephen Alexander Martin from 1980 to 1993.

The most indoor caps is 85, by Richard Clarke (England) from 1976 to 1987.

The highest attendance at an international match is 65,165, for the match between England and the USA at Wembley, London, UK, on 11 March 1978.

The greatest number of goals scored in international hockey is 267, by Paul Litjens (Netherlands) in 177 games.

The fastest goal in an international was scored seven seconds after bully-off, by John

HIGHEST SCORE IN AN INTERNATIONAL HOCK

French for England v. West Germany at Nottingham, UK, on 25 April 1971.

The greatest goalkeeping in international hockey was by Richard James Allen (India), who conceded no goals in the 1928 Olympics and only three in 1936.

International matches, women's
The most international appearances by a woman is 257, by Alison Ramsay, who played 150 matches for Scotland and 107 for Great Britain from 1982 to 1995.

The highest score in an international match was England's 23–0 defeat of France at Merton, Greater London, UK, on 3 Feb 1923.

British club hockey
The most goals scored by one player is 19, by M. C. Marckx during Bowdon second XI's

23–0 defeat of Brooklands second XI on 31 Dec 1910.

David Ashman has scored a record 2,164 goals, in games for Hampshire, Southampton, Southampton Kestrals and Hamble Old Boys from 1958 to 1996. He has scored 2,005 goals for the last—a record for one club.

The most goals in a women's club match is 21, by Edna Mary Blakelock during Ross Ladies' 40–0 defeat of Wyeside at Ross-on-Wye, Herefordshire, on 24 Jan 1929.

Lacrosse
Men's
The USA has won six of the seven World Championships, in 1967, 1974, 1982, 1986, 1990 and 1994. Canada beat the USA 17–16 in 1978 after extra time.

Most capped hockey player 286

The record for the highest individual score was set by Nick Rackard (Wexford), who scored seven goals and seven points against Antrim in the 1954 All-Ireland semi-final.

Lowest score
The lowest score in an All-Ireland final occurred when Tipperary (one goal, one point) beat Galway (nil) in the first championship at Birr, in 1887.

Largest crowd
The largest ever attendance for a hurling match was 84,865, for the All-Ireland final between Cork and Wexford at Croke Park, Dublin, in 1954.

Longest hit
The greatest distance for a 'lift and stroke' is 118 m (129 yd), credited to Tom Murphy of Three Castles, Kilkenny, in a 'long puck' contest in 1906.

Left
Great Britain won the first women's lacrosse world title in 1969. Since then the USA has dominated, winning four of the six competitions that have been held to date.

MOST INTERNATIONAL APPEARANCES IN WOMEN'S LACROSSE IS 86

Stockport won the English Club Championship 17 times between 1897 and 1989.

The highest ever score in an English Club Championship final is Stockport's 33–4 win over London University on 9 May 1987.

Peter Daniel Roden (Mellor) has made 42 international appearances, from 1976 to 1990.

The highest win in an international match is Scotland's 34–3 win over Germany at Greater Manchester, UK, on 25 July 1994.

Women's
The USA has won the world title four times: the World Championships in 1974, and the World Cup in 1982, 1989 and 1993.

Vivien Jones played in 86 internationals (74 for Wales, nine for the Celts and three for Great Britain) from 1977 to 1994.

Christy Ring and John Doyle also share the record for the most All-Ireland medals won, with a total of eight each. Ring's appearances on the winning side were 1941–44, 1946 and 1952–54, while Doyle's were 1949–51, 1958, 1961–62 and 1964–65.

Christy Ring also holds the record for playing in a record 22 inter-provincial finals, between 1942 and 1963, and was on the winning side 18 times.

Highest and lowest scores
The highest ever score in an All-Ireland final was attained in 1989, when Tipperary (four goals, 29 points) beat Antrim (three goals, nine points) by 41 to 18.

The highest ever aggregate score was achieved when Cork (six goals, 21 points) defeated Wexford (five goals, 10 points) by 39 to 25 in the 80-minute 1970 final.

Shinty
Most titles
Newtonmore, Highland, has won the Camanachd Association Challenge Cup a record 28 times, between 1907 and 1986.

David Ritchie and Hugh Chisholm have both won a record 12 winners' medals while playing for Newtonmore.

Most senior competitions
In 1984 Kingussie Camanachd Club won all five senior competitions, including the Camanachd Cup final. This was equalled by Newtonmore in 1985.

Highest scores
The highest Scottish Cup final score was achieved in 1909, when Newtonmore beat Furnace 11–3 at Glasgow. Dr Johnnie Cattanach scored eight hails or goals.

In 1938 John Macmillan Mactaggart scored a record 10 hails for Mid-Argyll in a Camanachd Cup match.

The record for the highest score by an international team was set by Great Britain and Ireland with their 40–0 defeat of Long Island during their 1967 tour of the USA.

Hurling
Most titles
The most All-Ireland Championships to have been won by one team is 27, by Cork between 1890 and 1990.

Cork also hold the record for the most successive All-Ireland Championship wins, with four, from 1941 to 1944.

Most appearances
Three players have appeared in the All-Ireland finals 10 times: Christy Ring for Cork and Munster, John Doyle for Tipperary and Frank Cummins for Kilkenny.

Left
The highlight of the hurling season is the All-Ireland final for the McCarthy Cup. In the 1987 final shown here, Galway (one goal, 12 points) beat Kilkenny (no goals, nine points).

Ball games

Right
Australia has won the World Netball Championships a record seven times. Seen here in action in the 1995 final, Australia defend against South Africa's Irene van Dyk. Van Dyk scored a record 543 goals during the Championships.

Netball

Most World titles
Australia has won the World Championships a record seven times, 1963, 1971, 1975, 1979, 1983, 1991 and 1995.

Most British titles
The greatest number of victories in the National Club's Championships is seven, by Sudbury Netball Club, 1968–69, 1970 (shared), 1971, 1973 and 1984–85.

The record number of wins in the County Championships is 21, by Surrey, 1949–64, 1966, 1969 (shared), 1981, 1986 (shared), 1991 and 1992.

Most international appearances
Kendra Slawinski (England) played in a record 128 international matches from 1981 to 1995.

Highest scores
The Cook Islands beat Vanuatu 120–38 on 9 July 1991, during the World Championships at Sydney, Australia.

The record number of goals by an individual at one World Championships tournament is 543, by Irene van Dyk (South Africa) in 1995.

Handball

Olympics
The USSR won a record five titles—the men's in 1976, 1988 and 1992 (by the Unified Team from the republics of the ex-USSR), and the women's in 1976 and 1980.

South Korea shares the record for the most women's titles, with wins in 1988 and 1992.

World Championships
The record for the greatest number of men's indoor titles is four, by Romania in 1961, 1964, 1970 and 1974.

Germany/West Germany won the outdoor title a record five times between 1938 and 1966 and have won the indoor title twice, in 1938 and 1978.

A record three women's titles have been won by: Romania in 1956, 1960 (both outdoor) and 1962; the GDR in 1971, 1975 and 1978; and the USSR in 1982, 1986 and 1990.

European Champions' Cup
Spartak of Kiev, USSR (now Ukraine), won a record 13 women's titles from 1970 to 1988.

Vfl Gummersbach of West Germany have won a record five men's titles, 1967, 1970–71, 1974 and 1983. They are also the only club team to have won all three European trophies: the European Champions' Cup, the European Cup Winners' Cup and the IHF Cup.

Highest international score
The highest score in an international match occurred when the USSR beat Afghanistan 86–2 in the 'Friendly Army Tournament' at Miskolc, Hungary, in Aug 1981.

British titles and scores
A record seven men's national championship titles has been won by Brentwood '72 (British Championship in 1974 and English National League, 1979–83; British League in 1985).

The most women's titles is eight, by Wakefield Metros (English National League from 1982 to 1987 and British League in 1988 and 1990).

The record score in a men's league match was set by Glasgow University when they beat Claremont 69–5 at Glasgow in March 1984.

The women's record is a score of 47–13 by Wakefield Metros against Ruslip Eagles at Featherstone, W Yorkshire, on 25 Feb 1990.

The highest score by an individual is 29, by Graham Hammond during Wakefield's 39–13 victory over Hull University at Eccles Recreation Centre in Nov 1990.

The women's record is 15 goals, by Donna Hankinson for Manchester United SSS against Arcton (26–9) at Kirkby on 12 Nov 1989; by Julie Wells for Wakefield Metros against Ruislip Eagles (47–13) at Featherstone, W Yorkshire, on 25 Feb 1990; and by Catherine Densmore for Halewood Town (23) against Ruislip Eagles (17) at Bristol on 25 May 1991.

Gaelic football

All-Ireland Championships
The greatest number of All-Ireland Championships to have been won by one team is 30, by Ciarraidhe (Kerry), between 1903 and 1986.

The greatest number of successive wins is four, by Wexford (1915–18) and by Kerry (twice, 1929–32 and 1978–81).

The most finals to have been contested by an individual is 10, including eight wins by the Kerry players Pat Spillane, Paudie O'Shea and Denis Moran, 1975–76, 1978–82 and 1984–86.

The highest team score in a final was the 27–15 victory by Dublin (five goals, 12 points) over Armagh (three goals, six points) on 25 Sept 1977. (One goal equals three points).

The highest combined score was 45 points, when Cork beat Galway 26–19 in 1973.

The highest individual score in an All-Ireland final is two goals (six points) by Jimmy Keaveney for Dublin v. Armagh in 1977, and Michael Sheehy for Kerry v. Dublin in 1979.

Largest crowd
A record crowd of 90,556 attended the Down v. Offaly final at Croke Park, Dublin, in 1961.

Volleyball

Most world titles
The USSR has won a record six men's titles (1949, 1952, 1960, 1962, 1978 and 1982) and five women's titles (1952, 1956, 1960, 1970 and 1990).

Most Olympic titles
The USSR has won a record three men's titles (1964, 1968 and 1980) and four women's titles (1968, 1972, 1980 and 1988).

The only player to have won four medals is Inna Valeryevna Ryskal (USSR), who won women's silver medals in 1964 and 1976 and gold medals in 1968 and 1972.

The men's record is held by Yuriy Mikhailovich Poyarkov (USSR), who won gold medals in 1964 and 1968 and a bronze in 1972, and by Katsutoshi Nekoda (Japan), who won gold in 1972, silver in 1968 and bronze in 1964.

Most internationals by British players
Ucal Ashman made a record 153 men's appearances for England from 1976 to 1986.

The most internationals by a woman is 171, by Ann Jarvis for England from 1974 to 1987.

Softball
World Championships
The USA has won the men's fast pitch World Championship a record five times, in 1966, 1968, 1976 (shared), 1980 and 1988.

The USA also holds the record for the greatest number of women's fast pitch titles, with a total of four victories, in 1974, 1978, 1986 and 1990.

The most runs scored in a men's World Championship tournament is 19, by Marty Kernaghan (Canada) in 1988.

The most runs to have been scored in a women's tournament is 13, by Kathy Elliott (USA) in 1974.

HIGHEST HANDBALL SCORE IN AN INTERNATIONAL MATCH IS 86-2

The best average in a men's tournament is .647, by Clark Bosch (Canada) in 1988.

The highest average in a women's tournament is .550, by Tamara Bryce (Panama) in 1978.

The most strikeouts in a men's tournament is 99, by Kevin Herlihy (New Zealand) in 1972.

The greatest number of strikeouts in a women's tournament is .76, by Joan Joyce (USA) in 1974.

European Championships
The record for the greatest number of women's European Championship titles is eight, by the Netherlands from 1979 to 1984 and in 1988 and 1990.

US National Fast Pitch Championships
The record for the greatest number of men's National Fast Pitch Championships is 10, by the Clearwater (Florida) Bombers, 1950, 1954, 1956–57, 1960, 1962–63, 1966, 1968 and 1973.

ELIC FOOTBALL MATCH WAS 90,556 AT CROKE PARK, DUBLIN, IN 1961

The greatest number of women's titles have been won by the Raybestos (Hi Ho) Brakettes of Stratford, Connecticut, with 23 wins (1958–60, 1963, 1966–68, 1971–78, 1980, 1982–83, 1985, 1988 and 1990–92).

US National Slow Pitch Championships
The record for the most men's slow pitch championships is three, by Skip Hogan A.C. of Pittsburgh, (1962 and 1964–65), and by Joe Gatliff Auto Sales of Newport, Kentucky, (1956–57 and 1963).

The most title wins in the men's super slow pitch is four, by Steele's Sports/Silver Bullets, Grafton, Ohio (1985–87 and 1990).

The most women's slow pitch wins is five, by the Dots of Miami, Florida, as the Converse Dots in 1969, the Marks Brothers in 1974, the N Miami Dots in 1975 and the Bob Hoffman Dots from 1978 to 1979.

Top
South Korea has won two Olympic women's handball titles.

Middle
Volleyball, originally known as 'Mintonette', was created as a non-contact alternative to basketball in 1895. It has become one of the most widely played games in the world.

Bottom
Softball was invented in 1887 as an indoor version of baseball and until 1926 was known as 'kitten-ball' or 'mush-ball'. The sport developed on an international level following the formation of the International Softball Federation in 1950.

Championship tennis

Right
The youngest winner of the men's singles title in the US Championships to date is Pete Sampras (b. 1971), who was 19 years 28 days old when he won in 1990.

slam, in 1988. She also won the women's singles Olympic gold medal in the same year.

Double's titles
Pamela Howard Shriver of the USA won a record eight successive women's titles with Navrátilová and 109 successive games in all events between April 1983 and July 1985.

The first doubles pair to win the grand slam were Frank Sedgeman and Kenneth McGregor (Australia) in 1951.

The most singles titles won in grand slam tournaments is 24,

The most men's singles wins since the abolition of the Challenge Round in 1922 is five (consecutive), by Björn Rune Borg (Sweden) from 1976 to 1980.

William Charles Renshaw (GB) won a record seven singles (1881–86 and 1889).

The men's record for mixed doubles titles is four, by: Elias Victor Seixas (USA), 1953–56; Kenneth Norman Fletcher (Australia), 1963, 1965–66 and 1968; and Owen Keir Davidson (Australia), 1967, 1971 and 1973 74.

Youngest players and champions
The youngest ever match winner was Jennifer Capriati (USA), at 14 years 89 days in 1990.

The Swiss player Martina Hingis became the youngest ever Wimbledon champion when she

by Margaret Court (11 Australian, five US, five French, three Wimbledon), 1960–73.

The greatest number of men's singles titles to have been won in grand slam tournaments is 12 (six Australian, two French, two US and two Wimbledon), by Roy Stanley Emerson (Australia) from 1961 to 1967.

The greatest number of grand slam tournament wins by one doubles partnership is 20 (five Wimbledon, three French, 12 US), by Althea Louise Brough (USA) and Margaret Evelyn Du Pont (USA) from 1942 to 1957, and by Martina Navrátilová and Pam Shriver (seven Australian, five Wimbledon, four French, four US) from 1981 to 1989.

won the women's doubles in 1996 at the age of 15 years and 282 days.

Charlotte 'Lottie' Dod was 15 years 285 days old when she won the singles title in 1887.

The youngest men's winner is Boris Becker (West Germany), who won the 1985 men's title at the age of 17 years 227 days.

Oldest champions
Margaret Evelyn du Pont was 44 years 125 days old when she won the mixed doubles in 1962 with Neale Fraser (Australia).

The oldest singles champion was Arthur Gore (GB) at the age of 41 years 182 days in 1909.

Most appearances
Arthur Gore (GB) made 36 appearances from 1888 to 1927.

Grand slam
Men's titles
In 1935, Frederick John Perry (GB) became the first man to have won all four major singles titles (Wimbledon, US, Australian and French Open).

The first man to hold all four championships simultaneously was John Donald Budge (USA) in 1938. (With Wimbledon and US in 1937, he won six successive grand slam tournaments).

The first man to achieve the grand slam twice was Rodney George Laver of Australia (as an amateur in 1962 and professional in 1969).

Women's titles
Six successive grand slam tournaments have been won by: Maureen Connolly (USA), in 1953; Margaret Court (Australia), in 1970; and Martina Navrátilová (USA) in 1983/4.

Stefanie Maria Graf (West Germany) is the only other woman to have won the grand

Wimbledon
Most titles won by women
Billie-Jean King (USA) won a record 20 titles between 1961 and 1979 (six singles, ten women's doubles and four mixed doubles).

Elizabeth Montague Ryan (USA) won a record 19 doubles titles (12 women's and seven mixed) from 1914 to 1934.

The record for women's singles titles is nine, by Martina Navrátilová (1978–79, 1982–87 and 1990).

The women's record for mixed doubles titles is seven, by Elizabeth Ryan (USA) from 1919 to 1932.

Most titles won by men
Hugh Laurence Doherty (GB) won a record 13 titles: five singles titles (1902–06) and a record eight men's doubles (1897–1901 and 1903–05) partnered by his brother Reginald.

Jean Borotra (France) played 35 times in the men's singles, from 1922 to 1964. He then played in the Veterans' Doubles until 1977, when he was 78 years old.

Greatest crowds

The record crowd for one day was 39,813, on 26 June 1986.

The record for the whole championship was 403,706, in 1989.

US Championships
Most wins

Margaret Evelyn du Pont won a record 25 titles between 1941 and 1960: a record 13 women's doubles (12 with Althea Brough), nine mixed doubles and three singles.

The most men's titles is 16, by William Tatem Tilden, including seven men's singles, from 1920 to 1925 and in 1929.

Tilden's record of seven singles is shared with Richard Dudley Sears, from 1881 to 1887,

Tracy Ann Austin was 16 years 271 days old when she won the women's singles in 1979.

French Open
Most wins (from international status 1925)

Margaret Court won a record 13 titles (five singles, four women's doubles and four mixed doubles) from 1962 to 1973.

The most men's titles is nine, by Henri Cochet of France (four singles, three men's doubles and two mixed doubles) from 1926 to 1930.

The oldest singles champion is Andrés Gimeno (Spain) in 1972, at 34 years 301 days old.

Australian Championships
Most wins

The player to have won the most titles is Margaret Court, who won a record total of 21 titles, including 11 women's singles finals (1960–66, 1969–71 and 1973).

A record six men's singles were won by Roy Stanley Emerson (Australia), in 1961 and from 1963 to 1967.

Thelma Dorothy Long won 12 women's doubles and four mixed doubles, making a record total of 16 doubles titles. She won her first titles in 1936 and her last in 1958, in a 22-year winning span.

Adrian Karl Quist won a record 10 consecutive men's doubles between 1936 and 1950 (the last eight with John Bromwich), as well as three men's singles.

Youngest champions

The youngest men's winner was Rodney W. Heath, who was 17 years old when he won the singles in 1905.

Monica Seles is the youngest woman ever to win a title. She won the 1991 singles final when she was 17 years 55 days old.

Oldest champions

Norman Everard Brookes won the 1924 men's doubles at the age of 46 years 2 months.

Kenneth Robert Rosewall became the oldest singles winner at the age of 37 years 62 days in 1972. He had first won the title 19 years previously, in 1953.

Grand Prix Masters
ATP Tour Championship

A record five titles have been won by Ivan Lendl, in 1982, and 1983, 1986 (two) and 1987. He appeared in nine successive finals from 1980 to 1988.

UBLES AT WIMBLEDON UNTIL HE WAS 78 YEARS OLD

LONGEST WINNING SPAN IN THE AUSTRALIAN CHAMPIONSHIP IS 22 YEARS

and by William A. Larned, from 1901 to 1902 and 1907 to 1911.

The record for women's singles is seven, by: Molla Mallory (1915–16, 1918, 1920–22 and 1926); and Helen Newington Moody (USA) (1923–25, 1927–29 and 1931).

Oldest champion

Margaret du Pont won the mixed doubles at the age of 42 years 166 days in 1960.

Youngest champions

Vincent Richards was 15 years 139 days old when he won the men's doubles in 1918.

The youngest ever men's champion is Pete Sampras, at 19 years 28 days in 1990.

The singles record is seven, by Chris Evert (1974–75, 1979–80, 1983, 1985–86).

Björn Borg won a record six men's singles (1974–75, 1978–81).

Youngest champions

Andrea Jaeger and Jimmy Arias were aged 15 years 339 days and 16 years 296 days respectively when they won the mixed doubles in 1981.

The youngest singles winner is Monica Seles (Yugoslavia), at 16 years 169 days in 1990.

Oldest champion

Elizabeth Ryan won the 1934 women's doubles at the age of 42 years 88 days.

James 'Jimmy' Scott Connors (USA) is the only player to qualify for 14 consecutive years, from 1972 to 1985. He chose not to play in 1975, 1976 and 1985, and won in 1977. He qualified again in 1987 and 1988, but did not play in 1988.

A record seven doubles titles were won by John Patrick McEnroe and Peter Fleming (both USA), from 1978 to 1984.

Virginia Slims Championship

Martina Navrátilová has a record six singles wins, between 1978 and 1986.

Martina Navrátilová has also won a record nine doubles titles (one with Billie-Jean King in 1980, and eight with Pam Shriver to 1991).

Tennis

Fastest service 222 km/h

Right
The successful 1995 US Davis Cup team (from left to right: Richey Reneberg, Jim Courier, Andre Agassi, Tom Gullickson, Pete Sampras and Todd Martin) celebrate their 3–2 victory over Russia in the final. The Davis Cup was instituted in 1900 and the USA have won it a record 31 times.

Below right
Spanish player Arantxa Sánchez Vicario earned a women's season's record of $2,943,665 (£1,920,325) in 1994, and is one of only three women to have won more than $10 million (£7 million) on the Tour. The others are Martina Navrátilová and Steffi Graf.

International team tennis
Davis Cup
The most wins in the Davis Cup, the men's international team championship, is 31 by the USA between 1900 and 1995.

The record for the greatest number of appearances for Davis Cup winners is eight, by Roy Emerson (Australia) from 1959 to 1962 and 1964 to 1967.

Bill Tilden (USA) played in a record 28 finals, winning a record 21 (17 out of 22 singles and four out of six doubles). He was in seven winning sides from 1920 to 1926 and four losing sides from 1927 to 1930.

Nicola Pietrangeli (Italy) played a record 163 rubbers (66 ties) between 1954 and 1972, winning 120. He played 109 singles (winning 78) and 54 doubles (winning 42).

The most rubbers by a Briton is 65 (with 43 wins) by Michael John Sangster, between 1960 and 1968.

The record for the greatest number of wins by a Briton is 45 from 52 rubbers, by Fred Perry, including 34 of 38 singles, between 1931 and 1936.

Wightman Cup
The annual women's match was won a record 51 times by the USA.

Sarah Virginia Wade (GB) played in a record 21 ties and 56 rubbers between 1965 and 1985, and won 19 times—a record for a British player.

Christine Marie Evert (USA) won all 26 of her singles matches between 1971 and 1985.

Including doubles, she achieved a record 34 wins from 38 rubbers played.

At 13 years 168 days old, Jennifer Capriati became the youngest ever Wightman Cup player when she beat Clare Wood (GB) 6–0, 6–0 at Williamsburg, Virginia, USA, on 14 Sept 1989.

Federation Cup (instituted 1963)
The most wins in the Federation Cup (Fed Cup from 1995), the women's international team championship, is 14 by the USA, between 1963 and 1990.

Virginia Wade (GB) played every year from 1967 to 1983 in a record 57 ties, playing 100 rubbers, including 56 singles (winning 36) and 44 doubles (winning 30).

Chris Evert won 40 out of 42 singles matches (1977–89), including her first 29.

Individual records
Olympic Games
A record four gold medals, as well as a silver and a bronze, were won by Max Decugis (France) between 1900 and 1920.

The record for the most women's medals is five, by Kitty McKane (GB), who won one gold, two silver and two bronze in 1920 and 1924.

Fastest tennis service
The fastest service to have been timed with modern equipment is 222 km/h (138 mph), by Steve Denton (USA) at Beaver Creek, Colorado, USA, on 29 July 1984.

The women's record for the fastest service timed with modern equipment is 196 km/h (121.8 mph), by Brenda Schultz-McCarthy (Netherlands) at the 1996 Australian Open at Melbourne on 22 Jan.

Highest season's earnings
Pete Sampras (USA) won a men's season's record of $5,415,066 (£3,430,949) in 1995.

Arantxa Sánchez Vicario (Spain) set a women's record of $2,943,665 (£1,920,325) in 1994.

Highest career earnings
The record for the highest career earnings by a male player is $21,859,428, by Pete Sampras (USA) to the end of 1995.

The women's record for the greatest career earnings is $20,065,290, by Martina Navrátilová to the end of 1994. Navrátilová won a world record 167 singles tournaments and 165 doubles titles.

The most first-place prize money ever won by a player is $2 million (£1,038,583), by Pete Sampras when he won the Grand Slam Cup at Munich, Germany, on 16 Dec 1990. In the final of the event he defeated Brad Gilbert (USA) 6–3, 6–4, 6–2.

The record for the highest ever total prize money is $10,893,890 (£7,200,000), for the 1996 US Open Championships.

Y PETE SAMPRAS IN 1995

Greatest crowd
A record-breaking 30,472 people were present at the Astrodome, Houston, Texas, USA, for the 'Battle of the Sexes' on 20 Sept 1973, when Billie-Jean King (USA) beat Robert Larimore Riggs (USA) 6–4, 6–3, 6–3.

The record attendance at an orthodox match is 25,578, for the Australia v. USA match in the Davis Cup Challenge Round (first day) in Sydney, NSW, Australia, on 27 Dec 1954.

Longest match
The record for the longest match in a grand slam tournament is 5 hr 26 min, between Stefan Edberg (Sweden) and Michael Chang (USA) for the semi-final of the US Championships from 12 to 13 Sept 1992. Edberg won 6–7, 7–5, 7–6, 5–7, 6–4.

Longest game
The longest known singles game lasted 31 minutes and consisted of 37 deuces (80 points). It was played between Anthony

Left
The 1992 US Championship semi-final between Swedish player Stefan Edberg, pictured here, and US player Michael Chang lasted 5 hr 26 min, making it the longest match ever played during a grand slam tournament.

Fawcett (Rhodesia) and Keith Glass (GB) in the first round of the Surrey Championships at Surbiton, UK, on 26 May 1975.

A game lasting a record-breaking 52 minutes was played between Noëlle van Lottum and Sandra Begijn in the semi-finals of the Dutch Indoor Championships at Ede, Gelderland, Netherlands, on 12 Feb 1984.

Longest tiebreak
A tiebreak for the fourth and ultimately decisive set of a first-round men's doubles match at Wimbledon on 1 July 1985 went to 26–24. Jan Gunnarsson (Sweden) and Michael Mortensen (Denmark) defeated John Frawley (Australia) and Victor Pecci (Paraguay) 6–3, 6–4, 3–6, 7–6.

Real tennis
Earliest title
The first recorded world tennis champion was Clergé (France) c.1740.

First titles
Jacques Edmond Barre (France) held the title for a record 33 years from 1829 to 1862.

Basque player Pierre Etchebaster holds the record for the greatest number of successful defences of the title, at eight, 1928–52.

The Women's World Championships has been won three times by Penny Lumley (GB), in 1989, 1991 and 1995.

The Amateur Championship of the British Isles has been won a record 16 times by Howard Rea Angus, from 1966 to 1980 and in 1982. Angus was also world champion from 1976 to 1981 and won eight Amateur Doubles Championships with David Warburg, from 1967 to 1970, 1972 to 1974 and in 1976.

Oldest court
The oldest active court in the United Kingdom is at Falkland Palace, Fife. It was built by King James V of Scotland in 1539.

Left
Falkland Palace has the oldest British tennis court that is still in use. Real (meaning 'royal') tennis was derived from the game *jeu de paume*, which was played in monastery cloisters in about the 11th century. The architecture of the cloisters is reflected in the features of purpose-built courts, such as the sloping roofs and side gallery. During play the ball can be hit against the roof-slopes. The basic scoring system is the same as that used in lawn tennis, which derived from real tennis in the late 19th century.

Racket sports

LONGEST BADMINTON RALLIES ON RECORD LASTED FOR MORE THAN 90 STROKES

Right
Squash, derived from the sport of rackets, became enormously popular in the 1970s, both as a competitive sport and as a fitness craze. The development of glass courts—such as this one used in the Al-Ahram International Championship in Egypt—has allowed for greater visibility for spectators, and some quite spectacular competition venues.

Below right
Jansher Khan has continued the success of the Khan dynasty from the Peshawar region of Pakistan, following men such as Jahangir, Hashim, Azam and Roshan.

Squash rackets
World Championships
Jansher Khan (Pakistan) has won seven World Open titles (1987, 1989–90 and 1992–95).

Jahangir Khan (Pakistan) won six World Open titles (1981–85 and 1988) and the International Squash Rackets Federation world individual title (1979, 1983 and 1985).

Geoffrey B. Hunt (Australia) won four World Open titles (1976–77, 1979–80) and three World Amateur titles (1967, 1969 and 1971).

The most women's World Open titles is five, by New Zealander Susan Devoy (1985, 1987, 1990–92).

The record for the most men's world team titles is six, by Australia (1967, 1969, 1971, 1973, 1989 and 1991) and Pakistan (1977, 1981, 1983, 1985, 1987 and 1993).

England (1985, 1987, 1989 and 1990) and Australia (1981, 1983, 1992 and 1994) have both won the women's team title four times.

Open Championship
The most wins in the Open Championship is 10 by Jahangir Khan, in successive years from 1982 to 1991.

Hashim Khan (Pakistan) won seven times (1950–55 and 1957) and also won the Vintage title six times (1978–83).

The most British Open women's titles is 16, by Heather Pamela McKay (Australia) from 1961 to 1977. She also won the World Open title in 1976 and 1979.

Amateur Championship
The most wins in the Amateur Championship is six by Abdelfattah Amr Bey (Egypt) (1931–33, 1935–37).

Longest championship match
Jahangir Khan beat Gamal Awad (Egypt) 9–10, 9–5, 9–7, 9–2 in the final of the Patrick International Festival at Chichester, W Sussex, UK, on 30 March 1983, in 2 hr 45 min. The first game lasted a record 1 hr 11 min.

Shortest championship match
Philip Kenyon (England) beat Salah Nadi (Egypt) 9–0, 9–0, 9–0 in 6 min 37 sec in the British Open at Lamb's Squash Club, London, UK, on 9 April 1992.

Highest speed
In British tests in Jan 1988, Roy Buckland hit a ball by an overhead service at a speed of 232.7 km/h (144.6 mph) over the distance to

WORLD'S FASTEST SPORT

the front wall—equivalent to an initial speed at the racket of 242.6 km/h (150.8 mph).

Badminton
World Championships
A record five individual titles have been won by Park Joo-bong (South Korea): men's doubles in 1985 and 1991 and mixed doubles in 1985, 1989 and 1991.

Three Chinese players have each won two individual world titles: Yang Yang won the men's singles in 1987 and 1989; and Li Lingwei and Han Aiping won the women's

S. RAMESH BABU COMPLETED 5,000 TABLE TENNIS VOLLEYS WITH TWO BATS

singles in 1983 and 1989 and in 1985 and 1987 respectively.

Indonesia have won the men's World Team Badminton Championships for the Thomas Cup 10 times (1958, 1961, 1964, 1970, 1973, 1976, 1979, 1984, 1994 and 1996).

The most wins at the women's World Team Badminton Championships for the Uber Cup is five, by Japan (1966, 1969, 1972, 1978 and 1981), and China (1984, 1986, 1988, 1990 and 1992).

All-England Championships
A record eight men's singles were won by Rudy Hartono Kurniawan (Indonesia), from 1968 to 1974 and in 1976.

The most titles (including doubles) is 21, by George Alan Thomas, 1903–28.

The most titles won by a woman is 17, by Muriel Lucas (later Mrs King Adams) from 1899 to 1910, and by Judith Margaret 'Judy' Hashman (USA), including a record 10 singles (1954, 1957–58, 1960–64, 1966–67).

Shortest game
Ra Kyung-min (South Korea) beat Julia Mann (England) 11–2, 11–1 in six minutes during the Uber Cup at Hong Kong, on 19 May 1996.

Longest rallies
In the 1987 All-England Championships men's singles final between Morten Frost (Denmark) and Icuk Sugiarto (Indonesia) there were two successive rallies of more than 90 strokes.

The country that has taken the most women's team titles (Marcel Corbillon Cup) is China, 1965, 1975–89 (biennially), 1993 and 1995.

English Open
Richard Bergmann (Austria, then GB) won a record six singles (1939–40, 1948, 1950, 1952, 1954).

Viktor Barna (Hungary, then GB) won the men's doubles title on a record seven occasions (1931, 1933–35, 1938–39 and 1949), and a record 20 titles in total.

The record for the most women's singles titles is six, by Maria Alexandru (Romania), 1963–64, 1970–72 and 1974.

Diane Rowe (now Scholer) won the women's doubles title on a record 12 occasions (1950–56, 1960, 1962–65) and a record 17 titles overall.

English Closed
The most titles is 26, by Desmond Hugh Douglas: a record 11 men's singles, (1976, 1979–87 and 1990), plus 11 men's doubles and four mixed doubles.

A record seven women's singles were won by Jill Patricia Hammersley (1973–76, 1978–79 and 1981).

Counter hitting
The greatest number of hits in one minute is 173, by Jackie Bellinger and Lisa Lomas at Northgate Sports Centre, Ipswich, Suffolk, UK, on 7 Feb 1993.

The most shares in Amateur Doubles Championship titles is 11, by William Boone between 1975 and 1994.

The most titles by one pair is 10, by David Sumner Milford and John Ross Thompson between 1948 and 1959.

Racketball
World Championships
The USA has won all seven team titles, in 1981, 1984, 1986 (tie with Canada), 1988, 1990, 1992 and 1994.

The most men's singles titles won is two, by Egan Inoue (USA) in 1986 and 1990.

The most women's singles titles won is two, by Cindy Baxter (USA) in 1981 and 1986, Heather Stupp (Canada) in 1988 and 1990, and Michelle Gould (USA) in 1992 and 1994.

British National Championships
Six titles have been won in the women's event by Elizabeth 'Bett' Dryhurst, 1985–87, 1988 (shared), 1989 and 1991.

The men's record is three by Nathan Dugan, from 1993 to 1995.

Fives
Eton Fives
One pair, Brian C. Matthews and John P. Reynolds, has won the amateur championship (Kinnaird Cup) 10 times, from 1981 to 1990. Reynolds won an 11th title with Manuel de Souza-Girao in 1991.

Rugby Fives
The most Amateur Singles titles is 22, by Wayne Enstone (1973–78 and 1980–95).

The record for the Amateur Doubles Championship is 10, by David John Hebden and Ian Paul Fuller (1980–85 and 1987–90). Wayne Enstone has won the title 12 times with three different partners.

Pelota Vasca (Jaï Alaï)
World Championships
Roberto Elias and Juan Labat of Argentina won the *Trinquete Share* four times, in 1952, 1958, 1962 and 1966. Labat won a record total of seven world titles in all between 1952 and 1966.

Riccardo Bizzozero (Argentina) won a record seven World Championship titles in various *Trinquete* and *Frontón corto* events between 1970 and 1982.

The most wins in the *Cesta Punta* is three by José Hamuy (Mexico), with two different partners, in 1958, 1962 and 1966.

Fastest speed
Pelota has the fastest projectile speed of any ball game, at about 302 km/h (188 mph), compared with 273 km/h (170 mph) for a golf ball driven off a tee (electronically timed).

Far left
Li Lingwei of China, the woman who has most recently won the women's world badminton championships twice.

Left
Pelota is the fastest of all ball games. The high speed at which the ball travels is generated by the curved wicker basket at the end of a player's arm, known as a *grand chistera* or *cesta*.

LOTA, WITH BALLS MOVING AT UP TO 302 KM/H

Table tennis
Most titles
G. Viktor Barna (Hungary, then GB) won five World singles titles (1930, 1932–35) and eight men's doubles (1929–35, 1939). With two more at mixed doubles and seven team, he had 22 world titles in all.

Angelica Rozeanu (Romania) won a record six women's singles, 1950–55.

Mária Mednyánszky (Hungary) won seven women's doubles, in 1928 and from 1930 to 1935, and a record total of 18 world titles.

The most men's team titles (Swaythling Cup) is 12, by Hungary (1927–31, 1933–35, 1938, 1949, 1952 and 1979).

With a bat in each hand, S. Ramesh Babu completed 5,000 consecutive volleys over the net in 41 min 27 sec at Jawaharal Nehru Stadium, Swargate, India, on 14 April 1995.

Rackets
World Championships
The longest reign is by Geoffrey Willoughby Thomas Atkins, who won the title by beating the professional James Dear in 1954, and defended it four times until retirement in 1972.

Most Amateur titles
The most titles won by an individual is nine, by Edgar Maximilian Baerlein between 1903 and 1923, and William Robin Boone between 1976 and 1993.

Championship golf

Right
One of the greatest golfers of all time, Jack Nicklaus is the only person to have won the Open, US Open, Masters, PGA and US Amateur titles more than once each.

Career earnings $9,592,628

British Open
Any round
The record is 63 strokes, by: Mark Hayes (USA) at Turnberry, S Ayrshire, on 7 July 1977; Isao Aoki (Japan) at Muirfield, E Lothian, on 19 July 1980; Greg Norman (Australia) at Turnberry on 18 July 1986; Paul Broadhurst (GB) at St Andrews, Fife, on 21 July 1990; Jodie Mudd (US) at Royal Birkdale on 21 July 1991; and Nick Faldo (GB) on 16 July and Payne Stewart (USA) on 18 July, both at Royal St George's, Sandwich, Kent, in 1993.

First 36 holes
Nick Faldo (GB) completed the first 36 holes at Muirfield in 130 strokes (66, 64) on 16 and 17 July 1992. He added a third round of 69 to equal his 54-hole record of 199 at St Andrews, Fife, in 1990 (67, 65, 67).

Total aggregate
The record aggregate is 267 (66, 68, 69, 64), by Greg Norman (Australia) at Royal St George's, from 15 to 18 July 1993.

US Open
Any round
The record for any round is 63, by: Johnny Miller (USA) at Oakmont Country Club, Pennsylvania, on 17 June 1973, and Jack Nicklaus (USA) and Tom Weiskopf (USA), both at Baltusrol Country Club, Springfield, New Jersey, on 12 June 1980.

First 36 holes
The record is 134, by: Jack Nicklaus (63, 71) at Baltusrol, on 12 and 13 June 1980; Chen Tze-Chung (Taiwan) (65, 69) at Oakland Hills, Birmingham, Michigan, in June 1985; and Lee Janzen (USA) (67, 67) at Baltusrol, on 17 and 18 June 1993.

Total aggregate
The record aggregate over 72 holes is 272, by Jack Nicklaus (63, 71, 70, 68) from 12 to 15 June 1980 and Lee Janzen (67, 67, 69, 69) from 17 to 20 June 1993, both at Baltusrol Country Club.

US Masters
Any round
The lowest score for a round is 63 by: Nick Price (Zimbabwe) in 1986 and Greg Norman (Australia) in 1996.

First 36 holes
Raymond Floyd holds the record of 131 (65, 66), which he set in 1976.

Total aggregate
The record for the total aggregate in the US Masters is 271, by: Jack Nicklaus (67, 71, 64, 69) in 1965 and Raymond Floyd (65, 66, 70, 70) in 1976.

US PGA
Any round
The record is 63, by: Bruce Crampton (Australia) at Firestone, Akron, Ohio, in 1975; Raymond Floyd (USA) at Southern Hills, Tulsa, Oklahoma, in 1982; Gary Player (South Africa) at Shoal Creek, Birmingham, Alabama, in 1984; Vijay Singh (Fiji) at Inverness Club, Toledo, Ohio, in 1993; and Michael Bradley (USA) and Brad Faxon (USA) at Riviera, Pacific Palisades, California, in 1995.

Total aggregate
The record is 267, by Steve Elkington (Australia) (68, 67, 78, 64) and by Colin Montgomerie (GB) (68, 67, 67, 65) at Riviera GC, Pacific Palisades, California, in 1995.

Youngest and oldest winners
Youngest Open winner
Tom Morris Jr won at Prestwick, S Ayrshire, UK, in 1868, aged 17 years 249 days.

Oldest Open champions
'Old Tom' Morris was 46 years 99 days old when he won at Prestwick, UK, in 1867.

The oldest Open champion this century is Roberto de Vincenzo (Argentina), who was 44 years 93 days old when he won in 1967.

Oldest US Open champion
Hale Irwin (USA) was 45 years 15 days old when he won on 18 June 1990.

Team competitions
World Cup (formerly Canada Cup)
The USA recorded a total of 21 wins between 1955 and 1995.

The only men to have been on six winning teams have been Arnold Palmer (USA) (1960, 1962–64 and 1966–67) and Jack Nicklaus (1963–64, 1966–67, 1971 and 1973).

Jack Nicklaus has taken the individual title a record three times (1963–64 and 1971).

The lowest aggregate score for 144 holes is 536 by the USA (Fred Couples and Davis Love III), at Dorado, Puerto Rico, from 10 to 13 Nov 1994. The lowest individual score is 265, by Couples on the same occasion.

Ryder Cup
The USA has won 23 times, drawn twice and lost six times to 1995.

Arnold Palmer has won the most matches, with 22 won, two halved and eight lost out of a total of 32.

The most contests played in is 10, by Christy O'Connor (Ireland), from 1955 to 1973, and Nick Faldo, from 1977 to 1995.

ND A RECORD 20 ALL TOLD

Walker Cup
The USA have won 30, Great Britain & Ireland four (1938, 1971, 1989 and 1995) and the 1965 match was tied.

Jay Sigel (USA) has won a record 18 matches, with five halved and 10 lost, between 1977 and 1993.

Joseph Boynton Carr (GB and Ireland) played in 10 contests between 1947 and 1967.

Curtis Cup
The USA have won the Curtis Cup a record 20 times to 1994.

Carole Semple Thompson (USA) has won a record 15 matches in nine contests between 1974 and 1996.

Individual records
Highest prizes
The highest first prize ever was $1 million (£660,000), for the Sun City Challenge, South Africa, between 1987 and 1991.

The highest total prize money is $2,700,000 (£1,800,000), for the Johnnie Walker World Championship at Tryall GC, Montego Bay, Jamaica, between 1992 and 1994.

Highest earnings
The US PGA career record is $10,592,628, by Greg Norman (Australia) from 1976 to June 1996, including a season's record of $1,654,959 in 1995. He has won more than $15.2 million worldwide (1976 to June 1996).

Colin Montgomerie won a season's record for a European tour of £835,051.40, in 1995 European Order of Merit tournaments.

Nick Faldo won a record £1,558,978 worldwide in 1992, and holds the European tour career earnings record, at £4,984,877 from 1976 to June 1996.

Most tournament wins
John Byron Nelson (USA) won 18 tournaments in a year, including a record 11 consecutive wins between 8 March and 4 Aug 1945.

Sam Snead won 84 official US PGA tour events between 1936 and 1965.

The women's record for PGA wins is 88, by Kathy Whitworth between 1959 and 1991.

The most career victories in European Order of Merit tournaments is 55, by Severiano Ballesteros (Spain) between 1974 and 1995.

Ben Hogan won the US Open a record four times.

MOST MAJOR GOLF TITLES

British Open: 6
Harry Vardon
1896, 1898–99, 1903, 1911, 1914

The Amateur: 8
John Ball
1888, 1890, 1892, 1894, 1899, 1907, 1910, 1912

US Open: 4
William 'Willie' Anderson
1901, 1903–05
Robert Tyre 'Bobby' Jones Jr
1923, 1926, 1929–30
William Benjamin Hogan
1948, 1950–51, 1953
Jack William Nicklaus
1962, 1967, 1972, 1980

US Amateur: 5
Robert Tyre Jones Jr
1924–25, 1927–28, 1930

US PGA: 5
Walter Charles Hagan
1921, 1924–27
Jack William Nicklaus
1963, 1971, 1973, 1975, 1980

US Masters: 6
Jack William Nicklaus
1963, 1965–66, 1972, 1975, 1986

US Women's Open: 4
Elizabeth 'Betsy' Earle-Rawls
1951, 1953, 1957, 1960
'Mickey' Wright
1958–59, 1961, 1964

US Women's Amateur: 6
Glenna Collett Vare
1922, 1925, 1928–30, 1935

British Women's: 4
Charlotte Cecilia Pitcairn Leitch
1914, 1920–21, 1926
Joyce Wethered
1922, 1924–25, 1929

Note: Nicklaus is the only golfer to have won five different major titles (British Open, US Open, Masters, PGA and US Amateur titles) twice and a record 20 all told (1959–86). In 1930 Bobby Jones achieved a unique 'Grand Slam' of the US and British Open and Amateur titles.

Colin Montgomerie won a record £835,051.40 on a 1995 European tour.

Golf

Right
There is evidence that golf has been played on the famous Old Course at St Andrews for almost 600 years. The course originally consisted of 12 holes, and a round was played over 22 (11 out, 11 in). In the late 18th century, four holes were turned into two and the round became 18 holes. This is now the standard around the world.

Longest hole-in-one 408 m

Courses and equipment

Most expensive golf club
A Scottish iron golf club of c. 1700 sold for £92,400 at Sotheby's sale of golfing memorabilia at Loretto School, Musselburgh, East Lothian, UK, held on 13 July 1992 to coincide with the 121st Open Championship. It was bought by Titus Kendall on behalf of the Valderamma Golf Club in Sotte Grande, Spain.

Most expensive golf ball
On 1 July 1995, Jaime Ortiz Patino (Spain) paid a record £19,995 at Edinburgh for a Victorian feathery ball.

Longest hole
The longest hole is the seventh hole (par-7) of the Satsuki GC, Sano, Japan, which measures 881 m (964 yd).

The longest hole in the United Kingdom is the second at Gedney Hill, Lincs, which extends for 613 m (671 yd).

Longest course
The longest course is the par-77, 7,612-m (8,325-yd) International GC in Bolton, Massachussetts, USA, from the 'Tiger' tees, remodelled in 1969 by Robert Trent Jones.

Best strokes and scores

Longest drives
The greatest ever recorded drive on an ordinary course is 471 m (515 yd), by Michael Hoke Austin of Los Angeles, California, USA, in the US National Seniors

Open Championship at Las Vegas, Nevada, on 25 Sept 1974. Austin, who stood 1.88 m (6 ft 2 in) tall and weighed 92 kg (203 lb), drove the ball to within a yard of the green on the par-4, 412-m (450-yd) fifth hole of the Winterwood Course, and it then rolled 59 m (65 yd) past the flagstick. He was aided by an estimated 56 km/h (35 mph) tailwind.

Longest putts
The longest holed putt in a major tournament is 33.5 m (110 ft), by Jack Nicklaus in the 1964 Tournament of Champions, and Nick Price in the 1992 US PGA.

Bob Cook (USA) sank a putt measured at 42.74 m (140 ft 2¾ in) on the 18th at St Andrews, UK, in the International Fourball Pro Am Tournament on 1 Oct 1976.

Lowest 18 holes, men's
At least four players have played a long course (over 5,490 m or 6,000 yd) in a score of 58, most recently Monte Carlo Money (USA) at the par-72, 6,041-m (6,607-yd) Las Vegas Municipal GC, Nevada, USA, on 11 March 1981.

Alfred Edward Smith achieved an 18-hole score of 55 (15 under par 70) on his 3,884-m (4,248-yd) home course, scoring four, two, three, four, two, four, three, four and three (29 out), and two, three, three, three, three, two, five, four and one (26 in), on 1 Jan 1936.

The US PGA Tournament record is 59, by: Al Geiberger in the second round of the Danny Thomas Classic, on the 72-par, 6,628-m (7,249-yd) Colonial GC course, Memphis, Tennessee, on 10 June 1977; and Chip Beck in the third round of the Las Vegas Invitational, on the 72-par, 6,381-m (6,979-yd) Sunrise GC course, Las Vegas, Nevada, on 11 Oct 1991.

Lowest 18 holes, women's
The lowest recorded score on an 18-hole course (over 5,120 m or 5,600 yd) is 62, by: Mary 'Mickey' Kathryn Wright (USA) on the Hogan Park Course (par 71, 5,747 m or 6,286 yd) at Midland, Texas, USA, in Nov 1964; Janice Arnold (New Zealand) at the Coventry Golf Club (5,317 m or 5,815 yd), W Midlands, UK, on 24 Sept 1990; Laura Davies (GB) at the Rail Golf Club (6,019 m or 6,583 yd), Springfield, Illinois, USA, on 31 Aug 1991; and Hollis Stacy at Meridian Valley, Seattle, Washington, USA, on 18 Sept 1994.

Lowest British score
The lowest score recorded in a professional tournament on a British course of more than 5,490 m (6,000 yd) is 60, by: Paul Curry, in the second round of the Bell's Scottish Open on the King's course (5,899 m or 6,452 yd), Gleneagles, on 9 July 1992; and Keith MacDonald in the third round of the Barratt Golf Mid Kent Classic at the Mid Kent GC (5,675 m or 6,206 yd) on 6 Aug 1993.

Lowest 72 holes
The lowest recorded score on a first-class course is 255 (29 under par), by Leonard Peter Tupling (GB) in the Nigerian Open at Ikoyi GC, Lagos, in Feb 1981. The score was made up of 63, 66, 62 and 64, with an average of 63.75 per round.

The lowest score in a US professional event is 257 (60, 68, 64, 65), by Mike Souchak in the 1955 Texas Open at San Antonio.

The 72-hole record on the European tour is 258 (64, 69, 60, 65), by David Llewellyn in the Biarritz Open from 1 to 3 April 1988. This was equalled by Ian Woosnam (Wales) (66, 67, 65, 60) in the Monte Carlo Open from 4 to 7 July 1990.

The lowest score for four rounds in a British first-class tournament is 262 (66, 63, 66, 67), by Bernard Hunt in the Piccadilly Tournament on the par-68, 5,655-m (6,184-yd) Wentworth East course, Virginia Water, Surrey, from 4 to 5 Oct 1966.

The lowest four-round total ever to be scored in a US LPGA Championship event is 267 (68, 66, 67, 66), by Betsy King (USA) in the Mazda LPGA Championship on the par-71, 5,735-m (6,272-yd) Bethesda Country Club course in Bethesda, Maryland, USA, from 14 to 17 May 1992. King won by 11 strokes and was 17 under-par, both of which are LPGA Championship records.

453 M, BY SHAUN LYNCH

Holes-in-one
Longest holes-in-one
The longest straight hole ever holed in one shot was the 10th (408 m or 447 yd) at Miracle Hills GC, Omaha, Nebraska, USA, by Robert Mitera on 7 Oct 1965. Mitera stood 1.68 m (5 ft 6 in) tall and weighed 75 kg (11 st 11 lb). He was a two-handicap player who normally drove 224 m (245 yd). An 80-km/h (50-mph) gust of wind carried his shot over a 265-m (290-yd) drop-off.

The longest 'dog-leg' hole achieved in one stroke is the 453-m (496-yd) 17th by Shaun Lynch at Teign Valley GC, Christow, near Exeter, Devon, UK, on 24 July 1995.

The longest hole-in-one by a woman is 359 m (393 yd), by Marie Robie on the first hole of the Furnace Brook GC, Wollaston, Massachusetts, USA, on 4 Sept 1949.

Most consecutive holes-in-one
There are at least 20 known cases of 'aces' being achieved in two consecutive holes. The greatest of these was Norman L. Manley's unique 'double albatross' on the par-4, 301-m (330-yd) seventh and the par-4, 265-m (290-yd) eighth holes on the Del Valle Country Club course, Saugus, California, USA, on 2 Sept 1964.

The first woman on record to score two consecutive 'aces' was Sue Prell, on the 13th and 14th holes at Chatswood GC, Sydney, Australia, on 29 May 1977.

The players who have come the closest to achieving three consecutive holes-in-one were Dr Joseph Boydstone, on the third, fourth and ninth holes at Bakersfield GC, California, USA, on 10 Oct 1962, and Rev. Harold Snider, who aced the eighth, 13th and 14th holes of the par-3 Ironwood course, Arizona, USA, on 9 June 1976.

Youngest and oldest to shoot holes-in-one
The youngest golfer on record to have shot a hole-in-one is Coby Orr of Littleton, Colorado, on the 94-m (103-yd) fifth at the Riverside Golf Course, San Antonio, Texas, USA, in 1975, at the age of five years.

The youngest girl was Kathryn Webb, who was 9 years 275 days old when she shot a hole-in-one on the 98-m (107-yd) eighth at Forbes GC, NSW, Australia, on 14 May 1972.

The oldest man to have shot a hole-in-one is Otto Bucher (Switzerland), on the 119-m (130-yd) 12th at La Manga GC, Spain, on 13 Jan 1985, at the age of 99 years 244 days.

The oldest woman was Erna Ross, on the 102-m (112-yd) 17th at The Everglades Club, Palm Beach, Florida, USA, on 23 April 1986, at the age of 95 years 257 days.

The longest throw on record is 120.24 m (394 ft 5 in), by Stefan Uhr (Sweden) at Prästholmen, Mora, Sweden, on 20 Aug 1992.

Fastest individual round
The record for the fastest round to have been played with the golf ball coming to rest before each new stroke is 27 min 9 sec, by James Carvill at the 18-hole, 5,628-m (6,154-yd) Warrenpoint Golf Course, Co. Down, UK, on 18 June 1987.

Fastest team round
The 35 members of the Team Balls Out Diving completed the 5,516-m (6,033-yd) John E. Clark course at Point Micu, California, USA, in a world record time of 9 min 39 sec on 16 Nov 1992.

Most holes in 24 hours, on foot
Ian Colston played a record 22 rounds and five holes (401 holes) at the par-73, 5,542-m (6,061-yd) Bendigo GC, Victoria, Australia, from 27 to 28 Nov 1971.

The British record for the most holes to be played on foot in 24 hours is 360 holes, by Antony J. Clark at Childwall GC, Liverpool, UK, on 18 July 1983.

Most holes in 24 hours, with golf carts
David Cavalier played a record 846 holes at the nine-hole, 2,755-m (3,013-yd) Arrowhead Country Club course, North Canton, Ohio, USA, from 6 to 7 Aug 1990.

Other records
World one-club record
Thad Daber (USA) played the 5,520-m (6,037-yd) Lochmore Golf Club, Cary, North Carolina, USA, with a six-iron in 70, to win the 1987 World One-Club Championship.

Throwing the golf ball
Joe Flynn (USA) threw a ball around 18 holes (over 5,490 m or 6,000 yd) with a record low score of 82, at the 5,695-m (6,228-yd) Port Royal course, Bermuda, on 27 March 1975.

The greatest number of holes played in 24 hours by a woman is 509, by Cyndy Lent (USA) at Twin Lakes Country Club, Wisconsin, USA, from 7 to 8 Aug 1994.

Most balls hit in one hour
The greatest number of balls to have been driven in one hour, over a distance of 91 m (100 yd) and into a target area, is 2,146, by Sean Murphy of Vancouver, Canada, at Swifts Practice Range, Carlisle, Cumbria, UK, on 30 June 1995.

Snooker, billiards and pool

LONGEST CONSECUTIVE RUN IN AN AMERICAN STRAIGHT POOL MATCH IS 625 BALLS

Snooker

World Championships

The World Professional Championship was won a record 15 times by Joe Davis, on the first 15 occasions it was contested, from 1927 to 1940 and in 1946.

The most wins in the Amateur Championships is two, by Gary Owen (England) in 1963 and 1966, Ray Edmonds (England) in 1972 and 1974, and Paul Mifsud (Malta) 1985–86.

Allison Fisher (b. 1968) has won the women's World Championships seven times, in 1985–86, 1988–89 and 1991–93.

Maureen Baynton won the women's Amateur Championships a record eight times between 1954 and 1968.

The youngest man to win a world title is Stephen O'Connor (b. 1972) of Ireland, who was 18 years 40 days old when he won the World Amateur Snooker Championship in Colombo, Sri Lanka, on 25 Nov 1990.

Stephen Hendry (b. 1969) of the United Kingdom became the youngest World Professional champion on 29 April 1990, at the age of 21 years 106 days.

Stacey Hillyard (b. 1969) of the United Kingdom won the women's World Amateur Championship in Oct 1984 at the age of 15.

Highest breaks

The first person to achieve the 'maximum' break of 147 in a game of snooker was the New Zealander E. J. 'Murt' O'Donoghue (1901–94) at Griffiths, NSW, Australia on 26 Sept 1934.

The first officially ratified break of 147 was by Joe Davis against Willie Smith at Leicester Square Hall, London, UK, on 22 Jan 1955.

The first break of 147 in a major tournament was by John Spencer on a table with outsized pockets at Slough, Berks, UK, on 13 Jan 1979. The first on a standard table was by Steve Davis in the Lada Classic at Oldham, Greater Manchester, UK, on 11 Jan 1982.

The youngest person to score a competitive maximum was Ronnie O'Sullivan (b. 1975)—aged 15 years 98 days—during the English Amateur Championship (Southern Area) at Aldershot, Hants, UK, on 13 March 1991.

Tony Drago (b. 1965) made a break of 149 in a witnessed practice frame at West Norwood, Greater London, UK, on 1 Feb 1995. The break involved a free ball, which created an 'extra' red, when all 15 reds were still on the table. In an exceptional case like this, the maximum break is 155.

The only '16 red' clearance ever completed in a tournament was by Steve James (b. 1961) who

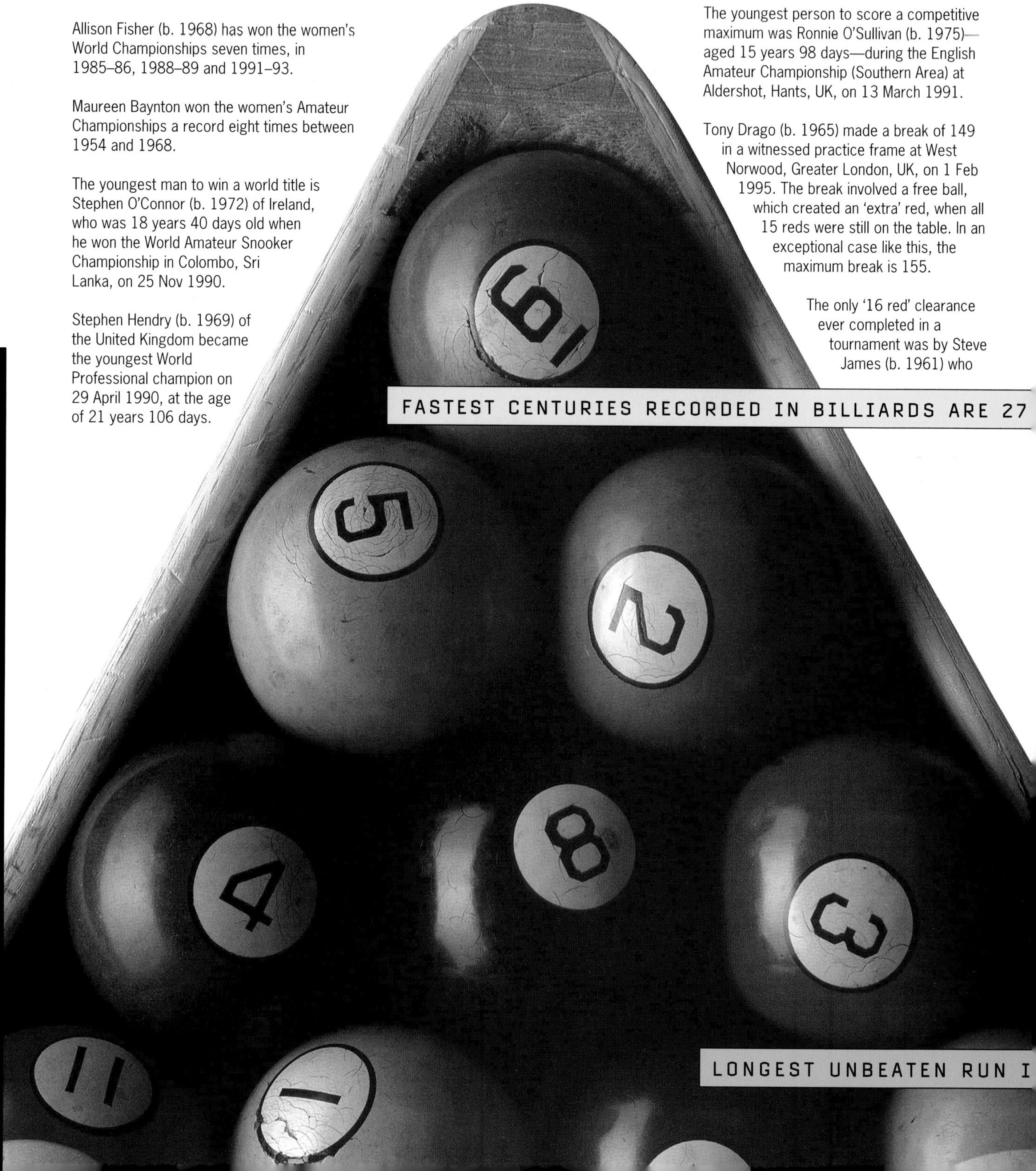

FASTEST CENTURIES RECORDED IN BILLIARDS ARE 27

LONGEST UNBEATEN RUN I

Highest snooker break 149

made 135 in the World Professional Championships at Sheffield, S Yorkshire, UK, on 14 April 1990.

The record world amateur break is 147, by Geet Sethi of India in the Indian Amateur Championships on 21 Feb 1988.

The highest break by a woman is 137, by Stacey Hillyard of the United Kingdom in the General Portfolio Women's Classic at Aylesbury, Bucks, UK, on 23 Feb 1992.

The record number of women's titles is nine, by Vera Selby (b. 1930) from 1970 to 1978.

Youngest champion
The youngest winner of the world professional title is Mike Russell (b. 1969), who was aged 20 years 49 days when he won at Leura, Australia, on 23 July 1989.

Highest breaks
Tom Reece (1873–1953) made an unfinished break of 499,135, including 249,152 cradle cannons (two points each) in 85 hr 49 min against Joe Chapman at Burroughes' Hall, Soho Square, London, UK, between 3 June and 6 July 1907. It is not recognized, because press and public were not continuously present.

The highest certified break made by the anchor cannon is 42,746, by William Cook of England from 29 May to 7 June 1907.

The official world record under the then baulk-line rule is 1,784, by Joe Davis in the United Kingdom Championship on 29 May 1936.

Walter Albert Lindrum (1898–1960) of Australia made an official break of 4,137 in 2 hr 55 min against Joe Davis at Thurston's on 19–20 Jan 1932, before the baulk-line rule was in force.

Geet Sethi of India made a break of 1,276 in the World Professional Championship in Bombay, India, on 1 Oct 1992.

1952. His official record is 46 seconds, set in Sydney, Australia, in 1941.

Three-Cushion
William F. Hoppe (1887–1959) of the USA won 51 billiards championships in all forms from 1906 to 1952.

Raymond Ceulemans (b. 1935) of Belgium has won 20 Three-Cushion World Championships (1963–73, 1975–80, 1983, 1985 and 1990).

Bar billiards
Keith Sheard scored 28,530 points in 19 min 5 sec at the Crown and Thistle, Headington, Oxford, UK, on 9 July 1984.

The highest score in 24 hours by a team of five is 1,754,730 by Les Green, Ricard Powell, Kevin Clark, Mick Lingham and Curt Driver of The Shipwrights Arms, Chatham, Kent, UK, on 26–27 May 1990.

Left
Joe Davis won the Snooker World Professional Championship a record 15 times.

Pool
Ball pocketing
The unoffical record for the longest consecutive run in an American straight pool match is 625 balls, held by Michael Eufemia at Logan's Billiard Academy, Brooklyn, New York, USA, on 2 Feb 1960. The official record is 526, by Willie Mosconi at Springfield, Ohio, in March 1954.

The record for the most balls pocketed in 24 hours is 16,497 by Paul Sullivan at the Abbey Leisure Centre, Selby, N Yorkshire, UK, on 16–17 April 1993.

Left
Pool-players in Kashgar City on the Silk Road, China. Since its invention in the USA, the game of pool has spread all over the world.

Longest unbeaten run
From 17 March 1990 to his defeat by Jimmy White (b. 1962) on 13 Jan 1991, Stephen Hendry won five successive titles and 36 consecutive matches in ranking tournaments.

In 1992, Ronnie O'Sullivan won 38 consecutive games in qualifying competitions.

Billiards
Most titles
The most World Championships won by one player is eight, by the Briton, John Roberts Jr (1847–1919), in 1870 (twice), 1871, 1875 (twice), 1877 and 1885 (twice).

The record for the most world amateur titles is four, by Robert James Percival Marshall (b. 1910) of Australia in 1936, 1938, 1951 and 1962.

The record for the most British professional titles is seven, by Joe Davis (1901–78), in 1934–39 and 1947.

The most English Amateur Championship titles won by one person is 15, by Norman Dagley (b. 1930) in 1965–66, 1970–75 and 1978–84.

The highest break in amateur competition is 1,149, by Michael Ferreira of India at Calcutta, India on 15 Dec 1978. Under the more stringent 'two pot' rule, the highest break is Ferreira's 962 unfinished, at Bombay, India on 29 April 1986.

Fastest century
Walter Lindrum made an unofficial break of 100 in 27.5 seconds in Australia on 10 Oct

Speed potting
The record time for potting all 15 balls is 32.72 seconds, by Paul Sullivan at the Excelsior Pool & Snooker Club, Leeds, S Yorkshire, UK, on 26 Sept 1995.

The record time by a woman is 42.28 seconds, by Susan Thompson at the Ferry Inn, Holmsgarth, Lerwick, Shetland, UK, on 28 Jan 1995.

Bowling, croquet, pétanque

DAVID BRYANT HAS WON A RECORD 15 WORLD CHAMPIONSHIP GOLD MEDALS

Right
It is believed that pétanque began in 1910 as a derivation of the ancient game of jeu provençal.

Outdoor bowls
World Championships
Briton David John Bryant has won a record three singles titles, in 1966, 1980 and 1988. With the triples in 1980 and the Leonard Trophy in 1980 and 1988, he has won a total of six World Championship gold medals.

Scotland has won the Leonard Trophy a record four times (1972, 1984, 1992, 1996).

Elsie Wilke of New Zealand won two women's singles titles, in 1969 and 1974.

Three women's gold medals have been won by: Merle Richardson of Australia for the fours in 1977 and the singles and pairs in 1985; Dorothy Roche of Australia for the triples in 1985 and 1988 and the fours in 1988; and Margaret Johnston of Ireland for the singles in 1992 and the pairs in 1988 and 1992.

English and British Championships
The record for the most English Bowls Association championship victories is 16, won or shared by David Bryant. The wins include six singles (1960, 1966, 1971–73 and 1975), three pairs (1965, 1969 and 1974), three triples (1966, 1977 and 1985) and four fours championships (1957, 1968, 1969 and 1971). He has also won seven British titles (four singles, one pairs, one triple, one fours) in the period 1957–86.

HIGHEST EVER PETANQUE SCORE IN 24 HOUR

Highest score
The highest score in an international match was by Swaziland, who beat Japan 63–1 in the World Championships at Melbourne, Australia, on 16 Jan 1980.

Indoor bowls
World Championships
The most singles titles is three, by both David Bryant (UK) from 1979 to 1981, and Richard Corsie (UK), in 1989, 1991 and 1993.

The pairs have been won six times by David Bryant and Tony Allcock (1986–87, 1989–92).

English Nationals
The most EIBA Singles Championship wins is nine, by David Bryant from 1964 to 1983.

Highest score
The highest total in fours is 59, by Eastbourne & District Indoor Bowls Club v. Egerton Park, at Eastbourne, E Sussex, UK, on 7 Feb 1989.

The greatest 'whitewash' was 55–0, by C. Hammond and B. Funnell against A. Wise and C. Lock in the second round of the EIBA National Pairs Championships at The Angel, Tonbridge, Kent, UK, on 17 Oct 1983.

Tenpin bowling
Highest scores
The highest individual score for three sanctioned games is 899 (from a possible 900), by Thomas Jordan at Union, New Jersey, USA, on 7 March 1989.

The highest individual score by a woman is 864, by Jeanne Maiden at Solon, Ohio, USA, on 23 Nov 1986. This series included a record 40 consecutive strikes (all pins down with one ball).

The maximum score of 900 for a three-game series was achieved by Glenn Richard Allison at the La Habra Bowl, Los Angeles, California, USA, on 1 July 1982, but this record was not recognized by the ABC due to the oiling patterns on the boards.

A score of 900 has also been recorded in five unsanctioned games in the USA, by: Leon Bentley at Lorain, Ohio, on 26 March 1931; Joe Sargent at Rochester, New York, in 1934; Jim Murgie in Philadelphia, Pennsylvania, on 4 Feb 1937; Bob Brown at Roseville Bowl, California, on 12 April 1980; and John Strausbaugh at York, Pennsylvania, on 11 July 1987. These series must have consisted of 36 consecutive strikes.

The record for the highest average for one season in sanctioned competition is 245.63, by Doug Vergouven of Harrisonville, Missouri, USA, in 1989/90.

The highest season's average by a woman is 232, by Patty Ann of Appleton, Wisconsin, USA, in 1983/4.

The record British score for a three-game series is 847, by Lawrence William Ellis, at the Airport Bowl, Hounslow, Greater London, on 30 Aug 1992.

The British three-game series record by a woman is 785, by Emma Barlow, at the Airport Bowl, Hounslow, Greater London, on 24 Nov 1994.

PBA records
Earl Roderick Anthony was the first player to win $1 million. He also won a record 41 PBA titles in his career.

The record earnings by a player in a single season are $298,237 (£163,328), by Mike Aulby in 1989.

The record for the highest earnings in an individual career is $1,715,423 to 10 July 1995, by Peter Weber.

Highest score within 24 hours
A team of six scored a record 242,665 within a 24-hour period at Dover Bowl, Dover, Delaware, USA, from 18 to 19 March 1995.

A member of the team, Ricard Ranshaw (USA), set an individual record of 51,064.

Croquet
Most championships
The record for the greatest number of victories in the Open Croquet Championships is 10, by John William Solomon in 1953, 1956, 1959, 1961 and from 1963 to 1968.

Solomon also won 10 Men's Championships (1951, 1953, 1958–60, 1962, 1964–65 and 1971–72), 10 Open Doubles with Edmond Patrick Charles Cotter (1954–55, 1958–59, 1961–65 and 1969), and one Mixed Doubles with Freda Oddie (1954).

Solomon also won the President's Cup (an invitation event for the best eight players) on nine occasions (1955, 1957–59, 1962–64, 1968 and 1971). He was Champion of Champions on all four occasions on which the competition was run, from 1967 to 1970.

George Nigel Aspinall has won the President's Cup a record 11 times (1969–70, 1973–76, 1978, 1980, 1982 and 1984–85).

Dorothy Dyne Steel, 15 times winner of the Women's Championship from 1919 to 1939, won the Open Croquet Championship four times, in 1925, 1933, and 1935–36. She also won five Doubles and seven Mixed Doubles titles, giving a total of 31.

World Championships
The greatest number of World Championship wins is three, by Briton Robert Fulford in 1990, 1992 and 1994.

International trophy
The MacRobertson Shield has been won by Great Britain a record 10 times (1925, 1937, 1956, 1963, 1969, 1974, 1982, 1990, 1993 and 1996).

Left
David Bryant has won 15 World Championship gold medals, 16 English Bowls Association titles and seven British titles over four decades, since his first success in 1960.

Pétanque
World Championships
To 1995, France had won a record 15 World Championship titles.

The women's World Championships have been won twice, by both Thailand (1988 and 1990), and France (1992 and 1994).

Highest score in 24 hours
Chris Walker and his son Richard scored a record 2,109 points in a total of 172 games at the Gin Trap, Ringstead, Norfolk, UK, from 24 to 25 June 1988.

2,109 IN 172 GAMES

Left
The Hurlingham Club is one of the centres of sporting tradition in the United Kingdom. As well as being the headquarters for both croquet and polo, it has been the venue at which various world records in atheletics have been set.

DOROTHY DYNE STEEL WON A RECORD 31 WOMEN'S CROQUET TITLES

Swimming and water sports

Right
American Matt Biondi matched the achievements of his legendary compatriot Mark Spitz when he gained his 11th medal, a silver, at the 1992 Olympic Games.

Below right
The traditional Polynesian sport of surfing in a canoe was first recorded by Captain Cook on his first voyage to Tahiti in 1711. The modern sport, using boards, has developed during the 20th century.

Swimming

Fastest swimmer
In a 25-yd pool, Tom Jager (USA) achieved a record average speed of 8.64 km/h (5.37 mph), when he swam 50 yd in 19.05 seconds at Nashville, Tennessee, USA, on 23 March 1990.

The fastest speed ever achieved by a female swimmer is 7.21 km/h (4.48 mph), by Yang Wenyi (China), during her world record swim in the 50-m sprint.

Most world records
The greatest number of men's world records set by one swimmer is 32, by Arne Borg (Sweden) between 1921 and 1929.

For currently recognized events (metric distances in 50-m pools), the greatest number of men's world records is 26, by Mark Andrew Spitz (USA) between 1967 and 1972.

The greatest number of women's world records by one swimmer is 42, by Ragnhild Hveger (Denmark) from 1936 to 1942.

For currently recognized events, the greatest number of womens' world records held is 23, by Kornelia Ender (GDR) from 1973 to 1976.

The most world records set in a single pool is 86 (including 48 over imperial distances), in the North Sydney pool, Australia, between 1955 and 1978.

Most world titles
Michael Gross (West Germany) won 13 World Championship medals: five gold, five silver and three bronze, between 1982 and 1990.

The most medals by a woman is 10, by Kornelia Ender, who won eight gold and two silver medals in 1973 and 1975.

The record for the greatest number of gold medals is six (two individual and four relay), by James Paul Montgomery (USA) in 1973 and 1975.

The most medals to have been won at a single championship is seven, by Matthew Nicholas Biondi (USA): three gold, one silver and three bronze (1986).

Most Olympic medals
The greatest number of men's gold medals ever to have been won by one swimmer is nine, by Mark Spitz (USA): 100-m and 200-m freestyle in 1972, 100-m and 200-m butterfly in 1972, 4 x 100-m freestyle in 1968 and 1972, 4 x 200-m freestyle in 1968 and 1972 and 4 x 100-m medley in 1972. All but the 1968 4 x 200-m freestyle medal were also new world records at the time.

Mark Spitz also won a silver (100-m butterfly) and a bronze (100-m freestyle) in 1968, making a record total of 11 medals.

Spitz's record of seven medals at one games in 1972 was equalled by Matt Biondi (USA) in 1988, when he won five gold, one silver and one bronze in 1988. Biondi also shares Spitz's record total of 11 medals, as he won a further gold in 1984 and two golds and a silver in 1992.

The record number of Olympic gold medals to have been won by a woman is six, by Kristin Otto (GDR) at Seoul, South Korea, in 1988 (100-m freestyle, backstroke and butterfly, 50-m freestyle, 4 x 100-m freestyle and 4 x 100-m medley).

Dawn Fraser (Australia) is the only swimmer to have won the same event on three successive occasions (100-m freestyle in 1956, 1960 and 1964).

The record for the greatest number of women's medals is eight, by: Dawn Fraser, with four golds and four silvers between 1956 and 1964; Kornelia Ender, with four golds and four silvers between 1972 and 1976; and Shirley Babashoff (USA), with two golds and six silvers between 1972 and 1976.

The greatest number of individual gold medals is four, by Charles Meldrum Daniels (USA), in the 100-m freestyle in 1906 and 1908, the 220-yd freestyle in 1904, and the 440-yd freestyle in 1904; by Roland Matthes (GDR), with the 100-m and 200-m backstroke in 1968 and 1972; and by Mark Spitz and Kristin Otto.

The most gold medals won by a British swimmer is four, by Henry Taylor (mile freestyle in 1906, 400-m freestyle in 1908, 1,500-m freestyle in 1908 and 4 x 200-m freestyle in 1908). He won a silver and three bronzes from 1906 to 1920 to make a record total of eight medals.

The most medals won by a British woman is four, by Margaret Joyce Cooper (now Badcock), with one silver and three bronze between 1928 and 1932.

Largest pools
The world's largest swimming pool is the seawater Orthlieb Pool, Casablanca, Morocco. It is 480 m (1,574 ft) long and 75 m (246 ft) wide, and has an area of 3.6 ha (8⁹⁄₁₀ acres).

The largest land-locked pool in current use is Willow Lake at Warren, Ohio, USA, which measures 183 m x 46 m (600 x 150 ft).

The largest British swimming pool in use is the Royal Commonwealth Pool, Edinburgh, which was completed in 1970 and has 2,000 permanent seats.

Diving
Most Olympic medals
The greatest number of medals to have been won by a diver is five, by Klaus Dibiasi (Italy), with three gold and two silver between 1964 and 1976; and by Gregory Efthimios Louganis (USA), with four gold and one silver in 1976, 1984 and 1988.

Klaus Dibiasi is the only diver to have won the same event at three successive Games (highboard in 1968, 1972 and 1976).

Two divers have won the highboard and springboard doubles at two games: Patricia Joan McCormick (USA) in 1952 and 1956 and Greg Louganis (USA) in 1984 and 1988.

Highest scores
Greg Louganis (USA) achieved record scores at the 1984 Olympic Games in Los Angeles, California, USA, obtaining a total of 754.41 points for the 11-dive springboard event and 710.91 points for the highboard.

The first diver awarded a perfect score of 10.0 by all seven judges was Michael Holman Finneran, for a backward 1½ somersault, 2½ twist, from the 10-m board in the 1972 US Olympic Trials in Chicago, Illinois, USA.

Greg Louganis was awarded 10.0 points by all seven judges for his highboard inward 1½ somersault in the pike position at the 1984 World Championships in Guayaquil, Ecuador.

Water polo
Most Olympic titles
Hungary has won a record six Olympic titles in 1932, 1936, 1952, 1956, 1964 and 1976.

The record for the most gold medals is three, by George Wilkinson (GB) in 1900, 1908 and 1912; by Paulo 'Paul' Radmilovic (GB) and Charles Sidney Smith (GB) in 1908, 1912 and 1920 (the former also won a gold medal for the 4 x 200-m freestyle swimming in 1908); and by Deszö Gyarmati (Hungary) and György Kárpáti (Hungary), 1952, 1956, 1964.

Most world titles
The USSR (1975 and 1982), Yugoslavia (1986 and 1991), and Italy (1978 and 1994) have all won the World Championships twice.

The highest placing by a Briton is a silver medal, by Beatrice Eileen Armstrong (later Purdy) in the 1920 highboard event.

The best placing by a British man is bronze, by Harold Clarke (plain high diving, 1924) and Brian Eric Phelps (highboard, 1960).

Youngest Olympic winner
Marjorie Gestring (USA) took the springboard diving title aged 13 years 268 days at the Berlin Olympics on 12 Aug 1936. This makes her the youngest person ever to have won any Olympic title.

Most world titles
Greg Louganis (USA) won a record five world titles (highboard in 1978 and highboard and springboard in 1982 and 1986), as well as four Olympic gold medals in 1984 and 1988. Three gold medals in one event have also been won by Philip George Boggs (USA), for the springboard in 1973, 1975 and 1978.

Most goals
The greatest number of goals to have been scored by one player in an international match is 13, by Debbie Handley during Australia's 16–10 defeat of Canada at the World Championship in Guayaquil, Ecuador, in 1982.

Most international appearances
The greatest number of international appearances is 412, by Aleksey Stepanovich Barkalov (USSR) between 1965 and 1980.

The most international appearances by a British player is 126, by Martyn Thomas between 1964 and 1978.

Surfing
Most World Amateur titles
The record for the most World Amateur Championships titles is three, by Michael Novakov (Australia), who won the Kneeboard event in 1982, 1984 and 1986.

Most World Professional titles
Mark Richards (Australia) had won the men's World Professional surfing title five times, in 1975 and from 1979 to 1982.

The most women's titles won is four, by Frieda Zamba (USA), from 1984 to 1986 and in 1988, and Wendy Botha (South Africa, then Australia), in 1987, 1989, 1991 and 1992.

Highest waves
Waimea Bay in Hawaii is generally believed to provide the most consistently high waves; they frequently reach 9–11 m (30–35 ft).

Longest sea wave ride
Waves that can be ridden for about 1,700 m (5,700 ft) break in Matanchen Bay near San Blas, Nayarit, Mexico, four to six times a year.

Longest ride
The longest ride on a surfboard is 4.73 km (2 miles 1,650 yd), on the Severn bore, UK, by Colin Kerr Wilson on 23 May 1982.

The official British Surfing Association record for riding a surfboard in a standing position is 4.2 km (2 miles 1,050 yd), by David Lawson, from Stonebeach to The Parting—also on the Severn bore—on 10 Aug 1995.

Above
Greg Louganis (USA) holds the diving records for both world titles (five) and US national titles (47).

Swimming records

SARAH HARDCASTLE HOLDS THE BRITISH 400-M, 800-M AND 1,500-M FREESTYLE RECORDS

Right
The earliest mention of swimming races dates back to 36 BC in Japan, but it may have been a popular sport long before that.

SHORT-COURSE WORLD RECORDS
(set in 25-m pools)

MEN

Freestyle
50 m: 21.50 Aleksandr Popov (Russia)
Desenzano, Italy, 13 March 1994
100 m: 46.74 Aleksandr Popov (Russia)
Gelsenkirchen, Germany, 19 March 1994
200 m: 1:43.64 Giorgio Lamberti (Italy)
Bonn, Germany, 11 Feb 1990
400 m: 3:40.46 Danyon Loader (New Zealand)
Sheffield, S Yorkshire, UK, 11 Feb 1995
800 m: 7:34.90 Kieren Perkins (Australia)
Sydney, Australia, 25 July 1993
1,500 m: 14:26.52 Kieren Perkins (Australia)
Auckland, New Zealand, 15 July 1993
4 x 50-m: 1:27.62 Sweden
Stavanger, Norway, 2 Dec 1994
4 x 100-m: 3:12.11 Brazil
Palma de Mallorca, Spain, 5 Dec 1993
4 x 200-m: 7:05.17 West Germany
Bonn, Germany, 9 Feb 1986

Backstroke
50 m: 24.37 Jeff Rouse (USA)
Sheffield, S Yorkshire, UK, 12 Feb 1995
100 m: 51.43 Jeff Rouse (USA)
Sheffield, S Yorkshire, UK, 12 April 1993
200 m: 1:52.51 Martin López-Zubero (Spain)
Gainesville, Florida, USA, 11 April 1991

Breaststroke
50 m: 27.00 Mark Warnecke (Germany)
Gelsenkirchen, Germany, 18 Feb 1995
100 m: 59.02 Frédéric Deburghgraeve (Belgium)
Bastogne, Belgium, 17 Feb 1996
200 m: 2:07.80 Philip Rogers (Australia)
Melbourne, Australia, 28 Aug 1993

Butterfly
50 m: 23.45 Mark Foster (GB)
Sheffield, S Yorkshire, UK, 15 Dec 1995
100 m: 52.07 Marcel Gery (Canada)
Leicester, UK, 23 Feb 1990
*51.94 Denis Pankratov (Russia)
Paris, France, 4 Feb 1996
200 m: 1:53.05 Franck Esposito (France)
Paris, France, 26 March 1994
*1:52.34 Denis Pankratov (Russia)
Paris, France, 3 Feb 1996

* Not ratified.

Medley
100 m: 53.10 Jani Sievinen (Finland)
Malmö, Sweden, 30 Jan 1996
200 m: 1:54.65 Jani Sievinen (Finland)
Kuopio, Finland, 21 Jan 1994
400 m: 4:06.03 Jani Sievinen (Finland)
Lappeenranta, Finland, 19 Jan 1996
4 x 50-m: 1:36.69 Auburn Aquatics
Auburn, New York, USA, 9 April 1996
4 x 100-m: 3:32.57 USA
Palma de Mallorca, Spain, 2 Dec 1993

WOMEN

Freestyle
50 m: 24.23 Le Jingyi (China)
Palma de Mallorca, Spain, 3 Dec 1993
100 m: 53.01 Le Jingyi (China)
Palma de Mallorca, Spain, 2 Dec 1993
200 m: 1:55.16 Claudia Poll (Costa Rica)
Rio de Janeiro, Brazil, 1 Dec 1995
400 m: 4:02.05 Astrid Strauss (GDR)
Bonn, Germany, 8 Feb 1987
800 m: 8:15.34 Astrid Strauss (GDR)
Bonn, Germany, 6 Feb 1987
1,500 m: 15:43.31 Petra Schneider (GDR)
Gainesville, Florida, USA, 10 Jan 1982
4 x 50-m: 1:40.63 Germany
Espoo, Finland, 22 Nov 1992
4 x 100-m: 3:35.97 China
Palma de Mallorca, Spain, 4 Dec 1993
4 x 200-m: 7:52.45 China
Palma de Mallorca, Spain, 2 Dec 1993

Backstroke
50 m: 27.64 Bai Xiuyu (China)
Desenzano, Italy, 12 March 1994
100 m: 58.50 Angel Martino (USA)
Palma de Mallorca, Spain, 3 Dec 1993
200 m: 2:06.09 He Cihong (China)
Palma de Mallorca, Spain, 5 Dec 1993

Breaststroke
50 m: 30.98 Han Xue (China)
Beijing, China, 11 Jan 1996
100 m: 1:05.70 Samantha Riley (Australia)
Rio de Janeiro, Brazil, 2 Dec 1995

WORLD RECORDS
(set in 50-m pools)

MEN

Freestyle
50 m: 21.81 Tom Jager (USA)
Nashville, Tennessee, USA, 24 March 1990
100 m: 48.21 Aleksandr Popov (Russia)
Monte Carlo, Monaco, 18 June 1994
200 m: 1:46.69 Giorgio Lamberti (Italy)
Bonn, Germany, 15 Aug 1989
400 m: 3:43.80 Kieren Perkins (Australia)
Rome, Italy, 9 Sept 1994
800 m: 7:46.00 Kieren Perkins (Australia)
Victoria, Canada, 24 Aug 1994
1,500 m: 14:41.66 Kieren Perkins (Australia)
Victoria, Canada, 24 Aug 1994
4 x 100-m: 3:15.11 USA (David Fox, Joe Hudepohl, Jon Olsen, Gay Hall)
Atlanta, Georgia, USA, 12 Aug 1995
4 x 200-m: 7:11.95 CIS (Dmitriy Lepikov, Vladimir Pyechenko, Venyamin Tayanovich, Yevgeniy Sadovyi)
Barcelona, Spain, 27 July 1992

Breaststroke
100 m: 1:00.95 Károly Güttler (Hungary)
Sheffield, S Yorkshire, UK, 3 Aug 1993

SHORT-COURSE 50-M BUTTERFLY RECORD IS 23.

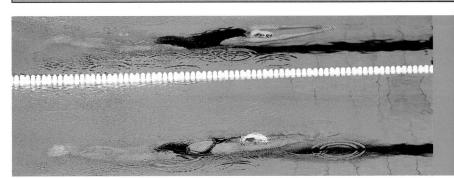

200 m: 2:20.85 Samantha Riley (Australia)
Rio de Janeiro, Brazil, 1 Dec 1995

Butterfly
50 m: 26.56 Angela Kennedy (Australia)
Sheffield, S Yorkshire, UK, 12 Feb 1995
100 m: * 58.68 Liu Limin (China)
Rio de Janeiro, Brazil, 2 Dec 1995
200 m: 2:05.65 Mary Terstegge Meagher (USA)
Gainesville, Florida, USA, 2 Jan 1981

* Slower than long-course best.

Medley
100 m: 1:01.03 Louise Karlsson (Sweden)
Espoo, Finland, 22 Nov 1992
200 m: 2:07.79 Allison Wagner (USA)
Palma de Mallorca, Spain, 5 Dec 1993
400 m: 4:29.00 Dai Gouhong (China)
Palma de Mallorca, Spain, 2 Dec 1993
4 x 50-m: 1:52.44 Germany
Espoo, Finland, 21 Nov 1992
4 x 100-m: 3:57.73 China
Palma de Mallorca, Spain, 5 Dec 1993

200 m: 2:10.16 Michael Barrowman (USA)
Barcelona, Spain, 29 July 1992

Butterfly
100 m: 52.32 Denis Pankratov (Russia)
Vienna, Austria, 23 Aug 1995
200 m: 1:55.22 Denis Pankratov (Russia)
Paris, France, 14 June 1995

Backstroke
100 m: 53.86 Jeff Rouse (USA) (relay leg)
Barcelona, Spain, 31 July 1992
200 m: 1:56.57 Martin López-Zubero (Spain)
Tuscaloosa, Alabama, USA, 23 Nov 1991

Medley
200 m: 1:58.16 Jani Sievinen (Finland)
Rome, Italy, 11 Sept 1994
400 m: 4:12.30 Tom Dolan (USA)
Rome, Italy, 6 Sept 1994
4 x 50-m: 3:36.93 USA (David Berkoff, Richard Schroeder, Matt Biondi and Christopher Jacobs)
Seoul, South Korea, 25 Sept 1988
3:36.93 USA (Jeff Rouse, Nelson Diebel, Pablo Morales and Jon Olsen)
Barcelona, Spain, 31 July 1992

100-m freestyle 46.74 seconds

WOMEN

Freestyle
50 m: 24.51 Le Jingyi (China)
Rome, Italy, 11 Sept 1994
100 m: 54.01 Le Jingyi (China)
Rome, Italy, 5 Sept 1994
200 m: 1:56.78 Franziska van Almsick (Germany)
Rome, Italy, 6 Sept 1994
400 m: 4:03.85 Janet Evans (USA)
Seoul, South Korea, 22 Sept 1988
800 m: 8:16.22 Janet Evans (USA)
Tokyo, Japan, 20 Aug 1989
1,500 m: 15:52.10 Janet Evans (USA)
Orlando, Florida, USA, 26 March 1988
4 x 100-m: 3:37.91 China
(Le Jingyi, Shan Ying, Le Ying and Lu Bin)
Rome, Italy, 7 Sept 1994
4 x 200-m: 7:55.47 GDR
(Manuela Stellmach, Astrid Strauss, Anke Möhring
and Heike Friedrich)
Strasbourg, France, 18 Aug 1987

Breaststroke
100 m: 1:07.46 Penny Heyns (South Africa)
Durban, South Africa, 4 March 1996
200 m: 2:24.76 Rebecca Brown (Australia)
Brisbane, Australia, 16 March 1994

BRITISH NATIONAL RECORDS
(Set in 50-m pools)

MEN

Freestyle
50 m: 22.43 Mark Foster
Sheffield, S Yorkshire, UK, 24 May 1992
100 m: 50.24 Michael Fibbens
Sheffield, S Yorkshire, UK, 22 May 1992
200 m: 1:48.84 Paul Palmer
Sheffield, S Yorkshire, UK, 3 Aug 1993
400 m: 3:48.14 Paul Palmer
Sheffield, S Yorkshire, UK, 6 Aug 1993
800 m: 7:59.48 Graeme Smith
Sheffield, S Yorkshire, UK, 22 March 1996
1,500 m: 15:03.43 Graeme Smith
Sheffield, S Yorkshire, UK, 22 March 1996
4 x 100-m: 3:21.41 GB (Michael Fibbens, Mark
Foster, Paul Howe, Roland Lee)
Barcelona, Spain, 29 July 1992
4 x 200-m: 7:22.57 GB (Paul Palmer, Steven
Mellor, Stephen Akers, Paul Howe)
Barcelona, Spain, 27 July 1992

Breaststroke
100 m: 1:01.33 Nicholas Gillingham
Sheffield, S Yorkshire, UK, 21 May 1992

WOMEN

Freestyle
50 m: 26.01 Caroline Woodcock
Bonn, Germany, 20 Aug 1989
100 m: 55.79 Karen Pickering
Rome, Italy, 5 Sept 1994
200 m: 1:59.74 June Croft
Brisbane, Australia, 4 Oct 1982
400 m: 4:07.68 Sarah Hardcastle
Edinburgh, UK, 27 July 1986
800 m: 8:24.77 Sarah Hardcastle
Edinburgh, UK, 29 July 1986
1,500 m: 16:39.46 Sarah Hardcastle
Edinburgh, UK, 31 March 1994
4 x 100-m: 3:45.52 GB (Susan Rolph, Alex
Bennett, Claire Huddart and Karen Pickering)
Rome, Italy, 7 Sept 1994
4 x 200-m: 8:09.62 England (Sarah
Hardcastle, Claire Huddart, Alex Bennett,
Karen Pickering)
Victoria, Canada, 20 Aug 1994

Breaststroke
100 m: 1:10.39 Susannah 'Suki' Brownsdon
Strasbourg, France, 21 Aug 1987
200 m: 2:30.63 Marie Hardiman
Crystal Palace, London, UK, 31 July 1994

:CONDS, BY MARK FOSTER

CHINESE SWIMMER LE JINGYI HOLDS FOUR INDIVIDUAL WORLD RECORDS

Butterfly
100 m: 57.93 Mary Meagher (USA)
Brown Deer, Wisconsin, USA, 16 Aug 1981
200 m: 2:05.96 Mary Meagher (USA)
Brown Deer, Wisconsin, USA, 13 Aug 1981

Backstroke
100 m: 1:00.16 He Cihong (China)
Rome, Italy, 11 Sept 1994
200 m: 2:06.62 Krisztina Egerszegi (Hungary)
Athens, Greece, 25 Aug 1991

Medley
200 m: 2:11.57 Lu Bin (China)
Hiroshima, Japan, 7 Oct 1994
400 m: 4:36.10 Petra Schneider (GDR)
Guayaquil, Ecuador, 1 Aug 1982
4 x 100-m: 4:01.67 China (He Cihong, Dai
Guohong, Liu Limin and Le Jingyi)
Rome, Italy, 11 Sept 1994

200 m: 2:11.29 Nicholas Gillingham
Barcelona, Spain, 29 July 1992

Butterfly
100 m: 53.30 Andrew Jameson
Seoul, South Korea, 21 Sept 1988
200 m: 1:58.50 James Hickman
Sheffield, S Yorkshire, UK, 23 March 1996

Backstroke
100 m: 55.00 Martin Harris
Sheffield, S Yorkshire, UK, 22 April 1995
200 m: 1:59.52 Adam Ruckwood
Sheffield, S Yorkshire, UK, 23 April 1995

Medley
200 m: 2:03.20 Neil Cochran
Orlando, Florida, USA, 25 March 1988
400 m: 4:24.20 John Davey
Crystal Palace, London, UK, 1 Aug 1987
4 x 100-m: 3:41.66 GB (Martin Harris, Nick
Gillingham, Michael Fibbens, Mark Foster)
Sheffield, S Yorkshire, UK, 8 Aug 1993

Butterfly
100 m: 1:01.33 Madeleine Scarborough
Auckland, New Zealand, 28 Jan 1990
200 m: 2:11.97 Samantha Paula Purvis
Los Angeles, California, USA, 4 Aug 1984

Backstroke
100 m: 1:03.27 Katharine Osher
Victoria, Canada, 21 Aug 1994
200 m: 2:13.91 Joanne Deakins
Barcelona, Spain, 31 July 1992

Medley
200 m: 2:16.41 Susan Rolph
Sheffield, S Yorkshire, UK, 23 March 1996
400 m: 4:46.83 Sharron Davies
Moscow, USSR, 26 July 1980
4 x 100-m: 4:11.88 England (Joanne Deakins,
Susannah 'Suki' Brownsdon, Madeleine
Scarborough, Karen Pickering)
Auckland, New Zealand, 29 Jan 1990

Long-distance swimming

English Channel

First crossings

There is good evidence to show that Jean-Marie Saletti, a French soldier, escaped from a British prison hulk off Dover, UK, and swam to Boulogne, France, in July or Aug 1815.

Paul Boyton (USA) swam from Cap Gris-Nez, France, to the South Foreland, UK, in his patent life-saving suit in 23 hr 30 min from 28 to 29 May 1875.

The first person to swim the English Channel from shore to shore without a life jacket was the Merchant Navy captain Matthew Webb, who swam an estimated 61 km (38 miles) to make the 33-km (21-mile) crossing from Dover, UK to Calais Sands, France, in a time of 21 hr 45 min from 12:56 p.m. to 10:41 a.m. on 24 and 25 Aug 1875.

The first crossing made from France to the United Kingdom without a life jacket was achieved by Enrico Tiraboschi, a wealthy Italian living in Argentina, in a time of 16 hr 33 min on 12 Aug 1923, to win the *Daily Sketch* prize of £1,000.

The first woman to swim the Channel was Gertrude Caroline Ederle (USA), who crossed from Cap Gris-Nez, France, to Deal, UK, on 6 Aug 1926 in 14 hr 39 min (then an overall record time).

First double and triple crossings

The first ever double crossing of the English Channel was made by Antonio Abertondo (Argentina), in a time of 43 hr 10 min from 20 to 22 Sept 1961.

The first triple crossing was by Jon Erikson (USA), in a time of 38 hr 27 min from 11 to 12 Aug 1981.

Hundeby of California, USA, who swam from Shakespeare Beach, Dover, UK, to Cap Gris-Nez, France, on 27 Sept 1994.

The fastest crossing time from France to the United Kingdom is 8 hr 5 min, by Richard Davey (GB) in 1988.

The fastest ever crossing time by a relay team is 6 hr 52 min (from the United Kingdom to France), by the US National Swim Team on 1 Aug 1990.

Fastest double and triple crossings

The fastest double crossing was achieved in a time of 16 hr 10 min, by Philip Rush (New Zealand) on 17 Aug 1987.

The fastest double crossing achieved by a female swimmer is 17 hr 14 min by Susie Maroney (Australia) on 23 July 1991.

The US National Swim Team completed the two-way relay in a record-breaking time of 14 hr 18 min on 1 Aug 1990.

Philip Rush (New Zealand) made the fastest ever triple crossing in a time of 28 hr 21 min from 17 to 18 Aug 1987.

Greatest number of crossings

The most Channel crossings by one swimmer is 32, by Alison Streeter (GB) between 1982 and 4 Sept 1995. This total includes a record seven crossings in one year, in 1992.

The most Channel crossings by a male swimmer is 31, by Michael Read (GB) from 24 Aug 1969 to 19 Aug 1984.

Oldest swimmer

The oldest person to have successfully swum across the English Channel is Bertram Clifford

Fastest crossing

The record time for crossing the Irish Channel is 9 hr 53 min 42 sec, by Alison Streeter on 22 Aug 1988. She was also the first person to complete the crossing from Scotland to Northern Ireland, in a time of 10 hr 4 min on 25 Aug 1989.

Lake swimming

Loch Ness

The fastest time taken to swim Loch Ness, UK, which is 36.5 km (22 miles 1,230 yd) long, is 9 hr 25 min 37 sec, by Rachel Rose Godburn on 20 Aug 1995.

David Trevor Morgan achieved a two-way crossing of Loch Ness in a record time of 23 hr 4 min on 1 Aug 1983. In 1988, Morgan also became the only person to have swum Loch Ness (on 16 July), the 34.6-km-long (21½-mile) Loch Lomond (on 18 July) and the English Channel (from 20 to 21 July). His times were 11 hr 9 min, 11 hr 48 min and 11 hr 35 min respectively.

Lake Windermere

The fastest time taken to swim the length of Lake Windermere, which extends for 16.9 km (10½ miles) from Fellfoot to Waterhead, UK, is 3 hr 49 min 12 sec, by Justin Palfrey on 7 Sept 1991.

Other distance swimming

Greatest distances

The longest ever swim on record covered 2,938 km (1,826 miles). It was made along the Mississippi River, USA, between Ford Dam near Minneapolis, Minnesota, and Carrollton

The first triple crossing made by a woman was by Alison Streeter (GB) in a time of 34 hr 40 min from 2 to 3 Aug 1990.

Earliest crossing

The earliest date in the year on which the English Channel has been swum is 30 May, by Kevin Murphy (GB) in 1990. He achieved this in a time of 13 hr 16 min, with the water at a temperature of 12°C (54°F).

Latest crossing

The latest date in the year on which a Channel crossing has been made is 28 Oct, by Michael Peter Read (GB) in 1979, in a time of 17 hr 55 min.

Fastest crossings

The official Channel Swimming Association record for a crossing is 7 hr 17 min, by Chad

Batt of Australia, who was 67 years 241 days old when he crossed from Cap Gris-Nez, France, to Dover, UK, between 19 and 20 Aug 1987. Batt achieved this feat in a time of 18 hr 37 min.

The oldest woman to swim the English Channel was Susan Fraenkel of South Africa, who completed the crossing in a time of 12 hr 5 min on 24 July 1994, at the age of 46 years 103 days.

Irish Channel

First crossing

The 37-km-wide (23-mile) North Channel between Donaghadee, Northern Ireland, and Portpatrick, Scotland, was first swum by Tom Blower of Nottingham, UK, in a time of 15 hr 26 min in 1947.

Ave, New Orleans, Louisiana, by Fred P. Newton of Clinton, Oklahoma. He was in the water for a total of 742 hours between 6 July and 29 Dec 1930.

In 1966, Mihir Sen of Calcutta, India, became the only person to have swum the Palk Strait from Sri Lanka to India (in 25 hr 36 min from 5 to 6 April), the Straits of Gibraltar (in 8 hr 1 min on 24 Aug), the entire length of the Dardanelles (in 13 hr 55 min on 12 Sept), the Bosphorus (in 4 hr on 21 Sept), and the length of the Panama Canal (in 34 hr 15 min from 29 to 31 Oct).

Greatest distances covered in 24 hours

Anders Forvass (Sweden) swam a total of 101.9 km (63 miles 560 yd) at the 25-m Linköping public swimming pool, Sweden, from 28 to 29 Oct 1989.

The greatest distance covered in 24 hours in a 50-m pool is 96.7 km (60 miles 150 yd), by Evan Barry (Australia) at the Valley Pool, Brisbane, Australia, from 19 to 20 Dec 1987.

The greatest distance that has been swum in 24 hours by a female swimmer is 93.625 km (58 miles 310 yd), by Susie Maroney (Australia) at Carss Park, Sydney, Australia, from 21 to 22 April 1995.

Long-distance relays

The New Zealand national relay team, consisting of 20 swimmers, swam a record distance of 182.807 km (113 miles 1,040 yd) in Lower Hutt, New Zealand, in 24 hours from 9 to 10 Dec 1983. They covered 160 km (100 miles) in 20 hr 47 min 13 sec.

The club record for the greatest distance covered by a team of five within 24 hours is

...AWAN AL AWAMI COVERED A RECORD 78.92 KM UNDERWATER IN 24 HOURS

162.52 km (100 miles 1,735 yd), by the Portsmouth Northsea Swimming Club at the Victoria Swimming Centre, Portsmouth, Hants, UK, from 4 to 5 March 1993.

The club record for the greatest distance covered by a team of five female swimmers in 24 hours is 143.11 km (88 miles 1,625 yd), by the City of Newcastle Amateur Swimming Club, UK, from 16 to 17 Dec 1986.

The greatest ever number of participants in a one-day swim relay is 2,375, at Liverpool High School, Liverpool, New York, USA, from 20 to 21 May 1994. Each participant swam one length.

Underwater swimming

Paul Cryne (GB) and Samir Sawan al Awami (Qatar) swam a record distance of 78.92 km (49 miles 68 yd) in a 24-hour period. This was achieved from Doha to Umm Said (both in Qatar) and back, from 21 to 22 Feb 1985. The men, who were using sub-aqua equipment, were swimming underwater for 95.5% of the time.

The greatest distance swum underwater by a relay team is 151.987 km (94 miles 773 yd), by six swimmers in a pool at Olomouc, Czechoslovakia, from 17 to 18 Oct 1987.

Sponsored swimming

The greatest amount of money ever to have been raised in a sponsored swim for charity was £122,983.19 in 'Splash '92'. The fund-raising event was organized by the Royal Bank of Scotland Swimming Club and held at the Royal Commonwealth Pool, Edinburgh, UK, from 25 to 26 Jan 1992. There was a total of 3,218 participants.

The greatest amount of money raised for charity at an event staged at several pools was £548,006.14, by 'Penguin Swimathon '88'. A total of 5,482 swimmers participated at 43 pools throughout London, UK, from 26 to 28 Feb 1988.

Top
In modern times, competitive swimming was popularized in the United Kingdom from at least 1791, and the first national swimming association was founded in 1869.

Middle
In 1926 American swimmer Gertrude Ederle became the first woman to cross the English Channel. As of May 1996, there had been 6,381 attempts to swim the Channel by 4,387 people. Of these, 485 individuals (321 men and 161 women) from 42 countries have made 761 successful crossings (708 single, 22 double and three triple).

Bottom
The Mississippi River in the USA extends for 3,780 km (2,350 miles) from northern Minnesota to the Gulf of Mexico beyond New Orleans and was the scene of the longest recorded swim, during which Fred P. Newton covered 2,938 km (1,826 miles).

...D WHEN HE SWAM FROM CAP GRIS-NEZ TO DOVER

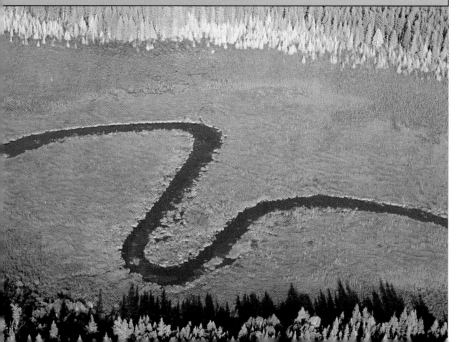

Rowing, powerboat racing

Rowing

Olympics and World Championships

Three gold medals have been won by: John Brenden Kelly (USA), single sculls in 1920 and double sculls in 1920 and 1924; Paul Vincent Costello (USA), double sculls in 1920, 1924 and 1928; Jack Beresford Jr (GB), single sculls in 1924, coxless fours in 1932 and double sculls in 1936, Vyacheslav Nikolayevich

The most women's single sculls wins is five, by Christine Hahn (GDR), 1974–75, 1977–78 and the 1976 Olympic title.

Boat Race

In the 142 races held between 1829 and 1996, Cambridge has won 73 times, Oxford 68 times and there was a dead heat on 24 March 1877.

Andrew Holmes), 1989 (with Simon Beresford), and 1991 and 1993–95 (with Matthew Pinsent). The record time is 6 min 56 sec, by Redgrave and Pinsent on 1 July 1995.

Longest race

The longest annual rowing race is the Tour du Lac Leman, Geneva, Switzerland, which is for coxed fours (the five-man crew taking turns as

Right
Steven Redgrave and Matthew Pinsent won Olympic gold in the coxless pairs in 1992. Since forming their partnership at the beginning of the 1990s, the pair have dominated all major rowing events.

Ivanov (USSR), single sculls in 1956, 1960 and 1964; Siegfried Brietzke (GDR), coxless pairs in 1972 and coxless fours in 1976 and 1980; Pertti Karppinen (Finland), single sculls in 1976, 1980 and 1984; and Steven Geoffrey Redgrave (GB), coxed fours in 1984 and coxless pairs in 1988 and 1992.

The record for the greatest number of gold medals won at World Championships and Olympic Games is nine, by: Giuseppe and Carmine Abbagnale (Italy) (World, 1981–82, 1985, 1987, 1989–91 and Olympic coxed pairs 1984 and 1988—all with the same cox, Guiseppe di Capua); and Steven Redgrave (GB) (three Olympic titles and world titles at coxed pairs 1986 and coxless pairs 1987, 1991, 1993–95).

Francesco Esposito (Italy) has won a record nine titles at lightweight events (coxless pairs 1980–84, 1988 and 1994 and coxless fours 1990 and 1992).

At women's events Yelena Tereshina (USSR) has won a record seven golds (eights, 1978–79, 1981–83 and 1985–86).

The most wins at single sculls is five by: Peter-Michael Kolbe (West Germany) in 1975, 1978, 1981, 1983 and 1986; Pertti Karppinen in 1979 and 1985 (plus three Olympic wins); and Thomas Lange (GDR/Germany) in 1987, 1989 and 1991, with two Olympics in 1988 and 1992.

The race record time for the 6.779-km (4-mile 374-yd) Putney to Mortlake course is 16 min 45 sec, by Oxford on 18 March 1984.

The smallest winning margin was by a canvas, by Oxford in 1952 and 1980.

The greatest winning margin (apart from sinking) is 20 lengths, by Cambridge in 1900.

Boris Rankov rowed in a record six winning boats, for Oxford from 1978 to 1983.

Susan Brown coxed a record two winning boats, for Oxford in 1981 and 1982.

Daniel Topolski coached Oxford to a record 10 successive victories, from 1976 to 1985.

Henley Royal Regatta

The most wins in the Diamond Challenge Sculls is six, by Guy Nickalls (GB), 1888–91 and 1893–94, and by Stuart Alexander Mackenzie (Australia and GB), 1957–62.

The record time is 7 min 23 sec, by Vaclav Chalupa (Czechoslovakia) on 2 July 1989.

The record time for the Grand Challenge Cup event is 5 min 58 sec by Hansa Dortmund, West Germany, on 2 July 1989.

The most wins in the Silver Goblets and Nickalls Challenge Cup (instituted 1845) is seven by Steve Redgrave (GB): 1986–87 (with

cox) over 160 km (99 miles). The best winning time is 12 hr 22 min 29 sec, by RG Red Bull Bonn, Germany, on 2 Oct 1994.

Highest speed

The world record time for 2,000 m (2,187 yd) on non-tidal water is 5 min 24.28 sec (a speed of 22.20 km/h or 13.79 mph), by an eight from Hansa Dortmund (Germany) at Essen, Germany, on 17 May 1992.

The women's fastest time is 5 min 58.50 sec, by the Romanian team at Duisberg, Germany, on 18 May 1996.

The single sculls speed record is 6 min 37.03 sec (18.13 km/h or 11.26 mph), by Juri Jaanson (Estonia) at Lucerne, Switzerland, on 9 July 1995.

The women's single sculls record is 7 min 17.09 sec by Silken Laumann (Canada) on 17 July 1994 at Lucerne.

Distance (24 hours)

The greatest distance (upstream and downstream) is 227.33 km (141 miles 450 yd), by six members of Dittons Skiff and Punting Club on the River Thames between Hampton Court and Teddington, Greater London, UK, from 3 to 4 June 1994.

River Thames (UK)

Five members of the Lower Thames Rowing Club rowed the navigable length of the

Thames (299.14 km or 185 miles 1,543 yd), from Lechlade Bridge, Glos, to Southend Pier, Essex, in 38 hr 43 min 20 sec in May 1993.

The fastest time from Folly Bridge, Oxford, to Westminster Bridge, London (180 km or 112 miles) is 14 hr 25 min 15 sec, by an eight from Kingston Rowing Club on 1 Feb 1986.

Canoeing
Most titles
Gert Fredriksson (Sweden) won a record six Olympic gold medals, 1948–60. He added a silver and a bronze for a record eight medals.

Longest race
The 1967 Canadian Government Centennial Voyageur Canoe Pageant and Race covered 5,283 km (3,283 miles) from Rocky Mountain House, Alberta, to Montreal, Quebec.

River Rhine
The fastest time, solo and supported, from official marker posts at Chur, Switzerland, to Willemstad, Netherlands—a distance of about 1,130 km (702 miles)—is 7 days 13 hr 56 min, by Roel Kimpe (Netherlands) in 1993.

The fastest woman is Tracy Anderson (GB), who took 12 days 15 hr 10 min in 1993.

Winnipeg, Manitoba, Canada, to Belem, Brazil, from 1 June 1980 to 1 May 1982. All portages were human powered.

Without any portages or assistance Richard H. Grant and Ernest 'Moose' Lassy circumnavigated the eastern USA via Chicago, New Orleans, Miami, New York and the Great Lakes from 22 Sept 1930 to 15 Aug 1931, covering 9,820 km (6,102 miles).

Largest canoe raft
A raft made up of 582 kayaks and canoes, organized by the Cleveland Metroparks, was held together by hands only, while free

Left
The start of the Cowes to Torquay powerboat race, which was instituted in 1961. The race was first run from Cowes to Torquay, but from 1968 it included the return journey and covered a distance of 320.4 km (199 miles).

ND MONTREAL, CANADA

The most Olympic medals won by a woman is four, by Birgit Schmidt (GDR) between 1980 and 1992.

The most gold medals at one Games is three, by Vladimir Parfenovich (USSR) in 1980 and Ian Ferguson (New Zealand) in 1984.

Including the Olympic Games, a record 25 world titles have been won by Birgit Schmidt, from 1979 to 1995.

The most men's world records is 13, by Gert Fredriksson from 1948 to 1960, Rüdiger Helm (GDR) from 1976 to 1983, and Ivan Patzaichin (Romania) from 1968 to 1984.

The most individual titles by a British canoeist is five, by Richard Fox at K1 slalom in 1981, 1983, 1985, 1989 and 1993. He also won five gold medals at K1 team, 1981–93.

Highest speed
The German four-man kayak champions at the Barcelona Olympics in 1992 covered 1,000 m in 2 min 52.17 sec in a heat on 4 Aug. The average speed was 20.90 km/h (12.98 mph).

The Hungarian four won the 200-m title at the 1995 World Championships in 31.227 seconds, at an average speed of 23.05 km/h (14.32 mph).

Distance (24 hours)
In Sept 1987 Zdzislaw Szubski paddled 252.9 km (157 miles 255 yd) on the River Vistula from Wlocklawek to Gdansk, Poland.

Marinda Hartzenberg (South Africa) paddled 220.69 km (137 miles 229 yd) without a current on Loch Logan, South Africa, in 24 hours from 31 Dec 1990 to 1 Jan 1991.

Eskimo rolls
Ray Hudspith achieved 1,000 rolls in 34 min 43 sec at the Elswick Pool, Newcastle upon Tyne, UK, on 20 March 1987 and 100 rolls in 3 min 7.25 sec at Killingworth Leisure Centre, Tyne and Wear, on 3 March 1991.

The women's record for 100 rolls is 3 min 47.54 sec, by Helen Barnes at Crystal Palace, Greater London, UK, on 18 Feb 1995.

Randy Fine (USA) executed 1,796 continuous rolls at Biscayne Bay, Florida, USA, in 1991.

Colin Brian Hill achieved 1,000 'hand rolls' in 31 min 55.62 sec at Consett, Co. Durham, UK, on 12 March 1987, 100 hand rolls in 2 min 39.2 sec at Crystal Palace, London, on 22 Feb 1987, and 3,700 continuous hand rolls at Durham City Swimming Baths, Co. Durham, on 1 May 1989.

Longest canoe journey
Father and son Dana and Donald Starkell paddled the 19,603 km (12,181 miles) from

floating for 30 seconds, on the Hinckley Lake, Cleveland, Ohio, USA, on 21 May 1995.

Powerboat racing
APBA Gold Cup
The most wins is 10, by Chip Hanauer (USA), 1982–88, 1992–93 and 1995.

The highest average speed for the race is 240.05 km/h (149.16 mph), by Chip Hanauer piloting *Miss Budweiser* in 1995.

Cowes to Torquay
The most wins is four by Renato della Valle (Italy), from 1982 to 1985.

The highest average speed for the race is 148 km/h (92 mph) by Sergio Mion (Italy), piloting *SM-Racer* in 1993.

Longest races
The longest offshore race was the Port Richborough, London—Monte Carlo Marathon Offshore international event over 4,742 km (2,947 miles) in 14 stages in 1972.

The longest circuit race is the 24-hour annual race on the River Seine at Rouen, France.

Transatlantic crossing
The fastest crossing from Ambrose Light Tower, New Jersey/New York, USA, to Bishop Rock Light, Isles of Scilly, is 2 days 14 hr 7 min 47 sec, by *Gentry Eagle* in July 1989.

FASTEST POWERBOAT ATLANTIC CROSSING WAS 2 DAYS 14 HR 7 MIN 47 SEC

Yachting

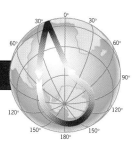

Fastest windsurfer 84.02 km/h

Yachting
Olympic titles

The first sportsman to win individual gold medals in four successive Olympic Games was Paul B. Elvstrøm (Denmark), in the Firefly class in 1948 and the Finn class in 1952, 1956 and 1960. He also won eight other world titles in a total of six classes.

The least penalty points by the winner of any class in an Olympic regatta is three (five wins, one disqualified and one second in seven starts), by *Superdocious* of the Flying Dutchman class, sailed by Lt Rodney Stuart Pattisson, RN, and Iain Somerled Macdonald-Smith, at Acapulco Bay, Mexico, in Oct 1968.

The only British yachtsman to win in two Olympic regattas is Rodney Pattisson in 1968 and in 1972 with *Superdoso*, crewed by Christopher Davies, at Kiel, Germany. Pattison also won a silver medal in 1976 with Julian Brooke Houghton.

Admiral's Cup and ocean racing

A record 19 nations competed in the Admiral's Cup in 1975, 1977 and 1979.

Great Britain holds the record for the most wins in the Admiral's Cup, with nine.

The first modern ocean race covered the 630 nautical miles (1,166 km) from Brooklyn, New York, USA, to Bermuda in June 1906. Organized by Thomas Fleming Day, editor of the magazine *The Rudder*, the race is still held in even numbered years, from Newport, Rhode Island, USA, to Bermuda.

Earliest race

The earliest race that is still regularly run (for any type of craft and on freshwater or saltwater) is the Chicago–Mackinac race on lakes Michigan and Huron, first sailed in 1898. It was held again in 1904, then annually until the present day, except for 1917–20. The record for the course, which covers 333 nautical miles (616 km), is 1 day 1 hr 50 min, at a mean speed of 12.89 knots (23.84 km/h), by the sloop *Pied Piper*, owned by Dick Jennings (USA), in 1987.

Longest race

The world's longest sailing race is the Vendée Globe Challenge, first raced from Les Sables d'Olonne, France, on 26 Nov 1989. The distance circumnavigated without stopping was 22,500 nautical miles (41,652 km). The race is for 50–60-ft (15–18-m) boats sailed single-handed. The record time on the course is 109 days 8 hr 48 min 50 sec, by Titouan Lamazou (France) in *Ecureuil d'Aquitaine*, which finished on 19 March 1990.

Oldest round-the-world race

The oldest regular round-the-world sailing race is the quadrennial Whitbread Round-the-World Race, originally organized by the Royal Naval Sailing Association in Aug 1973. It starts in England, and the course is varied from race to race. The distance for 1993–94 was 32,000 nautical miles (59,239 km), beginning and ending in Southampton, with the stops at

MOST BOATS TO START IN

Punta del Este, Uruguay; Fremantle, Australia; Auckland, New Zealand; Punta del Este; Uruguay; and Fort Lauderdale, Florida, USA.

America's Cup

There have been 29 challenges since 8 Aug 1870, and the USA has won on every occasion except 1983 and 1995, when it lost to Australia and New Zealand respectively.

In individual races sailed, American boats have won 81 races and foreign challengers have won 13.

Dennis Walter Conner (USA) has been in more cup races as a member of the afterguard than any other sailor, with six appearances since 1974, when he was starting helmsman with Ted Hood as skipper. He was winning skipper/helmsman in 1980, 1987 and 1989, and losing skipper in 1983 and 1995.

Charlie Barr (USA), who defended in 1899, 1901 and 1903, and Harold S. Vanderbilt (USA) in 1930, 1934 and 1937, each steered the winner three times in succession.

The closest finish in a race for the cup was on 4 Oct 1901, when *Shamrock II* (GB) finished two seconds ahead of the American *Columbia*.

Most competitors
The most boats ever to start in a single race was 2,072, in the Round Zeeland (Denmark) race on 21 June 1984, over a course covering 235 nautical miles (435 km).

The most boats to start in a British race was 1,781 keeled yachts and multihulls on 17 June 1989 from Cowes in the Annual Round-the-Island Race. The fastest time achieved in this annual event is 3 hr 55 min 28 sec, by the trimaran *Paragon,* sailed by its owner Michael Whipp on 31 May 1986.

The largest trans-oceanic race was the ARC (Atlantic Rally for Cruisers), when 204 boats out of 209 starters from 24 nations completed the race from Las Palmas, Gran Canaria, Canary Islands, to Barbados in 1989.

Oldest club
The world's oldest club, the Royal Cork Yacht Club, claims descent from the Cork Harbour Water Club, established in Ireland by 1720.

The oldest active British club is the Starcross Yacht Club at Powderham Point, Devon. Its first regatta was held in 1772.

The oldest existing club to have been formed as a yacht club is the Royal Yacht Squadron, Cowes, Isle of Wight, which was instituted as 'The Yacht Club' at a meeting at the Thatched House Tavern, St James's Street, London, UK, on 1 June 1815.

Highest speed
The highest speed reached under sail on water by any craft over a 500-m (1,640-ft) timed run is 46.52 knots (86.21 km/h), by trifoiler *Yellow Pages Endeavour,* piloted by Simon McKeon and Tim Daddo, both of Australia, at Sandy Point near Melbourne, Australia, on 26 Oct 1993.

The British record for men is 42.16 knots (78.13 km/h), by David White at West Kirby, Merseyside, UK, on 17 Oct 1991.

The British speed record for women is 37.21 knots (68.95 km/h), by Samantha Metcalfe at Sotavento Beach, Fuerteventura, Canary Islands, on 27 July 1995.

Ice and sand yachting
Highest speeds
The highest officially recorded speed is 230 km/h (143 mph), by John D. Buckstaff in a Class A stern-steerer on Lake Winnebago,

Wisconsin, USA, in 1938. Such a speed is possible in a wind of 115 km/h (72 mph).

The official world record for a sand yacht is 107 km/h (66.48 mph), by Christian-Yves Nau (France) in *Mobil* at Le Touquet, France, on 22 March 1981, when the wind speed reached 120 km/h (75 mph).

A speed of 142.26 km/h (88.4 mph) was attained by Nord Embroden (USA) in *Midnight at the Oasis* at Superior Dry Lake, California, USA, on 15 April 1976.

Largest yacht
The largest ice yacht was *Icicle,* built for Commodore John E. Roosevelt for racing on the Hudson River, New York, USA, in 1869. It was 21 m (68 ft 11 in) long and carried 99 m² (1,070 ft²) of canvas.

Windsurfing
Most titles
Stephan van den Berg (Netherlands) has won a record five world titles, from 1979 to 1983.

Speed records
The fastest speed for a windsurfer is 45.34 knots (84.02 km/h), by Thierry Bielak (France) at Saintes Maries de-la-Mer canal, Camargue, France, on 24 April 1993.

The women's speed record for any craft was set by windsurfer Babethe Coquelle (France), who achieved 40.38 knots (74.83 km/h) at Tarifa, Spain, on 7 July 1995.

Longest sailboards
The longest sailboard is 50.2 m (165 ft) in length. It was constructed at Fredrikstad, Norway, and first sailed on 28 June 1986.

The longest 'snake' of boardsails was set by 70 windsurfers in tandem at the 'Sailboard Show '89' event at Narrabeen Lakes, Manly, Australia, on 21 Oct 1989.

Left
The technique for sand, or land, yachting is similar to that for sailing. Land yachts can reach a speed of three or four times the wind velocity.

Left
Titouan Lamazou sails his way to first place in the 1990 Vendée Globe Challenge.

Skiing

Longest ski-jump 194 m

Skiing
World/Olympic Championships

The record for the most World Alpine Championship titles is seven individual (four slalom titles, in 1934 and 1937–39, and three downhill titles, in 1935, 1937 and 1939) and five combined titles (in 1934, 1935 and 1937–39) by Christl Cranz (b. 1914) of Germany. She also won gold for the combined in the 1936 Olympics.

The most World Alpine Championship titles won by a man is seven, by Anton 'Toni' Sailer (b. 1935) of Austria, who won all four titles (giant slalom, slalom, downhill and non-Olympic Alpine combination) in 1956, and the downhill, giant slalom and combined in 1958.

The most World Nordic Championship titles won by one man is 11, by Gunde Svan (b. 1962) of Sweden, who won seven individual titles (15 km in 1989, 30 km in 1985 and 1991, 50 km in 1985 and 1989, and Olympic 15 km in 1984 and 50 km in 1988) and four relay titles (4 x 10 km in 1987 and 1989 and Olympics in 1984 and 1988).

The most World Nordic Championship titles won by a woman is 11, by Yelena Välbe (b. 1968) of Russia, who won six individual and five relay titles between 1989 and 1995.

The most medals is 23 (seven gold), by Raisa Petrovna Smetanina (b. 1952) of the USSR/CIS, between 1974 and 1992.

The most titles won by a jumper is five, by Birger Ruud (b. 1911) of Norway, in 1931, 1932 and 1935–37. Ruud is the only person to win Olympic events in both Alpine and Nordic disciplines. In 1936, he won the ski-jumping and the Alpine downhill.

World Cup

The greatest number of individual event wins is 86 (46 giant slalom and 40 slalom) from a total of 287 races by Ingemar Stenmark (b. 1956) of Sweden, from 1974 to 1989. This included a men's record of 13 wins in one season (1978/9), of which 10 were part of a record 14 successive giant slalom wins between March 1978 and Jan 1980.

Franz Klammer (b. 1953) of Austria won a record total of 25 downhill races between 1974 and 1984.

Annemarie Moser-Pröll (b. 1953) of Austria holds the women's record for individual event wins, with a total of 62 victories from 1970 to 1979, including 11 consecutive downhill wins from Dec 1972 to Jan 1974.

Vreni Schneider (b. 1964) of Switzerland won a record 13 events (plus one combined event) in the 1988/9 season. This included victories in all seven slalom events.

Ski-jumping

The longest jump in the World Cup is 204 m (669 ft) by Andreas Goldberger of Austria, at Harrachov, Czech Republic, on 9 March 1996.

The longest dry ski-jump on record is 92 m (302 ft), by Hubert Schwarz of West Germany, at Berchtesgarten, Germany, on 30 June 1981.

Highest speed

The world speed record is 241.448 km/h (150.028 mph), by Jeffrey Hamilton (USA) at Vars, France, on 14 April 1995.

The British speed record is 219.914 km/h (136.684 mph) set by Graham Wilkie at Les Arcs, France, on 16 April 1988.

The fastest speed in a World Cup downhill is 112.4 km/h (69.8 mph), by Armin Assinger of Austria at Sierra Nevada, Spain, on 15 March 1993.

The women's speed record is 226.7 km/h (140.8 mph) by Karine Dubouchet (France) at Les Arcs, France, on 20 April 1996.

Above right
Jumps of over 150 m (490 ft)—from ramps up to 90 m (295 ft) high—are regularly achieved in Olympic and World Cup ski-jumping events.

SEPPO-JUHANI SAVOLAINEN COVERED A RECOR

Marc Girardelli has taken five overall World Cup Alpine titles.

Longest races
The longest skiing race in the world is the Vasaloppet in Sweden, an annual event covering 89 km (55¼ miles). The greatest number of people to start the race is 10,934, on 6 March 1977, while the greatest number of people to finish was 10,650 finishers, on 4 March 1979. The fastest time recorded for the race is 3:48:55, by Bengt Hassis of Sweden on 2 March 1986.

The longest downhill race is the *Inferno* in Switzerland, which covers the 15.8 km (9⅘ miles) from the top of the Schilthorn to Lauterbrunnen. There were a record 1,401 entrants in 1981, and the record time, 13:53:40, was set by Urs von Allmen of Switzerland in 1991.

Longest run
The longest all-downhill ski run is the Weissfluhjoch-Küblis Parsenn course, near Davos, Switzerland, which extends over a distance of 12.23 km (7⅔ miles).

Cross-country (Nordic)
In 24 hours, Seppo-Juhani Savolainen covered 415.5 km (258 miles 315 yd) at Saariselkä, Finland, on 8–9 April 1988.

The women's record is 330 km (205 miles), by Sisko Kainulaisen at Jyväskylä, Finland, on 23–24 March 1985.

Freestyle
Edgar Grospiron (b. 1969) of France has won World Championship titles on a record three occasions, for moguls in 1989 and 1995 and aerials in 1995. He also won an Olympic title in 1992.

The record for the most overall World Cup titles is 10, by Connie Kissling (b. 1961) of Switzerland, from 1983 to 1992.

The men's record for World Cup titles is five, by Eric Laboureix (b. 1962) of France, 1986–88 and 1990–91.

Ski-bob
The highest speed attained is 166 km/h (103.1 mph), by Erich Brenter (b. 1940) of Austria at Cervinia, Italy, in 1964.

The most individual combined titles in the World Championships is four, by Petra Tschach-Wlezcek of Austria, 1988–91.

The most World Championship titles by a man is three, by Walter Kronseil of Austria from 1988 to 1990.

Grass skiing
Most titles
The most World Championship titles won by one person is 14, by Ingrid Hirschhofer of Austria from 1979 to 1993.

The most World Championship titles won by a man is seven, by Erwin Gansner of Switzerland from 1981 to 1987, and Rainer Grossmann of Germany from 1985 to 1993.

Two men—Erwin Gansner (1987) and Rainer Grossmann (1991)—and two women—Katja Krey of West Germany (1989) and Ingrid Hirschhofer (1993)—have won all four titles in one year.

Highest speed
The recorded for the highest speed in grass skiing is 92.07 km/h (57.21 mph), by Klaus Spinka of Austria at Waldsassen, Germany, on 24 Sept 1989.

Snowshoeing
Fastest
The IASSRF (International Amateur Snowshoe Racing Federation) record for 1.6 km (1 mile) is 5:56.7, by Nick Akers of Edmonton, Alberta, Canada, on 3 Feb 1991.

The 100-m snowshoeing record is 14.07 seconds, by Jeremy Badeau at Canaseraga, New York, USA, on 31 May 1991.

MOST OLYMPIC TITLES
Men
Alpine – 3
Anton 'Toni' Sailer (Austria) (b. 1935)
Downhill, slalom, giant slalom (1956)
Jean-Claude Killy (France) (b. 1943)
Downhill, slalom, giant slalom (1968)
Alberto Tomba (Italy) (b. 1966)
Slalom, giant slalom (1988); *giant slalom* (1992)
Nordic – 5
Bjørn Dæhlie (Norway) (b. 1967)
15 km, 50 km, 4 x 10 km (1992); *10 km, 15 km* (1994)
Nordic (jumping) – 4
Matti Nykänen (Finland) (b. 1963)
70 m hill (1988); *90 m hill* (1984, 1988); *team* (1988)

Women
Alpine – 3
Vreni Schneider (Switzerland) (b. 1964)
Giant slalom, slalom (1988); *slalom* (1994)
Nordic – 6
Lyubov Yegorova (Russia) (b. 1966)
10 km, 15 km, 4 x 5 km (1992); *5 km, 10 km, 4 x 5 km* (1994)

MOST OLYMPIC MEDALS
Men (Nordic) – 9
Sixten Jernberg (Sweden) (b. 1929), four gold, three silver and two bronze in Nordic events (1956–64)
Women (Nordic) – 10
Raisa Smetanina (USSR/CIS) (b. 1952), four gold, five silver and one bronze in Nordic events (1976–92)
Alpine – 5
In addition to their three golds, Alberto Tomba won silver in the 1992 and 1994 *slalom*, and Vreni Schneider won silver in the *combined* and bronze in the *giant slalom* in 1994. Kjetil André Aamodt (Norway) (b. 1971) won one gold (*super giant slalom*, 1992), two silver (*downhill, combined*, 1994) and two bronze (*giant slalom*, 1992; *super giant slalom*, 1994)

MOST WORLD CUP ALPINE TITLES
Men
Overall – 5
Marc Girardelli (Luxembourg) (b. 1963)
1985–86, 1989, 1991, 1993
Downhill – 5
Franz Klammer (Austria) (b. 1953)
1975–78, 1983
Slalom – 8
Ingemar Stenmark (Sweden) (b. 1956)
1975–81, 1983
Giant Slalom – 7
Ingemar Stenmark (Sweden)
1975–76, 1978–81, 1984
Super Giant Slalom – 4
Pirmin Zurbriggen (Switzerland) (b. 1963)
1987–90

Women
Overall – 6
Annemarie Moser-Pröll (Austria) (b. 1953)
1971–75, 1979
Downhill – 7
Annemarie Moser-Pröll (Austria)
1971–75, 1978–79
Slalom – 6
Vreni Schneider (Switzerland) (b. 1964)
1989–90, 1992–95
Giant Slalom – 5
Vreni Schneider (Switzerland)
1986–87, 1989, 1991, 1995
Super Giant Slalom – 4
Carole Merle (France) (b. 1964)
1989–92
Katja Seizinger (Germany) (b. 1964)
1993–96

MOST WORLD CUP NORDIC TITLES
Men
Jumping – 4
Matti Nykänen (Finland) (b. 1963)
1983, 1985–86, 1988
Cross-Country – 5
Gunde Svan (Sweden) (b. 1962)
1984–86, 1988–89

Women
Cross-Country – 4
Yelena Välbe (USSR/CIS/Russia) (b. 1968)
1989, 1991–92, 1995

5.5 KM IN 24 HOURS AT SAARISELKÄ, FINLAND

Bjørn Dæhlie has won a record five Olympic gold medals.

Winter sports

Fastest Cresta Run 50.41 seconds

Ice hockey

World Championships/Olympic Games

The USSR won 22 world titles, including the Olympic titles of 1956, 1964 and 1968, between 1954 and 1990, and Russia won in 1993. It has won a record eight Olympic titles: the remaining five were won in 1972, 1976, 1984, 1988 and 1992 (as the CIS).

The most gold medals won by an individual is three, by Soviet players Vitaliy Semyenovich Davydov, Anatoliy Vasilyevich Firsov, Viktor Grigoryevich Kuzkin and Aleksandr Pavlovich Ragulin in 1964, 1968 and 1972, Vladislav Aleksandrovich Tretyak in 1972, 1976 and 1984, and Andrey Khomutov in 1984, 1988 and 1992.

National Hockey League

Gordon 'Gordie' Howe (Canada) played in a record 1,767 regular season games (and 157 play-off games) over 26 seasons, for the Detroit Red Wings. 1946–71, and the Hartford Whalers in 1979/80. He also played 419 games (and 78 play-off games) for the Houston Aeros and the New England Whalers in the World Hockey Association, 1973–79.

Wayne Gretzky (Edmonton Oilers/Los Angeles Kings/St Louis Blues) holds the NHL scoring records for the regular season as well as play-off games. He has scored 837 goals and 1,771 assists, resulting in a record 2,608 points from 1,253 games. He has also scored the most goals in one season—92 for the Edmonton Oilers in 1981/2.

Gordie Howe holds the North American career record for goals, with 1,071 (1,049 in NHL) between 1946 and 1980. It took him 2,204 NHL games to achieve his 1,000th goal.

Robert Marvin 'Bobby' Hull (Chicago Black Hawks and Winnipeg Jets) scored his 1,000th goal in his 1,600th National Hockey League game on 12 March 1978.

The most points in a North American major league game is 10, by Jim Harrison for Alberta in a WHA match at Edmonton, Canada, on 30 Jan 1973; and Darryl Sittler for Toronto Maple Leafs v. Boston Bruins in an NHL match at Toronto, Canada, on 7 Feb 1976.

The most goals in a game is seven, by Joe Malone for Québec v. Toronto St Patricks at Québec City, Canada, on 31 Jan 1920.

The most assists is seven, by Billy Taylor for Detroit against Chicago on 16 March 1947, and Wayne Gretzky for Edmonton: against Washington on 15 Feb 1980, Chicago on 11 Dec 1985, and Québec on 14 Feb 1986.

The Montreal Canadiens scored a record 132 points (60 wins and 12 ties) from 80 games in 1976/7.

The longest undefeated run in a season was 35 games by the Philadelphia Flyers between 14 Oct 1979 and 6 Jan 1980.

The most goals scored in one season is 446, by the Edmonton Oilers in 1983/4.

The highest aggregate score is 21: the Montreal Canadiens beat Toronto St Patrick's 14–7 at Montreal, on 10 Jan 1920; and the Edmonton Oilers beat Chicago Black Hawks 12–9 at Chicago, USA, on 11 Dec 1985. The highest score for a single team is 16, by Montreal Canadiens against Québec Bulldogs, at Québec City, Canada, on 3 Nov 1920.

Above
In the sport of lugeing, contestants sit up or lie back on sleds as they race downhill at speeds of more than 130 km/h (81 mph).

Right
The Detroit Red Wings hold the record for the most games won by a team in a single ice hockey season, with 62 victories in 1995/6. The most outstanding player in the team's history was Gordon 'Gordie' Howe, who holds the record for both the most games played and the most goals scored in in North America.

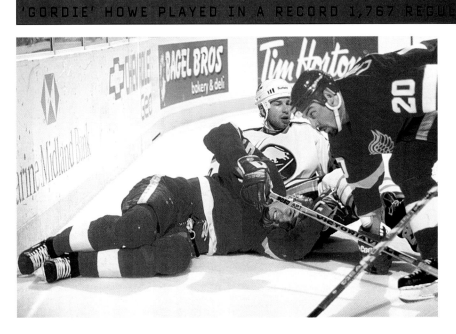

Stanley Cup

The Montreal Canadiens have won the Stanley Cup 24 times in a record 32 finals (1916, 1924, 1930–31, 1944, 1946, 1953, 1956–60, 1965–66, 1968–69, 1971, 1973, 1976–79, 1986, 1993).

Wayne Gretzky (Edmonton, Los Angeles and St Louis) has scored a record 362 points in Stanley Cup games, with a record 112 goals and 250 assists. He also holds the record for one season, with 47 points (16 goals and a record 31 assists) in 1985.

The most goals scored in one season is 19, by Reginald Joseph Leach for Philadelphia in 1976, and Jari Kurri for Edmonton in 1985.

A record five goals in a Stanley Cup game were scored by Maurice Richard for Montreal against Toronto on 23 March 1944; Darryl Glen Sittler for Toronto against Philadelphia

The most individual goals in a senior game is 18, by Rick Smith (Canada), helping the Chelmsford Chieftains to defeat the Sheffield Sabres 27–2 in an English League match on 3 March 1991.

Steve Moria (Canada) scored 13 assists for Fife Flyers in a match at Cleveland on 28 March 1987.

During the 1986/7 season Rick Fera (Canada) set a British season record of 318 points (including a record 165 goals) in 48 games for Murrayfield Racers.

Tim Salmon (Canada) achieved a record 183 assists in one season, in 47 games for Ayr Bruins in 1985/6.

The most points scored during a career in the Heineken League is 2,136 (875 goals and 1,281 assists) by Tony Hand (GB).

Franco Gansser (Switzerland), 1981, 1983–86, 1988–89 and 1991.

The most wins in the Curzon Cup is eight, by Nino Bibbia, 1950, 1957–58, 1960, 1962–64 and 1969.

Lugeing

The most World Championship titles (including Olympics) is five. This record is held by four people: Thomas Köhler (GDR), single-seater 1962, 1964 and 1967, two-seater 1967 and 1968; Hans Rinn (GDR), single-seater 1973 and 1977, two-seater 1976–77 and 1980; Stefan Krausse and Jan Behrendt (both GDR/Germany), two-seater 1989, 1991–93 and 1995. George Hackl (GDR/Germany) has won a record four single-seater titles, 1989–90, 1992 and 1994.

Margit Schumann (GDR) has won five women's titles, 1973–75, 1976 (Olympic) and 1977.

MOST MEN'S WORLD CHAMPIONSHIP CURLING TITLES IS 24, BY CANADA

---

on 22 April 1976; Reggie Leach for Philadelphia against Boston on 6 May 1976; and Mario Lemieux for Pittsburgh against Philadelphia on 25 April 1989.

A record six assists in a game was achieved by Mikko Leinonen for New York Rangers against Philadelphia on 8 April 1982; and Wayne Gretzky for Edmonton against Los Angeles on 9 April 1987.

The most points in a game is eight, by Patrik Sundström for New Jersey against Washington on 22 April 1988, and by Mario Lemieux for Pittsburgh against Philadelphia on 25 April 1989.

Other competitions

The English (later British) League Championship has been won by Streatham (later Redskins) a record five times (1935, 1950, 1953, 1960 and 1982).

The British Championship has been won a record four times by Durham Wasps (1987–88 and 1991–92).

The British League title has been won five times by Durham Wasps (1985, 1988–89 and 1991–92).

Most goals and points

The record for the most goals in a world championship match is 58, when Australia beat New Zealand 58–0 at Perth, Australia, on 15 March 1987.

The record for the highest score in a British League match was set by Medway Bears, when they beat Richmond Raiders 48–1 at Gillingham, Kent, in a Second Division fixture on 1 Dec 1985. The match total of 49 goals is the record for the highest aggregate in a British League match.

The fastest goal in a British League match was scored just four seconds after play started by Stephen Johnson, playing for Durham Wasps against Ayr Bruins at Ayr on 6 Nov 1983.

Bobsleigh and tobogganing
Bobsledding

The world four-man bob title has been won 20 times by Switzerland (1924, 1936, 1939, 1947, 1954–57, 1971–73, 1975, 1982–83, 1986–90 and 1993). This included a record five Olympic victories (1924, 1936, 1956, 1972 and 1988). Switzerland has also won the two-man title 17 times (1935, 1947–50, 1953, 1955, 1977–80, 1982–83, 1987, 1990, 1992 and 1994). This included a record four Olympic wins (1948, 1980, 1992 and 1994).

Eugenio Monti (Italy) was a member of 11 World Championship crews (eight two-man crews, three four-man crews) between 1957 and 1968.

The most Olympic gold medals won by an individual is three, by Meinhard Nehmer and Bernhard Germeshausen (both GDR) in the 1976 two-man event and the 1976 and 1980 four-man events.

Tobogganing

The fastest time recorded for the Cresta Run—a 1,212-m (3,977-ft) long course with a drop of 157 m (514 ft)—is 50.41 seconds, by Christian Bertschinger (Switzerland) on 23 Feb 1992. He achieved an average speed of 86.56 km/h (53.79 mph).

Prince Constantin von Liechtenstein (b. 1911) is the oldest person to have ridden the Cresta Run successfully, on 13 Feb 1996, aged 84.

The most Grand National wins is eight, by the 1948 Olympic Champion Nino Bibbia (Italy), 1960–64, 1966, 1968 and 1973; and by

Left
Curling, which is believed to have originated in Scotland, was originally played on frozen lakes and ponds. Today, however, it usually takes place indoors, on purpose-built rinks. The greatest distance that a curling stone has ever been thrown is 175.66 m (576 ft 4 in), by the Canadian Eddie Kulbacki at Park Lake, Neepawa, Manitoba, in 1989.

Curling
Most titles

Canada has won the men's World Championships a record 24 times (1959–64, 1966, 1968–72, 1980, 1982–83, 1985–87, 1989–90 and 1993–96).

The most women's World Championships titles is nine, by Canada (1980, 1984–87, 1989, 1993–94 and 1996).

The most Strathcona Cup wins is seven, by Canada (against Scotland) in 1903, 1909, 1912, 1923, 1938, 1957 and 1965.

Largest bonspiel

The Manitoba Curling Association Bonspiel held annually in Winnipeg, Canada, is the world's largest bonspiel. In 1988, there were 1,424 teams of four men using 187 sheets of curling ice.

Skating

Ice skating

Figure skating

The most Olympic gold medals is three, by Gillis Grafström (Sweden) in 1920, 1924 and 1928; Sonja Henie (Norway) in 1928, 1932 and 1936; and Irina Konstantinovna Rodnina (USSR) in 1972, 1976 and 1980.

The most men's individual world figure skating titles is 10, by Ulrich Salchow (Sweden) from 1901 to 1905 and from 1907 to 1911.

The record for womens' individual world figure skating titles is 10, by Sonja Henie (Norway) between 1927 and 1936.

Irina Rodnina won 10 pairs titles, four with Aleksey Nikolayevich Ulanov, from 1969 to 1972, and six with her husband Aleksandr Gennadyevich Zaitsev, from 1973 to 1978.

The most ice dance titles is six, by Lyudmila Alekseyevna Pakhomova and her husband Aleksandr Georgiyevich Gorshkov of the USSR, 1970–74 and 1976. They also won the first Olympic ice dance title in 1976.

The record for the most men's British titles is 11, by Jack Ferguson Page of Manchester SC, from 1922 to 1931 and in 1933.

The most women's British titles won is six, by Magdalena Cecilia Colledge of Park Lane FSC, London, 1935–36, 1937 (two titles), 1938 and 1946, and Joanne Conway, 1985–91.

The most pairs titles won by an ice dance couple is seven, by Jayne Torvill and Christopher Dean, 1978–83 and 1994.

Rintje Ritsma of the Netherlands set a record speed skating score of 156.201 points for the world overall title.

Karl Schäfer (Austria) and Sonja Henie (Norway) both achieved double 'Grand Slams' in 1932 and 1936. This feat was repeated by Katarina Witt (GDR) in 1984 and 1988.

The only British skaters to win the 'Grand Slam' of World, Olympic and European titles in the same year are John Curry in 1976 and Jayne Torvill and Christopher Dean in 1984.

The highest tally of maximum six marks awarded in an international championship is 29, to Jayne Torvill and Christopher Dean in the World Ice Dance Championships at Ottawa, Canada, in March 1984 (seven in the compulsory dances, a perfect set of nine for presentation in the set pattern dance and 13 in the free dance, including another perfect set from all nine judges for artistic presentation). They were also awarded a perfect set of nine sixes for artistic presentation in the free dance at the 1983 World Championships at Helsinki, Finland, and the 1984 Winter Olympics at Sarajevo, Yugoslavia.

The most sets of sixes by a soloist is seven, by Donald George Jackson (Canada) in the World Men's Championships in Prague, Czechoslovakia, in 1962; and by Midori Ito (Japan) in the World Women's Championships at Paris, France, in 1989.

Robin Cousins (UK) set a distance record of 5.81 m (19 ft 1 in) in an axel jump and 5.48 m (18 ft) with a back flip at Richmond Ice Rink, Surrey, UK, in Nov 1983.

Kurt Browning (Canada) was the first to achieve a quadruple jump (toe loop) in competition, at the World Championships in Budapest, Hungary, on 25 March 1988.

The first woman to achieve a quadruple jump was Surya Bonaly (France) in the World Championships at Munich, Germany, on 16 March 1991.

Speed skating

The most Olympic gold medals for speed skating is six (two in 1960, four in 1964), by Lidiya Pavlovna Skoblikova (USSR).

The men's record for Olympic gold medals is five, by Clas Thunberg (Finland) in 1924 and 1928 and Eric Arthur Heiden (USA) in 1980.

The most Olympic medals is eight by Karin Kania (GDR) (three gold, four silver, one

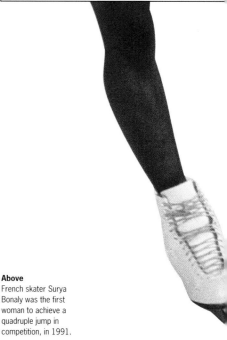

Above
French skater Surya Bonaly was the first woman to achieve a quadruple jump in competition, in 1991.

bronze), 1980–88. The men's record is seven, by Clas Thunberg (five gold, one silver, one bronze) and Ivar Ballangrud (Norway), (four gold, two silver, one bronze), 1928–36.

The record for the most world overall titles is five, by Oscar Mathisen (Norway), 1908–09 and 1912–14, and Clas Thunberg, 1923, 1925, 1928–29 and 1931.

The most women's titles is five, by Karin Kania (GDR), 1982, 1984 and 1986–88. She also won a record six overall sprint world titles (1980–81, 1983–84, 1986–87).

Igor Zhelezovskiy (USSR/Belarus) has won a record six men's sprint overall titles, 1985–86, 1989 and 1991–93.

The highest score for this world overall title is 156.201 points by Rintje Ritsma (Netherlands), at Hamar, Norway, from 7 to 9 Jan 1994.

The record time over the 200 km (124 miles) of the 'Elfstedentocht' ('Tour of the Eleven Towns') is 5:40:37 for men, by Dries van Wijhe (Netherlands), and 5:48:8 for women, by Alida Pasveer (Netherlands), both at Lake Weissensee, Austria, on 11 Feb 1989.

Martinus Kuiper (Netherlands) set a 24-hour record of 546.65 km (339 miles 1,183 yd) at Alkmaar, Netherlands, in Dec 1988.

Barrel jumping on ice skates
The official distance record is 8.97 m (29 ft 5 in) over 18 barrels, by Yvon Jolin at Terrebonne, Québec, Canada, in Jan 1981.

The most world pair titles is six, by Tammy Jeru (USA), partnered by John Arishita (1983–86) and by Larry McGrew (1990–91).

Speed skating
The fastest speed achieved in an official world record is 44.20 km/h (27.46 mph), by Luca Antoniel (Italy), who covered a distance of 300 m in 24.678 seconds on a road at Bello, Colombia, on 15 Nov 1990.

The women's speed skating record is 40.30 km/h (25.04 mph) over a distance of 300 m on a road at Grenoble, France, on 27 Aug 1987, by Marisa Canofoglia (Italy).

The men's world record for 10,000 m on a road or track is 14 min 55.64 sec, by Giuseppe De Persio (Italy) at Gujan-Mestras, France, on 1 Aug 1988.

The women's 10,000-m road or track record is 15 min 58.022 sec, by Marisa Canofoglia (Italy) at Grenoble, France, on 30 Aug 1987.

Land's End to John O' Groats
Damian Magee skated the length of the British mainland in 9 days 5 hr 23 min, in June 1992.

The fastest time from Land's End to John O' Groats by a woman is 12 days 4 hr 15 min, by Cheryl Fisher from 19 Sept to 1 Oct 1987.

Roller hockey
Portugal has won the most roller hockey World Championships, with 14 titles between 1947 and 1993. Portugal also won a record 18 European titles between 1947 and 1994.

Ice dancers Torvill and Dean scored a perfect set of nine sixes for artistic presentation at Helsinki in 1983 and Sarajevo in 1984.

IE LENGTH OF GREAT BRITAIN IN JUST OVER NINE DAYS

The women's record is 6.84 m (22 ft 5¼ in) over 13 barrels, by Marie-Josée Houle at Lasalle, Québec, Canada, on 1 March 1987.

Roller skating
Most titles
Alberta Vianello (Italy) has won 18 world speed titles: eight track and 10 road (1953–65). Annie Lambrechts (Belgium) matches this, with one track and 17 road titles (1964–81).

The most British individual men's titles won is 18, by John Edward Fry from 1967 to 1986.

Chloe Ronaldson won 40 individual and 14 team women's senior titles, 1958–85.

The records for the most figure titles are: five men's titles, by Karl Heinz Losch of West Germany (1958–59, 1961–62 and 1966) and by Sandro Guerra of Italy (1987–89 and 1991–92); and five women's titles, by Rafaella Del Vinaccio of Italy (1988–92).

Skateboarding
Fastest
Eleftherios Argiropoulos covered a record 436.6 km (271 miles 510 yd) in 36 hr 33 min 17 sec from 4 to 5 Nov 1993 at Ekali, Greece.

The highest speed recorded in a prone position is 126.12 km/h (78.37 mph), by Roger Hickey, on a course near Los Angeles, California, USA, on 15 March 1990.

The highest stand-up speed is 89.20 km/h (55.43 mph), also by Roger Hickey, at San Demas, California, USA, on 3 July 1990.

Best jumps
Tony Alva set a long-jump record of 5.18 m (17 ft), clearing 17 barrels at the World Professional Skateboard Championships at Long Beach, California, USA, in Sept 1977.

The high-jump record is 1.67 m (5 ft 5¾ in), by Trevor Baxter (UK) at Grenoble, France, on 14 Sept 1982.

SPEED SKATING

WORLD RECORDS, MEN
500 m – 35.39
Hiroyasu Shimizu (Japan), Calgary, Canada, 2 March 1996
1,000 m – 1:11.67
Manabu Horii (Japan), Calgary, Canada, 1 March 1996
1,500 m – 1:50.61
Hiroyuki Noake (Japan), Calgary, Canada, 2 March 1996
3,000 m – 3:56.16
Thomas Bos (Netherlands), Calgary, Canada, 3 March 1992
5,000 m – 6:34.96
Johann Olav Koss (Norway), Hamar, Norway, 13 Feb 1994
10,000 m – 13:30.55
Johann Olav Koss (Norway), Hamar, Norway, 20 Feb 1994

WORLD RECORDS, WOMEN
500 m – 38.69
Bonnie Blair (USA), Calgary, Canada, 12 Feb 1995
1,000 m – 1:17.65
Christa Rothenburger (GDR), Calgary, Canada, 26 Feb 1988
1,500 m – 1:59.30
Karin Kania (GDR), Medeo, USSR, 22 March 1986
3,000 m – 4:09.32
Gunda Niemann (Germany), Calgary, Canada, 25 March 1994
5,000 m – 7:03.26
Gunda Niemann (Germany), Calgary, Canada, 26 March 1994
10,000 m – 15:25.25 (not officially recognized)
Yvonne van Gennip (Netherlands), Heerenveen, Netherlands, 19 March 1988

WORLD RECORDS, MEN'S SHORT TRACK
500 m – 42.68
Mirko Vuillermin (Italy), Lake Placid, USA, 29 March 1996
1,000 m – 1:28.47
Michael McMillen (New Zealand), Denver, Colorado, USA, 4 April 1992
1,500 m – 2:18.16
Marc Gagnon (Canada), The Hague, Netherlands, 1 March 1996
3,000 m – 4:56.29
Chae Ji-hoon (South Korea), Gyovik, Norway, 19 March 1995
5,000-m relay – 7:04.92
Italy, The Hague, Netherlands, 3 March 1996

WORLD RECORDS, WOMEN'S SHORT TRACK
500 m – 45.25
Isabelle Charset (Canada), The Hague, Netherlands, 2 March 1996
1,000 m – 1:34.07
Nathalie Lambert (Canada), Hamar, Norway, 7 Nov 1994
1,500 m – 2:27.27
Marianella Canclini (Italy), Guildford, UK, 6 Feb 1996
3,000 m – 5:02.18
Chun Lee-kyung (South Korea), Gyovik, Norway, 19 March 1995
3,000-m relay – 4:21.50
Italy, The Hague, Netherlands, 3 March 1996

BRITISH RECORDS, MEN'S SHORT TRACK
500 m – 43.06
Nicholas Gooch, Obersdorf, Germany, 18 Jan 1996
1,000 m – 1:31.32
Nicholas Gooch, Gyovick, Norway, 18 March 1995
1,500 m – 2:18.30
Nicholas Gooch, The Hague, Netherlands, 1 March 1996
3,000 m – 4:59.01
Nicholas Gooch, Humberside, UK, 6 March 1994
5,000-m relay – 7:09.54
Great Britain, Guildford, UK, 6 Feb 1996
(Nicholas Gooch, Wilfred O'Reilly, Matthew Jasper, Robert Mitchell)

BRITISH RECORDS, WOMEN'S SHORT TRACK
500 m – 46.45
Debbie Palmer, Obersdorf, Germany, 18 Jan 1996
1,000 m – 1:39.81
Debbie Palmer, Gyovik, Norway, 16 Dec 1995
1,500 m – 2:30.03
Debbie Palmer, Guildford, UK, 6 Jan 1996
3,000 m – 5:34.81
Debbie Palmer, Graz, Austria, 21 Jan 1995
3,000-m relay in 4:51.75
Great Britain, Guildford, UK, 6 Feb 1996
(Debbie Palmer, Lucie Grimes, Sarah Lindsay, Renata Barnes)

Boxing

LONGEST BAREKNUCKLE FIGHT LASTED 6 HR 15 MIN AT FIERY CREEK, AUSTRALIA, IN 1855

Right
Rocky Marciano (left of picture), seen here fighting Roland la Starza, was born Rocco Francis Marchegiano in 1923, and died in 1969. He attained fame as the only world heavyweight boxing champion to retire undefeated, after 49 professional fights.

GREATEST NUMBER OF CONSECUTIVE KNOCK-OUTS IS 44 BY LAMAR CLARK, W

Fight durations

Longest fights
The longest recorded fight with gloves was between Andy Bowen and Jack Burke at New Orleans, Louisiana, USA, in April 1893. Lasting 7 hr 19 min and 110 rounds, it was declared a no contest but changed to a draw.

The longest bare-knuckle fight lasted 6 hr 15 min between James Kelly and Jack Smith at Fiery Creek, Dalesford, Victoria, Australia, on 3 Dec 1855.

The most rounds in one fight was 276 when Jack Jones beat Patsy Tunney in 4 hr 30 min in Cheshire, UK, in 1825.

Shortest fights
A knock-out in 10.5 seconds (including a 10 seconds count) occurred on 23 Sept 1946, when Al Couture struck Ralph Walton while the latter was adjusting a gum shield in his corner at Lewiston, Maine, USA. If the time was accurately taken, Couture must have been more than half-way across the ring from his own corner at the opening bell.

The shortest fight on record was in a Golden Gloves tournament at Minneapolis, Minnesota, USA, on 4 Nov 1947, when Mike Collins floored Pat Brownson with the first punch and the contest was stopped, without a count, four seconds after the bell.

The shortest world title fight was 20 seconds, when Gerald McClellan (USA) beat Jay Bell in a WBC middleweight bout at Puerto Rico on 7 Aug 1993.

The shortest heavyweight world title fight was the James J. Jeffries v. Jack Finnegan bout at Detroit, USA, on 6 April 1900, which was won by Jeffries in 55 seconds.

Most fights won

Most fights without a defeat
Edward Henry Greb (USA) (1894–1926) was unbeaten for 178 consecutive bouts, but these included 117 'no decision', of which five were unofficial losses, from 1916 to 1923.

Of boxers with complete records, Packey McFarland of the USA had a total of 97 fights (five draws) without a defeat between 1905 and 1915.

Pedro Carrasco (Spain) won 83 consecutive fights from 22 April 1964 to 3 Sept 1970, drew once and had a further nine wins before his loss to Armando Ramos in a WBC lightweight contest on 18 Feb 1972.

Most knock-outs
The most finishes classed as 'knock-outs' achieved is 145 (129 in professional bouts) by Archie Moore (USA) from 1936 to 1963.

Heavyweight champions

Longest reign
Joe Louis (USA) was the undefeated world heavyweight champion for 11 years 252 days, from 22 June 1937 until he announced his retirement from boxing on 1 March 1949. During his reign, he made a record 25 defences of his title.

Shortest reign
Tony Tucker (USA) was IBF champion for just 64 days from 30 May to 2 Aug 1987.

Undefeated career
Rocky Marciano (USA) is the only world champion at any weight to have won every fight of his entire completed professional career, from 17 March 1947 to 21 Sept 1955. Of his 49 fights, 43 were decided by knock-outs or stoppages.

YOUNGEST OLYMPIC CHAMPI

Oldest champion
George Foreman (USA) was 45 years 287 days old when he knocked out Michael Moorer at Las Vegas, USA, on 5 Nov 1994. He defended the IBF version in April 1995.

Youngest champion
Mike Tyson (USA) was 20 years 144 days old when he beat Trevor Berbick for the WBC title at Las Vegas, Nevada, USA, on 22 Nov 1986.

World champions

Longest reign
The heavyweight duration record of 11 years 252 days, set by Joe Louis from 1937 to 1949, stands for all divisions.

Shortest reign
Tony Canzoneri (USA) was light-welterweight champion for 33 days, from 21 May to 23 June 1933—the shortest period in which a boxer has won and lost the title in the ring.

Most rounds in one fight 276

Oldest champion
Archie Moore, who was recognized as light-heavyweight champion up to 10 Feb 1962, was believed to be aged 45–48 at that date.

Youngest champion
Wilfred Benitez of Puerto Rico was 17 years 176 days old when he won the WBA light welterweight title in San Juan, Puerto Rico, on 6 March 1976.

Most titles at different weights
Two boxers have won world titles at five different weights; Thomas Hearns (USA) (b. 18 Oct 1958), WBA welterweight (1980), WBC super welterweight (1982), WBC light heavyweight (1987), WBC middleweight (1987) and WBO super middleweight (1988); and Sugar Ray Leonard (USA) (b. 17 May 1956) WBC welterweight (1979 and 1980), WBA junior middleweight (1981), WBC middleweight (1987), WBC light heavyweight (1988) and WBC super middleweight (1988).

World titles at three different weights (featherweight, lightweight and welterweight) were held simultaneously by Henry Armstrong (USA) from Aug to Dec 1938.

Barney Ross (USA) may have simultaneously held the lightweight, junior-welterweight and welterweight world titles from 28 May to 17 Sept 1934, but there is some dispute as to when Ross relinquished his lightweight title.

Most title bouts
The record number of title bouts in one career is 37, of which 18 ended in 'no decision', by three-time world welterweight champion Jack Britton (USA) from 1915 to 1922. The record number of title bouts without any 'no decision' contests is 34, including a record 29 wins by Julio César Chávez (Mexico) between 1984 and 1996.

Most knock-downs in a title fight
Vic Toweel (South Africa) knocked down Danny O'Sullivan (GB) a record 14 times in 10 rounds during their world bantamweight fight at Johannesburg, South Africa, on 2 Dec 1950, before O'Sullivan retired.

Longest fight
The longest title fight under Queensberry Rules was between the lightweights Joe Gans and Oscar Matthew 'Battling' Nelson at Goldfield, Nevada, USA, on 3 Sept 1906. It was terminated in the 42nd round, when Gans was declared the winner on a foul.

Amateur
Most World Championship titles
Félix Savon of Cuba has won a record five World Championship titles (heavyweight in 1986, 1989 and 1991 and 91 kg in 1993 and 1995).

Most Olympic titles
Only two boxers have won three Olympic gold medals: southpaw (left-handed) László Papp (Hungary), who won the middleweight in 1948 and the light-middleweight in 1952 and 1956; and Teofilo Stevenson (Cuba), who won the heavyweight title in 1972, 1976 and 1980.

Youngest Olympic champion
Jackie Fields (USA) won the featherweight title at the age of 16 years 162 days in 1924. (The minimum age for competitors is now 17).

Oldest Olympic champion
Richard Kenneth Gunn (GB) holds the record for the oldest boxer ever to have won the

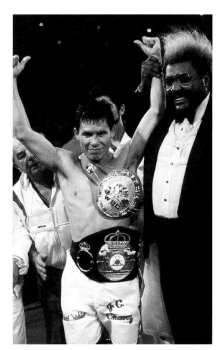

Left
Mexican boxer Julio César Chávez holds the record for the most title bouts without a single 'no decision' contest.

Olympic featherweight gold medal, at the age of 37 years 254 days on 27 Oct 1908 in London, UK.

British titles
Most British titles
The most defences of a British heavyweight title is 14, by 'Bombardier' Billy Wells between 1911 and 1919.

Lonsdale Belts
A Lonsdale belt is awarded to a boxer who wins three British title fights in one weight division. The only boxer to have won three Lonsdale Belts outright is heavyweight Henry Cooper, who retired after losing to Joe Bugner. Cooper held the heavyweight title from 12 Jan 1959 to 28 May 1969 and from 24 March 1970 to 16 March 1971.

The shortest time ever taken to win a Lonsdale Belt, is 95 days, by Michael Ayers in the lightweight division, from 18 Feb to 24 May 1995.

The longest time that it has taken a boxer to win a Lonsdale Belt outright is 8 years 236 days, by Kirkland Laing from 4 April 1979 to 26 Nov 1987.

Most British amateur titles
The greatest number of ABA titles to have been won by any boxer is eight, by John Lyon at light-flyweight from 1981 to 1984 and at flyweight from 1986 to 1989.

Alex 'Bud' Watson of Leith won a record 10 British amateur titles (the Scottish heavyweight title in 1938, 1942 and 1943 and the light-heavyweight championship from 1937 to 1939, from 1943 to 1945 and in 1947). Watson also won the ABA light-heavyweight title in 1945 and 1947.

SO KNOCKED OUT SIX OPPONENTS IN A SINGLE NIGHT

S JACKIE FIELDS, WHO WON THE FEATHERWEIGHT TITLE AT THE AGE OF 16 YEARS 162 DAYS

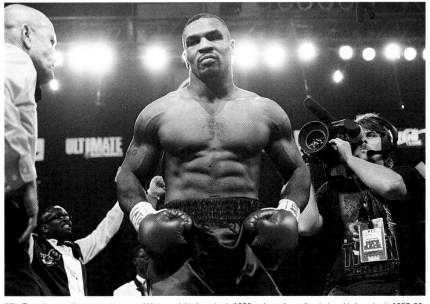

Mike Tyson became the youngest ever world heavyweight champion in 1986 and was the undisputed world champion in 1987–90.

Combat sports

LONGEST WRESTLING BOUT ON RECORD LASTED 11 HR 40 MIN

Centre
World Championship tug-of-war contests were held annually from 1975 to 1986, and have taken place biennially since then. The longest ever pull lasted 2 hr 31 min, but since the introduction of AAA rules, which forbid lying on the ground or entrenching the feet, the longest pull has been 24 min 45 sec.

Right
Hawaiian sumo wrestler Konishiki ('Dumptruck') is the heaviest ever *rikishi*. Competitors in Japan's national sport rarely weigh in at less than 130 kg (285 lb), maintaining their large size by over-consumption of a high-protein stew called *chankonabe*.

Wrestling

Most titles and medals

Three Olympic titles have been won by: Carl Westergren (Sweden) in 1920, 1924 and 1932; Ivar Johansson (Sweden) in 1932 (two) and 1936; and Aleksandr Vasilyevich Medved (USSR) in 1964, 1968 and 1972.

Four Olympic medals were won by: Eino Leino (Finland) at freestyle (1920–32); and by Imre Polyák (Hungary) at Greco-Roman (1952–64).

The freestyler Aleksandr Medved (USSR) won a record 10 World Championships at three weight categories (1962–64 and 1966–72).

The only wrestler to win the same title in eight successive years is Aleksandr Kareline (Russia), who won the World Championship and Olympic titles in the Greco-Roman 130-kg class between 1988 and 1995.

Most British titles

The most British titles won in one weight class is 14, by welterweight Fitzlloyd Walker from 1979 to 1992.

Most wins

In international competition, the 1964 Olympic freestyle 63-kg champion Osamu Watanabe (Japan) was unbeaten and did not concede a score in 189 consecutive matches.

Longest bout

Martin Klein (Estonia, representing Russia) beat Alfred Asikáinen (Finland) in an 11-hr 40-min bout for the Greco-Roman 75-kg 'A' event silver medal in the 1912 Olympics.

Sumo wrestling

Yokozuna (grand champion) Sadji Akiyoshi, alias Futabayama, set the all-time record of 69 consecutive wins from 1937 to 1939.

Yokozuna Koki Naya, alias Taiho ('Great Bird'), won the Emperor's Cup 32 times up to his retirement in 1971.

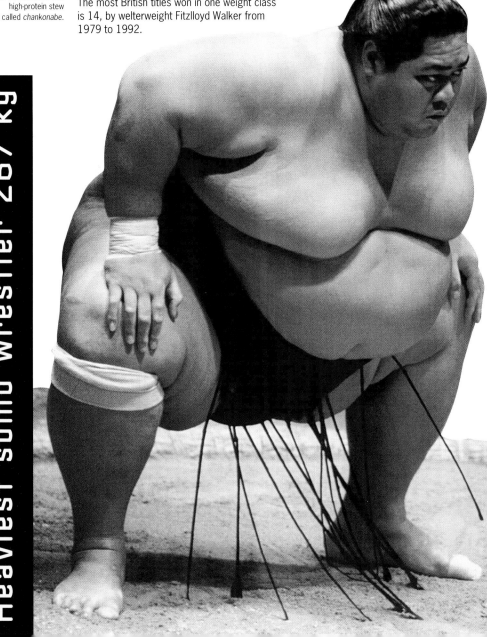

The *ozeki* Tameemon Torokichi, alias Raiden, won 254 bouts and lost 10 (a record 96.2% of wins) in 21 years, from 1789 to 1810.

Yokozuna Mitsugu Akimoto, alias Chiyonofuji, won the Kyushu Basho for eight successive years, from 1981 to 1988. He also holds the record for the most career wins (1,045) and the most *Makunouchi* (top division) wins (807).

In 1978, Toshimitsu Ogata, alias Kitanoumi, won a record 82 of the 90 bouts that top *rikishi* fight annually. In July 1974, aged 21 years 2 months, he became the youngest to attain the rank of *yokozuna*.

Hawaiian-born Jesse Kuhaulua, alias Takamiyama, was the first non-Japanese to

LONGEST EVER TUG OF W

win an official top-division tournament, in July 1972. In Sept 1981 he set a record of 1,231 consecutive top-division bouts.

In all six divisions, the greatest number of consecutive bouts is 1,631, by Yukio Shoji, alias Aobajo, from 1964 to 1986.

The most bouts in a career is 1,891, by Kenji Hatano, alias Oshio, from 1962 to 1988.

Hawaiian-born Chad Rowan, alias Akebono, became the first foreign *rikishi* to be promoted to the top rank of *yokozuna*, in Jan 1993. He is also the tallest (2.04 m or 6 ft 8 in) and heaviest (227 kg or 501 lb) *yokozuna* in sumo history.

The heaviest ever *rikishi* is the Samoan-American Salevaa Fuali Atisanoe, alias Konishiki, of Hawaii, who weighed in at 267 kg (589 lb) at Tokyo's Ryogoku Kokugikan on 3 Jan 1994.

Judo

Most World and Olympic titles

Yasuhiro Yamashita won nine consecutive Japanese titles from 1977 to 1985, and five world and Olympic titles (Over 95 kg in 1979, 1981 and 1983, Open in 1981, and Olympic Open in 1984). He retired undefeated after 203 successive wins from 1977 to 1985.

Two other men have won four world titles: Shozo Fujii (Japan) (Under 80 kg in 1971, 1973 and 1975 and Under 78 kg in 1979);

Heaviest sumo wrestler 267 kg

and Naoya Ogawa (Japan) (Open in 1987, 1989 and 1991 and Over 95 kg in 1989).

Four men have won two Olympic gold medals: Wilhelm Ruska (Netherlands) (Over 93 kg and Open in 1972); Peter Seisenbacher (Austria) (86 kg in 1984 and 1988); Hitoshi Saito (Japan) (Over 95 kg in 1984 and 1988); Waldemar Legien (Poland) (78 kg in 1988 and 86 kg in 1992).

Ingrid Berghmans (Belgium) has won a record six women's world titles: Open in 1980, 1982, 1984 and 1986 and Under 72 kg in 1984 and 1989.

Karen Briggs is the most successful British player, having won a total of four women's

and 1988); and José Manuel Egea (Spain) (Under 80 kg in 1990 and 1992).

Four women's kumite titles have been won by Guus van Mourik (Netherlands) at Over 60 kg in 1982, 1984, 1986 and 1988.

Three individual men's kata titles have been won by Tsuguo Sakumoto (Japan) in 1984, 1986 and 1988.

Three individual women's kata titles have been won by Mie Nakayama (Japan) in 1982, 1984 and 1986, and by Yuki Mimura (Japan) in 1988, 1990 and 1992.

Fencing
Most world titles
A record five individual world titles have been won by Aleksandr Romankov (USSR), at foil in 1974, 1977, 1979, 1982 and 1983.

Christian d'Oriola (France) won four world foil titles (1947, 1949 and 1953–54) and two individual Olympic titles (1952 and 1956).

Four women foilists have won three world titles: Helene Mayer (Germany), 1929, 1931 and 1937; Ilona Schacherer-Elek (Hungary), 1934–35 and 1951; Ellen Müller–Preis (Austria), 1947 and 1949–50; and Cornelia

Aladár Gerevich (Hungary) won seven golds (one individual and six team) from 1932 to 1960—a record Olympic span of 28 years.

The most gold medals by a woman is four (one individual, three team) by Yelena Dmitryevna Novikova (USSR), 1968–76.

Edoardo Mangiarotti (Italy) won a record 13 Olympic medals (six gold, five silver, two bronze) for foil and épée from 1936 to 1960.

Tug of war
Most titles
The most successful team at the World Championships has been England, with 16 titles in all categories from 1975 to 1993.

Sweden has won the 520-kg category three times and the 560-kg category at all five women's World Championships between 1986 and 1994.

The Wood Treatment team (formerly the Bosley Farmers) of Cheshire, UK, won 20 consecutive AAA Catchweight Championships (1959–78), two world titles (1975–76) and 10 European titles at 720 kg.

Record distance
The record distance for a tug-of-war contest is 3,623 m (3,692 yd), between Freedom Square and Independence Square at Lodź, Poland, on 28 May 1994.

STED 2 HR 41 MIN IN 1889, AT JUBBULPORE, INDIA

world titles: Under 48 kg in 1982, 1984, 1986 and 1989.

Adrian Neil Adams has the most successful international record of a British male player, having won two junior (1974 and 1977) and five senior (1979–80, 1983–85) European titles, four World Championship medals (one gold, one silver, two bronze) and two Olympic silver medals.

Most British titles
The most British titles won is nine, by David Colin Starbrook: Middleweight (1969–70), Light-heavyweight (1971–75) and Open division (1970–71).

Karen Briggs has won a record seven women's titles (Open, 1981–82, 1986–87, 1989–90 and 1992).

Karate
World Championships
Great Britain has been victorious in the World Championships at the Kumite team event on a record six occasions (1975, 1982, 1984, 1986, 1988, 1990).

Four men have won two men's individual kumite titles: Pat McKay (GB) (Under 80 kg in 1982 and 1984); Emmanuel Pinda (France) (Open in 1984 and Over 80 kg in 1988); Thierry Masci (France) (Under 70 kg in 1986

Hanisch (West Germany), 1979, 1981 and 1985. Ilona Schacherer-Elek also won two individual Olympic titles (1936 and 1948).

Most Olympic medals
The most individual Olympic gold medals is three, by Ramón Fonst (Cuba) in 1900 and 1904 (two), and by Nedo Nadi (Italy) in 1912 and 1920 (two).

Nedo Nadi also won three team gold medals in 1920; the five gold medals at a single celebration is the fencing record.

Longest pulls
The longest recorded pull (pre AAA rules) lasted 2 hr 41 min, when 'H' Company beat 'E' Company of the Second Battalion of the Sherwood Foresters (Derbyshire Regiment) at Jubbulpore, India, on 12 Aug 1889.

The longest tug-of-war pull ever recorded under AAA rules lasted for 24 min 45 sec. It was the first pull between the Republic of Ireland and England during the world championships (640-kg class) at Malmö, Sweden, on 18 Sept 1988.

Left
The different swords used in fencing are the foil, the épée and the sabre. Men's fencing has been part of the Olympic Games since 1896, while women's fencing was introduced in 1924, using foil only. The 1996 Games saw the introduction of épée events for women.

Target sports

Most Olympic shooting medals 11

Right
Archery has grown from the use of the bow and arrow in warfare to a competitive sport, of which the world governing body is the Fédération Internationale de Tir à l'Arc (FITA). In general, competitions are based on double FITA rounds, whereby 72 arrows are shot at targets from distances of 90, 70, 50 or 30 m for men and 70, 60, 50 or 30 m for women.

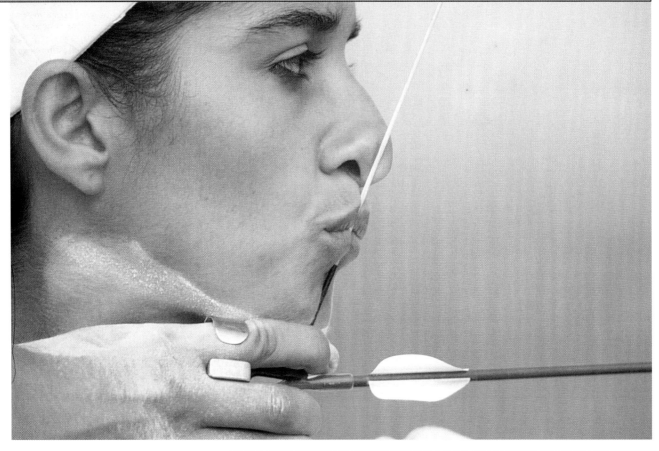

Archery
World Championships
The most titles won by a man is four, by Hans Deutgen of Sweden from 1947 to 1950.

The most titles won by a woman is seven, by Janina Spychajowa-Kurkowska of Poland in 1931–34, 1936, 1939 and 1947.

The USA has won a record 14 men's and eight women's team titles.

Olympic Games
Hubert van Innis of Belgium won six gold and three silver medals at the 1900 and 1920 Olympic Games.

British Championships
The record for the most men's titles is 12, by Horace Alfred Ford in 1849–59 and 1867.

The most women's titles is 23, by Alice Blanche Legh, in 1881, 1886–92, 1895, 1898–1900, 1902–09, 1913 and 1921–2. She could not win in 1882–85 because her mother was champion, or from 1915 to 1918, when WWI halted the championships.

Target archery over 24 hours
The highest score by a pair of archers over 24 hours by is 76,158, during 70 Portsmouth

Rounds (60 arrows per round at 20 yd, at 60-cm FITA targets) by Simon Tarplee and David Hathaway at Evesham, Worcs, UK, on 1 April 1991. Tarplee also set an individual record of 38,500 during this attempt.

Greatest draw
Gary Sentman, of Roseberg, Oregon, USA, drew a longbow weighing a record 79.83 kg (176 lb) to the maximum draw on the arrow of 72 cm (28¾ in) at Forksville, Pennsylvania, USA, on 20 Sept 1975.

Shooting
Most Olympic medals
Carl Townsend Osburn (USA) won 11 medals, in 1912, 1920 and 1924 (five gold, four silver and two bronze).

The only marksman to win three individual gold medals is Gudbrand Gudbrandsönn Skatteboe of Norway, in 1906.

Bisley
The Queen's (King's) Prize, shot since 1860, has only once been won by a woman, Marjorie Elaine Foster, who scored 280 in July 1930.

Arthur George Fulton (1887–1972) won three times (1912, 1926 and 1931). Both his father and his son also won the prize.

The highest score for the final of the Queen's Prize is 295 out of a possible 300, by Lindsay Peden of Scotland on 24 July 1982; and by Colin Brook of London & Middlesex RA on 24 July 1993. The latter was on targets with a smaller bullseye.

The record for the Silver Medals is 150 of a possible 150, by Martin John Brister of the City Rifle Club and Lord John Swansea of the South Wales Rifle Club on 24 July 1971. This was equalled by John Henry Carmichael of WRA Bromsgrove RC on 28 July 1979 and Robert Stafford of London & Middlesex RA on 26 July 1980, with the size of the bullseye reduced. Graham Robilliard, on 26 July 1991, and Colin Brook, on 23 July 1993, scored 150 with the size of the bullseye reduced even further.

Small-bore
The British individual small-bore rifle record for 60 shots prone is 597/600, held jointly by Philip Scanlon, Alister Allan and John Booker.

Clay pigeon

The record for the greatest number of world clay pigeion shooting titles is six, by Susan Nattrass of Canada, in 1974, 1975, 1977–1979 and 1981.

Bench rest shooting

The smallest group on record at 914 m (1,000 yd) is 10.058 cm (3²⁴⁄₂₅ in), by Frank Weber (USA) with a .308 Baer at Williamsport, Pennsylvania, USA, on 14 Nov 1993.

The smallest group on record at 500 m (546 yd) is 3.81 cm (1½ in), by Ross Hicks of Australia, using a rifle of his own design at Canberra, Australia, on 12 March 1994.

Darts

Most titles

Eric Bristow holds the record for the greatest number of wins in the World Masters Championship (five, 1977, 1979, 1981 and 1983–84), the World Professional Championship (five, 1980–81 and 1984–86) and the World Cup Singles (four, 1983, 1985, 1987 and 1989). John Lowe is the only other man to have won each of the three major titles: World Masters (1976 and 1980); World Professional (1979, 1987 and 1993); World Cup Singles (1981).

World Cup

England has had a record nine wins at the biennial World Cup tournament.

The biennial World Cup for women has been won a record four times by England.

/ER 24 HOURS IS 76,158

Biggest prize

John Lowe won £102,000 for the first 501 to be scored with the minimum nine darts (six successive treble 20s, treble 17, treble 18 and double 18) in a major event, on 13 Oct 1984 at Slough, Berks, UK, in the World Match-play Championships quarter-finals.

Speed

The fastest time taken to complete three games of 301, finishing on doubles, is 1 min 38 sec, by Ritchie Gardner on BBC TV's *Record Breakers,* on 12 Sept 1989.

Least darts

Roy Edwin Blowes (Canada) was the first to achieve a 501 in nine darts (bull, treble 20, treble 17, five treble 20s, double 20), 'double-on, double-off', at the Widgeons pub, Calgary, Canada, in March 1987. This was equalled (double 20, six treble 20s, treble 17, bull) by Steve Draper at the Ex-Serviceman's Club, Wellingborough, Northants, UK, in Nov 1994.

The least darts thrown for a score of 1,001 is 19, by Cliff Inglis, with 160, 180, 140, 180, 121, 180 and 40 at the Bromfield Men's Club, Devon, UK, on 11 Nov 1975; and by Jocky Wilson, with 140, 140, 180, 180, 180, 131 and bull at The London Pride, Bletchley, Bucks, UK, on 23 March 1989.

WORLD ARCHERY RECORDS
Men—single FITA rounds
FITA Oh Kyo-moon (South Korea) scored 1,368 points from a possible 1,440 in 1995
90 m Vladimir Yesheyev (USSR) scored 330 points from a possible 360 in 1990
70 m Hiroshi Yamamoto (Japan) scored 344 points from a possible 360 in 1990
50 m Han Seung-hoon (South Korea) scored 348 points from a possible 360 in 1994
30 m Han Seung-hoon (South Korea) scored 360 points from a possible 360 in 1994
Team South Korea (Oh Kyo-moon, Lee Kyung-chul, Kim Jae-pak) scored 4,053 points from a possible 4,320 in 1995
Women—single FITA rounds
FITA Kim Jung-rye (South Korea) scored 1,377 points from a possible 1,440 in 1995
70 m Cho Youn-jeong (South Korea) scored 338 points from possible 360 in 1992
60 m He Ying (China) scored 349 points from a possible 360 in 1995
50 m Lim Jung (South Korea) scored 340 points from a possible 360 in 1994
30 m Joanne Edens (GB) scored 357 points from a possible 360 in 1990
Team South Korea (Kim Soo-nyung, Lee Eun-kyung, Cho Yuon-jeong) scored 4,094 points from a possible 4,320 in 1992
Indoor (18 m)
Men
Magnus Pattersson (Sweden) scored 596 points from a possible 600 in 1995
Women
Natalya Valeyeva (Moldova) scored 590 points from a possible 600 in 1995
Indoor (25 m)
Men
Magnus Pattersson (Sweden) scored 593 points from a possible 600 in 1993
Women
Petra Ericsson (Sweden) scored 592 points from a possible 600 in 1991

DARTS SCORING RECORDS
24-hour
Men (eight players)
1,722,249 by Broken Hill Darts Club at Broken Hill, NSW, Australia on 28–29 Sept 1985
Women (eight players)
744,439 by a team from the Lord Clyde, Leyton, London, UK, on 13–14 Oct 1990
Individual
566,175 by Russell Locke at Hugglescote Working Men's Club, Leics, UK, on 17–18 Sept 1993
Bulls and 25s (eight players)
526,750 by a team at the George Inn, Morden, Surrey, UK, on 1–2 July 1994
10-hour
Most trebles
3,056 (from 7,992 darts) by Paul Taylor at the Woodhouse Tavern, Leytonstone, London, UK, on 19 Oct 1985
Most doubles
3,265 (from 8,451 darts) by Paul Taylor at the Lord Brooke, Walthamstow, London, UK, on 5 Sept 1987
Highest score (retrieving own darts) 465,919 by John Archer and Neil Rankin at the Royal Oak, Cossington, Leics, UK, on 17 Nov 1990
Bulls (individual)
1,320 by John Lowe at The Unicorn Tavern, Chesterfield, Derbys, UK, on 27 Oct 1994
6-hour
Men
210,172 by Russell Locke at the Hugglescote Working Mens Club, Coalville, Leics, UK, on 10 Sept 1989
Women
99,725 by Karen Knightly at the Lord Clyde, Leyton, London, UK, on 17 March 1991

INDIVIDUAL WORLD SHOOTING RECORDS

In 1986, the International Shooting Union (UIT) introduced new regulations for determining major championships and world records. The leading competitors now undertake an additional round with a target subdivided to tenths of a point for rifle and pistol shooting, and an extra 25, 40 or 50 shots for trap and skeet. Harder targets have since been introduced. The table below shows the world records, as recognized by the UIT at the end of 1995, for the 15 Olympic shooting disciplines to be contested at Atlanta in 1996, giving in brackets the score for the number of shots specified plus the score in the additional round.

MEN
Free Rifle 50 m 3 x 40 shots
1287.9 (1,186+101.9)
Rajmond Debevec (Slovenia)
Munich, Germany, 29 Aug 1992
Free Rifle 50 m 60 shots prone
703.5 (599+104.5)
Jens Harskov (Denmark)
Zürich, Switzerland, 6 June 1991
Air Rifle 10 m 60 shots
699.4 (596+103.4)
Rajmond Debevec (Yugoslavia)
Zürich, Switzerland, 7 June 1990
Free Pistol 50 m 60 shots
672.5 (575+97.5)
Sergey Pyzhyanov (Russia)
Milan, Italy, 16 June 1993
Rapid-Fire Pistol 25 m 60 shots
699.7 (596+107.5)
Ralf Schumann (Germany)
Barcelona, Spain, 8 June 1994
Air Pistol 10 m 60 shots
695.1 (593+102.1)
Sergey Pyzhyanov (USSR)
Munich, Germany, 13 Oct 1989
Running Target 10 m 30/30 shots
678.8 (579+99.8)
Jens Zimmermann (Germany)
Milan, Italy, 31 May 1994
Skeet 125 targets
149 (124+25)
Dean Clark (USA)
Barcelona, Spain, 20 June 1993
149 (124+25)
Andrea Benelli (Italy)
Fagnano, Italy, 29 May 1994
149 (124+25)
Andrea Benelli (Italy)
Lisbon, Portugal, 5 June 1994
Trap 125 targets
149 (125+24)
Giovanni Pellielo (Italy)
Nicosia, Cyprus, 1 April 1994
149 (124+25)
Marco Venturini (Italy)
Munich, Germany, 10 Sept 1994
Double Trap 150 targets
191 (143+48)
Joshua Lakatos (USA)
Barcelona, Spain, 15 June 1993
WOMEN
Standard Rifle 50 m 3 x 20 shots
689.3 (590+99.3)
Vessela Letcheva (Bulgaria)
Munich, Germany, 28 Aug 1992
Air Rifle 10 m 40 shots
500.8 (399+101.8)
Valentina Cherkasova (USSR)
Los Angeles, USA, 23 March 1991
Sport Pistol 25 m 60 shots
696.2 (594+102.2)
Diana Jorgova (Bulgaria)
Milan, Italy, 31 May 1994
Air Pistol 10 m 40 shots
492.4 (392+100.4)
Lieselotte Breker (West Germany)
Zagreb, Yugoslavia, 18 May 1989
Double Trap 120 targets
147 (112+35)
Deborah Gelisio (Italy)
Nicosia, Cyprus, 3 April 1994

Races and horses

Below right
The Kentucky Derby is held every year on the first Saturday in May at Churchill Downs, Louisville.

Centre right
The Grand National offers the greatest prize money of any race over jumps in the United Kingdom. In the 1996 race, *Rough Quest* claimed the biggest purse ever for a British race over jumps.

Far right
Desert Orchid has won more prize money than any other steeplechaser in the United Kingdom, a total of £652,802.

Prizes, prices and earnings

Largest prizes
The highest prize money for a single day's racing is $10 million (£8.4 million), for the Breeders' Cup series of seven races staged annually in the USA since 1984.

The largest single race purse was $4 million (£2.6 million), including a record first prize of $2.4 million (£1.6 million) won by *Cigar* for the Dubai World Cup on 27 March 1996.

Highest price
On 23 July 1985, Robert Sangster and partners paid $13.1 million (£9.5 million) for *Seattle Dancer* at Keeneland, Kentucky, USA.

Greatest winnings
The highest career earnings is $9,663,593 by the 1994 Japanese Triple Crown winner *Narita Brian* (foaled 1991) to June 1996.

Most wins in a year
Lenoxbar won 46 races from 56 starts in 1940 in Puerto Rico.

Most wins in the same race
Doctor Syntax won the Preston Gold Cup seven times in a row, between 1815 and 1821.

Triple Crown winners
The English Triple Cown (2,000 Guineas, Derby and St Leger) has been achieved 15 times, most recently by *Nijinsky* in 1970.

The American Triple Crown (Kentucky Derby, Preakness Stakes, Belmont Stakes) has been achieved 11 times, most recently by *Affirmed* in 1978.

World speed records
Big Racket reached 69.62 km/h (43.26 mph), in a ¼-mile (402-m) race at Mexico City,

Best win-loss record
Eclipse never lost a race in a total of 18 starts, in a career that lasted from May 1769 to Oct 1770.

Most races won in a season
Three-year-old *Fisherman* won 23 races (from 34 starts) in 1856.

Most career wins
Catherina recorded a total of 79 wins out of 176 starts in a career that lasted from 1832 to 1841.

Most Pattern-race wins
The most prolific British-trained winner of all time is *Brigadier Gerard*, with 13 wins in 1971 and 1972.

Biggest winning margin in a Classic
Mayonaise won by 20 lengths in the 1,000 Guineas on 12 May 1859.

Highest winnings
The greatest amount won by a British-trained horse is £1,283,794, by *Snurge*, between 1989 and 1994.

The most prize money earned in a year is $4,578,454 (£2,869,245), by *Sunday Silence* in the USA, in 1989. This included $1,350,000 (£846,024) from the Breeders' Cup Classic and a $1-million (£626,684) bonus for the best record in the Triple Crown races.

Winning horses

Longest winning sequence
Camarero was undefeated in 56 races in Puerto Rico from 19 April 1953 to his first defeat on 17 Aug 1955. In his career to 1956, he won 73 of a total of 77 races.

Best win-loss record
Kincsem, a Hungarian mare, was unbeaten in 54 races in Europe between 1876 and 1879.

Most career wins
Chorisbar won 197 of 324 races in Puerto Rico between 1937 and 1947.

Mexico, on 5 Feb 1945. *Onion Roll* achieved the same speed at Thistledown, Cleveland, Ohio, USA, on 27 Sept 1993.

Oldest winners
The oldest winners on the Flat are 18-year-olds *Revenge* at Shrewsbury in 1790, *Marksman* at Ashford, Kent, in 1826, and *Jorrocks* at Bathurst, Australia, in 1851. At the same age *Wild Aster* won three hurdle races in 1919, and *Sonny Somers* won two steeplechases in Feb 1980.

British Flat racing

Most runners
The most horses for a Flat race is 58, in the Lincolnshire Handicap on 13 March 1948.

Longest winning sequence
Meteor won 21 consecutive races from 1786 to 1788.

The record earnings for a season is £1,262,302 in 1995 by *Lammtarra* (foaled 1992), who won the Derby, the King George VI and Queen Elizabeth Stakes, and the Prix de l'Arc de Triomphe.

Highest-rated horses
Since the 1977 introduction of official ratings in the International Classifications, the highest rating is 141, for *Dancing Brave* in 1986.

The only horse to win two Horse of the Year awards is the filly *Dahlia*, in 1973 and 1974.

The Derby
Shergar won the Derby by a record margin of 10 lengths in 1981.

There have been two dead-heats in the history of the Derby: in 1828 *Cadland* beat *The Colonel* in the run-off, and in 1884 *St Gatien* and *Harvester* divided the stakes.

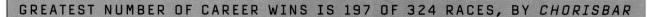

Best winning margin 20 lengths

The largest prize on the British Turf is £523,100, won by *Shaamit* for the Derby on 8 June 1996.

Jumping

Most successful horses

Sir Ken won a record 16 hurdle races in succession, from April 1951 to March 1953.

A record three Champion Hurdles have been won by four horses: *Sir Ken,* from 1952 to 1954, *Hatton's Grace* from 1949 to 1951, *Persian War* from 1968 to 1970, and *See You Then* from 1985 to 1987.

The horse that has won the Cheltenham Gold Cup most often is *Golden Miller*, with five wins from 1932 to 1936.

The mare *Dawn Run* is the only horse to have won both the Champion Hurdle (1984) and the Cheltenham Gold Cup (1986).

The greatest number of Horse of the Year awards is four, by *Desert Orchid*, from 1987 to 1990.

JBAI WORLD CUP IN 1996

Highest winnings

Desert Orchid won £652,802 between 1983 and 1991.

The highest prize won over jumps in the United Kingdom is £142,534, by *Rough Quest* in the Grand National on 30 March 1996.

Grand National

The highest number of horses in any race is 66, in the Grand National on 22 March 1929.

The only horse to have won the Grand National three times is *Red Rum*, in 1973, 1974 and 1977, from a total of five runs (he came second in 1975 and 1976).

Manifesto ran a record eight times, from 1895 to 1904. He won in 1897 and 1899 and came third three times and fourth once.

The highest weight ever carried to victory in the Grand National is 79.4 kg (12 st 7 lb), by *Cloister* (1893), *Manifesto* (1899), *Jerry M.* (1912) and *Poethlyn* (1919).

MAJOR BRITISH RACE RECORDS, FLAT

DERBY
Record time: 2 min 32.31 sec
Lammtarra in 1995
Most wins (jockey): 9
Lester Piggott in 1954, 1957, 1960, 1968, 1970, 1972, 1976, 1977, 1983
Most wins (trainer): 7
Robert Robson in 1793, 1802, 1809, 1810, 1815, 1817, 1823
John Porter in 1868, 1882, 1883, 1886, 1890, 1891, 1899
Fred Darling in 1922, 1925, 1926, 1931, 1938, 1940, 1941
Most wins (owner): 5
3rd Earl of Egremont in 1782, 1804, 1805, 1807, 1826
HH Aga Khan III in 1930, 1935, 1936, 1948, 1952

2,000 GUINEAS
Record time: 1 min 35.08 sec
Mister Baileys in 1994
Most wins (jockey): 9
Jem Robinson in 1825, 1828, 1831, 1833, 1834, 1835, 1836, 1847, 1848
Most wins (trainer): 7
John Scott in 1842, 1843, 1849, 1853, 1856, 1860, 1862
Most wins (owner): 5
4th Duke of Grafton in 1820, 1821, 1822, 1826, 1827
5th Earl of Jersey in 1831, 1834, 1835, 1836, 1837

1,000 GUINEAS
Record time: 1 min 36.71 sec
Las Meninas in 1994
Most wins (jockey): 7
George Fordham in 1859, 1861, 1865, 1868, 1869, 1881, 1883
Most wins (trainer): 9
Robert Robson in 1818, 1819, 1820, 1821, 1822, 1823, 1825, 1826, 1827
Most wins (owner): 8
4th Duke of Grafton in 1819, 1820, 1821, 1822, 1823, 1825, 1826, 1827

OAKS
Record time: 2 min 34.19 sec
Intrepidity in 1993
Most wins (jockey): 9
Frank Buckle in 1797, 1798, 1799, 1802, 1803, 1805, 1817, 1818, 1823
Most wins (trainer): 12
Robert Robson in 1802, 1804, 1805, 1807, 1808, 1809, 1813, 1815, 1818, 1822, 1823, 1825
Most wins (owner): 6
4th Duke of Grafton in 1813, 1815, 1822, 1823, 1828, 1831

ST LEGER
Record time: 3 min 1.6 sec
Coronach in 1926 and *Windsor Lad* in 1934
Most wins (jockey): 9
Bill Scott in 1821, 1825, 1828, 1829, 1838, 1839, 1840, 1841, 1846
Most wins (trainer): 16
John Scott in 1827, 1828, 1829, 1832, 1834, 1838, 1839, 1840, 1841, 1845, 1851, 1853, 1856, 1857, 1859, 1862
Most wins (owner): 7
9th Duke of Hamilton in 1786, 1787, 1788, 1792, 1808, 1809, 1814

KING GEORGE VI AND QUEEN ELIZABETH DIAMOND STAKES
Record time: 2 min 26.98 sec
Grundy in 1975
Most wins (jockey): 7
Lester Piggott in 1965, 1966, 1969, 1970, 1974, 1977, 1984
Most wins (trainer): 5
Dick Hern in 1972, 1979, 1980, 1985, 1989
Most wins (owner): 3
Sheikh Mohammed 1990, 1993, 1994

MAJOR BRITISH RACE RECORDS, JUMPING

GRAND NATIONAL
Record time: 8 min 47.8 sec
Mr Frisk in 1990
Most wins (jockey): 5
George Stevens in 1856, 1863, 1864, 1869, 1870
Most wins (trainer): 4
Fred Rimell in 1956, 1961, 1970, 1976
Most wins (owner): 3
James Machell in 1873, 1874, 1876
Sir Charles Assheton-Smith in 1893, 1912, 1913
Noel Le Mare in 1973, 1974, 1977

CHELTENHAM GOLD CUP
Record time: 6 min 23.4 sec
Silver Fame in 1951
Most wins (jockey): 4
Pat Taaffe in 1964, 1965, 1966, 1968
Most wins (trainer): 5
Tom Dreaper in 1946, 1964, 1965, 1966, 1968
Most wins (owner): 7
Dorothy Paget in 1932, 1933, 1934, 1935, 1936, 1940, 1952

CHAMPION HURDLE
Record time: 3 min 50.7 sec
Kribensis in 1990
Most wins (jockey): 4
Tim Molony in 1951, 1952, 1953, 1954
Most wins (trainer): 5
Peter Easterby in 1967, 1976, 1977, 1980, 1981
Most wins (owner): 4
Dorothy Paget in 1932, 1933, 1940, 1946

MAJOR INTERNATIONAL RACE RECORDS

PRIX DE L'ARC DE TRIOMPHE
Record time: 2 min 26.3 sec
Trempolino in 1987
Most wins (jockey): 4
Jacques Doyasbère in 1942, 1944, 1950, 1951
Frédéric Head in 1966, 1972, 1976, 1979
Yves Saint-Martin in 1970, 1974, 1982, 1984
Pat Eddery in 1980, 1985, 1986, 1987
Most wins (trainer): 4
Charles Semblat in 1942, 1944, 1946, 1949
Alec Head in 1952, 1959, 1976, 1981
François Mathet in 1950, 1951, 1970, 1982
Most wins (owner): 6
Marcel Boussac in 1936, 1937, 1942, 1944, 1946, 1949

VRC MELBOURNE CUP
Record time: 3 min 16.3 sec
Kingston Rule in 1990
Most wins (jockey): 4
Bobby Lewis in 1902, 1915, 1919, 1927
Harry White in 1974, 1975, 1978, 1979
Most wins (trainer): 9
Bart Cummings in 1965, 1966, 1967, 1974, 1975, 1977, 1979, 1990, 1991
Most wins (owner): 4
Etienne de Mestre in 1861, 1862, 1867, 1878

KENTUCKY DERBY
Record time: 1 min 59.4 sec
Secretariat in 1973
Most wins (jockey): 5
Eddie Arcaro in 1938, 1941, 1945, 1948, 1952
Bill Hartack in 1957, 1960, 1962, 1964, 1969
Most wins (trainer): 6
Ben Jones in 1938, 1941, 1944, 1948, 1949, 1952
Most wins (owner): 8
Calumet Farm in 1941, 1944, 1948, 1949, 1952, 1957, 1958, 1968

IRISH DERBY
Record time: 2 min 25.60 sec
St Jovite in 1992
Most wins (jockey): 6
Morny Wing in 1921, 1923, 1930, 1938, 1942, 1946
Most wins (trainer): 6
Vincent O'Brien in 1953, 1957, 1970, 1977, 1984, 1985
Most wins (owner): 5
HH Aga Khan III in 1925, 1932, 1940, 1948, 1949

Jockeys, trainers and owners

Right
Horse racing dates back some 3,000 years, when the Ancient Egyptians are believed to have participated in the sport. It was certainly part of the ancient Olympic Games. Races were recorded in England *c.* AD 200 using Arab horses imported by the Romans.

Below right
Peter Scudamore is the most successful National Hunt jockey ever, but he was never able to emulate the achievement of his father, Michael, in winning a Grand National. Michael Scudamore rode *Oxo* to victory in 1959.

World records
Most wins by jockeys
The 1.50-m-tall (4-ft 11-in) Billie Lee 'Bill' Shoemaker (USA), who had a racing weight of 44 kg (97 lb), rode a record 8,833 winners out of 40,350 mounts from his first ride on 19 March 1949 and first winner on 20 April 1949 to his retirement on 3 Feb 1990.

The greatest number of races won by one jockey in a year is 598 from 2,312 rides, by Kent Jason Desormeaux (USA) in 1989.

The most winners ridden in one day is nine, by Chris Wiley Antley (USA) on 31 Oct 1987 (four at Aqueduct, New York, USA, and five at The Meadowlands, New Jersey, USA).

The most winners ridden on one card is eight by six riders, most recently (and from the fewest rides) by Patrick Alan Day, from nine rides at Arlington International, Illinois, USA, on 13 Sept 1989.

The longest winning streak is 12, by Sir Gordon Richards in 1933 (one at Nottingham, UK, on 3 Oct, six out of six at Chepstow, UK, on 4 Oct and the first five races the following day at Chepstow); and by Pieter Stroebel at Bulawayo, Southern Rhodesia (now Zimbabwe), from 7 June to 7 July 1958.

Highest winnings by jockeys
The highest amount won in one year is 3,133,742,000 yen (£18,795,310), by Yutaka Take in Japan in 1993.

Christopher McCarron (USA) has earned a career record total of $192 million from 1974 to 1996.

Most wins by trainers
Jack Charles Van Berg (USA) had the greatest number of wins in a year, at 496 in 1976.

The career record is 6,950 wins, by Dale Baird (USA) from 1962 to the end of 1996.

The only trainer to saddle the first five finishers in a championship race is Michael William Dickinson of Dunkeswick, W Yorkshire, UK, in the Cheltenham Gold Cup on 17 March 1983. He won a record 12 races in one day on 27 Dec 1982.

Highest winnings by trainers
The greatest amount of earnings won by a trainer in a single year is $17,842,358 (£10,026,050), by Darrell Wayne Lukas (USA) in 1988. He has also won a record of $140,024,750 during his career.

Most wins by owners
The most career wins by an owner is 4,775, by Marion H. Van Berg in North America over a period of 35 years from 1937 to 1971.

The most wins by an owner in a year is 494, by Dan R. Lasater (USA) in 1974.

Highest winnings by an owner
The greatest amount won by an owner in a year is $6,881,902 (£3,847,647), by Sam-Son Farm in North America in 1991.

British flat racing
Most wins by jockeys
Sir Gordon Richards won 4,870 races out of 21,815 mounts from his first mount at Lingfield Park, Surrey, on 16 Oct 1920 to his last at Sandown Park, Surrey, on 10 July 1954. His first win was on 31 March 1921. In 1953, at his 28th and final attempt, he won the Derby, six days after being knighted. He

was champion jockey 26 times between 1925 and 1953 and won a record 269 races (from 835 rides) in 1947.

Lester Keith Piggott won 4,513 races in the United Kingdom between 1948 and 1995, and his global total exceeds 5,300.

The greatest number of wins in one day is seven, by Patrick James John Eddery at Newmarket and Newcastle on 26 June 1992.

The greatest number of Classic races to have been won by one jockey is 30, by Lester Piggott from his first victory on *Never Say Die* in the 1954 Derby to the 2,000 Guineas on *Rodrigo de Triano* in 1992. He won the Derby nine times, the St Leger eight times, the Oaks six times, the 2,000 Guineas five times and the 1,000 Guineas twice.

Highest winnings by jockeys
The most prize-money ever won in a single year is £2,924,854, by Lanfranco 'Frankie' Dettori in 1995.

Left
HH Aga Khan III leads in the second of his record five Derby winners, *Bahram*. The 1935 winner won all nine of his races, including the English Triple Crown.

RNED IN A BRITISH SEASON BY ONE TRAINER IS £2,018,748, IN 1995

Most wins by trainers
The most wins in a season is 182 (from 1,215 starts) by Richard Michael Hannon of East Everleigh, Wilts, in 1993.

John Scott of Malton, Yorkshire, won 40 Classics between 1827 and 1863.

Henry Richard Amherst Cecil of Newmarket has been the champion in terms of races won a record nine times, between 1978 and 1989.

Highest winnings by trainers
The highest prize money to have been earned in a single season is £2,018,748, by John Leeper Dunlop in 1995.

In 1986 trainer Michael Ronald Stoute of Newmarket set a new record for worldwide earnings, at £2,778,405.

Alexander Taylor of Manton, Wilts, was champion trainer in terms of money won a record 12 times between 1907 and 1925.

Most wins by owners
HH Aga Khan III was the leading owner a record 13 times between 1924 and 1952.

The most Classics won is 20, by George Fitzroy, 4th Duke of Grafton, between 1813 and 1831, and Edward Stanley, 17th Earl of Derby, between 1910 and 1945.

Highest winnings by an owner
The record prize money won in one season is £2,666,730, by Sheikh Mohammed bin Rashid al Maktoum of Dubai in 1994.

Jumping
Most wins by trainers
William Arthur Stephenson of Leasingthorne, Co. Durham, won 2,644 races over jumps,

plus 344 on the flat, to make a record total of 2,988 victories in the United Kingdom between 1946 and 1992.

Martin Charles Pipe has been champion trainer in terms of races won a record 11 times, between 1986 and 1996.

Highest winnings by trainers
Martin Pipe won a record-breaking £1,203,014 in prize money in 1990/1, when his horses won a record 230 races from a total of 782 starts.

In terms of the amount of money won, Frederick Thomas Winter of Lambourn, Berks, was the champion trainer a record eight times between 1971 and 1985.

Most wins by jockeys
Peter Scudamore won a record 1,678 races over jumps—out of a total of 7,521 mounts—between 1978 and 1993.

The record for the greatest number of wins in one season is 221 (from a total of 663 rides), by Peter Scudamore in 1988/9.

The greatest number of wins in a single day is six, by two amateurs: Edward Potter Wilson at Crewkerne, Somerset, on 19 March 1878 and Charles James Cunningham at Rugby, Warks, on 29 March 1881.

The record for the greatest number of successive victories is 10, by John Alnham Gilbert, from 8 to 30 Sept 1959, and by Philip Charles Tuck, from 23 Aug to 3 Sept 1986.

The jockey who has won the greatest number of championships is Peter

Scudamore, with eight (one shared), in 1982 and from 1986 to 1992.

Highest winnings by jockeys
The most prize money won in one season is £1,235,170, by Norman Williamson in 1994/5.

Below
Billie Lee Shoemaker has ridden more winners than any other jockey. He won the Kentucky Derby four times—his last in 1986 on *Ferdinand*, when, aged 54, he was the oldest jockey ever to win the race.

Equestrian sports

Right
The British Open Championship for the Cowdray Park Gold Cup was instituted in 1956 and has been won most often by Stowell Park and Tramontana. Polo originated in central Asia, and is now popular around the world. The pitch on which it is played can be as large as 274 x 182 m (300 x 272 yd), the biggest of any sport.

The official record for the long jump over water is 8.40 m (27 ft 6¾ in), by *Something*, ridden by André Ferreira (South Africa) at Johannesburg, South Africa, on 25 April 1975.

The indoor high-jump record is 2.40 m (7 ft 10¾ in), by *Optibeurs Leonardo*, ridden by Franke Sloothaak (Germany) at Chaudefontaine, Switzerland, on 9 June 1991.

The British high-jump record is 2.32 m (7 ft 7¼ in) by the 16.2-hands (165-cm) grey gelding *Lastic* ridden by Nick Skelton at Olympia, London, UK, on 16 Dec 1978.

Three-day eventing
Olympics and World Championships
Charles Ferdinand Pahud de Mortanges (Netherlands) won a record four Olympic gold medals: team in 1924 and 1928 and individual (riding *Marcroix*) in 1928 and 1932.

Bruce Oram Davidson (USA) is the only rider to have won two individual world titles, on *Irish Cap* in 1974 and *Might Tango* in 1978.

Richard John Hannay Meade is the only British rider to win three Olympic gold medals: team in 1968 and 1972 and individual in 1972.

Show jumping
Olympic Games
The most Olympic gold medals to have been won by one rider is five, by Hans Günter Winkler (West Germany): four team medals in 1956, 1960, 1964 and 1972 and the individual Grand Prix in 1956. He also won team silver in 1976 and team bronze in 1968 for a record seven medals overall.

The greatest number of team wins in the Prix des Nations is six, by Germany in 1936, 1956, 1960, 1964, 1972 and 1988 (the last two as West Germany).

The lowest score obtained by a winner is no faults, by Frantisek Ventura (Czechoslovakia) on *Eliot* in 1928; by Alwin Schockemöhle (West Germany) on *Warwick Rex* in 1976; and by Ludger Beerbaum (Germany) on *Classic Touch* in 1992.

Pierre Jonquères d'Oriola (France) is the only person to have won the individual gold medal twice, in 1952 and 1964.

World Championships
The men's World Championships have been won twice by Hans Günter Winkler (West Germany) from 1954 to 1955 and Raimondo d'Inzeo (Italy) in 1956 and 1960.

The women's World Championships were won twice by Jane 'Janou' Tissot (France) on *Rocket* in 1970 and 1974.

The greatest number of team wins in the World Championships is three, by France in 1982, 1986 and 1990.

President's Cup
The President's Cup has been won a record 14 times by Great Britain (1965, 1967, 1970, 1972–74, 1977–79, 1983, 1985–86, 1989 and 1991).

David Broome represented Great Britain a record 106 times in Nations Cup events between 1959 and 1994.

World Cup
Double World Cup winners have been Conrad Homfeld (USA) in 1980 and 1985, Ian Millar (Canada) from 1988 to 1989, and John Whitaker (GB) from 1990 to 1991.

King George V Gold Cup and Queen Elizabeth II Cup
David Broome (GB) has won the King George V Gold Cup a record six times, on *Sunsalve* in 1960, on *Mister Softee* in 1966, on *Sportsman* in 1972, on *Philco* in 1977, on *Mr Ross* in 1981 and on *Lannegan* in 1991.

The Queen Elizabeth II Cup for women has been won five times by Elizabeth Edgar, on *Everest Wallaby* in 1977, on *Forever* in 1979, on *Everest Forever* in 1981 and 1982, and on *Everest Rapier* in 1986.

The only horse to have won both trophies is *Sunsalve*, in 1957 and 1960.

Jumping records
The official *Fédération Equestre Internationale* high-jump record is 2.47 m (8 ft 1¼ in), by *Huasó*, ridden by Capt. Alberto Larraguibel Morales (Chile) at Viña del Mar, Santiago, Chile, on 5 Feb 1949.

Badminton three-day event
The Badminton Home Trials have been won six times by Lucinda Jane Green, on *Be Fair* in 1973, *Wide Awake* in 1976, *George* in 1977, *Killaire* in 1979, *Regal Realm* in 1983 and *Beagle Bay* in 1984.

Dressage
Olympics and World Championships
Germany (as West Germany, 1968–90) have won eight team golds at the Olympics (1928, 1936, 1964, 1968, 1976, 1984, 1988 and 1992) and seven at the World Championships.

Nicole Uphoff has won two individual Olympic dressage titles.

Dr Reiner Klimke (West Germany) has won a record six Olympic golds (team from 1964 to 1988 and individual in 1984). He is also the only rider to have won two world titles, on *Mehmed* in 1974 and *Ahlerich* in 1982.

Henri St Cyr (Sweden) won a record two individual Olympic gold medals, in 1952 and 1956. This was equalled by Nicole Uphoff (Germany), who won in 1988 and 1992.

World Cup
The only double winners are Christine Stückelberger (Switzerland) on *Gauguin de Lully*, 1987–88; Monica Theodorescu (Greece) on *Ganimedes Tecrent*, 1993–94; and Anky van Grunsven (Netherlands) on *Camelion Bonfire*, 1995–96.

Carriage driving
World Championships
A record three World Championship team titles have been won by: Great Britain, in 1972, 1974 and 1980; Hungary, in 1976, 1978 and 1984; and the Netherlands, in 1982, 1986 and 1988.

Two individual titles have been won by: György Bárdos (Hungary) in 1978 and 1980;

NDRE FERREIRA IN 1975

Tjeerd Velstra (Netherlands) in 1982 and 1986; and Ijsbrand Chardon (Netherlands) in 1988 and 1992.

British titles
To 1994, George Bowman had won a record 17 Horse Teams titles at the National Driving Championships in the United Kingdom.

Polo
Highest handicap
The highest handicap to be based on six 7½-minute 'chukkas' is 10 goals, introduced in the USA in 1891 and in the United Kingdom and Argentina in 1910. A total of 56 players have received 10-goal handicaps. For the 1996 season, there are nine playing in the United Kingdom (seven Argentinians and two Mexican). The last (of six) 10-goal handicap

Most titles
The British Open Championship for the Cowdray Park Gold Cup has been won a record five times by Stowell Park (1973–74, 1976, 1978 and 1980) and by Tramontana (1986–89 and 1991).

Highest score
The highest ever aggregate number of goals scored in an international match is 30, attained when Argentina beat the USA by 21–9 at Meadowbrook, Long Island, New York, USA, in Sept 1936.

Most chukkas
The greatest number of chukkas to have been played on one ground in a single day is 43. This was achieved by the Pony Club on the Number 3 Ground at Kirtlington Park, Oxon, UK, on 31 July 1991.

Left
British show jumper David Broome won the King George V cup for a record sixth time on *Lannegan*. Broome was world champion in 1970 and represented Great Britain a record 106 times in Nations Cup events. His sister Elizabeth Edgar has won the Queen Elizabeth II Cup a record five times.

BRITISH HIGH JUMP RECORD OF 2.32 M WAS SET BY NICK SKELTON ON *LASTIC*

players from the United Kingdom was Gerald Matthew Balding, in 1939.

The highest handicap of a current British player is eight, by Howard Hipwood (who had a handicap of nine in 1992).

Claire J. Tomlinson of Gloucestershire, UK, attained a handicap of five, the highest ever by a woman, in 1986.

A match of two 40-goal teams has been staged on three occasions at Palermo, Buenos Aires, Argentina, in 1975, in the USA in 1990, and in Australia in 1991.

Field sports

LARGEST FRESHWATER FISH EVER CAUGHT WAS A STURGEON WEIGHING 212.28 KG

Right
On 9 May 1992 Howard L. Collins caught a record-breaking 18.25-kg (40-lb 4-oz) brown trout while fishing at Heber Springs, Arkansas, USA.

Far right
A black marlin weighing a record 707.61 kg (1,560 lb) was caught by Alfred C. Glassell Jr at Cabo Blanco, Peru, on 4 Aug 1953.

Below
Angling, which is one of the most popular British participant sports, includes both freshwater and marine fishing. The International Game Fish Association (IGFA) recognizes world records for a large number of species of game fish, both freshwater and saltwater.

Angling

Largest single catch
The largest officially ratified fish caught on a rod was a 5.13-m-long (16-ft 10-in) man-eating great white shark (*Carcharodon carcharias*) weighing 1,208.38 kg (2,664 lb), caught on a 59-kg (130-lb) test line by Alf Dean at Denial Bay, Ceduna, South Australia, in April 1959.

A 1,537-kg (3,388-lb) great white shark was caught by Clive Green off Albany, Western Australia, on 26 April 1976, but the record is unratified, since whale meat was used as bait.

The biggest fish caught on a rod by a British angler was a 620-kg (1,366-lb) great white shark, by Vic Samson at The Pales, South Australia, on 8 April 1989.

In 1978 a 6.2-m (20-ft 4-in) great white shark weighing more than 2,268 kg (5,000 lb) was harpooned and landed by fishermen in the harbour of San Miguel, Azores.

IGFA world records
New records recognized by the IGFA reached an annual peak of 1,074 in 1984. The heaviest freshwater category recognized is for the sturgeon, and a specimen with a record weight of 212.28 kg (468 lb) was caught by Joey Pallotta III on 9 July 1983 off Benicia, California, USA.

World Freshwater Championship
France won 13 world titles between 1959 and 1995 and the European title in 1956.

The individual title has been won a record three times by Robert Tesse (France), in 1959, 1960 and 1965, and by Bob Nudd (England), in 1990, 1991 and 1994.

The record weight (team) is 34.71 kg (76 lb 10⅕ oz) in three hours, by West Germany on the River Neckar at Mannheim, Germany, on 21 Sept 1980.

The record weight by an individual is 16.99 kg (37 lb 9 oz), by Wolf-Rüdiger Kremkus (West Germany) at Mannheim on 20 Sept 1980.

LARGEST FISH CAUGHT ON A ROD WAS A GREAT WHIT[E]

In 1967, Belgian Jacques Isenbaert caught a record 652 fish at Dunaújváros, Hungary.

Casting
The longest ever freshwater cast under ICF rules is 175.01 m (574 ft 2 in), by Walter Kummerow (West Germany), for the Bait Distance Double-Handed 30-g event at Lenzerheide, Switzerland, in 1968. On the same occasion, Andy Dickison set a British national record of 148.78 m (488 ft 1 in).

At the currently contested weight of 17.7 g—known as

18-g bait distance—the longest double-handed cast is 139.31 m (457 ft ½ in), by Kevin Carriero (USA) at Toronto, Canada, on 24 July 1984.

The British record for the fixed-spool reel is 138.79 m (455 ft 3 in), by Hugh Newton at Peterborough, Cambs, UK, on 21 Sept 1985.

The British record for the multiplier reel is 108.97 m (357 ft 6 in), by James Tomlinson at Torrington, Devon, UK, on 27 April 1985.

The longest fly distance double-handed cast is 97.28 m (319 ft 1 in), by Wolfgang Feige (West Germany) at Toronto, Canada, on 23 July 1984.

Hywel Morgan set a British national record of 91.22 m (299 ft 2 in) at Torrington, Devon, UK, on 27 April 1985.

The British Surfcasting Federation record is 257.32 m (844 ft 3 in), by Neil Mackellow at Peterborough, Cambs, UK, on 1 Sept 1985.

Fly fishing, World Championships
The most team titles is five, by Italy in 1982, 1983, 1984, 1986 and 1992.

The most individual titles is two, by Brian Leadbetter (GB) in 1987 and 1991.

Best freshwater cast 175.01 m

Hunting

Largest pack
When hunting six days a week, the Duke of Beaufort's hounds, maintained at Badminton, Glos, UK, since 1786, had 120 couples of hounds. The 10th Duke was Master of Foxhounds for a record 60 years (1924 until his death in 1984) and hunted on 3,895 days from 1920 to 1967.

Longest hunt
In Jan or Feb 1743, a hunt held by Squire Sandys is reputed to have covered 128 km (80 miles) from Holmbank, Lancs, to Ulpha, Cumbria, UK, in six hours.

Charlton Hunt (W Sussex, UK) ran from East Dean Wood to a kill more than 92 km (57¼ miles) away in 10 hr 5 min in Jan 1738.

Game shooting

Largest tally to a single sportsman
A record 556,813 head of game fell to the guns of the 2nd Marquess of Ripon between 1867 and the morning of 22 Sept 1923, when he dropped dead on a grouse moor after shooting his 52nd bird.

Thomas, 6th Baron Walsingham, bagged a one-day record for a single gun of 1,070 grouse in Yorkshire, UK, on 30 Aug 1888.

Beagling
Jean Bethel 'Betty' McKeever was sole Master of the Blean Beagles in Kent, UK, from the age of eight in 1909 until her death in 1990.

HARK WEIGHING 1,208 KG

WORLD ANGLING RECORDS

FRESHWATER AND SALTWATER FISH:
A selection of All-Tackle records ratified by the International Game Fish Association at Nov 1995

Barracuda, Great: 38.55 kg (85 lb)
John W. Helfrich
Christmas Island, Kiribati, 11 April 1992
Bass, Striped: 35.6 kg (78 lb 8 oz)
Albert R. McReynolds
Atlantic City, New Jersey, USA, 21 Sept 1982
Catfish, Flathead: 41.39 kg (91 lb 4 oz)
Mike Rogers
Lake Lewisville, Texas, USA, 28 March 1982
Cod, Atlantic: 44.79 kg (98 lb 12 oz)
Alphonse J. Bielevich
Isle of Shoals, New Hampshire, USA, 8 June 1969
Conger: 60.44 kg (133 lb 4 oz)
Vic Evans
Berry Head, Devon, UK, 5 June 1995
Halibut, Pacific: 166.92 kg (368 lb)
Celia H. Dueitt
Gustavus, Alaska, USA, 5 July 1991
Mackerel, King: 40.82 kg (90 lb)
Norton I. Thomton
Key West, Florida, USA, 16 Feb 1976
Marlin, Black: 707.61 kg (1,560 lb)
Alfred C. Glassell Jr
Cabo Blanco, Peru, 4 Aug 1953
Pike, Northern: 25 kg (55 lb 1 oz)
Lothar Louis
Lake of Grefeern, Germany, 16 Oct 1986
Sailfish (Pacific): 100.24 kg (221 lb)
C. W. Stewart
Santa Cruz Island, Ecuador, 12 Feb 1947
Salmon, Atlantic: 35.89 kg (79 lb 2 oz)
Henrik Henriksen
Tana River, Norway, 1928
Shark, Hammerhead: 449.5 kg (991 lb)
Allen Ogle
Sarasota, Florida, USA, 30 May 1982
Shark, Porbeagle: 230 kg (507 lb)
Christopher Bennett
Pentland Firth, Caithness, UK, 9 March 1993
Shark, Thresher: 363.8 kg (802 lb)
Dianne North
Tutukaka, New Zealand, 8 Feb 1981
Shark, Great White: 1,208.38 kg (2,664 lb)
Alfred Dean
Ceduna, South Australia, 21 April 1959
Sturgeon, White: 212.28 kg (468 lb)
Joey Pallotta III
Benicia, California, USA, 9 July 1983
Swordfish: 536.15 kg (1,182 lb)
L. Marron
Iquique, Chile, 17 May 1953
Trout, Brook: 6.57 kg (14 lb 8 oz)
Dr W. J. Cook
Nipigon River, Ontario, Canada, July 1916
Trout, Brown: 18.25 kg (40 lb 4 oz)
Howard L. Collins
Heber Springs, Arkansas, USA, 9 May 1992
Trout, Lake: 30.16 kg (66 lb 8 oz)
Rodney Harback
Great Bear Lake, NWT, Canada, 19 July 1991
Trout, Rainbow: 19.1 kg (42 lb 2 oz)
David Robert White
Bell Island, Alaska, USA, 22 June 1970
Tuna, Bluefin: 679 kg (1,496 lb)
Ken Fraser
Aulds Cove, Nova Scotia, Canada, 26 Oct 1979
Tuna, Yellowfin: 176.35 kg (388 lb 12 oz)
Curt Wiesenhutter
San Benedicto Island, Mexico, 1 April 1977
Wahoo: 70.53 kg (155 lb 8 oz)
William Bourne
San Salvador, Bahamas, 3 April 1990

BRITISH ANGLING RECORDS

COARSE FISH:
A selection of fish recognized by the National Association of Specialist Anglers

Barbel: 7.314 kg (16 lb 2 oz)
P. Woodhouse
River Medway, Kent, 1994
Bleak: 0.120 kg (4 oz 4 dr)
B. Derrington
River Monnow, Wye Mouth, 1982
Bream: 7.512 kg (16 lb 9 oz)
M. McKeown
Southern water, 1991
Bream, Silver: 0.425 kg (15 oz)
D. E. Flack
Grime Spring, Lakenheath, Suffolk, 1988
Carp: 25.06 kg (55 lb 4 oz)
A. White
Mid Northants water, 1995
Carp, Grass: 11.453 kg (25 lb 4 oz)
D. Buck
Honeycroft Fisheries, Canterbury, Kent, 1993
Catfish (Wells): 25.968 kg (57 lb 4 oz)
R. Coote
Withy Pool, Beds, 1995
Chub: 3.912 kg (8 lb 10 oz)
P. Smith
River Tees, 1994
Dace: 0.574 kg (1 lb 4 oz 4 dr)
J. L. Gasson
Little Ouse, Thetford, Norfolk, 1960
Eel: 5.046 kg (11 lb 2 oz)
S. Terry
Kingfisher Lake, Ringwood, Hants, 1978
Gudgeon: 0.141 kg (5 oz)
D. Hall
River Nadder, Salisbury, Wilts, 1990
Orfe, Golden: 3.373 kg (7 lb 7 oz)
D. Smith
Horton Pool, 1995
Perch: 2.523 kg (5 lb 9 oz)
J. Shayler
Private water, Kent, 1985
Pike: 21.236 kg (46 lb 13 oz)
R. Lewis
Llandefgfedd Reservoir, Pontypool, Gwent, 1992
Roach: 1.899 kg (4 lb 3 oz)
R. N. Clarke
Dorset Stour, 1990
Stickleback: 0.005 kg (3 dr)
M. Drinkwater
River Calder, Brighouse, W Yorkshire, 1995
Tench: 6.548 kg (14 lb 7 oz)
G. Bevan
Southern stillwater, 1993
Zander (Pikeperch): 8.448 kg (18 lb 10 oz)
R. Armstrong
River Severn, 1993

FRESHWATER GAME FISH:
Salmon: 29.03 kg (64 lb)
Miss G. W. Ballantine
River Tay, Scotland, 1922
Trout, American Brook: 2.65 kg (5 lb 13 oz 8 dr)
A. Pearson
Avington Fishery, Hants, 1981
Trout, Brown: 11.51 kg (25 lb 6 oz)
A. Finlay
Loch Awe, Argyll and Bute, 1996
Trout, Rainbow: 10.96 kg (24 lb 2 oz 13 dr)
J. Moore
Pennine Trout Fishery, Littleborough, Lancs, 1990
Trout, Sea: 10.2 kg (22 lb 8 oz)
S. Burgoyne
River Leven, 1989

Animal sports

Fastest pigeon 177.14 km/h

Right
The first greyhound race meeting was held at Hendon, London, UK, in Sept 1876. The sport was revolutionized by perfecting the use of a mechanical hare in 1919. The fastest speed achieved by a greyhound is 67.32 km/h (41.83 mph).

Below
Racing pigeons are expected to achieve an average speed of 56–64 km/h (35–40 mph) during a race. In favourable conditions, however, speeds in excess of 145 km/h (90 mph) can be attained.

Greyhound racing
Derby
Two dogs have won the English Greyhound Derby twice: *Mick the Miller*, on 25 July 1929 (when owned by Albert H. Williams) and 28 June 1930 (owned by Arundel H. Kempton), and *Patricia's Hope*, on 24 June 1972 (owned by Gordon and Basil Marks and Brian Stanley) and 23 June 1973 (owned by G. and B. Marks and J. O'Connor).

Grand National
The only dog to win the Grand National three times is *Sherry's Prince* (owned by Joyce Mathews of Surrey, UK), from 1970 to 1972.

Derby 'triple'
The only dogs to win the English, Scottish and Welsh Derby 'triple' are *Trev's Perfection*, owned by Fred Trevillion, in 1947; *Mile Bush Pride*, owned by Noel W. Purvis, in 1959, and *Patricia's Hope* in 1972.

Fastest greyhound
The highest timed speed is 366 m (400 yd) in 19.57 sec, or 67.32 km/h (41.83 mph), by *Star Title* on the straightaway track at Wyong, NSW, Australia, on 5 March 1994.

The highest speed recorded in the United Kingdom is 63.37 km/h (39.38 mph), by *Ravage Again*, when it covered a two-bend, 250-m (273-yd) course in 14.2 seconds at Belle Vue, Greater Manchester.

The fastest automatically timed speed for a full four-bend race is 62.59 km/h (38.89 mph) at Hove, E Sussex, UK, by *Glen Miner* on 4 May 1982. It covered 515 m (563 yd) in 29.62 sec.

The top speed over hurdles is 60.58 km/h (37.78 mph), by *Lord Westlands*, at Hove, E Sussex, UK.

Most wins
The most career wins is 143 by the American greyhound *JR's Ripper* from 1982 to 1986.

The most consecutive victories is 37, by *JJ Doc Richard*, owned by Jack Boyd, at Mobile, Alabama, USA, to 29 May 1995.

The British best is 32, including 16 track record times, from Aug 1984 to 9 Dec 1986, by *Ballyregan Bob*, owned by Cliff Kevern and trained by George Curtis. His race wins were by an average of more than nine lengths.

Top earnings and prizes
The career earnings record is $297,000 (£162,535), by *Homespun Rowdy* (1984–87).

The highest first prize for a race is $125,000 (£84,079), won by *Ben G Speedboat* in the Great Greyhound Race of Champions at Seabrook, New Hampshire, USA, in Aug 1986.

Harness racing
Most successful driver
In North American harness-racing history, Hervé Filion of Québec, Canada, has achieved a record 14,685 wins to 17 May 1995.

The most wins in a year is 843, by Walter Case (USA) in 1992.

The top career earnings are $130,945,655 (£82,547,850), by John D. Campbell (USA) to 17 May 1995. This includes a record of $11,620,878 (£18,434,199) in one year in 1990, when he won 543 races.

Top prices, winnings and prizes
The most expensive pacer is *Nihilator*, which was syndicated in 1984 by Wall Street Stable and Almahurst Stud Farm for the sum of $19.2 million (£16,171,145).

The highest price ever paid for a trotter is $6 million (£3,281,917) for *Mack Lobell*, by John Erik Magnusson of Vislanda, Sweden, in 1988.

The greatest ever winnings is $4,907,307 (£3,158,668), by the trotter *Peace Corps* from 1988 to 1993.

The greatest amount won by a pacer is $3,225,653 (£2,230,588), by *Nihilator*, from 1984 to 1985.

The single season records are $2,264,714 (£1,907,449) by pacer *Cam's Card Shark* in 1994 and $1,878,798 (£1,028,183) by trotter *Mack Lobell* in 1987.

The largest ever purse was $2,161,000 (£1,644,597), for the Woodrow Wilson two-year-old race over one mile at the Meadowlands, New Jersey, USA, on 16 Aug 1984. Of this, a record $1,080,500 (£822,298) went to the winner *Nihilator*.

Pigeon racing

Longest flights
The official British duration record (flying into the United Kingdom) is a distance of 1,887 km (1,173 miles) in 15 days, by *C.S.O.*, in the 1976 Palamos Race.

The longest homing flight was claimed for a pigeon owned by the first Duke of Wellington. Released from a ship off the Ichabo Islands, West Africa, on 8 April 1845, it dropped dead a mile from its loft at Nine Elms, Wandsworth, Greater London, UK, on 1 June, 55 days later, having apparently covered about 8,700 km (5,400 miles), but possibly 11,250 km (7,000 miles) to avoid the Sahara Desert.

In 1990 it was reported that a pigeon owned by David Lloyd and George Workman of Nantyffyllon, Bridgend, UK, had flown a distance of 10,860 km (6,750 miles) from Lerwick, Shetland, UK, to Shanghai, China—possibly the longest non-homing flight ever.

Highest speeds
The highest race speed on record is 177.14 km/h (110.07 mph), in an East

Highest-priced
The highest sum paid is £110,800, to Jan Herman of Waalre, Netherlands, in July 1992 by Louella Pigeon World of Markfield, Leics, UK, for a four-year-old cock bird. The pigeon, subsequently named *Invincible Spirit,* had won the 1992 Barcelona International race.

Biggest mass release
The largest ever simultaneous release of pigeons was at Orleans, France, in Aug 1988, when more than 215,000 pigeons were released for a Dutch National race.

The biggest release in the United Kingdom took place at Beachy Head near Eastbourne, E Sussex, on 11 May 1991, when 42,500 birds were released for the Save The Children Fund Eastbourne Classic.

Rodeo

Largest rodeo
The National Finals Rodeo, organized by the Professional Rodeo Cowboys Association (PRCA) and the Women's Professional Rodeo Association (WPRA) had a paid attendance of

The most prize money won in a season is $297,896 (£199,877), by Ty Murray in 1993.

Youngest champions
The youngest world titleholder is Anne Lewis, who was 10 years old when she won the WPRA barrel racing title in 1968.

Ty Murray is the youngest cowboy to win the PRCA All-Around Champion title, at the age of 20 in 1989.

Bull riding
The highest score was 100 points of a possible 100, by Wade Leslie on *Wolfman Skoal* at Central Point, Oregon, USA, in 1991.

The top bucking bull *Red Rock* dislodged 312 riders between 1980 and 1988, and was finally ridden to the eight-second bell by Lane Frost on 20 May 1988.

Saddle bronc riding
The highest score in a saddle bronc ride is 95 of a possible 100, by Doug Vold on *Transport* at Meadow Lake, Saskatchewan, Canada, in 1979.

TOP BUCKING BULL *RED ROCK* DISLODGED A TOTAL OF 312 RIDERS

Left and far left
Rodeo developed from the ranching skills used in the North American cattle industry. In the bull-riding event, as for all riding events in professional rodeo, the aim is to ride the bull until a bell is rung, after eight seconds.

Anglian Federation Race from E Croydon, Surrey, UK, on 8 May 1965. The 1,428 birds were backed by a powerful south-south-west wind, and the winner was owned by A. Vigeon & Son.

The highest speed ever recorded in a race over a distance of more than 1,000 km (621⅖ miles) is 133.46 km/h (82.93 mph), by a hen in the Central Cumberland Combine race over a distance of 1,099.316 km (683 miles 147 yd) between Murray Bridge, South Australia, and North Ryde, Sydney, Australia, on 2 Oct 1971.

Career record
The greatest competitive distance flown in a single career is 32,318 km (20,082 miles), by *Nunnies*, a chequer cock owned by Terry Haley of Abbot's Langley, Herts, UK.

171,414 for 10 performances in the 1991 Finals, when a record $2.6 million (£1,400,000) in prize money was offered.

Most world titles
The record number of all-around titles (awarded to the leading money winner in a single season in two or more events) in the PRCA World Championships is six, by: Larry Mahan (USA), 1966–70 and 1973; Tom Ferguson (USA), 1974–79; and Ty Murray (USA), 1989–94.

Jim Shoulders of Henrietta, Texas, USA, won a record 16 World Championships at four events between 1949 and 1959.

Top earnings
Roy Cooper achieved record career earnings of $1,510,795 (£968,893), 1975–94.

Bareback riding
Joe Alexander of Cora, Wyoming, USA, scored 93 of a possible 100 on *Marlboro* at Cheyenne, Wyoming, in 1974.

Sled dog racing

Oldest
The oldest established sled dog trail is the 1,688-km (1,049-mile) Iditarod Trail from Anchorage to Nome, Alaska, USA, which has existed since 1910 and been home to an annual race since 1967. The fastest time for the race was set by Doug Swingley (USA) in March 1995, with 9 days 2 hr 42 min 19 sec.

Longest
The world's longest race is the 2,000-km (1,243-mile) Berengia Trail from Esso to Markovo, Russia.

Motor racing

FASTEST OVERALL AVERAGE SPEED REACHED IN A GRAND PRIX IS 242.623 KM/H

Grand Prix

Most successful drivers

The World Drivers' Championship has been won a record five times by Juan-Manuel Fangio (Argentina), in 1951 and from 1954 to 1957. He retired in 1958, having won 24 Grand Prix races (two shared) from 51 starts.

Alain Prost (France) holds the record for both the most Grand Prix points in a career (798.5) and the most Grand Prix victories (51), from a total of 199 races between 1980 and 1993.

The most Grand Prix victories in a year is nine, by Nigel Mansell (GB) in 1992 and Michael Schumacher (Germany) in 1995.

The most Grand Prix starts is 256, by Ricardo Patrese (Italy) from 1977 to 1993.

on 14 July 1946, at the age of 53 years and 240 days.

The oldest Grand Prix driver was Louis Alexandre Chiron (Monaco), who finished sixth in the Monaco Grand Prix on 22 May 1955, aged 55 years 292 days.

The youngest to qualify for a Grand Prix was Michael Thackwell (New Zealand), in Canada on 28 Sept 1980, aged 19 years 182 days.

Most successful manufacturers
Ferrari of Italy have won a record eight manufacturers' World Championships (1961, 1964, 1975–77, 1979 and 1982–83).

Ferrari also hold the record for the most race wins, at 106 by June 1996.

Closest finish
The smallest ever winning margin in a World Championship race was when Peter Gethin (GB) beat Ronnie Peterson (Sweden) by just 0.01 seconds in the Italian Grand Prix at Monza on 5 Sept 1971.

Ayrton Senna (Brazil) beat Nigel Mansell (GB) by 0.014 seconds in the Spanish Grand Prix on 13 April 1986. (Since 1982 timing for all races has been to thousandths).

British Grand Prix
Fastest speed
The fastest time is 1 hr 18 min 10.436 sec, at an average speed of 235.405 km/h (146.274 mph), by Alain Prost in a McLaren at Silverstone on 21 July 1985.

WORLD'S LONGEST EVER RALLY, THE SINGAPORE AIRLINES LONDON–SYDNE

The greatest number of pole positions is 65, by Ayrton Senna (Brazil), from a total of 161 races (41 wins) between 1985 and 1994.

Oldest and youngest drivers
The youngest world champion was Emerson Fittipaldi (Brazil), who won his first title on 10 Sept 1972 at the age of 25 years 273 days.

The oldest world champion was Juan-Manuel Fangio, who won his last World Championship on 4 Aug 1957, aged 46 years 41 days.

The youngest Grand Prix winner was Bruce Leslie McLaren (New Zealand), who won the United States Grand Prix at Sebring, Florida, on 12 Dec 1959, aged 22 years 104 days.

Troy Ruttman (USA) was 22 years 80 days old when he won the Indianapolis 500 (then part of the World Championships) on 30 May 1952.

The oldest Grand Prix winner (pre-World Championship) was Tazio Giorgio Nuvolari (Italy), who won the Albi Grand Prix in France

The most successes by one team since the institution of the Constructor's Championship in 1958 was 15 of the 16 grands prix, by McLaren in 1988. Ayrton Senna had eight wins and three seconds, Alain Prost had seven wins and seven seconds, and McLaren amassed more than three times the points of its nearest rival, Ferrari.

Excluding the Indianapolis 500 race, then included in the World Drivers' Championship, Ferrari won all seven races in 1952 and the first eight (of nine) in 1953.

Fastest race
The fastest overall average speed for a Grand Prix race is 242.623 km/h (150.759 mph), by Peter Gethin (GB) in a BRM in the Italian Grand Prix at Monza on 5 Sept 1971.

The record for the fastest ever qualifying lap is 1 min 05.59 sec at an average speed of 258.802 km/h (160.817 mph), by Keke Rosberg (Finland) in a Williams–Honda in the British Grand Prix on 20 July 1985.

Most wins
The most wins by one driver is five, by Jim Clark (1962–65 and 1967) in Lotus cars.

Jim Clark and Jack Brabham (Australia) have both won the race on three different circuits: Brands Hatch, Silverstone and Aintree.

The most wins by a manufacturer is 10, by Ferrari (1951–54, 1956, 1958, 1961, 1976, 1978 and 1990).

Le Mans
Greatest distance
Dr Helmut Marko (Austria) and Gijs van Lennep (Netherlands) covered 5,333.565 km (3,314 miles 216 yd) in a Porsche 917K in the 24-hour Grand Prix d'Endurance at Le Mans, France, on 12 and 13 June 1971.

Fastest race lap
The fastest time over the 13.536-km (8-mile 723-yd) lap is 3 min 21.27 sec, at an average speed of 242.093 km/h (150.429 mph), by

Alain Ferté (France) in a Jaguar XRJ-9 on 10 June 1989.

On 14 June 1985, Hans Stück (West Germany) achieved the fastest practice lap speed of 251.664 km/h (156.377 mph).

Most wins
The race has been won by Porsche cars a record 14 times (1970–71, 1976–77, 1979, 1981–87, 1993 and 1996).

The greatest number of wins by one driver is six, by Jacques Bernard 'Jacky' Ickx (Belgium), 1969, 1975–77 and 1981–82.

Indianapolis 500
Most successful drivers
The most wins is four, by Anthony Joseph 'A. J.' Foyt Jr (USA) in 1961, 1964, 1967 and 1977; Al Unser Sr (USA) in 1970, 1971,

Highest prizes
The highest prize fund is $8,028,247 (£5,086,642), in 1995.

The individual prize record is $1,373,813 (£896,218), by Al Unser Jr in 1994.

Rallying
Longest
The Singapore Airlines London–Sydney Rally covered a total distance of 31,107 km (19,329 miles) from Covent Garden, London, UK, to Sydney Opera House, Australia, between 14 Aug and 28 Sept 1977. It was won by Andrew Cowan, Colin Malkin and Michael Broad in a Mercedes 280E.

The longest annual race is Kenya's Safari Rally, won a record five times by Shekhar Mehta (1973, 1979–82). The 17th Safari, in 1971, covered 6,234 km (3,874 miles).

Drag racing
Piston-engined (NHRA events)
The lowest elapsed time on record by a piston-engined dragster from a standing start for 440 yd (402 m) is 4.445 seconds, by Larry Dixon (USA) at Englishtown, New Jersey, USA, on 19 May 1995.

The highest terminal velocity at the end of a 440-yd run is 506.07 km/h (314.46 mph), by Kenny Bernstein (USA), at Pomona, California, USA, on 30 Oct 1994.

The lowest elapsed time for a petrol-driven piston-engined car is 6.988 seconds, by Kurt Johnson (USA), at Englishtown, New Jersey, USA, on 21 May 1994.

The highest terminal velocity for a petrol-driven, piston-engined car is 318.32 km/h (197.80 mph), by Darrell Alderman (USA) at Somona, California, USA, on 27 July 1994.

Far left
Damon Hill (GB) sprays Michael Schumacher (Germany) after winning the 1996 San Marino Grand Prix. Schumacher had the most to celebrate in 1995, winning a record nine races in the season.

Below left
Colin McRae, driving a Subaru Impreza, became the youngest winner of the rallying world championship, clinching the title by winning the last event of the 1995 season, the RAC Rally.

SMALLEST WINNING MARGIN IN A WORLD CHAMPIONSHIP RACE IS 0.014 SECONDS

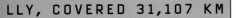

LLY, COVERED 31,107 KM

1978 and 1987; and Rick Ravon Mears (USA) in 1979, 1984, 1988 and 1991.

A. J. Foyt Jr started in a record 35 races, between 1958 and 1992.

Rick Mears has started from pole position a record-breaking six times (1979, 1982, 1986, 1988, 1989 and 1991).

Fastest time
The record time is 2 hr 41 min 18.404 sec (299.307 km/h or 185.981 mph), by Arie Luyendyk (Netherlands) driving a Lola-Chevrolet on 27 May 1990.

The record average speed for four-laps qualifying is 381.392 km/h (236,986 mph) by Arie Luyendyk in a Reynard-Ford-Cosworth on 12 May 1996. This included a one-lap record of 382.216 km/h (237.498 mph).

The track speed record is 385.051 km/h (239.260 mph), set by Arie Luyendyk on 9 May 1996.

Monte Carlo
The rally has been won a record four times by Sandro Munari (Italy), in 1972, 1975, 1976 and 1977; and Walter Röhrl (West Germany), in 1980, 1982, 1983 and 1984.

RAC Rally
Hannu Mikkola (Finland), with co-driver Arne Hertz (Sweden), has had a record four wins, in a Ford Escort in 1978 and 1979 and an Audi Quattro in 1981 and 1982.

World Championship
Juha Kankkunen (Finland) has won the World Championship on a record four occasions (1986–87, 1991 and 1993).

The most wins in World Championship races is 21, by Juha Kankkunen (Finland).

The most wins in a season is six, by Didier Auriol (France) in 1992.

A record eleven manufacturers' titles were won by Lancia between 1972 and 1992.

The youngest winner is Colin McRae (GB), at the age of 27 years 89 days in 1995.

The lowest elapsed time for a petrol-driven piston-engined motorcycle is 7.532 seconds, by David Schultz (USA) at Reading, Pennsylvania, USA, on 18 Sept 1993. The highest terminal velocity for this type of vehicle is 292.66 km/h (181.85 mph), achieved by David Schultz (USA), at Reading on 19 Sept 1993.

Other races
Oldest races
The oldest race that is still regularly run is the RAC Tourist Trophy on the Isle of Man, which was first staged on 14 Sept 1905.

The oldest continental race is the French Grand Prix, first held on 26 and 27 June 1906.

The Coppa Florio in Sicily has been held on an irregular basis since 1906.

Fastest race
The fastest race is the Busch Clash at Daytona, Florida, USA, on a 4-km (2½-mile) 31-degree banked track over 80.5 km (50 miles). Bill Elliott averaged 318.331 km/h (197.802 mph) in a Ford Thunderbird in 1987.

Motorcycling and speedway

BARRY SHEENE LAPPED THE 14.12-KM FRANCORCHAMPS CIRCUIT IN A RECORD 3 MIN 50.3 SEC

Right
In speedway competitions, four riders compete over four laps of dirt track in a series of heats. League racing was introduced to British speedway in 1929 and consisted of a Southern League and a Northern Dirt Track League. The World Championship was inaugurated at Wembley, London, UK, in 1936.

Below right
Giacomo Agostini (b.1942) is the only rider to have won two motorcycle racing world titles in five consecutive years (the 350 cc and 500 cc titles between 1968 and 1972).

Motorcycle racing

Oldest race and longest circuit
The oldest annually contested motorcycle races are the Auto-Cycle Union Tourist Trophy (TT) series, which were first held on the 25.44-km (15-mile 1,425-yd) 'Peel' (St John's) course on the Isle of Man on 28 May 1907. Since 1911 they have been run on the 'Mountain' circuit, which at 60.72 km (37 mile 1,285 yd) is also the longest circuit used for any motorcycle race. It has 264 curves and corners.

Fastest circuits
The highest average lap speed attained on any closed circuit is 257.958 km/h (160.288 mph), by Yvon du Hamel (Canada) on a modified 903 cc four-cylinder Kawasaki Z1 at the 31-degree banked 4.02-km (2½-mile) Daytona International Speedway, Florida, USA, in March 1973.

The fastest road circuit was the 14.12-km (8-mile 1,355-yd) Francorchamps near Spa, Belgium, which was lapped in 3 min 50.3 sec, at an average speed of 220.721 km/h (137.150 mph), by Barry Sheene (GB) on a 495 cc four-cylinder Suzuki. This was during the Belgian Grand Prix in 1977, when he set a record time of 38 min 58.5 sec for this 10-lap, 141.20-km (87-mile 1,302-yd) race.

The fastest British circuit was the 4.453-km (2.767-mile) outer circuit at the Brooklands Motor Course near Weybridge, Surrey, which was open from 1907 to 1939. The lap record was 80 seconds (giving an average speed of 200.37 km/h or 124.51 mph), by Noel Baddow 'Bill' Pope (GB) on a Brough Superior powered by a supercharged 996 cc V-twin '8-80' JAP engine developing 110 bhp in 1939.

The fastest British circuit in current use consists of the public roads over which the

Ulster Grand Prix is held at Dundrod, Co. Antrim. In Aug 1990 Steve Hislop (Scotland) set an overall average speed of 195.48 km/h (121.46 mph) for the 'King of the Road' race and in Aug 1994 Jason Griffiths (Wales) set a lap record of 202.94 km/h (126.10 mph).

Most World Championship titles
The most world titles is 15, by Giacomo Agostini (Italy): seven at 350 cc, from 1968 to 1974, and eight at 500 cc, from 1966 to 1972 and in 1975.

Angel Roldan Nieto (Spain) won a record seven 125 cc titles (1971–72, 1979 and 1981–84), and a record six titles at 50 cc (1969–70, 1972 and 1975–77).

British motorcyclist Phil Read won a record-breaking four 250 cc titles, in 1964, 1965, 1968 and 1971.

Rolf Biland (Switzerland) won a record seven world side-car titles, 1978–79, 1981, 1983 and 1992–94.

Giacomo Agostini (Italy) won 122 races (68 at 500 cc, 54 at 350 cc) in the World Championship series between 24 April 1965 and 25 Sept 1977, including a record 19 in 1970—a season's total also achieved by Mike Hailwood in 1966.

The record number of career wins for any one class is 79, by Rolf Biland at side-car.

Youngest World Champion
Italian rider Loris Capirossi was 17 years 165 days old when he won the 125 cc title on 16 Sept 1990.

Oldest World Champion
Hermann-Peter Müller (West Germany) won the 250 cc title in 1955 at the age of 46.

Most successful machines
Japanese Yamaha machines won 45 World Championships between 1964 and 1992.

Most Tourist Trophy wins
The most wins in the Isle of Man TT races is 21, by William 'Joey' Dunlop (Ireland) from 1977 to 1996.

The first man to win three consecutive TT titles in two events was James A. Redman (Rhodesia), who won the 250 cc and 350 cc events from 1963 to 1965.

The most events won in one year is four (Formula One, Junior, Senior and Production) by Philip McCallen (Ireland), in 1996.

Fastest Tourist Trophy speed
The Isle of Man TT circuit speed record is 198.93 km/h (123.61 mph), by Carl George

GREATEST NUMBER OF CAREER WINS IN ONE CLASS IS 7?

Moto-cross
Most World Championships
Joël Robert (Belgium) won a record-breaking six 250 cc Moto-cross World Championship titles, in 1964 and from 1968 to 1972. Between 25 April 1964 and 18 June 1972 he also won a record 50 250 cc Grand Prix races.

Belgian motorcyclist Eric Geboers (Belgium) is the only person to have won each of the three categories of the Moto-Cross World Championships: 125 cc in 1982 and 1983, 250 cc in 1987 and 500 cc in 1988 and 1990.

Youngest champion
The youngest ever winner of the Moto-Cross World Championships was Dave Strijbos (Netherlands), who rode to victory in the 125 cc title at the age of 18 years 296 days on 31 Aug 1986.

Speedway
Most appearances and points
Barry Briggs (New Zealand) made a record 18 appearances in the world finals between 1954 and 1970 and in 1972. He won the world title in 1957, 1958, 1964 and 1966 and scored a record total of 201 points from 87 races.

Most world titles
The record for the greatest number of wins in the World Championship is six, by Ivan Gerald Mauger (New Zealand) from 1968 to 1970 and in 1972, 1977 and 1979.

The World Pairs Championships (renamed the World Team Championships in 1994) have been won a record nine times by Denmark, in 1979, from 1985 to 1991 and in 1995.

The former World Team Cup was won a record nine times by both England/Great Britain (as Great Britain in 1968 and from 1971 to 1973 and as England from 1974 to 1975 and in 1977, 1980 and 1989) and by Denmark (in 1978, 1981, from 1983 to 1988 and in 1991).

Hans Hollen Nielsen (Denmark) is the most successful rider in World Championship competitions, with eight Team (formerly Pairs), nine Team and four individual world titles for a record total of 21.

In 1985 Erik Gundersen (Denmark) became the first person to ever hold world titles for the individual, pairs, team and long-track events simultaneously.

Most British league titles
The Wembley Lions hold the record for the greatest number of National League victories, with eight, in 1932, from 1946 to 1947 and from 1949 to 1953.

In 1965, the National League was replaced by the British League, which Belle Vue (who had six National League wins, from 1933 to 1936 and in 1939 and 1963) have won a record five times, including three consecutive times from 1970 to 1972.

Belle Vue (Manchester) had a record nine victories (1933–37, 1946–47, 1949 and 1958) in the National Trophy Knock-out Competition (held from 1931 to 1964).

The National Trophy Knock-out Competition was replaced in 1965 by the Knock Out Cup, which has been won a record eight times (one shared) by Cradley Heath.

Most consecutive British league wins
Oxford set a record of 28 successive wins in the British League in 1986.

Highest British league scores
The highest score recorded in league racing was when Berwick beat Exeter 78–18 in the 16-heat formula for the National League on 27 May 1989.

A maximum possible score was achieved by Bristol when they defeated Glasgow (White City) 70–14 on 7 Oct 1949 in the National League Division Two.

The highest score in the Knock Out Cup was 81–25, when Hull beat Sheffield in 1979.

Individual score for a season
The record for the highest number of league points scored by an individual in one season is 563, by Hans Nielsen for Oxford in the British League in 1988.

Highest career score
The league career scoring record is 6,471 points by Nigel Boocock, from 1955 to 1980.

British League Rider's Championship
Ivan Mauger holds the record for the most appearances, at 15, and the most points scored, at 146, between 1965 and 1979.

The record for the greatest number of wins is six by Barry Briggs, from 1965 to 1970.

Leicester are the only team to have used the same seven riders in a complete league programme. This was in 1969 when the same seven riders rode in all of the 36 matches.

Tests
The only rider to have scored maximum points in every match of a Test series was Arthur 'Bluey' Wilkinson, in five matches for Australia against England in Sydney in the 1937/8 season.

Left
Irish motorcyclist Joey Dunlop (b. 1952) has won a record 21 victories in Isle of Man TT races.

Y ROLF BILAND AT SIDE-CAR

Fogarty on 12 June 1992. On the same occasion Steve Hislop set the race speed record of 1 hr 51 min 59.6 sec, with an average speed of 195.18 km/h (121.28 mph), to win the 1992 Senior TT on a Norton.

The fastest woman around the 'Mountain' circuit is Sandra Barnett (GB), who achieved a speed of 179.86 km/h (111.76 mph) in the Senior TT on 10 June 1994.

Most World Trials Championships
The record for the most World Trials Championships titles is six, by Jordi Tarrès (Spain), in 1987, 1989, 1990, 1991, 1993 and 1994.

HANS HOLLEN NIELSEN HAS WON A RECORD 21 WORLD SPEEDWAY TITLES

Cycling

HIGHEST SPEED EVER ACHIEVED ON A BICYCLE IS 268.831 KM/H, BY FRED ROMPELBERG

Right
The Tour de France, the world's greatest cycle race, was first held in 1903. Riders cover the course, which varies each year, over a three-week period. More than 2 million spectators watch the race each year.

Highest altitude 6,960 m

Speed and distance

Highest speed
The highest speed ever achieved on a bicycle is 268.831 km/h (166.944 mph), by Fred Rompelberg (Netherlands) behind a windshield at Bonneville Salt Flats, Utah, USA, on 3 Oct 1995. Considerable help was provided by the slipstreaming effect of the lead vehicle.

The British speed record is 158.05 km/h (98.21 mph) over 200 m, by David Le Grys on a closed section of the M42 at Alvechurch, Warks, on 28 Aug 1985.

Michael Secrest covered 1,958.196 km (1,216 miles 1,349 yd) in 24 hours behind pace, at Phoenix International Raceway, Arizona, USA, on 26 and 27 April 1990.

Cross-America
The men's trans-America solo record is 8 days 8 hr 45 min, by Paul Selon over 5,000 km (3,107 miles) in the Race Across America from Costa Mesa, California, to New York, in Aug 1989.

The women's trans-America solo record is 9 days 9 hr 9 min, by Susan Notorangelo, also in the 1989 Race Across America.

Daniel Buettner, Bret Anderson, Martin Engel and Anne Knabe cycled the length of the Americas from Prudhoe Bay, Alaska, USA, to the Beagle Channel, Ushuaia, Argentina, between 8 Aug 1986 and 13 June 1987. They covered a total distance of 24,568 km (15,266 miles).

Endurance
In 1939 Thomas Edward Godwin (GB) covered 120,805 km (75,065 miles) in 365 days—an average of 330.96 km (205 miles 1,150 yd) per day. He then completed 160,934 km (100,000 miles) in 500 days to 14 May 1940.

From 1922 to 25 Dec 1973, Tommy Chambers of Glasgow, UK, rode a verified total of 1,286,517 km (799,405 miles).

Jay Aldous and Matt DeWaal cycled a distance of 22,997 km (14,290 miles) in 106 days on a round-the-world trip from This is the Place Monument, Salt Lake City, Utah, USA, from 2 April to 16 July 1984.

Tal Burt of Israel circumnavigated the world by bicycle, covering a total distance of 21,329 km (13,253 road miles) from Place du Trocadero, Paris, France, in a time of 77 days 14 hr, from 1 June to 17 Aug 1992.

Nick Sanders cycled a distance of 7,728 km (4,802 miles) around the United Kingdom in 22 days, between 10 June and 1 July 1984.

Cycle tours
The greatest authenticated number of people to have participated in a bicycle tour is 31,678, in the 90-km (56-mile) London to Brighton Bike Ride, UK, on 19 June 1988.

It has been estimated that in excess of 45,000 people participated in the 75-km (46-mile) Tour de l'Ile de Montréal, Canada, on 7 June 1992.

NARROWEST WINNING MARGI

Races

Most Olympic titles
The most gold medals won is three, by Paul Masson (France) in 1896, Francisco Verri (Italy) in 1906, Robert Charpentier (France) in 1936 and Daniel Morelon (France) in 1968 (two) and 1972.

In the 'unofficial' 1904 cycling programme, Marcus Latimer Hurley (USA) won four events.

World Championships
The most wins at one event is 10, by Koichi Nakano (Japan) for professional sprint from 1977 to 1986.

The greatest number of wins at a men's amateur event is seven, by Daniel Morelon (France), for sprint (1966–67, 1969–71, 1973 and 1975) and by Leon Meredith (GB) for the 100-km motor-paced race (1904–05, 1907–09, 1911 and 1913).

The record for the greatest number of women's titles is nine, by Jeannie Longo (France) for pursuit (1986 and 1988–89), road (1985–87, 1989 and 1995), points (1989) and time-trial (1995).

Most British titles
Beryl Burton was 25 times British all-round time-trial champion from 1959 to 1983, and won 72 individual road TT titles, 14 track-pursuit titles and 12 road-race titles to 1986.

Ian Hallam won a record 25 men's titles from 1969 to 1982.

Tour de France
The most wins is five by Jacques Anquetil (France), 1957 and 1961–64; Eddy Merckx (Belgium), 1969–72 and 1974; Bernard Hinault (France), 1978–79, 1981–82 and 1985; and Miguel Induráin (Spain), 1991–95.

In the closest Tour de France, Greg LeMond (USA) completed the race in 87 hr 38 min 35 sec, beating Laurent Fignon (France) by eight seconds after 3,267 km (2,030 miles) over 23 days (1–23 July 1989).

Giro d'Italia
The record for the greatest number of wins in the Giro d'Italia is five, by Alfredo Binda (Italy), in 1925, 1927–29 and 1933; by Fausto Coppi (Italy), in 1940, 1947, 1949 and from 1952 to 1953; and by Eddy Merckx (Belgium), 1968, 1970 from 1972 to 1974.

The fastest average speed was 40.663 km/h (25.266 mph), achieved by Tony Rominger (Switzerland) in 1995.

Vuelta a España
The record for the greatest number of wins in the Tour of Spain is three, by Tony Rominger (Switzerland), from 1992 to 1994.

The fastest average speed is 42.185 km/h (26.213 mph) over 1,714 km (1,065 miles), by Joey McLoughlin (GB) in 1986.

Six-day races
The most wins is 88 out of 233 events, by Patrick Sercu (Belgium) from 1964 to 1983.

Longest one-day race
The longest one-day 'massed start' road race is the 551–620-km (342–385-mile) Bordeaux–Paris event, France.

Cyclo-cross
Most titles
Eric De Vlaeminck (Belgium) won both the Amateur and Open in 1966 and six Professional titles from 1968 to 1973.

Fastest Three Peaks
In 1980, Stephen Poulton cycled from sea level at Caernarvon, Gwynedd, via Snowdon, Scafell Pike and Ben Nevis, to sea level Fort William, Highland, UK, in 41 hr 51 min.

Highest altitude
Canadians Bruce Bell, Philip Whelan and Suzanne MacFadyen cycled on the peak of Mt Aconcagua, Argentina, on 25 Jan 1991, at an altitude of 6,960 m (22,834 ft) . This was equalled by Mozart Hastenreiter Catão

WORLD CYCLING RECORDS
These records are those recognized by the Union Cycliste Internationale (UCI). Since 1 Jan 1993 their reduced list no longer distinguishes between professional and amateur records, indoor and outdoor records, or records set at altitude and sea level.

MEN
Unpaced standing start
1 km: 1:00.613 Shane Kelly (Australia) Bogota, Colombia, 26 Sept 1995
4 km: 4:20.894 Graeme Obree (GB) Hamar, Norway, 19 Aug 1993
4 km, team: 4:03.840 Brett Aitken, Stuart O'Grady, Tim O'Shaunessy, Billy Joe Shearsby (Australia), Hamar, Norway, 20 Aug 1993
1 hour (kms): 55.291 Tony Rominger (Switzerland), Bordeaux, France, 5 Nov 1994

Unpaced flying start
200 m: 9.865 Curtis Harnett (Canada) Bogota, Colombia, 28 Sept 1995
500 m: 26.649 Aleksandr Kirichenko (USSR) Moscow, USSR (now Russia), 29 Oct 1988

WOMEN
Unpaced standing start
500 m: 34.604 Felicia Ballanger (France) Hyeres, France, 3 July 1994
3 km: 3:31.924 Antonella Bellutti (Italy) Cali, Colombia, 7 April 1996
1 hour (kms): 47.411 Yvonne McGregor (GB) Manchester, UK, 17 June 1995

Unpaced flying start
200 m: 10.831 Olga Slyusareva (Russia) Moscow, Russia, 6 Aug 1990
500 m: 29.655 Erika Salumäe (USSR) Moscow, USSR (now Russia), 6 Aug 1987

BRITISH ROAD RECORDS
100 MILES
Men's bike: 3:11:11
Ian Cammish, 10 Aug 1993
Men's trike: 3:39:51
Dave Pitt, 18 Oct 1991
Women's bike: 3:49:42
Pauline Strong, 18 Oct 1991

LONDON TO BRIGHTON AND BACK
Men's bike: 4:15:08
Phil Griffiths, 20 July 1977
Men's trike: 4:51:07
Dave Pitt, 25 July 1979
Women's bike: 4:55:28
Gill Clapton, 15 July 1972

LONDON TO BATH AND BACK
Men's bike: 9:03:07
John Woodburn, 13 June 1981
Men's trike: 10:19:00
Ralph Dadswell, 22 June 1991
Women's bike: 10:41:22
Eileen Sheridan, 22 Aug 1952

LAND'S END TO JOHN O' GROATS
Men's bike, one day: 21:02:18
Andy Wilkinson, 29 Sept–1 Oct 1990
Men's trike, two days: 5:29:01
Ralph Dadswell, 10–12 Aug 1992
Women's bike, two days: 6:49:45
Pauline Strong, 28–30 July 1990

THE TOUR DE FRANCE IS EIGHT SECONDS, IN 1989

The fastest average speed is 39.896 km/h (24.773 mph) by Eric Caritoux (France), 1984.

Tour of Britain (Open)
Four riders have won twice: Bill Bradley (GB), 1959–60; Leslie George West (GB), 1965 and 1967; Fedor den Hertog (Netherlands), 1969 and 1971; and Yuriy Kashurin (USSR), 1979 and 1982.

The closest race was in 1976, when Bill Nickson (GB) won by five seconds after 1,665.67 km (1,035 miles) over 14 days.

(Brazil) on 11 March 1993 and Tim Sumner (GB) and Jonathon Green (GB) on 6 Jan 1994.

Cycle speedway
Most British Campionships
The greatest number of British Senior Team Championships titles is nine, by Poole, in 1982, 1984 and from 1987 to 1993.

Most individual titles
Derek Garnett took four individual titles, in 1963, 1965, 1968 and 1972.

Above far left and above left
Eddy Merckx (b. 1945) and Miguel Induráin (b. 1964) are two of the four riders to have won the Tour de France a record five times. In 1992, Induráin also set the record for the fastest average speed for the race, at 39.504 km/h (24.547 mph).

Aerial sports

HIGHEST ABSOLUTE ALTITUDE BY A WOMAN IN A SINGLE-SEATER GLIDER IS 12,637 M

Right
Hang gliding is a form of flying using only air currents. The World Team Championships were officially instituted in 1976 and have been won a record four times by Great Britain.

Most outside loops 208

Gliding
Most titles
The most World Individual Championship titles won by one person is four, by Ingo Renner (Australia) in 1976 (Standard class), 1983, 1985 and 1987 (Open).

The British National Championship has been won eight times by Ralph Jones.

Women's altitude records
The record for the greatest height gain is 10,212 m (33,504 ft), by Yvonne Loader (New Zealand) at Omarama, New Zealand, on 12 Jan 1988.

The women's single-seater world record for absolute altitude is 12,637 m (41,460 ft), by Sabrina Jackintell (USA) in an Astir GS on 14 Feb 1979.

The British single-seater absolute altitude record is 10,550 m (34,612 ft), set by Anne Burns in a Skylark 3B over South Africa on 13 Jan 1961, when she set a British record (then a world record) for height gain of 9,119 m (29,918 ft).

Hang gliding
Most World Team Championships
The World Team Championships were won by Great Britain in 1981, 1985, 1989 and 1991.

World records (men)
The greatest distance in a straight line and the greatest declared goal distance is 488.2 km (303 miles 622 yd) by Larry Tudor

(USA) from Hobbs Airpark, New Mexico, USA, to Elkhart, Kansas on 3 July 1990.

The greatest height gain is 4,343 m (14,250 ft), by Larry Tudor, at Owens Valley, California, USA, on 4 Aug 1985.

The greatest out and return distance is 310.3 km (192 miles 1,428 yd) by Larry Tudor and Geoffrey Loyns (GB), at Owens Valley, California, on 26 June 1988.

The greatest triangular course distance covered is 196.1 km (121 miles 1,390 yd), by James Lee (USA) at Wild Horse Mesa, Colorado, USA, on 4 July 1991.

World records (women)
The distance record is 335.8 km (208 miles 1,155 yd), by Kari Castle (USA) at Owens Valley, California, USA, on 22 July 1991.

The greatest height gain attained is 3,970 m (13,025 ft) by Judy Leden (GB) at Kuruman, South Africa, on 1 Dec 1992.

The greatest out and return distance covered via a single turn is 292.1 km (181 miles 884 yd), by Kari Castle (USA) at Hobbs Airpark, New Mexico, USA, on 1 July 1990.

The greatest declared goal distance is 212.50 km (132 miles 70 yd), by Liavan Mallin (Ireland) at Owens Valley, California, USA, on 13 July 1989.

RECORD DURATION FOR AN INVERTED FLIGHT IS 4 H

The greatest triangular course distance is 114.1 km (70 miles 1,581 yd), by Judy Leden (GB) at Kössen, Austria, on 22 June 1991.

British distance record
The British hang glider Geoffrey Loyns covered a record distance of 312.864 km (194 miles 712 yd) in Flagstaff, Arizona, USA, on 11 June 1988.

The record distance covered within the British Isles is 244 km (151 miles 1,091 yd), by Gordon Rigg from Lords Seat to Witham Friary, Somerset, on 4 June 1989.

Microlighting
World records
The greatest distance covered in a straight line is 1,627.78 km (1,011 miles 792 yd), by Wilhelm Lischak (Austria) from Volsau, Austria, to Brest, France, on 8 June 1988.

The greatest distance in a closed circuit is 2,702.16 km (1,679 miles 70 yd), by Wilhelm Lischak at Wels, Austria, on 18 June 1988.

The greatest altitude reached is 9,720 m (31,890 ft), by Serge Zin (France) at Saint Auban, France, on 18 Sept 1994.

The highest speed to have been attained over a 500-km (310-mile) closed circuit is 293.04 km/h (182 mph), by C. T. Andrews (USA) on 3 Aug 1982.

British altitude record
David Cook ascended to 8,249 m (27,064 ft) on 28 April 1990 at Aldeburgh, Suffolk.

Longest flights
Eve Jackson flew from Biggin Hill, Kent, UK, to Sydney, Australia, from 26 April 1986 to 1 Aug 1987. The flight took 279 hr 55 min and covered 21,950 km (13,639 miles).

From 1 Dec 1987 to 29 Jan 1988, Brian Milton (GB) covered a distance of 21,968 km (13,650 miles) from London, UK, to Sydney, Australia. His flying time was 241 hr 20 min.

Aerobatics
World Championships
The men's team competition has been won a record six times by the USSR.

Petr Jirmus (Czechoslovakia) is the only man to have become world champion twice, in 1984 and 1986.

Lyubov Nemkova (USSR) won a record five medals, coming first in 1986, second in 1982 and 1984 and third in 1976 and 1978.

The oldest ever world champion is Henry Haigh (USA) in 1988, at the age of 63.

Inverted flight
The longest inverted flight was 4 hr 38 min 10 sec, by Joann Osterud, from Vancouver to Vanderhoof, Canada, on 24 July 1991.

Loops
Joann Osterud achieved 208 outside loops in a 'Supernova' Hyperbipe over North Bend, Oregon, USA, on 13 July 1989.

On 9 Aug 1986, David Childs performed 2,368 inside loops in a Bellanca Decathalon over North Pole, Alaska.

Brian Lecomber completed 180 consecutive inside loops in a Jaguar Extra 230 on 29 July 1988 over Plymouth, Devon, UK.

4 MIN 10 SEC

Raymond Conte holds the unofficial world record for the most loops achieved in a microlight, with 21.

WORLD AND BRITISH GLIDING SINGLE-SEATER RECORDS
Straight Distance
1,460.8 km (907 miles 1,232 yd)
Hans-Werner Grosse (West Germany)
Lübeck, Germany, to Biarritz, France, 25 April 1972
Straight Distance, British
949.70 km (590 miles 176 yd)
Karla Karel
Australia, 20 Jan 1980
Declared Goal Distance
1,254.26 km (779 miles 634 yd)
Bruce Lindsey Drake, David Napier Speight,
Sholto Hamilton Georgeson (New Zealand)
Te Anau to Te Araroa, New Zealand, 14 Jan 1978
Declared Goal Distance, British
859.2 km (534 miles)
M. T. Alan Sands
Ridge soaring to Chilhowee, Virginia, USA, 23 April 1986
Goal and Return
1,646.68 km (1,023 miles 352 yd)
Thomas L. Knauff (USA)
Gliderport to Williamsport, Pennysylvania, USA, 25 April 1983
Goal and Return, British
1,127.68 km (700 miles 1,267 yd)
M. T. Alan Sands
Lock Haven, Pennysylvania, to Bluefield, Virginia, USA, May 1985
Absolute Altitude
14,938 m (49,009 ft)
Robert R. Harris (USA)
California, USA, 17 Feb 1986
Absolute Altitude, British
11,500 m (37,729 ft)
H. C. Nicholas Goodhart
California, USA, 12 May 1955
Height Gain
12,894 m (42,303 ft)
Paul F. Bikle (USA)
Mojave, Lancaster, California, USA, 25 Feb 1961
Height Gain, British
10,065 m (33,022 ft)
David Benton
Portmoak, Scotland, UK, 18 April 1980

SPEED OVER TRIANGULAR COURSE
100 km
195.3 km/h (121.35 mph)
Ingo Renner (Australia), Tocumwal, Australia, 14 Dec 1982
100 km, British
166.38 km/h (103.38 mph)
Bruce Cooper, Australia, 4 Jan 1991
300 km
169.50 km/h (105.32 mph)
Jean-Paul Castel (France), Bitterwasser, Namibia, 15 Nov 1986
300 km, British
146.8 km/h (91.2 mph)
Edward Pearson, SW Africa (now Namibia), 30 Nov 1976
500 km
170.06 km/h (105.67 mph)
Beat Bünzli (Switzerland), Bitterwasser, Namibia, 9 Jan 1988
500 km, British
141.3 km/h (87.8 mph)
Bradley James Grant Pearson, South Africa, 28 Dec 1982
750 km
158.41 km/h (98.43 mph)
Hans-Werner Grosse (W Germany), Alice Springs, Australia, 8 Jan 1985
750 km, British
109.8 km/h (68.2mph)
Michael R. Carlton, South Africa, 5 Jan 1975
1,000 km
169.72 km/h (105.46 mph)
Helmut Fischer (Germany), Hendrik Verwoerd Dam, South Africa, 5 Jan 1995
1,000 km, British
112.15 km/h (69.68 mph)
George Lee, Australia, 25 Jan 1989
1,250 km
133.24 km/h (82.79 mph)
Hans-Werner Grosse (W Germany) Alice Springs, Australia, 9 Dec 1980
1,250 km, British
109.01 km/h (67.73 mph)
Robert L. Robertson, USA, 2 May 1986

Paragliding and parachuting

Right
The women's world record free-fall formation involved 100 women from 20 countries over France in Aug 1992. When parachuting, it is estimated that the human body reaches 99% of its low-level terminal velocity after falling 573 m (1,880 ft), which takes 13–14 seconds. This is 188–201 km/h (117–125 mph) at normal atmospheric pressure in a random posture, but can be up to 298 km/h (185 mph) in a head-down position.

Greatest height gain 4,526 m

Paragliding

Longest flights (tow-launched)
The greatest distance ever flown is 285 km (177¹⁄₁₀ miles), by Kat Thurston (GB) from Kuruman, South Africa, on 25 Dec 1995.

The greatest distance flown by a male paraglider is 283.9 km (176 miles 700 yd), by Alex François Louw (South Africa) from Kuruman, South Africa, on 31 Dec 1992.

Longest flights
The greatest distance to have been flown is 253 km (157 miles), by Robby Whittal at Kuruman, South Africa, on 22 Jan 1993.

The greatest distance flown within the United Kingdom is 175.4 km (108 miles 1,580 yd), from Long Mynd, Shrops, to Pulloxhill, Beds, by Steve Ham on 19 May 1994.

Greatest height gain (tow-launched)
The record for the greatest height gain is 4,526 m (14,849 ft), by Robby Whittal (GB) at Brandvlei, South Africa, on 6 Jan 1993.

The greatest height gain by a woman is 2,971 m (9,747 ft), by Verena Mühr (Germany) at Bitterwasser, Namibia, on 13 Dec 1991.

Parachuting

First attempts
Faustus Verancsis is said to have parachuted with a framed canopy in Hungary in 1617.

In 1687 the King of Ayutthaya in Siam (now Thailand) was reported to have been entertained by an ingenious athlete parachuting with two large umbrellas.

Louis-Sébastien Lenormand demonstrated a quasi-parachute—a braced conical canopy—from a tower in Montpellier, France, in 1783.

Longest duration fall
Lt. Col. William H. Rankin (USMC) took 40 minutes to fall in North Carolina, USA, on 26 July 1956. The record duration of the fall was due to thermals.

Longest delayed drop
The world's longest delayed drop by a man was 25,820 m (84,700 ft or 16 miles 73 yd) from a balloon at 31,330 m (102,800 ft), by Capt. Joseph W. Kittinger at Tularosa, New Mexico, USA, on 16 Aug 1960. The maximum speed reached in rarefied air was 1,006 km/h

(625.25 mph) at 27,400 m (90,000 ft), which is just faster than the speed of sound.

The longest delayed drop by a woman is 14,800 m (48,556 ft), by Elvira Fomitcheva (USSR) over Odessa, USSR (now Ukraine), on 26 Oct 1977.

The longest delayed drop over the United Kingdom by male civilians is 10,180 m (33,400 ft) from a balloon at 10,850 m (35,600 ft), by M. Child and R. McCarthy over Kings Lynn, Norfolk, on 18 Sept 1986.

The longest delayed drop to have been achieved by female civilians over the United Kingdom is 6,520 m (21,391 ft), from an aircraft at 7,600 m (24,900 ft), by Francesca Gannon and Valerie Slattery over Netheravon, Wilts, on 11 March 1987.

The longest delayed drop made by a group over the United Kingdom is 11,943 m (39,183 ft) from an aircraft at 12,613 m (41,383 ft), by S/Ldr. J. Thirtle, Fl. Sgt. A. K. Kidd and Sgts L. Hicks, P. P. Keane and K. J. Teesdale over Boscombe Down, Wilts, on 16 June 1967.

Base jump
The highest base jump was made by Nicholas Feteris and Dr Glenn Singleman from a mountain ledge (the 'Great Trango Tower') at 5,880 m (19,300 ft) in the Karakoram range, Pakistan, on 26 Aug 1992.

Mid-air rescue
The first mid-air rescue took place when Miss Dolly Shepherd brought down Miss Louie May

Cross-Channel (lateral fall)
Sgt. Bob Walters accompanied by three soldiers and two Royal Marines parachuted 35.4 km (22 miles) from 7,600 m (25,000 ft), from Dover, Kent, UK, to Sangatte, France, on 31 Aug 1980.

Total sport parachuting descents
The greatest number of descents made is 22,000, by Don Kellner (USA), at various locations in the USA to May 1996.

The most descents made by a woman is 10,900, by Cheryl Stearns (USA), mainly over the USA to May 1996.

24–hour total
The most descents made in 24 hours (in accordance with United States Parachute Association rules) is 352, by Cheryl Stearns (USA) at Raeford, North Carolina, on 8 and 9 Nov 1995.

Largest canopy stack
The world record for the most people ever to form a canopy stack is 46, by an international team at Davis, California, USA. The stack was held for 37.54 seconds on 12 Oct 1994.

Largest free-fall formations
The world's biggest ever free-fall formation (not recognized by the FAI) consisted of 216 people representing 23 countries and was held for 8.21 seconds from a height of 6,400 m (21,000 ft) over Bratislava, Slovakia, on 19 Aug 1994.

The world record for the number of people to make up an official (recognized by the FAI)

free-fall formation is 200. Parachutists representing 10 different countries held the formation for 6.47 seconds, from a height of 5,030 m (16,500 ft), over Myrtle Beach, South Carolina, USA, on 23 Oct 1992.

The largest all-female free-fall formation consisted of 100 women representing 20 countries and was held for 5.97 seconds, from a height of 5,200 m (17,000 ft) at the Aérodrome du Cannet des Maures, France, on 14 Aug 1992.

The largest free-fall formation undertaken over the United Kingdom involved 60 people and was held for four seconds, from 4,600 m (15,000 ft), over Peterborough, Cambs, on 8 June 1989.

Oldest parachutist
The oldest ever parachutist was Edwin C. Townsend, who, on his 89th birthday, made a jump over Vermillion Bay, Louisiana, USA, on 5 Feb 1986.

The oldest woman to make a jump was Sylvia Brett (GB), who was 80 years 166 days old when she parachuted over Cranfield, Beds, UK, on 23 Aug 1986.

The oldest person to make a tandem jump was Hildegarde Ferrera (USA), who parachuted at Mokuleia, Hawaii, USA, at the age of 99, on 17 Feb 1996.

The oldest man to make a tandem jump was Edward Royds-Jones, who was 95 years 170 days old when he parachuted over Dunkeswell, Devon, UK, on 2 July 1994.

AY ON HER SINGLE PARACHUTE IN 1908, IN THE FIRST EVER MID-AIR RESCUE

on her single parachute from a balloon at 3,350 m (11,000 ft) over Longton, Staffs, UK, on 9 June 1908.

The lowest mid-air rescue occurred when Eddie Turner saved Frank Farnan, who had been injured and rendered unconscious in a collision after jumping out of an aircraft at 3,950 m (13,000 ft). Turner pulled Farnan's ripcord at 550 m (1,800 ft), less than 10 seconds from impact, over Clewiston, Florida, USA, on 16 Oct 1988.

Highest escape
Flt. Lt. J. de Salis (RAF) and Flying Officer P. Lowe (RAF) made the highest ever escape, at 17,100 m (56,000 ft) over Monyash, Derby, UK, on 9 April 1958.

Lowest escape
S/Ldr. Terence Spencer (RAF) achieved the lowest ever escape, at a height of 9–12 m (30–40 ft) over Wismar Bay in the Baltic Sea on 19 April 1945.

Highest landing
Ten USSR parachutists (four of whom were killed) landed at a record altitude of 7,133 m (23,405 ft) at Lenina Peak, USSR (now the Tajikistan/Kyrgyzstan border), in May 1969.

Left
Members of a Sea Air Land (SEAL) team practise parachuting from an aircraft over Puerto Rico. Many hours of practice are required in order to perfect skills.

The Olympic Games

History of the Games
First Games
The ancient Olympics may date back to c. 1370 BC, but the earliest Games of which there is definite record took place in July 776 BC, when Coroibos, a cook from Elis, won the foot race.

The Olympic Games of the modern era were inaugurated in Athens, Greece, on 6 April 1896, at the instigation of Pierre de Fredi, Baron de Coubertin.

Countries attending the most Games
Five countries have been represented at all 24 Summer Games held from 1896 to 1996: Australia, France, Greece, Great Britain and Switzerland (the latter only contested the 1956 Equestrian events in Sweden and did

competitor is seven, by Vera Caslavska-Odlozil (Czechoslovakia) in 1964 and 1968.

The most gold medals by a British competitor is four by: Paul Radmilovic in water polo in 1908, 1912 and 1920 and in the 4 x 200-m freestyle relay in 1908; the swimmer Henry Taylor in 1906 and 1908; and Steven Geoffrey Redgrave in the coxed fours in 1984 and coxless pairs in 1988, 1992 and 1996.

The only Olympians to win four consecutive individual titles in the same event are Alfred Adolph Oerter (USA), who won the discus from 1956 to 1968, and Frederick Carleton 'Carl' Lewis, who won the long jump from 1984 to 1996. If the Intercalated Games of 1906 are included, Raymond Clarence Ewry (USA) won both the standing long jump and

The most medals by a man is 15, by Nikolay Yefimovich Andrianov (USSR), 1972–80.

The most medals at one Games is eight, by gymnast Aleksandr Nikolayevich Dityatin (USSR) in 1980.

Youngest and oldest gold medallists
A French boy (name not on record) coxed the Netherlands pair in 1900 at 7–10 years of age, in place of Dr Hermanus Gerhardus Brockmann, who was too heavy for the final.

The youngest ever female champion, Kim Yoon-mi (South Korea), was in the winning team in the 1994 women's 3,000-m short-

not attend the Games in Melbourne). Of these only France, Great Britain and Switzerland have been present at all Winter celebrations (1924–94) as well.

Participants and spectators
Most participants
The record for the most competitors at a Summer Games is 10,768, representing all 197 nations of the International Olympic Committee, at Atlanta, USA, in 1996.

The most competitors at a Winter Games is 1,737 (1,216 men, 521 women) from 67 countries, at Lillehammer, Norway, in 1994.

Most medals
In the ancient Games, where victors were given a chaplet of wild olive leaves, Leonidas of Rhodos won 12 running titles, 164–152 BC.

The most individual gold medals by a male competitor in the modern Games is 10, by Raymond Clarence Ewry (USA), 1900–08.

The record for the greatest number of gold medals to have been won by a female

the standing high jump at four games in succession (1900, 1904, 1906 and 1908). Paul Bert Elvstrøm (Denmark) won four successive gold medals at monotype yachting events (1948–60), but with a class change.

Swimmer Mark Andrew Spitz (USA) won a record seven golds at one Games, including three in relays, at Munich, Germany, in 1972.

The most gold medals in individual events at one Games is five, by speed skater Eric Arthur Heiden (USA) at Lake Placid, USA, in 1980.

The only man to win a gold medal in both the Summer and the Winter Games is Edward Patrick Francis Eagan (USA), who won the 1920 light-heavyweight boxing title and was a member of the winning four-man bob in 1932.

Christa Luding (GDR) was the first woman to win a medal at both Summer and Winter Games, with silver in the 1988 cycling sprint event. Earlier medals were for speed skating.

The record for the most medals by a woman is 18, by gymnast Larisa Semyonovna Latynina (USSR) from 1956 to 1964.

track speed skating relay event at the age of 13 years and 85 days.

The oldest ever medallist, Oscar Swahn, won a silver in shooting at the age of 72 years 280 days in 1920.

Youngest and oldest British competitors
Magdalena Cecilia Colledge skated in the 1932 Games at the age of 11 years 73 days.

Hilda Lorna Johnstone was 70 years 5 days old when she participated in the equestrian dressage in the 1972 Games.

Longest Olympic careers
The record for the longest career is 40 years by: Dr Ivan Joseph Martin Osiier (Denmark) in fencing, 1908–32 and 1948; Magnus Andreas Thulstrup Clasen Konow (Norway) in yachting, 1908–20, 1928 and 1936–48; Paul Elvstrøm (Denmark) in yachting, 1948–60, 1968–72 and 1984–88; and Durward Randolph Knowles (GB in 1948, then Bahamas) in yachting, 1948–72 and 1988.

The longest career of a female Olympian is 28 years, by Anne Jessica Ransehousen

(USA) in dressage in 1960, 1964 and 1988, and by Christilot Hanson-Boylen (Canada) in dressage, 1964–76, 1984 and 1992.

The longest Olympian career of a British competitor is 32 years, by Enoch Jenkins, in clay pigeon shooting, 1920, 1924 and 1952.

The longest career by a British woman is 20 years, by Dorothy Tyler (high jump 1936–56), and Tessa Sanderson (javelin 1976–96). Davina Galicia participated over 28 years, in alpine skiing from 1964 to 1972 and speed skiing in 1992 (demonstration sport).

The record for the greatest number of Olympic Games competed in by any one participant is nine, by yachtsman Hubert Raudaschl (Austria) from 1964 to 1996.

Kerstin Palm (Sweden) competed in a women's record of seven Games, 1964–88.

The record for the greatest number of appearances by a British competitor is six, by the swimmer and water polo player Paul Radmilovic from 1906 to 1928, and fencer Bill Hoskyns from 1956 to 1976.

The most appearances for Great Britain by a woman is six, by javelin thrower Tessa Sanderson from 1976 to 1996.

Largest crowds
The biggest crowd at an Olympic site was 104,102, at the 1952 ski-jumping at the Holmenkollen, outside Oslo, Norway.

Estimates of the number of spectators watching the marathon race through Tokyo, Japan, on 21 Oct 1964 range from 500,000 to 1.5 million.

The official total spectator attendance at Los Angeles, USA, in 1984 was 5,797,923.

The 1996 Olympic Games
Countries
A record 79 countries and territories won medals at the Games, the following for the first time: Armenia, Azerbaijan, Burundi, Czech Republic, Ecuador, Georgia, Hong Kong, Moldova, Mozambique, Slovakia and Tonga. Belarus, Kazakhstan, Ukraine and Uzbekistan also won medals at the Summer Games for the first time, having previously won medals at the Winter Games.

Participants
The most successful individual participant at the Atlanta Games was the Russian gymnast Aleksey Nemov, who won a total of six medals. The most gold medals won by an individual was four, by the US swimmer Amy van Dyken.

Below
The 1996 Games saw the introduction of new cycling events (men's and women's individual road time trials and mountain bike racing and women's points races) and of men's and women's beach volleyball. Other sports with new events were: athletics (women's 5,000 m and women's triple jump); badminton (mixed doubles); fencing (women's epée and epée team); football (women's); swimming (women's 4 x 200-m freestyle); rowing (men's and women's lightweight double sculls and men's lightweight coxless fours) and shooting (men's and women's Olympic double trap). Softball also appeared for the first time.

JUNTRIES WON MEDALS AT THE ATLANTA GAMES

MOST MEDALS IN THE 1996 GAMES

USA 101: 44 gold, 32 silver, 25 bronze
Germany 65: 20 gold, 18 silver, 27 bronze
Russia 63: 26 gold, 21 silver, 16 bronze
China 50: 16 gold, 22 silver, 12 bronze
Australia 41: 9 gold, 9 silver, 23 bronze
France 37: 15 gold, 7 silver, 15 bronze
Italy 35: 13 gold, 10 silver, 12 bronze
South Korea 27: 7 gold, 15 silver, 5 bronze
Cuba 25: 9 gold, 8 silver, 8 bronze
Ukraine 23: 9 gold, 2 silver, 12 bronze
Canada 22: 3 gold, 11 silver, 8 bronze
Hungary 21: 7 gold, 4 silver, 10 bronze
Romania 20: 4 gold, 7 silver, 9 bronze
Netherlands 19: 4 gold, 5 silver, 10 bronze
Poland 17: 7 gold, 5 silver, 5 bronze
Spain 17: 5 gold, 6 silver, 6 bronze
Bulgaria 15: 3 gold, 7 silver, 5 bronze
Brazil 15: 3 gold, 3 silver, 9 bronze
Great Britain 15: 1 gold, 8 silver, 6 bronze
Belarus 15: 1 gold, 6 silver, 8 bronze
Japan 14: 3 gold, 6 silver, 5 bronze
Czech Republic 11: 4 gold, 3 silver, 4 bronze
Kazakhstan 11: 3 gold, 4 silver, 4 bronze
Greece 8: 4 gold, 4 silver
Sweden 8: 2 gold, 4 silver, 2 bronze

MOST OLYMPIC MEDALS

The total medals, for leading nations, in all Olympic events (including discontinued events but excluding medals won in Official Art competitions, 1912–48).

Summer Games (1896–96)
USA 2,015: 833 gold, 634 silver, 548 bronze
Soviet Union (includes CIS [Unified team] in 1992) 1,234: 485 gold, 395 silver, 354 bronze
Great Britain 635: 177 gold, 233 silver, 225 bronze
France 562: 176 gold, 181 silver, 205 bronze
Germany (1896–1964 and 1992–94) 516: 151 gold, 181 silver, 184 bronze
Sweden 459: 134 gold, 152 silver, 173 bronze
Italy 444: 166 gold, 136 silver, 142 bronze
Hungary 425 : 142 gold, 128 silver, 155 bronze
German Democratic Republic (1968–88) 410: 153 gold, 130 silver, 127 bronze
Australia 294: 87 gold, 85 silver, 122 bronze
Finland 292: 99 gold, 80 silver, 113 bronze
Japan 280: 93 gold, 89 silver, 98 bronze
Romania 239: 63 gold, 77 silver, 99 bronze
Poland 227: 50 gold, 67 silver, 110 bronze
Canada 217: 49 gold, 77 silver, 91 bronze
Federal Republic of Germany (1968–88) 200: 56 gold, 64 silver, 80 bronze
Netherlands 187: 49 gold, 57 silver, 81 bronze
Switzerland 174: 46 gold, 68 silver, 60 bronze
Bulgaria 182: 43 gold, 76 silver, 63 bronze
China 164: 52 gold, 63 silver, 49 bronze

Winter Games (1924–94)
Soviet Union (includes CIS [Unified team] in 1992) 217: 87 gold, 63 silver, 67 bronze
Norway 214: 73 gold, 77 silver, 64 bronze
USA 146: 53 gold, 56 silver, 37 bronze
Austria 128: 36 gold, 48 silver, 44 bronze
Finland 123: 36 gold, 45 silver, 42 bronze
German Democratic Republic (1968–88) 110: 39 gold, 36 silver, 35 bronze
Sweden 99: 39 gold, 26 silver, 34 bronze
Germany (1896–1964 and 1992–94) 87: 34 gold, 29 silver, 24 bronze
Switzerland 85: 27 gold, 29 silver, 29 bronze
Italy 67: 25 gold, 21 silver, 21 bronze
Canada 64: 19 gold, 20 silver, 25 bronze
France 53: 16 gold, 16 silver, 21 bronze
Netherlands 50: 14 gold, 19 silver, 17 bronze
Federal Republic of Germany (1968–88) 39: 11 gold, 15 silver, 13 bronze
Czechoslovakia (includes Bohemia) 26: 2 gold, 8 silver, 16 bronze
Russia (includes Czarist Russia) 24: 12 gold, 8 silver, 4 bronze
Great Britain 23: 7 gold, 4 silver, 12 bronze
Japan 19: 3 gold, 8 silver, 8 bronze
Korea 10: 6 gold, 2 silver, 2 bronze
Liechtenstein 9: 2 gold, 2 silver, 5 bronze

Athletics

KENNY HARRISON OF THE USA SET A NEW OLYMPIC TRIPLE-JUMP RECORD OF 18.09 M

World record 🌐
Olympic record 🏛
British record 🏴

Below right
Donovan Bailey (far left of picture) on his way to victory in the 100-m gold in a world record time of 9.84 seconds. The other runners are, from left to right: Frankie Fredericks, who came second; Dennis Mitchell, who came fourth; and Ato Boldon, who came third.

Far right
Michael Johnson became the first male athlete in Olympic history to win the double of 200 m and 400 m when he covered 200 m in a world record time of 19.32 seconds.

MEN

100 m 🌐
Gold: Donovan Bailey (Canada) 9.84 seconds
Silver: Frankie Fredericks (Namibia) 9.89
Bronze: Ato Boldon (Trinidad & Tobago) 9.90

200 m 🌐
Gold: Michael Johnson (USA) 19.32 seconds
Silver: Frankie Fredericks (Namibia) 19.68
Bronze: Ato Boldon (Trinidad & Tobago) 19.80

400 m 🏛
Gold: Michael Johnson (USA) 43.49 seconds
Silver: Roger Black (GB) 44.41
Bronze: Davis Kamoga (Uganda) 44.53

800 m 🏛
Gold: Vebjoern Rodal (Norway) 1 min 42.58 sec
Silver: Hezekiel Sepeng (South Africa) 1:42.74
Bronze: Fred Onyancha (Kenya) 1:42.79

400-m hurdles
Gold: Derrick Adkins (USA) 47.54 seconds
Silver: Samuel Matete (Zambia) 47.78
Bronze: Calvin Davis (USA) 47.96

4 x 100-m
Gold: Canada 37.69 seconds
Silver: USA 38.05
Bronze: Brazil 38.41

4 x 400-m
Gold: USA 2 min 55.99 sec
Silver: GB 2:56.60 🏴
Bronze: Jamaica 2:59.42

Steeplechase
Gold: Joseph Keter (Kenya) 8 min 7.12 sec
Silver: Moses Kiptanui (Kenya) 8:08.33
Bronze: Alessandro Lambruschini (Italy) 8:11.28

Triple jump 🏛
Gold: Kenny Harrison (USA) 18.09 m
Silver: Jonathon Edwards (GB) 17.88
Bronze: Yoelbi Quesada (Cuba) 17.44

Shot
Gold: Randy Barnes (USA) 21.62 m
Silver: John Godina (USA) 20.79
Bronze: Oleksandr Bagach (Ukraine) 20.75

Discus 🏛
Gold: Lars Riedel (Germany) 69.40 m
Silver: Vladimir Dubrovshchik (Belarus) 66.60
Bronze: Vasiliy Kaptyukh (Belarus) 65.80

Hammer
Gold: Balazs Kiss (Hungary) 81.24 m
Silver: Lance Deal (USA) 81.12
Bronze: Oleksiy Krykun (Ukraine) 80.02

1,500 m
Gold: Noureddine Morceli (Algeria) 3 min 35.78 sec
Silver: Fermin Cacho (Spain) 3:36.40
Bronze: Stephen Kipkorir (Kenya) 3:36.72

5,000 m
Gold: Venuste Niyongabo (Burundi) 13 min 07.96 sec
Silver: Paul Bitok (Kenya) 13:08.16
Bronze: Khalid Boulami (Morocco) 13:08.37

10,000 m 🏛
Gold: Haile Gebrselassie (Ethiopia) 27 min 07.34 sec
Silver: Paul Tergat (Kenya) 27:08.17
Bronze: Salah Hissou (Morocco) 27:28.59

Marathon
Gold: Josia Thugwane (South Africa) 2 hr 12 min 36 sec
Silver: Lee Bong-ju (South Korea) 2:12:39
Bronze: Eric Wainaina (Kenya) 2:12:44

110-m hurdles 🏛
Gold: Allen Johnson (USA) 12.95 seconds
Silver: Mark Crear (USA) 13.09
Bronze: Florian Schwarthoff (Germany) 13.17

20-km walk
Gold: Jefferson Perez (Ecuador) 1 hr 20 min 07 sec
Silver: Ilya Markov (Russia) 1:20:16
Bronze: Bernardo Segura (Mexico) 1:20:23

50-km walk
Gold: Robert Korzeniowski (Poland) 3 hr 43 min 30 sec
Silver: Mikhail Shchennikov (Russia) 3:43:46
Bronze: Valentin Massana (Spain) 3:44:19

High jump 🏛
Gold: Charles Austin (USA) 2.39 m
Silver: Artur Partyka (Poland) 2.37
Bronze: Steve Smith (GB) 2.35

Pole vault 🏛
Gold: Jean Galfione (France) 5.92 m
Silver: Igor Trandenkov (Russia) 5.92
Bronze: Andrei Tivontchik (Germany) 5.92

Long jump
Gold: Carl Lewis (USA) 8.50 m
Silver: James Beckford (Jamaica) 8.29
Bronze: Joe Greene (USA) 8.24

FASTEST EVER PERSON OVE

Javelin
Gold: Jan Zelezny (Czech Republic) 88.16 m
Silver: Steve Backley (GB) 87.44
Bronze: Seppo Raty (Finland) 86.98

Decathlon
Gold: Dan O'Brien (USA) 8,824 points
Silver: Franke Busemann (Germany) 8,706
Bronze: Tomas Dvorak (Czech Republic) 8,664

MARIE-JOSE PEREC SET A NEW WOMEN'S 400-M RECORD OF 48.25 SECONDS

Fastest ever 200 m 19.32 sec

4 x 100-m
Gold: USA 41.95 seconds
Silver: Bahamas 42.14
Bronze: Jamaica 42.24

4 x 400-m
Gold: USA 3 min 20.91 sec
Silver: Nigeria 3:21.04
Bronze: Germany 3:21.14

10-km walk
Gold: Yelena Nikolayeva (Russia) 41 min 49 sec
Silver: Elisabetta Perrone (Italy) 42:12
Bronze: Wang Yan (China) 42:19

High jump
Gold: Stefka Kostadinova (Bulgaria) 2.05 m
Silver: Niki Bakogianni (Greece) 2.03
Bronze: Inga Babakova (Ukraine) 2.01

Long jump
Gold: Chioma Ajunwa (Nigeria) 7.12 m
Silver: Fiona May (Italy) 7.02
Bronze: Jackie Joyner-Kersee (USA) 7.00

...0 M IS DONOVAN BAILEY (CANADA), WHO COVERED THE DISTANCE IN 9.84 SECONDS

WOMEN

100 m
Gold: Gail Devers (USA) 10.94 seconds
Silver: Merlene Ottey (Jamaica) 10.94
Bronze: Gwen Torrence (USA) 10.96

200 m
Gold: Marie-Jose Perec (France) 22.12 seconds
Silver: Merlene Ottey (Jamaica) 22.24
Bronze: Mary Onyali (Nigeria) 22.38

400 m
Gold: Marie-Jose Perec (France) 48.25 seconds
Silver: Cathy Freeman (Australia) 48.63
Bronze: Falilat Ogunkoya (Nigeria) 49.10

800 m
Gold: Svetlana Masterkova (Russia) 1 min 57.73 sec
Silver: Ana Fidelia Quirot (Cuba) 1:58.11
Bronze: Maria Lurdes Mutola (Mozambique) 1:58.71

1,500 m
Gold: Svetlana Masterkova (Russia) 4 min 00.83 sec
Silver: Gabriela Szabo (Romania) 4:01.54
Bronze: Theresia Kiesl (Austria) 4:03.02

5,000 m
Gold: Wang Junxia (China) 14 min 59.88 sec
Silver: Pauline Konga (Kenya) 15:03.49
Bronze: Roberta Brunet (Italy) 15:07.52

10,000 m
Gold: Fernanda Riberio (Portugal) 31 min 1.63 sec
Silver: Wang Junxia (China) 31:02.58
Bronze: Gete Wami (Ethiopia) 31:06.65

Marathon
Gold: Fatume Roba (Ethiopia) 2 hr 26 min .05 sec
Silver: Valentina Yegerova (Russia) 2:28.05
Bronze: Yuko Arimori (Japan) 2:28.39

100-m hurdles
Gold: Ludmila Enquist (Sweden) 12.58 seconds
Silver: Brigita Bukovec (Slovenia) 12.59
Bronze: Patricia Girard-Leno (France) 12.65

400-m hurdles
Gold: Deon Hemmings (Jamaica) 52.82 seconds
Silver: Kim Batten (USA) 53.08
Bronze: Tonja Buford-Bailey (USA) 53.22

Triple jump
Gold: Inessa Kravets (Ukraine) 15.33 m
Silver: Inna Lasovskaya (Russia) 14.98
Bronze: Sarka Kasparkova (Czech Republic) 14.98

Shot
Gold: Astrid Kumbernuss (Germany) 20.56 m
Silver: Sui Xinmei (China) 19.88
Bronze: Irina Khurdoroshkina (Russia) 19.35

Discus
Gold: Ilke Wyludda (Germany) 69.66 m
Silver: Natalya Sadova (Russia) 66.48
Bronze: Ellina Zvereva (Belarus) 65.64

Javelin
Gold: Heli Rantanen (Finland) 67.94 m
Silver: Louise McPaul (Australia) 65.54
Bronze: Trine Hattestad (Norway) 64.98

Heptathlon
Gold: Ghada Shouaa (Syria) 6,780 points
Silver: Natasha Sazanovich (Belarus) 6,563
Bronze: Denise Lewis (GB) 6,489

Above left
Carl Lewis, who won the men's long jump for a fourth consecutive time, is one of only two Olympians to have won an individual event at four successive Games. The other is discus thrower Al Oerter, who won from 1956 to 1968.

Above
Marie-Jose Perec (right of picture) also succeeded in winning the 200-m and 400-m double, equalling the achievement of Valerie Brisco-Hooks (USA) in 1984. Merlene Ottey (centre) won silver in the 200 m and went on to win a seventh Olympic medal, equalling the women's record. In the 100 m she was denied gold by a photo finish.

Swimming, yachting

World record 🜨
Olympic record ⌂
British record 🏴

Below right
Hungarian Krisztina Egerszegi won the women's 200-m backstroke for a third successive time in 1996. Egerszegi is only the second swimmer to have won the same event at three Games, equalling the achievement of Australian Dawn Fraser. It was Egerszegi's fifth individual swimming gold, which is also a record.

Far right
Ireland's Michelle Smith had an exceptional Games in 1996, achieving a double in the 200-m and 400-m medley and winning a total of three golds and one bronze.

Swimming

MEN

50-m freestyle
Gold: Aleksandr Popov (Russia) 22.13 seconds
Silver: Gary Hall (USA) 22.26
Bronze: Fernando Scherer (Brazil) 22.29

100-m freestyle
Gold: Aleksandr Popov (Russia) 48.74 seconds
Silver: Gary Hall (USA) 48.81
Bronze: Gustavo Borges (Brazil) 49.02

200-m freestyle
Gold: Danyon Loader (New Zealand) 1 min 47.63 sec
Silver: Gustavo Borges (Brazil) 1:48.08
Bronze: Daniel Kowalski (Australia) 1:48.25

200-m breaststroke
Gold: Norbert Rozsa (Hungary) 2 min 12.57 sec
Silver: Karoly Guttler (Hungary) 2:13.03
Bronze: Andrey Korneyev (Russia) 2:13.17

100-m backstroke
Gold: Jeff Rouse (USA) 54.10 seconds
Silver: Rodolfo Falcon Cabrera (Cuba) 54.98
Bronze: Neisser Bent (Cuba) 55.02

200-m backstroke
Gold: Brad Bridgwater (USA) 1 min 58.54 sec
Silver: Tripp Schwenk (USA) 1:58.99
Bronze: Emanuele Merisi (Italy) 1:59.18

100-m butterfly 🜨
Gold: Denis Pankratov (Russia) 52.27 seconds
Silver: Scott Miller (Australia) 52.53
Bronze: Vladislav Kulikov (Russia) 53.13

WOMEN

50-m freestyle
Gold: Amy van Dyken (USA) 24.87 seconds
Silver: Le Jingyi (China) 24.90
Bronze: Sandra Volker (Germany) 25.14

100-m freestyle ⌂
Gold: Le Jingyi (China) 54.50 seconds
Silver: Sandra Volker (Germany) 54.88
Bronze: Angel Martino (USA) 54.93

200-m freestyle
Gold: Claudia Poll (Costa Rica) 1 min 58.16 sec
Silver: Franziska van Almsick (Germany) 1:58.57
Bronze: Dagmar Hase (Germany) 1:59.56

400-m freestyle
Gold: Danyon Loader (New Zealand) 3 min 47.97 sec
Silver: Paul Palmer (GB) 3:49.00
Bronze: Daniel Kowalski (Australia) 3:49.39

1,500-m freestyle
Gold: Kieren Perkins (Australia) 14 min 56.40 sec
Silver: Daniel Kowalski (Australia) 15:02.43
Bronze: Graeme Smith (GB) 15:02.48 🏴

4 x 100-m freestyle ⌂
Gold: USA 3 min 15.41 sec
Silver: Russia 3:17.06
Bronze: Germany 3:17.20

4 x 200-m freestyle
Gold: USA 7 min 14.84 sec
Silver: Sweden 7:17.56
Bronze: Germany 7:17.71

100-m breaststroke
Gold: Frédéric Deburghgraeve (Belgium) 1 min 00.65 sec (1:00.60 🜨 in qualifying)
Silver: Jeremy Linn (USA) 1:00.77
Bronze: Mark Warnecke (Germany) 1:01.33

200-m butterfly
Gold: Denis Pankratov (Russia) 1 min 56.51 sec
Silver: Tom Malchow (USA) 1:57.44
Bronze: Scott Goodman (Australia) 1:57.48

200-m medley ⌂
Gold: Attila Czene (Hungary) 1 min 59.91 sec
Silver: Jani Sievinen (Finland) 2:00.13
Bronze: Curtis Myden (Canada) 2:01.13

400-m medley
Gold: Tom Dolan (USA) 4 min 14.90 sec
Silver: Eric Namesnik (USA) 4:15.25
Bronze: Curtis Myden (Canada) 4:16.28

4 x 100-m medley 🜨
Gold: USA 3 min 34.84 sec
Silver: Russia 3:37.55
Bronze: Australia 3:39.56

400-m freestyle
Gold: Michelle Smith (Ireland) 4 min 07.25 sec
Silver: Dagmar Hase (Germany) 4:08.30
Bronze: Kirsten Vlieghuis (Netherlands) 4:08.70

800-m freestyle
Gold: Brooke Bennett (USA) 8 min 27.89 sec
Silver: Dagmar Hase (Germany) 8:29.91
Bronze: Kirsten Vlieghuis (Netherlands) 8:30.84

4 x 100-m freestyle ⌂
Gold: USA 3 min 39.29 sec
Silver: China 3:40.48
Bronze: Germany 3:41.48

4 x 200-m freestyle
Gold: USA 7 min 59.87 sec
Silver: Germany 8:01.55
Bronze: Australia 8:05.47

100-m breaststroke
Gold: Penny Heyns (South Africa) 1 min 7.73 sec (1:07.02 🜨 in qualifying)
Silver: Amanda Beard (USA) 1:08.09
Bronze: Samantha Riley (Australia) 1:09.18

200-m breaststroke
Gold: Penny Heyns (South Africa) 2 min 25.41 sec
Silver: Amanda Beard (USA) 2:25.75
Bronze: Agnes Kovacs (Hungary) 2:26.57

100-m backstroke
Gold: Beth Botsford (USA) 1 min 1.19 sec
Silver: Whitney Hedgepeth (USA) 1:01.47
Bronze: Marianne Kriel (South Africa) 1:02.12

200-m backstroke
Gold: Krisztina Egerszegi (Hungary) 2 min 7.83 sec
Silver: Whitney Hedgepeth (USA) 2:11.98
Bronze: Cathleen Rund (Germany) 2:12.06

100-m butterfly
Gold: Amy van Dyken (USA) 59.13 seconds
Silver: Liu Limin (China) 59.14
Bronze: Angel Martino (USA) 59.23

200-m butterfly
Gold: Susan O'Neil (Australia) 2 min 7.76 sec
Silver: Petria Thomas (Australia) 2:09.82
Bronze: Michelle Smith (Ireland) 2:09.91

Diving

MEN

Springboard
Gold: Xiong Ni (China) 701.46 points
Silver: Yu Zhoucheng (China) 690.93
Bronze: Mark Lenzi (USA) 689.49

Platform
Gold: Dmitriy Saoutine (Russia) 692.34 points
Silver: Jan Hempel (Germany) 663.27
Bronze: Xiao Hailiang (China) 658.20

WOMEN

Springboard
Gold: Fu Mingxia (China) 547.68 points
Silver: Irina Lashko (Russia) 512.19
Bronze: Annie Pelletier (Canada) 509.64

Platform
Gold: Fu Mingxia (China) 521.58 points
Silver: Annika Walter (Germany) 479.22
Bronze: Mary Ellen Clark (USA) 472.95

Yachting

Laser
Gold: Robert Scheidt (Brazil) 26 points
Silver: Ben Ainslie (GB) 37
Bronze: Peer Moberg (Norway) 46

Tornado
Gold: Jose Luis Ballester/Fernando Leon (Spain) 30 points
Silver: Mitch Booth/Andrew Landenberger (Australia) 42
Bronze: Lars Grael/Kiko Pellicano (Brazil) 43

Soling
Gold: Germany
Silver: Russia
Bronze: USA

Star
Gold: Torben Grael/Marcelo Ferreira (Brazil) 25 points
Silver: Hans Wallen/Bobbie Lohse (Sweden) 29
Bronze: Colin Beashel/David Giles (Australia) 32

OMEN'S 100-M BREASTSTROKE IS 1 MIN 7.02 SEC, BY SOUTH AFRICAN PENNY HEYNS

PANIARDS JOSE LUIS BALLESTER AND FERNANDO LEON

200-m medley
Gold: Michelle Smith (Ireland) 2 min 13.93 sec
Silver: Marianne Limpert (Canada) 2:14.35
Bronze: Li Lin (China) 2:14.74

400-m medley
Gold: Michelle Smith (Ireland) 4 min 39.18 sec
Silver: Allison Wagner (USA) 4:42.03
Bronze: Krisztina Egerszegi (Hungary) 4:42.53

4 x 100-m medley
Gold: USA 4 min 2.88 sec
Silver: Australia 4:05.08
Bronze: China 4:07.34

Synchro swimming

Gold: USA 99.720 points
Silver: Canada 98.367
Bronze: Japan 97.753

Water polo

Gold: Spain
Silver: Croatia
Bronze: Italy

Finn
Gold: Mateusz Kusznierewicz (Poland) 32 points
Silver: Sebastien Godefroid (Belgium) 45
Bronze: Roy Heiner (Netherlands) 50

Europe
Gold: Kristine Roug (Denmark) 24 points
Silver: Margriet Matthijsse (Netherlands) 30
Bronze: Courtenay Becker-Dey (USA) 39

470 (Men)
Gold: Yevhen Braslavets/Igor Matviyenko (Ukraine) 40 points
Silver: Ian Walker/John Merricks (GB) 61
Bronze: Vitor Rocha/Nuno Barreto (Portugal) 62

470 (Women)
Gold: Begona Via Dufresne/Theresa Zabell (Spain) 25 points
Silver: Yumiko Shige/Alicia Kinoshita (Japan) 36
Bronze: Olena Pakholchik/Ruslana Taran (Ukraine) 38

Mistral (Men)
Gold: Nikolaos Kaklamanakis (Greece) 17 points
Silver: Carlos Espinola (Argentina) 19
Bronze: Gal Fridman (Israel) 21

Mistral (Women)
Gold: Lee Lai Shan (Hong Kong) 16 points
Silver: Barbara Kendall (New Zealand) 24
Bronze: Alessandra Sensini (Italy) 28

Above left
Belgian Frédéric Deburghgraeve, the winner of the men's 100-m breaststroke title, achieved a world record time of 1 min 00.6 sec in qualifying for the final.

Above
Action from the men's 470 yachting class, which was won by Ukrainians Yevhen Braslavets and Ivor Matviyenko. British pair Ian Walker and John Merricks won silver from the Portuguese pair by just one point.

Canoeing, rowing

REDGRAVE AND PINSENT SET A NEW OLYMPIC RECORD OF 6:20.09 IN THE COXLESS PAIRS

World record ✪
Olympic record ⌂
British record ⌂

Below right
French C2 pair Frank Addison and Wilfrid Forgues in action on the Ocoee River in Tennessee, USA. The pair, who had won bronze in Barcelona in 1992, went on to win the gold medal.

Far right
An emotional Steven Redgrave with his record fourth Olympic gold medal. Redgrave is the only rower in Olympic history to have won four golds.

Canoeing

MEN
Slalom K1
Gold: Oliver Fix (Germany) 141.22 points
Silver: Andraz Vehovar (Slovenia) 141.65
Bronze: Thomas Becker (Germany) 142.79
Slalom C1
Gold: Michal Martikan (Slovakia) 151.03 points
Silver: Lukas Pollert (Czech Republic) 151.17
Bronze: Patrice Estanguet (France) 152.84
Slalom C2
Gold: Frank Addison/Wilfrid Forgues (France) 158.82 points
Silver: Jiri Rohan/Miroslav Simek (Czech Republic) 160.16
Bronze: Andre Ehrenberg/Michael Senft (Germany) 163.72
500 m (K1) ⌂
Gold: Antonio Rossi (Italy) 1 min 37.42 sec
Silver: Knut Holmann (Norway) 1:38.33

1,000 m (K4) ⌂
Gold: Germany 2 min 51.52 sec
Silver: Hungary 2:53.18
Bronze: Russia 2:53.99
1,000 m (C1) ⌂
Gold: Martin Doktor (Czech Republic) 3 min 54.41 sec
Silver: Ivan Klementyev (Latvia) 3:54.95
Bronze: Gyorgy Zala (Hungary) 3:56.36
1,000 m (C2)
Gold: Andreas Dittmer/Gunar Kirchbach (Germany) 3 min 31.87 sec
Silver: Antonel Borsan/Marcel Glavan (Romania) 3:32.29
Bronze: Csaba Horvath/Gyorgy Kolonics (Hungary) 3:32.51

WOMEN
Slalom K1
Gold: Stepana Hilgertova (Czech Republic) 169.49 points

Bronze: Piotr Markiewicz (Poland) 1:38.61
500 m (K2)
Gold: Kay Bluhm/Torsten Gutsch (Germany) 1 min 28.69 sec
Silver: Beniamino Bonomi/Daniele Scarpa (Italy) 1:28.72
Bronze: Danny Collins/Andrew Trim (Australia) 1:29.40
500 m (C1) ⌂
Gold: Martin Doktor (Czech Republic) 1 min 49.93 sec
Silver: Slavomir Knazovicky (Slovakia) 1:50.51
Bronze: Imre Pulai (Hungary) 1:50.75
500 m (C2) ⌂
Gold: Csaba Horvath/Gyorgy Kolonics (Hungary) 1 min 40.42 sec
Silver: Nikolai Juravschi/Victor Reneischi (Moldova) 1:40.45
Bronze: Gheorghe Andriev/Grigore Obreja (Romania) 1:41.33
1,000 m (K1) ⌂
Gold: Knut Holmann (Norway) 3 min 25.78 sec
Silver: Beniamino Bonomi (Italy) 3:27.07
Bronze: Clint Robinson (Australia) 3:29.71
1,000 m (K2) ⌂
Gold: Antonio Rossi/Daniele Scarpa (Italy) 3 min 09.19 sec
Silver: Kay Bluhm/Torsten Gutsche (Germany) 3:10.51
Bronze: Milko Kazanov/Andrian Dushev (Bulgaria) 3:11.20

Silver: Dana Chladek (USA) 169.49
Bronze: Myriam Fox-Jerusalmi (France) 171.0
500 m (K1) ⌂
Gold: Rita Koban (Hungary) 1 min 47.65 sec
Silver: Caroline Brunet (Canada) 1:47.89
Bronze: Josefa Idem (Italy) 1:48.73
500 m (K2) ⌂
Gold: Agneta Andersson/Susanne Gunnarsson (Sweden) 1 min 39.32
Silver: Ramona Portwich/Birgit Fischer (Germany) 1:39.68
Bronze: Katrin Borchert/Anna Wood (Australia) 1:40.64
500 m (K4) ⌂
Gold: Germany 1 min 31.07 sec
Silver: Switzerland 1:32.70
Bronze: Sweden 1:32.91

Rowing

MEN
Single sculls ⌂
Gold: Xeno Mueller (Switzerland) 6 min 44.85 sec
Silver: Derek Porter (Canada) 6:47.45
Bronze: Thomas Lange (Germany) 6:47.72
Double sculls
Gold: Davide Tizzano/Agostino Abbagnale (Italy) 6 min 16.98 sec
Silver: Kjetil Undset/Steffen Stoerseth (Norway) 6:18.42
Bronze: Frederic Kowal/Samuel Barathay (France) 6:19.85

Double sculls (lightweight)
Gold: Markus Gier/Michael Gier (Switzerland) 6 min 23.47 sec
Silver: Maarten van der Linden/Pepjin Aardewijn (Netherlands) 6:26.48
Bronze: Anthony Edwards/Bruce Hick (Australia) 6:26.69
Quad sculls
Gold: Germany 5 min 56.93 sec
Silver: USA 5:59.10
Bronze: Australia 6:01.65
Coxless pairs ⌂
Gold: Steven Redgrave/Matthew Pinsent (GB) 6 min 20.09 sec

Silver: David Weightman/Robert Scott (Australia) 6:21.02
Bronze: Michel Andrieux/Jean-Christophe Rolland (France) 6:22.15
Coxless fours
Gold: Australia 6 min 6.37 sec
Silver: France 6:07.03
Bronze: GB 6:07.28
Coxless fours (lightweight)
Gold: Denmark 6 min 9.58 sec
Silver: Canada 6:10.13
Bronze: USA 6:12.29
Eights
Gold: Netherlands 5 min 42.74 sec
Silver: Germany 5:44.58
Bronze: Russia 5:45.77

WOMEN
Single sculls
Gold: Yekaterina Khodotvich (Belarus) 7 min 32.21 sec
Silver: Silken Laumann (Canada) 7:35.15
Bronze: Trine Hansen (Denmark) 7:37.20
Double sculls
Gold: Marnie McBean/Kathleen Heddle (Canada) 6 min 56.84 sec
Silver: Cao Mianying/Zhang Xiuyun (China) 6:58.35
Bronze: Irene Eijs/Eeke van Nes (Netherlands) 6:58.72

Target sports, equestrian

NEW OLYMPIC RECORD FOR THE MEN'S FREE PISTOL IS 666.4 POINTS, BY BORIS KOKOREV

Double sculls (lightweight)
Gold: Constanta Burcica/Camelia Macoviciuc (Romania) 7 min 12.78 sec
Silver: Teresa Bell/Lindsay Burns (USA) 7:14.65
Bronze: Rebecca Joyce/Virginia Lee (Australia) 7:16.56

Quad sculls
Gold: Germany 6 min 27.44 sec
Silver: Ukraine 6:30.36
Bronze: Canada 6:30.38

Coxless pairs
Gold: Megan Still/Kate Slatter (Australia) 7 min 1.39 sec
Silver: Missy Schwen/Karen Kraft (USA) 7:01.78
Bronze: Christine Gosse/Helene Cortin (France) 7:03.82

Eights
Gold: Romania 6 min 19.73 sec
Silver: Canada 6:24.05
Bronze: Belarus 6:24.44

Small-bore rifle-three positions
Gold: Jean-Pierre Amat (France) 1,273.9 points
Silver: Sergey Beliaev (Kazakhstan) 1,272.3
Bronze: Wolfram Waibel (Austria) 1,269.6

Olympic trap
Gold: Michael Diamond (Australia) 149 points
Silver: Josh Lakatos (USA) 147
Bronze: Lance Bade (USA) 147

Olympic double trap
Gold: Russell Mark (Australia) 189 points
Silver: Albano Pera (Italy) 183
Bronze: Zhang Bing (China) 183

Skeet
Gold: Ennio Falco (Italy) 149 points
Silver: Miroslaw Rzepkowski (Poland) 148
Bronze: Andrea Benelli (Italy) 147

WOMEN
Sport pistol
Gold: Li Duihong (China) 687.9 points
Silver: Diana Yorgova (Bulgaria) 684.8

Team (men)
Gold: USA
Silver: South Korea
Bronze: Italy

Team (women)
Gold: South Korea
Silver: Germany
Bronze: Poland

Equestrian sports

SHOW JUMPING
Individual
Gold: Ullrich Kirchhoff (Germany) 1.0 point
Silver: Willi Melliger (Switzerland) 4.0
Bronze: Alexandra Ledermann (Netherlands) 4.0

Team
Gold: Germany 1.75 points
Silver: USA 12.0
Bronze: Brazil 17.25

AUSTRALIA WON THE TEAM THREE-DAY EVENT WITH A TOTAL OF 203.85 POINTS

Shooting

MEN
Free pistol
Gold: Boris Kokorev (Russia) 666.4 points
Silver: Igor Basinski (Belarus) 662.0
Bronze: Roberto Di Donna (Italy) 661.8

Rapid-fire pistol
Gold: Ralf Schumann (Germany) 698.0 points
Silver: Emil Milev (Bulgaria) 692.1
Bronze: Vladimir Vokhmyanin (Kazakhstan) 691.5

Air pistol
Gold: Roberto Di Donna (Italy) 684.2 points
Silver: Wang Yifu (China) 684.1
Bronze: Tanu Kiriakov (Bulgaria) 683.8

Air rifle
Gold: Artem Khadzhibekov (Russia) 695.7 points
Silver: Wolfram Waibel (Austria) 695.2
Bronze: Jean-Pierre Amat (France) 693.1

Running game target
Gold: Yang Ling (China) 685.8 points
Silver: Xiao Jun (Japan) 679.8
Bronze: Miroslav Janus (Czech Republic) 678.4

Small-bore rifle-prone
Gold: Christian Klees (Germany) 704.8 points
Silver: Sergey Beliaev (Kazakhstan) 703.3
Bronze: Josef Gonci (Slovakia) 701.9

Bronze: Marina Logvinenko (Russia) 684.2

Small-bore rifle
Gold: Aleksandra Ivosev (Yugoslavia) 686.1 points
Silver: Irina Gerasimenok (Russia) 680.1
Bronze: Renata Mauer (Poland) 679.8

Air pistol
Gold: Olga Klochneva (Russia) 490.1 points
Silver: Marina Logvinenko (Russia) 488.5
Bronze: Mariya Grozdeva (Bulgaria) 488.5

Air rifle
Gold: Renata Mauer (Poland) 497.6 points
Silver: Petra Horneber (Germany) 497.4
Bronze: Aleksandra Ivosev (Yugoslavia) 497.2

Olympic double trap
Gold: Kim Rhode (USA) 141 points
Silver: Susanne Kiermayer (Germany) 139
Bronze: Deserie Huddleston (Australia) 139

Archery

Individual (men)
Gold: Justin Huish (USA)
Silver: Magnus Petersson (Sweden)
Bronze: Oh Kyo-moon (South Korea)

Individual (women)
Gold: Kim Kyung-wook (South Korea)
Silver: He Ying (China)
Bronze: Olena Sadovnycha (Ukraine)

DRESSAGE
Individual
Gold: Isabell Werth (Germany) 235.09 points
Silver: Anky van Grunsven (Netherlands) 233.02
Bronze: Sven Rothenberger (Netherlands) 224.94

Team
Gold: Germany 5,553 points
Silver: Netherlands 5,437
Bronze: USA 5,309

THREE-DAY EVENT
Individual
Gold: Blyth Tait (New Zealand) 56.8 points
Silver: Sally Clark (New Zealand) 60.4
Bronze: Kerri Millikin (USA) 73.7

Team
Gold: Australia 203.85 points
Silver: USA 261.1
Bronze: New Zealand 268.55

Combat, strength, gymnastics

FIRST WOMEN'S INDIVIDUAL EPEE GOLD MEDAL WAS WON BY LAURA FLESSEL OF FRANCE

World record ⊕
Olympic record �
British record ⟨Ω

Below right
Turkish lifter Naim Suleymanoğlü achieved an unprecedented third Olympic gold when he won the 64-kg bodyweight class in 1996. He won the title with a world record total of 335 kg.

Below far right
Gymnast Li Xiaoshuang of China, the winner of the men's combined title, won silver for both floor and team events.

World 54-kg snatch record 132.5

Combat

BOXING
48 kg
Gold: Daniel Petrov Bojilov (Bulgaria)
Silver: Mansueto Velasco (Philippines)
Bronze: Oleg Kiryukhin (Ukraine)
Bronze: Rafael Lozano (Spain)
51 kg
Gold: Maikro Romero (Cuba)
Silver: Bulat Dzumadilov (Kazakhstan)
Bronze: Albert Pakeev (Russia)
Bronze: Zoltan Lunka (Germany)
54 kg
Gold: Istvan Kovacs (Hungary)
Silver: Arnaldo Mesa (Cuba)
Bronze: Raimkul Malakhbekov (Russia)
Bronze: Vichairachanon Khadpo (Thailand)
57 kg
Gold: Somluk Kamsing (Thailand)
Silver: Serafim Todorov (Bulgaria)
Bronze: Pablo Chacon (Argentina)
Bronze: Floyd Mayweather (USA)
60 kg
Gold: Hocine Soltani (Algeria)
Silver: Tontcho Tontchev (Bulgaria)
Bronze: Terrance Cauthen (USA)
Bronze: Leonard Doroftei (Romania)
63.5 kg
Gold: Hector Vinent (Cuba)
Silver: Oktay Urkal (Germany)
Bronze: Bolat Niyazymbetov (Kazakhstan)
Bronze: Fathi Missaoui (Tunisia)
67 kg
Gold: Oleg Saitov (Russia)
Silver: Juan Hernandez (Cuba)
Bronze: Marian Simion (Romania)
Bronze: Daniel Santos (Puerto Rico)
71 kg
Gold: David Reid (USA)
Silver: Alfredo Duvergel (Cuba)
Bronze: Ezmouhan Ibzaimov (Kazakhstan)
Bronze: Karim Tulaganov (Uzbekistan)
75 kg
Gold: Ariel Hernandez (Cuba)
Silver: Malik Beyleroglu (Turkey)
Bronze: Mohamed Bahari (Algeria)
Bronze: Rhoshii Wells (USA)
81 kg
Gold: Vasiliy Jirov (Kazakhstan)
Silver: Lee Seung-bae (South Korea)
Bronze: Antonio Tarver (USA)
Bronze: Thomas Ulrich (Germany)
91 kg
Gold: Felix Savon (Cuba)
Silver: David Defiagbon (Canada)
Bronze: Nate Jones (USA)
Bronze: Luan Krasniqi (Germany)
91+ kg
Gold: Vladimir Kichko (Ukraine)
Silver: Paea Wolfgram (Tonga)
Bronze: Aleksey Lezin (Russia)
Bronze: Duncan Dokiwari (Nigeria)

FENCING
Men
Foil, individual
Gold: Alessandro Puccini (Italy)
Silver: Lionel Plumenail (France)
Bronze: Franck Boidin (France)
Foil, team
Gold: Russia
Silver: Poland
Bronze: Cuba

Epée, individual
Gold: Aleksandr Beketov (Russia)
Silver: Ivan Perez Trevejo (Cuba)
Bronze: Geza Imre (Hungary)
Epée, team
Gold: Italy
Silver: Russia
Bronze: France
Sabre, individual
Gold: Stanislav Pozdnyakov (Russia)
Silver: Sergey Sharikov (Russia)
Bronze: Damien Touya (France)
Sabre, team
Gold: Russia
Silver: Hungary
Bronze: Italy
Women
Foil, individual
Gold: Laura Badea (Romania)
Silver: Valentina Vezzali (Italy)
Bronze: Giovanna Trillini (Italy)

Foil, team
Gold: Italy
Silver: Romania
Bronze: Germany
Epée, individual
Gold: Laura Flessel (France)
Silver: Valeriy Barlois (France)
Bronze: Gyoengyi Szalay Horvathne (Hungary)
Epée, team
Gold: France
Silver: Italy
Bronze: Russia

JUDO
Men
60 kg
Gold: Tadahiro Nomura (Japan)
Silver: Girolamo Giovinazzo (Italy)
Bronze: Dorjpalam Naramandakh (Mongolia)
Bronze: Richard Trautmann (Germany)
65 kg
Gold: Udo Quellmalz (Germany)
Silver: Yukimasa Nakamura (Japan)
Bronze: Israel Hernandez Plana (Cuba)
Bronze: Henrique Guimaraes (Brazil)
71 kg
Gold: Kenzo Nakamura (Japan)
Silver: Kwak Dae-sung (South Korea)
Bronze: James Pedro (USA)

Bronze: Christophe Gagliano (France)
78 kg
Gold: Djamel Bouras (France)
Silver: Toshihiko Koga (Japan)
Bronze: Soso Liparteliani (Georgia)
Bronze: Cho In-chul (South Korea)
86 kg
Gold: Jeon Ki-young (South Korea)
Silver: Armen Bagdasarov (Uzbekistan)
Bronze: Marko Spittka (Germany)
Bronze: Mark Huizinga (Netherlands)
95 kg
Gold: Pawel Nastula (Poland)
Silver: Kim Min-soo (South Korea)
Bronze: Miguel Fernandes (Brazil)
Bronze: Stéphane Traineau (France)
95+ kg
Gold: David Douillet (France)
Silver: Ernesto Perez (Spain)
Bronze: Harry van Barneveld (Belgium)
Bronze: Frank Moeller (Germany)

CHINESE WEIGHTLIFTER ZHAN XUGANG BROKE THRE

Women
48 kg
Gold: Kye Sun (North Korea)
Silver: Ryoko Tamura (Japan)
Bronze: Amarilis Savon Carmenaty (Cuba)
Bronze: Yolanda Soler (Spain)
52 kg
Gold: Marie-Claire Restoux (France)
Silver: Hyung Sook-hee (South Korea)
Bronze: Noriko Sugawara (Japan)
Bronze: Legna Verdecia (Cuba)
56 kg
Gold: Driulis Gonzalez (Cuba)
Silver: Jung Sun-yong (South Korea)
Bronze: Isabel Fernandez (Spain)
Bronze: Marisabel Lomba (Belgium)
61 kg
Gold: Yuko Emoto (Japan)
Silver: Gella Vandecaveye (Belgium)
Bronze: Jenny Gal (Netherlands)
Bronze: Jung Sung-sook (South Korea)
66 kg
Gold: Cho Min-sun (South Korea)
Silver: Aneta Szczepanska (Poland)
Bronze: Wang Xianbo (China)
Bronze: Claudia Zwiers (Netherlands)
72 kg
Gold: Ulla Werbrouck (Belgium)
Silver: Yoko Tanabe (Japan)

Bronze: Yienia Scapin (Italy)
Bronze: Diadenis Luna (Cuba)
72+ kg
Gold: Sum Fuming (China)
Silver: Estela Rodriguez (Cuba)
Bronze: Johanna Hagn (Germany)
Bronze: Christine Cicot (France)

WRESTLING
Freestyle
48 kg
Gold: Kim Il (North Korea)
Silver: Armen Mkrchyan (Armenia)
Bronze: Alexis Vila Perdomo (Cuba)
52 kg
Gold: Valentin Dimitrov Jordanov (Bulgaria)
Silver: Namik Abdullayev (Azerbaijan)
Bronze: Maulen Mamyrov (Kazakhstan)
57 kg
Gold: Kendall Cross (USA)
Silver: Giuvi Sissaouri (Canada)
Bronze: Ri Yong Sam (North Korea)
62 kg
Gold: Tom Brands (USA)
Silver: Jang Jae-sung (South Korea)
Bronze: Elbrus Tedeyev (Ukraine)
68 kg
Gold: Vadim Bogiyev (Russia)

ORLD RECORDS AT 70 KG

Silver: Townsend Saunders (USA)
Bronze: Zaza Zazirov (Ukraine)
74 kg
Gold: Buvaysa Saytyev (Russia)
Silver: Park Jang-soon (South Korea)
Bronze: Takuya Ota (Japan)
82 kg
Gold: Khadzhimurad Magomedov (Russia)
Silver: Yang Hyun-mo (South Korea)
Bronze: Amir Reza Khadem Azghadi (Iran)
90 kg
Gold: Rasull Khadem Azghadi (Iran)
Silver: Makharbek Khadartsev (Russia)
Bronze: Eldari Kurtanidze (Georgia)
100 kg
Gold: Kurt Angel (USA)
Silver: Abbas Jadidi (Iran)
Bronze: Arawat Sabejew (Germany)
130 kg
Gold: Mahmut Demir (Turkey)
Silver: Aleksey Medvedev (Belarus)
Bronze: Bruce Baumgartner (USA)

Strength

Greco-Roman
48 kg
Gold: Sim Kwon-ho (South Korea)
Silver: Aleksandr Pavlov (Belarus)

Bronze: Zafar Gulyov (Russia)
52 kg
Gold: Armen Nazaryan (Armenia)
Silver: Brandon Paulson (USA)
Bronze: Andriy Kalashnikov (Ukraine)
57 kg
Gold: Yuri Melnichenko (Kazakhstan)
Silver: Dennis Hall (USA)
Bronze: Sheng Zetian (China)
62 kg
Gold: Wlodzimierz Zawadzki (Poland)
Silver: Juan Luis Maren Delis (Cuba)
Bronze: Mehmet Pirim (Turkey)
68 kg
Gold: Ryszard Wolny (Poland)
Silver: Ghani Yolouz (France)
Bronze: Aleksandr Tretyakov (Russia)
74 kg
Gold: Feliberto Ascuy Aguilera (Cuba)
Silver: Marko Asell (Finland)
Bronze: Josef Tracz (Poland)
82 kg
Gold: Hamza Yerlikiya (Turkey)
Silver: Thomas Zander (Germany)
Bronze: Valeriy Tsilent (Belarus)
90 kg
Gold: Vyacheslav Oleynyk (Ukraine)
Silver: Jacek Fafinski (Poland)
Bronze: Maik Bullman (Germany)
100 kg
Gold: Andrzej Wronski (Poland)
Silver: Sergey Lishtvan (Belarus)
Bronze: Mikael Ljungberg (Sweden)
130 kg
Gold: Aleksandr Karelin (Russia)
Silver: Siamak Ghaffari (USA)
Bronze: Serguei Moureiko (Moldova)

Figures (total in kg)
54 kg
Gold: Halil Mutlu (Turkey) 287.5 (Snatch: 132.5 ⬤)
Silver: Zhang Xiangsen (China) 280
Bronze: Sevdalin Minchev (Bulgaria) 277.5
59 kg ⬤
Gold: Tang Lingsheng (China) 307.5
Silver: Leonidas Sabanis (Greece) 305
Bronze: Nikolai Peshalov (Bulgaria) 302.5
64 kg ⬤
Gold: Naim Suleymanoğlü (Turkey) 335
Silver: Valerios Leonidis (Greece) 332.5
(Clean and jerk: 187.5 ⬤)
Bronze: Xiao Jiangang (China) 322.5
70 kg ⬤
Gold: Zhan Xugang (China) 357.5 (Snatch: 162.5 ⬤;
Clean and jerk: 195 ⬤)
Silver: Kim Myong-nam (North Korea) 345
Bronze: Attila Feri (Hungary) 340
76 kg ⬤
Gold: Pablo Lara (Cuba) 367.5
Silver: Yoto Yotov (Bulgaria) 360
Bronze: Jon Chol (North Korea) 357.5
83 kg ⬤
Gold: Pyrros Dimas (Greece) 392.5 (Snatch: 180 ⬤)
Silver: Marc Huster (Germany) 382.5
(Clean and jerk: 213.5 ⬤)
Bronze: Andrzej Cofalik (Poland) 372.5
91 kg
Gold: Alexey Petrov (Russia) 402.5
(Snatch: 187.5 ⬤)
Silver: Leonidis Kokas (Greece) 390
Bronze: Oliver Caruso (Germany) 390
99 kg ⬤
Gold: Kakhi Kakhiasvilis (Greece) 420
(Clean and jerk: 235 ⬤)
Silver: Anatoliy Khrapaty (Kazakhstan) 410
Bronze: Denis Gotfrid (Ukraine) 402.5
108 kg
Gold: Timur Taimazov (Ukraine) 430
(Clean and jerk: 236 ⬤)
Silver: Sergey Syrtsov (Russia) 420
Bronze: Nicu Vlad (Romania) 420

+108 kg
Gold: Andrey Chemerkin (Russia) 457.5
(Clean & Jerk: 260 ⬤)
Silver: Ronny Weller (Germany) 455
Bronze: Stefan Botev (Australia) 450

Gymnastics

MEN
Team
Gold: Russia 576.778 points
Silver: China 575.539
Bronze: Ukraine 571.541
Combined
Gold: Li Xiaoshuang (China) 58.423 points
Silver: Aleksey Nemov (Russia) 58.374
Bronze: Vitaliy Scherbo (Belarus) 58.197
Floor
Gold: Ioannis Melissanidis (Greece) 9.85 points
Silver: Li Xiaoshuang (China) 9.837
Bronze: Aleksey Nemov (Russia) 9.8
Parallel bars
Gold: Rustam Sharipov (Ukraine) 9.837 points
Silver: Jair Lynch (USA) 9.825
Bronze: Vitaliy Scherbo (Belarus) 9.8
Horse
Gold: Li Donghua (Switzerland) 9.875 points
Silver: Marius Urzica (Romania) 9.825
Bronze: Aleksey Nemov (Russia) 9.787
Rings
Gold: Yuri Chechi (Italy) 9.887 points
Silver: Szilvestzter Csollany (Hungary) and Dan
Burinca (Romania) 9.812
Horizontal bar
Gold: Andreas Wecker (Germany) 9.85 points
Silver: Krasimir Dounev (Bulgaria) 9.825
Bronze: Vitaliy Scherbo (Belarus), Aleksey Nemov
(Russia) and Fan Bin (China) 9.8
Vault
Gold: Aleksey Nemov (Russia) 9.787 points
Silver: Yeo Hong-chul (South Korea) 9.756
Bronze: Vitaliy Scherbo (Belarus) 9.724

WOMEN
Team
Gold: USA 389.225 points
Silver: Russia 388.404
Bronze: Romania 388.246
Combined
Gold: Lilia Podkopayeva (Ukraine) 39.255 points
Silver: Gina Gogean (Romania) 39.075
Bronze: Simona Amonar (Romania) and Lavinia
Milosovici (Romania) 39.067
Asymmetric bars
Gold: Svetlana Chorkina (Russia) 9.85 points
Silver: Bi Wenjiing (China) and Amy Chow (USA)
9.837
Floor
Gold: Lilia Podkopayeva (Ukraine) 9.887 points
Silver: Simona Amonar (Romania) 9.85
Bronze: Dominique Dawes (USA) 9.837
Beam
Gold: Shannon Miller (USA) 9.862 points
Silver: Lilia Podkopayeva (Ukraine) 9.825
Bronze: Gina Gogean (Romania) 9.787
Vault
Gold: Simona Amonar (Romania) 9.825 points
Silver: Mo Huilan (China) 9.768
Bronze: Gina Gogean (Romania) 9.750
Rhythmic (individual)
Gold: Ekaterina Serebryanskaya (Ukraine)
39.683 points
Silver: Ianina Batyrchina (Russia) 39.382
Bronze: Elena Vitrichenko (Ukraine) 39.331
Rhythmic (team)
Gold: Spain 38.933 points
Silver: Bulgaria 38.866
Bronze: Russia 38.365

Team sports, racket sports

World record ⊕
Olympic record ⊡
British record ⚲

Below right
The football final between Nigeria and Argentina was won 3–2 by Nigeria, who scored twice in the last 15 minutes. A public holiday was declared by the Nigerian government to honour the team's success.

Below far right
Chinese pair Deng Yaping and Qiao Hong won the women's table tennis doubles title for the second successive Games. Yaping went on to win the singles title for a second successive time, and in doing so achieved a record fourth gold medal in total.

Team sports

BASEBALL
Gold: Cuba
Silver: Japan
Bronze: USA

BASKETBALL
Men
Gold: USA
Silver: Yugoslavia
Bronze: Lithuania
Women
Gold: USA
Silver: Brazil
Bronze: Australia

FOOTBALL
Men
Gold: Nigeria
Silver: Argentina

SOFTBALL
Gold: USA
Silver: China
Bronze: Australia

VOLLEYBALL
Men
Gold: Netherlands
Silver: Italy
Bronze: Yugoslavia
Women
Gold: Cuba
Silver: China
Bronze: Brazil

BEACH VOLLEYBALL
Men
Gold: Kent Steffes and Karch Kiraly (USA)
Silver: Mike Whitmarsh and Michael Dodd (USA)
Bronze: John Child and Mark Hesse (Canada)

Mixed doubles
Gold: Kim Dong-moon and Gil Young-ah (South Korea)
Silver: Park Joo-bong and Ra Kyung-min (South Korea)
Bronze: Liu Jianjun and Sun Man (China)

TABLE TENNIS
Men's singles
Gold: Lui Guoliang (China)
Silver: Wang Tao (China)
Bronze: Joerg Rosskopf (Germany)

Men's doubles
Gold: Kong Linhui and Lui Guoliang (China)
Silver: Lu Lin and Wang Tao (China)
Bronze: Lee Chun-seung and Yoo Nam-kyu (South Korea)

Women's singles
Gold: Deng Yaping (China)

Bronze: Brazil
Women
Gold: USA
Silver: China
Bronze: Norway

HANDBALL
Men
Gold: Croatia
Silver: Sweden
Bronze: Spain
Women
Gold: Denmark
Silver: South Korea
Bronze: Hungary

HOCKEY
Men
Gold: Netherlands
Silver: Spain
Bronze: Australia
Women
Gold: Australia
Silver: South Korea
Bronze: Netherlands

MODERN PENTATHLON
Gold: Aleksandr Parygin (Kazakhstan) 5,551 points
Silver: Eduard Zenkova (Russia) 5,530
Bronze: Janos Martinek (Hungary) 5,501

Women
Gold: Jackie Silva Cruz and Sandra Pires Tavares (Brazil)
Silver: Monica Rodrigues and Adriana Samuel Ramos (Brazil)
Bronze: Natalie Cook and Kerri Ann Pottharst (Australia)

Racket sports

BADMINTON
Men's singles
Gold: Poul-Erik Hoyer-Larsen (Denmark)
Silver: Dong Jiong (China)
Bronze: Rashid Sidek (Malaysia)

Men's doubles
Gold: Rexy Mainaky and Ricky Subagja (Indonesia)
Silver: Cheah Soon Kit and Yap Kim Hock (Malaysia)
Bronze: Denny Kantono and S. Antonius (Indonesia)

Women's singles
Gold: Bang Soo-hyun (South Korea)
Silver: Mia Audina (Indonesia)
Bronze: Susi Susanti (Indonesia)

Women's doubles
Gold: Ge Fei and Gu Jun (China)
Silver: Gil Young-ah and Jang Hye-ock (South Korea)
Bronze: Qin Yiyuan and Tang Yongshu (China)

Silver: Jing Chen (Taiwan)
Bronze: Qiao Hong (China)

Women's doubles
Gold: Deng Yaping and Qiao Hong (China)
Silver: Liu Wei and Qiao Yunping (China)
Bronze: Park Hae-jung and Ryu Ji-hae (South Korea)

TENNIS
Men's singles
Gold: Andre Agassi (USA)
Silver: Sergi Bruguera (Spain)
Bronze: Leander Paes (India)

Men's doubles
Gold: Todd Woodbridge and Mark Woodforde (Australia)
Silver: Neil Broad and Tim Henman (GB)
Bronze: Marc-Kevin Goellner and David Prinosil (Germany)

Women's singles
Gold: Lindsay Davenport (USA)
Silver: Arantxa Sanchez Vicario (Spain)
Bronze: Jana Novotna (Czech Republic)

Women's doubles
Gold: Gigi Fernandez and Mary Joe Fernandez (USA)
Silver: Jana Novotna and Helena Sukova (Czech Republic)
Bronze: Conchita Martinez and Arantxa Sanchez Vicario (Spain)

Top 1,000-m time trial 1:02.712

Cycling

COLLINELLI SET A NEW WORLD INDIVIDUAL PURSUIT RECORD OF 4:19.153

MEN

1,000-m time trial ⛃
Gold: Florian Rousseau (France) 1 min 2.712 sec
Silver: Erin Hartwell (USA) 1:02.940
Bronze: Takanobu Jumonji (Japan) 1:03.261

Sprint (200 m)
Gold: Jens Fiedler (Germany)
Silver: Marty Nothstein (USA)
Bronze: Curtis Harnett (Canada)

Individual pursuit
Gold: Andrea Collinelli (Italy) 4 min 20.893 sec
(🕒4:19.153 in qualifying)
Silver: Philippe Ermenault (France) 4:22.714
Bronze: Bradley McGee (Australia) 4:26.121

Team pursuit ⛃
Gold: France 4 min 5.93 sec
Silver: Russia 4:07.73
Bronze: Australia 4:07.57

Points race
Gold: Silvio Martinello (Italy) 37 points
Silver: Brian Walton (Canada) 29
Bronze: Stuart O'Grady (Australia) 27

Road race
Gold: Pascal Richard (Switzerland) 2 hr 53 min 56 sec
Silver: Rolf Sorensen (Denmark) 2:53:56
Bronze: Max Sciandri (GB) 2:53:58

Road time trial individual
Gold: Miguel Induráin (Spain) 1 hr 4 min 5 sec
Silver: Abraham Olano (Spain) 1:04:17
Bronze: Chris Boardman (GB) 1:04:36

Mountain bike
Gold: Bart Jan Brentjens (Netherlands) 2 hr 17 min 38 sec
Silver: Thomas Frischknecht (Switzerland) 2:20:14
Bronze: Miguel Martinez (France) 2:20:36

WOMEN

Sprint (200 m)
Gold: Felicia Ballanger (France)
Silver: Michelle Ferris (Australia)
Bronze: Ingrid Haringa (Netherlands)

Individual pursuit ⛃
Gold: Antonella Bellutti (Italy) 3 min 33.595 sec
Silver: Marion Clignet (Canada) 3:38.571
Bronze: Judith Arndt (Germany) 3:38.744

Points race
Gold: Nathalie Lancien (France) 24 points
Silver: Ingrid Haringa (Netherlands) 23
Bronze: Lucy Tyler Sharman (Australia) 17

Road race
Gold: Jeannie Longo-Ciprelli (France) 2 hr 36 min 13 sec
Silver: Imelda Chiappa (Italy) 2:36:38
Bronze: Clara Hughes (Canada) 2:36:44

Road time trial individual
Gold: Zulfiya Zabirova (Russia) 36 min 40 sec
Silver: Jeannie Longo-Ciprelli (France) 37:00
Bronze: Clara Hughes (Canada) 37:13

Mountain bike
Gold: Paolo Pezzo (Italy) 1 hr 50 min 51 sec
Silver: Alison Sydor (Canada) 1:51:58
Bronze: Susan De Mattei (USA) 1:52:36

Below left
Women's mountain biking gold medallist Paolo Pezzo of Italy. Mountain biking was one of the new events held at the 1996 Olympic Games.

Below
On his way to winning the individual pursuit title, Italian Andrea Collinelli achieved a new world record time for 4,000 m.

Events

Right
In April 1996 David Huxley set a new world record by pulling a 187-tonne Boeing 747-400 a distance of 54.7 m (179 ft 6 in) during the *Record Breakers* trip to Australia. He has also pulled Concorde (weighing 105 tonnes) in the past, achieving a top distance of 143 m (469 ft 2 in) in Oct 1994.

Middle right
On the same trip Grant Edwards set a new train-pulling record, when he succeeded in moving a 201-tonne train a distance of 36.8 m (120 ft 9 in).

Far right
The day after Huxley set his plane-pulling record he gave a further demonstration of his strength by pulling the 387-tonne HMAV *Bounty* 25 m (82 ft).

Largest paper plane 13.97 m

Record Breakers: 25 years
The Anniversary series

In 1996 *Record Breakers*, the BBC's celebration of everything superlative, launched its 25th Anniversary series, clocking up its own record as the longest surviving television embodiment of *The Guinness Book of Records* anywhere in the world. It started life as a relatively unambitious series of six shows presented by the late Roy Castle. Since then, literally hundreds of records have been attempted in front of the *Record Breakers* cameras.

Shooting for the anniversary series of *Record Breakers* took place throughout the year, but the programme's trip to Australia early in 1996 was a prime example of what it takes to capture records as they fall. When David Huxley (already a plane-pulling record-holder) announced his intention to single-handedly pull a jumbo jet down a taxi-way at Sydney Airport, the *Record Breakers* team was sceptical but threw all their resources at such an event. Director Linda Ross positioned four cameras around the Qantas 747-400 and filmed the plane's weighing in and the additional fuelling that brought its weight to the Guinness-stipulated 187 tonnes, matching the only previous attempt to pull a plane of this class—an attempt that produced no more than 12.7 cm (5 in) of movement in its front wheel. On 2 April, Huxley succeeded in pulling the plane a record 54.7 m (179 ft 6 in).

Later that week, Canberra strongman Grant Edwards pulled a 201-tonne antique steam train 36.8 m (120 ft 9 in) to set a new world record, beating the previous Guinness train-pulling record of 12 m (39 ft 4 in).

The producer of the *Record Breakers* programme, Greg Childs, explains why the programme goes to such lengths in its coverage of record attempts: "*Record Breakers* faces a unique set of problems in television terms. There's none of the usual 'Can we go again?' for us. If we fail to capture the moment when the record's broken, the entire drama is missing its climax. We owe it to our contributors to produce the very best images of their struggle and their achievement. That's why we put months of planning into an event like the plane-pull. We negotiate every fine detail so that we can get as close as possible to the record-breaker, both in camera terms and emotionally, because we need to be able to share their moment of triumph, as it happens."

The 25th Anniversary series of *Record Breakers* transmits in its traditional Friday afternoon slot on BBC1 in the autumn of 1996. The continuing success of the longest running record-breaking action programme in the world is a tribute to 25 years of co-operation between the BBC and *The Guinness Book of Records*. Jan 1997 sees the launch of a new series celebrating the very best of that excitement and adventure, *Record Breakers Gold!*

Record-breaking in 1996
Plane-pulling

On 2 April 1996, Australian David Huxley succeeded in breaking the world record for pulling a jumbo jet when he moved a 187-tonne Qantas Boeing 747-400 a distance of 54.7 m (179 ft 6 in) down the runway at Sydney Airport, NSW, Australia.

Train-pulling

On 4 April 1996, Grant Edwards broke the record for train-pulling when he single-handedly pulled a 201-tonne train over a distance of 36.8 m (120 ft 9 in) at Thirlmere, NSW, Australia.

Card-memorizing

On 6 June 1996, Dominic O'Brien of Furneux Pelham, Herts, UK, broke a world record in

front of the *Record Breakers* cameras when he recalled an entire pack of cards after looking at them only once. The time taken to memorize the cards, 38.29 seconds, beat the previous record of 42.01 seconds (set in Nov 1994) by 3.72 seconds.

Paper aircraft
Duration

The world record for the longest level flight by a hand-launched paper aircraft is a time of 18.8 seconds. It was set by Ken Blackburn in a hangar at JFK airport, New York, USA, on 19 Feb 1994.

The British record for level flight duration is 15.5 seconds. It was set by by Philip Wright of Cranfield University, Beds, on 22 March 1996 at Alexandra Palace, London, UK.

Distance
The greatest distance ever covered by a paper aircraft indoors is 58.82 m (193 ft). This feat was achieved by Tony Felch at the La Crosse Center, Wisconsin, USA, on 21 May 1985.

Largest paper aircraft
The largest flying paper aeroplane in the world had a wingspan of 13.97 m (45 ft 10 in). It was constructed by a team of students from the Faculty of Aerospace Engineering at Delft University of Technology, Netherlands, and was flown on 16 May 1995. It was launched indoors and flew a distance of 34.8 m (114 ft 2 in).

Paper aircraft challenge
Andrew Little of the Royal Aeronautical Society wrote to 'Megalab', the contribution of the BBC's *Tomorrow's World* to *National Science Week*, to suggest a large-scale attempt on the record for keeping a paper plane aloft. The event was filmed at Alexandra Palace, London, UK, on 22 March 1996.

Left
'Memory Man' Dominic O'Brien is congratulated by record-breaking athlete Kriss Akabusi and senior Guinness editor Clive Carpenter in the Elephant House at London Zoo, UK, where O'Brien set a new record for card-memorizing on 6 June 1996.

201-TONNE TRAIN 36.8 M

Facts and figures:
• A total of 10,000 A4 sheets of paper were bought for the event and an estimated 6,000–7,000 of them were used
• Prior to the event the heating at Alexandra Palace was switched off to reduce the likelihood of flight durations being extended by artificially created rising thermals
• There were 11,000 entrants in the competition and a TV audience of 4.4 million
• A total of 27 teams competed, from places as varied as British Aerospace and Rolls Royce to Oaklands Primary School in West London, UK

Main rules:
• The flight must be made indoors, where the general public may view
• The plane must be made from a single sheet of A4 paper, which can be folded and cut
• Minimal use of glue or sellotape is permitted

Ken Blackburn holds the world record for keeping a paper aircraft aloft for the greatest possible duration. He first broke the record on 29 Nov 1983, achieving a time of 16.9 seconds at North Carolina State University, USA. He beat his own record in 1987, with a flight of 17.2 seconds, and then did so again on 18 Feb 1994, with a flight of 18.8 seconds in a hangar at JFK airport, New York, USA. On 22 March 1996, Blackburn failed in his most

recent attempt to beat his own record again, although he did record the best flight of the day, with a time of 17.3 seconds.

A new British paper aircraft record was set at the event when Philip Wright, a postgraduate student from Cranfield University, Beds, achieved a flight time of 15.5 seconds.

Ken Blackburn's advice for potential paper aircraft throwers: "There are a couple of secrets to setting the record. One is designing the right plane; the second is that you have to throw it almost exactly straight up, within about 10° of vertical, which is why I've spent one-and-a-half months getting my arm in shape."

Below far left
At Alexandra Palace the British Aerospace team work on the design of their aircraft with the aid of lap-top computers.

Below left
Ken Blackburn of St Peter's, Missouri, USA, the current record-holder, shows off the aircraft he used for his 17.3-second throw.

Below
Entrants practise their throwing techniques before making their official attempts.

ORLD RECORD FOR KEEPING A PAPER AIRCRAFT IN THE AIR IS CURRENTLY 18.8 SECONDS

Index

JOIN YOUR RECORD-BREAKING FRIENDS IN CYBERSPACE:

GUINNESSWORLDS.COM WILL BE THE ADDRESS OF THE NEW GUINNESS INTERNET CLUB TO BE LAUNCHED SOON. REGISTER NOW AND RECEIVE ADVANCE NOTICE OF THE LATEST DEVELOPMENTS WE ARE PLANNING—INCLUDING AMAZING CHAT ROOMS, BROADCAST COVERAGE OF RECORD-BREAKING EVENTS AROUND THE WORLD AS THEY HAPPEN, THE RULES AND REGULATIONS THAT YOU NEED TO FOLLOW IF YOU WISH TO BREAK RECORDS, GUINNESS EXPERTS ON-HAND TO ANSWER YOUR DETAILED QUESTIONS, AND MUCH MUCH MORE.

IT'S EASY—JUST FILL IN THE FORM BELOW AND SEND IT TO US COMPLETELY FREE OF CHARGE USING OUR FREEPOST ADDRESS:

GUINNESS PUBLISHING
FREEPOST
NW5750
33 LONDON ROAD
ENFIELD
MIDDLESEX EN2 6BR

ALTERNATIVELY, THOSE OF YOU ALREADY WIRED CAN E-MAIL US AT WEBMASTER@GUINNESSWORLDS.COM

Tell us what you thought

In its 41-year history *The Guinness Book of Records* has kept in close touch with its audience— a simple result of the letters and communications we get from you our readers. As part of our programme of continuous improvement, we wish to know in detail what you think of this year's edition. By filling in the form below, we can ensure that we create an even better book next year. Send us the form below free to our Freepost address (see above):

Name

Address

Postcode

Signature of parent/guardian (if under 18)

QUESTION 1: Your favourite items from the 1997 *Guinness Book of Records*

Which items did you find very interesting?   p.   p.   p.   p.   p.

Which items did you find quite interesting?   p.   p.   p.   p.   p.

Which items were of no interest to you at all?   p.   p.   p.   p.   p.

QUESTION 2: Your favourite illustrations

Please write in the boxes the page numbers of your favourite three pictures/photographs etc   p.   p.   p.

QUESTION 3: How do you rate the 1997 *Guinness Book of Records?*

Please give *The Guinness Book of Records* marks out of 10

(Score 10 if you think it is wonderful, 0 if you are very disappointed with it)

QUESTION 4: When did you last read a *Guinness Book of Records?*

QUESTION 5: Here are some of the statements that different people make about *The Guinness Book of Records.* **Do you agree?**

Please tick one box for each statement that best describes your view.

	Agree a lot	Agree a bit	Disagree a bit	Disagree a lot
I enjoy reading it on my own				
I enjoy reading it with friends and relations of my own age				
I enjoy reading it with my parents				
It helps me with homework and school projects				
I usually just browse without looking for anything specific				
I usually know in advance what I am looking for				
I hope to get more editions of *The Guinness Book of Records* in future years				
I love looking for really crazy records				
I prefer books that explain things in more detail				
I look for laughs when I read a book at home				
There is too much in *The Guinness Book of Records*				

QUESTION 6: Other editions of *The Guinness Book of Records*

Have you got any of these other editions of *The Guinness Book of Records* (please tick)

1996	1995	1994	1993
1992	1991	before 1990	

QUESTION 7: About yourself Your age? ☐   Your sex? ☐ male ☐ female

Your occupation?

Who bought *The Guinness Book of Records* for you?

Yourself	Mother	Father	Partner
Brother	Sister	Other relative	Friend

If you are in full-time education, please tell us your favourite subjects.

Do you own, or have access to, a PC/Mac at home?

Own	Owned by family	School
At Home	At school	At work

Do you have access to the Internet?

In 1759 Arthur Guinness founded the Guinness Brewery at St James' Gate, Dublin, and by 1833 the brewery was the largest in Ireland. Arthur Guinness Son & Co. Ltd became a limited liability company in London in 1886, and by the 1930s Guinness had two breweries in Britain producing its special porter stout. The slogans 'Guinness is good for you', 'Guinness for strength' and 'My Goodness, My Guinness' appeared everywhere. Guinness was in a unique position in the brewing trade in Britain in that it was the only beer on sale in every public house, yet Guinness did not actually own any of the pubs—except for the Castle Inn on its hop farms at Bodiam, Sussex. Thus the company was always on the look-out for promotional ideas.

Whilst at a shooting party in Co. Wexford, Ireland, in 1951, Sir Hugh Beaver, the company's managing director, was involved in a dispute as to whether the golden plover was Europe's fastest game bird. In his host's library at Castlebridge House, Sir Hugh could not confirm the answer in any of the reference books. Again in 1954, an argument arose as to whether grouse were faster than golden plover. Sir Hugh realized that such questions could arise amongst people in pubs and that a book that answered these questions would be helpful to licensees.

Chris Chataway, the record-breaking athlete, was then an underbrewer at Guinness' Park Royal Brewery. When he heard of Sir Hugh's idea, he recommended the ideal people to produce the book—the twins Norris and Ross McWhirter, whom he had met through athletics events, both having won their Blues for sprinting at Oxford. The McWhirters were running a fact-finding agency in Fleet Street and so impressed the Board that they were immediately commissioned to compile what was to become *The Guinness Book of Records*.

After a busy year of research, the first copy of the 198-page *Guinness Book of Records* was bound by printers on 27 August 1955. It was an instantaneous success and became Britain's No 1 best-seller before Christmas.

The British success was soon replicated elsewhere. *The Guinness Book of Records* English edition is now published in 40 different countries with another 37 editions in foreign languages. Total sales of all editions passed 50 million in 1984, 75 million in 1994 and will reach the 100 million mark early in the next millennium.

Records are constantly changing and few survive from the first edition in 1955. As in 1955, our hope remains that this book can assist in resolving enquiries on facts, and may turn the heat of argument into the light of knowledge.